CRUEL APRIL

CRUEL APRIL

The Fall of Saigon

OLIVIER TODD

Translated from the French by
STEPHEN BECKER

W·W·NORTON & COMPANY

New York   London

Fiction
Tod

Printed in the United States of America.

The text of this book is composed in Times Roman,
with display type set in Fenice Regular.
Composition by PennSet, Inc.
Manufacturing by Haddon Craftsmen, Inc.
Book design by Jacques Chazaud

Library of Congress Cataloging-in-Publication Data

Todd, Olivier.
   [Cruel avril. English]
   Cruel April : the fall of Saigon / Olivier Todd :
translated from the French by Stephen Becker.
      p.   cm.
   Translation of: Cruel avril.
   Includes bibliographical references.
   1. Vietnamese Conflict. 1961–1975—Vietnam—Ho Chi Minh City.
   2. Ho Chi Minh City (Vietnam)—History. I. Title.
   DS559.9.S24T6313   1990
   959.704'3—dc20   89-38584
   ISBN 0-393-02787-2

W. W. Norton & Company, Inc., 500 Fifth Avenue, New York, N.Y. 10110
W. W. Norton & Company Ltd., 10 Coptic Street, London WC1A 1PU

1 2 3 4 5 6 7 8 9 0

To the memory of Tran Van Ba,
for Chantal Charpentier

Contents

———◆———

April is the cruellest month, breeding
Lilacs out of the dead land, mixing
Memory and desire, stirring
Dull roots with spring rain.

T. S. Eliot

CRUEL APRIL

Preface

◆

Here are some of the human dramas, diplomatic maneuvers, military strategy and political manipulations, from Hanoi to Washington via Moscow, Paris and other great cities, that culminated in the fall of Saigon on April 30, 1975—twenty-one years after the battle of Dien Bien Phu.

This account covers the first four months of that cruel year.

Often in the poetic collective memory of a people, sometimes under the colder and more stringent gaze of historians, the capture, loss or recapture of a city casts a dark shadow over a whole epoch. When a city becomes the capital, the nerve center of administrative, financial, cultural and military networks, to capture that city is to seize power. The sack of Corinth by the Romans in 146 B.C. marks the end of the Greeks' independence and preeminence in the ancient Mediterranean world. The sack of Rome by the Visigoths in A.D. 410, though the Empire had long been falling apart, stands like a milestone between two epochs. Off to liberate the Holy Sepulchre, the Crusaders, urged on by the Venetians in 1204, cheerfully pillage Constantinople, the most prestigious Christian city of the time; history takes a strange turn. Granada is torn from the Moorish grasp in 1492; a civilization ebbs. Napoleon abandons Moscow in 1812; French defeat seems assured. Capitals occupied more than once, like Paris in 1814 or 1940, stand more heroic when successfully defended—as at the battle of the Marne—than when yielded to the enemy. In 1939, Madrid falls; the Spanish War is over, prelude to or rehearsal for World War II. For Europe that war will end with Stalin's soldiers raising the Red flag on the Reichstag

3

in Berlin. In 1942, when the Japanese took over in Singapore, the West seemed to bow before the Orient, Europe before Asia.

Fifteen years after its fall, Saigon too is emblematic of a fundamental historic moment, and a true first: with the support of the Soviet Union, Red China and other satellite states, in 1975 a small totalitarian country, Vietnam, forced a powerful democracy, the United States, to beat a retreat—the triumph of a closed society over an open society, and thus over *all* democracies. When I finished this book, I wondered whether that triumph was a "definitive victory." In 1987, communism seemed irreversible. Then came Gorbachevism—whatever that turns out to be. Even in Vietnam, one of the staunchest Stalinist régimes with China, North Korea, Romania, and Albania, leaders *talked* about glasnost and perestroika. The Hanoi gerontocrats and their heirs have always promised reforms but never delivered them. *Perhaps* Vietnam will also turn into another democratic society. Perhaps the whole of Asia, including red—or bloody—China, will see "the end of history." About Vietnam, I can only state my hopes. Like many of my Vietnamese friends, left and right, I doubt whether bloodshed will be avoided *there*.

No chronicle is pure and incorrupt. Events are not altogether reducible to words. Even using documents, testimonies, reports, cables, dispatches, radio broadcasts, films, letters, diaries, a journalist recreating a day, or a historian piecing together a year in the past, cannot abandon all subjectivity—he selects and orders events, and sets them in perspective to tell a story of History. This by no means proves that "objectivity does not exist," as a currently overworked phrase has it.

The journalistic approach and historical method are essentially no different. The historian steps back, keeps his distance and has plenty of time. But the journalist can ask questions of the living. Each filters truth through his own sensibilities, which he must know well and control. Raymond Aron has written, "Each of us is for himself the nearest and most mysterious of beings." Why did I want to investigate and reexamine this complex chain of events in 1975?

I covered that war from 1965 to 1973. It affected me, in all meanings of that word, more than any other war, as it did my colleagues. I was granted visas—journalist's privilege—for Hanoi grudgingly, for Saigon easily; and most important, in 1973 I made my way into the Provisional Revolutionary Government's (PRG) zone down by Ca Mau, along with my friend Ron Moreau, a *Newsweek* Saigon correspondent.

We arrived unannounced, so worked without benefit of a carefully guided tour. Ron speaks Vietnamese so well that his jokes entertained these revolutionary guerrillas; I knew North Vietnam; we worked together. My views of the war changed radically. The uneasiness I'd felt during my visit to North Vietnam the previous year precipitated out, as if chemically.

I came back convinced that I'd been wrong. With a few faint reservations in the *Nouvel Observateur*, a French weekly, I had defended what seemed a movement of national liberation and the last stage of an anticolonialist battle; I discovered, a bit late, that the PRG in the South was the secular and ideological arm of the communist government in Hanoi. Had I been to some extent a victim of what Jean-François Revel calls "the totalitarian temptation"?

To paraphrase Edgar Morin, I had at any rate militated to establish a regime in Saigon that I condemned in Prague or Budapest. By their sympathy for at first the PRG and then Hanoi, partisans of the noncommunist left were blinded by anger. Then our perception of communist systems, mainly the North Vietnamese, verged on the spiritual. Our assessment of anticommunist regimes, mainly the South Vietnamese, verged on demonology. We did not think of Uncle Ho as the Holy Ghost, but Thieu was Lucifer. We were dreaming, you see, of "socialism with a human face" in Southeast Asia.

Some are still dreaming of it.

At the word "Vietnam" innumerable images and faces rush in on me, pell-mell, insistent. That contract American officer on Black Virgin Mountain, commanding a company of Cambodian mercenaries . . . Nguyen Minh, my interpreter in Hanoi during my first stay in the austere because poverty-stricken capital. Minh pulled us out of bad trouble, Gerard Chaliand and me, on Route 1 with U.S. fighter bombers prowling above . . . Thieu, sleek and smiling, taking a shot of me with his Polaroid in Independence Palace . . . The horrors of war . . . South Vietnamese wounded at Danang, North Vietnamese wounded at Phat Diem . . . Progressive priests here, crusader priests there . . . Everywhere orphaned babies, unloved, endlessly rocking from side to side, a syndrome familiar to pediatricians . . . Soldiers of all armies, in gut-wrenching fear but impassive—in short, brave, all of them . . . The warmth of meals shared with American or South Vietnamese soldiers, North Vietnamese or Vietcong. One side offered Winstons, the other Dien Bien Phus . . . Pham Van Dong, lordly, calling you "cher ami" in a Quai d'Orsay tone . . . Peasants and city folk, all waiting for peace but not the same peace their governments awaited. Ah, the bitter mauve mildness of twilights and dawns, north and south, during respites from the war . . . Political expert Ton That Thien between his quiet analyses and his exotic fish in Saigon, public relations expert Nguyen Khac Vien propagandizing his visitors in Hanoi. Both wonderfully fluent in French . . .

I hope my account was written with the detachment that time and distance inevitably impose, but with passion also. I wanted to understand, and also to make my excuses without absolving myself.

I have not, I hope, reduced the North Vietnamese to the role or dimensions of dehumanized marionettes. We must render unto Caesar the things that are Hanoi's: an inordinate will, megalomaniacal, a kind of heroism, implacable and unquestionable, along with a fabulous ignorance of the world beyond its borders.

On one side the collective leadership in Hanoi functions like a cold diehard monster, "the State's intelligence personified," in Clausewitz's phrase, master of the three symbiotic war fronts, diplomacy, politics and combat. On the other side in Saigon we see the decline and fall of a regime obstructed and then abandoned, whose leaders, sometimes pathetic, often unaware, are caught in the multiple snares of American democracy's political and bureaucratic intrigues.

You may be surprised at accounts of certain deliberations, almost always secret, among Hanoi's civilian and military leadership: these conversations, decisions and arguments were passed along by communist writers, and most of all by North Vietnamese generals Van Tien Dung and Tran Van Tra. When they are not tongue-tied by doctrine, these two officers are gifted with a literary style and, sometimes, a frankness, even a sense of humor, rare among communist leaders, at least in public or in writing. Some former Vietnamese communists, once stationed in Hanoi or embassies, also enlightened me. I have almost always noted my sources. Certain informants insisted on anonymity: several Vietnamese, mainly because they feared reprisals against their families; Poles, Americans, Frenchmen, others too. Discretion, modesty, a preference for anonymity or professional caution were overriding.

About names, given names and patronymics: at the risk of offending Vietnamese who have adopted the Occidental system, I have not been consistent. We say *Thieu, Big Minh, Pham Van Dong, Ho Chi Minh.* In a Vietnamese's full name, the last word is his given name. *Thieu, Minh, Dong* are given names. When we say *Thieu* it is a bit as if we wrote *Charles* when speaking of General de Gaulle or *Margaret* for Mrs. Thatcher. An added difficulty for the Western eye and ear: there are few given names and patronymics in Vietnam. You will meet Nguyen Cao *Ky*, the dashing marshal of the South Vietnamese air force, but also Nguyen *Ky*, a political prisoner in the North. I ease the reader's way by specifying always who precisely is in question. When a character appears for the first time, I give his full name: *Can Van Vien*, chairman of the joint chiefs of staff; from then on I use his given name: *Vien*. Vietnamese readers will understand that I could not use the five Vietnamese accents without risking unintentional humor. In Vietnamese, not only does the meaning of a word change according to accent, but even with the same accent a word can take more than one meaning, depending on the phrase in which it occurs.

One wish: that those who read this chronicle, "right" or "left" or elsewhere, question their own attitudes, their opinions yesterday and today on Vietnam—Vietnam, pretty well forgotten now except when a junk overloaded with boat people finds a port or a ship that will accept these admirable but indeed troubling passengers. Who can flatter himself that his conscience is perfectly clear? Reread, certain articles in the conservative press of 1975 would astonish even their authors. There were anti-Americans everywhere.

Apropos of the Spanish Civil War, Malraux said that the communists supported the communists, and the fascists supported Franco, but democracies never helped the democrats. European democrats forgot about Vietnamese democrats. There were no fascists in South Vietnam. Did the West think any deeper than European clichés about the Saigon regime, a semi-democracy?

The fall of Saigon was not classic, but it remains instructive, whatever happens in the communist world, with or without Gorbachev.

Preface to the English Language Edition

Like the Berlin wall, the bamboo wall will fall: the question is not *if* but *when*. In one month, or ten years, revolution against communism will come to Hanoi and Ho Chi Minh City as it did to Warsaw, Budapest, Prague, and Bucharest. It would not be completely illogical to claim that China, North Korea, Vietnam, and Albania will remain socialist and Stalinist until doomsday but it is highly unlikely.

Western powers, especially the United States and France, had better prepare. Think-tanks must put to themselves and to their governments a question: what should we do about Vietnam today or tomorrow, when the Vietnamese rebel?

In Paris and London and Washington, it seems bureaucrats and diplomats think the West should help the Hanoi gerontocrats to "liberalize" the régime. What they don't understand is that communist systems are by nature totalitarian. Their rulers don't decide to change: the people do. Communist systems do not reform themselves: economic bankruptcy and the "masses" push the leaders forward. For all his virtues, events have moved Gorbachev, not vice versa.

Direct economic aid to Hanoi would only prolong the survival of another communist government. Vietnamese families may be helped by sending money and parcels directly to them. We can help the people, but we should not prolong the agony of communism in Vietnam by helping the existing government. There is no such thing as democratic communism, or socialism with a human face.

What will Westerners do when the Vietnamese revolt? In 1989, Roland

9

Dumas, French foreign affairs minister—a bit late, after events in Romania—suggested that the international commonwealth of free nations should invent a new legal concept, the right and "duty to interfere"—*le devoir d'ingérence*. How and when in Vietnam? Now in 1990, M. Dumas is less sanguine about the practical implications of his conceptual speculations.

Many writers—Peter Braestrup, David Butler, Frank Snepp, among other Americans—have described the 1975 debacle from various different political and moral points of view. I once heard Raymond Aron say that Americans like Paxton had no business studying Vichy France. Anglo-Saxons, I hope, will allow a Frenchman to offer still another view on Hanoi's victory of fifteen years ago.

If they are not destroyed, sooner or later, Hanoi's archives will allow us all to dig deeper into Vietnamese history. I stand by my account, ready to be corrected some day by documents and witnesses to be revealed in Moscow, Budapest, and Warsaw, perhaps even in Beijing.

Americans, notwithstanding My-Lai and other abominations, should not feel ashamed of their efforts in Vietnam. The United States probably should not have gone in alone, and the war should have been conducted differently, but Americans must not allow Hanoi to work on an American guilt complex. Had the South Vietnamese and the Americans won the war, the anticommunist revolution would have spread to North Vietnam in 1989 or 1990. Cambodia might have been spared the Red Khmer bloodbath. A united Vietnam would be developing politically and economically.

The American withdrawal or defeat postponed the democratic process in the whole of "Indochina."

Olivier Todd
1990

Some Important Dates
Before 1975

After a thousand years of Chinese occupation, innumerable internecine conflicts and a century of independence, the Vietnamese are conjoined to the "Indochinese Union" by the French in 1887. The Union comprises Tonkin, Annam and Cochin-China, as well as part of Cambodia. In 1893 the French add Laos.

1930

Ho Chi Minh founds the Indochinese Communist Party in Hong Kong.

1944

December 22: Vo Nguyen Giap begins operations against the French.

1945

August 16: Ho Chi Minh creates a Committee of Vietnamese National Liberation. Emperor Bao Dai abdicates. Ho Chi Minh forms a provisional government.

September 2: Flanked by American officers in Hanoi, Ho Chi Minh proclaims the Democratic Republic of Vietnam.

September 24: General Leclerc arrives in Saigon.

1946

Ho Chi Minh signs an agreement with France which recognizes the Democratic Republic of Vietnam, an integral part of the French Union within the framework of an Indochinese federation.

June 1: The Fontainebleau Conference, attended by Ho Chi Minh, is to clarify the status of the new nation. The conference bogs down because Admiral Thierry d'Argenlieu proclaims a separate Cochin-Chinese government.

November: The "pacification," or bombardment, of Hanoi by French Admiral Thierry d'Argenlieu.

December 19: In Hanoi, Ho Chi Minh's troops attack the French. The first Indochinese war begins.

1947

April: The Vietminh, losing all their cities in Tonkin and Annam, withdraw to the mountains north of Hanoi.

1948

June 5: Treaty of the Baie d'Along (Halong Bay). Bao Dai becomes Vietnamese chief of state, but none of his successive governments wins popular support.

1950

January 14: Ho Chi Minh announces that the only legal government in Vietnam is his Democratic Republic of Vietnam.

February: For practical purposes, Vietnam is divided in two.

August 3: The 35-man U.S. Military Assistance Advisory Group arrives in Vietnam.

1954

May 7: Dien Bien Phu falls.

May 8: The conference convenes in Geneva. The Chinese and Soviets put pressure on Ho Chi Minh's envoys to accept partition at the 17th parallel.

July 20: While Pierre Mendès-France is prime minister, the French and the Vietnamese communists sign the Geneva Accord on "a cease-fire and cessation of hostilities in Vietnam." The Americans do not ratify the final declaration. After almost eight years of war, there is a cease-fire throughout Indochina. There are 342 Americans in South Vietnam.

August: One million refugees, most of them Catholic, flee the North.

August 8: The National Security Council in Washington concludes that the Geneva Accord is "a disaster" that may lead "to the loss of Southeast Asia."

November 20: Pierre Mendès-France returns from Washington. The command of the Vietnamese national army is transferred to the Vietnamese government, and the Americans assume responsibility for its training. The French expeditionary force pulls out.

1955

October 26: Ngo Dinh Diem proclaims the Republic of South Vietnam. He is president, prime minister, minister of defense and commander in chief of the armed forces.

December: Except for coal mines and Hanoi's transport system, almost all the 150 French corporations in North Vietnam are nationalized without compensation.

1956

April 28: The last French soldier leaves Vietnam. The French military mission for the navy and the air force will leave a year later.

1959

May: U.S. military advisers are assigned to the South Vietnamese army at regimental level.

1960

December 20: Hanoi announces the establishment of the National Front for the Liberation of South Vietnam (the NLF).

1961

December 11: The first U.S. helicopters arrive in Vietnam, with 400 men.

1962

October 15: U.S. helicopters and crews go into battle against Vietcong units.

1963

November 2: President Ngo Dinh Diem is assassinated. The coup has U.S. Ambassador Henry Cabot Lodge's prior blessing. There follows a series of putsches and South Vietnamese governments.

1964

July 14: North Vietnamese officers take command of some Vietcong units.

September 18: Two companies of North Vietnamese infantry intervene in Quang Tri province, south of the 17th parallel.

1965

February 22: General Westmoreland requests two battalions of U.S. marines to protect U.S. bases at Danang.

April 7: President Johnson announces that he is ready to open peace talks "without preconditions."

June: The first Australian contingent arrives.

November 27: The Pentagon informs President Johnson that U.S. forces in Vietnam will have to be increased from 120,000 to 400,000. They will eventually number over half a million.

1966

February 15: In response to a letter from Ho Chi Minh asking that he use his influence, President de Gaulle outlines the French position on Vietnam: the Geneva Accord of 1954 should be applied, and the Vietnamese government should pursue a policy of strict neutrality.

September 4: Through spokesman William Bundy the United States rejects de Gaulle's proposal that America announce the unilateral withdrawal of its troops.

1967

January 24: Orders from the Pentagon: American pilots are forbidden to bomb targets within nine kilometers of Hanoi.

September 3: Nguyen Van Thieu is reelected president of the Republic of Vietnam.

1968

January 30: On the first day of the Tet holiday, Vietcong troops, supported by a large number of regular North Vietnamese units, attack thirty-seven big cities. They take Hue, Dalat, Kontum, Quang Tri. Nineteen Vietcong hold part of the U.S. Embassy in Saigon for six hours. On February 10 the general offensive is largely repulsed, though the recapture of Hue takes a month. Militarily the offensive is a check to North Vietnam, but politically and psychologically it is a disaster for the Americans.

May: The North Vietnamese arrive in Paris for negotiations.

May 5: A second large-scale communist offensive.

May 9: Thieu announces that even if the United States negotiates with the enemy, he will never recognize the NLF.

1969

June 10: Creation of the Provisional Revolutionary Government (PRG) of South Vietnam.

1972

January 25: Richard Nixon discloses that Henry Kissinger has been negotiating secretly with the North Vietnamese in France since 1969.

February 21: President Nixon visits China, to Hanoi's intense dissatisfaction.

March 30: The North Vietnamese launch a major offensive in South Vietnam.

April 4: The United States renews the bombing of North Vietnam after a pause of three and a half years.

May 22: Nixon visits the Soviet Union.

October 8: In Paris North Vietnamese negotiator Le Duc Tho accepts, for the first time, a plan that does not exclude President Thieu.

November 7: Nixon is reelected.

December 12: Thieu still opposes the "false peace" detailed in Paris.

December 16: Kissinger announces that the Paris talks are stalled.

December 18: Renewal of raids on North Vietnam by B-52s and other aircraft.

1973

January 8: Kissinger and Le Duc Tho come to an agreement in Paris.

January 15: An end to all bombing of North Vietnam.

January 21: Thieu agrees to sign the Paris Agreement.

March 15: The United States protests to Hanoi about the illegal infiltration of troops and materiel into South Vietnam. Kissinger advises Nixon to resume the bombing of North Vietnam. Nixon refuses.

March 29: The last American prisoners are released in Hanoi.

April 3: Presidents Nixon and Thieu meet at San Clemente in California.

April 25: Discussions among the Vietnamese factions in Paris on the future of their country. Impasse.

August 15: Implementation of a congressional resolution interdicting all American bombing or "military action" in Southeast Asia.

October 16: The Nobel Peace Prize is awarded jointly to Kissinger and Le Duc Tho; the latter declines it.

1974

August 9: Richard Nixon ceases to be president of the United States. Vice-President Gerald Ford succeeds him.

December 3: South Vietnamese intelligence agencies predict that the communists will resume fighting.

December 31: The South Vietnamese government announces that 80,000 people have been killed during the past year—more than in any other year of the war.

A Few Useful
Abbreviations

AFP: Agence France-Presse.

ARVN: Army of the Republic of South Vietnam.

DIA: Defense Intelligence Agency (Pentagon).

DMZ: Demilitarized Zone along the 17th parallel.

DRV: Democratic Republic of Vietnam—North Vietnam.

GVN: Government of (South) Vietnam.

ICCS: International Commission of Control and Supervision. It comprises Hungarians, Poles, Indonesians and Iranians. Established by the Paris Agreement of 1973 and assigned to assure implementation of the cease-fire.

MR: Military region. South Vietnam was divided into four of these, MR 1, etc. They were also known as I Corps, II Corps, etc.

NLF: National Liberation Front. Under Hanoi's control, but in theory independent. Battles for the "liberation" of the South from 1960 on.

NVA: North Vietnamese Army.

NVG: North Vietnamese government.

PRG: Provisional Revolutionary Government (of South Vietnam). A product of the NLF; replaces it nationally and internationally starting in 1969. Like the Algerians, the Vietnamese substitute a *government* for a *front*, but the PRG is teleguided by the North. Hanoi has always refused to create a permanent governmental structure representing South Vietnam, as that would ratify the partition of Vietnam.

    The fictive presence of the PRG will prove extremely useful—as will be seen—in 1975.

VC: Vietcong. The NVG's South Vietnamese partisans.

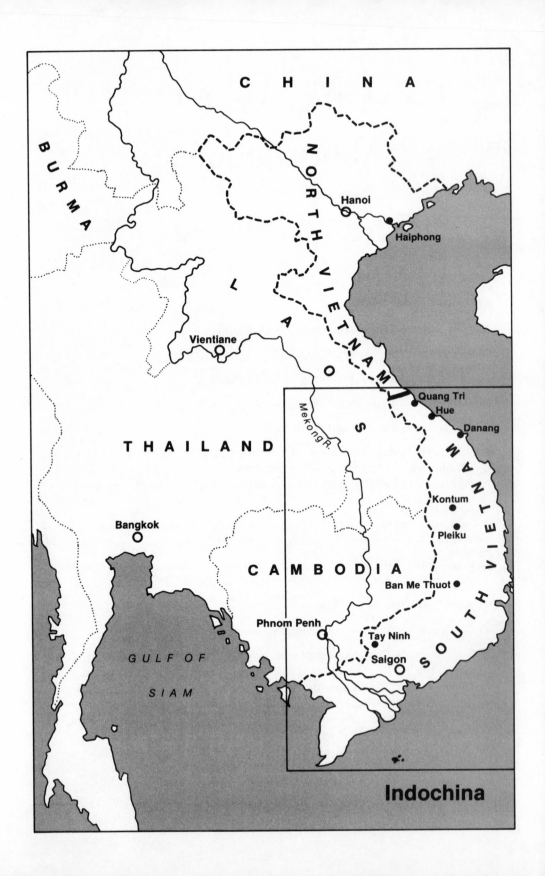

Indochina

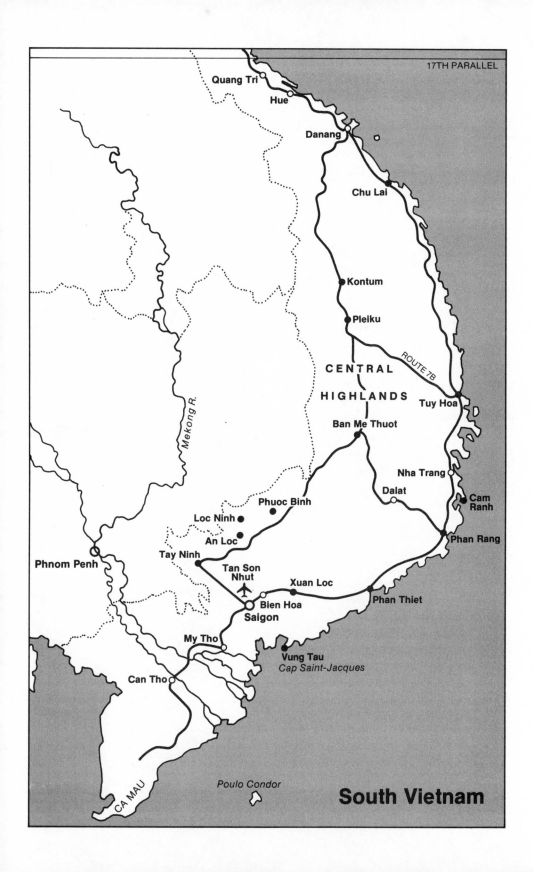

Quang Tri

Hue

Danang

Chu Lai

Kontum

Pleiku

C E N T R A L

H I G H L A N D S

Tuy Hoa

ROUTE 7B

Ban Me Thuot

Nha Trang

Dalat

Cam
Ranh

Phuoc Binh

Loc Ninh

An Loc

Phan Rang

Tay Ninh

Mekong R.

Tan Son
Nhut

Xuan Loc

Phan Thiet

Bien Hoa

Saigon

Phnom Penh

My Tho

Vung Tau
Cap Saint-Jacques

Can Tho

CA MAU

Poulo Condor

South Vietnam

1

Hanoi-Saigon:
1789 Kilometers

Toward 6 A.M. Saigon time, on January 1, 1975—year of the Tiger, month of the Buffalo, hour of the Cat, by the Vietnamese lunar calendar—nineteen rockets of Soviet manufacture detonate in Bien Hoa province, about twenty kilometers north of Saigon. One rocket blasts through the thatched roof of a house where Nguyen Van Be is sleeping. Killed immediately, this young man of sixteen is the first official civilian death in South Vietnam that year. Be was hoping to become a biologist.

In theory, since midnight Greenwich Mean Time on January 27, 1973, as fixed by the Paris Agreement on "the end of the war and the re-establishment of peace in Viet-nam,"* a cease-fire is in place—the most murderous truce this century. In 1974, 14,000 South Vietnamese soldiers and 7,000 civilians died in the course of military operations, according to carefully tabulated statistics issued by the U.S. Embassy in Saigon. The body count of North Vietnamese was 57,000, more corpses, more testimony to this phony armistice.

At the U.S. Embassy (a concrete block adjoining the French Embassy) on this New Year's Day, no cable of any importance arrives from the White House or the State Department. President Gerald Ford and his wife are frolicking in the snow near a chalet high in the Rocky Mountains. U.S. Secretary of State Henry Kissinger is ending a sunny vacation at Vice-President Nelson Rockefeller's house in Puerto Rico. In Saigon, diplomats

---

* See Appendix I.

of the political section on the first floor of the embassy, and CIA officials on the top floor, are debating possibilities. Some think the year will be calm; others are more worried. In December the consolidated intelligence report justified any forecast: "Communist military forces in South Vietnam are more powerful than ever before. . . . We believe that the communists will commit part of their strategic reserve to exploit major vulnerabilities in the South Vietnamese position. . . . It is even possible that . . . the communists will move to an all-out offensive."[1] So much for the defeatists.

"But our best judgment now," explains the same report, "is that they will not do so. . . . Hanoi prefers to achieve its dry season goals through a military-political campaign that avoids the risks and losses of an all-out offensive." So much for the optimists.

Analysts in the intelligence community take many factors into account, primarily the weather. For centuries decisive battles in Vietnam have taken place before the rainy season. The monsoon begins in May. Torrents rise in spates in the Central Highlands. Beneath the triple canopy of jungle, the soil becomes spongy. Paddy on the plain is drowned. Everywhere trucks, heavy artillery and tanks bog down. Leaden cloud cover grounds helicopters often and fighters almost always. Earth, air and water conspire to bar men from hunting down and killing one another. The monsoon gives enemies time to pull themselves together. For thirty years of war, brotherly adversaries have ignored the siesta, but both sides bow before the monsoon. Patrick Hays, 6'1" tall, short hair, clear blue eyes, a graduate of St. Cyr and a sublieutenant active in the Algerian putsch, suffers real nostalgia for his First Overseas Airborne Regiment. Twelve years ago Hays came to Vietnam as an assistant on a plantation. Now he directs all Michelin's operations. His Vietnamese wife was a television star. Hays speaks Vietnamese fluently. He travels the countryside often. He is well informed. His position naturally suggests, to super-shrewd journalists or diplomats, that he is an agent of the French secret service; this Hays denies with a laugh. For several days he has had no radio contact with the smallest of the Michelin plantations—3,000 hectares, 1.4 million rubber trees, 500 employees—in the province of Phuoc Long, about a hundred kilometers north of the capital. The communist troops—"les Viets," says Hays, like most of the French in Indochina—have taken two outposts on Route 311, south of the plantation and the provincial capital, Phuoc Binh.

In mid-December Hays held long talks there with the plantation foreman and the district chief. Their hearts were in their boots. They talked about mass troop movements of North Vietnamese regulars, not about the usual guerrilla resistance, the Provisional Revolutionary Government of South Vietnam, or PRG.

In Saigon, in his office near the Cercle Sportif, the athletic club he serves as general secretary, Hays noted: "The communists may very well attack the weak spot in Phuoc Binh, namely the old city . . . and the runway for heavy aircraft. . . . Defense is complicated by the presence of 25,000 civilians. . . . The government's resources are much feebler than in 1972."[2]

Well, it's not the first time a garrison has fallen. Contact with the plantation has often been broken. The Sino-Vietnamese foreman is a wily one; he'll pull through one more time. Part of this forsaken province, backed up against Cambodia, belongs to the communists by night and the Saigon government by day. Let's keep cool and set this minor incident in a larger perspective. Vietnam has taught us never to give up hope. For Hays the Paris Agreement offered reasonable hope of survival for free Vietnam: If the communists "pulled the plug" the Americans would send them B-52s. For Hays the war was won in 1970. Before that the province swarmed with guerrillas. In 1971 there were hardly any left. You could drive country roads in safety. After that the situation deteriorated again, little by little. Now to reach Saigon Hays must send his latex convoys by way of Ban Me Thuot to the north. A 1,000-kilometer detour. The trucks can proceed from the plantation straight to the capital only when the road has been "opened" by an operation that requires a whole battalion.

Nguyen Van Thieu, president of the Republic of Vietnam, holds audience at Independence Palace, of banal but comfortable modern architecture. Agustini Manglia, ambassador from the Philippines, dean of the diplomatic corps, is speaking: "There's a feeling of optimism now. An acceptable accommodation brightens our horizon."

Approving nods from the audience.

This month the Iranian delegate presides over the International Commission of Control and Supervision, the ICCS. He proves less cheerful: "I hope the Paris Agreement will be observed."

Equally approving nods.

Iranian, Indonesian, Polish and Hungarian soldiers and civilians on the ICCS are under orders to report violations of the cease-fire. They know that Hanoi's troops, like Saigon's, observe Article 2, on the cease-fire, no more than they do most of the twenty-three articles in the agreement signed in 1973. Both sides proceed with caution. They gain ground gnawing and nibbling. They take, lose, retake a hamlet or a paddy. Nevertheless the level of combat remains "acceptable"—above all to the Americans, who have no more combat troops in Vietnam.

In Saigon itself peace reigns, strictly speaking. No attempted assassinations, no rockets. Tourists arrive by Air France, Thai International, Cathay Pacific Airways. Some take advantage of a week's tour offered by Air Vietnam. For 27,000 piastres they can hop as far as Dalat, a truly beautiful city in a gentle climate. At the Saigon track there are eight races on the card. A hot horse: Phuong Dung. Ten days ago a new restaurant opened: the New Carina. Saigon is not burning.

A good part of le tout-Saigon cocktails, sups, dances, but not in the International House nightclub, closed for repairs. Its management apologizes by an announcement in the *Saigon Post*, the English-language daily subsidized by the CIA: "We are redecorating, and replacing the air-conditioners." Investors are busy in the capital. U.S. embassy personnel sometimes discuss a serious problem: where to build the future Hyatt luxury hotel.

At the CIA club in the Hotel Duc groups dine at small tables. Among the guests are Graham Martin, the patrician American ambassador, and his counterparts Nara of Japan and Aran of Israel. The anagrams are amusing: Aran, Nara. Thomas Polgar is there too, chief of the CIA mission in Vietnam, the most complex listening post in the world; and Frank Snepp, a young analyst with "the Company," traditional nickname for the CIA. They're talking economics. South Vietnam's economy would hold up well if not for the sharp rise in oil prices.

They jeer at the misadventures of the South Vietnamese Fifth Division's former commander. He broke and fled in Cambodia. They're flying him back to Phnom Penh. He and fourteen other officers will be tried for bribery. Around the tables at the Hotel Duc there is more talk of the Saigon government's tortuous political problems than of military matters. For the first time in four years Catholic students are demonstrating in the city, distributing leaflets. After a shoving match, the police drive a hundred or so back toward a church.

In its editorial the *Song Than*, a Vietnamese daily, states, "1975: [presidential] election year. One way or another, our system of leadership must be improved."

They comment on news items. A captain assigned to general headquarters, Le Van Nga, has put a bullet through his head, leaving a note for President Thieu. It seems the captain killed himself "to support the Buddhist cause." According to a military spokesman, the officer "acted for purely religious reasons." Doubtless the captain was excessively moved by recent deliberations of the Sixth Buddhist Congress. This congress expressed regret that the authorities were "not making greater efforts to promote the national reconciliation and concord provided for by the Paris Agreement."

Ordinary people—those whom Joinville would have called "Our Lord's humble folk"—are not partying. The Vietnamese New Year's Day, Tet, comes in February. The middle and upper-middle classes, Westernized, Frenchified, Americanized, celebrate January 1st less boisterously than the Americans, French, Poles and Hungarians on duty in Vietnam. Friends foregather and gossip. The young people play records; they adore the popular singer Trinh Con Son:

> *At night cannon fire reaches the city,*
> *The street cleaner stops to listen.*
> *Cannon fire wakes the mother.*

Cannon fire wakes the child,
Who gazes sadly at the mountain lit up by flares.

Chez Givral, across from the Hotel Continental, the Three Musketeers—as Saigon's reporters call them—meet over a good cup of coffee: charming M. Vuong, dignified Pham Xuan An and Cao Giao, whose goatee reminds everyone of Ho Chi Minh. Giao freelances for *Newsweek*. An, on the regular payroll at *Time*, the only Vietnamese journalist drawing an American salary, is very well informed and highly respected. The Three Musketeers wonder aloud. "A friend of mine has a cousin who works on the Michelin plantation," says Cao Giao, "and this cousin claims the North Vietnamese have tanks, T-72s and T-54s."

An has his doubts: "I think the communists are mounting an attack on Tay Ninh."[3]

Tay Ninh is the Holy See of the Cao Dai sect. They venerate Victor Hugo and Sun Yat-sen, among other saints, in their kaleidoscopic rococo wedding cake of a temple.

Three thousand kilometers from Saigon, on the island of Okinawa, between Formosa and Japan, Captain Cyril Moyher is bored.

A marine, thirty years old, assigned now to logistics, Moyher ordinarily commands a combat training unit at Camp Lejeune. His wife and children are in Jacksonville, North Carolina. The Marine Corps is close with its money. Families do not accompany officers. Thirteen months on Okinawa is not much fun. The island is host to ground installations, an air base, port facilities. With a little help from routine, a career soldier far from his family can turn into a drunk, a woman chaser or a religious fanatic, Moyher thinks. Because the U.S. armed forces like their officers to plug away at college courses, Moyher is studying for his bachelor's degree. He's majoring in systems analysis. That's all the rage. If his outfit, the Seventh Signal Battalion, takes part in maneuvers scheduled for February in the Philippines, the captain will leave his textbooks behind. Vietnam is no longer on his horizon. In Saigon a detachment of 159 Marines is in charge of security. Moyhers doesn't envy them.

The captain trains his recruits and crams for his college courses. In the mess they're saying the maneuvers will probably be postponed until March.

Twenty-two thousand kilometers from Saigon, the White House in Washington signs into law S.3418, reinforcing the right to privacy.

Gerald Ford has been president since the resignation five months before, in August 1974, of Richard Nixon, drowned by Watergate. The new president has inherited a shaky economy, high rates of inflation and interest, a demoralized Stock Exchange and 5 million unemployed. Ford seems to be a victim of Murphy's Law: what can go wrong will go wrong.

Vietnam is almost the private preserve of the secretary of state, Henry Kissinger.

Over this New Year's the ongoing serial in Washington is the CIA's illegal activities. They planned to assassinate Castro in the 1960s. They have no right to operate within the United States; nevertheless, they've established files on 10,000 American citizens. They've engaged in "electronic surveillance," a euphemism for bugs on your phone. They've also ferreted through private correspondence. These dubious practices, the family skeletons, fascinate the press, and somewhat less readers and television viewers. In his Oval Office, the president often receives the head of the CIA, William Colby, a subtle man with a pastor's face, a Princeton graduate and hero of World War II. Colby spends more time explaining his agents' "mistakes" than analyzing the situation in Vietnam. Ford himself is busier with the fallout from Watergate than with Vietnam. He hoped to defuse the scandal by pardoning Nixon. Week after week the capital wallows in Watergate. After deliberating for fifteen hours, a jury finds three former close associates of Nixon—John Ehrlichman, Bob Haldeman and John Mitchell—"guilty of conspiracy to obstruct justice." The capital is living in the immediate past and present.

Harried by reporters as well as congressmen and senators, Ford pays little attention to problems in distant Vietnam. To investigate the CIA's activities he has appointed a commission, chaired by Vice-President Nelson Rockefeller. Ronald Reagan, who has just completed a term as governor of California, is on the commission.

Intelligence reports are rewritten, condensed, the cream skimmed to produce abstracts for the president's desk. There are too many competing reports and agencies. The CIA[4] reports to the White House and to the National Security Council, directed by General Brent Scowcroft, Kissinger's ally.

The Pentagon's intelligence service[5] is responsible to Secretary of Defense James Schlesinger, on bad terms with Kissinger, and to the Joint Chiefs of Staff at the Pentagon.

Each arm—air force, navy, army and marines—supervises its own intelligence bureau. The State Department also has a bureau, more political.[6] Decoding and interception of allied or enemy communications are Defense's responsibility.

In principle these bureaucracies are coordinated by the director of central intelligence.[7] From the common effort emerge syntheses. The last one, December's, read by Ford, is an ambiguous and prudent compromise. Nothing alarmist: "All things considered," it does not seem that the North Vietnamese are about to launch a grand offensive.

No one in Washington has paid any attention to a cable from Wolfgang Lehmann, minister-counselor and second in command at the U.S. Embassy in Saigon.[8] Lehmann emphasizes the presence of General Viktor Kulikov, a Soviet deputy minister of defense, in Hanoi in December.

Lehmann does not believe that this Soviet is visiting the North Vietnamese capital simply to represent Moscow at the thirtieth anniversary of the North Vietnamese army. "It is doubtful that Kulikov will spend the rest of his time singing Christmas carols." In South Vietnam there are now numbers of dead and wounded recalling "the daily average casualty rate during the 1972 offensive." Lehmann notes that "Soviet deputy defense minister [Pavel] Batitsky led a group of Soviet anti-aircraft experts on visits to Hanoi one week before the opening of the NVA 1972 spring offensive." At that time the North Vietnamese mounted massive attacks that failed. Classified "confidential," the counselor's cable remains just that.

Another of the embassy staff is also dissatisfied with Washington's views on Vietnam. Head of the CIA in Saigon, Thomas Polgar has read through the first version of December's synthesis. To his mind, Washington's analysts are not "with it." They seem to predict a long-term general offensive by North Vietnam "1914-style," across the demilitarized zone on the 17th parallel, between the two Vietnams: "We fear that the authors [of the synthesis], trying to arrive at a balanced judgment, have underestimated the potential—indeed, the probability—of intense communist activity in the coming months." Polgar adds, "There is no reason to believe that the next big offensive will resemble that of 1972. . . . Several factors indicate that there will be a large-scale military operation."[9] Polgar bases his view on concentrations of North Vietnamese troops, convoy movements along the whole network of the Ho Chi Minh trail and interrogations of prisoners.

In Washington they're assuming the North Vietnamese will mount a large-scale military operation in 1976, year of the U.S. presidential election. The last two big offensives by Hanoi, in 1963 and 1972, seem to establish an implicit precedent in communist politico-military strategy.

This opinion prevails at the State Department, too. On the seventh (Kissinger's) floor, Douglas Pike, a gruff bearish man and distinguished Vietnamese specialist, thinks, like most of the secretary's advisers, that in the months to come the North Vietnamese will wage limited war. The "war of flags" continues: the nationalists try to plant theirs, red and yellow, in the countryside; the communists try to hoist the PRG's, blue and red, over the villages and hamlets. This bloody and underhanded game has been under way since the Paris Agreement was signed.[10]

Kissinger is not too worried. More serious problems require his attention. These last six months he has been busy mainly with the Middle East and the unstable peace that has reigned there since the Yom Kippur War. The Arabs have embarked on an arms race. Planes and missiles for Israel have had to be extracted from Congress. Kissinger is also playing mediator between the Turks and Greeks over Cyprus. The secretary of state must hold together a constantly squabbling NATO. He does not believe that Vietnam will collapse in 1975.[11]

Kissinger is quick to remind anybody that an American secretary of state considers or confronts four priorities every day: (1) the possibility of war with the Soviet Union; (2) the question of energy resources and the status of pipelines; (3) nuclear proliferation; (4) the unforeseen hot spots, the flash points.

Vietnam is no longer a priority.

Kissinger remains convinced that heating up the war in Vietnam is not in the interest of either the Soviets or the Chinese communists. The brush-fire war is guttering. It will not flame up again. In geopoliticians' jargon, the conflict will remain at "low intensity." The Soviets were easing their way toward détente before this miserable little war in Vietnam. In poor health, Leonid Brezhnev has just postponed a trip to Egypt. As for the Chinese, they have never wanted a powerful, unified Vietnam on their southern border. The New China Agency, summing up the Beijing hierarchy's attitudes in its roundup of 1974, mainly stresses Europe, the "bone of contention" disputed by the two superpowers. In the course of his trips to Beijing, Kissinger never saw the least real Chinese interest in Vietnam's welfare, despite the compulsory rhetoric.[12]

"Sixteen to eighteen hours a day," says Kissinger, "it's all you can do to keep up with these four [priorities]."

Agencies and various think tanks worry about the rest. In Southeast Asia the problem right now is Cambodia. The Khmer Rouge are closing in on Phnom Penh. No longer is the Mekong open all the way to the capital. That's probably a serious matter. Operations in Cambodia and Vietnam should not automatically be linked. Ties between the North Vietnamese communists and the Khmer Rouge are loose and difficult, as Nguyen Duc Cuc, assigned to liaison with the Khmer Rouge by the Central Committee, emphasizes in Hanoi when he chats with diplomats.[13] In the current international context, the North Vietnamese have no desire to embark on large-scale military operations, even if their final objective does remain the reunification of the two Vietnams. Kissinger has never doubted this.

Hanoiology is an art even more complex than Kremlinology or Beijingology.

In the suburbs of Hanoi, along former colonial Route 1, stands an old red and white milestone that no Frenchman can ever forget: "Saigon 1789 km."

Hanoi's climate is harsher than Saigon's. On this New Year's Day it's cold. Kieu Xuan Tien,[14] twenty-two years old, is going to the movies on Hai Ba Trung near the little lake. At 8 P.M. they're showing the first part of a Soviet film, *The Month of August*. The film's message: victory in World War II was more the Soviets' doing than anyone else's. The film is hard to follow; it's shown in its original version, with the sound too low, and behind the screen a monotonous voice translates the dialogue.

Tien, son of a doctor in the PRG—that Provisional Revolutionary Government which controls communist resistance in the South—arrived in Hanoi four years ago, after a punishing trek on foot up the Ho Chi Minh trail. His mother lives in the South. In Hanoi the young man joined his father. A film buff, he'll be sent to apprentice in East Berlin or Moscow if he pulls down good marks at the special school he's enrolled in. He dreams of becoming the Vietnamese Eisenstein. They give him passes for one dong; he can scalp them for fifteen on the black market. Tiresome, this Soviet film, but a man must improve his mind.

As he does every day—a scholarly duty—the young man has scanned the *Nhan Dan*, daily newspaper of the Lao Dong, the Workers' Party, the Vietnamese C.P. The editorial foresees "great revolutionary successes" in the year to come. Unlike his father, the young man is not a communist. Nevertheless, he trusts the newspapers and radio in the Democratic Republic of Vietnam. Nowadays they emphasize the "competition campaign." Hanoi's streets and boulevards and factories flaunt immense, superb frescoes, as naive as they are socialist realist, in faded colors: blue workers work, green soldiers fight, pink women and children cheer on workers and fighters in their "anti-imperialist battle."

In Hanoi you meet fewer foreign diplomats than in Saigon, and social life is less festive. Diplomats cannot leave the capital without official permission. They have few contacts with the Vietnamese, so live like an isolated clan. One of the loneliest is surely Mr. John Fawcett, the British ambassador. To the North Vietnamese, Great Britain is an American Trojan horse. This month Fawcett completes his one-year tour of duty in the Democratic Republic of Vietnam. He will be replaced by a chargé d'affaires, Mr. John Stewart. With suave obstinacy the authorities in Hanoi have refused, for the last twelvemonth, to accept the ambassador's letters of credit: Her Majesty's Government does not choose to recognize the Provisional Revolutionary Government of South Vietnam. For the British, the PRG is not independent. There is no good reason to establish ties with it, since doing so would only displease the Americans. The Hanoi government accepts the presence of the British diplomat without fully accrediting him: the North Vietnamese need a British representative in Hanoi to issue visas for London and above all Hong Kong. John Fawcett polishes his final report. He devotes a paragraph to the competition campaign. It is

by no means the first. Workers are invited to vie with each other in productivity and avoidance of waste. The campaign may have had some slight effect. When, however, I made a little speech, through the office interpreter, to a gang of workmen who for a week had been going conspicuously slow in the making and hanging of new doors for my outhouses—Is

this how you vie with each other to set new production records, gentlemen? Is this the way you practise thrift to speed
the building of socialism? Is this how you hope to qualify for
the honourable title of Socialist Labour Team?—they
thought it an even better joke than I did, and went even
slower for a day or two whilst they recovered from their
merriment.[15]

In this report, nothing of substance about North Vietnamese leaders'
intentions. Prudent, the British diplomat thinks these leaders will be . . .
prudent. Up against North Vietnamese communism, diplomats often take
their desires for reality. Their analyses are steeped in wishful thinking.

North of Hanoi, thirty kilometers from Lao Kay and fifty from the
Chinese frontier, a thousand prisoners spend an ordinary day in the Phong
Quang detention camp. Common felons mingle with politicals.

Political prisoner Nguyen Ky came north in 1958, fleeing the Southern
regime. Professor in a secondary school, he was a writer. They accused
him of "bourgeois nationalism" and reproached him for a "naturalist tendency." He has been imprisoned several times, last in 1964. He has just
been transferred from barracks A to barracks B. Today he is planting
cassava stems. In his short-sleeved shirt and sweater he shivers. Soldiers
armed with rifles and militiamen, pistol at the belt, watch over his group,
thirty prisoners. Ky works eight hours a day. He is racked by hunger. A
bad worker earns nine kilos of potatoes, cassava or rice per month; a good
one, fifteen kilos. Ky's production, average, earns him thirteen kilos. January 1st is not a holiday. Ky hates Sundays and holidays. Restricted to the
camp those days, you can steal nothing. Working outside you may run
across a vegetable or a few greens.[16]

In another hut in the same camp lives another prisoner, Nguyen Chi
Thien, arrested and imprisoned as often as Ky. They do not know each
other. Thien recites poems that he composes but is forbidden to set down:

> Friend, when I see you
> I will speak to you
> of cassava, of yams
> My story is tragic
> because it speaks of chains
> of firing squads
> of shame
> of treason
> This story,
> friend, will hurt your feelings
> But it will frighten the enemy
> for it is eternal

for it lasts indefinitely
for it moves the heart to pity
It is a story
Of cassava, of yams. . . .

In all the camps, from North to South, at Phong Quang as at Poulo Condor, hunger obsesses the prisoners.

Lemon Banana Orange Sugar
Peanut Beans Rice Potato
once touched by the grace
of the Party
are glorified
glorified. . . .[17]

In Saigon, diplomats estimate that prisons and camps hold between 5,000 and 30,000 political prisoners. In Hanoi, diplomats, from the East or from the West, haven't the faintest notion of the number of political detainees. In the South, the Red Cross or international commissions of inquiry can sometimes visit certain camps. In the North, never.

There is a large port-wine stain close to the arch of his left eyebrow, clearly visible below his bare forehead. His comrades have nicknamed Tran Van Ba "Coxcomb." He is not good-looking. Other friends call him "Toad." Since 1973 Ba has been president of the general association of Vietnamese students in Paris. Very anticommunist, it mocks the Saigon government, which co-opts some of its members by buying them. Ba has decided to reform the association. In a bulletin a Vietnamese student writes that Ba "is casting a ray of honesty onto a pile of shit." Ba seems as suspicious of Saigon's generals as of Hanoi's civilians. His father, Tran Van Van, was assassinated when Ba was twenty-one, no one knows by whom—agents from Hanoi or generals from Saigon? So Ba was disinclined to join the army. In principle all the young men did their military service. Exempt were war orphans, the unfit, deferred students abroad, often mon-eyed young men like Cao Anh Dung: this son of the chairman of the joint general staff is in Switzerland. 1967: Ba joins his brother in France. Living in a maid's room, he enters the first form at the Lycée Carnot and goes through the events of May 1968 in Paris amused and amazed.

At the Sorbonne and elsewhere portraits of Mao, Che and Ho Chi Minh hang like icons. To his brother, student at the national school of statistics, Ba says during the riots, "Suppose we could do this—what do you say? For our own people, in Saigon!"

Ba took a degree in economics at the college in Assas, and was assigned to practical work in Nanterre, a leftist bastion. There, a nationalist Viet-namese like him was quickly classified "fascist."

Ba is obsessed: he will work for Vietnam's salvation. To avoid the label of "rich young man" he turns ascetic. Encased in a filthy fur-lined jacket and gray jeans turning black, chewing his pipe, he lives meanly. He rejects romantic attachments. He jokes to a young woman: "If a girl could clear up this red stain on my temple, I'd marry her."

In his apartment in Bourg-la-Reine, transformed into a dormitory for his friends, he comments on day-to-day events in Saigon over sweet potatoes or plates of rice and sesame seed. At first his money was on Thieu: "With all his faults, Nyugen Van Thieu does the best possible job for the South."

But after meeting the president of the Vietnamese republic in Germany, Ba will be disillusioned: "Thieu's playing sorcerer's apprentice. With him in charge we're down the drain."

Ba takes on all comers, and is a very moralistic political militant. He explains his point of view to everybody, ignoring labels—"left," "right"— which only annoy him. To a young politician, Jacques Toubon, as to a young philosopher, André Glucksmann. Ba wants to resist disorganized hatred and blind violence, but to fight just the same. He speaks little and reads much. He walks alone in the streets of Paris. Cheerfully sarcastic about religion and religious hierarchies in Vietnam, he stops before a church, then enters. He loves churches when they're empty. He is often to be found in the rue Monge, at the offices of the student association. He listens to newcomers and old-timers alike, and works on their material problems. Many of the students are poor. Ba sways them to his beliefs: the communists are implacable and believe only in force. The PRG is only a foil, useful in packaging Hanoi politics. Forging himself a political philosophy, Ba begins with a few simple principles: to fight misery, we must create happiness; to fight poverty, we must create wealth; to confront oppression, lovers of liberty need a united front. Shy but warm, obliging, fraternal, Ba unmakes and remakes Vietnam with other students over beer in the chalet at the Parc Montsouris. Or with his brother at a billiard table in the café-tabac Le Lion at Denfert-Rochereau.

Ba ponders Adam Smith—Vietnam is wealthy; it is a nation but with no tradition of public service. Ba loves photography, pinball machines, films of friendship and solidarity in wartime—*La Grande Illusion, For Whom the Bell Tolls, The Bridge on the River Kwai.*

In January 1975, Ba and some students prepare a large evening party for the Tet holiday. Parisians, the French, Europeans, whatever their political opinions, are no longer interested in Vietnam. Ba bitterly resents this apathy, the collective mask of a bad conscience.

2

---◆---

Even the Gods Weep
for Phuoc Long

In Vietnam the names of certain cities recall a whole history, legends, an atmosphere: hectic Saigon, austere Hanoi, imperial Hue, Catholic Phat Diem. . . .

The town of Phuoc Binh, close to the Cambodian border in Phuoc Long province, means nothing, except perhaps exile for bureaucrats.

Ten years ago, a Vietcong commando unit attacked Phuoc Binh. Five American soldiers were killed and a dozen wounded. Now, since mid-December, two divisions of North Vietnamese regulars, the Third and the Seventh, are advancing on Phuoc Binh, a provincial capital, a pleasant large village in the bend of a river in the foothills of the Central Highlands. With the river lapping at steep slopes on three sides, the setting is spectacular. The province numbers no more than 50,000 inhabitants. Most of them, Montagnards, belong to the Man and Hmong tribes. No paddy here. The Montagnards live on the forest, rubber and cassava.

To the Saigonese, Phuoc Binh, 115 kilometers to the north, is like the Far West. The town is huddled along a main drag that also serves as landing strip. At the end of the strip stands city hall, topped by a spire. To either side of the street-airstrip the garrison—3,000 South Vietnamese regulars and 1,000 militiamen—is installed in barracks and straw huts.

All roads to the provincial capital are cut. The North Vietnamese have occupied the four county seats surrounding the town and are tightening the noose.

In Saigon, South Vietnamese headquarters notes these developments.

The theoretical head of the army, General Cao Van Vien, chairman of the joint general staff, is worried: northeast of Phuoc Binh rises Ba Ra Mountain, a hill 723 meters high that protects a communications center.[1]

For a long time now choppers and prop planes have been resupplying the town. Every month the airlift delivers 500 tons of rice, sugar and salt, along with gasoline and ammunition. The government and the military establishment in Saigon live by one formula—whoever holds the capital holds the province—and one statistic—the communists occupy 18 percent of Vietnamese territory and control 10 percent of the population. Check it out—after thirty years of war, no recent census, and all these peasants and refugees coming and going!

The troops converging on Phuoc Binh are unquestionably North Vietnamese (NVA) regulars. You can tell by their arms, their uniforms, green or tan, their pith helmets, their accent. The Vietcong, the PRG's troops, are turned out less formally: they lean to straw hats and black pyjamas and wear a checked terrycloth towel as a kind of ascot.

Surprising provincial headquarters as well as Saigon, the North Vietnamese commit about forty T-54 tanks south of the town at 7 A.M. on January 1. ARVN regulars stop them.

A handsome beast, seven meters long, an efficient mechanical monster, the T-54 is a medium tank. Sturdy, fairly easy to repair, weighing thirty-six tons, it can make 48 kilometers an hour and has a range of 500 kilometers. With auxiliary gas tanks it covers 700 kilometers. It carries thirty-four shells for its 100 mm. guns. The Soviets haven't supplied their allies with the more sophisticated tanks, the T-62, the T-72 or the fifty-ton T-10 with 210 mm. guns. For starters they sent the North Vietnamese their amphibious fourteen-ton PT-76. ARVN's American M-48s are far more powerful. But the T-54 is a match for the M-48.

Hanoi does not trust its tanks to the PRG's Vietcong.

North Vietnamese infantry encircles then attacks Ba Ra Mountain despite efforts at interdiction by South Vietnamese aircraft. Their pilots must come down to 1,500 meters. Shy of the dense North Vietnamese flak, they rarely fly under 3,000 meters. This is not a matter of courage. The pilots are under strict orders. They mustn't take chances with their aircraft. Visibility is good, without the mist that often hangs over the town just after dawn. The NVA sets up heavy artillery close by Ba Ra, 130 mm. guns. Soon eight ARVN 105s and four 155s are knocked out.

The day after the attack President Thieu—flanked by his vice-president, old Tran Van Huong, more lawyer than strategist, and his prime minister, the silent Tran Thien Khiem—calls together his generals. Should they reinforce Phuoc Binh? With how many troops? Or pull out?

In forty-eight hours of combat, the provincial capital's defenders knock out fifteen tanks. Nonetheless the communist infantry advances. Their tactics are a surprise. Squads of soldiers cling to the rear of the tanks. The T-54 moves up, the soldiers jump off. Often the tanks dash back to return with a new load of infantry. They fight from house to house, from straw hut to straw hut. The T-54s are reinforced with exterior armorplate. Between the armor and the body of the tank, the blast of the hollow armor-piercing shell is diffused. The South Vietnamese M-72 antitank rockets are ineffective. Sometimes the combatants are too close for time-fused rockets; they ricochet off the tank and explode harmlessly. The T-54s' crews are safe inside. The ARVN infantry can't toss grenades through the turrets.

Pounded by artillery, the emplacement's barracks, bunkers and trenches collapse.

Phuoc Binh is part of Military Region 3. Regional headquarters is at Bien Hoa, a large air base thirty kilometers north of Saigon. Its commanding officer, General Du Quoc Dong, decides to retake the town and demands reinforcements of Saigon. He wants to drop paratroops from helicopters north of the provincial capital and resupply the defenders. Thieu refuses. Dong offers his resignation. Thieu does not accept it.

Frantic discussions in Bien Hoa and Saigon. Is the attack on Phuoc Binh perhaps a diversion? The communists seem ready to mount an assault on Bien Hoa, home base for the fighter bombers that support operations in MR 3. The communists can thrust toward Phuoc Binh and simultaneously commence major operations in the other three military regions. Thieu doesn't want to weaken any of the garrisons. The commander of MR 3 is demanding several airborne regiments. He is authorized to take over two companies of rangers, 200 men, volunteers, trained commandos from the 81st Group, stationed in Bien Hoa.

On January 4 the ceiling at Phuoc Binh is low, the horizon leaden. Moreover it's raining in gusts. Helicopters full of rangers try to land them; try again; fail twice. Only one weak radio contact links Bien Hoa and the besieged town.

At 0800 on January 5 choppers land 120 rangers east of the town. Some of the choppers take flak but manage to fly out. The rangers make contact with the defenders and retake positions, most important the provincial chief's residence. Their antitank weapons seem effective against the T-54s, but the rangers don't have enough of them.

At 2100 Bien Hoa and Saigon learn that half the rangers are out of action. Impossible to evacuate the wounded. The Montagnards, militiamen of the regional forces, know how to fight, but their loyalty to the Saigon government fluctuates. The rangers signal that their "situation is desperate." They establish a defensive perimeter around the administrative center and the residence.

Next morning the North Vietnamese throw more tanks and fresh infantry units into the battle. Fierce combat rages all day.

On January 6 at midnight some rangers and other survivors, outflanked, escape from the town. Taking advantage of darkness they proceed in small groups, without radio, without air support, some without arms or ammunition. They plunge into the jungle and the countryside.

The military appraisal of this affair is gloomy, even if strategically this town and this province, now lost, are of small importance out there at the far end of Vietnam. South Vietnamese headquarters counts 850 survivors; they lose 5,400 officers and men, half a division. Two C-130 transports have been shot down. Saigon has thirty-two C-130s in all. A bad political blow, too: the communists have taken a province and its capital before, but this is the first time the South Vietnamese do not retake them.

For the first time, too, there has been no U.S. participation in a major engagement. Since the signing of the Paris Agreement two years ago, the commanders of the four military regions have paid regular visits to headquarters of the U.S. air force in Southeast Asia, at Nakhon Phanom in Thailand. The big base is in direct contact with Saigon and the South Vietnamese military regions. Procedure for launching strategic U.S. air support is always outlined to the commanders of the four military regions. So the Vietnamese generals have no reason to doubt their right to U.S. bombers. Where were they this time?

Thieu announces three days of national mourning; he closes the night-clubs, dance halls, theaters and cinemas. He bans soccer matches and horseracing. New banners appear in the capital: "Our army will avenge these losses in blood." Demonstrators, some conscripted, others sponta-neous, parade outside headquarters of the International Commission of Control and Supervision. During this battle of Phuoc Binh the members of the ICCS have, one more time, displayed their amiable impotence. They could not even negotiate a truce to evacuate civilians. These civilians, businessmen, civil servants, peasants and two New Zealand nuns in charge of 400 orphans, somehow make it to Saigon.

The Americans in Saigon also draw up a gloomy account. In his report, Colonel William LeGro, head of the military attaché's intelligence service, states that South Vietnamese losses are dizzying. His Vietnamese driver sighs:

"Even the gods weep for Phuoc Long."[2]

On January 7 Kissinger meets with his Special Action Group[3] in Wash-ington. His experts ask themselves several questions about Phuoc Long. Was it an important military operation? No, says CIA director William Colby. How can we save the situation in MR 3? By sending U.S. fighter bombers, and better yet strategic bombers, B-52s. An inadmissible answer: American public opinion will see it as a fresh commitment that no one wants. Yet the North Vietnamese attack is the most serious violation of the Paris Agreement since 1973. The Americans are the only ones who honor the agreement, by and large. They did ignore Article 6, which provides for "the dismantlement of all [U.S.] bases in South Vietnam" within sixty days of ratification. By legal sleight of hand, the Americans did not dismantle their bases. They "transferred" them to the South Vi-etnamese. The Americans are fussy about fine print. Also, U.S. observation planes fly over North Vietnamese territory from time to time. There's no way to disguise that violation.

President Ford's inner circle wants to forget Vietnam. With a presidential election coming up in 1976, Ford has nothing to gain by associating his "image" with a renewal of U.S. intervention. Everyone wants a president pure as the driven snow. At the Pentagon they've written Vietnam off. Since the U.S. troops came home from the South and the American prisoners from the North, Washington has been shrouded in a sour guilt over Vietnam, a self-anesthesia. Basic rule of bureaucracy: the less one talks about a problem, the sooner it's forgotten. This Vietnamese war is supposed to disappear in the bright sunshine of détente.

The Special Action Group makes no decision. Kissinger is despondent. Since the Paris Agreement was signed he's said more than once that if Hanoi negotiated in bad faith, and it was proved, the U.S. response would be swift and vigorous.

On his way out of the SAG meeting, Kissinger asks aloud, in his slow, gravelly bass, with the residual German accent, "What kind of people are we?"[4]

Civilians and military alike are bemused. What's on the secretary of state's mind? The credibility of the United States, to be sure.

Short, portly, the most famous of U.S. secretaries of state, admired, vilified, Kissinger, fifty-two years old, has been involved in Vietnamese affairs for ten years and more.[5] Directing foreign affairs since Richard Nixon's election in 1968, first as special security adviser, then as secretary of state, a brilliant academic and a persuasive statesman, a geopolitician and a man of action, choreographer and dancer of his own diplomacy, Kissinger has a tendency to moralize. Now at the beginning of January, his morality, which he identifies with the honor of the United States, sweeps him along. A pragmatic Spenglerian, a manipulator of nations and politicians, a cabinet secretary who often bypasses his own bureaucracy and cherishes secrets as much as glory, Kissinger lets himself go. He commands a global political vision. Above all things he has sought to consolidate a "structure of peace," a new balance of power through control of strategic weapons. Détente among the superpowers was stalled by this sorry war in Vietnam. He all but agrees with Galbraith and others who say ironically, "If we hadn't made so many mistakes, that little country would never have emerged from the obscurity it so richly deserved." Kissinger devoted eight harrowing years to Vietnam. President Ford has left foreign affairs largely in his hands. Unlike Nixon, Ford has never overflowed with ideas in that area. He is incapable of the "conceptual breakthroughs" that enchant his secretary of state. A twisted personality but an imaginative political man, Nixon too had a vision on the planetary scale. Not so his successor, of whom Kissinger said, "On the personal level I feel closer to Ford than I was to Nixon."[6] From which we may infer that intellectually . . .

Subject to shifting moods and often depressed, Kissinger spent three and a half years negotiating an agreement with Hanoi that would preserve U.S. prestige. His public debates and private conversations with Le Duc Tho, special adviser to the North Vietnamese delegation in Paris, led directly to the Paris Agreement. Admittedly imperfect (according to Kissinger), it enabled U.S. troops (according to the secretary of state) to leave Vietnam with dignity and honor, whatever his critics on the American far right said. For a long time Thieu refused to sign the agreement. Kissinger sometimes gives his colleagues the impression that he has more respect for Hanoi's representatives than Saigon's. In the South Vietnamese capital they nickname Kissinger "the midnight diplomat" and the "king of camouflage," when they are not privately calling him a hypocritical son of a bitch. In 1975 Kissinger is physically and psychologically far from Vietnam. He has not set foot in the country since October 1972. And even that is a bad memory: Kissinger wanted to persuade Thieu to agree to his plan for a treaty. Their exchanges were harsh. Thieu called Kissinger "the bastard," *thang cho de*. Before leaving, the secretary of state said, "They've insulted me so thoroughly that I will never return to Saigon." One of the conferees, Hoang Duc Nha, cousin and information adviser to Thieu, irritated Kissinger with a critique of the Paris Agreement article by article.

Thieu and Nha are still convinced that in signing the agreement of January 27, 1973, Kissinger acted with utter cynicism: the Americans were recovering their prisoners of war and leaving Vietnam, knowing very well that Hanoi would never give up the idea of forced reunification.

Still, Kissinger and his colleagues had reason to believe that the fragile agreement would hold: up to a point the Vietnamization of Saigon's army, which Nixon favored even more than Kissinger did, had proved successful. Thieu's troops could hold their own against low- or medium-strength attacks up to the regimental level. Thieu could not hold off many North Vietnamese divisions. But Hanoi would not launch a general offensive. The Politburo was afraid of Nixon's reaction: he had never hesitated to send out the B-52s. He brought the North Vietnamese to the conference table by bombarding the Hanoi area in December 1972. In a nutshell, dissuasion would work. Moreover, this South Vietnamese government, beyond its internal problems, is showing a certain dynamism, above all economically. It isn't popular, but the people of South Vietnam aren't rebelling. Lastly, the North Vietnamese leaders, plunging their people into a long war and demonstrating extraordinary endurance, rule over a powerful military and police state but a civilian society bled white. These North Vietnamese leaders are hoping for reparations, over $3 billion in U.S. aid. In Paris they insisted on Article 21 of the agreement, which provides for "reconciliation" and stipulates that in accord with its "traditional policy" the United States will contribute to "healing the wounds of war and to postwar reconstruction of the Democratic Republic of Vietnam." "Healing the wounds of war," pure North Vietnamese boilerplate, pops up often in

Hanoi's propaganda. Kissinger believes that countries and their leaders act in self-interest. Does he underestimate the force of ideology among North Vietnam's leaders?

Weighing the advantages and disadvantages, Kissinger set the Paris Agreement in the context of the triangular détente with the Soviet Union and the People's Republic of China. He could count on Moscow and Beijing to apply pressure: they supplied the North Vietnamese with materiel and money. In Kissinger's mind, it all hung together: he was establishing a direct connection between détente and the steady extinction of the war in Vietnam.

On November 23 and 24, 1974, six weeks before the fall of Phuoc Binh, Ford and Brezhnev met at Vladivostok, determined to improve U.S.–Soviet relations. It is neither possible nor rational that Vietnam prejudice arrangements between the superpowers. Kissinger, author and practitioner of the politics of linkage, must show the Soviets as well as the Chinese that the road to détente runs via reduction of the Vietnamese problem. He bought Soviet cooperation by granting them most-favored-nation status. Alas, a few months ago in the autumn of 1974, Senator Henry Jackson, a potential presidential candidate, pushed through an amendment: it links détente to Jewish emigration from the Soviet Union. Another amendment limits credits to Moscow. All that, unfortunately, inspires little moderation in the Soviet Union. In 1975, what interest have the Soviets in checking their North Vietnamese comrades?

In 1974 the climate seemed favorable until Nixon's departure. Soviets and Chinese, in their capitals and their foreign embassies, let it be known that they were continuing economic aid to the DRV but would deliver fewer weapons.

Kissinger understands the principal weakness of the Paris Agreement from the military point of view: as Saigon did not realize until too late in the game, it does not specifically stipulate withdrawal of North Vietnamese troops from South Vietnam. They are still in place. Moreover, the North Vietnamese have never honored the clauses about both sides' war materiel: each worn rifle, each heavy gun, each jeep—everything—can only be replaced item for item. These replacements have never been made properly, supervised by the ICCS at designated locations.

Another flaw in the plan, this one political: the South's future governmental organisms are to be be worked out by the two Vietnamese parties. Kissinger knows that this clause is unrealistic, like the establishment of a National Council of Reconciliation and Concord. Can anyone seriously imagine these bitter enemies administering or jointly governing even a town, much less half a country? But Kissinger knew that he had made a point: until the summer of 1972, Hanoi wanted to tie—to each his linkage—the cease-fire to the political settlement. A diplomatic victory for Kissinger, an uncoupling: Hanoi drops its demand for Thieu's departure, which permits the continuance of "a solid political structure in South Vietnam."

South Vietnamese like Thieu and Nha have never agreed that the Paris
Agreement tacitly ratifies the presence of North Vietnamese regulars in
the South. In the province of Phuoc Long, regiments and divisions of
Hanoi's troops are maneuvering in great sweeps. With this offensive, even
if it is limited, the complex house of cards that Kissinger built falls apart.
What now? Ask supplemental appropriations for Vietnam? This Congress,
and especially the House of Representatives, is now full of Democrats in
the style of Senator George McGovern, a confirmed man of peace, un-
methodical and generous. In 1974 Congress reduced the military appropriation for South Vietnam from $1 billion to $750 million, of which $300
million went to civil and military salaries for agencies under the U.S.
military attaché in Saigon. During the Yom Kippur War, the Israelis obtained over $2 billion in military aid from the United States. To many
elected U.S. officials it seems more important to defend Israel than Vietnam. Looking closer, and factoring in the rise in oil prices due to the Arab
embargo, aid to Saigon was doubly reduced in 1974.

For Kissinger the Vietnam War's second front is Washington, in Congress, even at the heart of the administration. Some on the highest levels
once gloried in the name of hawk. Now they favor an end to the war, and
let it be known, like Secretary of Defense James Schlesinger. Outside the
government, a Robert McNamara, a Clark Clifford, a McGeorge Bundy,
powerful diehards under Johnson, now believe the country must wriggle
free of the quagmire. This, even though they believe that the PRG is only
Hanoi's arm in South Vietnam and that the Vietnamese communists are
as totalitarian as any. Influential senators, too, anticommunists, John Sten-
nis or Richard Russell. Former hawks join the most celebrated senatorial
doves, George McGovern, Frank Church, Albert Gore, Wayne Morse,
Edward Kennedy. Even at the White House, Kissinger cannot count on
those who ought to be his natural allies. Some of the praetorians around
Gerald Ford think the Vietnamese problem will dissolve by itself.

Tired, like a man under siege, Kissinger keeps asking, "What kind of
people are we?"

His colleagues notice that he's biting his nails.

On the morning of January 7 General Vien telephones Thieu: the
chairman of the South Vietnamese joint general staff is reporting to the
president. Aerial reconnaissance patrols over Phuoc Binh indicate that all
resistance has ceased.

At Independence Palace Thieu calls a special meeting,[7] which General
Vien does not attend. Those present include the vice-president, the prime
minister, the two deputy prime ministers Tran Van Don and Nguyen Van
Hao, the presidents of the Senate and of the National Assembly, the chief
justice of the Supreme Court and the very stout general Dang Van Quang,
Thieu's special assistant for security.

The terrain and the logistical difficulties, says Thieu, favor the communists. It will be hard for our army to retake the province.

Fat Quang, who rarely takes part in meetings, says flatly: "Phuoc Long and its capital are indefensible. So are An Loc and Kontum."

An Loc, to the west, and Kontum, in the northeast, are large towns and provinces. Quang adds brutally: "The communists can take them any time they want to."

No one reacts. As if he has not understood, or attaches no importance to the words, Thieu goes on: "We can protest, and try to influence world opinion. Let's protest to the United Nations! And to the signatories of the Paris Agreement! Nothing will come of these gestures. Most countries are preoccupied with the energy crisis. But this government must have an increase in military and economic aid from the United States."

Thieu addresses the presidents of the National Assembly and the Senate: "We must send a delegation to the United States to put pressure on Congress. Before that, we invite a few hand-picked American senators and congressmen here. We can work out just who with the American Embassy people."

The president of the National Assembly approves: "But American congressmen have problems with their constituents," he says. "We need to influence public opinion in the United States through other organizations and institutions."

"For example?"

"The unions, the American Legion, the Red Cross."

Thieu seems unconvinced. They have to work on American senators. He goes on to U.S. domestic policy. How can they inspire a grass-roots surge?

"The government feels isolated," Thieu says, looking at his prime minister as if he, Thieu, did not control that government. He lets the pause run on, waiting for Khiem to answer. As so often, the prime minister has nothing to say. Thieu goes on: "During serious crises in the past, several opposition parties supported the government."

None of them is really active except the Democratic Party that Thieu created. The president wants to broaden the government's political base by quickly passing a rather liberal law aimed precisely at political parties. All but the Communist Party should be legalized. That will impress Washington favorably. Thieu gives his instructions to the presidents of the National Assembly and the Senate. In South Vietnam the executive branch controls the legislative.

The deputy prime ministers present propose that Thieu meet with notables of national stature and seek their support. Thieu nods, but neither suggests nor requests any names. He also hopes the Vietnamese Assembly and Senate will put the finishing touches on a law about freedom of the press. They must let him know!

The council broaches economic questions, reviewing points discussed in a cabinet meeting four days earlier. The prime minister said then that they had to gain time. In 1976, South Vietnam will export oil. Ordinarily Khiem does not interfere in military matters or internal political affairs, at any rate in public or among the ministers. He makes do with economic and social questions. Today he ventures out of his specialties. According to him, international public opinion on Vietnam is "frozen." He ventures the prediction that the United States will not intervene militarily. Ford is "inflexible."

Thieu listens, does not agree with his prime minister, seems ill at ease.

"We can survive a difficult interim period," says Khiem, "precisely because we'll have oil resources in 1976."

He compares the country's situation to a poker player's. With oil, we raise. Hanoi will have to fold. To bring in gushers as soon as possible, the companies must see a quick profit. We have to encourage them, offer them part of the government's percentage: "That will encourage them to drill faster. We can't afford the luxury of a maximum long-term percentage."

Khiem reminds them that he has asked Hao, deputy prime minister for economic affairs, to put pressure on the oil companies. The prime minister expects more positive results within six months. He seems optimistic and insists, "If we can export a lot of oil in 1977, we'll be in good shape."

At this economic bombshell, the committee almost forgets the loss of Phuoc Long province.

That same night, two detailed reports of this meeting reach the U.S. Embassy. One comes from Thieu's special security aide. On request General Quang relays summaries from the presidential palace. Thieu knows this. He encourages Quang to pose as a CIA agent in the palace. Through him, Thieu can manipulate certain Americans in the embassy who think they're manipulating him. Vietnamese of whatever party have a thousand years' experience in spying, in double and triple agentry. The Americans' experience is more recent. The second report is based on confidential information from other members of the council. There are just as many leaks in Saigon as in Washington and plenty of informers around the president, the prime minister and civilian and military leaders. The CIA has bugged the presidential palace extravagantly. They're convinced that one of Thieu's close colleagues is a mole reporting to Hanoi. Who? Quang, Hao or someone else?

The chairman of the joint chiefs of staff is advised of the council's decisions. He receives his instructions. The general must prepare to brief important American visitors.

On January 9, in the large conference room at headquarters, the "gold room," Vien gives his officers the abstract of an eleven-page report.[8] It announces a "large-scale military offensive" by North Vietnamese troops, a conclusion the president has been waiting for.

In Vietnamese military slang, they say that Vien is *che du*, he "opens the umbrella." Vien possesses neither the spirit of initiative nor the talent for synthesis and analysis that his functions imply. He was too quick to agree that headquarters function as an advisory command post. The merest colonel knows it. Was that the price Vien paid to keep his job? He looks dashing in his red paratrooper's beret, but prefers yoga to lightning inspections at the front. He carries obedience, or obsequiousness, too far. General Quang, the stout security counselor, prepares cursory strategic or tactical plans for Thieu. When the president approves them, Quang orders headquarters to execute them. It was Quang who ordered the rangers sent to encircled Phuoc Binh.

On January 17 Vien receives a report from General Tran Van Trung, head of psychological warfare. Relayed to the prime minister and the president, the report reaches the U.S. Embassy next day. It analyzes the communists' plans for 1975: "The object of this campaign, which will doubtless end in June, is to occupy a certain number of districts and provinces, principally Tay Ninh, Phuoc Long [a prediction already fulfilled], Binh Long, Kien Tuong and Kien Phong." The communists will "attempt to cut the Republic of Vietnam in two along a line beginning north of Kontum and hitting the coast at Quang Nam. In coming months they will do what they can to weaken the economy." They will attack bridges, warehouses, arsenals and the physical plant of the new oil industry. They will work carefully, as "they want to preserve the infrastructure for use when they have seized power." They will create a situation that requires the Saigon government to "take in a million refugees." To stir up trouble, "female cadres will infiltrate refugee camps," those that already exist and those that will be needed. The communists will wage anti-Thieu campaigns to keep him from running in the October [1975] presidential election. They'll revive an old slogan: "As long as Thieu rules, the war will go on." Communist youth, women's and intellectual organizations—says this report from psychological warfare—are to work with American peace movements to keep Ford from sending further military aid to Saigon. In this campaign the communists hope to use American ex-POWs. "If these plans succeed, in June 1975 the Republic of Vietnam will be forced to sign another agreement and form a coalition government." Propaganda teams will then try to "break up South Vietnamese military units." Communist delegates to the coalition government will create many difficulties "for a year or two." This government "will prove ineffective." The communists will resign. Another government, "the independent, national and democratic government of the Republic of South Vietnam," will emerge and will be "radical, socialist and proletarian." Three or four years later, "a dictatorial government which will complete reunification of North and South" will replace this "proletarian" government.

Around Thieu they think the enemy is working two or perhaps three years ahead. The South Vietnamese government seems isolated but solid. Mainly it must improve the economic situation. Government ministers multiply their inspiring declarations. Running the economy, Hao affirms that exports are increasing. Pressed for proof, he talks about wood and fish to the tune of $100 million a year. It is an optimistic view. In 1974, for $929 million in imports, there was only $76 million in exports. The government is accused of mismanaging the economy, of tolerating currency traffic and a black market. Hao lays out morality campaigns and makes personal appearances.

Accompanied by the mayor of Saigon, he scours the markets where contraband is piled up—cigarettes, alcohol, hi-fi systems. He tries to persuade the amused and gaping vendors that this illegal commerce must cease. In his candor Hao seems sincere. Buyers or sellers, the Saigonese laugh. The press comes down hard on this vice prime minister and his televised promenades: "Exhibitionistic behavior," writes the daily *Dien Tin*.

Decent people know that the real corruption—gross misappropriation of public funds, juicy import licenses, improper construction permits, traffic in currency—is not cooked up at the markets.

At the Thieves' Market, a hodgepodge of flea market and open-air discount stores, they sell or resell transistors and typewriters, battle dress and khaki skivvies, canned goods, combat rations, electric drills made in California, crocodile shoes from Formosa. Boxes of soap and helmets are jumbled together on open display. Around the market you can buy grass or heroin cheap—less than those claim who take Pigalle for Paris or Soho for London and call Saigon the world capital of vice, but more than the minions of Admiral Chung Tan Cang, longtime czar of the war on drugs, will admit. Since 500,000 American soldiers went home, business is not so good.

All kinds and classes crisscross the Thieves' Market without meeting— Saigon's bourgeoisie, upper, middle and lower; peasants who came in carts from Can Tho in the Delta, or from Tay Ninh, close to the Cambodian frontier; employees and workers of a thousand businesses with offices in the capital; Vietnamese soldiers in uniform; soldiers and officers of the International Commission of Control and Supervision in civilian clothes. There is much talk about the hundreds of "cowboys," young men in pointed boots who, riding pillion on a Vespa, pluck purses or a Leica from tourists in passing. There are hundreds of thousands of honest or just about honest Saigonese going about their lawful occasions and surviving. Too often foreigners see only the picturesque, exotic and shady surface of the city. For every opium den in Saigon there are over a hundred ordinary businesses, and for every bordello a thousand restaurants or grocery stores. Saigon leaves a wake of history and legend. Greater Saigon, with Gia Dinh, Cholon, its sprawling suburbs and outskirts, counts 3.5–4 million souls. Rural folk flow to the cities and the capital, settle in, vanish, spring up again.

Tourists, benevolent or hostile, mainly keep to the heart of the city, around the presidential palace, the main post office, the pink cathedral,

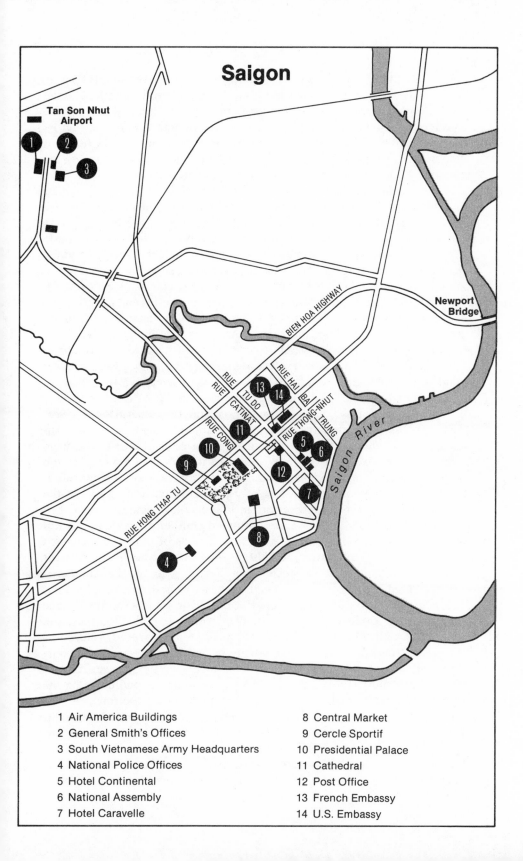

Saigon

Tan Son Nhut Airport

BIEN HOA HIGHWAY

Newport Bridge

RUE TU DO

RUE CATINAT

RUE CONG

RUE HAI BA

RUE THONG-NHUT

TRUNG

Saigon River

RUE HONG THAP TU

1 Air America Buildings
2 General Smith's Offices
3 South Vietnamese Army Headquarters
4 National Police Offices
5 Hotel Continental
6 National Assembly
7 Hotel Caravelle

8 Central Market
9 Cercle Sportif
10 Presidential Palace
11 Cathedral
12 Post Office
13 French Embassy
14 U.S. Embassy

and Tu Do Street, the city's belly, running toward the river and its floating restaurants. Visitors stroll near the central market and the hotels, like the old Continental, whose owner, Philippe Franchini, painter and writer, used to rule discreetly. Here hovers the shadow of Graham Greene, and across the way is the modern air-conditioned Caravelle. The tourists frequent restaurants owned by Frenchmen, often Corsican, and branches of the eighteen Vietnamese banks and fourteen foreign banks.[9]

The international set knows mainly the fancy neighborhoods, the first and third arrondissements with their well-planned avenues, their luxurious houses safe within fences or walls, with hedges of shrubs, oleanders, rows of teak and tamarind trees. There, in the great bourgeois tradition, reside the upper civil servants, Europeans, Japanese, Americans. As if embedded in one long siesta, the boulevards are calm, passersby rare. During the American war, which the communists call "the second resistance," 100,000 Americans, civilian and military, lived in Saigon in hotels and camps. They also lived in rented or purchased houses in these spacious and tranquil enclaves, a lovely heritage of French colonialism and architecture.

Most of the Saigonese live elsewhere, in the fifth and sixth arrondissements, noisy, swarming, overcrowded, in unpaved alleyways and stinking dead-ends. This is not Calcutta or Dacca, not atrocious poverty. Saigonese who cannot rent one, two, or three rooms in an HLM (middle-income housing project) on the outskirts, and who do not own a permanent house, occupy plank or cardboard huts, shacks on stilts, shanties, or sampanhouses. Everywhere is the buzz of family potteries or plastics as a cottage industry, that pox of the Third World as of the developed world. In the people's Saigon they repair and cannibalize bicycles, motorbikes, refrigerators under temporary palm-leaf roofs. Corrugated iron gleams in the sun. Near the canals and ditches of black and yellow water are encrusted the slums, the "rats' nests." Bare-bottomed children play amid sacks of wood and paddy, amid garbage, tin cans, lengths of pipe and reclaimed boxes. In these shantytowns the kids eat their fill, but the health services have not conquered vitamin deficiency or malaria. War and the Americans have secreted a kind of artificial and temporary prosperity; the fallout has wafted down to the lowest classes. Except in the refugee camps no one dies of hunger in South Vietnam. In 1975 even in scientific journals, you read that South Vietnam is 80 percent "peasant." Not true. Displaced by the war, attracted by the salaries, many peasants have become not only domestic servants but masons, carpenters, mechanics, machinists, electricians. The American experts and sociologists who swooped down on the country haven't had time to see this phenomenon up close, busy as they were laying plans for pacification and interrogating Vietcong prisoners. At its very core Vietnamese society is changing, progressing, entering the twentieth century, some say; exploding, rotting, others say. The war scatters families; it makes prostitutes but also skilled employees and workers, doctors, computer scientists, high-level specialists; and leaves in its wake tens of thousands of unemployed, some of whom join the army to survive. There is more of a working class in Saigon than in Hanoi!

More of a community, the 500,000 Chinese who live in Cholon comprise proportionately fewer unemployed. In theory they have long been forbidden to do business in fish, meat, cloth, metals, cereals and rice. Nor have they the right to own stores and service stations or transport merchandise or passengers.[10] But in Vietnam theory rarely dictates practice. The Chinese control networks and guilds from which all secret services (the CIA tries hard) have bad luck recruiting agents. Entrepreneurs, workers, in cahoots with Vietnamese front men, the Chinese in fact own rice mills, flour mills, oil mills, canneries and, quasi-legally, sauce factories, mediocre hotels and excellent restaurants, hardware stores and groceries. The city swarms with their peddlers, their bars, their cheap eateries. They are partners in countless import-export houses; they conduct business wholesale and retail. Their agreements and deals hold up because in business the word of a Chinese, even without a signed contract, is good as gold. They keep in close contact with banks and financial institutions in Bangkok, Singapore, Hong Kong and Taipei. There's nothing like a Chinese for a friendly transfer of funds abroad, to convert piastres into dollars, marks or Swiss francs regardless of exchange regulations.

In Cholon you see fewer government slogans than elsewhere. "Phuoc Long will be retaken": this fresh banner now decorates the capital. Brand new, it hangs with others across the façades of public buildings. Who cares about Thieu's four No's? "No negotiations with the enemy": comical after the interminable debates and long tragi-comedy of the Paris Agreement. "No recognition of communists in South Vietnam": political necessity for the South Vietnamese president. "No coalition government": flat negation of the agreement, which provides for a council of reconciliation. "No territorial concessions to the communists": a bitter bluff these days, after the fall of Phuoc Binh.

Like the North Vietnamese, the South Vietnamese are offered an anthology of slogans, painted on walls or pasted up: "No sale of rice to the communists," which says plenty about rural trafficking. "Never mind what the communists say, look at what they do," bears the stamp of Confucian wisdom. "An alliance with the communists is a sugar-coated poison pill," Thieu's phrase, which he quotes eagerly to the people and to visitors.

If not for this propaganda, if not for radio and television news, daily papers, rumors, gossip circulating through every neighborhood, if not for the uniformed soldiers, you could almost forget the war in Saigon; sometimes you hear distant artillery, but there are no more raids or explosions in the capital. The barbed wire is rolled up, the sandbags are split and the sentries forlorn, often sitting easy outside police stations, barracks, government buildings. Spared, capital of a curious peace-in-war, Saigon takes advantage of its good luck, uses up its energies, gives off a warm and lilting charm.

Beginning at velvety dawn the city opens like those paper flowers that you drop in water. As do almost all the big cities of Asia. Suburbanites head for the center of town. Policemen in gray uniforms wake the many who sleep in the open on mats or ponchos. Pigeons coo. Women light their braziers. The smell of charcoal dissolves into the smell of spicy soups and gasoline, and the strong odor of *nuoc mam*. In immaculate pants and short-sleeved shirts, clerks and workmen stroll among old ladies in conical hats, young ladies in silk *ao dai*. Squalling young men and legless beggars fight over a corner of the sidewalk. Bicycles and motorbikes jam the streets. Stalls offer chewing gum, cigarettes, vases, sunglasses, toothpaste, teapots, ballpoint pens, tongs, bowls, birds. The whole range of cheap Western plastic goods in electric colors has conquered the Orient. They buy, barter, resell, repair. Here it smells of mint, there of urine. The markets, especially the central market, swarm with people and overflow with strawberries, oranges, litchi nuts, grapefruit, pimentoes, potatoes, watercress, onions, carrots. Buyers bargain, as much for pleasure as for price. Morning and evening traffic is prodigious, staggering, joyful. Its chaos dictates its laws. It obeys live cops more than red lights. Buses and cars repainted ten times are jam-packed. Bicycles, motorbikes, scooters fart their way among the taxis, old blue and cream 4 hp. Renaults with meters that don't work. The drivers start up in second. Saigon is Hondaville, Peugeotville, Renaultville. Toward 8 A.M. you see Vietnamese chauffeurs at the wheels of black Ford Pintos. Almost everyone knows that the American beside the driver belongs to the CIA. The black Pinto is the Company's preferred or regulation car. Other Occidentals, often French, drive around in Dalats or Méharis. Three-wheeler bikers deliver boxes and bound packages, balancing like circus performers. You are constantly held up by traffic jams. Horns blow. Cars accelerate abruptly. Shouted arguments erupt for form's sake. A child, two babies, three, smile from a baggage rack. In the center of the city especially you notice the Indians. Three or four thousand live in Saigon. The Hindus come from Coromandel, from Malabar, from the French trading posts in India. They examine currency, snap it up, exchange it. Moneylenders, their rates are fearsome. Hindus often have French passports, like Annamale, night porter at the Hotel Continental. A few Sikhs, stern in their turbans, are guards and watchmen.

Boys of twelve and thirteen still accost foreigners: "Change money? Boom-boom girl? Boom-boom dirty picture?"

Others, older, walk the streets hawking opium dens. The connoisseurs find the hotel Hung Dao, where girls in t-shirts welcome them, Hung Dao No. 1, Hung Dao No. 2. An enormous machine running in neutral most of the time, the war looses Vietnamese upon the heart of the city, in combat fatigues, without weapons, shopping or at loose ends. Buck privates often hold hands or hook little fingers—like many soldiers in Hanoi. Officers, looking important, drive around in jeeps or command cars. In mid-morning the heat shimmers along the paving stones. The heavy air is like a sauna.

An ambulance siren screams. Chez Givral, the Three Musketeers sip their first cup of coffee. Vuong and Cao Giao listen to An with friendly respect, although frightened by the range of his cold and precise views.

After noon the cinemas fill up. War films are popular—even though you can see and hear real combat thirty or forty kilometers down the road. Why this fascination? Perhaps because the films come to an end. The good win out over the bad. In Saigon, you live on the fringe of the war, but you cannot forget it. Everyone knows that it is not over, and no one can picture its end.

The audience is smaller at shows organized by the embassies' cultural attachés, which also use movies to draw customers. The French Institute is showing *Jules and Jim* on the 9th, *César and Rosalie* on the 10th. In its architecture the center of Saigon is indeed, like Hanoi, a French colonial city. But the students no longer speak French. In recent years English has been more useful in making your way through the ranks, civilian or military.

Refugees from Phuoc Binh who came in small groups, on foot, by car, some in army trucks, are no problem to the capital. Saigon more than other large cities—Danang or Hue—seems truly remote from the war being waged far from the capital, in the Vietnam of the Central Highlands, jungles, rice paddies, villages and hamlets. Out there they have as much plastic but no electricity or neon lights. Children fish for carp in the ponds, or, from the dikes, watch over white buffalo, blue-gray really, lacquered and shiny when they emerge from the water. In Saigon, the least rifle shot draws a crowd. In the countryside a bomb or shell has to explode quite close before the kids pay any attention. They judge the danger by ear. The villagers also try to live outside the war, in a patient and essential need to slip between firefights, to work and fetch water, to plant and replant, to live and survive. With black pigs and skinny chickens dashing about under wooden bedsteads, with straw huts and a few solid buildings, with transistor radios blatting different news but similar music, nothing so much resembles a village in the South as a village in the North. At least from afar, now in 1975 as in 1965 or 1955. In North Vietnam the villages are more picturesque: corrugated iron roofs are less common.

3

───◆───

Nixon's Letters

$\mathbb{A}$merican combat troops, advisers
to ARVN units, technical personnel and paramilitary organizations have
been out of Vietnam since March 1973. The United States is complying
with Article 5 of the Paris Agreement, which stipulated that they withdraw
those forces within sixty days. American public opinion, Congress and that
often stupefying obsession with fine print all militate against any obvious
violation of the agreement. Before its ratification, finagling with the spirit
if not the letter during operation "Enhance Plus," the Americans supplied
Vietnam with plenty of arms and ammunition, more or less modern—the
Pentagon tried to avoid stockpiling sophisticated weapons there. Right
now 8,000 U.S. citizens are living in South Vietnam. The embassy phone
book lists 2,300 names.[1] The American is no longer father; he is just barely
tutor, with fewer rights and duties. The nerve center of the American
establishment, the embassy a few hundred meters from Thieu's residence
at the presidential palace, is like a fortress. Communist troops penetrated
for several hours during the Tet offensive in 1968.

From his second-floor suite of offices, between the political and economic sections, Ambassador Graham Martin rules over a superabundance
of agencies in Saigon, and over the four consulates. At U.S. listening posts
in the countryside,[2] certain "vice-consuls" are CIA agents. They report to
their boss, Thomas Polgar, who works on the fourth floor of the embassy,
close to a sophisticated communications center. Also answering to the
embassy are the U.S. Information Service (USIS) above the Lincoln Li-

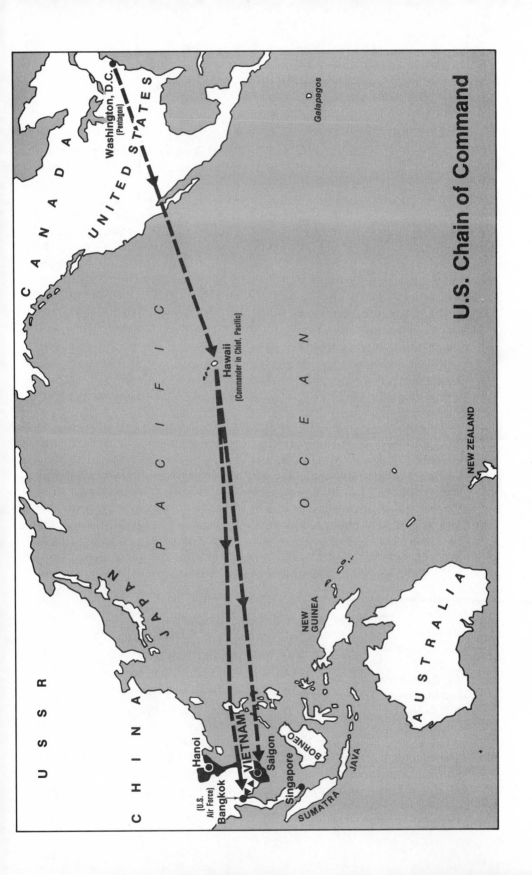

U.S. Chain of Command

brary, and the development agency (USAID) in buildings near the Cercle Sportif.

Two branches of the embassy are important for the number and function of their employees: the CIA and the Military Attaché's Office. In Saigon alone, counting secretaries and cryptographers, the CIA employs 300 civil servants. Some of them lodge at the Hotel Duc. Its bar, solarium and swimming pool are popular.

The Defense Attaché's Office (DAO, distinct from the embassy's military attaché), the only such organization in the world, is the largest of these agencies. Fifty officers and twelve hundred civilians work under the command of General Homer Smith, specialist in logistics. Some of the civilians—about a hundred—are soldiers temporarily discharged and hired by contract. As a special military attaché, Smith answers to the ambassador. As a general, he also answers to the Commander in Chief, Pacific, at Hawaii (CINCPAC), who in turn reports to the Joint Chiefs of Staff[3] at the Pentagon. This ponderous system, which dissipates orders in time and space, has been operating since the war began. General Smith and Martin get along well. Alan Carter, head of USIS, is on bad terms with his ambassador, who accuses him of talking too much to reporters. This diplomatic microsociety secretes lasting hates and sympathies—of which the Vietnamese in power, in Hanoi as well as Saigon, are well aware.

General Smith's offices and agencies have moved into the former headquarters buildings of the U.S. forces in Vietnam, with its annexes, cafeterias, movie and swimming pool, at Tan Son Nhut airport. Smith keeps busy coordinating the flow of military supplies for the army and sends his aides out to inspect South Vietnamese troops. A complicated job. The North Vietnamese lie to the Soviets and Chinese about the level of their supplies, and the South Vietnamese lie to the Americans. After reports from the ten provincial listening posts,[4] General Smith's office writes up accounts of any cease-fire violations. These are more numerous and detailed than the ICCS's.

The CIA is equally present at the airport, highly visible with one of its airlines'—Air America's—dark blue and white planes and helicopters. In the late 1960s, the good old days, Air America counted 5,600 employees. Its pilots, many of them ex-officers, know Vietnam well. They are paid $45,000 a year, half of it tax-free.

Since the Paris Agreement, Air America transports the ICCS personnel, which includes Hungarians and Poles. When the commission was established, Polgar explained that if all its members, Canadians (later replaced by Iranians), Indonesians, Poles and Hungarians, brought in their own planes, life would be one long series of accidents. He proposed the use of Air America. Everyone knows it belongs to the CIA. The first Polish ambassador to the ICCS—a former general manager of Lot, the Polish airline—understood the problem and persuaded his Hungarian colleagues to accept Polgar's offer. It was economical, too; the Eastern bloc is short of hard currency. On the whole there have been few accidents. But one day PRG troops shot down two ICCS helicopters. There was a North Vietnamese officer aboard one of them.

The ICCS has its headquarters in town and access to various services at Tan Son Nhut airport. This international commission of so-called control and supervision controls nothing and supervises little. In no time at all the Canadians translated ICCS as "I can't control shit." The Vietnamese suggest another translation: *"Im cho coi sao,"* to wait in silence for whatever will happen. The Paris Agreement devoted eighteen articles to the legal structure of the ICCS, successor to the ICC, the International Control Commission, which, from 1954 to 1973, operated in low gear at Saigon and Hanoi. Noting the ICCS's inefficiency, the Canadians withdrew early on. Iranians took their place. The Shah saw it as a way to make an entrance onto the international scene. The Hungarians and Poles refuse to investigate complaints made by Saigon. Sometimes the Indonesians and Iranians, listless and weary, investigate alone. The exercise is academic. Their reports have no legal value.

On January 10, 1975, a Pole and a Hungarian, with their Iranian and Indonesian colleagues, countersign a report critical of the Provisional Revolutionary Government in Long Khanh district, eighty kilometers northeast of Saigon. Back in the capital, called to order by their superiors, the Hungarian and the Pole announce that they were forced to sign a text they didn't understand.

The Paris Agreement called for seven regional ICCS teams, to inspect war materiel that the belligerents replace.[5] The ICCS knows that most of these teams were never established or have never been at full strength on their assigned ground. The ICCS was supposed to number 3,000 at the start. It became an enormous bureaucracy feeding on itself and never stationed any observers in Phuoc Long province. Classic scenario: the South Vietnamese asked them to move in; the Hungarians and Poles took cover behind a "lack of information"; the Iranians and the Indonesians suggested sending teams in; the Hungarians and Poles refused, "as security cannot be assured." In Saigon no one is surprised.

Hosting cocktail parties and dinners, playing tennis, swimming in the pool at the Cercle Sportif, the officers of the ICCS are bit players in the juridical show. Complaints are blocked by vetos. At their plenary sessions they don't discuss Phuoc Long except to decide quickly and solemnly that nothing can be done. At great length they settle practical problems: Why isn't the pool at Tan Son Nhut refilled every day? What are the gas rations this week? Isn't the price of dinner at the mess too high? Who will represent his delegation tonight at the French Embassy, tomorrow at Australia's? What films are the delegations showing at the movie?

For many of the Poles and Hungarians this is their first trip abroad. Dazzled by their salaries paid in dollars, they move around the city in buses protected by antigrenade screens, visit the temples, buy gold and jewels, chase skirts, learn the rules of American football. At soirées in Saigon, General Czeslaw Dega, very heavy, and Ambassador Fijalkowski, very slim, seem quite popular. With such charm, such elegance, do they kiss hands in the Polish manner! General Dega is a surprise. He sings the praises of the "Shah of Iran's white revolution" and his "ambitious projects."[6] Dega sympathizes with the French military attaché, Colonel Yves Gras, a scrupulous historian of the French war in Indochina but sometimes less well informed on the current war. The two officers discuss Napoleon, Mme. Walewska, Foch. Not bad, this French colonel! He has confided to the Pole, "The Vietnamese problem is too complicated to be solved by dollar diplomacy."

The Poles know Vietnam better than the Hungarians; they've had representatives in both North and South for twenty years. Many Poles travel on the ICCS plane, a curious shuttle that links Saigon and Hanoi every Friday. Perhaps because they have so much background to catch up on, the Hungarians specialize in intelligence. Cameras in hand, they wander about bridges, barracks, air bases, and munitions depots. The South Vietnamese are enraged, and complain. To no avail: members of the ICCS, you see, enjoy diplomatic immunity. The Iranians are deliciously hospitable. They offer everyone caviar, which marries well with Polish vodka or Hungarian wines. Only the Indonesians operate fully in the spirit of the Paris Agreement. They venture out exposed to shot and shell, and they evaluate and compare the forces in person, adding up the violations.

"Why are you so active?" Polgar asks a high Indonesian officer.

"We'll have to fight the Vietnamese. Not in my lifetime, perhaps, but some day."

In two years, Poles, Hungarians and Americans, civilian or military, have formed bonds. They are all white, in contrast to these Vietnamese, nationalist or communist, so difficult to grasp when one comes from Budapest, or Warsaw, or Washington. And there are natural affinities between the higher bureaucracy and the career military. What does ideology matter, or if one side tries to corrupt the other! The ICCS delegations are riddled with intelligence officers looking for moles or renegades, with little success. On the ICCS they hardly watch the Vietnamese war, but they watch each other well enough. Polish and Hungarian officers pass information to the communists, which bothers the CIA very little. Polgar says: "There's plenty of work for everybody. When you piss in the ocean, you're bound to raise the water level."

Ambassador Graham Martin treats the Poles with distant courtesy. On his arrival, their ambassador paid a formal call on his American colleague. The Hungarian, that lout, neglected this formality. So Martin never sees him.

On the other hand, Polgar maintains the best of relations with the Hungarians, above all with Colonel Janos Toth and the political adviser, Anton Tolgyes. Polgar is of Hungarian origin. Toth directs Hungarian intelligence. Colleagues, Polgar and Toth sympathize even as they mistrust. To make sense of this "ocean" of information and for mutual aid, they've perfected an ingenious and original system: at the same hour, in two different parts of Saigon, a CIA agent and a Hungarian officer brief the other side. A watertight system: the Americans and the Hungarians can't deceive each other or pass disinformation, or trot out again what their counterparts have confided to them. Hearing about this arrangement, the Poles too wanted to profit by it. Their officers, in mufti to be sure, go to the U.S. Embassy. They're received by one of Polgar's colleagues, young Frank Snepp.

In private with the Americans, the Poles make fun of the Hungarians, and vice-versa. Returning the courtesy, the Americans complain about the South Vietnamese. The Polish and Hungarian officers, high-living men of the world, admit their perplexity over the Vietnamese communists: "Our Vietnamese comrades are very courageous, very obstinate and very determined. And very hard to understand."

Despite insistent queries, the Poles and Hungarians have not managed to extract any substantial information from the Vietnamese communists on the invasion of Phuoc Long province. Considerately, the Americans have kept the ICCS informed—because Vietnamese communist comrades too have been installed in Saigon, bag and baggage and well armed, at Tan Son Nhut airport since 1973: 250 Vietcong officers and men—that is, from the PRG forces—and 50 or so NVA officers and men, inscrutable, as quick with a smile as with a slogan. In geometrically aligned barracks, behind barbed wire and sandbags, in the shadow of watchtowers where South Vietnamese sentinels watch over them, the communist enemy belongs to two other commissions created by the Paris Agreement in nineteen articles. The PRG soldiers wear loose green uniforms and Hanoi's men tan uniforms of somewhat better cut. PRG representatives often have distinctly northern accents.

A Four-Party Joint Military Commission comprises the United States, the Saigon government, the Hanoi government, and the Provisional Revolutionary Government. Its mission is to find the missing and dead.

A Two-Party Joint Military Commission comprises only representatives of Saigon and the PRG.

These two commissions were to accompany ICCS teams on their official rounds. For two years they have been frozen in place. When the Poles and Hungarians ask for news of the battle of Phuoc Long from the Vietcong and North Vietnamese officers, they're answered with the usual smile: "We're not up to date on that."

The communists seldom leave the barracks in their camp, "Camp Davis," named for one of the first American soldiers killed in Vietnam. In their documents, newspapers or books, the communists always call it "Camp David." There are two rows of grouped barracks, one for the PRG, one for the DRV. When they arrived, the communists—especially the

PRG chief, General Tran Van Tra, since risen to command the Phuoc Long campaign—found their living rooms, bedrooms and baths seeded with American microphones.

The affable General Tra was replaced by the more brusque General Hoang Anh Tuan. In truth, the important man at Camp Davis in 1975 is Colonel Vo Dong Giang. Bolshevik diplomatic principle: the number two official is more important than the number one. The communist soldiers grow flowers and vegetables, plant trees and spy. The chief of staff of the North Vietnamese army, General Van Tien Dung, says it all: "Our comrades at Tan Son Nhut had their own particular position, standing proudly and publicly in the midst of the enemy. That position not only symbolized the revolution and its political cause, but also helped the party better understand the feelings of the people about liberation, and helped us understand the enemy during the days of their death throes."[7]

The detachment at Camp Davis is in constant radio contact with Hanoi. General Dung is perfectly frank: "The joint military commission, under the command of General Hoang Anh Tuan," keeps Hanoi "quickly informed of news . . . and also troop movements" that it succeeds in "discovering on the spot by various means, including direct observation." Indeed, there could be no better post for monitoring air traffic.

The main worry of the Vietnamese at Camp Davis, their obsession, is that the Americans may break their codes. Their principal public activities, press conferences, take place Saturday mornings beneath portraits of their leaders, most prominently that of Ho Chi Minh. Journalists learn nothing from them. After offering tea, orangeade and cigarettes—blue-pack dark tobacco, red-pack light tobacco, brand Dien Bien Phu—the communist soldiers set forth their protests in the traditional wooden language: Saigon and Washington are violating the agreement. They are responsible for the violations of the cease-fire. They do not respect the spirit of the agreement. They do not permit the communists free passage in and out of Camp Davis. "At Phuoc Long," they announce, "our army of liberation has responded to the provocations of the Saigon regime."

Yet in this province North Vietnamese troops have by all evidence violated the principal clauses of the Paris Agreement. Not since 1973 have they shown so little respect for the cease-fire. Hanoi has "infiltrated" its troops and introduced undeclared materiel. The North Vietnamese army is using Laotian and Cambodian bases. Only one clause has not been not violated: the demilitarized zone on the 17th parallel has not been crossed, as in 1972.

A bizarre situation, sanctioned and confirmed by the Paris Agreement. These communists at Camp Davis, patient and tough, posted in from Hanoi and the jungle, are saying that day is night when they talk about Phuoc Long. For almost two years they've been living here a few hundred meters from General Homer Smith's office and the housing reserved to South Vietnamese generals. A strange imbroglio, Saigonese enough. Imagine an

American or Soviet military listening post in Berlin before the end of World War II. Or several Wehrmacht signal companies installed in London in 1944.

In Hanoi you run across Poles and, for a few hours now and then, American liaison officers; and that's about it.

It's easy to imagine how the presence of those men at Camp Davis irritates Thieu. When these communist soldiers arrived in March 1973, the South Vietnamese authorities wanted them to fill out landing cards. To affirm nonrecognition of the Saigon government, the communists refused. So they had no right to disembark. After hours of waiting and pressure from the Americans, the Hanoi and PRG delegations settled in at Camp Davis.

Thieu has lost the whole province of Phuoc Long and wants to take it out on the men at Camp Davis. The only possible reprisal is to cut off their water. He decides against it.

The president has other pressing needs, civilian and military. What is the Hanoi Politburo planning? How can he galvanize South Vietnam's latent energies?

Round face, hair slicked back, his bulging brow unwrinkled, he never shows his fatigue, and he maintains an air of self-assurance. He acts as if he had a mandate from Heaven to preserve and defend his country, underwritten by a mandate from the Americans. He's proved that he's as anticommunist as they are. Ill at ease with American politicos, he feels closer to two statesmen who have confronted the communist armies as he has, Park Chung Hee of South Korea and Chiang Kai-shek on Taiwan. Thieu has sent his brother, Nguyen Van Kieu, as ambassador to the Generalissimo.

Thieu has one absolute conviction: Washington will not abandon him whatever happens. But he knows that American leaders can betray their allies. Didn't they let President Diem go in 1963? Thieu saw Diem's corpse. In 1968 Thieu even feared that he in turn would be assassinated with Washington's consent.

Born in 1924—the hour, day, month and year of the Rat, a bad omen— Nguyen Van Thieu carries his fifty-two years well. Uniquely successful in this country of coups d'état, Thieu has been in power for over eight years. His stability indicates a shrewdness that the Americans—most of all Ambassador Martin—appreciate.

The youngest of seven children in a modest Southern family, Thieu joined the Vietminh communists for several months in 1944. Then he chose the nationalist side. He almost became a naval officer. Trained at Coëtquidan in France, Thieu worked his way up to the top of the military hierarchy, and thus, in Vietnam, to the top of the political hierarchy after President Diem's assassination. Martin's predecessor in Saigon, U.S. Ambassador Ellsworth Bunker, chose Thieu as a presidential candidate in preference to the dashing aviator Nguyen Cao Ky. Thieu seemed more mature and more flexible. Brave in combat, a competent general officer, ambitious, he avoids outbursts, and he temporizes. A Buddhist, Thieu converted to Catholicism under Diem, himself a fanatical Catholic. In his palace library the president has a collection of *L'Annuaire du Vatican* bound in red leather, inherited from Diem. Thieu's Catholicism is convenient. He seems to have converted mainly in order to marry Nguyen Thi Mai Anh, daughter of a prominent Catholic. Talkative, self-controlled, Thieu shelters behind cascades of laughter, a rather Confucian approach: "To show anger is vulgar," said Confucius. "To laugh is the best way to keep them guessing." From Saigon to Hanoi, Vietnamese leaders emit this protective and often indecipherable laughter.

Every day in the press and on the radio the North Vietnamese communists call Thieu a "puppet," a "traitor," a "fascist" or "an American lackey." In contrast to many political figures in Saigon, the president has little to do with the Americans. He knows none of them intimately, unlike his more worldly cousin, Nha. Thieu receives Ambassador Martin, Lehmann, a few delegations. This lackey is obviously short on servility.

A current dilemma: If Thieu says too much about the recent North Vietnamese aggression at Phuoc Long, he'll scare off the foreign investors he counts on, mainly the Americans and the Japanese. If he says too little about it, public opinion and the Congress in Washington won't see the danger menacing his country. First of all a military man, then political, and a mediocre diplomat, Thieu never elaborates an international strategy despite the insistent advice of his cousin Nha and his roving ambassador, Bui Diem. In two years, save for American visitors, only *one* ranking foreigner, an African minister, has been seen in Saigon. In the capital, only two embassies matter: the American and the French (the French vastly less, whatever the Quai d'Orsay and the Elysée Palace may think, numbed as they are by devalued memories). Washington insists that the British, Germans, Italians and Belgians be represented in Saigon. Their embassies are inert.

Thieu gives the government newspapers a permanent assignment: when they speak of the Paris Agreement, they must also cry treason, a fool's bargain. It was a death warrant, a surrender! Thieu wants not so much to bypass or exploit the agreement as to deny it. To the diplomats this is short-sighted. Both friends and enemies agree that even if you don't love the president, you can respect him. Cunning and suspicious, he is authoritarian, not totalitarian. Opponents speak freely in the National Assembly, the Senate, the entire judicial apparatus, the thirty daily and weekly papers. Thieu is a paternalistic condottiere of anticommunism; what he lacks is a public charisma, in sad contrast to legends cast in bronze about North Vietnamese leaders. Of General Vo Nguyen Giap, North Vietnamese defense minister, Thieu says that he "wants to play at being the Vietnamese Napoleon" and that he is "really a superannuated professor."

The top man in North Vietnam, Comrade Le Duan, secretary of the

Communist Party, shrouds himself in mystery. Thieu rarely receives journalists; Le Duan, never. In Hanoi, leadership seems monolithic and hides
its intramural differences. In Saigon, known and public rivalries burst like
bubbles in broad daylight. Thieu, general-president and president-general,
mistrusts his collaborators and often despises them. For prime minister he
chose another four-star general, Khiem. A presidential election is coming
up in October 1975. Thieu wonders whether Khiem plans to run against
him. In Saigon the liberal middle classes are saying aloud that South Vietnam is "a half country in all ways, half-democracy, half-dictatorship, with
a government delivering half-measures." Thieu doesn't electrify the citi-
zenry. The refugees arriving from Phuoc Long are clear evidence that there
was no uprising in favor of the North Vietnamese. Hanoi's consolation is
that the civilian population has never risen against them or for Thieu and
his regime.

A product of the officer caste, Thieu doesn't control his army as the
Party controls its own in the North. He named General Vien chairman of
the Joint General Staff because Vien shows no political ambition. Furthermore he lets the president command directly. Thieu knows how to
command; he does not know how to control. He lives in constant fear of
a coup d'état by the military. He himself played a part in the putsch against
President Diem. After Phuoc Long, the generals hold consultations, and
every time Thieu's security adviser reports that two- and three-star generals
are meeting, the president worries. By nature he prefers inaction to action.
To his collaborators' suggestions he often answers "Maybe" or "We'll see,"
which reveals nothing of his mind. Like so many military heads of government in the Third World, he thinks democratic freedoms should be
granted in small doses.

Thieu lacks political savvy. Despite lectures on constitutional rights
inflicted by his cousin Nha, this president does not understand how the
government in Washington functions. Despite the existence of a bicameral
legislature, President Thieu can release millions of piastres at his own
convenience. Unthinkable that the American president cannot do the same
with dollars, cannot bypass the Senate and the House of Representatives
in Washington! In case of a hard blow, and the loss of Phuoc Long is a
very hard blow, Thieu is counting on President Gerald Ford.

Thieu has confidence in fat Quang, adviser, confidant, general political
watchdog, a very intelligent servant of his master. When the aviator Ky
was prime minister, Quang was relieved as commander of MR 4 in the
Delta. They accused him of corruption. Thieu appointed him minister of
planning, then assistant or special adviser on national security. Enormous,
a Buddha with piercing eyes, Quang looks like the traitor in a B movie.
There's no proof, but it's one of Saigon's clichés that Quang is abominably
corrupt. Curious: he wanted to send his daughter to an American university, but couldn't pay the fees. He applied for a scholarship from the

American cultural agencies, was turned down, and his daughter left for Australia, where she lived with one of Quang's relatives and worked at the Vietnamese Embassy. Mme. Quang never appears dripping jewels and never buys or sells. Quang roams the presidential palace at will, saluted by white-gloved guards in gold-trimmed uniforms. Quang is part of the furnishings, lacquered tables and sideboards, crystal vases, inlaid folding Chinese screens, modern desks, leather armchairs, a gaudy and ill-assorted mix of old and new.

Quang keeps Thieu informed. A new campaign against him is in the making. It will be aimed at the president's family and harp on the usual string, corruption. Mme. Thieu buys and sells—her right as a citizen. The moral code nevertheless demands that the country's first lady, or any dignitary's spouse, keep her distance from the confused wheeling and dealing often disguised as philanthropic activities. Mme. President works with civilians, above all with Ly Long Than, a Chinese merchant of Cholon, owner of Vinatexco, an influential textile company. The word is that Mme. Thieu and M. Than have invested heavily in the recovery of copper, steel and aluminum scrap. The war leaves plenty of ruins and a lot of scrap metal that's exported on Korean or Panamanian ships. Mme. Thieu is accused of manipulating the piastre. On Soviet advice, the North Vietnamese have quit printing counterfeit currency; their creation, their protégé, the PRG needs South Vietnamese money, and the best place to find that money is Hong Kong.

And Mme. Thieu was once a bit too close to Nguyen Cao Thang, director of the Vietnamese Pharmaceutical Bureau, which has a monopoly on the importation of many specialities. This Thang, one of Thieu's closest cronies, influenced or manipulated senators and deputies. He used arguments or bribes. A vote might cost $1,000–$2,000. Thieu feels that the problem of corruption can be solved after the war. There's talk often about the corruption in South Vietnam, rarely about the same problem up North.

The question agitates the international press, but Thieu knows that the American ambassador will defend an original thesis: what Westerners call corruption is, for Martin, a manifest sign of economic health and an inevitable phenomenon in time of war. Is there any more of a black market in Vietnam today than in Europe during World War II? Thieu can rest easy. The good Quang reports that Martin has forbidden the embassy's agencies to send Washington any ill-considered reports on this problem. The ambassador demands absolute proof. Traffickers, liars, embezzlers do not sign receipts, are not photographed doing business. They use false names and untraceable channels.

Quang hardly thinks the new anti-Thieu campaign will amount to much.

In his bedroom at the palace, Thieu keeps a secret dossier, a weapon in reserve: twenty-seven letters from President Richard Nixon[8] and originals or copies of cables dispatched by an American diplomat. For Thieu, the texts of these letters, and certain of Nixon's statements, are more important than the Paris Agreement. Without divulging their content to his ministers, Thieu alludes to undertakings made by Nixon. Thieu taps his hip pocket as though the letters were in it: "I have his promise here!"

When the South Vietnamese president refused to sign the first version of the Paris Agreement, Nixon, furious, yelled at Kissinger: "Brutality is nothing. You have never seen it, if this son of a bitch doesn't go along, believe me." Despite Nixon's low blows, Thieu is self-confident. He distrusts Kissinger, still in office. Nixon promised to react in case of a serious North Vietnamese offensive. Thieu rereads these letters often.

October 16, 1972, Nixon to Thieu: "You can be completely assured that we will continue to provide your Government with the fullest support, including continued economic aid and whatever military assistance is consistent with the ceasefire provisions." Later in the same letter, apropos of the North Vietnamese: "I can assure you that we will view any breach of faith on their part with the utmost gravity; and it would have the most serious consequences."

Thieu thinks Kissinger pulled a fast one by implicitly accepting the continued presence of North Vietnamese troops in the South after the cease-fire. Thieu is convinced that Kissinger deceived Nixon about the gist of conversations in Paris and conceded more to the North Vietnamese than he would admit to Nixon. All the same, what counts for Thieu is what Nixon, commander in chief of the U.S. armed forces, wrote and said.

On November 14, 1972, General Alexander Haig, sent to Saigon by Nixon and Kissinger, demands that Thieu yield on certain clauses of the agreement. In a letter Nixon lectures Thieu, then writes: "Far more important than what we say in the agreement . . . is what we do in the event the enemy renews its aggression." Nixon and Thieu are on the same wavelength. Content means more than form. What do the articles of the agreement matter! Thieu sees primarily the personal commitment of an American president as opposed to the legalisms of a text. There is no possible misunderstanding. Nixon adds: "You have my absolute assurance that if Hanoi fails to abide by the terms of this agreement it is my intention to take swift and severe retaliatory action."

The same refrain on January 14, 1973. Nixon has bombed North Vietnam and mined its ports. He does not hesitate to act harshly. Nixon shakes a mailed fist at Thieu, telling him that the United States will sign the agreement in Paris with or without the Republic of Vietnam, but he writes: "We do not recognize the right of foreign troops to remain on South Vietnamese soil. . . . The U.S. will react vigorously to violations of the Agreement."

Five days later, another letter from Nixon to Thieu. The American president restates these two themes and adds, to Thieu's satisfaction: "We recognize your government as the only legitimate government of South Vietnam."

Sure of himself, imperious, imperial, Nixon cajoled Thieu then threatened to depose him. To force a signature from him, Nixon did not hesitate to wave a red flag: the suppression of all aid from Congress. But Nixon promised, always, reprisals against the North Vietnamese.

Seeking certainty, Thieu reviews these memories after the signature of the Paris Agreement: invited to the little White House in San Clemente, California, in April 1973—to avoid demonstrations he was not invited to Washington—Thieu meets Nixon, who says to him: "You can count on us." The wily Kissinger adds that there will be "massive and brutal retaliation" if Hanoi breaks the agreement. Roving ambassador Bui Diem was also at San Clemente. Also Martin, who since then has often given the South Vietnamese president to understand that the Americans would continue to assist him. In case of a massive attack, the reply would be explosive.

This is fundamental: in his letter of June 13, 1973, Nixon writes: "This has ceased to be a matter between negotiators, or lawyers, or experts. This is now a matter directly between the two of us."

". . . or lawyers . . ." Thieu translates: The Paris Agreement is a scrap of paper. He knows how orthodox communists, Leninists and Stalinists, view treaties. If they violate them, others may. Nixon has understood, and Thieu understands Nixon. Repeated written and oral guarantees, explicit or implicit, and Richard Nixon's pledged word to Nguyen Van Thieu transcend the agreement; reprisals, reactions, those words underlined by Thieu on the original letters from the American president, imply to the South Vietnamese president the intervention of American bombers at the very least.

Further proof: NKP, for Nakhon Phanom, a code name familiar to all South Vietnamese corps commanders for headquarters of the Seventh U.S. Air Force in Thailand. NKP, magic formula. Despite Cousin Nha's acid comments and cruel cautions, Thieu thinks that America will charge to his rescue at the last moment. At Nakhon Phanom, the B-52s are waiting.

In Thieu's mind, Ford has inherited Nixon's functions and commitments. The whole of Richard Nixon's correspondence commits him. And Thieu also fears that a badly advised Ford will not think the fall of Phuoc Long critical.

Thieu wonders. Is this the moment to go public with these letters? Perhaps respect for what ought to remain confidential also holds him back.

4

The Flames of Hanoi

The American Frances FitzGerald, now visiting Hanoi, wrote once that "many Americans concluded that Thieu, personally, held the extreme right-wing position in the Vietnamese political spectrum."[1] An academic and journalist, FitzGerald published *Fire in the Lake* in 1972, an extremely interesting book on the Vietnamese and Americans in Vietnam. A great success, it has become required reading for American diplomats and military personnel. Several copies are still lying about the embassy in Saigon, in the library of the information service and the offices of the military attaché, with other classics: Bernard Fall, Sir Robert Thompson, Mao, Giap. . . . Without disguising the Vietnamese communists as angelic progressives, FitzGerald criticized the Americans' attitudes, means and ends in Vietnam and analyzed the contradictions and incompatabilities, pressed to the extreme, between Western and Oriental culture. For FitzGerald, the Vietnamese communists were—alas!—hard, but—so much the better!—pure. They are much less corrupt than their brothers in the South, she thinks, as do so many progressives and liberals. She is aware of the organic ties between the PRG and Hanoi, but supposes that the PRG enjoys a certain independence. She wrote, in elegant and sinister abstraction, that liberation will mean "the moment has arrived for the narrow flame of revolution to cleanse the lake of Vietnamese society from the corruption and the disorder of the American war."

Mai Van Bo, a ranking official in the Ministry of Foreign Affairs in Hanoi, once a skillful ambassador to Paris, familiar with American public opinion, appreciated *Fire in the Lake*. FitzGerald, a well-intentioned middle-class intellectual, concluded: "If Vietnam is to be independent, it must have a national government. . . . Today, peace implies revolution." She approved of revolutionary reunification. Mai Van Bo thinks Fitz-Gerald's attitude is healthy, useful and correct. She deserves her visa. After a long wait, she obtains it. At the beginning of January she roams Hanoi with a delegation which includes Fred Bransman, codirector of Indochinese Resources, a pacifist group and a bête noire of Ambassador Graham Martin.

In Hanoi strangers are often lodged in the Hotel Thong Nhat. It is much like the Continental in Saigon; once it was part of the same chain. The same spacious rooms, charming and old-fashioned, the same fans gently stirring the air. At the Thong Nhat, no roof terrace like the Continental's. The plumbing works badly, the sheets are darned and the whole ground floor is occupied by security services. They watch the guests' comings and goings. The guests are well fed, but quickly notice that coffee, butter and meat are scarce. Shown every attention, privileged, the foreigners never lack for cigarettes. A delegation is a smoothly running, isolated organism, always accompanied by a driver, an organizer (the customary euphemism for policeman) and an interpreter—at the outset M. Long, for this American group.

"Hanoi," FitzGerald writes, "does not look impressive . . . seemed half lethargic, tropical."[2] In the northern capital, where the façades are crazed and the roughcasts crumbling, bicyclists "have as little faith in the rules and as much in their own prowess as the Honda drivers of Saigon."[3] The old French heart of Hanoi seems clean.

The crowds in this capital don't mill about like Saigon's, but seem denser—though no more disciplined. There are few cars and soldiers on the main arteries. Innumerable cyclists pedal Russian Phoenixes, Chinese Mirs. Peugeot bicycles are prized. From dawn to dusk swarms of military vehicles circulate. Here is a vehicular melting pot of all the people's democracies: trucks, tank trucks, tow trucks, Russian jeeps and command cars, Molotovas, Zis, Zil, huge Aurochs. But you can also find the Chinese Giafong with the long rounded hood, the Polish Stars, 20s, 25s and 27s, the Czech Pragas and Tatras, Iphas from the German Democratic Republic and Korean Hirondelles. Overloaded antique tramways, green and blue or red, pass buffalo carts.

In the residential neighborhoods of this ancient colonial capital, and also in the working-class quarters, cement holes two meters deep, individual shelters, are full of muddy water. Is there no fear that U.S. bombers will return? Here and there teams of workmen are scouring the shelters. Are they afraid the U.S. bombardment will be renewed?

If not for obvious rationing, armed soldiers, anti-aircraft guns, visible SAM rockets, and conversations hanging on the war like clothes on a line, you might, even here, forget the war. The Americans have never targeted the center of Hanoi. A few bombs went astray, killing a French diplomat or a sergeant of the ICCS. The heart of Hanoi has always been protected. The war begins in the suburbs, as at Saigon.

Near the Little Lake, young people drink beer on the café terraces. In the old Chinese neighborhood, home to artisans, less frantic than Cholon, hard by the Long Bien bridge—the old Doumer bridge, repaired, destroyed, and rebuilt twenty times—on the avenue leading to Bach Mai hospital, ubiquitous and insistent loudspeakers blare slogans and, from six in the morning, broadcast Radio Hanoi's dreary programs.

FitzGerald suffers from a "slight claustrophobia." Guest of the Committee of Solidarity with the American People, the delegation sees only "what officials take one to see." An immutable ritual, an atmosphere of extreme courtesy and patience: all the delegations are subjected to an interminable series of expositions, the *bao cao*, Confucian-Marxist exercises. On an old table in the French style of the 1930s or 1940s the hosts offer tea, bananas, cookies, candies, cigarettes, with gracious gestures, as if the tea and candies were indispensable medications. The hosts inquire after the guests' health, their families, their friends, spinning a spider's web of sympathizers from New York to Paris or Stockholm. The hosts note for the tenth time that Hanoi is cooler than Saigon. You make a stab at political chat with the caution of a cat testing cold water.

Occasionally the escort changes. So this American group discovers that the interpreter at the Institute of Southeast Asia is the wife of the minister of defense himself, General Giap. No, unfortunately, the delegation does not meet Giap.

The most fascinating official, to FitzGerald, is Hoang Tung. A small man, round and lively with white hair in a crewcut, often wrapped in his scarf and overcoat, director of *Nhan Dan*, the Party's hard-line daily newspaper, and alternate on the Central Committee, Tung seems to be an obligatory stop for noted intellectuals visiting Hanoi. He's in direct contact with Party and government hierarchies.

In Hanoi, the latter assigns visitors and propaganda duties. Le Duan, secretary of the Party, receives important members of brother Communist Parties. Prime Minister Pham Van Dong welcomes diplomats, professors, priests, ministers, journalists. Hoang Tung specializes in the eminent intellectual. His direct manner, his apparent simplicity, his irony do not mask his ideological firmness: Tung makes one think of *lim* wood, the hardest in Vietnam's forests. In contrast to many officials here, Tung doesn't burden himself with circumlocutions. Speaking of the guerrillas, the PRG and the North Vietnamese regulars in the South, he does not use the sacred trope "the forces of liberation." To these American visitors Tung says, "Some people call them 'the North Vietnamese,' others call them 'the Vietcong'— you can call them anything you like."

Tung admits by implication that North Vietnamese divisions make up the bulk of combat troops in the South.

Tung retails anecdotes expansively. He's fascinated by Henry Kissinger, "that doctor of philosophy [sic] who has lately been more inclined to espionage." He goes on: during the Paris negotiations Le Duc Tho, special adviser to the North Vietnamese delegation, asked Kissinger if it would be hard to push a law through Congress for aid to North Vietnam. "But you don't understand us at all," answered Kissinger, and explained that the U.S. government is often hard pressed to obtain small sums for precise projects, for example, in social welfare, but that each year Congress voted a huge budget for the Pentagon, and the administration could use some of that money for aid to North Vietnam.

Apocryphal, this story, but enlightening: the idea of reparations haunts North Vietnamese leaders. The communist Tung, like the nationalist Thieu, is persuaded that every American president can manipulate Congress financially.

Tung tackles theoretical problems with gusto. Fitzgerald asks him what role the Vietnam War has played in History. Learned and modest, he believes that it has helped to change the balance of forces in the world.

Doctrinaire themselves, Hanoi's communists know that a world revolution is in progress. Vietnam becomes one of its prime movers, like Cuba. The Democratic Republic of Vietnam constitutes "the avant-garde of the world proletariat." According to Moscow the avant-garde is the Soviet Union. Vietnamese communists never forget that the USSR was in no hurry to recognize their republic at its birth; and they haven't forgiven the Chinese for their reconciliation (thanks to Nixon and Kissinger) with the Americans. Nor has Hanoi forgotten that at the time of the Geneva Accords in 1954 the Soviets and Chinese forced the 17th parallel on their little Vietnamese brother as the border between communist and nationalist Vietnam. Nor has Hanoi's leadership forgiven the Soviets their spineless reaction to the American blockade of Haiphong in April 1972 and the American bombings of December 1972. During that critical phase of the battle, of brinkmanship between Hanoi and Washington, the Soviets stood prudently by. In the Brezhnev–Nixon summit of May 1972 the North Vietnamese press sees a meeting "contrary to principle." The North Vietnamese leadership knows that Moscow and Beijing manipulate détente and leave world revolution for tomorrow. By subtle touches, people like Tung make clear to foreigners what divides Hanoi from Beijing and Moscow. The dispute runs deep.

Sometimes Tung uses general discussion to evoke differences and similarities. So the communist world's theoretical circles are haunted by a question considered fundamental: On the road to glorious socialism, can political consciousness be more advanced than economic development? Vietnam not being industrialized, the Vietnamese communists should be aligned with the Chinese. According to the latter, political consciousness can surge ahead of industrial development. Ho Chi Minh's heirs, according to Tung, take a position close to Soviet orthodoxy: the country will be socialist when it is developed economically. Tung remarks that in his writings Le Duan insists on the importance of technological development. In Hanoi, Maoism is treated with a cold and distant respect cloaked in self-conscious smiles. The Chinese embassy is full of *The Little Red Book* in Vietnamese. By some odd chance, they never leave the embassy.

With Tran Phuong, economist and social scientist, FitzGerald raises the less ideological and more delicate problem of changes within the Party. Which means more to a communist, ideological conviction or expertise? "The approach we take is different in emphasis from that of the Chinese," says Phuong. "We believe that the first priority is skill and technique. Will is necessary but not sufficient."

At the heart of the Party, Hoang Tung explains, there is debate not schism. It is a matter of generations. At all levels, the Party and the state include veterans of the first Indochinese war. They haven't the necessary skills to modernize the country. "There is a tendency," he says, "to look into past history for guidance and to lack the capacity for present tasks. . . . I joke with Le Duan about the subject. I tell him that if we lived under the old regime, I'd give lots of people noble status—you know, honorary titles."

In nineteen days, the American delegation visits Hanoi, its monuments, its museums, and some provinces in the Red River Delta. From start to finish they are told of the need to increase production of rice, coal, iron, electricity, cement, chemical fertilizers. There has been serious work on the transition period to follow reunification, they are told. Businessmen of the South will be welcome to buy coal in the North or sell rice. This reunification will take a while, five years, perhaps ten. The timetable is recited wherever they go, even by Pham Van Dong himself. To these Americans, whom he receives briefly, the prime minister declares, "Reunification will come, for who can prevent it? Go and ask Gerald Ford. But the Paris Agreement must be implemented first. There must be peace, democracy, national concord and a new government in Saigon. Reunification will come. I will go back to the South."

Pham Van Dong, born near Hue, in the Quang Ngai region, is sixty-nine; has superb eyes, deep, gleaming with the intense flame of malaria; fleshy lips; swarthy skin; long thin hands; he speaks French in a voice that charms foreigners. His silhouette is slim in an outfit half civilian, half military. What a seductive mix of methodical realism and contained romanticism is this prime minister, who quotes Diderot, Victor Hugo, Zola! "Exalting" is one of his favorite words. Apparently postponing reunification to some unpredictable but distant day, he adds, smiling, "But as for the date, I must visit an astrologer."

The members of the delegation were at no time aware of the intensity or importance of the battle of Phuoc Long; for that matter neither were numerous diplomats posted in Hanoi.

* * *

In a memorandum, Australian chargé d'affaires G. C. Lewis draws no dramatic conclusions from military developments in the South.[4] He recently spoke with his Russian and Polish colleagues in Hanoi, who assured him that the Democratic Republic of Vietnam "now envisages full integration of the two halves of Vietnam only as a very long-term objective, if they really envisage it at all." South Vietnam controlled by the PRG and South Vietnam controlled by Saigon "could be gradually linked in some form of association, and perhaps eventually federation, with the North."

Soviet diplomats explain to the Australians that the Vietnamese communists are truly at a stand: "the two economies [North and South] alone have grown too far apart for amalgamation to be possible, although cooperation between the agricultural South and industrial North should be practicable." Playfully, the Australian continues: "We would add the comment that as seen from here the digestion by the DRV of the Honda society of South Vietnam would hardly seem a practicable proposition." Furthermore, according to Lewis, the North Vietnamese leaders are wary of the Southerners' influence on the Northerners.

The Australian diplomat is repeating what the North Vietnamese tell their Soviet comrades.

Two counselors at the Soviet Embassy, MM. Trigubemko and Markov, circulate among the diplomatic colony, confiding that the Soviet Union has decreased its military aid to Hanoi in 1974. The jingoes and diehards, explain the Soviets, are the Chinese. *They* are encouraging Hanoi to mount an offensive in the South. Trigubemko adds that the Chinese might "commit troops." You understand, he assures all, this is only a personal opinion. He considers that Hanoi's more realistic leaders are dreaming more of a Vietnamese confederation than a reunification. He speaks of two Vietnams as of two Koreas, and two Germanys. He lays into China, "the new colonial power," which exerts such a bad influence on the Cambodian revolutionaries. The most important thing, for the Soviet counselor, is this: "Our friends here must concentrate their resources on the construction or reconstruction of socialism."

No Vietnamese higher-ups in contact with Westerners in Hanoi will rule out the possibility of an attack by the Southern "forces of liberation" in 1975. Nor an intervention by the American bombers. These leaders say they want to avoid an excessive American response. "We don't want to desecrate the thirtieth anniversary of our republic's foundation, in September 1975."

These analyses, adding richness if not consistency with each repetition, circulate through Hanoi and arrive in Western capitals. The soothing talk takes on substance in even the least receptive spirits. Westerners take Soviet and North Vietnamese talk with a grain of salt, but the incessant plugging away, in the closed and incestuous little world of Hanoi's diplomats, leaves its mark. All the more so as there is something perfectly reasonable about the good intentions advertised by the North Vietnamese communists: it would be more in their interest to make peace than to make war. As Clausewitz said, conquerors prefer peace. They like to invade your territory unresisted. The North Vietnamese are prepared to wait.

Now at the start of the new year, they complain of being badly resupplied by their allies. They let slip to Eastern and Western diplomats alike that convoys from China are late. They refer to savage strikes by Chinese railway workers. The tone of Western diplomatic dispatches from Hanoi suggests that the communist leadership is implementing a policy of small steps. All reports tally: the Politburo is putting the economy ahead of politics. It is preparing for a war protracted over several years.

Two diplomats at least, one from the East and one from the West, disagree with this analysis. Since September 1974 the Pole Domogola, posted to Hanoi three years ago, thinks that the North Vietnamese are preparing to launch an offensive. He sees no possible political solution, no moderate leader who might emerge to replace Thieu. Domogola keeps in touch with the Polish civil and military brass in the South, more up to date than others on North Vietnamese troop movements.

Another skeptic is Philippe Richer, French ambassador to Hanoi, once deported to Buchenwald, later an officer who spent two years with Laotian troops. Graduate of the Ecole National d'Administration, a diplomat, he knows Moscow and Bucharest well and arrived at Hanoi in January 1975[5] with no illusions about the possibility of a stable government in the South. Several weeks previously Prime Minister Pham Van Dong had demanded, via François Missoffe, special French envoy in Asia, that France pressure the Americans to force Thieu out of office. But the Paris Agreement implicitly confirmed Thieu in place. The North Vietnamese are nevertheless trying to oust him. By all evidence, they don't intend to let up.

Pham Van Dong receives Richer for the first time in January and says to him: "I hope you've brought me an answer." The French diplomat has no precise instructions. He is confused, and leaves it all rather vague.

With few exceptions, information converging from all over—from Hanoi and North Vietnamese diplomatic posts throughout the world,[6] the powerful communist network of information or disinformation—indicates no one should attach much importance to this notable incident at Phuoc Long. The Politburo is maintaining a certain pressure in the South and is letting the military amuse itself, that's all. Few experts seem to notice that the source of *all* news, emanating from the East or the West, is always the same: Hanoi.

In the middle of January, moreover, all specialists have in their hands a document dating from December 1974, Resolution 08/CT74, mimeographed by the PRG military command in the South.[7] It analyzes many elements of the battle "for the year to come. Nguyen Van Thieu's government and puppet army, if they are not yet near collapse, continue to struggle against increasing difficulties in all areas and are weakening stead-

vely and qualitatively." The communists are crazy for pa-
t often they keep their cadres in the field well informed.
well that communist cadres knew the substance of discussions
n Kissinger and the North Vietnamese before Thieu did—
to his great anger.

In Saigon, intelligence services carefully examine documents found on
prisoners or enemy dead. A notebook taken from a Vietcong cadre in
January comments on Resolution 08/CT74: "Our members must never
forget the enemy's stubborn desire to eliminate the working class—the
reason for the present conflict. In consequence, we must multiply our effort
three to five times in 1975. We must be self-sufficient in the field, because
we have to fight a prolonged war."

The communists will never abandon their final goal, the unification of
Vietnam; but for the moment, evidently, they foresee a long war.

On the international scene, the Democratic Republic of Vietnam and
the Provisional Revolutionary Government appear to be two distinct ent-
ities. They let the world know of their differences and disagreements, but
they speak with one voice. In diplomacy and mediation the Americans,
on the other hand, stand in disarray at all levels of the military and civilian
hierarchies.

On January 8 Admiral Noel Gayler, commander in chief of U.S. forces
in the Pacific—subsuming the theater of operations in Vietnam—tapes a
television interview at Camp Smith in Honolulu. The Americans are the
pioneers of television but the medium often gets away from them.

Before the interview is broadcast, Colonel Sheldon Godkin lets it be
known that Gayler does not exclude U.S. intervention to prevent the
"collapse" of South Vietnam after the defeat at Phuoc Long. The interview
runs on NBC's very popular *Today* show. The admiral proves more subtle
than expected. He first states that the United States will use American
equipment, not *soldiers*, to reinforce Thieu's regime. An intervention, says
the admiral, is "possible though the circumstances that would lead to it
appear remote." The admiral hesitates, stammers. South Vietnamese must
be given all the material help "that they can reasonably use. I don't mean
extravagantly—there's no prospect of that anyway—but I mean enough
ammunition so that they are fighting for their lives—they can save themselves—enough food so that they can eat, and their families can eat, ponchos to keep the rain off."

This powerful officer's suggestions make a bad impression in Saigon.
Ponchos against T-54 tanks? Washington is hardly happier. Any allusion
to a U.S. military intervention has to be handled with care. Not long ago
Kissinger mentioned intervention in the Middle East. Facing an enemy
one must never proclaim that one will *not* to do this or that, *not* send
soldiers. . . . Twenty-five years earlier, North Korea attacked South Korea.

The secretary of state, Dean Acheson, had just said that the American line of defense did *not* include Korea.

At the State Department most experts have settled on their belief: the Phuoc Long incident, an aberration that will not be repeated, occurred in a limited military campaign. No one can extrapolate from it or draw strategic conclusions. Certainly South Vietnamese resistance could have been tougher. The Policy Planning Council, a group of Kissinger's experts concerned with the long term,[8] think that intervention would be useful, but is impossible. The Pentagon also thinks they cannot send bombers, even if contingency plans are in place. The Pentagon hatches plans for everything, interventions in Vietnam, the Middle East, Germany, the occupation of Antarctica.

Why *impossible?* President Ford, commander in chief of the armed forces, is bound by Laws 93-50 and 93-52 and Joint Resolution (of the House and Senate) 542, passed in November 1973 by the Congress.[9] The president cannot commit troops for any length of time except after a declaration of war by Congress, and in precisely defined circumstances—after an attack against the territory or armed forces of the United States. Congress must be informed within forty-eight hours of any military intervention ordered by the president. That intervention is limited to sixty days. Kissinger advocates sending warships into Vietnamese waters to make Hanoi understand that the communists must halt. Ford, naturally inclined toward caution, opposes him there. The whole ballet within the U.S. government is visible, public. The Soviet Embassy in Washington, via Moscow, keeps Hanoi up to date on the tensions and disagreements at the heart of the American power structure.

U.S. policy is made and unmade at the White House, in Congress, and in the cabinet. And on television. Nixon shunned it. Ford's advisers want him to appear. The president does appear on several TV channels in his ritual State of the Union address on January 13. His advisers insisted: Vietnam still seems "a negative factor," so not a word on this subject. The advisers' strategy is clear. Either this incident, an obscure Vietnamese province fallen into communist hands, will blur to oblivion, in which case silence is the order of the day, or the situation in Vietnam will deteriorate, in which case let Kissinger pick up the pieces. Right now the voters, senators and congressmen are preoccupied with the economy, not with Saigon's fate.

In Congress the influential pressure groups, where Vietnam is concerned, are doves, not Thieu's backers.

On January 16, having left Hanoi, Frances FitzGerald's delegation stops in Laos. Fred Bransman reports on his trip to the U.S. Embassy in Vientiane. An adviser composes an ironic cable for Washington: "[Bransman was] impressed by trip to Hanoi, country was harmonious, the government was fulfilling the people's needs, no one in the Politburo had profiteered from enrichment [sic], countryside happily collectivised . . . The North Vietnamese are not at all ideological but pragmatic . . . they want a political solution."

Upon their return to Washington on January 19, Bransman and the others besiege the corridors of Congress and lobby against any aid to the Saigon government. Bransman does his work well.

Ford takes the congressional climate into account, and reactions in the press. A State Department study of editorial opinions in thirty-six daily newspapers shows that sixteen of them are "firmly opposed" to aid to Saigon, and thirteen "are sympathetic," if not to the regime in Saigon, at least to the idea of aid.[10]

President (accidentally) for less than six months, a decent man (too soon to say how courageous he is), a big fellow with a broken nose and a square jaw, Gerald Ford, "Gerry," smacks of health, probity, chewing gum. He does not look his sixty-two years. Before his accession to the presidency, the press said repeatedly, "Gerry is honest." They wanted him so much to be honest. No hanky-panky or chicanery on his record. Before he is sworn in as president, 350 investigators pass his life under the microscope. In Washington's collective legend, Nixon loved money and despised people. Ford gets along well with everyone. His bank account and portfolio of stocks add up to about $250,000. This president hides nothing. Because he has nothing to hide—above all intellectually? ask the wiseguys. His rather bland personality is transparently lackluster and hygienic and simple. Ford embraces no historic vision. About Gerry they use one word repeatedly: decent. His Boy Scout aspect charms some and reassures others. No imagination, but shrewd skill. His presence in the House of Representatives for over twenty-five years testifies to that. He had sufficient sense of compromise to become the Republican minority leader. Will he grow in stature, Gerry? Harry Truman, not at all promising to start with, became an excellent president. The White House, like the Elysée Palace or 10 Downing Street, needs character most of all. During his first months, Ford profited by the honeymoon. The press went easy on him and protected him. If Ford had not existed, he would have been invented. He knows that everybody expects a "low profile" presidency of him, as opposed to imperial presidencies from Roosevelt to Johnson, from Kennedy to Nixon. In the fine-screening of polls, as in editorials, Ford comes off well for a conservative Republican.[11] A supporter of the war in Vietnam, he nevertheless criticized the way it was conducted under Johnson; the means, not the ends. Ford accepts dissension even in his family. His two sons, Mike and Jack, opposed the war vigorously. Gerry has never claimed competence in foreign—to him—affairs. A few weeks earlier, Ford met with Valéry Giscard d'Estaing in the Antilles. Sheltering behind Kissinger when necessary, Ford came off pretty well. Giscard suggested that an accommodation with Hanoi might be possible. Kissinger seemed skeptical. One could always try.[12]

Ford doesn't want to be dragged into a renewal of the war. The War Powers Act of Congress all but takes care of that. The president is also under pressure from James Schlesinger: at this stage, the secretary of defense does not favor intervention. During a press conference on January 14 Schlesinger says,

> Now, the situation appears to be that the North Vietnamese are not likely to launch a massive countrywide offensive. What they are attempting to do is weaken the control the SVN regime has over the country. . . . I am not anticipating a major 1972-type offensive. . . . I believe the North Vietnamese continue to have an abiding respect for American power.

Then, a loyal cabinet member whatever happens, Schlesinger continues: "American opinion, historically, has reacted in anger to outright aggression. . . . The President has the power to approach the Congress; under these circumstances it might well authorize the use of American power."

For geopolitical comments on the consequences of a disaster in Vietnam, Schlesinger, with false candor, refers the public to the State Department, that is, to Kissinger.

In the political backwaters of Washington, Kissinger and Schlesinger are like two hostile crocodiles, suspicious and respectful of each other. In the cabinet Schlesinger is Kissinger's only intellectual rival, and the latter is careful to distance him from important decisions. There are Vietnam veterans working in the two departments. Diplomats lack the perspective of career soldiers. The former want to preserve the United States' credibility in the world community. The latter would rather evacuate the last American officers and men still stationed in Vietnamese villages. Schlesinger, secretary of defense for only eighteen months, does not embody the war in Vietnam. Kissinger, coauthor of the Paris Agreement, cannot be so detached. To public opinion, he carries Vietnam on his shoulders.

Ford proposes to ask Congress for $300 million in supplemental aid for Vietnam.[13]

On the night of January 23 the president is interviewed on NBC television by two stars, John Chancellor, commentator, and Tom Brokaw, anchorman. The talk comes to Vietnam. Brokaw asks the simplest question: "Mr. President, what is your objective in Southeast Asia, and Vietnam particularly?"

The president, awkward but seemingly frank:

In Vietnam, after all the lives that are lost there, Americans, over fifty thousand, and after the tremendous expenditures that we made in American dollars, several times more than $30 billion a year, uh, it seems to me that we ought to try and give the South Vietnamese the opportunity through military assistance, uh, uh, to protect their way of life.

When Ford speaks, on television and after banquets, it feels as if music is blurring his remarks, a medley of religious hymns and department store elevator music.

There follow general considerations on American traditions since World War II and aid due its allies. Ford distinguishes between humanitarian aid and military assistance. The president offers pompous prophecies about American traditions and virtues. Brokaw steers him back to the subject at hand. How long will the American involvement last, how deep is the commitment?

The president:

I don't think that there is any long-term commitment. As a matter of fact, the American ambassador there, Graham Martin, has told me, as well as Dr. Kissinger, that he thinks if adequate dollars which are translated into arms and economic aid—if that was made available that within two or three years the South Vietnamese would be over the hump militarily as well as economically.

The remarks are not very original. Ford is aware of this: "I am sure we have been told that before, but they [the South Vietnamese] had made substantial progress until they began to run a little short of ammunition, until inflation started in the last few months [sic] to accelerate."

Ford gives his ambassador full marks. Graham Martin, the president affirms, is "a very dedicated man and very realistic." Defect and virtue, President Ford is sweet and simple as apple pie.

To both professional politicians and voters, these controversies, debates and tensions within the U.S. government are striking. To Hanoi also. In a special message to Congress—a solemn occasion—on January 28, Ford asks for supplemental financial aid, $300 million to South Vietnam and $222 million to Cambodia. The president does not claim that with this aid the war will be won in Cambodia or Vietnam. Nevertheless, in the military chess game under way they can force the adversary into stalemate, according to him, and thus force him to the table for political negotiation.[14] Gerald Ford, whose inner circle hoped he would be the president of après-Vietnam, is up to his neck in the quagmire, but he doesn't know it.

"Ford is up shit creek," says a ranking young diplomat from the State Department, far out of Kissinger's earshot.

5

A Stroke of the Ax
at the Base of the Trunk

United States and South Vietnam-
ese intelligence services know that the Politburo and Central Military Committee, supreme authorities in North Vietnam's war effort, are meeting in
Hanoi. The Politburo has been in almost constant session there from December 18, 1974, to January 8, 1975.

On January 8 Hanoi concludes, as Saigon has, that the battle of Phuoc
Long is over. All the bigwigs attend important meetings with representatives of the North Vietnamese chiefs of staff and of COSVN [Central Office
for South Vietnam], military and political headquarters of the PRG in the
South. Among the politicians: Le Duan, Truong Chinh, president of the
National Assembly, Pham Van Dong, Le Duc Tho. Among the military:
Generals Vo Nguyen Giap, legendary minister of defense, Van Tien Dung,
commander in chief, Le Ngoc Hien, in charge of headquarters operations,
and Tran Van Tra, commander of zone B2, in the South.[1]

All but the last two are members of the Politburo. The Party controls
the army and the principal generals are part of the political apparatus. A
putsch is impossible. You don't rebel against yourself. The military share
political power and so are not frustrated. All these panjandrums elaborate
a strategic plan covering two years, 1975 and 1976. "Everything hinges on
our assessment of the situation at home and abroad," writes Dung. "How
would the Americans and the chieftains of the puppet army and administration react?"[2] American reactions are a primary problem: Will they
dare intervene? Have they other plans, other schemes? What are the best

revolutionary measures to take over the next two years? The discussions
are lengthy.

Pham Van Dong paces the floor as he speaks: "In evaluating the enemy,
we have to answer a lot of questions and avoid old-fashioned notions.
We're in a new phase. The United States has pulled out its troops to
conform with the Paris Agreement. They see the agreement as a victory.
But they were often beaten."

The conferees announce to the public that the North Vietnamese victory
was complete. Among themselves, opinions are more moderate.

"Now," Pham Van Dong continues, "whatever happens, they [the
Americans] can't intervene again with infantry. They could supply air or
naval support. That wouldn't be enough for either victory or defeat." He
laughs: "I'm joking but telling the truth too when I say the Americans
won't come back, even if you offer them candy."

By cables from the Soviets in Washington, relayed from Moscow, and
simply by reading the American press, the North Vietnamese prime minister knows that the United States won't commit ground troops.

Truong Chinh, massive, doctrinaire even in the eyes of his most orthodox companions, speaks slowly. Solemn, he holds a notebook and im-
provises from his notes deliberately, as if he were setting commas between
his phrases by careful little brushstrokes: "Pressure is applied to the enemy
in three ways: by our military assaults, by economic and technical difficulties, by the struggle of the masses."

The leadership has a fair idea of the limits to this participation of the
masses. The slogan is part of their credo. Reports and archives must include
such pious declarations. An uprising of the South Vietnamese people
against the Saigon regime is the flying saucer of this war: much talked
about but never seen.

"As a consequence," Truong Chinh goes on, "the enemy is weakening
rapidly. Their army has not been able to resolve the contradiction between
holding territory or populations and fighting a mobile war, but it's still an
army. Their losses haven't been too heavy and they can still recruit."

Correct. In the South's various theaters of operations, the North Vietnamese army—350,000 regulars—can group and concentrate its attacks
on a few points. The South Vietnamese army and militia—1,300,000 men—
are scattered, everywhere thin on the ground.

Truong Chinh also considers a future U.S. intervention, a major obsession: "The United States still has 25,000 military advisers in the South."

Do the North Vietnamese brass come to believe the false figures they
fabricate? There is such a thing as self-intoxication. Here too they engrave
legend in the archives: thus it becomes History. For a communist, History
is not the complex sum of real events but whatever conforms to the line,
predictions and statements of the Part, to the whole petrified Marxist
Vulgate. Truong Chinh seems less aware than Pham Van Dong of developments on the American political scene.

"If the United States senses danger," he says, "they'll intervene. But they'll have a hard time fighting a land war, and they'll have to be frugal and careful with their navy and air force." From the official notes of these discussions there emerges a muted quarrel between the more nimble Pham Van Dong and the more dogmatic Truong Chinh—even if their language is similar.

During the meetings, everyone offers an opinion, going on for hours as if the repetition of a statement would lend it substance and even accuracy. No one hesitates to repeat a colleague's words, even in insinuating disagreement. A consensus arises about the worst-case scenario, U.S. intervention, possible but not probable. The offensive must continue. Le Duan, secretary general of the Party and thus the most powerful of North Vietnamese leaders, draws their conclusions: "Two years is a little and a lot. . . . We have to take military, political and diplomatic action at an equal pace; that is our special approach, our originality." How right he is! It is the politics of three simultaneous fronts, the North Vietnamese trident, the three converging arrows, *ba mui giap cong*.

They consider choosing a city in the South as capital, to consolidate the PRG's political and diplomatic position. Tay Ninh or An Loc? They postpone the decision, partly because the destruction of a new "capital" by American bombers would be politically awkward.

Unanimously of course Le Duan's conclusions are adopted and included in the final resolution: "Never have military and political conditions been so favorable for us . . . to proceed toward peaceful reunification." NVA divisions have just swallowed up a South Vietnamese province. The phrase "peaceful reunification" is not without humor or cynicism. The communist rulers don't know yet if they're going to start off with politics, diplomacy or the military. "We have the will and the way to win, and to keep the United States from saving the administration in Saigon." The will is incontestable, the determination still obsessive.

In Washington a government of global power, active or influential on all continents, is laboring under innumerable worries and obligations. Its leaders' attention is spread permanently thin. They have to keep an eye on the Middle East, Europe, Central America and Africa, a bit neglected by Kissinger. In Hanoi the government, apparently united, has been concentrating on one objective for thirty years, the only goal on its political horizon: to free all Indochina from the foreign presence, reunite the two Vietnams and build "socialism." The North Vietnamese rulers have accomplished a minor miracle: they have persuaded themselves, and by 1975 much of international public opinion, that the survival of communist Vietnam in the North is inextricably linked to reunification of the two Vietnams.

The final declaration reads: "We have a responsibility to our people and the people of the world." We sense here the fine hand of Le Duan, the most evangelistic of the leaders. He often uses that phrase, which is not simply rodomontade.

Heavy in his movements as in his style, his complexion matte, Le Duan is one of the historic founders of the Party but lacks Ho Chi Minh's charisma, Pham Van Dong's charm, Giap's amiability. Theoretician, strategist, intelligence officer, bureaucrat in the Vietnamese communist movement, Le Duan was born in central Vietnam and knows both North and South, where he fought the French during "the first resistance." Head of the Party for fifteen years, he replaced Truong Chinh, demoted to the presidency of the National Assembly and held responsible for a bloody "agrarian reform" that claimed around 50,000 victims in 1956. The Vietnamese communists liquidate their adversaries, Trotskyite or nationalist, but do not liquidate one another.

Le Duan turns up in Moscow and Beijing. He does not know the Western world. A professor of revolution, in a style influenced by Stalin's slogans and litanies, he never ceases to repeat that the Vietnamese communists are responsible to all the world's peoples and that they must take advantage of "contradictions in the enemy camp." For him the dialectic, a quasi-metaphysical force, universal law of political gravity, kneads and shapes the world. In this first month of 1975, victory is sure; but how to assure it finally, to avoid the checks and disappointments of the offensives in 1968 and 1972?

The process of contradiction is not yet consummated. For Le Duan social change in Vietnam must come via military transformation: 1968, 1972, 1976 are so many moments in the dialectic. Thieu's regime cannot *not* fall. The Tet offensive in 1968 was a political victory for the communists though a military defeat. By Giap's own admission it cost the National Liberation Front 40,000 men—which, in one sense, resolves the problem of the front's quantitative importance. Even in that massacre of the NLF's cadres Le Duan sees History on the march. In him more than in any other historic leader an Oriental fatalism merges into a sort of Western determinism. More vigorously than Ho Chi Minh, more profoundly than Pham Van Dong, Le Duan seems cast in the prophetic mold of the *Communist Manifesto*. All his writings testify to that. The "objective conditions of the triumphant revolution" are nigh in Vietnam, despite the Party's weaknesses here, the army's difficulties there and the masses' apathy everywhere. After all these decades, victory looms, inexorable.

The Paris Agreement? No more than legalisms, buying time, their inexhaustible raw material, for the communists and effecting the departure of American troops, next-to-last stage of the process. Le Duan can display a marked arrogance even toward his communist partners, the Soviets, Chinese, Romanians, East Germans. In his coded messages he never hesitates to criticize Moscow and Beijing for dragging their feet vis-à-vis Washington. He persuades his party cadres that the Vietnamese are the true stewards of Marxist method. He has never believed in "peaceful coexistence," Khrushchev's nauseating invention. Messianic, Le Duan proclaims that world revolution is at hand. "The Vietnamese people's struggle" is the "spearhead of the army of the world revolution."[3] Le Duan navigates between Soviet deviations and Chinese errors and holds his course.

This resolution of January 1975 proclaims the "historic mission" of Vietnamese communists to the people of the world. When Pham Van Dong receives foreign visitors, he presents himself primarily as a nationalist. Le Duan, addressing himself exclusively to other communists, does not hide what he thinks, and acts primarily as an international communist.

After the political meetings, the conclave at Hanoi takes up manifold military problems. General Tra makes no bones about past and present difficulties: "Because they'd been in action since April 1972, our cadres and men were exhausted. We had no time to replace our personnel."[4] Unusual candor for the top brass. "All our units were in disarray, and we were suffering from a lack of manpower and a shortage of food and ammunition. So it was hard to stand up under enemy attacks. Sometimes we had to withdraw and let the enemy retake control of the population." This is apropos of the political and military climate after the Paris Agreement.

General Le Quang Dao's contribution—he is the army's principal political commissar—harps on traditional themes: (1) We must resolve the occasional contradictions that still divide military commanders and political commissars in the army. This sort of tirade irritates Giap, who is happier with Dao's second point: (2) A large number of officers lack technical know-how for warfare in the 1970s. When the North Vietnamese troops began large-scale tank operations in 1972, they made mistakes. They underestimated the South Vietnamese troops' fighting spirit. (3) North Vietnamese regulars in the South, 90 percent of the troops on the ground, have to master combined operations, using artillery, infantry and tanks in one battle. (4) They must improve logistics and standardize equipment. North Vietnam does not manufacture war materiel. Her sister socialist democracies deliver ammunition higgledy-piggledy, and it is not always the same caliber as the arms shipped. And (5) they must perfect training techniques on all levels, ordinary soldiers, noncoms and officers.

Ten years earlier, in 1965, the NVA counted one cadre for eight men; now it's one for six. Quality has to catch up with quantity. Since January 1973 the number of North Vietnamese in the South has doubled, and the commander in chief now commands seven times more armored vehicles and seven hundred tanks, mostly T-54s and T-55s.

Logistics: the Ho Chi Minh trail—what the North Vietnamese call Network or Route 559 because its construction began in 1959—is in good shape. Certain stretches are hard to navigate after the month of April because of the rains.

They decide to transfer several of the engineer units defending the Ho Chi Minh trail southward to Laos and Cambodia, incorporating them into combat units. Another crucial decision: in the months to come General Dung will direct operations in the South.

Tactical disagreements surfaced during the battle of Phuoc Long. Gen-

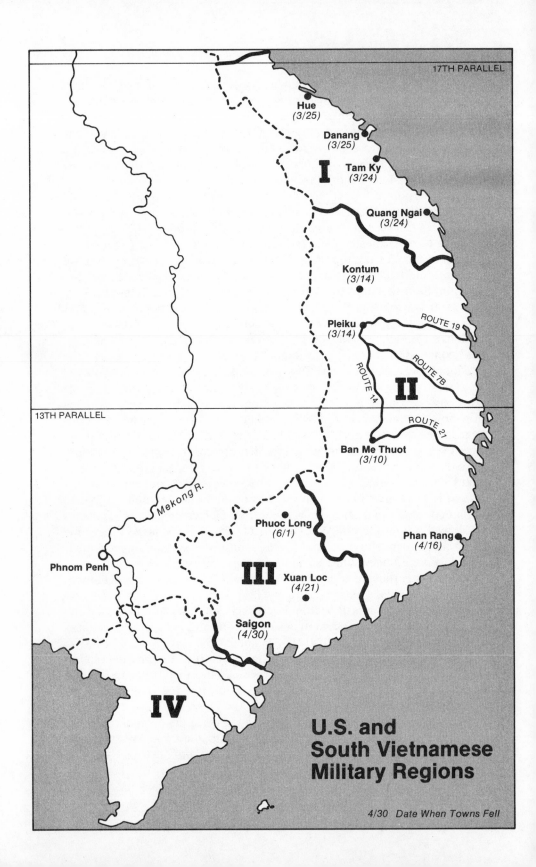

17TH PARALLEL

Hue
(3/25)

Danang
(3/25)

I Tam Ky
(3/24)

Quang Ngai
(3/24)

Kontum
(3/14)

Pleiku
(3/14)

ROUTE 19

ROUTE 7B

ROUTE 14

II

ROUTE 21

13TH PARALLEL

Ban Me Thuot
(3/10)

Mekong R.

Phuoc Long
(6/1)

Phan Rang
(4/16)

Phnom Penh

III Xuan Loc
(4/21)

Saigon
(4/30)

IV

U.S. and South Vietnamese Military Regions

4/30 Date When Towns Fell

eral Tra was not granted all the armor he wanted. Like some South Vietnamese generals, General Le Ngoc Hien hoards his stocks of arms and ammunition, especially tanks and big guns. Dung, with an eye to 1976, supported his chief of operations.

So Hanoi's strategists chop the year 1975 into three phases: the first, through February, centers on Zone B2, in the South; the second, from March to June, covers the rest of the South, where several attacks must be mounted; the third, starting in August, will be a time of reduced activity in preparation for 1976.[5]

In the context of "the large-scale and victorious offensive and insurrection of 1976," Hien laid down a schedule for the delivery of high-caliber ammunition: 10 percent in 1975, 45 percent in 1976, the rest kept stockpiled. The North Vietnamese are beavers. But the confirmed victory at Phuoc Long demands modification of these figures. Tra obtains more munitions than expected for his southern front, 27,000 tons instead of 11,000 in 1975.

The scale of the victory at Phuoc Long persuades the North Vietnamese rulers to extend their meetings past January 8.

Stating the general staff's views in Hanoi, Dung proposes to concentrate a large force, a steamroller, to open a corridor to Kontum, where they'll crush the enemy and liberate the province. Then they'll assault MR 2 headquarters in Pleiku. They'll liberate most of the Central Highlands. Pleiku and Kontum are fairly close to the 17th parallel, the border between the two Vietnams, and very close to the North Vietnamese rear bases, less than 100 kilometers away. They can easily and quickly concentrate tanks in that area.

Dung wants to keep his supply lines as short as possible. Hence his choice of Pleiku and Kontum. Tra, a North Vietnamese general but speaking for Southern combat troops, has a different perspective: "What toy soldiers you are!" he says. "You imagine battles fought by human waves and tons of munitions. What's that to us, barefoot soldiers counting our cartridges on a miserable faraway front? If you attack Pleiku and Kontum you're throwing your men against the enemy's strongest point. He's been dug in there for a long time, and he's waiting for us on solid ground."

Tra proposes another solution: "An assault on Ban Me Thuot would be a surprise to the enemy. We could take it from the wrong side, from the rear, where he's not watching. . . . That would be attacking the tree with a stroke of the ax at the base of the trunk. The branches and foliage will fall later."

Discussions continue on military options after the victory at Phuoc Long. On January 15 General Tra and Pham Hung, party secretary in the South and thus political brass, meet with Le Duan (the reports use his code name, *Ba*). Still undecided, Le Duan nevertheless plumps for a campaign in the Delta, south of Saigon, starting primarily with the cities. Implicitly he acknowledges that a civilian uprising is still a problem: "About the cities—we have to pay close attention to the masses' reactions, and build them to a tidal wave. As spearheads we must use women, youngsters, students, union members."

Again Tra calls for an attack on Ban Me Thuot. Once more the Politburo meets.

On the general staff, in the Central Military Committee, debate also rages. One thing is sure: the Americans won't send troops in. On January 20, PRG representatives Pham Hung and Tra meet with Le Duc Tho. He tells them the final decision. The primary attack will be against Ban Me Thuot: "I attended a meeting of the Central Military Committee to let them know that the Politburo had decided on that operation. . . . The international situation is very complicated. In 1975, we must limit our combat."

The politicians decide. The military gears up to execute the decision. For Dung and the general staff, their troops will be far enough from the large air bases in the Saigon region. North Vietnam has an air force but has never ordered it below the 17th parallel.

On January 24 General Tra heads south to his headquarters in Zone B2. He and Pham Hung fought hard to win this decision: an attack on Ban Me Thuot.

They almost missed the Hanoi meetings altogether. In December the chief of operations wired them not to come to the capital. They never received the message. On their way north they took the Ho Chi Minh trail and missed the messenger, Luong Van Nho, assigned to deliver that order as well as directives "relating to the plan for 1975"—which directives did not, early on, provide for any major campaign.

Tra has been allotted supplementary arms and ammunition and is well satisfied.[6] His advice won the day. He is a two-star general in the regular North Vietnamese army but he represents the PRG, and he advocates their line and their interests. He is fifty-seven years old, of medium height, round face, playful humor, and during his stay at Camp Davis in 1973 he all but pawed the ground impatiently, even as he amused himself watching the antics of the ICCS and the Two-Party and Four-Party commissions.

He coordinated the attack on Saigon in 1968 and has been fighting in the South since 1959. In the PRG's operations there, Tra is in fact second in command after Pham Hung. On the higher levels of Vietnamese communism, political officers take precedence over military in all areas. But when we shift to the battlefield, at divisional, regimental, battalion, company and platoon levels, the military prevail over the politicals. During his stay at Camp Davis, Tra answered Western journalists' questions as much by jokes as by wooden formulas. Like Thieu, he loves photography. Greedily he snatched up two Polaroids in Saigon, cameras unknown in Hanoi. In the coming campaign he will make do with black and white film.[7]

Shortly after his several months' stay at Camp Davis, Tra dropped out of sight. American and South Vietnamese intelligence files on him contain columns of question marks. A fisherman's son, he worked on the railroads. He served the Party in the South, was "regrouped" to the North after the Geneva Accords of 1954 and attended military colleges, finally becoming commandant of the 330th Division. He is a member of the Central Military Committee, but not the Politburo. A need for mystery is engrained in the traditions of Vietnamese secret societies, and it impels the communists, most notably Ho Chi Minh, to hide behind pseudonyms. Tra used many— Tu Chi, Muoi Tri. . . . Sometimes, to cover his tracks, he allowed himself the luxury of borrowing other North Vietnamese generals' names, Tran Nam Trung for one.

Heading back to his headquarters, he observes that 559, the Ho Chi Minh trail, is functioning almost perfectly. At the start, in the early 1950s, the trail was a dirt road. Since 1959 it has become a vast transportation system.

Two wide parallel arteries plunge southward. During the last three years North Vietnamese engineers have also built lateral east-west roads, access to Hue and Danang on the coast. Some routes were laid to skirt urban areas and South Vietnamese garrisons. In sixteen years the trails have become paths, the paths roads, and the roads highways. Trucks roll three or four abreast. Walkways parallel the highways. Small garrisons and rest camps mark intervals of eight hours' march. To protect this infrastructure, especially after January 1974, headquarters deployed several batallions of anti-aircraft.

"North Vietnam," says General Dung, "has thousands of mechanized vehicles of all sorts like bulldozers, and tens of thousands of soldiers, workers, engineers, youth volunteers." Voluntary or not, this mass of laborers, sappers and electricians faced enormous difficulties—bombings by B-52s, the monsoon, inadequate supplies and malaria, as North Vietnam is short of quinine. With prodigious endurance and patience, this phalanx of workers cut through mountains, leveled ways reputed impassable, hauled rocks and stones, felled trees, built bridges, established ferries, dug shelters. Vietnamese are tough, resistant to fatigue. Trained, exhorted, supervised, subjected to rigorous discipline, the Northerners are fiercer or more malleable than others. Fanatically dedicated,[8] the men and women of the Ho Chi Minh trail are successors to those who transported stripped-down artillery—on their backs, through the jungle—to Dien Bien Phu.

Proudly describing improvements to 559, Dung says (and his statements are confirmed by U.S. and South Vietnamese aerial reconnaissance photos): "This road is eight meters wide. Big rigs and heavy military vehicles . . . travel at high speed in both directions. Day and night they have transported thousands of tons . . . to the battlefield to support major campaigns." North Vietnamese staff headquarters seems exceptionally happy about the procedure for transporting gasoline: "All along this strategic road" runs "a pipeline linking Quang Tri to Loc Ninh that can supply fuel to the tens of thousands of vehicles . . . traveling the route." A paradox:

the army of a small underdeveloped country, lacking everything, has one of the best military pipelines in the world.

Giap and Dung are above all supply officers of genius, served by troops who accept unprecedented sacrifices. The Americans have never succeeded in neutralizing the famous trail—one of their major strategic frustrations.[9] Against so resolute an enemy it proved impossible, despite all the technology employed, to cut 559, a 10,000-kilometer network of flexible communication routes. From 1959 on the Americans never managed to cut the Ho Chi Minh trail, even using state-of-the-art electronics. How could the South Vietnamese do it in 1975?

The last week of January 1975: in Hanoi, Le Duan receives General Dung. The secretary of the Party asks the commander in chief if his combined forces are sufficient to assault Ban Me Thuot.

"We have enough troops," Dung tells him. "If we know how to use them we can gain the advantage."

The secretary general is not so sure.

Afterward Dung meets with Le Duc Tho. The Politburo has decided to send the former Paris negotiator south after the commander in chief. The same old story: a politician keeping an eye on the military. Speaking of the planned attack, which in his view is not the final offensive, Tho says: "If we win this big battle, we'll certainly create a new situation, one extremely favorable to us." Never short on courtesy, he adds: "Remember to take care of your health."

Le Duc Tho is very important in the Party now, one of Le Duan's possible successors. He is sixty-four years old. During a little under five years of secret and open negotiations in Paris as Kissinger's almost complicitous adversary, he fascinated the secretary of state—who nevertheless noted a rare insolence in him. Le Duc Tho allowed himself patronizing airs. During a secret meeting in Jean Sainteny's apartment, the professorial Kissinger raised his voice: "I tell you that . . . President Nixon wants . . . he demands . . ." Lordly and snug in his collared tunic, impassive, Tho heard Kissinger out. Then he answered gently: "Mr. Kissinger, you see my white hair. My life is behind me. Your hair is dark. You have much to learn. What you just said to me, I have already heard in another language." Meaning: Long ago the French said that to me. "I have heard all that. I will hear it again." Kissinger lowered his voice and said "Your Excellency" to an amused Le Duc Tho.

U.S. elected officials keep their jobs for a few years. Like all North Vietnamese leaders, Le Duc Tho is in place for the long term. The Catholic Church works in centuries; the Communist Church, as Ho Chi Minh so often stated, works in ten-, twenty-, thirty-, fifty-year periods. The North Vietnamese leadership has avoided bloody internecine purges. Its obviously monolithic unity, solidified by war, stands in sharp contrast to the succession of civilians and military men ruling Saigon. Well known in the West since his very successful public appearances in Paris—he captivated the media—Le Duc Tho, born in the North, has been a militant since he was sixteen. Le Duan directed the war in the South until 1953; then Tho succeeded him. Member of the Politburo since 1955, Le Duc Tho coordinates a global strategy in line with the North Vietnamese formula, "Fight and negotiate, negotiate and fight," *danh danh dam dam*. A sign of his rise: his name preceded Giap's on the roster of the committee for Ho Chi Minh's funeral.

The opportune moment, the *thoi co*, comes in 1975. Nothing unusual in sending a man of his caliber to the South. More than anyone else in Hanoi, he is a master of shifting international variables.

According to his official biographies, Tho is "of rural origin." He is among the mandarins, but his pseudonym suggests rather a bourgeois origin: *Duc* means virtue, and *Tho* longevity. His prose writings seem shorter but just as heavy as Le Duan's. In the party hierarchy, only Uncle Ho and the official poet To Huu were as openly devoted to socialist realist poetry as Le Duc Tho.[10] He publishes his works regularly:

> *Often in the past thirty years*
> *We have known as much glory as hardship.*
> *Armed with the Party's teachings*
> *We have struggled against cruel aggressors*
> *And spread humanitarian notions.*
> *Much time has passed,*
> *But our pen remains as young as springtime,*
> *Our writings are still sharp*
> *And our love for the profession is still strong.*
> *The course of life is still rough*
> *But, braving the waves and the storms,*
> *We row on, and move our boat forward.*

Before Le Duc Tho leaves for the South's battlefields, Le Duan says to him: "Don't come back without a victory. . . . We have an historic chance now that won't come again in 10,000 years."[11]

At least that's what the hagiography tells us.

The West is still talking about Giap. In 1975, gravely ill, for practical purposes he drops to the second level of military operations. Dung, younger at fifty-eight, earned his fourth star the year before. (Giap also has four stars.) Clearly more "of rural origin" than Le Duc Tho—you can hear it in his accent—Dung has worked in a textile factory as an electrician, a skilled worker, the aristocrat of the proletariat. In the natural course of things, Dung early joins the Indochinese Communist Party. He is arrested, imprisoned, released, arrested again; during a transfer in 1941 he escapes and hides in a pagoda, where he lives for two years as a Buddhist monk. After that he is a political commissar, and then he commands one of the most celebrated Vietminh divisions, the 320th. A member of the Politburo in 1972, he directs the sweeping campaign that begins with the capture of Quang Tri. But the South Vietnamese, supported by B-52s, push the North Vietnamese back. Since then, Dung has modernized the NVA, learned lessons from his setbacks and taken several upper-level courses in Soviet war colleges. He has instituted unified command of the various services at the division level. In Hanoi the military attachés speak of him as friendly, but less imaginative and cultivated than Giap. In the game of labels ("pro-Soviet," "pro-Chinese"), a pathetic if not dangerous pastime, diplomats murmur that Dung, like Giap, leans *rather* toward Moscow. Dung is first and foremost a career soldier. The Soviets supply 95 percent of the heavy war materiel, planes, artillery, tanks: Dung draws the necessary and obvious conclusions, inescapable to a commander in chief. Interminable arguments divide the advocates of military professionalism from ideological true believers. Like the majority of his corps and generals, Dung takes his stand with the former: military proficiency is more important to him than Marx's collected works. Before leaving for the South, he conducted a seminar on "regularizing the army," that is, on professionalism: "After studying the characteristics of modern warfare," he said,

> Lenin insisted on the need to organize a regular army of the proletarian state. At the Eighth Congress of the Communist Party of the Soviet Union, Lenin defeated the military's enemies within the Party, those who stood for a system of elected commanders, of guerrilla style and behavior, of scorn for strict military discipline . . . —all those opposed to the organization of a regular army of workers and peasants, the Red Army championed by Lenin.[12]

In quoting Lenin, Dung is taking precautions; an officer has to be a professional first—better expert than Red. Operative words: "regular army." The rest, "proletarian state," "army of workers and peasants," is only padding. Dung takes a clear stand. To avoid charges of deviationism, he concludes with a bizarre sentence: "The regular army quality of any army reflects above all the class structure of that army."

Like all soldiers of high rank, North or South, Dung knows the works of the Chinese Sun Tzu, who, two millenia earlier, composed *The Art of War*, codifying the rules of an art which is not a science but is based more and more on scientific data. Sun Tzu was Chinese. Most Vietnamese hate to acknowledge their debt to Chinese culture. So Dung is happier referring to Karl von Clausewitz, a modern who rejoices in Lenin's imprimatur, as in Marx's and Engels'.[13] They cherish orthodoxy fiercely in Hanoi. And aside from orthodoxy and tradition, Clausewitz is studied in the Soviet academies. The Prussian general's combination of politics and soldiering is immensely attractive to a Vietnamese communist, especially the idea of "war as a continuation of policy by other means or by a combination of other means."

Sun Tzu said: "Take an indirect route and divert the enemy by attracting him with a lure. That way you may leave after him and arrive before him. He who is capable of acting thus understands the strategy of the direct and the indirect."[14]

Clausewitz writes: "Victory is not merely winning on the battlefield, but physical and moral destruction, a destruction most often achieved only by hot pursuit and mopping up."[15]

Dung is an attentive reader of Sun Tzu and Clausewitz.

6

Asleep
on Their Feet

To freeze South Vietnamese troops in place, the North Vietnamese launch diversionary attacks. On January 22 a police station is blown up in Nguyen Van Que, the heart of a middle-income residential area in suburban Saigon. Four policemen are wounded in the attack. For the first time since 1972, war comes to greater Saigon. Are the communists making ready to disrupt the Tet festivities? The Vietnamese new year begins February 11.

Nha is worried. Four months ago Thieu's cousin gave up his post at Information. One of his last proposals as quasi-minister and privileged presidential adviser was the emphatic suggestion that Thieu talk directly with the PRG. Despite his public statements, the president was intrigued by the idea. But what would the Americans think of it? In 1963 the Americans had eliminated Diem largely because his closest kin, the Ngo brothers, wanted to negotiate directly with Hanoi. A lesson there that haunts Thieu . . . Some accuse Nha of veering to the left. He calls himself a realist: "It's a matter of survival." He doesn't believe that what's good for the United States is necessarily good for Vietnam. Ambassador Graham Martin demanded Nha's head and got it; Nha vacated his office on the third floor of the presidential palace.

Nicknamed "the anti-American kid," thirty-three years old, Nha never minces words. Yielding to Martin and firing Nha lie heavy on Thieu's conscience; he has not lost confidence in Nha. The young man lectures the president: "You have to shake up your administration. Your Prime Minister Khiem has lost his punch. At Phuoc Long the communists were jabbing at our defenses. They want to see how the Americans will react. And the Americans won't lift a finger."[1]

Thieu doesn't believe that. Talking to Thieu, Nha calls him "elder brother." At this time Thieu has only one daughter. He treats Nha like an independent but respectful son. When the president was commanding the military school at Dalat, the young Nha, a boarder at the lycée, spent many hours at Thieu's home. Nha is fluent in French and English. After four years' study at the University of Oklahoma he takes his degree in engineering; he then goes on to the University of Pittsburgh. Toward East Coast Americans like Kissinger, Nha harbors all the distrust of a Midwesterner. Few Vietnamese know the Americans as well as Nha. With "elder brother" he expresses at least 90 percent of what he thinks. Before the president, his courtiers and entourage, that's a lot. With no inferiority complex about the Americans, with, on the contrary, a sense of superiority, Nha doesn't cultivate the traditional Vietnamese respect for the elder and wiser. He has all it takes to charm or displease, depending on the need. He is five feet nine, large for a Vietnamese, and elegant in his famous alpaca safari outfits. His intellectual agility now overjoys and now infuriates American diplomats. He has also advised Thieu to dump his chief of staff.

When Martin arrived in Saigon, a diplomat asked Nha: "Would you like us to introduce you to the ambassador?" Nha forced the issue boldly: "No. I am a minister. It is the ambassador who should be presented to me." Martin was not amused and never forgave that cocky shot from a patriotic nationalist too sure of himself and protocol. Kissinger and Martin decided that this young man lacked experience. And doesn't he owe his influence to nepotism? His life style is exasperating. He drives Mustangs and Mercedes. In his living room he's built a wood-burning fireplace, American-style, doubtless the only one in Saigon. He controls a worldwide network of informers. Before the signing of the Paris Agreement, he often clashed violently with Kissinger.

Nha presses Thieu: "Ford doesn't have a free hand with the budget. The Americans tell you what they want you to hear. But I tell you we can't count on Big Brother."

Thieu sighs: "You exaggerate. You're too harsh. Martin's making our case and backing us all the way."

Since his arrival in Saigon, the ambassador has personally guaranteed U.S. aid to the president, who needs to believe him. Thieu trusts Martin. The ambassador gives strict orders to his departments. They must frustrate any plots aimed at destabilizing or overthrowing Thieu. And in the ambassador's view, the least opposition to Thieu is an embryonic plot. The instructions take broad effect: U.S. diplomats make little contact with the noncommunist opposition in South Vietnam, above all the "Third Force" and its potential chief, General Duong Van Minh, called Big Minh. For

After the fall of Phuoc Long early in January, South Vietnamese survivors regroup at Bien Hoa, north of Saigon. "Even the Gods Weep for Phuoc Long." *(Photo Associated Press)*

The Ho Chi Minh Trail: a network of highways. North Vietnamese supplies flowed surely and steadily. In this U.S. photo, trucks are proceeding three abreast. *(Photo U.S. Department of Defense)*

37MM AAA

TRUCKS 3 ABREAST

From the moment it was established in 1973, the International Commission of Control and Supervision was powerless. The Canadians withdrew almost immediately and were replaced by the Iranians. "What's the fuel ration this week?" *(Photo Chantal Charpentier)*

Graham Martin, U.S. ambassador to Saigon: "Within every diplomat lurks an actor." *(Photo UPI/Bettmann Newsphotos)*

Thomas Polgar, CIA chief of station: "Why, single men in barracks don't grow into plaster saints." *(D.R.)*

Frank Snepp, CIA analyst: "South Vietnam is not short of munitions." *(Photo Associated Press)*

Philippe Richer, French ambassador to Hanoi, on April 30: "I follow customary usage, and hang out flags only for *our* national holidays." *(Photo Marc Riboud/Magnum)*

Jean-Marie Merillon, French ambassador to Saigon. Never does succeed in establishing Big Minh. "Our own people are unharmed." *(Photo Agence France-Presse)*

At left, Patrick Hays, Michelin in Vietnam: "Deal with the matter at hand."
At right, Pierre Brochand, second secretary in the French Embassy at
Saigon: "It's already too late." *(Photo Jean-Claude Labbe)*

The author with Nguyen Van Thieu at the presidential palace in 1973:
"You must not confuse astrologers and horoscopists." *(Photo Jean-Claude
Labbe)*

General Pham Van Phu, one of the ARVN's worst commanders: "Let's get the hell out of here." *(D.R.)*

General Ngo Quang Truong, one of the ARVN's finest commanders: "Looting will cease." *(Photo Lafontan/ SIPA Press)*

Tran Van Houng, next-to-last South Vietnamese chief of state: "I'd like to have been president for a whole week." *(Photo Dieter/SIPA Press)*

At left, Hoang Duc Nha, Thieu's cousin and confidant: "The Americans will let us go." At right, Tran Thien Khiem, prime minister: "Go ask the president." *(D.R.)*

Mme Tran Thi Nga, secretary, Pham Xuan An, reporter for *Time*—and North Vietnamese agent: "The communists want to negotiate." *(Photo Time)*

Cao Giao, stringer for *Newsweek*: "Friendship means more than politics." *(Photo Der Spiegel)*

the Americans, this Third Force consists mainly of weaknesses. It is represented by a handful of notables and small groups in the capital and a few towns. No use seeking a political solution there.

On January 24 nine American civilians, three women and six men, demonstrate before the U.S. Embassy, waving a banner: "Americans want peace in Vietnam. U.S. end the war." Passersby notice these demonstrators with curiosity and amusement.

Called to the scene, journalists film the show and interview the participants. NBC, the AP, UPI, television networks and press agencies cover the story. These demonstrators, peaceniks that Martin detests, landed in Saigon with tourist visas good for one week. They distribute tracts. A freelance journalist laughs: "Could these cats demonstrate in Hanoi?"

The police order the activists to disperse. They refuse. The chief of police doesn't want to arrest them in public. Whatever happens let's have no arrests on American television! Later, the demonstrators are picked up at their hotel. They're treated with exquisite courtesy, escorted to the airport, and hustled aboard a plane for Bangkok at 9:30 P.M.

Martin exults. These activists' trip was paid for by Fred Bransman's organization,[2] the same man who was in Hanoi several days earlier with Frances FitzGerald. The peaceniks were to meet members of the Third Force, Buddhists, in Saigon for another demonstration before the embassy.

Martin is sure that the intent was to provoke scuffles filmed and broadcast in the United States. The pacifists would show the world that this repressive regime in Saigon does not deserve economic or military aide. Martin rejoices. The militants, American citizens after all, were well treated and expelled in masterly fashion.

Kind souls, intermediaries real or phony, earnest gossips who claim to have a political solution for Vietnam, all multiply and converge on Washington.

On January 27, in Room 6209 at the Department of State, Robert Miller, right hand of the assistant secretary of state for Southeast Asia and the Pacific, receives Tran Van Huu. Twenty years before, at Pau, this former South Vietnamese prime minister negotiated his country's independence. Like former French prime ministers, their Vietnamese counterparts dream of a presidential future. Huu was recommended to the State Department by Donald Heath, ambassador to Saigon from 1950 to 1954. Not so highly recommended as to be received by Kissinger himself. Installed at the Hilton in New York City, Huu moves heaven and earth: he can, he assures all, serve as negotiator between the two Vietnams, nationalist and communist. Byzantine, Huu swears he has Thieu's authority "to negotiate in his own name, not as an agent for Thieu whom Hanoi hates." Huu claims Hanoi is encouraging him because he's always advocated economic aid to North Vietnam. A rich man, an anticommunist,

Huu now opposes the Third Force, that political unicorn, after having played an ambiguous game with the NLF. He explains to Miller that Thieu would stoutly resist resigning to help another general into his still-warm presidential seat, and no more for Prime Minister Khiem than for Big Minh. On the other hand, Thieu would leave if Huu managed the impossible, an acceptable peace. Thieu could then depart with his head high. He would leave behind him the image of a man who, in 1972, had beaten the North Vietnamese. "The Southern general," Huu emphasizes, "defeated the Northern hero, Giap. Thieu cares deeply about his warrior's place in History."

Toward the end of the interview, Huu introduces two colleagues to Miller: Le Quoc Tuy, ex-colonel in the South Vietnamese army, and Mai Van Hanh, a former French army pilot with dual citizenship, French and Vietnamese. Miller summarizes the American view: "We still hold to the Paris Agreement, which stipulates that all Vietnamese parties together will determine South Vietnam's future. We propose to continue material aid to the government of the Republic of Vietnam, as long as that is necessary to resist military pressure from the North."

Miller composes a note to Kissinger: "Essentially, Mr. Huu thinks that North Vietnam is admitting its inability to take the South by force and wishes to find a political solution. [Huu] says he has every reason to believe that President Thieu is disposed to step down in favor of someone who could establish a real peace in Vietnam."[3]

The United Nations looms large among serious potential intermediaries. After the fall of Phuoc Long, the U.S. ambassador to the U.N. protests. Kurt Waldheim answers by letter. He presents his compliments and remarks with a touch of acerbity that he, the secretary-general of the United Nations, played no part in the preparation or signing of the Paris Agreement. Waldheim regrets the loss of human life after "the intensification of fighting in Vietnam." He can do nothing but transmit his fears and disquiet to the government of the Democratic Republic of Vietnam in Hanoi and offer the U.S. representative renewed assurances of his highest esteem. On Vietnam the U.N., under Kurt Waldheim, sits on the sidelines, formidably useless, very much a "*machin*," as de Gaulle would say, a crazy contraption. Is Waldheim knowingly playing Hanoi's game?

With Kissinger and Schlesinger beside him, President Ford receives the congressional leadership for an hour and a half on January 30. To put across his request for supplemental financial aid, Ford is working the legislative crowd. Congressmen are mainly watching the Middle East. Ford, developing Kissinger's thesis, explains that the United States cannot demonstrate its internationalism at one point on the globe and its isolationism at another, in Vietnam. The leaders listen but make no commitment.

The House and Senate are both frosty. Ford is not surprised when Democratic Senator Edward Kennedy accuses the administration of "dragging its feet" on the diplomatic level. The Democratic political opposition

remains in opposition. Ford and his inner circle are more surprised when
Senator Henry Jackson, an impeccable anticommunist, states publicly:
"The U.S. should wind up the war."

The ponderous, precise legislative machine cranks into action. On January 30 the House Appropriations Committee will meet. An important
meeting in the Senate's and House's mazes of committees and subcommittees. Money bills must originate in the House. Solemn, meticulous,
gathered in imposing settings of marble and woodwork, the committees
sit behind bouquets of microphones and interrogate high officials. The
Appropriations Committee hears several witnesses, among them Erich von
Marbod, colleague of the undersecretary of defense, in charge of logistics.
Von Marbod says the Pentagon foresees a communist offensive within six
months. General A. Graham, head of the Defense Intelligence Agency,
states: "We do not think Hanoi will try to win a complete victory in the
next six months. . . . We foresee serious difficulties for the South Vietnamese. We expect attacks around Kontum and Pleiku."

Kontum and Pleiku—precisely where the North Vietnamese general
staff has decided *not* to attack. All the communist embassies in Washington
follow the congressional debates. When the debates are public they read
the verbatim accounts, and when the committees go into executive session,
leaks abound for the truly curious. So Hanoi is forewarned. An open
society—too open?—has no secrets, even at the decision-making level. In
the United States, it is almost impossible to take secret action of any real
scope.

Graham's testimony and von Marbod's do not seem strictly contradictory: an offensive may not aim at total victory. Nevertheless these statements trouble the congressmen. Robert Gialmo, Democrat, Connecticut,
says: "The count of the opposing forces that you give us shows that the
South Vietnamese outnumber the North Vietnamese in South Vietnam."

A myth and a monster for ten years now—this riddle, how many combat
troops on both sides; numbers hard to pin down. You have to distinguish
between regulars and irregulars, the PRG's communist guerrillas and South
Vietnamese militiamen. President Ford has just said that right now there
are 298,000 North Vietnamese in the South. In Washington spokesmen
claim, file folders in hand, that the South Vietnamese army—regulars,
regional and local forces—comprises 1.3 million men. So the lawmakers
think, Let's look hard at this: which side does the balance of forces favor?
General Graham knows that the South Vietnamese army doesn't have
500,000 truly operational troops in the field. It's modeled on the American
system: for every soldier in a combat unit, there are five, ten, sometimes
twenty in the rear, in the depots, at headquarters, on airbases. To admit
that would be to question longstanding American military policy. The
object is not to explain the structural weaknesses of Saigon's army but to
show the conjectural strength of Hanoi's troops. The general falls back on
the Ho Chi Minh trail. ". . . paved much of it. It used to take them [North

Vietnamese reinforcements] seventy days on foot. Now they do that in three weeks, usually riding most of the way."

Philip Habib, assistant secretary of state for Southeast Asia, appears before the Committee. Habib was one of Kissinger's aides in Paris. Gialmo asks him: "Has the United States any legal obligation to continue arming South Vietnam?" And answering his own question, the congressman adds: "While there is a moral obligation, there is no legal obligation."

Habib, quite pleased: "That is a very precise way of putting it."

The marathon of committees grinds on.

Perhaps by shrewd coincidence, Thieu (Nha is teaching him how to play the media) gives an interview to the most influential daily in the American capital, the *Washington Post*. The South Vietnamese president does not think that the United States will abandon its ally. Nevertheless, we have to prepare for the worst: "If the United States let Saigon down, the Republic of Vietnam would continue to fight," Thieu declares. Bad tactics: Thieu would be better advised to announce that without financial aid the South Vietnamese would have to quit the fight. Inadvertently Thieu has suggested that Saigon could struggle on without U.S. aid. The interview misfires.

To prove its determination, the Saigon government announces an end to demobilization. No more will common soldiers be mustered out at thirty-eight, noncoms at forty-two and junior officers at forty-five. To show its government's pugnacity, the ambassador in Washington passes this news to senators and congressmen, many of whom reflect, Well then, if *our* Vietnamese can manage by themselves . . .

When by chance Congress does take an interest in Southeast Asia, it tends to concentrate on the situation in Cambodia, which seems serious. The television news alone persuades them of that. To be taken seriously in 1975, a battle has to be televised. There were few films of the battle at Phuoc Long.

The Khmer Rouge occupy 80 percent of the country, firing rockets at will into Phnom Penh. It hasn't come to that in Saigon. Cambodian battalions have been reduced from 300 to 100 men. The South Vietnamese army is not dissolving. On the Cambodian Mekong, the Khmer Rouge are sinking tankers; the last freighter reaches Phnon Penh on January 23. The Vietnamese Mekong remains navigable. The only umbilical cord between the Cambodian capital and the outside world is an airlift.

On a cold afternoon in Washington, Vietnam expert Douglas Pike, author of a book on the Vietcong, strolls on the Mall, the immense avenue bordered by museums, monuments, and ministries. Pike is a level-headed specialist and has always resisted excessive emotional involvement in this Vietnamese affair, even when he was posted to the embassy in Saigon. During the Tet offensive—South Vietnam was put to fire and the sword—Pike surprised some visitors; he was cataloguing his stamp collection, and said, "This too shall pass." Sam Burger, formerly with the embassy in

Saigon, is walking with him on the Mall. They have just been sitting on an academic jury. A colonel was defending his doctoral thesis, "Is the South Vietnamese Defense Viable Without the Americans?" The candidate seemed optimistic. These two members of the jury are less so. Heading toward the State Department, Sam Burger says softly to Pike: "It's all over, isn't it?"

Pensive, Pike, after a few steps: "Yeah, it is."[4]

In Pike's mind, conviction preceded formulation of the idea. I've been kidding myself, he thinks. He cannot now bring himself to say, South Vietnam can survive. In official circles, men like Burger and Pike seem hard to find.

Around Kissinger, everyone is obsessed with the Middle East. "Nothing is more dangerous than the situation in the Mideast," says Kissinger; he wants to bring about an agreement on the Sinai. The Egyptian Sadat seems more accommodating than the Israeli Rabin. The latter, with a slim majority in the Knesset, has not much room to maneuver. These days Kissinger follows the twists and turns of Israel's internal politics more than he does South Vietnam's. He plans a ten-day journey to the Mideast in February. He wants the Israelis to agree to withdraw some fifty kilometers in the Sinai. Top civil servants, decoding diplomatic documents or hunched over maps, devote more time to Mitla Pass in the Sinai than to Cloud Mountain near Danang.

In Washington, few public servants can imagine that the North Vietnamese are ready to advance several hundred kilometers in the Central Highlands. Bureaucracies lack imagination.

In Brussels, Nguyen Phu Duc, South Vietnam's ambassador, pays a visit to General Alexander Haig, supreme commander of the allied forces in NATO. Thieu detests Kissinger but has happy memories of Haig, who, at the White House under Nixon, discussed the Paris Agreement with the South Vietnamese president in 1972. Haig put pressure on Thieu, but most courteously. Soldiers understand one another. Haig promises Duc that he'll intervene personally with Gerald Ford.

Since Marshall and Eisenhower there has not been a rise as meteoric as Haig's. In four years he has jumped from colonel to four-star general. At fifty, he holds a prestigious position in Europe. Early on he understood that a successful military career comes by way of good relations in the political jungle. General officers must show themselves as competent in diplomacy as in strategy. Haig earned a degree in international relations at the University of Washington. A Vietnam veteran, commander in chief of NATO, sensitive to reactions in European capitals, he too feels that American credibility is at risk. Haig knows that History shapes men and that certain individuals—Nixon, Kissinger—can change its course. Is Ford a man to take a firm grasp of History?

In Washington, the confused climate stuns Haig. He considers resigning to jolt public opinion. He is received at the White House. Haig is famous for giving free rein to bombastic utterance, preferring abstract Latinate paraphrases to stony Anglo-Saxon words. Carried away by emotion, he speaks simply: "Mr. President, you must resume the bombing. Even if Congress refuses."

"Al, I can't do it," Ford answers. "The country is fed up with the war."

Haig insists. Ford must send B-52s, on principle and in his own interest. If not, he won't be reelected, Haig says. "You've got to show leadership now, before it's too late."

Ford is concerned but not swayed. Ron Nessen and Donald Rumsfeld, members of his inner circle, reassure him: "Haig has lost contact with realities here in Washington. These days he reacts more like a soldier than a politician." And the coup de grâce: "Haig picked up some bad habits under Nixon—covert operations, and the White House bypassing Congress."

Ford must keep to the straight and narrow as president, to erase the memory of the secret bombing of Cambodia ordered by Nixon. Besides, White House staffers, asleep on their feet, believe there will be no North Vietnamese offensive before 1976.

7

---◆---

The Dragon's Vein

The second anniversary of the Paris Agreement, January 27, passes almost unnoticed in Saigon. A hundred or so Buddhists, among them about twenty mendicant sisters, try to march, starting from the An Quang pagoda. The police disperse them rudely. The Saigonese adopt Saigon's and Washington's official view, which soaks into the body politic like maple syrup on a pancake: the loss of Phuoc Long is nothing dramatic.

"Hanoi wants to establish a new balance of power for negotiating," says M. An, principal Vietnamese contributor to *Time*, always well informed. At the Café Givral he lays out his analysis for the other two musketeers, Cao Giao and Vuong. He develops it more succinctly for Mme. Tran Thi Nga, administrative secretary at the *Time* office. Mme. Nga takes no interest in politics. She wants peace and would love to revisit the North of her childhood, where she knew famine and Japanese occupation and was forced to marry a Chinese Kuomintang general by whom she had two children. The general was killed. Mme. Nga lived with her brother-in-law. Now she has four children. After working at the Ministry of Social Affairs, she settled in at *Time*.

There are fewer foreign journalists than before in Saigon. *Time*'s bureau chief asks Mme. Nga why she seems so sad. "The communists will keep on coming," says Mme. Nga. Then, to her own surprise: "I think I'm going to kill myself."

"You might think about some other way out," the bureau chief replies. Leave?

Writer Duyen Anh, like Mme. Nga a Northerner who fled to Saigon, is not so gloomy. A journalist nicknamed "the young people's writer," he has published about fifty novels, essays, volumes of poetry. He left his parents up North with his five brothers and sisters. His mother was killed in a bombing raid. A long time ago the writer belonged to a party opposed to President Diem, the French, the Americans, the Vatican, to all Vietnamese "who follow foreigners." He does not care for—no longer cares for—politics. In his stories he describes the confusion and isolation of young Vietnamese. Unless you're paid in dollars, like Mme. Nga at *Time*, you have to sell Vietnamese papers a lot of column-inches to make a living. The writer is not too unhappy: Nguyen Van Hao, deputy prime minister for the economy, has offered him a job as editor-in-chief of three newspapers. Distributed in Saigon, Danang and Can Tho, they cover the economy and education.

"I've accepted," Anh says, "because even if they're subsidized, these papers don't kiss official ass." He will also work for a magazine, *Green Revolution*, devoted to agrarian reform. Thieu comes off fairly well there. For March the writer is preparing a "day" called "Paddy for the Peasants."

Monk Thien Hue, twenty-three, lives with other young monks around a pagoda northeast of Saigon, ten minutes by car from the airport. He learns about the fall of Phuoc Long from the newspapers. Most Buddhist priests don't talk politics. But this group's pagoda, Quan The Am, three stories high and of no architectural interest, knew a moment of fame. In June 1963, under President Diem, a venerable priest committed suicide here to protest against Diem's anti-Buddhist policies. He doused himself with gasoline and lit a match. Mme. Nhu, Diem's sister-in-law, called it a "bonze barbecue." Today An Quang is the most famous pagoda in the country; journalists and politicians visit. There the Venerable Thich Tri Quang devotes much of his time to politics.

To lose one battle is no serious matter, thinks Engineer Van. He's met refugees, soldiers pouring back from Phuoc Long. Officers and men alike complain that they lack arms to retake the province and its capital. Some of them claim that all they could throw against North Vietnam's armored cars was Molotov cocktails. The engineer only half-believes them. During his studies in Paris, concentrating in public works, he met Nguyen Khac Vien, communist official of the Vietnamese League, who was recruiting cadres for the North. The engineer dreamed of establishing an egalitarian society. He almost left for Hanoi. A Northern propaganda film on agrarian reform showed people's tribunals and landowners' heads crushed by plows. Much troubled, the engineer returned to Saigon. For many Vietnamese it was a toss-up between North and South during the 1950s.

Employed at the Ministry of Public Works, Van hopes his compatriots will tend toward the Confucian logic of the happy medium. Neutralism and reconciliation represent that happy medium. The engineer belongs to the alumni association of the major schools: Petrus-Ky, Marie-Curie, Chasseloup-Laubat. The association admires two neutralists. One, Trinh Dinh Thao, president of the National Alliance for Peace and Democracy, survives in PRG territory. The other neutralist, Big Minh, lives in Saigon.

"Why don't the two neutralists cooperate, the one from the city and the one from the country?" asks the engineer. "We have to go beyond political differences, and reunite families."

So many middle-class Southerners have relatives in the North, and vice-versa! We're all Vietnamese. Big Minh himself has a brother up north, Duong Minh Nhut, a general in the supply corps. Even at the highest levels there exists a dense tangle of invisible ties. In Saigon they say President Thieu's wife is sponsoring the daughter of an important member of the PRG, and sent her, paying all expenses, to a university in the United States. During their war the Americans complained plenty about arrangements between the Vietcong and Saigon's troops at the local level. Why not work things out now on higher levels? The Americans can't understand that kind of thinking.

Despite communist massacres of South Vietnamese at Hue in 1968, the engineer thinks "communism is a subspecies—or a part—of nationalism." In one way it would be logical to have communists running the country. They've made great sacrifices. The road to the happy medium seems economically inevitable: the Northerners need the South's rice paddies as much as the Southerners need the North's minerals.

In the rue Le Loi the minister of public works and communications[1] calls a meeting of his bureau heads and the directors of companies answerable to the ministry—Air Vietnam, Vietnam Electric, and maritime, riverine and truck transport outfits. What can we learn from Phuoc Long?

"It's a communist trial balloon," says the minister. "They want to see if the Americans will intervene and if we South Vietnamese are going to fight." The minister leaves his subordinates free to act independently: "according to your conscience."

Meetings, informal or formal, are being held in most ministries and businesses. At Public Works, they adjourn in high spirits. In the babble you can hear, "The Americans have too much invested in South Vietnam to let us down." And "The Americans know the North Vietnamese can't administer the South's infrastructure."

Engineer Van is not so sure.

Like Mme. Nga, and the writer, and the monk, like all the Saigonese, like all the Vietnamese, the engineer is making ready for the Tet holiday, a good time to read the future. The year of the Cat will succeed the year of the Tiger. President or peasant, businessman or soldier, student or taxi driver, artisan or teacher, educated in the West or never left home, a

Vietnamese plunges into the occult with an intensity that surprises Europeans and makes Americans bristle. Argue about the supernatural and the irrational, and a Vietnamese answers: "*You* believe in scientific predictions. *We* are determinists in our own way. To reveal the future, we have methods that decipher omens and portents."

So they seek consultations. In the South as in the North, where authorities and press try to combat these customs. They hie themselves to the soothsayer. By analyzing the heads and tails of four coins in a bowl, the seer answers his client's questions. Blind soothsayers are much prized. Often palmists and physiognomists are the most expensive. A few Americans, even some of the researchers at the Rand Corporation, think physiognomy deserves more than polite condescension. A face speaks. According to some doctors, changes in pigmentation presage cardiac troubles. Well . . .

In Saigon they go on investing. Before you add a wing to your villa or rebuild your straw hut, make sure the new construction won't cut a vein of the Dragon that sleeps underground. A geomancer's opinion is essential. The wisest advice, and the most expensive, comes from astrologers. President Thieu often puts himself in their hands. If a Westerner asks him why he, a Catholic, consults astrologers, the president hides his annoyance behind a burst of laughter: "I don't consult astrologers, but horoscopists. Casting horoscopes is a very precise science. But all horoscopists aren't seers."

In 1974 Thieu asked a famous astrologer, "If I leave, quit the presidency, who can replace me? Don't forget Big Minh."

The considered response: "No one will replace you if you resign."

"Well then, the communists will replace me."

Before a military operation generals too seek consultations, which does not amuse their U.S. advisers. North Vietnamese officers do not seek consultations, but the PRG never hesitates to manipulate seers for disinformation, in Vietnam or in foreign parts among the diaspora.

Sun Tzu says: "What they call foreknowledge cannot be obtained from the spirits, nor from the gods, nor by analogy with past events, nor by calculation. It must come from men who know the enemy's situation."

Every year in Saigon Huynh Lien publishes a horoscope manual. He sells over 50,000 of them. The manual is a hot item even among overseas Vietnamese in Paris.

Lien is one of those highly valued horoscopists who cast for nations as for individuals. He is consulted on Vietnam's future.[2] This year of the Cat will be hard for Thieu. By his age, the president has close ties with the Mouse. The tiniest illiterate urchin, peddling cigarettes, knows that Cat and Mouse are not friends. Those who live under the sign of the Mouse need ties to those born in a year of the Horse. Everyone understands the reference to Mme. Thieu. To ward off evil, you devote yourself to charitable occupations and if possible make a retreat in a Buddhist monastery. Lien foresees many conflicts between Water and Fire. It would be good if the leaders took rather long vacations.

Before Tet people buy talismans and amulets, especially in the provinces.

Administrative services purr along in the tranquil capital. On February 1 the minister of posts, telephone and telegraph announces that he is now linked telephonically, via Paris, with the Republic of South Africa, Botswana, Lesotho and Rhodesia. *Prestige oblige*: for several days it's easier to call Pretoria than Paris.

Tourists wander the city. Gossip says there will be even more of them next year. Here's a classified ad February 2 in the *Saigon Post*, the English-language daily that's swiped many readers over the years from the French daily *Le Courrier de l'Extrême-Orient*:

> German boy 27 years old, wishes to
> make friend with a Vietnamese girl with
> a view to marriage. Girl with a picture
> will be appreciated.
> (Come back to Saigon next years 1976)
> Mr. Hartensuen, 7000 Stuttgart
> Wannenstrasse 88, Allemagne

The director of the Saigon Zoo proudly announces "137,200 visitors of whom 98,000 were adults and 38,400 children."[3] Doubtless 800 were eaten by crocodiles. In Vietnam, numbers and statistics, whether of dead, wounded, refugees or zoophiles, are often bizarre or dubious.

President Thieu prepares the traditional message to the people, to be broadcast on the eve of Tet. Thieu insists on three points: We must support the military front "to the maximum." How many fronts are there in this country? We must increase production. The two enemy Vietnamese republics are in harmony on this theme, even if the North harps louder on it. And last, Thieu demands a "general stabilization behind the lines": he wants more coherence and unity on the political level.

So the government must negotiate three crises in domestic policy.

The Hoa Hao have settled south of Saigon. This sect's philosophy is akin to Buddhism. But the Hoa Hao have a paramilitary organization that smacks of the large outlaw gang, or of a private militia. Heading it up are warlords and religious fanatics. The Hoa Hao's commitment, in contrast to the Cao Dai's, is political, nationalistic, and flatly anticommunist. The French, the Americans and Saigon's successive governments have therefore used or tolerated the Hoa Hao. The Vietminh, then the Vietcong, never flourished in zones of the Delta the sect controlled. With 1.5 million faithful and about 50,000 armed men, the Hoa Hao are a force to be reckoned with. They've always aspired to autonomy and they're agitating for it again.

Now they want to name their own province and district chiefs. Thieu will not yield his prerogatives. The heads of provinces and districts are officers who owe him fealty. With them the president maintains his authority over both civilian and military society.

Emissaries of the Hoa Hao come to the presidential palace and negotiate. Luong Trong Tuong, head of the Hoa Hao church, obscure and devious, asks Thieu to be responsive "to the aspirations of his faithful," whose loyalty he guarantees.

To reinforce their claims these men, armed with bamboo poles (not serious) but also with M-16 rifles and 81 mm. mortars (more impressive), cut the roads. They set up altars on the main highways in Long Xuyen province. The army clears a few roadblocks. Score: three dead. Thieu maneuvers but will not give in to any of the centrifugal forces tearing Vietnam apart. He gains time, parleys with the leaders and thumps the faithful. These Hoa Hao are immobilizing troops that could be used elsewhere. The situation is all the more dangerous because for the last ten years, thanks to them, the Delta has been the calmest area of Vietnam. With hazy promises and shrewd bribes, the higher-ups are appeased. A certain autonomy will be granted—when peace returns.

In Saigon itself Thieu has to deal with the noncommunist opposition, more restless than numerous. It comprises Buddhists, also Catholics. Though a convert himself, the president does not count on his coreligionists. Catholics who came from the North by whole villages after 1954, following their crusader priests, were reliable. These days there are some wavering "progressives" among Southern Catholics. Thieu thinks the Catholic Church is tainted all the way to the Vatican. John XXIII was firmly against communism. When Thieu was granted an audience in Rome, Paul VI advised him to come to some agreement with the Vietnamese communists. Paul VI also received Mme. Nguyen Thi Binh, the PRG's minister of foreign affairs. The Catholics are by no means exempt from Thieu's morbid suspicions.

The Redemptorist priest, Father Tran Huu Thanh, a small, nervous and cranky man, president of the People's Movement Against Corruption, looses a few incendiaries at the president. Duplicated, his messages are distributed in Vietnamese editors' offices and among foreign journalists. This priest accuses Thieu of rigging elections yesterday to seize power and encouraging corruption today. For Father Thanh, the president is "a man born of the war, who wants to perpetuate the war." Among the notables in Saigon backing the People's Movement Against Corruption are Senator Truong Tien Dat, and other priests like Father Thanh Lang, influential in intellectual circles, president of the PEN Club, president of the Vietnamese Press Council and Vietnamese Journalists Association.

This Redemptorist wields a clever and mischievous pen. He edits and publishes a text with the unequivocal title "Accusation Number One," which strikes sparks in his readers, especially in the working classes. His incendiary diatribes don't bother much with proofs. He charges that Thieu enjoys a sizable landed inheritance in Vietnam and abroad. That the president is involved in the drug traffic. That the People's Hospital, under Mme. Thieu's supervision, has become a hotbed of nepotism. That relatives of both the president and his wife have insinuated themselves into hundreds of businesses. Doesn't a brother-in-law of Mme. Thieu hold a monopoly on the importation of fertilizer? The sale of fertilizers brings in scandalous profits. Cautious, Thieu reacts in his usual crafty fashion. He shows no anger at the author of "Accusation Number One," nor does he prosecute him for defamation, a misdemeanor spelled out in Vietnamese law. The president swoops down on the newspapers that published the text. The charge: procommunist activities.

But Thieu commits a political error: at the same time he lashes out at several religious and political personalities, and also some journalists.

The government's tactics require explanation. The minister of the interior—flanked by the minister of information and the commandant of the National Police, who is also head of the secret service—holds a press conference[4] quite typical of this half-authoritarian, half-legalistic regime. The minister of the interior announces, "Sixteen reporters and two owner/editors have been arrested. They were working for the communists. They were plotting President Thieu's overthrow. They cannot be considered loyal opposition."

Five papers were shut down.[5] Others were seized because their directors refused to cleanse their editorials of phraseology offensive to the chief of state. The government unfurls a grandly vague accusation: "These publications tried deliberately to poison public opinion." During the press conference the minister presents two unconvincing "guilty parties." To Minh Trung says that he was acting "under Le Duan's orders." Vu Trong Luong states that they "ordered him to make the most of news unfavorable to the government." In the audience, composed mostly of journalists, there is tumult and laughter. They can hardly imagine the head of Hanoi's Communist Party giving orders to a Saigon journalist. "To make the most of" is a vague expression; there's no lack of bad news, and to make anything of it, a conscientious and critical journalist has no need of orders.

Representing the Journalists Association, Father Lang interrogates the minister in a strong, calm tone: "Why have you waited so long to make these arrests when, as you've just said, you've known about the defendants' activities for quite some time?"

Embarrassed, the minister ducks the question: "We are operating in the framework of a democratic government. The press must be free, but we cannot permit communist agents to transform it into an instrument of propaganda."

No one is deceived by this lofty statement of principle. A representative of the daily *Dien Tin* gently defends the journalist Luong, who works for his paper: "The accused covered cultural events for us. Before that he worked for a poetry program on Radio Saigon. If the government didn't know he was a communist agent, how could we be expected to know it?"

The audience clamors. A shout: "Who's been arrested?"

"Names, names!"

The top cop reads a list of arrested journalists, known or suspected communists.

Cao Giao, one of the Three Musketeers, asks: "And Choe?"

He is a famous cartoonist and he has disappeared. His cartoons are equally venomous toward Saigon and the communists. He goes underground briefly; he is not arrested. In Hanoi they arrest anybody. In Saigon the authorities have to be more careful.

This affair has the capital in an uproar. Meetings are held, motions of solidarity voted. A spokesman for the militant Buddhists of the An Quang pagoda announces: "We are ready to support the press." Four papers that had not been bothered decide not to publish for one day. Three dailies subsidized by the government[6] publish the official communiqué as gospel: the arrested reporters are communist secret agents.

The agitation reaches a heated National Assembly. Forty-eight members of groups representing part of the noncommunist opposition denounce the seizure of the papers, scrawl graffiti on the walls, accuse Thieu of employing "corrupt elements." A letter drawn up by protesters in parliament zeroes in on the president's security counselor among others, stout General Quang. Shrewd and careful, these protesters do not accuse the chief of state himself of personal corruption. To hallow the solemn occasion, each signatory dips his pen in his own blood.

The U.S. ambassador lets it be known that the arrest of these journalists will have a damaging effect on Washington. Consulted by Thieu, Cousin Nha concurs firmly. The government retreats. Ministers explain that there has been a misunderstanding. Most of the arrested journalists are perhaps not, doubtless not, probably not, communists. We shall see, we shall release certain of them, we shall release most of them, "victims of communist brainwashing."

Big Minh rallies his friends. The Third Force leader commits himself:

> By arresting editors-in-chief and journalists, by closing newspapers that support our struggle, the government has struck out at us. . . . An insolent and contemptuous attitude toward the people . . . This tyrannical government is trying to silence us. We cannot relax and enjoy our Tet holiday. We must continue our arduous battle. Ladies and gentlemen, friends all, I have long advocated reconciliation . . . the only realistic way to bring about peace.

Without going into detail, Minh refers to the need to transfer power to men "supported by the people" and to political movements "derived from the people."

Modest, Big Minh does not put himself forward. He too is prudent, and he attacks tyranny without naming names. Minh is slick. Between the two men Thieu and Minh there is something like a gentlemen's agreement. Or an ancient complicity: twelve years before, with others they worked together to overturn President Diem. Tradition demands that Thieu respect Minh, older and formerly his superior; interest demands that he handle Minh with care. For Thieu, to tolerate Minh is to accept a rival on the political scene, at least a potential rival, and to show the Americans a semblance of pluralism. Minh mutes his dissent, or formulates it in terms sufficiently veiled to preserve him from arrest and exclusion.

At fifty-nine, a tall and hefty man (whence his nickname Big), Duong Van Minh plays a curious role. He is impressive. But even his inner circle concedes that he has no flair for politics. Is it, as Karl Marx thought, that in flat countries the hills look like mountains? An odd "acknowledged leader" of the Third Force, this Minh who never declares himself! He was a doormat for others more ambitious and less popular than he. Just what is this popularity his friends claim for him? In Saigon they don't use public opinion polls. Minh has always hesitated to run in elections almost surely rigged. His destiny? Perhaps one of glorious near-misses. Son of a teacher, he dreamed of being a civil servant, of assimilating Europe. He could not attend the Sorbonne any more than he could Saint-Maixent. He enlists at the start of World War II and becomes a soldier in Vietnam. Emerging from a Japanese prison camp, he is imprisoned by the Vietminh, then certified a teacher. A lieutenant colonel in 1954, in the service of the Fourth French Republic, Minh, this man of feeling, brutally liquidates the frenzied Binh Xuyen sect. A protégé of President Diem, Minh earns his fourth star in 1957. In 1963 he takes part in the American-approved coup. Diem is assassinated—on Minh's personal order? Briefly head of the Revolutionary Committee formed, honorary chief of state, Minh falls victim to another coup d'état, fomented by young lions, and is sent to Bangkok. He returns to Saigon in October 1968. His former subordinate Thieu, now president, offers him a post as special counselor. To neutralize him by honoring him, compromising him by co-opting him? Minh declines the sticky offer, just as he refuses to head up a Buddhist party. Many boast of Minh's honesty and wisdom, but his transparency sometimes seems opaque. At 3 rue Tran Quy Cap, in his house, modest for a four-star general, he receives government higher-ups; unknown diplomats; famous editorial writers; agents, open or secret, of intelligence services. In 1971 his followers do well in Saigon's elections. For a long time he's been saying, shrewdly, "The Saigon government and the National Liberation Front [later the PRG], whatever they're worth, have their own army and their own police. The Third Force has nothing. It has only the people's support."[7] What do these "people" think? May Minh be more famous than popular, especially in the cities, and above all in Saigon?

In 1971 the presidential election had to be, or seem to be, open. The U.S. Embassy suggested that Minh run against Thieu. Minh hesitated, then refused. Tired of him, the Americans ceased courting him. These days, the only person of any importance at the U.S. Embassy to keep in touch with him is General Charles Timmes, a retired career officer recruited by the CIA, a Vietnam veteran, assigned to liaison with all Vietnamese generals.

Pierre Brochand, second councillor at the French Embassy, saw a lot of Minh. Easygoing and affable, the general adores exotic fish and orchids and plays tennis at the Cercle Sportif, where Brochand often goes. Minh murmurs, "I have no ambitions." And it is easy to believe. He repeats, "For me, politics is first and foremost morality. . . . My morality is often Confucian." The Americans discern no plan of action in this Confucian lack of ambition; they see it as a lack of drive. Many come to ask Minh's opinions and leave asking themselves, like Stalin about the Vatican, how many divisions does the Third Force have? A question that Minh asks himself, too. The general walks a line equidistant from the PRG and the Saigon government.

Minh is everywhere and nowhere. Placid, he remains on good terms with the prime minister, too: Khiem also has four stars. Among Minh's followers are dilettantes and men of distinction. One of his advisers, the political expert Ton That Thien, lists the general's trump cards: "Minh is a Southerner and a Buddhist. He has support in all of South Vietnam, at Hue as well as at Saigon. He's a complete soldier, his prestige in the army is intact, and he has no conceit." Can a political man do without ambition and conceit?

Around Minh are men waiting for him to make up his mind, or for events that will force him to take power. Vu Van Mau, doctor of laws, was minister of foreign affairs; rather a pacifist, he favors "the forces of reconciliation"—a movement, a trend, more than a party. Nguyen Van Huyen, more fervent Catholic than politician, more mystic than realist, resigned from the Senate to protest Thieu's policies; Huyen had been elected to the presidency of the Senate against Thieu's candidate. Minh and his men are always respected and rarely feared. In his slow voice, or in hackneyed phrases, Minh demands the right of peaceful assembly, the right of political organizations to exist truly, and on both sides. He enter-tains no illusions about the Hanoi regime. But in the name of reconciliation he avoids head-on clashes with the communists in his public speeches. Minh does not neglect details very important to the Vietnamese middle and upper-middle classes. He calls for the right to a passport and an end to entry and exit visas, which the Vietnamese have been subjected to. In trying to be Mr. Everybody, Minh is nobody.

Is he perhaps advancing one step at a time? Is he waiting for the propitious moment? In theory the Saigon government and the PRG are still negotiating at La Celle-Saint-Cloud. In practice, the meetings drowse along. What would he do if the two parties there came to an agreement on Minh's name? His response is never clear. He murmurs something to the effect that "I would like to serve my country with the support of my people." They take him as he is, a man of good will and so far ineffective. In the matter of the seizure of newspapers, Big Minh has committed himself with what, for him, is impetuosity. Thieu ignores his statements.

The traditional firecrackers, forbidden, burst and thunder here and there. Saigon is celebrating Tet. The pagodas are full. Joy is moderate. No Vietnamese can help remembering Tet in 1968. Then, contrary to previous strategy, the communists launched their offensive all across South Vietnam. On the eve of every holiday the question looms: Will they start up again? Forehanded, the government forbids civil servants to take vacations and soldiers to take long leaves. They must content themselves with a day and a half. The careful minister of national education allows the students a two-week vacation, to avoid demonstrations in favor of the journalists.

On February 17 the government withdraws some of its charges against the newspapers. On February 18 a court acquits the dailies charged with violating the press code, which Thieu admits should be revised. South Vietnamese justice is not entirely in the hands of the executive: the court fines the minister of the interior 200,000 piastres damages, to be paid to the daily *Song Than*.

When all is said and done, the government negotiates this crisis fairly well. The uproar dies away. These last judicial decisions will make a good impression on the committee of U.S. senators and congressmen that Thieu and his ministers await impatiently.

To mark the metes and bounds, to clarify Saigon's position, a South Vietnamese delegation roams the antechambers of the State Department and the corridors of Congress. Kissinger left Washington February 13 for a long journey that will take him to Egypt, Syria, Israel, Saudi Arabia, West Germany, and finally Geneva, where he is to meet Andrei Gromyko. This trip may serve Saigon's purposes. King Faisal admires the South Vietnamese stand. There's been talk of a loan from Saudi Arabia to South Vietnam.

The head of the South Vietnamese delegation in the U.S. capital, Tran Van Lam, president of the Senate, a bright and informed diplomat, is received by Gerald Ford, who says to him, "I must express my admiration for the chivalrous battle you and your compatriots are waging to remain free. . . . I'm sure you know what efforts I'm making to supply sufficient aid and assistance to your country. . . . I hope that North Vietnam, in view of the tenacity and determination of the South Vietnamese, will end by accepting the Paris Agreement."

Does Ford believe what he says? Thieu's envoy and his colleagues have the feeling that most of their hosts in Washington don't want to talk about Vietnam. Tired sighs and vague speeches deceive no one.

Lam speaks at the National Press Club: "The real problem is not only supplemental aid. A few years ago you spent a hundred million dollars a day when there were [in Vietnam] half a million American soldiers. . . . Three hundred million dollars [the amount Ford sought] is not exorbitant."

In Washington, as Lam knows only too well, they go on and on about the authoritarian nature of the Saigon regime. The peacenik lobby hammers away at this argument. Some of the congressional delegation about to fly to Saigon, Bella Abzug (D., N.Y.) especially, want to investigate the matter of political prisoners in the South.

Lam says: "Our country was practically born in the war. It has never had a chance to practice true democracy. . . . Whatever our system's flaws, at least it allows for possible change."

Lam's plea never reaches beyond a tight circle of Saigon sympathizers. In the end he is saying that quasi-dictatorships or dictatorships of the right, as opposed to dictatorships of the communist left, can alter.

Lam and his colleagues are an annoyance. Those in Washington who care at all about Southeast Asia are worrying about Cambodia.

On February 13 the CIA's consolidated daily intelligence report[8] offers two predictions. The communists intend "to overrun all of Tay Ninh province as [they] did in Phuoc Long province last month" and "Saigon will make strenuous efforts to defend Tay Ninh province."

For twenty years in the United States, experts in government and private institutions have made prophecy a national sport. These experts are driven by a desire to reduce war to easily manipulated banks of scientific data. What is not quantifiable is not science. To quantify human behavior—and therefore war—is the dream of all social science, indeed of all humane sciences, often neither scientific nor humane. Since Robert McNamara's reign at the Pentagon, that desire has become a constant.

This obsession leaps off the pages of a report by a researcher, Warren Phillips, presented during the annual meeting of the International Studies Association in Washington, February 18–23, 1975. Title of the report: "Could Henry Have Done It Alone?" Could Henry Kissinger have forced the North Vietnamese to negotiate? Phillips uses Markov analysis and estimating techniques. He enunciates the fundamental banality: "The way to predict what a nation will do toward another is to project into the future what it has done in this regard in the recent past." It is assumed that the variables and indicators reflecting past activities will serve to predict future behavior. Fascinated by the reduction of war to a mathematical game, part of the American intellectual establishment goes hog wild with exponential curves, logarithms, autocatalytic curves, parabolas. They postulate hyperbolic curves and sinusoids. Heads of state and civilian think tanks relish these diagrams and histograms and plunge into the analysis of correlations, regression of residuals, multivariate analysis, even factor analysis.

Once in stride, Phillips, examining North Vietnamese behavior between 1971 and 1973 to clarify the present and future, attempts to establish some fairly pathetic equations: "Imagine a highly stylized nation, S, with inputs, X, and outputs, Y, as in figure 1."

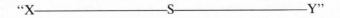

"X————————————————S————————————————Y"

Then Phillips sets values to grade North Vietnamese reactions to the Americans, Soviets and Chinese:

$$-3 = \text{very unfriendly}$$
$$-2 = \text{unfriendly}$$
$$-1 = \text{mildly unfriendly}$$
$$0 = \text{neutral}$$
$$+1 = \text{mildly friendly}$$
$$+2 = \text{friendly}$$
$$+3 = \text{very friendly}$$

There follow thirty-one pages of equations and diagrams, working up to the conclusion, an enormous platitude: "The important findings here are that the North Vietnamese response patterns are different from period to period during the time frame studied." The candid Phillips adds: "What is not well understood, as yet, is what makes the North Vietnamese shift from one strategy to another." Why do they negotiate briefly only to renew the battle, and vice versa? Precisely! Phillips admits, "More information is necessary about domestic decision processes in North Vietnam before the direct impact of international operations can be ascertained."

Many studies of this type, terrorist and tautological, have flourished in the past few years. Warren Phillips' study is not taken seriously at the State Department or the Pentagon. It caricatures one tendency among American intellectuals at grips with the Vietnamese problem.

Clausewitz:

> So it comes to pass that our theoretical and critical books, instead of being sensible treatises, clear and simple, in which the author knows what he is saying and the reader what he is reading, teem with technical terms, obscure points of intersection where author and reader part company. But they are often something even worse, that is, hollow shells. The author himself is no longer sure what they mean, and falls back on vague ideas which if expressed in plain language would be unsatisfactory even to himself.

The Americans have a stronger sense of optimism than of tragedy: they want History, in war as in peace, to be rational. During the 1970s the United States is living in an age of technological discoveries and decisive developments in data processing. Come on! We've sent a man to the Moon and we can't even whup this tiny little underdeveloped country, North Vietnam?

Computers produce interesting results as long as the input is based on simple Newtonian parameters, for example, the law of gravity. They should also provide—more, they *must* provide—data for understanding societies and political decisions. This explosion of data-processing methods and techniques is obvious throughout the Western world, but above all in the United States, where computer science took off early. Here and there a Warren Phillips or a computer processes information either false or so simplified that it makes no sense. The computer has no contact with reality. For a Phillips who claims to create a model of the North Vietnamese "nation's" behavior via Markov analysis, the war is not real, any more than a medieval war is for a twentieth-century historian.

No one knew what the North Vietnamese were going to do in 1963, 1965, 1968, 1972, 1973. No more does anyone know what they are going to do now, in February 1975. With a minimum of political savvy, after even a superficial reading of Lenin, we know, we can foresee, that they won't honor the Paris Agreement. American researchers, at the CIA or elsewhere, work from detailed information; but like them, Phillips cannot penetrate the minds of Secretary General Le Duan in Hanoi or of the North Vietnamese generals. One factor is fundamental: the monolithic will, the demented obstinacy, of Hanoi's leadership. It is not reducible, and cannot be fed into an equation or a computer.

At the International Studies Association's last session on February 23, James Schlesinger will not rule out American intervention. On ABC-TV[9] the secretary of defense is discreet: "It's a remote possibility." He too is thinking mainly about Cambodia: it seems certain to him that Cambodia will fall to the communists if Congress doesn't vote additional aid.

Next day Gerald Ford replies to Thieu's letters of January 24 and 25.[10] Thieu asked about American intentions after the fall of Phuoc Long. Ford sticks to generalities that do not commit him: "I share your concern. . . . I wish to assure you that this Government will continue to press for the full implementation of [the Paris] Agreement." To speak of implementing the agreement after the loss of a whole South Vietnamese province betrays either naive hypocrisy or unrealistic ignorance. Ford continues:

> Once again the South Vietnamese people and armed forces are effectively demonstrating their determination to resist Hanoi's attacks. Despite your existing limitations on am-
> munition . . . I was particularly impressed by the performance

of your forces at the Phuoc Long province capital and at Ba
Den Mountain, where they were overwhelmed only by
greatly superior numbers.

Ford accepts the idea that South Vietnam's main problem is a lack of
firepower. In Tay Ninh province, close to the Cambodian border, Black
Virgin Mountain, actually a hill protecting an important radio station, has
been taken. The North Vietnamese command and especially General Tra
have carefully orchestrated their diversionary operations to create the
impression that major assaults are being mounted in that region.

If the war is being prolonged, Ford explains to Thieu, who is already
more than convinced, the fault lies with the North Vietnamese. "We continue to believe that implementation of the Paris Agreement, with direct
negotiations between the Vietnamese parties, is the quickest, most appropriate, and most effective way to end the bloodshed."

A repetitive and imprecise letter: "We . . . will make every effort to
provide the assistance that is so necessary to your struggle until peace
comes." No question of sending B-52s or Phantoms, much less ground
troops. Ford makes one commitment only: to ask Congress for aid. Thieu
cannot see an end to his war; Ford talks as if peace were just around the
corner, even if he writes, "The path to peace is never easy. It has been
extraordinarily long and difficult in Vietnam." *Has been?* Won't it go on
being?

On February 27 the White House has the usual Daily Intelligence
Bulletin[11] to hand: "North Vietnam appears about to move one of its
reserve divisions—the 341st—to the south."

8

———◆———

Campaign 275

Nㅤorth Vietnam has done more than
that in the last three weeks. It has "transferred to the South" General
Dung, officially chief of staff, operationally commander in chief.

In a closed and militarized society like North Vietnam, a division's
movements can be tracked, but not a man's. Dung leaves 33 rue Pham
Ngu Lao on February 5 at 10 A.M., heading for the airport. He notes that
the peach trees are beginning to flower. He considers the disposition of
his armies, and his diversionary tactics. He signs messages ahead of time
for Mongolia, the German Democratic Republic, and the Soviet Union,
congratulating them on their armed forces' anniversaries. After Dung
leaves, the Hanoi papers publish reports of his activities, inspections, meetings with officers. . . . Every day at 7 A.M. and 2 P.M. the general's Volga,
curtains drawn, leaves his house for headquarters. It returns at noon and
at 5 P.M. It is common knowledge that Dung plays volleyball with the
soldiers of his personal guard. Late in the afternoon, therefore, these men
jump about ostentatiously in his courtyard. Even better, on the eve of his
departure the general's secretary is—officially and no less visibly—taken
sick. An ambulance comes for him.

Dung takes off secretly in an Antonov 24. The Americans will not know
until April that the chief of staff of the North Vietnamese army is in the
South. Code name of Dung's detachment: A-75.[1] Dung's code name: Tuan,
the Excellent. Giap's code name: Chien, the Battler. Who is more important, the Excellent or the Battler?[2]

The plane lands at Dong Hoi in North Vietnam. There, Detachment
A-75 leaves matters to command units of "559," headquarters for the Ho
Chi Minh trail. Dung and his escort roll along rutted roads, using motor-
boats to cross the river between North and South on the 17th parallel.
Detachment A-75 overtakes and passes innumerable convoys. Some of the
trucks are the army's, others have been placed at its disposition by the
Ministry of Transport.

What he sees along the roads and trails delights the general: "One thing
that was especially exciting was to see our fighters using motorized transport." Day after day, month after month, Dung says, the North Vietnamese
have economized and hoarded reserves all along the southern front, in
preparation for the great day. Accumulating stocks for ten years, the North
Vietnamese have succeeded in hiding them as well from the Americans
and South Vietnamese as from the Soviets and Chinese. Soviet and Chinese
officers travel with difficulty in the North and not at all in the South. Their
estimates are all the more uncertain as the Vietnamese communists are
given to dispersal, to *so tan*. They prefer to cache a ton of munitions here
and two tons there, in well-camouflaged hamlets and villages. There are
also large depots, these more easily pinpointed. But they can hide thousands of scattered tons from their Soviet and Chinese friends as from their
American and South Vietnamese enemies.

Arriving at 559's HQ, Dung settles into a straw hut but cannot sleep.
Questions circle in his mind: How could we carry out the Politburo's resolution on liberating the South? How would we win in the Central Highlands? And especially, how should we attack Ban Me Thuot so the enemy
would collapse quickly?" Dung also meditates on combat techniques "traditional with the Vietnamese" for over thirty years, and his own preference:
"Surprise attack, striking a powerful blow to the nerve center."

Sun Tzu:

> The enemy must not know where I wish to give battle. For,
> if he does not know where I will give battle, he must be
> prepared in many places. And if he is prepared in many
> places, those that I must fight against will not be numerous.
> For if his van is prepared, his rear will be weak, and if his
> rear is prepared, his van will be vulnerable. If he is prepared
> on the left, his right will be vulnerable. And if he is prepared
> on the right, he will not be numerous on the left. When he
> is prepared everywhere, he will be weak everywhere.

Clausewitz, more succinctly: "We say surprise is the basis of all operations, without exception."

The military originality of the North Vietnamese lies not so much in
surprise itself as in arranging the circumstances of surprise over years and

not just months. One of their imponderable weapons is time, the other is patience.

Dung is a careful supply officer, and everywhere he goes he makes sure his divisions have sufficient gasoline, vehicles, arms and ammunition. He must and wants to "think big." He is not at all sure yet of his options. "Is a powerful blow possible under these circumstances?" They add "TS 50" to his car's number plate to facilitate his travels; it gives him top priority and also makes the car easy to spot. Here, teams of female volunteers, or of designated volunteers, are repairing the road. Dung stops. The volunteers tell him, "Tet's almost here, chief, but we never see any mail!"

The Vietnamese give gifts for Tet. One of Detachment A-75 offers the soldiers a package . . . of hairpins.

At another stop, the group meets empty trucks headed north. A driver shouts, "Chief, it's the eve of Tet but we don't have any cigarettes left!"

Dung's entourage has plenty of cigarettes, and he passes them out. At another spot they catch up with the fully motorized 316th Division. Aside from its tanks and armored cars, it comprises over 500 trucks. For Dung, who began a war thirty years before with single-shot rifles, it is prodigiously satisfying to see these Zil 31s pulling 122 mm. and 130 mm. guns, all these T-54s and the batteries of SA-2 rockets. The officers of the 316th have been ordered to maintain complete radio silence. It isn't easy to keep over 10,000 men quiet, but the North Vietnamese army is disciplined. A wartime commander can achieve a double surprise: not having his forces spotted where they are, and making the enemy believe they're elsewhere. The name of the current operation is simple and not poetic: Campaign 275.

Nobody is predicting *the* victory, either in combat now south of the line or in Hanoi's newspapers. This is a good year for propaganda. The party newspaper, the *Nhan Dan*, repeats: "1975 is a year that marks important steps in the Vietnamese revolution: our party is 45 years old, our Nation 30, and this year we celebrate the 85th birthday of the founder of both our party and our Nation."

Portraits of the founding father, Ho Chi Minh, are not too common either at the front or in the rear, from which it may be inferred that unlike some elsewhere—obviously in Moscow and Beijing—Hanoi does not encourage the cult of personality. Uncle Ho's maxims and poems are quoted so often that the cult has been internalized. All officers and men have heard, and repeated a thousand times, "Nothing is more precious than independence and liberty."

Uncle Ho was born in May.

Gerald Ford cherishes a very American conviction: he is persuaded that if he presents the facts in a new light, especially to Congress, those facts can alter first public opinion and then votes. A delegation of senators and congressmen is headed for Saigon, and Ford is counting on them to convert a majority of lawmakers.

Invitations go out from the undersecretary of state for Southeast Asia, Philip Habib, who expects a group of twenty or so. American elected officials, like their counterparts everywhere, ordinarily love junkets at the taxpayers' expense. But after much triangular negotiating among the State Department, the White House and Congress, they barely managed to round up a group of ten: a Democratic senator, Dewey Bartlett, playing pilot fish, and nine representatives—John Flynt, chairman of the delegation, Bella Abzug, William Chappell, Donald Fraser, John Murtha, Samuel Stratton, Democrats, and Millicent Fenwick, Jack Kemp and Paul Mc-Closkey, Republicans.[3] For the White House this is not an ideal mix. Among the nine representatives, four Democrats have signed a letter (with seventy-eight other members of Congress) urging a progressive reduction in U.S. aid to Vietnam.

In Saigon both the palace and the U.S. Embassy view the delegation as a last shot at the $300 million Ford seeks. Philip Habib and Ambassador Martin detest each other cordially. Graham Martin, ready to give his all for the cause, is not happy to hear that Habib will accompany the group, along with Erich von Marbod.

Thieu prepares his welcome and receptions with as much curiosity as anxiety. Carefully he reads biographical notes on the delegates, supplied by the U.S. Embassy. Bella Abzug, New Yorker, important for her influence and her pacifism, will be tough. Millicent Fenwick, a *grande dame*, likes to smoke a small pipe. . . .

A whole cabinet meeting is devoted to this incursion. Prime Minister Khiem plumps for an organized tour, accentuating the positive, in the communist style of Potemkin village, or almost. Thieu vetoes that and decides to answer all the delegates' questions. Joking, the president urges Vuong Van Bac, his charming and elegant minister of foreign affairs, a handsome man, to target and seduce Abzug. Guffaws all around. Of Ford's letters Thieu retains only the general tone of commitment. He is unaware that the U.S. president has not seen all of Nixon's letters. Nor does Thieu grasp the extent to which Watergate has eroded the power of the presidency in Washington; he does not see that Congress is out to retrieve its power in foreign affairs from the White House, or that Ford's advisers want to isolate the president from the Vietnamese problem. Over and above American institutions, Thieu seems to sense a mystical continuity: Ford is Nixon: the one like the other represents and commits the United States absolutely.[4]

Will Thieu, should Thieu, divulge Nixon's and Ford's letters?

At the embassy the visit begins badly. There's no electricity. A dozen aides have come along with the delegation. Not included in the program organized by Graham Martin's offices, these young aides roam Saigon, digging and ferreting. Some of them meet staffers at the embassy who don't share the bosses' optimism. Some CIA men, like Frank Snepp, have long thought that the Paris Agreement was an ill-disguised defeat for the United

States. Furthermore, Snepp doesn't believe that the South Vietnamese lack arms and ammunition.

The ambassador has the feeling, at times justified, that several members of the delegation have already made up their minds. They already know, especially the truculent Bella Abzug, what they came to find. They don't keep open minds. Even the more hawkish congressmen find Martin peremptory and unrealistic. In the nature of things, the delegation suffers many briefings by various American agencies. The ambassador and his deputy, Wolfgang Lehmann, often preside. These briefings are studded with incident. At the start of one meeting Bella Abzug, looking for the CIA's top man, cries out, "Which one is Polgar?"

The ambassador is annoyed. He doesn't want them in direct contact with his subordinates. He knows that the congressional aides are seeking and finding other contacts than those provided by the embassy.

In the office of the military attaché, the delegation meets with Colonel William LeGro. They pay close attention to a document submitted by the colonel, on "estimating the North Vietnamese threat." It abounds with reservations. Paragraph 18: it is expected that the coming campaign will be nationwide. There are a certain number of indications that the North Vietnamese will commit divisions of the strategic reserve. The congressmen are accustomed to pessimistic estimates, especially from the military. In the United States it's a classic syndrome: several weeks before debate on the military budget there appears, quite by accident, a crescendo of newspaper articles estimating or overestimating the Soviet menace. Why shouldn't it be the same here with the North Vietnamese menace? But if the situation were truly irreversible, they would never vote an aid appropriation. In his report LeGro modulates his views carefully. Paragraph 46: over the short term the communists will probably enjoy prolonged success and take certain district capitals; nevertheless, increasing communist losses may turn out to be prohibitive over the long term.

When the investigators leave placid Saigon and scatter about the countryside, they still can't form any settled opinion about military operations. Paul McCloskey, a sturdy Californian and a former marine officer, visits familiar battlefields in central Vietnam. The situation seems much better than it was in his day. That doesn't square with Frank Snepp's view.

In estimating Thieu's hold on the public, the delegation parts company with Martin, Lehmann and Polgar. These three say that the president has matters well in hand. Bella Abzug and Dewey Bartlett are interested in political prisoners and the affair of the arrested journalists. Haven't they all been released? Undaunted, Martin says there are no political prisoners in South Vietnam. Saigon's judicial system, he says enthusiastically, is as effective as New York's, if not more so. They ask him about the famous tiger's cages where prisoners are confined at Poulo Condor. He claims that in a tropical climate they're healthier and airier than cells. The embassy doesn't give an inch: there are 35,000 prisoners in South Vietnam—all common criminals. Paul McCloskey answers, "More than half these prisoners are being held without trial. You have to consider then that half of them are political prisoners."

The ambassador throws a dinner party for the delegation. Some of the group boycott it. Bella Abzug brims with vociferous criticisms that the reporters collect happily. "This government is corrupt," she flashes. "Nobody wants to fight. We have to find some way to get rid of Thieu."

Encouraged by some middle-level diplomats, a few delegates confide to American correspondents, "Martin is too committed to Thieu to assess the political climate accurately." Or: "This ambassador is a catastrophe."

Followed by reporters, Bella Abzug goes to the house of Mme. Ngo Ba Thanh, prominent in the noncommunist opposition and the Third Force. The police don't allow Mme. Thanh to leave her house, but visitors are free to speak with her. The Saigon regime has placed her under civil house arrest.

Unannounced, Abzug turns up at ICCS headquarters. The South Vietnamese police guards will not admit her. After other contretemps, she finally finds two officers, one Hungarian and one Indonesian, who have nothing to say.

Martin snorts, "Publicity stunt!"

Bartlett and McCloskey are stubborn. They obtain permission to interview the imprisoned journalists. Saigon's chief of police hovers; he will not leave them alone. Three prisoners admit they're Vietcong agents. Bartlett and McCloskey are angry and demand to see the prisoners alone. Then one prisoner murmurs: "They've beaten us very much."

The delegation multiplies its political contacts. Father Thanh, crusader against corruption, declares, "A third of whatever aid you send us will be stolen. The arms will be sold to the opposition. The money will be used to pay soldiers who exist only on paper."

A visit to the prime minister is disappointing. Khiem and his minister of foreign affairs, also present, seem paralyzed. At Senator Vu Van Mau's, Bella Abzug and Donald Fraser meet with Buddhists of the National Force for Reconciliation as well as three senators and five deputies of the opposition. The Buddhists insist, "You must not vote money to build prisons."

Bella Abzug grumbles: "I will only vote for humanitarian aid."

Flamboyant Air Marshal Nguyen Cao Ky, former prime minister, receives Senator Bartlett. Ky's remarks are brief: "Until we find an acceptable solution, we'll need American aid badly."

Flynt, Chappell, Fraser and Fenwick talk at length with Tran Quoc Buu, president of the Confederation of Vietnamese Workers and a solid anticommunist since 1954, when Hanoi hounded, imprisoned or executed members of his union. His CVW, he emphasizes, is the only organization in Vietnam that can call a strike. To this trade unionist, Father Thanh and Senator Vu Van Mau don't count for much. But Thieu must try to co-opt them politically, or he'll push them into the communist camp. Dumping Thieu, Buu says, would be no solution: "When we got rid of President Diem, we set off a series of crises. We need continuity *and* drastic change in our domestic policies."

Buu hands out mimeographed copies of a speech he made five months before, in which he denounced the prevalent corruption. He thinks some of the arrested journalists are indeed communists. He's not sure they've been beaten: "All over the world," he sighs, "the police are hard-boiled."

Apropos of Mme. Ngo Ba Thanh, Buu becomes emotional. "I've known her for a long time! I supported her father for minister of labor in 1954. Like many women, she goes from one extreme to another."

Buu will not be a candidate in the presidential election: "We Vietnamese set a goal in life early on. We stick to it. My vocation is unionism, not politics."

The delegation makes a sudden twelve-hour visit to Phnom Penh. In the Cambodian capital the situation is deteriorating. During lunch, a rocket explodes 800 meters from the delegates. American Ambassador John Dean seems pessimistic. According to him, Cambodian president Lon Nol will resign "if he is thought to be a barrier on the road to peace." And he adds, "The United States is not committed to any one leader."

And 200 kilometers from Phnom Penh, in Vietnam, at Saigon, is the United States committed to Thieu?

The Cambodian refugees' fate is atrocious. The whole delegation returns from Cambodia convinced that humanitarian aid must be voted.

On the evening of March 1, Thieu hosts a dinner in honor of the delegates. In his toast, he recalls that several American presidents have promised him their support, but he makes no allusion to Nixon's letters. "This solemn promise was renewed when we signed the Paris Agreement," says the president slowly. "Are the United States' commitments valid? Can we trust in the United States' word? That is the message I would like to see you pass along to the members of the 94th Congress."

Thieu notes Bella Abzug's obvious hostility. During his toast, she pretends not to listen. The conversation, restrained and tedious, limps along in an uneasy, depressed atmosphere. Senator Bartlett is sympathetic to Saigon, but he relays the responses of prisoners he questioned. Thieu, clumsy according to some, brutal according to others, dismisses all that: "Yes, communists would say they'd been tortured."

Neither the embassy nor the palace, it would seem, "gets the message."

Until 1973 American public opinion seethed over the fate of prisoners of war in North Vietnam. The POWs came home. Now public concern has swung to the officers and men who have disappeared,[5] and the delegation intends to discuss the MIAs with the DRV and PRG staff in their ghetto at Camp Davis. For some congressmen this will also mean extensive newspaper coverage in their constituencies and states. A U.S. congressman, up for reelection every two years, is permanently greedy for favorable publicity.

From the moment they arrive at Camp Davis, the U.S. delegation feels that Hanoi's spokesmen are transforming a possibly constructive discussion into a propaganda exercise for the seventy journalists—reporters, cameramen and sound men—assembled there. The communist officers are seated at the end of a long table, under a yellow-gray bust of Ho Chi Minh apparently carved from a block of lard. A North Vietnamese lieutenant colonel, deputy chief of the Hanoi delegation, opens fire immediately. He would prefer to give a general response rather than take a series of questions. A battle over procedure ensues. The lieutenant colonel reads a bombastic text for twenty minutes: the Ford administration is responsible for continuing the war, thus rendering impossible any application of article 8(b) of the Paris Agreement concerning the MIAs. . . .

To cut short these turgid generalities, Senator Bartlett displays an MIA bracelet bearing the name of Captain Clifford Fieszel, 462-56-6781, shot down over North Vietnam and reported lost September 30, 1968.

The senator wants to know what happened to the captain. By a resolution of the General Assembly at the United Nations, the Democratic Republic of Vietnam is obliged to provide details. The lieutenant colonel refuses to answer.

"I go back to Oklahoma in about two weeks." The senator's voice rises. "Now what am I going to tell Mrs. Fieszel when we're paying a lot of money to send a flight from here to Hanoi once a week with the express purpose of providing information on MIAs, and we haven't received one bit of information?" The primary duty of the U.S. officers on this flight is to discuss the search for MIAs with North Vietnamese authorities. The senator ends his passionate blast: "We have a term in Oklahoma that covers your answers. It is hogwash."

Cao Giao, one of the reporters present, asks his colleague An what that means. An translates: "That means to talk rot. Hogwash is the mash they feed pigs."[6]

The senator looks this North Vietnamese officer in the eye and concludes, "All right! I take it by your silence that you want me to tell her that you've refused to answer. I'll do just that."

Millicent Fenwick picks up the lieutenant colonel's arguments. He has declared his government ready to settle all problems by negotiation. Well then, how? To several questions, the lieutenant colonel answers, "We will convey your demand to our government."

Acrimonious and futile, the discussion proceeds in an almost uninterrupted wrangle. A brisk row is worth filming. You can hear the whirr of cameras, reporters' orders to the cameramen, and from time to time Millicent Fenwick's exclamations: "He has not answered my question, he has not answered my question!"

McCloskey explains to the lieutenant colonel that some members of Congress don't want to continue aid to South Vietnam. If the DRV opposes the search for American MIAs, the wind may veer again.

It's a dialogue of the deaf, even if Fraser, putting a good face on it, says later that the conversations were useful.

The lieutenant colonel hews to his propaganda line: "You must go back to the United States and urge the people and the Congress to reject the Ford administration's policies and to cease all support for Thieu's clique."

Congressman Chappell speaks slowly and firmly. "I came to Vietnam . . . with as much objectivity as I know how to . . . exercise . . . to go back to America and . . . better foster peace. . . . Since coming to this meeting today you have made up my mind pretty solidly on what I shall do with my vote when I go back to the U.S. Congress. . . . I don't believe you people ever intended in the first place to abide by the agreement which was made in Paris," or their pledge on the MIAs. "You complain, and claim that nobody respects your diplomatic immunity here in Saigon. You say they cut your water and electricity. But I see you living very comfortably here." The congressman points to the ceiling fans, the trees and lawns outside the barracks—all that at the expense of the U.S. and Vietnamese governments. "When I go back to the States, I intend to vote for the $300 million in supplemental aid."

The Vietnamese reporters note, to their amusement, that the interpreter omits this last sentence.

To cool them off, Bella Abzug announces, "They sent back the bodies of twenty-three POWs who died in DRV camps, and Lieutenant Colonel Bao has agreed to ask his government about Captain Fieszel—that shows some willingness to ease the pain of the MIAs' families." She might hope that the DRV would supply more information about the MIAs: "It would be a big step . . . good will . . . normal relations . . ."

What neither the U.S. Embassy nor the presidential palace could settle—the delegates' state of mind—the communists have settled willy-nilly in an hour and a half. The members of the U.S. delegation are angry.

They move to PRG barracks, fifty meters further along. General Hoang Anh Tuan, member of the bipartite military commission, receives the Americans. Stating that the meeting has begun later than planned, he asks: "Do you want a whole hour?"

Bartlett and Flynt confer. "No, a half-hour will be enough."

The general wants to read a prepared text. Once is enough. The senator interrupts the general. "Why hasn't the PRG helped implement the article in the Paris Agreement about MIAs?"

The general sets about reading: "It is the fault of the United States that the Paris Agreement is not observed and that there has been no resolution of the MIA problem. . . ."

The Americans ask specific questions. Like his North Vietnamese counterpart, Tuan answers in generalities. Flynt wants details on forty-one American bodies that have not been sent back to the United States.

General Tuan: "After the signing of the Paris Agreement, the United States continued the war. . . . Impossible to implement the treaty . . . thousands of Vietnamese die every week. . . ."

Flynt interrupts: "I'm sorry but I don't want to hear this. I want to know where the forty-one bodies are. . . ."

Tuan: "I will not be forced to answer such a question and I believe the American people will understand." The general looks at his watch: "Our thirty minutes have passed."

On that, he rises and goes.

On her way out, Millicent Fenwick confides to reporters that she will now vote for humanitarian aid *and* military aid.

Radio Hanoi and Radio Liberation shortly announce that the senator and congressmen made statements "less than serious and unworthy of their rank."

During the American delegates' stay in Vietnam, there is a marked pause in the fighting. There has been no operation above company level, at most local firefights.

Before emplaning for Washington on Sunday, March 2, Senator Bartlett holds a press conference at the airport. To bring the war to an end, the delegation will recommend that President Ford urge Kissinger to start negotiations with the Soviets, Chinese and North Vietnamese. Has the senator forgotten that the secretary of state dislikes negotiating from weakness? The delegates prepare to board the plane. Ambassador Graham Martin breaks in: "May I fly back to Washington with you?"

The congressmen have seen only too much of Martin these last few days; the prospect of several more hours with him is less than enchanting. But how can they refuse?

After their departure, the embassy shoots off a cable to the secretary of state in Washington that ends, "The embassy believes that at least a few members of the congressional delegation managed to grasp a useful, if new [to them], dimension in the overall Vietnamese scene."

Back in Washington, Graham Martin senses a poisoned atmosphere even in the State Department offices. The last intelligence bulletin issued by the CIA and the department states that North Vietnamese troops south of the DMZ are stronger than ever but that they will not be able to bring South Vietnamese government forces to a decisive battle. The notion is taken up everywhere: Saigon's troops will not be defeated during the current dry season.[7] Staying at his daughter's house on 42nd Street, Martin plunges into lobbying. The department puts an automobile at his disposal, and junior officers of the Southeast Asia Section set up meetings for him. In Saigon he is, after Thieu, the most important person. In Washington, he is one ambassador among many, stripped of pomp and ceremony. In the department, civil servants seem to feel that no one's going to shoot up the ladder by meddling in Vietnamese affairs. Martin says: "They don't want to raise their heads, for fear of being slapped down by Jane Fonda."[8] Martin doesn't waste time preaching to already converted Republicans. Yet he runs across reluctance among them. Robert Gialmo, a Republican on the powerful Budget Committee, seems undecided.

Who are Martin's allies? Some senators, among them Barry Goldwater. Martin long ago lost hope of persuading one of his old friends, Mike Mansfield, Senate majority leader. How hard it is to make himself heard and understood! Martin maneuvers through a minefield. All these young men in senators' and congressmen's offices are peacemongers and defeatists, he thinks. Martin is rowing against the current.

The ambassador knows that several members of the delegation have criticized him often and sharply. Donald Fraser says frankly and openly, "As long as the American ambassador to Saigon walks hand in hand with Thieu's government, it will be difficult to discern the real nature of American interests."

Graham Anderson Martin, who has an acute sense of his dignity and his prerogatives, feels almost humiliated in Washington. Posted to Saigon in March 1973, he delayed his arrival several days, demanding an official plane to set him down in the South Vietnamese capital. That alone was suitable for an American ambassador, personal representative of the president.

Sixty-three years old, tall, keen of eye and gray of hair, in fragile health, smoking several packs of cigarettes a day, with an aristocratic air that impresses some as arrogance, others as good manners, Martin might have sprung from one of the better-known East Coast families, the Cabots, the Lodges, the Kennedys. Of more modest origin, he was born in North Carolina. His preacher-father taught him—Martin is proud of this—that it is "easier and more useful to tell the truth than to lie." Before senators and congressmen the ambassador alludes freely to his integrity and is not modest about his expertise.

He went not to Harvard, Princeton or Yale but to Wake Forest, a less famous university. Studying history, Latin and Greek gave him, he thinks, "a sense of the past." He quotes Thucydides easily. Studying ancient history, Anglo-Saxons identify themselves naturally with the Athenians. In this era of their own history, they've cast the doctrinaire North Vietnamese in the role of the austere Spartans.

Moving up to Washington, Martin was briefly a journalist, long enough to detest the profession, not long enough to understand it. In Saigon he divides the media into two categories: the majority, who do not parrot the embassy's official line; and the others. A good reporter, Martin insists, won't jeopardize American interests in any way. If the truth is unfavorable, it must be suppressed.

Martin embodies the permanent conflicting relationship between two vocations, diplomacy and journalism, but also a generation gap. In Vietnam and elsewhere older ambassadors are rarely in harmony with young reporters. Simplifying, Martin persuades himself that on the whole journalists, a wildly heterogeneous bunch, in Washington and Saigon are "pro-Hanoi." Perhaps it should be "anti-Thieu." That's different. Graham Martin has few friends now in the press corps. Once upon a time Cyrus Sulzberger, a VIP at the *New York Times*, was his friend. These days the *Times* harasses the ambassador, or at least Martin honestly thinks so. In Saigon he agreed to see *one* reporter, George McArthur, correspondent for the *Los Angeles Times* and a close friend of the ambassador's secretary. Martin can stand up for freedom of the press and on occasion defend its minions. When James Markham infiltrates a Vietcong zone and is almost deported by cousin Nha, the ambassador pleads his cause with Thieu. But nowadays Martin is in no mood to defend these bastards. He has issued strict orders. No leaks, no unofficial contact with the press. His subordinates in Saigon are letting him down. That was obvious during the congressional delegation's visit, and in Washington the ambassador suffers the fallout.

Martin began his career working in social security under Roosevelt. He's an avowed Democrat. Because he was an intelligence officer, a colonel and Southeast Asian specialist during the war, brushed up against Churchill and George Marshall, and frequently saw Allen Dulles, founder of the CIA, Martin flatters himself he knows more about the chiaroscuro world of intelligence than a Polgar or a Snepp. All the ambiguous reports on North Vietnamese intentions irritate the ambassador. After all, *he* grasps the overall picture. Representing the administration at the U.S. Embassy in Paris from 1947 to 1955, he knows these North Vietnamese. He watched Pham Van Dong at close range in Geneva in 1954. Above all, he watched the French government negotiate with the Vietminh, and lose. In Paris, Martin had close contacts with Special Services, in particular the DST (Direction de la Surveillance du Territoire—Intelligence Service). It was a profitable friendship. Martin is privy to information on the American pacifists and activists that crisscross Europe, information that the CIA has missed. During this last round of visits with lawmakers, the ambassador's first and only satisfaction was learning that the authorities in Saigon had refused to let one of these pacifists, Don Luce, accompany the senator and congressmen.

In his way Martin is still a Francophile—rarer in the American diplomatic establishment since General de Gaulle's speech at Phnom Penh. Not overly social, Martin sees only one counterpart in Saigon, French Ambassador Jean-Marie Mérillon.

An exemplary career: as ambassador in Thailand from 1963 to 1967, Martin acquired a port and six military airfields from Bangkok without once officially signing an agreement or a treaty. Outspoken in his scorn for the "narrow military mind," Martin opposed an attempt by the Pentagon to introduce troops into Thailand and brought about the recall of General William Stillwell, who did not share his convictions. In Bangkok Martin met Thieu.

An adopted son of the ambassador, a helicopter pilot, was killed in Vietnam. Some say Martin hardened after that. Convinced that the United States should not send marines to Thailand—or certain other spots—he fired venomous cables at the State Department, cables unacceptable to then Secretary of State Dean Rusk, who relieved Martin of his post, naming him special assistant for refugees and immigration. A job on the turkey farm. Fortunately, the ambassador rolled out the red carpet one day in Bangkok for a Coca-Cola lawyer, a political has-been, Republican Richard Nixon.

As president, Nixon recalls Martin's courtesies and sends him to Rome. Martin speaks no more Italian there than he did French in Paris, but he refines his procedures as chief of mission, directing all agencies closely, including the CIA, and supervising distribution of funds among Italian political parties, including Bettino Craxi's small socialist party.[9] Satisfied that he kept the Italian communists from power, Martin will proceed similarly with the Vietnamese communists. Let's see, then—who in Washington or Saigon knows more than he does about Vietnamese subtleties and complexities? Maybe Kissinger—one of whose aides Martin was during negotiation of the agreement in Paris. Sitting across from Le Duc Tho, Martin beheld in him "a true believer, a man of total conviction, inflexible." Biblically, Martin says, "The communists are convinced that they will inherit the earth." During tea breaks in Paris, Martin and Le Duc Tho talked about their grandchildren. Martin esteemed Le Duc Tho, but less than Kissinger did.

Martin bought a farm in Tuscany and prepared to retire. In December 1972, Alexander Haig informs him that President Nixon wants to post him to Saigon. Martin hesitates. He is ending his career. In Saigon he will take plenty of heat. Haig invokes duty and honor: "If the president says he needs you, you go. You cannot spend eight years in Paris, four in Rome, and then turn down a tough job."

Martin agrees. During his confirmation by the Senate in June 1973 he says, "We must wind up the American commitment in Vietnam as soon as possible, but the way we do it is extremely important. . . . We must end it by leaving an economically viable Vietnam." Aboard the plane carrying him to Washington on March 2, the ambassador, still splitting hairs, encouraged the congressional delegation about Saigon's economic future.

Here and there in Washington he tells his story, without much success. Rumors spread by Saigon's reporters and diplomats from Saigon precede him, surround him, neutralize him. No one accuses Martin of not working hard, but of working hard to ill effect. Precise, niggling, he reads all cables; everybody knows that. He can't see the forest for the trees, some say.

Others insist he plumps too hard for Thieu and his government even as he says confidentially that the prime minister is a mediocrity. If you mention the endemic corruption, he suggests that it "oils the machinery of economic development. . . . With the war, it's inevitable." He counts on the export of oil and fish to give South Vietnam "a good chance of survival."[10] Martin has descended on Washington too often these last months. For him it's the second front of the war in Vietnam. He trusts his deputy in Saigon, Wolfgang Lehmann, to keep things running smoothly. In Washington the ambassador fights rearguard battles, to his mind crucial, for $300 million in supplemental aid. Weary, exhausted by his trials and tribulations, in pain from an abscessed tooth, Martin leaves for a rest at the home of a cousin in North Carolina.

A long way from Washington, and even farther from Saigon.

9

"Little Head, Big Butt"

General Dung, NVA commander in chief, sets up headquarters in a leafy green patch of jungle near a forest of *khoocs* thirty-five kilometers west of the city of Ban Me Thuot and ten kilometers from the Cambodian border.

In the highlands he can easily conceal patrols, even a regiment or a division. The country is wild and outsize all along an immense plateau rising 400–1,500 meters, higher in places, reaching 2,598 meters on Ngoc Ninh Mountain, near Kontum, where the Americans expect an attack.

The Central Highlands glisten with rivers, lakes and waterfalls. The roads follow the valleys. An army needs to control, or at least dominate, those ancient French colonial routes, strategic highways now. The region is sparsely populated but rich in lush wild stands of forest and bamboo. Drawn up from the plains over the course of centuries, settled around fields of corn, squash or potatoes, are the Montagnards, citizens of Vietnam who do not speak the national language. More or less settled, they cultivate rice, hunt and raise livestock, but remain alien communities within the nation.[1] South or North, the Vietnamese have always had "problems" with the Montagnards.

General Dung likes the picturesque countryside. He loves the sound of dry yellow leaves crunching at his step. These pretty *khoc* leaves go up in flames at the slightest spark. Combat troops are less enchanted by this bucolic setting: after every frequent scattered little fire that breaks out the signal corps has to repair telephone lines.

Troops of elephants amble through the jungle. Wires are run very high, but the elephants rip them out over hundreds of meters. There are tigers in this jungle too. To keep his three emplaced divisions from being spotted, Dung issues orders to communicate by telephone, never by radio.

Dung gauges the balance of his forces over the whole theater of operations. "Because we had concentrated most of our forces in the main zone of the campaign, we had the advantage over the enemy in that area. In infantry we had 5.5 soldiers to the enemy's 1; in tanks and armored cars we had 1.2 to the enemy's 1; in heavy artillery we had 2.1 to the enemy's 1." In his memoirs the general does not dwell on his difficulties, mired tanks and cannons, shortage of competent mechanics, several lost companies forbidden to use their radios. He deplores certain deficiencies. The North Vietnamese had "little experience in attacking cities, and large-scale combined operations were still new to some of the branches."

Dung draws two conclusions from the 1968 and 1972 offensives. The combat troops, led by the Vietcong, were gritty and tough, but could not hold the cities in 1968.[2] Coordination of infantry, tanks and artillery was bad in 1972. The communists practice self-criticism. For three years North Vietnamese headquarters has been criticizing past operations.

In 1972, and even more in 1968, communist units . . . simply got lost! Soldiers from the North lost their way in unfamiliar towns. Vietcong recruits, mainly peasants, did no better at mastering big-city topography. In 1975, whether for Saigon or Ban Me Thuot, the North Vietnamese chief has at his disposal the latest Soviet materiel, but lacks . . . ordnance survey maps. Dung wants "to know more about Ban Me Thuot, capital of Darlac province." He sends a cadre, an officer in civilian clothes, and a few men to infiltrate the town.

They come back alarmed. The officer is dazzled. "This town is big!" he says. "It's almost as big as Haiphong city."

The patrol was impressed by the suburbs, and buildings "aglow with neon lights." At North Vietnamese headquarters, others jeer. The comparison won't hold up. Ban Me Thuot's population is 150,000 at most, Haiphong's a million at least. The information is rounded out by reports "from members of the revolutionary structure in town." They also interrogate a prisoner.

Dung outnumbers the enemy; he wants to add surprise. He limits patrols even now, to keep them from being spotted. He notes that at Ban Me Thuot "the enemy, even if feeble and isolated, occupies a vast range of urban buildings, which complicates matters terribly. They've organized their defenses." The communists have taken and held Phuoc Binh. Now they have to do as well with Ban Me Thuot, a larger town. "Attacking big cities, and large-scale combined operations, are new to us," Dung has admitted, conveniently forgetting that in 1972 North Vietnamese troops assaulted big cities but could never hold them.[3] Dung worries about the "many obstacles, rivers or fortified positions" the heavy artillery and tank units must surmount. The commander in chief has a tactical objective: "In combat, the best way to win fast is to destroy enemy headquarters and capture the commanders." So Dung wants his motorized shock troops to advance quickly. On a modest scale, but for the first time in Vietnam, blitzkrieg strategy is in order. As a ranking member of the Politburo, Dung considers problems of "liberation" or rather of occupation: "Ban Me Thuot is the political, economic, national and religious center of the Central Highlands. The presence of Montagnard tribes, Catholics, Protestants, Buddhists, large bourgeois families, planters and foreign nationals who have lived for decades in a climate of neocolonialism poses very complex problems." A promising mix . . . North Vietnamese troops must "show a correct attitude." He issues orders to that effect at all levels. Dung plans to "apply our program correctly" to "middle-class holdings." Here the general seems vague. On the other hand, he plans the immediate use of "prisoners of war in the front lines." The Democratic Republic of Vietnam has never signed the international convention on this matter.

Ban Me Thuot is capital of one of the dozen provinces of South Vietnam's Military Region 2, almost as large itself as the other three together, and also the least populated. Its people's loyalty to Saigon is uncertain. There were Montagnards at Phuoc Binh. There are some here in the reserves. One sure rule in this war: the farther from the capital and big cities, the less loyal the civilians. The wait-and-see peasants are in the habit of digging ditches at night to cut the roads, by order of the Vietcong, and filling them in during the day, by order of the ARVN. All this works in Dung's favor—rugged terrain; rocky peaks; narrow valleys; ravines smothered by jungle, hard to defend by land and harder to counterattack by air. It's easier to hide in this country than in the rice paddies of the South.

What a military blueprint for Dung! Across from him, the South Vietnamese 23rd Division and six ranger outfits. He has three divisions deployed, the 320th, 316th and 10th; they'll tighten like a vise on Ban Me Thuot. Dung has a weakness for his old division, the 320th. In 1952 he led a similar operation with it, on a smaller scale, a raid. He attacked the Catholic town of Phat Diem in Tonkin. Slipping between French outposts into the heart of the city, he blew up the enemy command post and held the town for twenty-four hours. Withdrawing, his troops harassed French posts for fifteen miles around. This time Dung does not intend to withdraw; he is going to revise the operation, which he's given a pretty name: Flowering Lotus.[4]

For the brief prebattle oration that every commander in chief must bequeath to posterity, Dung addresses the officers and men of the 316th: "There are lines from a poem which burn in my heart. I cannot remember the author, but they express the resentment, suffering and bitterness which every Vietnamese must reckon with:

For thirty years our land has been under arms,
And the round of the moon is still split in two,
Half shining on the North, half on the South."

To reinforce the enemy suspicion that he will attack Pleiku, seat of the military command for MR 2, Dung launches three diversionary operations. The South Vietnamese police receive disinformation from the PRG bureaucracy, ordering the resistance to prepare meetings at Pleiku and Kontum to welcome their "future liberators." Dung himself takes a hand in the second: the enemy learns that the 968th, in Laos, is advancing on Pleiku. Dung's order: "Raise all the rumpus you can to attract notice." Third, near Pleiku, he organizes a radio hoax: it gives the impression that the elite 320th is dug in nearby. A transmitter, a generator and a handful of men are enough to keep the airwaves humming.

In Saigon, the CIA falls into the trap. Analyst Frank Snepp keeps a close eye on the situation and notes significant North Vietnamese troop movements to the west and north of Ban Me Thuot. His only prediction is that the communists will isolate the city. At this point the CIA has little operational intelligence on the Central Highlands. A year and a half before, one of the agents running the region embezzled all the funds. There's no more money to pay spies. Moreover, the CIA post in Ban Me Thuot was shut down in a burst of economy. They have to count on Vietnamese in the pay of Saigon's agencies. There are plenty of double agents working that region; all in all they work mostly for Hanoi and the PRG. Snepp's report of March 7 is "a monumental error," the young analyst acknowledges today. Snepp no more than others believes the story of a North Vietnamese deserter who assures them that in reality the 320th is slipping from Pleiku toward Ban Me Thuot.[5]

Snepp is one of the most interesting CIA people in Vietnam. Like Ambassador Martin, he hails from North Carolina. At Columbia University's School of International Affairs in 1968, one of his professors, Philip Mosley, a specialist in Soviet affairs, told him, "You're not vivacious enough for the State Department. The CIA would suit you better." Mosley made that point even as Snepp was deciding that the best way to stay out of Vietnam was to cast his lot with the CIA. The night before signing on he went to see the James Bond film *Doctor No* and told himself, I too will drive a sports car. The luck of the draw sent him to Saigon for several years. Young and handsome, with a remarkable memory, he speaks and writes with a talent that Thomas Polgar, his chief, and Graham Martin, his boss, appreciate. They often use him for briefings. Martin sometimes finds him a bit theatrical, but in the long run has confidence in him. The ambassador invites him home frequently. Snepp dates one of Martin's daughters, Janet, a charming divorcee. A political moderate, Snepp knows that in intelligence the dangerous man is the one who overcommits himself morally. He does not question the legitimacy of the U.S. government's Vietnamese policy.

NVA troop movements leave the ARVN perplexed and divided. Like the Americans in Saigon, General Phan Van Phu, commander of MR 2, thinks Pleiku will be the primary North Vietnamese target. Reports from Saigon say the main assault will aim at Ban Me Thuot. Intelligence, radio intercepts, captured documents, prisoner interrogations accumulate and contradict. In the final analysis General Phu decides the North Vietnamese are going to attack Pleiku. Anyway, messages from Saigon suggest that an offensive against Ban Me Thuot is only "probable." Phu tells his officers: "That's too many targets, Ban Me Thuot and Kontum and Pleiku. . . ."

It seems logical to him that the enemy should focus its efforts on Pleiku, the nerve center. The ARVN inherited American headquarters there. Once upon a time French headquarters in the Central Highlands were at Ban Me Thuot, more in the middle of things. Shrugging off geography, the Americans preferred Pleiku, farther north, far from the heart of the Central Highlands. Highly mobile, rich in their armada of helicopters, the Americans could ignore distances.

Phu has commanded MR 2 since 1974. Thieu dismissed several general and superior officers then for corruption, among them three of the four regional commanders. Phu is a product of the French army. He was taken prisoner at Dien Bien Phu and is obsessed by the possibility that the North Vietnamese will recapture him. He admits that he's primarily "a field officer." At this juncture the field officer hesitates again. He doesn't want to strip his defensive deployment around Pleiku for the sake of Ban Me Thuot. Pleiku, on flat ground, seems more vulnerable to tanks. Politically, it would be disastrous to lose Pleiku. As Dung issues orders to attack several posts around Pleiku and Kontum, Phu persuades himself that Pleiku will be the primary target. If it proves to be Ban Me Thuot, he'll ask for air support and send reinforcements by chopper. Phu still bases his strategy on American models, in which large units can be moved long distances by helicopter. Uneasy, Phu senses that the enemy is creating a diversion. But where?

In the afternoon of March 9, Dung notifies the Politburo, the Central Military Committee and Giap, minister of defense, in Hanoi: "We will attack Ban Me Thuot March 10." His troop strength, he says, his stores and his armaments are satisfactory. His soldiers' morale seems excellent. The same day at 7 P.M. he telephones the commanders of his major units and confirms that they're ready to move out. He has resolved the last logistical problems. To cross the Sre Pok River, he ships the artillery on immense bamboo rafts.[6] "In the false calm of darkness fallen on the mountain, tens of thousands of men are marching toward their objective. The unit commanders, some of whom are already white-haired, [huddle] over maps to review their plans one last time."

First, Dung cuts the roads to Ban Me Thuot, particularly Route 14 linking it to Pleiku. To avoid effective intervention by South Vietnamese air units and to profit by nighttime, which confuses defenders more than attackers, Dung opens his offensive at 2 A.M. Supported by artillery barrages, the Tenth Division's infantry and armor move forward smoothly. Dung has 25,000 men, Ban Me Thuot's defenders 1,200. At 7:30 A.M. the first columns of North Vietnamese tanks surge out of the north and west. Rapidly they take and partially destroy a large weapons depot and a lot full of enemy armor. They bypass the radio station. Forty-five minutes later, the tanks are firing by eye at headquarters of the South Vietnamese 23rd Division. Elements of the South Vietnamese 53rd Regiment defend the airport west of town fiercely. The "lotus flowers": Dung bypasses it to seize the smallest airport, north of the city.

South Vietnamese aircraft enter the fray. The North Vietnamese have still sent up no planes.[7] The attackers' anti-aircraft is formidable. The South Vietnamese are still flying too high and, the worst kind of luck, their bombs devastate their own 23rd Division's communications center, which disorganizes the entire defense of Ban Me Thuot. No more contact with regional headquarters at Pleiku—where now they know what the North Vietnamese primary objective is! Phu decides to reinforce Ban Me Thuot, first with the 44th Infantry Regiment, part of the 23rd Division. To transfer two battalions Phu discovers that he has only seven large Chinook helicopters. Each can carry forty men. And very shortly two, three, then five helicopters break down.

At the U.S. Embassy in Saigon the mood is tense, and they consider lending General Phu CIA helicopters, Air America's. But it would be too flagrant a violation of the Paris Agreement. It's impossible to reinforce Ban Me Thuot by road. And hard to transfer enough men with two helicopters. There seems no solution to Phu's logistical problem.

Most South Vietnamese regular units, officers and men both, are used to having their families nearby, at the command base behind the lines. For a long time Ban Me Thuot has been command base for the 23rd Division and units defending the city, like the 53rd Regiment, and also depot for those *arriving* from Pleiku, like the 44th Regiment. Only the shock troops, paratroops, rangers and marines—the South Vietnamese have marines, too—don't ship their families along when they're deployed to new provinces or regions. American advisers have accepted the presence of these families, mainly because the soldiers' pay is low. A private earns about 20,000 piastres, less than $30, a month. To take care of their families, to bring them military rations, or chickens "found" during an operation, they must be nearby.[8]

Reinforcements helicoptered from Pleiku land on the outskirts of Ban Me Thuot and search frantically for their wives, their children, all their relatives. When they find them, many soldiers discard weapons and uniforms, slip into civilian clothes and try to make their way out of town. Only the rangers maintain discipline and keep fighting.

General Le Trung Tuong, commander of the 23rd Division, picked up a habit during the American war: he directs operations from a helicopter aloft. That gives him a fine view of the battlefield but no rapport with his men. General Tuong's wife and children are waiting for him at the training camp southeast of Ban Me Thuot. The general orders a ranger unit to prepare a landing zone near the training camp. He too is more worried about his family than about the battle. A burst of machinegun fire stitches his helicopter. Slightly wounded on the cheek, Tuong has himself hospitalized.

The NVA commander in chief had allowed himself a week at least to neutralize Ban Me Thuot fully and occupy the city. But for practical purposes he considers the town his by 5:30 P.M. on March 10.

On the first day Dung's troops undergo 200 sorties by the South Vietnamese air force; in the following days, 60. A few South Vietnamese companies, mostly rangers, fight on. South Vietnamese pilots, badly briefed, don't know where the NVA units are, or can't operate effectively because the combattants are too tightly locked. Or again, these pilots hesitate to drop their bombs on a city and suburbs jammed with civilians. The regional detachments of Montagnards play little part in the defense. Some of the Montagnards belong to the Unified Front for the Liberation of Oppressed Races (FULRO in French)—an irredentist and neutralist movement, weaker than Hanoi claims and stronger than Saigon admits— and have served as scouts for the North Vietnamese units. Around Ban Me Thuot, as elsewhere, the regular ARVN troops treat these Montagnards, of the Mong tribe, at best like dubious auxiliaries, at worst like filthy barbarians.

Thieu orders Phu to retake Ban Me Thuot. He even orders Colonel Le Vinh Hoa, director of Saigon Television, to send in a team to film the reconquest.[9] Phu has other projects in mind.

In Ban Me Thuot, North Vietnamese regulars take eight American Protestant missionaries, men and women, an Australian, a Filipino, and an American consular employee, Paul Struharik, among other foreign prisoners. These are well treated and begin a trek to North Vietnam.[10]

Agence France-Presse is the only Western news agency with offices in both Saigon and Hanoi. The Saigon bureau is run by Jean-Louis Arnaud. During the battle of Ban Me Thuot, Arnaud is in Bangkok. A dispatch from the Saigon office, signed by Paul Léandri, reveals that the Montagnards of FULRO are serving as scouts for the communist troops. Picked up by the international press, this report angers Prime Minister Khiem and President Thieu. They see it as implying an active opposition in the Central Highlands collaborating with the communists.

In Vietnam for over a year, Léandri, like many reporters, criticizes the Saigon regime often. He gets his information from a colleague, Loc, who wants to remain anonymous. Two police officers march into the AFP office.[11] Who is this journalist? Léandri refuses to reveal his sources. The police order him to appear at the Bureau of Immigration. He notifies friends at the French Embassy.

Thirty-eight years old, with a rather handsome, craggy face, of Corsican origin, obstinate, Léandri is furious. Late in the afternoon, in a chauffeur-driven company Peugeot, he goes to the Immigration Offices in Cholon, which are almost across the street from National Police headquarters. One of those same two officers insists again on the name of Léandri's informant. Léandri protests and demands to see a superior. Colonel Pham Kim Quy, director of criminal investigation? Maybe, sure, why not . . . The colonel is not in his office at police headquarters but across the street. Is he in the Immigration Offices? Léandri paces, hangs round, heads for town again, stops off at the AFP, returns to Immigration. Still no colonel. Léandri crosses the street, and parks his car in an alley by police headquarters. At 7 P.M. the French consul, Patrice Le Carruyer de Beauvais, arrives at the Immigration Offices. No one tells him that Léandri is waiting a few hundred meters off, at police headquarters.

Léandri cools his heels in a courtyard, grows impatient, works himself into a fury. Are they going to keep him there all night? 9 P.M. Abruptly the reporter slips into his car, slams the door, starts the engine, backs up and then moves forward. In the darkness policemen shout and rush out. Léandri accelerates. At the gate a guard fires on the Peugeot; it crashes against a wall. Léandri traveled about 300 meters. He took a bullet in the temple, and he is dead. Afterward the French, Americans and South Vietnamese come up with different stories. The Vietnamese were under the impression that Léandri was Eurasian. Would the police have fired if they'd thought they were dealing with a "pure" white man? Léandri was comparatively sympathetic to the Saigon regime.

Bad news travels fast. At the U.S. Embassy everyone is ordered to keep mum about this deplorable event. All the same, Thomas Polgar helps the South Vietnamese chief of police polish the explanatory communiqué. The South Vietnamese swear that Léandri was challenged aloud and that the guard fired at the Peugeot's tires. Léandri's death makes a bad impression in Washington, Paris, Saigon. Some see it as the South Vietnamese police taking revenge on Léandri. Or on the press in general. Or on France.

Thieu's and the nationalists' relations with France, or with the French community in Vietnam, are equivocal. Nationalists of Thieu's generation speak French much better than English, but politically Thieu is no Francophile. He thinks French presidents left him in the lurch. De Gaulle, too anti-American, was almost hostile. Indeed Pompidou, only the year before, recalled an ambassador accredited to Saigon. Today, President Valéry Giscard d'Estaing and his diplomats are openly toying with the idea of a solution that would grant an important role to the Third Force, crypto-communist according to the Vietnamese president. Thieu and many civilian and military bureaucrats don't understand the media's systematic hostility toward them. Nevertheless, if reporters aren't communists they enter Vietnam with no trouble and travel freely wherever they like. The ARVN supplies them with transport, less than the Americans used to, but as much as they can. There is no censorship of the foreign press.[12] But these journalists carp constantly at the Saigon regime, while they display unlimited tolerance toward Hanoi. They write about the PRG's courage and tenacity, forgetting that these troops are most often North Vietnamese regulars. They never miss a chance to point out the manifold weaknesses, e.g., chronic cowardice, of South Vietnamese soldiers. Always they stress desertions in the South, never in the North. But Thieu is proud of these troops, who often fight furiously. Who has ever given these soldiers the credit they deserve? In 1972 they retook Quang Tri after a forty-five-day battle. Cousin Nha urges the president to mollify the international press, especially the French press. But Thieu has been disappointed too often.

Relations with French residents of South Vietnam are better than with journalists from Paris. Still, they're ambiguous. Heads of companies, like Michelin's Patrick Hays, are generally anticommunist. But most take an apolitical stance on internal matters. Yet some Frenchmen (as stressed in fat General Quang's police reports to Thieu) are still anti-American. The enemies of my friends are my enemies. It's as if these French, though anticommunist, were saying: we couldn't beat the Vietminh, so why should the Americans finish off the Vietcong and North Vietnamese? Thieu sees himself as anticolonialist, and he suspects that the French want to reestablish themselves in Vietnam. These simpletons think they can compromise with the PRG and Hanoi!

The journalistic community gives plenty of publicity to the Léandri affair (*solidarité oblige*), which embarrasses the president. Many foreign reporters have died in Indochina, but this is the first time South Vietnamese police have killed a French correspondent.

The French ambassador requests an audience at the palace. Thieu receives Jean-Marie Mérillon. The president is very sorry. It was all a horrible misunderstanding. He seems to be apologizing to Mérillon. Despite his mistrust, it is not in Thieu's interest to antagonize the French. The ambassador notes that Thieu has a kind heart. The proof? He has never been able to bring himself to order the execution of prisoners on death row.

Hanoi newspapers and radio comment on the Léandri affair: the South Vietnamese are "fascists."

Nhan Dan in Hanoi publishes a report on the liberation of Ban Me Thuot:

> City streets are decked with flags, streamers, pictures and signs. . . . Everywhere in the street . . . people are welcoming the new authorities. . . . Students and professors from secondary schools . . . trade schools and normal schools are meeting joyfully in their institutions. They're calling out,

"What happiness!" Truly, Saigon's propaganda is as different
from reality as day from night! Hundreds of students and
villagers comb the streets, removing all cultural traces of the
Americans . . . and seeking out pigheaded enemies who still
foment trouble. At Bo De secondary school, thousands of
officers, soldiers and employees of the puppet apparatus have
gathered.[13]

On March 11 Thieu invites three generals, Prime Minister Khiem,
Chairman of the Joint Chiefs Vien, and National Security Adviser Quang,
to the palace for breakfast. The servants lay a table in the third-floor
hallway—out of range of American microphones, according to the president. He doesn't seem troubled by the course of the battle in Ban Me
Thuot: "We can't defend the whole country with our present forces. If we
try to hold every isolated post, we'll be nibbled to death."

Thieu sketches a new strategy on a map of Vietnam: they must hang
on to the "useful Vietnam" and beef up its forces, mainly in MR 4 in the
Delta and MR 3 around Saigon. Here are the country's riches, rice and
offshore oil wells. The president explains: we must redraw the northern
front, especially in MR 2. Farther north, we'll have to give up a lot of
territory. But we'll leave strong enclaves in Hue, Danang, Chu Lai. They'll
have symbolic as well as strategic value. The fortified base at Danang will
be important. The U.S. marines landed there in 1965. If they come back,
in a month or a year, they must be able to count on that base.

In a bizarre flight of fancy, Thieu compares the three enclaves to American bridgeheads in the Normandy campaign. Is he confusing the invaded
with the invaders?

Thieu asks his prime minister and his chief of staff to work out a new
defensive deployment: the new front he has selected will run from Tay
Ninh through Dalat to Nha Trang on the coast. Khiem is not surprised.
This reorganization was in the air. The president said a few quick words
about it some days before, to the commander of MR 1, General Ngo Quang
Truong. For three months General Charles Timmes and Admiral Cang
have also been considering this "option." In an offhand manner the president has already raised the possibility of a "new strategy," of a "strategic
revision," before his general officers. One of his occasional advisers, Ted
Sarong, a retired Australian general mistrusted by some at the U.S. Embassy, has proposed a variation of this retrenchment to Thieu.

For what may be modestly called a redeployment Thieu finds a financial
rationale. With his prime minister and his chief of staff, the general-
president does his arithmetic. Before, with $1.5 billion, we could defend
the four military regions. Therefore with $700 million we can only hold
MR 3 and 4. Also Thieu thinks, or hopes, that in yielding terrain, half the
whole country, he will effect two psychological shocks. First, the Americans
will be alarmed and more likely to vote supplemental aid. The minister of

planning, Nguyen Tien Hung, assures Thieu that there are considerable hidden funds in America, substantial secret war chests: the Pentagon must have some $850 million in reserve. (Some in Saigon confuse Vietnamese regimental paybooks and American public accountability.) American public opinion, quite volatile, can change. There must be a sort of Pearl Harbor in reverse. Second useful shock: South Vietnam, currently stunned, will be reassured. Major disadvantage: abandoning territory is a tacit renunciation of one of Thieu's "four no's": "not an inch of land to the communists."

In this new context, Thieu proposes to order his elite troops back to Saigon—the division of marines and the division of paratroopers that hold MR 1, just below the 17th parallel. The paratroops were created by the French, the marines by the Americans.

This notion percolates through the Vietnamese military command, not the American. Generals and colonels stroke their chins: Thieu wants primarily to keep his best troops at hand in the capital, to discourage potential putschists. He wants to be sure of military and political stability. From a military point of view, his plan is not absurd. It would offer the advantage of regrouping South Vietnamese troops up against more and more North Vietnamese divisions. In theory the possibilities seem reasonable. But in practice? Ban Me Thuot is part of "useful Vietnam." The city must be retaken.

American General James Gavin suggested enclaves long ago: but enclaves in which American troops were billeted—a strategy to avoid stretching these troops thin in combat.

Thieu has not disclosed his plan to the Americans. He might have told Martin if the latter had been in Saigon; the ambassador is the president's usual confidant. Thieu does not trust the embassy personnel in general: too many of them are hostile. Moreover, he wants to prevent leaks.

Dan Ellerman, economic adviser at the embassy, analyzes the situation with the deputy prime minister for economic affairs. Hao makes casual mention of a contraction in South Vietnamese deployment. Ellerman served in Vietnam as an intelligence officer in the marines. The military and political implications of Hao's remarks are not lost on him. He immediately reports his conversation to Wolfgang Lehmann, who asks Ellerman for a written report and makes sure it reaches Martin in the United States. The ambassador doesn't pay much attention to it.[14]

On March 12 Thieu summons Nguyen Ba Can, a member of Thieu's Democratic Party and president of the National Assembly. Thieu wants his two houses of parliament to declare a state of emergency, to shock South Vietnamese public opinion.

Then Thieu returns to military problems. He wants to visit the front, at MR 2 headquarters in Pleiku. His security adviser dissuades him. North Vietnamese anti-aircraft is dangerous, with plenty of undetected batteries here and there. And who knows, the presidential plane might be attacked by North Vietnamese fighters based at airfields north of the 17th parallel. Thieu will meet General Phu, commander of MR 2, halfway between Pleiku and Saigon, at Cam Ranh on the coast.

In the morning of March 14, with his prime minister, chief of staff and security adviser, Thieu boards his DC-6. They meet General Phu, but no other generals, at Cam Ranh. The meeting is held in a little white house refurbished for a visit from Lyndon Johnson in 1966.

Cam Ranh is a long way from Saigon's political currents or Pleiku's military hubbub. Once a huge U.S. air and naval base, Cam Ranh plays a strategic double role. With Cam Ranh you control part of Vietnam. But on the global scale, the Japanese, Americans and Soviets, each in turn, have cast a covetous eye on Cam Ranh. It is a deep-water port. The Americans built fifty-five large airports in Vietnam; Cam Ranh's is one of the best equipped. Today it lacks some of its customary radar coverage: that used to start at Ban Me Thuot. A superb site, peaceful, exquisite, miles of white sand, coral . . . Here the Americans established a rest and rehabilitation center for their soldiers. They surfed; went to the movies; devoured sixteen-ounce steaks, lobsters, crabs, oysters, mussels; relaxed in air-conditioned rooms with showers, stereo and television. Some of the buildings have decayed since the Americans left, but on the whole, at Cam Ranh, the atmosphere is delightfully calm.

First off, General Phu, nervous and even demoralized, runs through his order of battle, maps at the ready. All over the Central Highlands, he says, the situation is bad. The main highways have been cut. Ban Me Thuot has fallen. Pleiku, where he makes his headquarters, is now under siege. More NVA divisions are springing up. Phu cannot hold out more than a month or six weeks in Pleiku.

Thieu considers his new strategy, which he calls "small top and big bottom," *dau be dit to*. Americans will say "light on top, heavy on the bottom"; the French, "petite tête, gros cul"—little head, big butt. The president asks Phu: "As matters stand, can we retake Ban Me Thuot?"

Phu is evasive, asks for reinforcements, transport, ammunition. Thieu turns to General Vien. The chief of staff has no reserves and is fresh out of helicopters. On paper he has 430 of them, more than half useless. There are no spare parts. Other choppers have been shot down or damaged by the new Soviet Strella missiles in the battles of Phuoc Long, Ban Me Thuot and elsewhere.

The way Thieu sees it, if the South Vietnamese retake Ban Me Thuot and he executes his grand withdrawal, they could temporarily evacuate Pleiku and Kontum but quickly retake them. A confusing discussion follows. Thieu will depart under the impression that he has ordered Phu to reoccupy Ban Me Thuot. Phu will be under the impression that he has been asked primarily to withdraw from Pleiku and Kontum. It is a commonplace that conversations with Thieu tend to be imprecise. The president often answers questions with his customary vague formulas: We'll see, Why not, It's not impossible.

Certainly the evacuation of Pleiku has been decided. Neither the prime minister nor the chief of staff opposed it. Thieu has agreed to lose Pleiku to save Ban Me Thuot, Phu to lose Pleiku to save his headquarters, which he will transfer elsewhere.

They debate withdrawal routes. The best, Route 19, between Pleiku and the coast, is not practicable. The North Vietnamese have cut it and have massed artillery to either side, anti-aircraft guns and rockets, troops with antitank weapons. Phu proposes an old interprovince road, 7B. Used by loggers, it rises and falls and meanders for 200 kilometers to the coastal town of Tuy Hoa. The North Vietnamese never patrol it, or hardly ever. For once surprise will be on the South Vietnamese side. The engineers will lead off. They'll repair or buttress several bridges. Another advantage: the area is sparsely populated. The Saigon government has never had serious problems with the populace. To assure the defense of Pleiku—and Kontum—they won't evacuate local and regional South Vietnamese troops. And lastly, to avoid panic or flight, they'll leave the civil servants in place. The prime minister, in charge of these last, does not flinch. Khiem, in his eternal dark blue suit, blue shirt and red tie—his lucky suit, his wife swears—looks like a proper head accountant. As so often, he seems sullen and morose, while he is in fact prudent, little given to expressing opinions or imposing orders. He works so slowly and beats about the bush and temporizes so much that he seems reflective, impenetrable or immobile. Some impute presidential ambitions to him. But he settles for the second rank, sheltering behind the president. He may be a four-star general, but here he wears the prime minister's hat. His two favorite answers are "Speak directly to the president about it" and "Check with the Americans about it." The U.S. Embassy and the palace appreciate that.[15]

The chief of staff states his reservations: Vien recalls that in Indochina the French always got into trouble when they withdrew. The retreat from Lang Son ended in a massacre. Two columns of troops and vehicles, under the command of Colonels Lepage and Charton, were annihilated at the foot of the hills along colonial Route 4. On terrain something like forest Route 7B a celebrated French outfit, the Groupe Mobile 100, was smashed. It suffered the coup de grâce on National Route 14, at Chu Drek pass. Phu argues. Of course, any second lieutenant knows it, a withdrawal is the most difficult military operation. But the topography, here on 7B, seems better than along 19. Moreover, the South Vietnamese have solid air support.

Anyway there's no choice.

The meeting is about to end. Insistently, Phu demands that one of his aides, ranger commander Colonel Pham Van Tat, be promoted to brigadier general. This officer has never shown himself capable of high command. Vien does not know him, Thieu hesitates. Phu is Khiem's protégé, and this colonel is Phu's. The general in command of MR 2 must be allowed some slack, margin for independence and even error. The president and the chief of staff give up.

On his return to Saigon that same evening, Thieu dines with his cousin Nha. He sketches his new strategy, the advantages and disadvantages. "Phu," he says, "asked me for a brigade of paratroops and a brigade of marines. We barely have a full airborne brigade in reserve. Phu will have to manage with what he has."

Nha detests Khiem and has no liking for Phu, the prime minister's protégé. Weary, Thieu admits: "Phu is a good divisional general. I don't know if he can make it as a corps commander."

The next day Thieu receives Wolfgang Lehmann; he says nothing of the serious decisions taken at Cam Ranh. The president wants to use the Ban Me Thuot battlefield to annihilate the principal enemy units.

Lehmann: "Can you concentrate enough of your forces around Ban Me Thuot without stripping other regions?"

"It is indeed a tough problem," Thieu concedes. "We'd have to strip the northern Central Highlands substantially."

This disturbs the embassy's second in command.

"The battle for Ban Me Thuot will be hard," Thieu continues. "It will last a long time."

Since the Paris Agreement, South Vietnamese leaders have tended to economize on munitions. Thieu tells Lehmann that he has issued an order to supply combat troops in MR 2 with *all* the arms and ammunition they need. Thieu also expects big North Vietnamese pushes around Hue and Danang, and he believes the NVA will mount an assault on Tay Ninh, 150 kilometers northwest of Saigon.

Back at the embassy, Lehmann asks the U.S. military attaché to see the ARVN chief of staff. What do the South Vietnamese really need?

In a cable to General Brent Scowcroft at the White House, Lehmann reports his interview with Thieu. He includes predictions: "Kontum will probably fall when it is attacked . . . if the attack against Pleiku is made by two divisions of North Vietnamese forces . . . it may be lost as well." General Phu, Lehmann says specifically, is withdrawing his headquarters to Nha Trang.

Lehmann arranges for all Americans in Kontum and Pleiku to shift to Nha Trang. Last words of his cable to Scowcroft: "Prisoners including a warrant officer . . . have been identified as being from NVA 341st Division, one of the strategic [reserve] divisions."

Thomas Polgar also drafts a cable to the CIA in Washington: "South Vietnam is confronted with its biggest military and psychological crisis. Not comparable with 1972, because at that time Saigon had U.S. military support. North Vietnamese can today achieve more with less, but in fact they are achieving more with more. North Vietnamese advances faster and more impressive than at any time in 1972."

Polgar has met with General Nguyen Khac Binh, chief of the National Police and also head of intelligence, the CIO (Central Intelligence Organization), Vietnamese equivalent of the CIA and the FBI. Binh says North Vietnamese control of the Central Highlands is inevitable. According to him, neither Thieu nor his government "as presently constituted could digest" this loss. General demoralization looms on the horizon. Polgar adds that the first week of general offensive "has upset ammunition and fuel conservation plans. Ammunition reserves will run out well before end of fiscal year." The U.S. fiscal year runs from October to October. Polgar is thinking of congressional debates and decisions on supplemental aid. "South Vietnam is in deep trouble because of the interaction of North Vietnamese determination to bring about a military solution and the congressional attitude to unilaterally terminate or limit assistance to South Vietnam regardless of what the communists are doing. Ultimate outcome hardly in doubt, because South Vietnam cannot survive without U.S. military aid as long as North Vietnam's war-making capacity is unimpaired and supported by Soviet Union and China. Chief of Station."

Neither civilian nor military Americans in Saigon are officially forewarned of Thieu's decision. Shortly they will learn of the fait accompli, and General Homer Smith will complain bitterly to Vien. The South Vietnamese chief of staff will absolve himself: "It was the president's orders. He wanted to keep the whole operation secret."

10

◆

Route 7B

Ⅰn Brussels on March 8, just before the battle of Ban Me Thuot, Kissinger is discussing Cyprus with Dimitrios Bitsios, Greek minister of foreign affairs. The Americans already know the battle is over when on March 15, in Damascus, President Assad tells the U.S. secretary of state, "You lost Cambodia, you gave up Formosa [for Beijing]. You'll give in to Israel."

This round of jet diplomacy is a failure. Aboard the presidential plane, *Air Force One*, which flew Kissinger to both Cairo and Tel Aviv, reporters talk about his future. He's not the permanent miracle man these days. His most likely successor at State, they murmur, is Elliot Richardson, ambassador to London. On this trip Kissinger has ignored events in Vietnam. Ban Me Thuot? A marginal note.[1]

To strengthen Kissinger's hand, Ford announces that he'll stay on at State at least until January 1976.

In Saigon, Polgar is waiting for the congressional debates. He has confidence in the secretary of state.

Thomas Polgar sports an impressive title, "special assistant to the ambassador." Everybody recognizes the station chief when he visits the Cercle Sportif or ICCS headquarters, or when he makes the rounds of receptions and cocktail parties. A Hungarian journalist, officially on their delegation to the ICCS, says, "Polgar is our favorite Yank."[2]

Fifty-three years old, portly and bald, with thick horn-rimmed glasses, Polgar, born in Budapest, retains traces of a Hungarian accent in his polished English. He says "vas" for was, "tink" for think, "anyting" for anything. You may get the impression—inaccurate—that he uses his accent as Kissinger does.

A bank manager in Budapest, Polgar's father sends his son to the United States at sixteen. Polgar studies at a small university that trains students for the business world. Working as runner for an uncle who specializes in brokerage, Thomas learns his way around New York. The war interrupts his studies. He joins the U.S. army at the age of twenty. He speaks German. Like Sergeant Kissinger, he is assigned to intelligence, in the form of the OSS (Office of Special Services), embryo of the future CIA. A lot more fun than shooting craps with the 310th Infantry Regiment! The Allies occupy Germany. Polgar tracks down the assets and bank accounts of I. G. Farben, the industrial monolith. In Berlin he works under the command of men he admires, Allen Dulles, chief of American intelligence in Germany, and Richard Helms, station chief in Berlin.

Discharged in 1946, Polgar thinks about journalism, a crowded profession. He stays in intelligence, an excellent substitute, according to him, "especially during the emotional years of the Cold War and the Berlin blockade."[3] Not yet thirty, he finds himself in the secret service with a rank equivalent to colonel.

In Saigon he often runs into Colonel Toth, his favorite Hungarian delegate. Polgar learned long ago how to "chat with the other side." During a moment of tension in Berlin he arranged a meeting with the chief of the Soviet NKVD. "Whatever happens," Polgar tells him, "we won't take it out on each other's women and children." The Russian answers, "Agreed." At a certain level of the international intelligence community, the profession becomes a game. These spylords set the rules and, barring the odd exception, respect them.

In America success at this trade is well rewarded. Polgar's career thrives in Germany, then in Austria. In Argentina he is on intimate terms with the head of the junta. Hijackers seize a plane at the Buenos Aires airport. The chief of police holds firm on principle: no negotiating with hijackers. Called in for consultation, Polgar suggests telephoning the president. At 3 A.M., the latter lets himself be persuaded: "My policy of no negotiations applies only to Argentines. Why don't you as an American negotiate?" Polgar boards the plane and offers the air pirates doped Coca-Cola. They conk out. Next day Polgar wakes up famous.

He flatters himself that he's a realist with no illusions about human nature. He likes to quote Kipling: "Single men in barracks rarely live like plaster saints." Helms, promoted to Washington as CIA director, cables Polgar in July 1971. Handing him the wire, the cryptographer says, "As long as you're already sitting down, I'll give it to you straight." Text of the cable: "Unless there are reasons of which I do not know, can you relieve Ted Shackley as COS [chief of station] in VN [Vietnam] on 1st of October?" Mrs. Polgar is less than overjoyed. The oldest of their three children is just entering college in the United States. Hesitant, Polgar cables in reply: "Maybe I had better come home and talk to you about it."

To Helms he says firmly, "I don't know anything about East Asian operations." Helms answers, "Then you'll see it with a fresh eye," adding, "Never mind, you won't have time for operations. You'll have to worry about the Congress, the press, the State Department and the U.S. army in that order."

The military situation being what it is in March 1975, Congress is indeed one of Polgar's main preoccupations. The CIA mission chief thinks the United States is bogged down in a fearful quagmire in Vietnam. They have "a very, very handicapped child" on their hands. According to Polgar there was never any question of total military victory over Hanoi. And now the fighting is certainly not at "an acceptable level." Obviously Gerald Ford does not thrill to Vietnam as Richard Nixon or Lyndon Johnson did. Polgar sat in at various meetings in San Clemente, where he saw Graham Martin for the first time.

Nixon did indeed tell Thieu: "As long as I'm president, you can count on $1.6 billion a year in military aid, and between $600 million and a billion in economic aid."

Since Martin's arrival in Saigon, relations between ambassador and CIA head are good. Graham Martin, an eminent member of the white Anglo-Saxon Protestant establishment, has high esteem for this station chief, Jewish, emigré and atheist. Polgar has proved himself. In the civil service hierarchy he is now a GS-17, equivalent to a major general in the army. Martin and Polgar relish their importance, have a good sense of humor and love language. Because they appreciate well-written cables, Frank Snepp is one of their protégés.

Just now Polgar's Hungarian, Colonel Janos Toth, and political adviser Anton Tolgyes have no news for him. Nor have the Poles. After an ARVN victory one day, Polgar teased a Pole: "Our South Vietnamese friends fight back pretty well!" The Pole retorted, "So I see. But you'll lose the war in Washington."

In Washington the government's aid proposals for Vietnam meet a cool reception. Their advocates are disappointed during the first two weeks of March. American public opinion is not optimistic. The last Gallup poll[4] shows that 78 percent oppose supplemental aid to Vietnam and Cambodia. Republicans are almost as hostile as Democrats. Letters from voters pile up on senators' and congressmen's desks. Between sessions there are phone calls, letters, polls. No one wants to let down our allies in Indochina. But no one wants to be let down by his constituents either.

For Cambodia as for Vietnam there runs a gamut of possibilities: (1) give Ford all or part of the money he wants; (2) grant the military and humanitarian aid the president wants, but with conditions; (3) grant humanitarian aid but not military assistance; (4) grant only supplemental military aid; (5) reject all the government's demands.

Methodical and meticulous, senators and congressmen detach the Cambodian problem from the Vietnamese. The lawmakers revert to their natural tendency, too little understood in Saigon and elsewhere: isolationism.[5] Opposition to Ford's policy is most obvious in the House of Representatives. Government requests come up before committees and subcommittees. Philip Habib, assistant secretary of state for Southeast Asia, holds the fort. He explains to all those committees that neither government, U.S. or Cambodian, is after a military victory. Anyway, that would be hard. On paper the Cambodian army numbers 240,000. There are surely no more than 50,000 operational. The goal is to hold out for a few months, until September. Then the floods on the Mekong will allow them to relieve the blockade of Phnom Penh. And the Khmer Rouge will find it much harder to set ambushes on the roads and rivers.

Representative Don Fraser, one of the delegation to Saigon, says openly in political circles that the war in Cambodia is lost. There's only one way for the United States to pull out: they'll have to make contact with the French government and the secretary general of the United Nations and ask the Khmer Rouge what terms they want to end the war. Humanitarian aid to Cambodia would be acceptable. Representative Paul McCloskey, another of the Saigon delegation, says his point of view shifted after his visit to Phnom Penh. He'd been opposed to any military aid; that's no longer true. In Cambodia, he argues, both sides execute prisoners. If the Phnom Penh government runs out of weapons and ammunition, the reprisals will be horrible. Refugees have told him that when the Khmer Rouge take villages they order summary executions. Propaganda or reality? McCloskey favors limited military aid.

The president's requests proceed through normal channels. A presidential proposal must be passed by subcommittees, committees and the full House. The same in the Senate. If there's disagreement between the two bodies, a committee drawn from both houses works out a compromise. On March 10 William Colby, director of the CIA, told Congress, "I doubt if Cambodia can survive, even with additional aid." Some of the lawmakers say they're ready to vote favorably if the government explores a diplomatic opening. How? In Congress they talk about the Manac'h Plan.

Etienne Manac'h, then French ambassador to Beijing, was helpful to all factions—Americans, South Vietnamese, North Vietnamese, Vietcong—in 1973 during negotiations for the Paris Agreement. He even found a table shaped to all parties' satisfaction. His plan, as Washington sees it: the United States deposes Lon Nol and lets Prince Sihanouk return to Phnom Penh. Back in power, Sihanouk, always a sort of barometric bobber in Southeast Asian politics, forms a coalition government to include the Khmer Rouge. The only problem: the Khmer Rouge, as far as their intentions are known, haven't the least desire to negotiate. Victory is within range of their rifles and mortars. Besides, Sihanouk entertains no illusions about his influence over the Khmer Rouge. This pseudo-plan, stillborn a long time ago, draws support from the ill-informed and naive. There are a few such in Congress. A coalition government in South Vietnam is at least imaginable, if only because the PRG keeps suggesting it. In Cambodia the idea of a coalition is based on nothing at all. The Khmer Rouge never mention it. The U.S. ambassador in Phnom Penh has long been saying that a "controlled solution" must be found. U.S. senators and congressmen have the feeling that in Cambodia the United States doesn't control much. That's surely not true in Vietnam.

On the morning of March 12 the Democratic Caucus votes a resolution presented by five members, among them Bella Abzug, who had handled Martin and Thieu so roughly a few days before in Saigon. The caucus announces its opposition to "any further military assistance to Vietnam and Cambodia for the fiscal year 1975," a motion passed by 189 votes to 49.

The Senate, too, wants to shake off the Cambodian question, but they wonder how to reconcile American honor, the electorate's pessimism and the fate of an ally. A subcommittee of the Senate Foreign Relations Committee, responsible for foreign aid and economic policy, votes (by a bare majority, 4–3) to grant Cambodia $125 million in arms and ammunition.

Over and above the Indochina question, in the labyrinth of debates and amendments some legislators are primarily trying to limit any president's power in foreign and military policy. Whatever the pretext, they want to reclaim lost rights and privileges.

They have not yet broached the problem of Vietnam when the Cambodian problem is solved, if you can call it that, by a vote—to adjourn. The stubborn opposition played a shrewd hand with the congressional calendar. Congress takes its Easter vacation starting March 27. The committee that rules on this serious matter consists of twenty-three members. A close vote: eighteen for adjournment, fifteen against. Among those for adjournment—temporary burial of the problem and of Cambodia—are eight Republicans. For a Republican president like Ford, that's a serious blow. And eight Democrats voted against adjournment! The senators are voting not the party line but their souls and consciences, in doubt and disquiet. The fact remains that at a critical moment Republicans haven't upheld their president on a proposal Ford considers highly important.

In government as elsewhere people tend to shuck responsibility. At State they say the White House inner circle misjudged Congress's state of mind. In the White House they say bureaucrats at State should have presented the president's requests and proposals more convincingly.

Gerald Ford was minority leader of the House; he knows all the moves, and he returns to the charge. Those people at State led Congress to believe the government was all out for war. Ford makes it clear that he does not, absolutely not, stand for all or nothing. He would happily accept immediate military aid to Cambodia of—let's say—$82.5 million. To facilitate matters, arms and ammunition would be appropriated from existing stocks. That way they won't exceed the annual budget.

March 15: Charles Percy and Jacob Javits, in their very powerful Senate Foreign Relations Committee, propose approval of military aid for Cambodia of exactly $82.5 million. They carry the day, 9–7. But the committee stipulates that all military aid be suspended by June 30, 1975.

On March 15 Washington learns that the South Vietnamese are mounting strange operations in the Central Highlands, more precisely on Route 7B.

In Saigon it takes engineer Van a while to learn that the North Vietnamese have attacked and captured Ban Me Thuot.

At Public Works and Communications the minister has stopped conferring with his associates. The engineer's army friends claim the men at the front lack arms, ammunition and food. Van doesn't doubt his friends' courage. They also mention a massacre of civilians at Ban Me Thuot. Perhaps a memory of the executions at Hue in 1968 is still too lively. Officers and men returning to Saigon reproach the capital's populace for "living the good life." Thieu orders the "massage parlors" closed; small consolation for combat troops.

The engineer believes in a political solution. "They" will sort out a neutralist solution.

He doesn't see how the Americans can be indifferent to this new ordeal, any more than the Soviets or the Chinese. After all, the United States forced concessions from Thieu in 1973 and obliged him to sign the Paris Agreement. Now in 1975 the Soviet Union and China will surely put pressure on Hanoi. Some in Saigon remember that in 1956 the Soviet Union wanted to admit both Vietnams to the United Nations. And the United States opposed it! It's not just Saigon that overestimates Soviet influence on Hanoi.

The bonze Thien Hue, the young monk in his pagoda, doesn't care too much about towns and provinces falling, and there is a natural delay in radio and newspaper reports. Big battles have been commonplace for a long time. This one is like 1972, South Vietnam regaining lost ground. The evacuation of Ban Me Thuot, like that of Phuoc Binh, is no doubt part of an overall strategy. The nationalist troops will retake all those towns and provinces.

Writer Duyen Anh, like engineer Van, thinks Saigon will reach agreement with the communists. The latter will halt, at Qui Nhon . . . maybe. There will be a buffer zone between what the North Vietnamese take and what's left to the South Vietnamese. Then a government of reconciliation will be set up, in conformity with the Paris "accords." Vietnamese, North and South, often speak of the agreement in the plural.

Duyen Anh is convinced that the Americans have invested too much money in Vietnam to want or allow its downfall. When the capture of Ban Me Thuot is confirmed in Saigon, the writer is deeply perplexed. And if all South Vietnam fell? We depend too much on the United States. In the countryside corruption has created injustices. Memories of it will lead the people to support the communists. The poor forgotten people! The younger generation is only good for cannon fodder. Bad news: the magazine *Green Revolution*, to which the writer devotes much time, will suspend publication. His "day," "Paddy for the Peasants," will also be cancelled. Rumors fly: our soldiers are about to evacuate MR 2. They're talking about a withdrawal. A withdrawal is a retreat. To fight in retreat is to lose. Before the Geneva Accords in 1954 the French staff pulled back its troops; then too there was talk of strategic withdrawal. Then there was Dien Bien Phu. There in the hollow vale fought hardly a tenth of the French expeditionary corps. That was enough. . . . A defeat of little military importance can become a political disaster. And Thieu explains that he needs hundreds of millions of dollars! The angry writer works for the government but does not like Thieu. Or Americans. Or the Russians who support the North Vietnamese. The writer hopes and despairs.

Dalat, 300 kilometers north of Saigon: its populace seems hardly even worried.

In the center of town, near the hilltop, cafés, restaurants and the Hoa Binh cinema are jammed. After school adolescent students crowd around billiard tables and baby-foot. A lot of young Saigonese live here during the school and university year. You recognize girls from the Couvent des Oiseaux (Convent of the Birds), in navy blue skirt and light blue shirt. Weekends, middle-class young men from Saigon, boarding students at the Lycée Yersin, gather with cadets in the beige uniform of the Interservice Military Academy and the School of Psychological Warfare. They stroll around the lake, play tennis, rent pedalos. At night they flow back toward the center of town, to the bandstands; they listen gravely to Trinh Con Son's songs, the "rain ballads." The neighborhood is awash with scents: spicy soups, fried fish, strawberries. Small boutiques are very busy—mostly, late in the evening, Indians' shops offering perfume or yard goods shot with color.

Almost as small as the average Vietnamese, forty years old, with bushy eyebrows, Jean Maïs, priest of the Overseas Missions, teaches at the Catholic University visible high on the hill. The college of political science at Dalat attracts students from all over. In Vietnam for seven years, the ultimate authority in granting French degrees, speaking fluent Vietnamese, living on campus, Father Maïs has close contacts with students of all creeds. He receives confidences. A professor must advise and a foreign professor is doubtless unprejudiced. With Maïs the students let themselves go, even if many wonder how this Frenchman can really understand them. Some are interested in Father Thanh's movement against corruption, for the welfare of the country and the reestablishment of peace. He is much talked about. Others, often children of civil servants or the military, tell Father Maïs that Thanh is playing the communists' game. Maïs thinks Thanh's partisans come from families close to the NLF, or the PRG. Vietnamese talk more about the *Front* than the PRG. Maïs has a hard time distinguishing Third Force people who steer clear of the NLF from those who have solid ties to it. The professor considers himself impartial. But of course he tells them about the 1950s up North, the exodus of Catholics, agrarian reform. . . . He tries to understand the students' anguish and heartbreak. It seems to him that their parents play the major role in their political choice. Blood is thicker than ideology, he thinks. Maïs wonders about his colleagues, too. His assistant in French, Ngu, confides that his family sympathizes with the NLF's maquisards.

After the Tet holidays the students came peacefully back to Dalat. Since then parents, mostly from Saigon, have cabled their children: Come home. Children of the well-to-do are talking more and more about study abroad. Students come to say goodbye to Maïs. Last to go is the daughter of a pharmacist in Nha Trang. On March 1, Jean Maïs gave his lecture on metaphor to a half-empty hall. He believes that Ban Me Thuot, 100 kilometers from Dalat by forest trails, will be retaken.

Father Darricault, head of the missions, gathers his clergy at the regional rectory. Two young priests, in Vietnam only a short time, are ordered back to France. The other priests are free to do as they wish. Most of them will leave.

Little by little the university administration disappears. Some professors hie themselves to the American Cultural Center. The Americans are evasive, and shortly disappear. The rector of the university asks the provincial chief, the ultimate authority, for permission to shut the place down; after several days of shifts he is told, "Do what you want."

The authorities shrug off responsibility. The rector closes the university "temporarily"—about as definite here as the Spanish *mañana*. The rector sends for Father Maïs: "You're French. Your country keeps up good relations with Hanoi. If you can, stay here to maintain a presence at the university."

Students pack. The most influential or resourceful leave on military planes. The military airport is fifteen minutes from the center of town. Some buy tickets on Air Vietnam and go to the commercial airport, a half hour from Dalat. Others cram into cars and head for the coast. Jean Maïs' Citroën 2CV is always full. The priest's assistant does not leave. Nor does the young woman who heads the French club as well as the Buddhist Student Union. Most of those outside the university's petite or grande bourgeoisie, the employees, maids, artisans, stay in place, in Dalat as elsewhere. For thirty years they've been in the habit of waiting.

They wait some more.

* * *

Saturday, March 15, 10 A.M.: Polgar is at his desk in the U.S. Embassy. One of his agents telephones from Pleiku: "The Second Corps is pulling out!"

The CIA chief prides himself on knowing South Vietnamese troop movements in advance. Dumbfounded, he sends one of his assistants to the palace, another to staff headquarters.

At the palace General Quang says flatly, "Nothing is happening in Pleiku."

Quang gives everyone the impression that Thieu, no less, has asked General Phu to prepare plans. The offices at headquarters seem deserted. Polgar's colleague turns up just one brigadier general, Tho. "What's going on at Pleiku?"

"Nothing," the general says.

Polgar chews on a few nasty ideas. No chief of staff—what does that mean? Vien, officially absent for the day, is meditating.

In Graham Martin's absence, Wolfgang Lehmann is running the embassy. They hunt for him. He's at the dentist's. What shall they say to Washington, where no one's understood since the first of the year how serious matters are? There are still some Americans up there in MR 2. Can't afford to let them fall into communist hands. Polgar is directly responsible for the CIA's agents and personnel, but not for other U.S. officials.

Dalat is a dulcet word. In Vietnamese, English or French, Pleiku sounds harder and summons up bad memories. There the North Vietnamese, attacking an encampment of U.S. military advisers ten years ago, killed nine of them and wounded seventy-six. That was the first direct confrontation. Then U.S. planes bombed installations north of the 17th parallel. And after that, hundreds of thousands of American soldiers landed.

In Pleiku General Phu elaborates his plans for a withdrawal spread out over four days:

March 16, engineer units, arms and ammunition, fuel supplies, the first artillery batteries, 200 trucks convoyed by armored cars.

March 17, last artillery batteries, engineers, medical supplies, 250 trucks, armored cars.

March 18, personnel of MR 2 staff and provincial headquarters, military police, 200 men of the 44th Infantry Regiment, armored cars.

March 19, rear guard, a ranger unit, last armored elements.

Beginning March 15, jeeps and trucks leave Pleiku in groups of five. News of the pullback filters out.

In Saigon the prime minister presides over a cabinet meeting. One minister alludes to developments in the Central Highlands, in reproachful tones: "I heard the news by foreign radio, the BBC and the Voice of America."[6]

Sitting beside the prime minister, Dr. Nguyen Luu Vien[7] hears Khiem murmur: "Me too. . . ."

"What? *You?*"

"It's true," Khiem breathes. "I was not told."

"Well, who's making all these decisions?"

"They make the decisions down there," Khiem answers, jerking a thumb toward the presidential palace. "Three people knew about it."

"Who?"

"The president, General Vien and General Phu."

Thieu receives Bui Diem, former ambassador to Washington and for two years a roving ambassador. Competent, cultivated, with a degree from the University of Hanoi, he was at one time a mathematics teacher in a Vietminh zone. Fleeing the communists, he made it to Saigon and participated in the 1954 Geneva negotiations on the nationalist side. A permanent secretary for foreign affairs, member of several Vietnamese delegations, he observed Johnson and Nixon, at Honolulu, Manila, Guam, Midway and San Clemente. In Washington Bui Diem knows almost everyone and everyone knows him. Tireless, he keeps trying to explain Saigon's position, in Malaysia, Singapore, Indonesia, Japan, India and especially in France and the United States. With Cousin Nha, Bui Diem is one of the rare Vietnamese who truly understand American institutional and constitutional mechanisms. In Washington, where on the whole Nha is not liked, they do trust Bui Diem, more a civil servant or academic than a politician.

Bui Diem appears in Thieu's office together with a former minister of foreign affairs[8] and the president of the Confederation of Vietnamese Workers. "This is the crunch," Bui Diem says. "We have to rally all nationalists."

Thieu listens to the improvised delegation: "Put that in writing for me and come back with names."

This isn't the first time someone has delicately suggested that he modify his government. He seems unconvinced. A built-in dilemma: Thieu has to expand his political base, but any expansion, any compromise with the opposition, is in his eyes a concession to the communists. Still, he says he's ready to talk. Eternal pilgrim in a lost cause, Bui Diem must leave for Paris and Washington. Thieu tells him, "The main thing is, squeeze that aid out of the Americans."

Even to his special envoy, the president says nothing about the decision to withdraw from Pleiku! Worse: Does Thieu even realize how important his decision was?

Next day Bui Diem visits Vien, an old friend. Bui Diem has friends in all capitals. The chairman of the Joint General Staff is worried: "We have a little more than a month's worth of ammunition. After that it'll be hard to ask the men to fight."

Bui Diem knows there's not much chance of supplemental American credits. In Saigon they're thinking about other sources, even aid from the moderate Arab countries.[9] With long-term loans they could buy arms. On higher levels, civilian or military, they take it for granted that the services are short of arms and ammunition. But too often they underestimate the problem of morale.

That day Thieu, unaware or playing a part, seems sure of himself. The general-president, who naturally considers Giap a "false Napoleon," prepares to become a true Kutuzov. Pulling back, he'll let the enemy extend their lines of communication and bog down, not in Russian snow and winter, but in Indochinese monsoon and mud. The South Vietnamese will shorten their lines. Then the North Vietnamese will face intractable problems of supply.

Wolfgang Lehmann takes the U.S. Embassy in hand. He cables State in Washington: "I have ordered the consul general at Nha Trang to withdraw all American personnel from Kontum, Pleiku and Quang Duc. They will arrive at Nha Trang at the end of the afternoon."

Details trickle in: North Vietnamese sappers have blown up an arsenal in Kontum. Rockets put the city's airport out of action.

On the same day in Hanoi, the Politburo and Central Military Committee agree to a proposal by General Dung: the commander in chief suggests following up briskly. Given the green light, he issues orders. In 1968 and 1972 the North Vietnamese also fought major battles in the area. But, says Dung, "our victories were not as quick, or as brilliant, or as decisive as this year." All things considered, Thieu's armies won the day during those earlier major offensives. Now in March 1975 the North Vietnamese supply dumps, transport network and pipelines are larger and more efficient. Dung repeats: their job is to "hit hard and keep hitting . . . before the rainy season."

At Pleiku the South Vietnamese pullback is heavy going but continues steadily for three days, March 15–18. It is no small matter to redeploy an army corps, its men, trucks and armored cars, 20,000 tons of artillery shells, a month and a half's fuel reserves and two months' rations. All this has to be shifted to the coast, to Nha Trang, where they will mount the counterattack on Ban Me Thuot. Suddenly they understand why General Phu demanded a promotion for Tat. A new-minted general, Tat is assigned by Phu to "direct" the operation. Another general, longer in grade, must "supervise the whole." Hazy orders, incomprehensible in fact: a powerful source of misunderstandings.[10]

The staff at Pleiku never sent competent scouts to reconnoiter Route 7B, riddled with potholes and often impassable.

The first large units leave Pleiku, headed by the 20th Engineers. Their ranks are rapidly swelled by refugees from Kontum and Pleiku—Kontum is only about forty kilometers north of Pleiku.

On this road, not maintained for years, the M-48 tanks—forty-seven tons—advance laboriously. The regional forces receive contradictory orders. Phu says, "The regional forces are all Montagnards, so let's give them back to the mountains."

Other officers ask them to protect stretches of 7B. Knowing themselves abandoned, the Montagnards naturally scatter. Bridges on 7B have been blown. They have to be repaired. The work takes time. Still, the troops move along.

Until March 16 North Vietnamese intelligence botches the analysis. It is Western radio that supplies information of "extreme importance," says General Dung, "despite its fragmentary nature." Certain details alert the North Vietnamese. The American news agency UPI announces that "the price of an airplane ticket from Pleiku to Saigon has risen to 40,000 piastres." Why this run on the airport and this sudden explosion in price?

That afternoon the North Vietnamese monitor radio messages from South Vietnamese pilots. They took off from Pleiku and landed at Nha Trang, and they are not returning to base even though the North Vietnamese have not shelled it. Why? Dung understands: Phu has settled in at Nha Trang. Dung hears that the 450 Americans at Pleiku and some of their Vietnamese employees are leaving.

A helicopter shuttle is set up between the center of town and the airport. C-46s and C-47s establish an airlift to Nha Trang. To Pleiku's populace and Dung's spies alike, it's obvious: they're evacuating the city.

In Pleiku the CIA agents lose their cool. They "forget" a certain number of their South Vietnamese employees, among them their principal informers. Most important, they don't burn all their files.

A small group from the ICCS also leaves in a curious manner. The Americans feel an obligation toward the Indonesians and Iranians, none toward the Hungarians and Poles. These last, those "bastards," are in radio contact with the PRG and the North Vietnamese. Delightful codes: "It's a nice day. . . . The sky is clear. . . . Our friends are up early. . . ."[11]

Polgar and Lehmann find a way. By rotation, an Indonesian is now presiding over the ICCS in Saigon. He is notified. He tells only the Indonesians and Iranians.

Finally the Polish and Hungarian comrades, who have no desire to linger awaiting their North Vietnamese comrades, are evacuated by Air America.[12] Three cheers for the CIA!

Toward 7 P.M. on March 16 a lively discussion breaks out at North Vietnamese staff headquarters. They have the impression "that the enemy is plotting something in the Central Highlands, after losing their shirts at Phuoc Binh and Ban Me Thuot." Dung's staff is intrigued: Is it the whole ARVN Second Army Corps that's trying to disengage? "If it's a retreat, how will he go about it? By what route?" Dung wonders. To begin with he sets himself two priorities: "First, crush the counteroffensive quickly." Dung, like Thieu, thinks it will come. "Also, make urgent preparations to move our forces into position to encircle Pleiku."

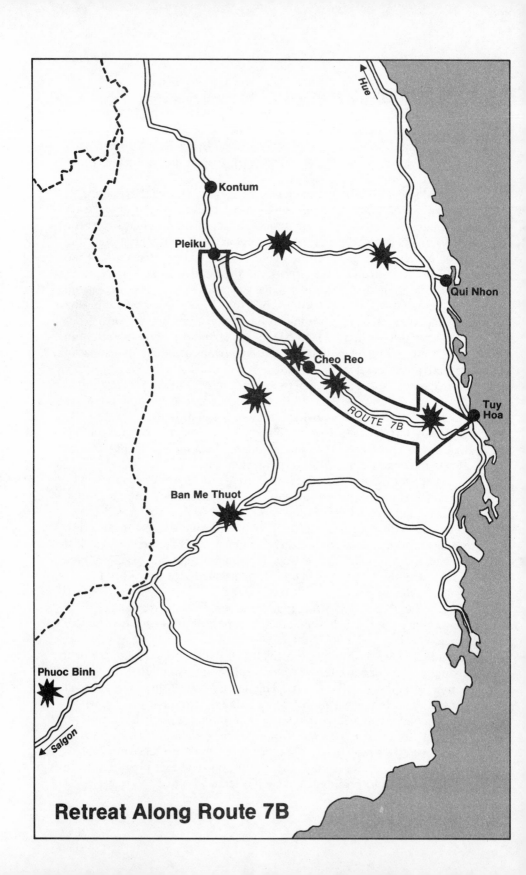

Hue

Kontum

Pleiku

Qui Nhon

Cheo Reo

ROUTE 7B

Tuy Hoa

Ban Me Thuot

Phuoc Binh

Saigon

Retreat Along Route 7B

The town empties hour by hour. Dung has cut strategic routes in the region, Routes 19, 14, 21. He doesn't bother with 7B. They assure him it's unusable, bridges in ruin and no ferries anywhere. At 9 P.M. he learns that all troops have been ordered to evacuate Pleiku. It's confirmed. So there's no garrison dug in, as intelligence from Hanoi had assumed. And now Dung also knows that for forty-eight hours most of the Second Army Corps has been converging on Route 7B, reported impassable. Dung is furious; vigorously, and for posterity, he reprimands General Kim Tuan, commander of the famous 320th Division, who had insisted that no unit, Northern or Southern, with artillery and armored cars could use the road: "That's dereliction, negligence that deserves a reprimand," barks Dung on the telephone. "Right now if you waver at all, are at all negligent, hesitate at all, are at all late, you've botched your job. If the enemy escape it'll be one big crime, and you'll have to bear responsibility for it."

For the first time a whole ARVN army corps is abandoning a strategic position during a major campaign, and carrying out a retreat in unfavorable circumstances.

Dung was once a foot soldier, and today brings back thirty years of memories. Like the ARVN chief of staff, he's thinking of the French retreat. And also of U.S. marines evacuating Khe Sanh in 1968. That wasn't a disaster; but it was certainly no victory for the Americans. More recently, in 1971, there was the South Vietnamese retreat along Route 9 in Laos, a catastrophe for Saigon. And the withdrawal of the ARVN Third Division at Quang Tri in 1972. But there the South Vietnamese retook the city. Dung notes: "Every time the enemy had to pull back fast in the face of an attack, he employed a variety of ruses for security."

Where's the trap? What's Thieu's stratagem? He has one, that's for sure.

During the night of March 16–17 the 320th Division moves forward. Racing through forests, its units prepare to attack the retreating South Vietnamese columns. The 320th's tanks and artillery will arrive March 18. Dung orders his 968th Division to advance on Pleiku, to cut through or bypass the city and drop down to take the retreating ARVN column on the other flank.

In Pleiku the sky is an explosion of blue and orange flames. The ARVN burns and abandons a major part of its fuel supplies.

On Route 7B cars and civilian trucks, bumper to bumper, mingle with convoys, breaking up military formations. The army's Dodge trucks are crammed with soldiers and their families, their furniture, baskets, chickens. Tanks and armored vehicles skid and slide. An ambulance follows mobile artillery. Batallions and companies stretch, sprawl, dissolve. Officers lose contact with their men. Captains shout at majors, demanding the right of way. Majors refuse colonels' orders. Messages, often incomprehensible, crackle from one end to the other of this enormous, slow, wheeled caterpillar. Radio sets break down, fall silent. There are bursts of fire from automatic weapons, the crump and blast of departing and arriving mortar shells. On March 18 officers with the column hear by radio about the loss of An Loc, a town only 100 kilometers north of Saigon, and 300 kilometers southeast of Route 7B.

More bad news trickles in from MR 1, the northernmost.

The withdrawal becomes a retreat, and the exodus a debacle. By day the refugees trudge through red dust and dry heat. By night they wilt in the humidity, in the musty odor of the jungle where North Vietnamese patrols prowl. The men are broken, the women weary, the children and elderly bewildered. There is not enough food or water. They pass more and more dead and dying, the dead eyes aswarm with insects. Mosquitoes batten on the living.

The soldiers left Kontum and Pleiku under good discipline but rapidly become demoralized. Yet most of them hang on to their guns. Civilians and soldiers alike are prisoners of distrust, confusion, disorder. An officer who loses his men in the chaos or the darkness comes under immediate suspicion of abandoning them and is then accused of desertion. At the roadside lie shapes wrapped in ponchos sodden with rain and mud. Odors of hot steel, grease and gasoline hang heavy over the column. At dawn, they await true daylight, when helicopters can land to pick up the wounded and the mothers and their children, and fighter bombers can strafe North Vietnamese units. But some mornings reveal sheets of fog striped gray and saffron. The refugees discover bridges, pagodas and small temples smashed open or in ruins. They stumble over wounded men and corpses they cannot take time to bury or send down the road. Often the bodies are folded, or bowed down, or strangely twisted. The whole country seems fugitive and petrified.

Yet at moments, day or night, an extraordinary tranquility descends on the column. Distant artillery falls silent, the phosphorescent flare of rockets dims. Voices calling, bats' squeaks, birds' cries . . . In hollows among the roots of trees lies tepid water. Dripping and lapping sounds drown out the buzz of insects. Here they stir up braziers to boil gluey rice. Elsewhere officers hunt down fires and lights; they must not be spotted; flashlights glimmer nonetheless, and truck drivers leave one or two headlights on. Faces are gaunt with fatigue, hunger, thirst. They are all hoping to reach the coast. And to reach Saigon. And then?

Noncoms tramp against the grain of the convoy, seeking a squad or a family. The column advances, skirting here a dead truck, a jeep, an old Citroen smoking, there motorbikes, Vespas, Lambrettas burning or abandoned for lack of fuel. Mortar and artillery fire picks up again, approaches. To dress their fire, North Vietnamese gunners deploy spotters close to the road. If a section of the convoy proceeds unmolested between two attacks, it's only because the North Vietnamese want to create obstructions and bottlenecks farther along. To magnify the next traffic jam—and the next massacre.

Most of the civilians in the endless convoy are city folk, but there are a few peasants.

Why are they fleeing? They're afraid. They dread socialist discipline. People of the Central Highlands dislike the Tonkinese, hard Northerners. The refugees suspect that Saigon has abandoned its basic policy, which for twenty years consisted of holding every square kilometer possible. Civil servants are convinced they'll be punished and bullied for having collaborated, willy-nilly, with the Americans. Merchants fear to see their shops nationalized. Others have heard talk of confiscated property, plundered lands, peasant revolts suppressed, people's tribunals and summary public executions. They can all imagine their province occupied by the North Vietnamese, then bombed by Thieu's air force. And if the Americans come back with B-52s? Some of the refugees are Catholic. And some of those who, in 1954, left Catholic towns like Phat Diem to the north, have joined this second exodus. Others are Buddhists and do not believe the communist promise of religious freedom.

In 1954 Pham Van Dong, negotiator at Geneva and a leader in the Hanoi government, said—sincerely or cynically—of the refugees, "We come to bring them happiness and they flee. Do you understand that?" In 1954 departures were organized; French and American warships helped in the evacuation. In 1975, on Route 7B, the Saigon government has made no provision for civilians.

March 20: overloaded trucks and tanks clog the ford on the Ba River. The head of the column is stopped dead. A delay. Helicopters fly in sheet metal to lay a new ford. Trucks in groups of five or ten, one group after another, are immobilized. The bottlenecks cannot be cleared.

Officers demand air support to protect the road. North Vietnamese heavy machineguns and artillery are firing on the convoy. South Vietnamese pilots dive, mistake their targets, bomb their own people and inflict enormous losses on a battalion of the Seventh Rangers. For quicker passage tank commanders bypass the new metal ford. Quicksand swallows their vehicles. There is chaos everywhere. Soldiers drown trying to cross the river.

In Saigon Polgar ponders this operation along Route 7B. No information from Vietnamese sources. No data from the satellites: for their scientific proprietors in Washington, Vietnam lost its priority long ago. Nor can Polgar demand an SR-71, a high altitude spy plane, a sort of improved U-2. A photo snapped by an SR-71 would show a damaged tank blocking a bridge. Though not, some claim, if its crew were smoking Winstons or Dien Bien Phus. If the CIA in Vietnam did acquire one of these reconnaissance planes, the snapshots would reach them several weeks later. And the military attaché at the U.S. Embassy can't send one of his planes because the Paris Agreement forbids any intervention of that kind. But the CIA has its prerogatives: a right to take the initiative on the margins of international legalism—at any rate as expressed in the Paris Agreement. Polgar sends an Air America plane.

The plane returns, and the photos show a retreat going as badly as possible. To his colleagues Polgar says, "It looks like a circus parade gone crazy. The elephants are in front. And the other animals are walking in their shit."

Polgar goes to see the prime minister. He asks Khiem to show these CIA photos to the president, and adds, "As an operational military unit, and from the point of view of equipment, your Second Army Corps has ceased to exist."

Even during the great North Vietnamese offensives of 1968 or 1972 they never saw anything like this. On 7B vehicles are burning, cadavers accumulate at the roadside. A cold rain follows the heat that parched hands and faces. Civilians and soldiers alike are shivering. Now bad weather precludes air support. Some units abandon their heavy weapons, then their lighter arms. Others, in the rear guard or flanking, continue to fight. But where *is* the rear? Where *are* the flanks?

March 21: The larger part of the column is clumped around fords and bridges east of Cong Son. Battalions of the NVA 320th Division cut the convoy to pieces, isolating the 6th, 7th, and 22nd ranger groups, the most obdurate fighters. Even worse, the NVA moves fast and blocks the convoy forty kilometers from the coast. Two battalions of rangers, the 35th and the 51st, supported by fifteen light M-41 tanks and eight medium M-48s, repulse a violent attack by the NVA 64th Regiment, on the night of March 23. The weather clears, and two CH-47 helicopters resupply the rangers with food and ammunition. They cut through the enemy lines. The sky closes in again. The rangers wipe out North Vietnamese positions before them, one after another, the last one on March 25. The rangers are at the head of the column that makes it to Tuy Hoa on the coast.

About 200,000 civilians swelled the column; 60,000 reach Tuy Hoa. The Second Corps' chief of staff, Colonel Khac Ly, estimates that of the support troops who left Pleiku only 5,000 reached their destination. Some units lost half their men, killed or wounded.

At headquarters in Saigon they add it up. The butcher's bill is heavy: they've lost an armored brigade and seven regiments. Thieu blames Phu and announces that Phu received no order to evacuate. Later he says the commander of the Second Corps should have prepared his withdrawal more carefully. The chief of staff in Saigon takes a more reasonable view: Phu had only forty-eight hours to deploy his troops. The problems were unimaginable. They could not foresee masses of civilians clinging to the soldiers and materiel, paralyzing any counterattack. Perhaps worst of all, they sadly underestimated the North Vietnamese command's ingenuity and adaptability. They had thought it ponderous, incapable of improvisation in maneuvering large conventional units.

Some South Vietnamese soldiers and junior officers behaved admirably.

But the lieutenants and captains were badly commanded. And certain orders and intelligence never arrived where they were needed. Before 1973, for example, the South Korean expeditionary corps had mined a stretch of roadside along 7B. The mines had never been cleared.

There is always misfortune in a defeat, plain bad luck, but here it was mainly a problem of command, of outmoded or incompetent field officers and generals.

The surviving units regroup at Tuy Hoa, consoling themselves by a recital of their high deeds. In defeat as in victory there is a fraternity, even more bitter because the dead and wounded, often abandoned, fell in vain.

In Tuy Hoa isolated groups of soldiers search for the remains of their units, which no longer exist. The rout has become a sleepwalk.

Sun Tzu says: "Order and disorder depend on organization; courage and cowardice, on circumstances; strength and weakness, on character." Sun Tzu also writes: "When a falcon's swoop destroys his prey, it is because his moment was well chosen."

Clausewitz remarks: "Every lost battle is a matter of weakness and dispersal. The most urgent need is to concentrate and by concentration to recover order, courage and confidence."[13]

11

What Are Moscow and Beijing up To?

Thieu wants primarily to save Saigon, to assure the "compact" defense of a viable Vietnam, roughly MR 3 and MR 4.

For several weeks the general-president has been expecting an attack northwest of the capital, around Tay Ninh, and so have the U.S. and South Vietnamese intelligence services. This attack could spearhead a general offensive. The battles of Ban Me Thuot, Kontum, Pleiku and Route 7B may have been diversions. Sometimes the NVA, at company or battalion level, jabs at Saigon's defenses fifty kilometers from the city's outskirts. As commander in chief, Thieu wants to hold back his reserves. His best troops, his division of marines and the airborne division commanded by a first-rate officer, General Quang Luong, have been dug in for a long time in MR 1, in South Vietnam's far north.

MR 1 is commanded by another highly esteemed general, Ngo Trang Truong. As capable as he is respected, forty-six years old, short and thin, with a dark, smooth, emaciated face and a large beauty mark under his right eye, Truong has a remote gaze, almost empty. He expresses himself in simple words and short sentences, without emphasis. When he stresses a point, his delivery quickens. In civilian clothes he passes for a laborer. In the countryside he could be taken for a peasant. His popularity with enlisted men and his legend, already entering History, rest on his deeds. During the battle for Hue in 1972, Truong held out for weeks. When the South Vietnamese were looting he made a public appeal by radio: "Soldiers and citizens of the First Military Region: this is General Truong speaking.

I have taken command. Tomorrow morning, deserters will rejoin their units. Looting will cease." And it ceased. And Truong retook Quang Tri, with three divisions against six NVA divisions.

Under harassing fire since the second week in March, Truong believes firmly that he can hold MR 1, where he has five divisions. He's sure of his marines and paratroops. His First Division? One of the best. The Third? Not bad. Only the Second, near Chu Lai, is weak. Truong and his staff will stand fast against any attack, even if Hanoi throws reserves into the battle. In contrast to General Phu, Truong prepares a withdrawal strategy based on a series of enclaves, potential retrenchments at Hue, Danang and Chu Lai.

Thieu[1] tells Truong to be ready to send his airborne division back to the Saigon area. Truong protests to staff headquarters in Saigon. Vien, overwhelmed and exhausted, answers that the president won't go back on his decision. Furious, Truong emplanes for Saigon to plead his cause. Thieu won't give in. Annoying, these generals who only see *their* region and not the greater national interest! Thieu "forgets" to notify Truong that he's also going to appropriate the marine division.

Truong returns to his headquarters in Danang and considers resigning.

He reorganizes his defenses. Thieu's new deal forces him to strip his outposts along the demilitarized zone, the length of the 17th parallel, the northern edge of his region.

Truong hears that the communist force he faces is larger than expected. His men will be up against North Vietnamese shock troops, Divisions 325C, 324B, 304. And the 711th and the 2nd. A reserve division, the 341st, is coming south. Finally, mixed units of NVA regulars and PRG guerrillas are regrouping at both ends of his military region, some in the north around Quang Tri, others in the south near Chu Lai. The guerrillas there are better armed and trained than before. If his marines and paratroops are pulled out, Truong may have to fight the equivalent of six divisions with only three of his own. His adversaries can attack "massed in depth." So he has to keep his divisions deployed, extended and diluted.

As the retreat from Pleiku begins on March 15, the 369th Marine Brigade evacuates Quang Tri.

Up there on the border the marines represent a solid presence, a strong force and a victory, the triumph at Quang Tri in 1972. These marines are disciplined and tough, and don't campaign with their families and furniture. Their departure is a blow to civilian morale. In all of Quang Tri province, as elsewhere, civilians listen to foreign radio, mostly the BBC and the Voice of America, easy to tune in. Beginning March 16 they hear precise and hair-raising reports of events along Route 7B. Townsfolk in MR 1 quickly grow nervous, then lose their heads, then leave, preceded by VIPs and civil servants. In Quang Tri the provincial chief himself, Lieutenant Colonel Do Ky, advises civil servants to evacuate their families. Quang Tri's people flee to Hue, and Hue's to Danang. In a few days Danang's population swells from 600,000 to 1 million.

On March 18 the prime minister meets with General Phu at Nha Trang, the new, and totally disorganized, headquarters of MR 2. Overwhelmed, Phu doesn't even seem coherent. He's Khiem's protégé but Khiem suggests that Thieu dismiss him. The president refuses. Besides, what good would it do, if the Second Army Corps no longer exists?

The prime minister goes to Danang. He promises assembled civil authorities that the government will take care of the flood of refugees and will appropriate funds. At headquarters in MR 1 Khiem meets Truong. No question of leaving him the marines or the airborne, even less of sending reinforcements.

Truong returns to Saigon. He no longer understands Thieu's strategy at all. What about his policy of enclaves? It seems he must hold Hue. After that ruinous retreat in MR 2, Thieu doesn't much want to allow another in MR 1.

At 11 A.M. on March 19 the president meets with the prime minister, his chief of staff and his security adviser. Vice President Tran Van Huong joins Khiem, Vien and Quang. They call in General Truong. They talk about two enclaves, maybe three. Truong says flatly that he can hold Hue and Danang. Thieu will await Truong's return to Danang before making an important radio broadcast on the defense of Hue.

But when he reaches Danang, Truong hears that the communists are attacking Hue in force. He calls Vien in Saigon. True to character, the chief of staff refers him to Thieu. Truong says: "Better put off your broadcast on Hue. The city may be untenable."

That same day Wolfgang Lehmann cables Brent Scowcroft at the White House. Lehmann asks him to "pass [the cable on to] Ambassador Martin," who is still recuperating in North Carolina: "Things here are happening rather quickly. . . . President scheduled to speak to the country tonight to explain government strategy . . . although not announced, everything shows the government has decided to abandon Quang Tri." According to Lehmann, they plan to let Hue go, too. Evidence? Tank units are withdrawing.

Lehmann tests the waters at staff headquarters in Saigon via Homer Smith. The general reports that officers are unhappy at the precipitous decision to evacuate Pleiku and Kontum. "The grumbling is not about the decision itself, which appears to be endorsed by the . . . majority" of officers, but about the manner in which it was executed: "far too much ammunition and equipment had to be left behind or destroyed."

Lehmann adds that he has found a "growing tendency among the Vietnamese, including the military, to blame the Americans. . . . We will watch it carefully and take the necessary action to prevent it from getting out of hand." He has already suggested to Scowcroft that it "is not too early to think of moving large numbers of people by sea lift. . . . Refugees are already crowding into Danang."[2] Lehmann is also thinking of his flock; that's his job. American officials stationed in Hue no longer sleep there. At night they travel several kilometers south to sleep near the airport; in an emergency they can be evacuated from there. Some Quakers from a charitable organization have made it clear that whatever happens they'll stay. The U.S. government watches over its citizens, but when they're not civil servants, they're not given orders.

Lehmann no longer believes in a South Vietnamese counterattack: "It now seems the GVN has dropped the idea of forcing a major battle in the Ban Me Thuot area."

An interesting military equation: the Americans don't know what the South Vietnamese are going to do, and the South Vietnamese don't know what the North Vietnamese are up to. These last are digesting their successes in astonished delight. Dung writes: "Our victory in the Central Highlands was immense, beyond all expectations."

By all evidence, the North Vietnamese commander in chief presented the Politburo and the Party's Central Military Committee with one fait accompli after another, like the hot pursuit along Route 7B, and exceeded his instructions. Nothing succeeds like success. Dung wants more: he asks Hanoi for authority to keep the offensive rolling. He has a fistful of trump cards. Despite occasional delay in the convoys, he has no serious problems with troops, rations, arms or ammunition. He can transport his men quickly, with his own vehicles or those taken intact from the enemy.

The general technical administration in Hanoi detaches 300 engineers, mechanics and specialists to restore hundreds of trucks to service. Repairing captured tanks and artillery isn't as easy, but they do it. Dung controls the main highways running down to the coastal plain. Despite his natural prudence, and Hanoi's too—they fear he may fall into a trap— the commander in chief wants to press on. It's all too tempting.

His staff officers circulate a line that becomes a classic joke overnight: "We can't draw maps fast enough to keep up with our troops!"

March 19: Polgar, who wonders if the prime minister ever did send the president those photos of the debacle on Route 7B, polishes a cable for the director of the CIA in Washington. The situation, he explains, has deteriorated "dramatically" in MR 1 as in MR 2. The mission chief predicts that Thieu will also lose Hue.

In his cables, Polgar likes to step back and set events in perspective, even if it means selective emphasis. That is surely necessary; no one in Washington seems to grasp the realities of the situation. "Geographic concept of the Republic of South Vietnam which emerged from the Geneva Accords [in 1954] . . . kept alive, if not intact, through massive American support, is no more." Polgar is thinking of that damned congressional debate on aid, back in Washington. He wants to supply his boss with ammunition: William Colby must be able to testify officially before committees and unofficially in conversations with important senators and congressmen that "survival of independent South Vietnam," as Polgar continues, "depends in large measure on U.S. actions. There is no doubt that a lack of U.S. determination in the Vietnam context will kill the nation which earlier U.S. efforts helped to create. . . . Additional aid is indispensable."

In Washington they're still not paying excessive attention to Vietnam. They're preoccupied by Cambodia. Bureaucracies usually yield to a natural tendency, claiming success when it occurs and criticizing one another in difficulty or failure: it's the White House's business, that's the State Department's job, this is in the Defense Department's bailiwick. History buffs among Pentagon officers are comparing Thieu's routed troops on 7B to Napoleon's before Moscow in 1812, to the French retreat in 1940, to the collapse of Nationalist Chinese armies in 1949.

No one in Saigon or Washington knows that a fundamental decision was made in Hanoi on March 20 in response to General Dung's requests: Politburo and Central Military Committee agree with the commander in chief. He must continue the offensive. For Dung the important thing is not to let Thieu "pull his troops together and concentrate them in the Saigon area and part of the Mekong Delta. . . . So we have to run a real race against the clock . . . to implement our plans for the liberation of Saigon faster than we expected."

Medical Corps Colonel Jean Fourré, surgeon, a forthright, direct man who served three "Indo" years in Laos, arrives to take over as head of the Grall Hospital, showcase of the French presence in Saigon. Grall is self-financing, and only the French doctors are paid by Paris. Fourré notes, to his surprise, that the French colony has remained calm.

At the embassy he confers with military attaché Colonel Yves Gras. The latter explains to the doctor that "the Viets,"[3] the North Vietnamese, are going to regroup and bide their time. They could take the South Vietnamese capital but they won't. Good. You know, in Asia, you mustn't lose face. Good. Hanoi has no desire to humiliate Saigon. Good. Perhaps the Viets will resume their offensive after the rainy season.

Surely, Fourré tells himself, our embassy people must know what's going on; this Colonel Gras is a veteran of the old days. In fact, the military attaché, a firebrand, has never impressed intelligence circles in Saigon, except the Poles, by his politico-military intuitions.

While disintegration begins in MR 1 and MR 2, President-General Thieu has his hands full on the political level too.

On Tuesday March 25 at 4:30 P.M., in the little conference room attached to his office on the first floor of the palace, he gathers his cabinet. His security counselor, General Quang, reports on domestic politics. He details the activities of various parties, opposition movements, some meetings here, some demonstrations there. Then Nguyen Van Hao, deputy prime minister for economic affairs, broaches problems of resupply, prices, foodstuffs and gasoline. The president listens and takes notes.

Thieu addresses his prime minister, to his left: "Khiem, I think it's time to reshuffle your cabinet and face up to the situation. We need a fighting cabinet—*noi cac chien dau*—made up of sure patriots, dynamic, decisive."

So the members of the present government aren't?

Thieu goes on. "I'll announce that this evening. We need to work fast, and cut the ground from under the enemy's feet. There's not a moment to lose."

The president has not said a word about the military situation! Does he consider that his private concern? Khiem rarely contradicts Thieu, but for once he says aloud what all the ministers present are thinking: first and foremost we have to slow the communist offensive, stabilize the front and take care of the refugees. Khiem is not a sentimental man, but what he saw at Danang, all those confused wandering civilians, moved him. Hao cries, "Mr. President, we can't go on retreating forever like this! We have to stop the North Vietnamese advance. Where do you think we can do that?"

Soft pencil in hand, Thieu steps to a map of Vietnam hanging on the wall. He traces two semicircles and a straight line on the transparent plastic overlay, saying confidently, "We don't retreat another step! In the First Military Region we hold an enclave here, at Danang. In the Second Region another enclave, there, at Qui Nhon. We dig in along a stable front on this line, from Deo Ca Mountain north of Nha Trang, to just above Dalat. You'll see: Danang will be our Stalingrad. Even better, because it's easier to defend and resupply."

Thieu has his comparisons badly tangled, surely forgetting that the besieged Germans in the Stalingrad enclave were *defeated*.

The president sits down: "Furthermore, I'm issuing an order that from now on we resist to the death, *tu thu*."

Thieu seems to believe his own statements. Is he taking words for deeds, verbs for victory? He writes a little oration with a pen and reads it aloud. Vice-President Huong, who wasn't a teacher for nothing, suggests a few improvements in style. The president sends for his private secretary, Colonel Cam, and orders him to transmit the text without delay to division and corps generals, also to the province chiefs, colonels.

That night, radio and television make much of the president's resolve: "to mobilize all the nation's energies . . . to stop the communist offensive . . . to bring aid to the refugees."

As if it were only a cabinet shakeup in peacetime or truce, the prime minister consults and receives some thirty VIPs over the next week. Khiem seems to be imitating a prime minister of the Fourth French Republic the day after a ministerial crisis. Doctor Nguyen Luu Vien composes a report summarizing the views of these thirty-odd advisers.

Thieu doesn't give a damn about South Vietnamese public opinion, but he listens to a few prominent advisers. Doctor Vien sets out four headings: the need to restore the people's confidence, to establish broad national unity, to change the government's ways, and to make an overture for peace—all the while inspiring the troops to check the communist offensive.

There are three possibilities:

> (1) If the army, for whatever reason—shortage of material or lack of morale—cannot halt the communist offensive, then the whole Republic of Vietnam will be invaded, and the world will have to accept a fait accompli. (2) If the communist offensive is stopped but we remain politically weak, then a procommunist coalition government will be installed. The communization of the Republic of Vietnam will be only a matter of time. (3) If the communist offensive is halted and we stand fast politically, then there could be a third Vietnam. This is the least bad solution. It is not realistic to think of reconquering lost provinces.

Then, and very strangely, Vien writes, "On the contrary, such language might frighten the Americans and close the door to the communists."

Over the last month, Thieu's political situation has not worsened. In fact, he can hope for some action by Vietnamese fence-sitters. Most who dislike the president and his regime mistrust the North Vietnamese even more and have no desire to be communized. Whatever Radio Hanoi and Radio Liberation say, so far there's been no groundswell of support for the advancing North Vietnamese troops. People are beginning to hear more than vague rumors on the communists' conduct when they occupy towns and villages.

Refugees from Phuoc Long, Ban Me Thuot and other "liberated" provinces testify that on the whole North Vietnamese soldiers show courtesy toward peasants and townspeople. There are no signs of pillage or rape. But the occupiers, usually after contact with the NLF or the PRG, hunt down and arrest South Vietnamese civil servants, especially police and security personnel. Cases of arrests followed by execution are clearly attested. The victors register the population everywhere. In the Central Highlands the Montagnards are separated from the Vietnamese. There's tight control everywhere. They assign a Vietcong to watch three, five, or ten families, depending on the number of NLF members available. The populace is encouraged to practice self-criticism and "to criticize others"; in short, to denounce them. People foresee courses of "retraining" and political reorientation. The occupiers are obsessed by cleanliness; they mobilize civilians to scour hamlets, villages and towns, as if it were necessary to purify the provinces physically and morally. In some places men and women are assigned to reconstruction and repair by the inspiring and time-honored system of obligatory and designated volunteers.

Prisoners of war are sorted out; here common soldiers; there noncoms; further along, officers. Treatment of common soldiers varies from one province to the next. They are released, or detained in improvised camps, or sent on their way north in small groups. The occupiers hang on to officers and noncoms from regional forces and militias. The prisoners' fate is wholly in the hands of North Vietnamese cadres or, when they surface, those of the PRG. Cadres are often from the North. Refugees testify that the PRG's Southern cadres prove more easygoing than those from the Center or North. A few Southerners even advise some residents, mainly minor civil servants, to disappear and let themselves be forgotten. In Ban Me Thuot 3,000 people were assembled at the marketplace after the North Vietnamese victory. Crisscrossing the crowd, PRG cadres plucked out 300 employees of the South Vietnamese government, some of them policemen. These were denounced as "enemies of the people, American lackeys and spies." They were marched out of town. Some were executed. Despite several examples of this kind, there was nowhere the "bloodbath" announced by the Saigon government. The system seems repressive, not bloody, for the moment at least, despite isolated cases of torture and atrocity. By word of mouth, Saigon's propaganda agencies exploit as best they can any rumors of repression in the new communist zones.

Part of the population flees before the NVA, but still no one is rushing to support the Saigon regime. No volunteers flock to enlist in the army, navy or air force.

Thieu was hoping for a huge burst of national energy; it never comes.

In Hanoi on March 22, Pham Van Dong hosts a grand diplomatic banquet. Halfway through dinner—everyone notices—an aide approaches the French ambassador: "The prime minister would like to speak to you, now."

Pham Van Dong takes Philippe Richer aside. The prime minister is full of charm and knows how to use it, quoting Hugo or Zola as usual and talking about the strong ties between France and Vietnam. There is more than one string to his bow. Right now he wants to tell Richer, who already has a fairly clear notion, what's happening in the South. Conversation with a North Vietnamese leader is always serpentine, and bristles with clichés. To decode it and extract the important points, you have to pick your way through stands of wooden phrase.

Richer asks, "What do you think of the Third Force [in South Vietnam]?"

"They're your friends," the prime minister answers. Then he says, "The situation is irreversible now. . . . France must do something. Thieu must go."

During the discussions that led to the Paris Agreement, Washington and Saigon insisted on one concession: that Thieu stay on.

And just how shall he interpret Pham Van Dong's remarks? They certainly mean that the French had better act before it's too late. Too late to restore very good terms with Hanoi.

Philippe Richer ponders Pham Van Dong's remarks for forty-eight hours before he cables the Quai d'Orsay.

Hue is smaller than the two enemy capitals or Danang, but is the most prestigious of all Vietnam's cities after Hanoi and Saigon. Capital of the central region, a cultural hub, Hue is symbolic on several levels. Once it was the capital of a unified Vietnam. In 1972 the Americans and South Vietnamese lost and retook it. They found charnel houses, and Hanoi's admirers never disputed the reports. They blamed the systematic executions on the NLF.

In a country ravaged by war and modernism, by sheet metal and plastic, Hue preserves all the charm of an ancient imperial capital. Vietnamese who have never seen Hue imagine it melancholy, often drowning in drizzle. Even during the dry season, fog shrouds the peaks of Mount Ngu or blankets the sluggish waters of the Perfume River. The town is built along the river. On the left bank stands the imperial city, a rectangle of fortifications in Vauban's style with walls six meters high enclosing tombs of Annamite emperors, palaces and temples pocked by mortar and artillery fire. The old city is crowded now with refugees finding their way around the marketplace among restaurants and shops and checking out sampan-hotels where, in normal times, night-people foregather.

Waves of vehicles, trucks, vans, civilian and military cars, motorbikes, carts, bicycles, jam the bridges and disgorge their passengers toward the government palace and the European quarter to the east. There cluster foreign consulates and the homes of their European employees. These foreigners, mostly Americans now, as well as upper civil servants and the town's middle classes, abandoned the Cercle Nautique early in the month, with its tennis courts and beaches. On every lawn are refugees mingling with soldiers who may be either regular patrols or refugees themselves. Civilians and soldiers alike are claiming squatter's rights at the university.

No one can say for sure that President Thieu was responsible for the loss of Phuoc Long or Ban Me Thuot, or for the catastrophic retreat from Kontum and Pleiku. But he is wholly responsible for the loss of Hue.

When General Truong, after conferring with the president in Saigon, returned to First Army Corps headquarters at Danang, seventy-five kilometers south of Hue, the news was bad. Communist tanks had made a clean sweep of the regional troops at Quang Tri, fifty kilometers north of Hue.

Truong goes up to Hue on March 20. There he orders General Lam Quang Thi to prepare at the same time to defend Hue *and* to evacuate his heavy equipment to Danang, his 175 mm. half-track howitzers and his M-48 tanks. At 1:30 in the afternoon he hears a speech by Thieu ordering the defense of the city at any cost. Back at headquarters in Danang by 7:30, Truong receives a cable signed by Vien: Hue will not be defended. At the same hour, national radio rebroadcasts Thieu's historic speech calling for the defense of Hue to the last man! The presidency forgot to relay orders to Le Vinh Hoa, director of radio, television and cinema.

A cryptic cable:

EXPRESS

Deliver personally #20/545 H/3-1975 T20.3/758.
From: Joint General Staff.
To: Commander in chief 1st Corps 1st Region.
Text #9.428/F 341.
Ref.: Message #9.424/JGS/F 342 or 20/145 11/3/1975 from JGS.

Following above message, the JGS respectfully transmit to your command the following instructions from the President of the Republic of Vietnam.

Firstly: Available air and naval units can support only one enclave. Consequently, you must initiate [*mener*, in French in the text] delaying actions toward Hai Van pass if situation requires it.

Secondly: Acknowledge receipt of these instructions.
General Can Van Vien, president JGS/Armed Forces of the Republic of Vietnam.

Furthermore, South Vietnamese intelligence services are circulating the up-to-date NVA order of battle. Five of its seven reserve divisions are said to have crossed to the South, and it commands, according to Saigon intelligence, over 800 tanks—fully armed and victualed—and nineteen divisions, fourteen of infantry. If there was the least doubt in the world, everybody knows now that for Hanoi this is it.

Thieu believes he left Truong a certain flexibility. Truong, weary and nervous, chain-smoking, believes he has none—a confusion deepened by the lack of coordination among the presidency, general headquarters and the First Corps command.

Thieu is sure Truong told him their only possible course was to hold Hue, because coastal Route 1 from Hue to Danang was cut. Rumor says the president ordered Hue evacuated because Truong had lost confidence. Rumor then says the general commanding the First Division abandoned Hue without warning Truong or Vien or Thieu. One and all decline any responsibility for orders, counterorders or the ensuing chain reaction.

Late at night on the 23rd, General Thi pays a call on the Archbishop of Hue, Monsignor Nguyen Kim Dien. The archbishop returned only two days ago from a seminar at the Vatican. With no electricity, he receives the general in his living room by candlelight. They sip tea.

The archbishop says, "I'm not surprised to see Hue abandoned; I hear from a reliable source that the First and Second Military regions will be given up to the communists. The new South Vietnam will consist of the Third and Fourth regions only."

The general gets the impression that these reliable sources include the Vatican. A couple of days later in Danang he will see Monsignor Pham Ngo Chi. This archbishop has come to protest the whole idea of defending Danang. It's useless. The prelate is equally sure that an agreement has already been reached with the communists. What's the use of fighting over scraps of territory and towns already ceded? In all civilian circles, as in some military circles, the most defeatist rumors become certain fact.

The archbishops apparently believe that if a soldier does his duty, he becomes a frivolous criminal.

On March 24 at 6 A.M. Truong issues the order to evacuate Hue. He has fine-tuned a daring plan.

The long Vinh Loc peninsula extends southeast of Hue for thirty kilometers. Marines, rangers and men of the First Division will cross to it, abandoning heavy equipment that can't be loaded on ferries or small boats. Between the southern tip of the peninsula and the mainland, engineers will improvise a bridge for access to the coast and Danang. At the same time, troops will be evacuated by sea. From Saigon, Admiral Cang has sent a vast flotilla that can rescue either civilians or soldiers as needed.

At first the maneuver goes fairly well despite a pounding by North Vietnamese artillery. Rearguard troops slow the enemy advance. But on March 25 civilians and soldiers—as in the retreat from Pleiku—start mingling. The soldiers of the First Division have their families in tow. Little by little the division dissolves. Officers and men hear that their commander, General Nguyen Van Dien, blurted, "We must abandon Hue. We've been betrayed."

On the beaches, some wait for the ships cruising offshore. Others press farther south, where engineers are supposed to build the bridge. The sea is rough. They have a hard time scuttling boats to support the bridge. Discipline turns to indiscipline, then rebellion. Frantic, some of the soldiers take boats by force, boats intended as underpinnings. Others try to reach solid ground on foot and are drowned by the rising tide. The rescue ships still don't approach the shore, either because their crews don't know how to maneuver them or because they fear the North Vietnamese artillery. Still other soldiers drown trying to swim out to the ships.

On March 23 Thieu had a letter from Gerald Ford.[4] The U.S. president never telephones Thieu, not even to boost his morale. This letter, which will be the last, seems admirably hazy and of a generality touching on the absurd: "It is my point of view," writes Ford, "that Hanoi's attack represents nothing less than an abrogation by force of the Paris Agreement."

Ford says he's following events closely. One would expect no less of him. He wants to honor America's responsibilities. But how? He will try anything to satisfy "materiel needs on the field of battle." Here and there Thieu underlines certain phrases which once more, in his view, commit the United States through its president: "American resolve to support a friend . . . America stands firmly behind the Republic of Vietnam at this crucial time." For Thieu, this letter is a lucky charm, a grigri. Since Ford has mentioned the United States' responsibilities, Thieu must specify what he needs. He asks one of his ministers, the distinguished economist Nguyen Tien Hung, to prepare an answer that will go off two days thence.

Thieu reminds Ford that the South Vietnamese signed the Paris Agreement not because they "believed naively" in their communist enemies' good will but because they counted on the United States' solemn commitment. Intentionally or not, Thieu repeats Nixon's and Kissinger's phrases: "firm promise," "rapid and vigorous measures of reprisal." For Thieu, the U.S. president's word is fundamental. Nixon promised, *has pledged his word*. Pledge: promise, commitment; it connotes good faith, honor. Not for a moment does Thieu distinguish the public, official Paris Agreement from Nixon's personal guarantees, which he thinks Ford must inherit. After three months of North Vietnamese offensive action, the president of the Republic of Vietnam asks the president of the United States, for the first time, to come to a decision. Ford must, in Thieu's view, "order a brief but intensive aerial bombing by B-52s against enemy concentrations and logistical bases in South Vietnam."

Having signed this letter, Thieu calls in his vice-president, his prime minister, his foreign minister, his chief of staff, his security advisor, to tell them about it.

The U.S. Embassy receives Thieu's letter early in the afternoon. Ford will not respond directly.

On March 25 Gerald Ford and Henry Kissinger receive a delegation from Saigon led by South Vietnam's ambassador to Washington, Tran Kim Phuong. The Vietnamese are inundated by good intentions; Ford will do anything—anything in his power—to wring supplemental aid from Congress. He'll send his army chief of staff to Saigon.

The South Vietnamese are gloomy when they leave. They have reason: only the night before, the Senate passed a general foreign aid bill appropriating $3.7 billion—which, on the military side, excludes South Vietnam. Gerald Ford's good will cannot prevail against congressional votes.

The U.S. president looks for international support; or rather, tries to reassure his friends and allies. He dispatches letters to heads of state in Southeast Asia and elsewhere. To Souvanna Phouma, prime minister of Laos; to Tun Razak, prime minister of Malaysia; to Lee Kuan Yew, prime minister of Singapore; to Suharto in Indonesia, to Marcos in the Philippines, to Park Chung Hee in South Korea, to President Chiang Ching-kuo in Formosa, to Kukrit Pramodj in Thailand, and, for good measure, to the prime ministers of Australia and New Zealand. Much of a muchness, these notes are not personalized. North Vietnam, says Ford, is "openly invading South Vietnam." He assures Their Excellencies that "the United States remains determined to give South Vietnam the tools it must have to resist."

Tools: an ambiguous word, or intentionally ill chosen? Credits, arms, ammunition? Ford is not considering B-52 raids, as Thieu is. In America only a handful are clamoring for a resumption of the bombings, like General William Westmoreland, former commander in chief in Vietnam.

In this letter to his colleagues, Ford announces that General Frederick Weyand, army chief of staff, will return to Saigon. "Unequivocally" Ford assures those whose security depends on Washington that the United States will honor its commitments. The country "will remain true to its traditions, to its obligations, and to its allies and friends in Asia and elsewhere." This pontification doesn't make much impression on the letter's recipients, least of all the Thais, a front-line nation well informed on developments throughout Indochina. American politicians and experts, like the president, often mention American "credibility," the superpower's determination to respect all commitments in the framework of its alliances. In Southeast Asia, a number of countries consider Vietnam a test case. They'll wait and see.

Communist China is one signatory to the Paris Agreement. To counterpoint and supplement Ford's letters, Kissinger protests to Beijing and Moscow. He sends almost the same message to Ch'iao Kuan-hua (Kissinger transliterated the old-fashioned way), minister of foreign affairs in the People's Republic of China, successor to the lamented (by Kissinger, at any rate) Chou En-lai; and to Andrei Gromyko, his eternal and lugubrious counterpart in the Soviet Union:

> Mr. Foreign Minister:
>
> I am writing to inform you that we are deeply concerned and disturbed by the recent military actions of the North Vietnamese authorities. Their total lack of restraint can only indicate a purposeful decision to throw aside the Paris Agreements on Vietnam.

Kissinger never believed that Hanoi would show perfect restraint, but he's over his threshold of tolerance. Now he's convinced the NVG has mounted a full-scale military campaign. The very wording of his letter indicates that in his view the general offensive started not at Phuoc Long but at Ban Me Thuot: "Beginning on March 10, 1975, North Vietnamese forces in South Vietnam launched attacks against a number of military bases and district and provincial capitals." Just back in Washington, Kissinger (or whoever writes the rough drafts of his letters) has carefully scanned intelligence reports. Kissinger adds: "North Vietnam has also sent elements of its reserve divisions directly into South Vietnam across the Demilitarized Zone."

He writes his Chinese and Soviet counterparts that this is a "policy of military escalation. Our intelligence reveals that the North Vietnamese plan to continue these acts of aggression, including attacks on the ancient capital of Hue [Kissinger is right] and on Tay Ninh province near Saigon [Kissinger is wrong]." Six days ago the North Vietnamese commenced operations in the region of Tay Ninh, but they were diversionary. Kissinger recalls the Chinese minister to a sense of his responsibilities.

> The recent blatant attacks by North Vietnamese forces, led by tanks and anti-aircraft weapons supplied by outside powers, one of which has hegemonistic ambitions toward the Asian region [friendly allusion to the USSR], represent a complete abrogation of the Paris Agreement of which you are a signatory. These developments are now returning the Indochina war to the level of a major international issue.

The attacks, he notes, took place just after the recent visit to Hanoi of a Chinese military delegation. "The most serious questions are raised about the willingness of outside powers to urge restraint on the authorities in Hanoi. . . . The North Vietnamese must be counseled . . . to engage in no further escalation, and to return to the cease-fire."

The secretary of state has established good relations with Beijing. When he signs these letters, is he under any illusion that the Chinese can possibly stop Hanoi at this stage? Moscow supplies the NVG with heavy armament, tanks, artillery, formidable anti-aircraft. Over the years Beijing has supplied infantry weapons, AK-47s, grenades, machineguns, mortars, and vehicles (not armored) with spare parts. The Chinese have also helped Hanoi survive by sending them rice, cloth and all the little items of daily life, crockery, needles, flashlights, lightbulbs. . . .

According to Kissinger, when he mooted Vietnam with Beijing's leaders, they "muttered two or three things in favor of Hanoi,"[5] but that was mere ritual. The context of Kissinger's talks with the Chinese communists was always the four-part division of Indochina: two Vietnams, one Cambodia and one Laos. To the Chinese, the United States would never accept defeat in Vietnam. A superpower acts like one. A unified Vietnam does not serve communist China's interests. The antagonism between China and Vietnam is age-old, and the divergences between Hanoi's and Beijing's theoreticians are growing. Mao was once a strong advocate of confrontation. But according to analyses by the U.S. National Security Council,[6] the Great Helmsman probably changed his views toward the end of the 1960s. Besides, his influence is waning. He was not seen at the party congress a few weeks before, in January 1975. The Chinese have noted that the North Vietnamese communists, despite grandiloquent allusions to popular uprisings, are applying a conventional military strategy of Soviet inspiration. And finally, for Peking a prolongation of the Vietnamese conflict risks an augmentation of Soviet influence and presence in the region. There is evidence of a sympathetic Chinese interest in the PRG and Khmer Rouge, as useful counterweights to Hanoi. In a word, to maintain their revolutionary image in the Third World the Chinese support their Vietnamese comrades vociferously, but do not want to see them set foot in Saigon. The Chinese are so fond of Vietnam that they want two of them.

In August 1974, the Chinese provoked the Paracel Islands incident with the aim of initiating direct negotiations with Saigon. Thieu understood China's devious scheme, but fear of the Americans kept him from grasping the proffered hand. Thieu still believes in a monolithic communist world.

Peking has tried cautiously to establish contact with Thieu. Through the intervention of Chinese Nationalists, who shuttle between Beijing and Taipei, the Chinese have been in touch with Thieu's brother, South Vietnam's ambassador to Taiwan. At Hong Kong in December 1974, an official of the South Vietnamese Central Intelligence Organization talked to Jim Eckes, Saigon manager for a major private airline. The official had a message from one of many communist notables in Hong Kong.[7] Eckes knows Thieu's inner circle well. Thieu's own minister of foreign affairs, Bac, also served as intermediary. One of his friends, a British Conservative M.P., again at the end of 1974, made overtures to the deputy minister of foreign affairs, Ch'iao Kuan-hua, in Beijing. The Chinese bet on the PRG but prove reticent when it comes to pressuring Hanoi.

Thieu has never wanted to embark on talks with Beijing, even secretly: the Chinese are communists, the PRG is only a fiction and above all, Thieu is always—and doubtless wrongly—afraid of the Americans' wrath.[8]

For Kissinger, the Chinese attach more importance to their new links with Washington than to their ties with Hanoi. But they're stuck with their ideological image and cannot disavow North Vietnam, or not yet. Washington knows there are tensions between Beijing and Hanoi. The North Vietnamese continuously complain of slow deliveries from China. At the turn of 1974–75, the Chinese did not cut off food and munitions, but their trains were woefully late. Strikes? Bureaucratic disorganization? A way to show Moscow and Hanoi Beijing's disapproval? Or disinformation?

Whatever it was, Kissinger must protest to Beijing as to Moscow.

His letter to Gromyko begins harshly: "I am writing to express very frankly my deep concern over . . ." When the Soviets use the word "frank" it indicates profound disagreement. They will understand. This letter to the Soviets is heavy with accusations:

> As these attacks occurred immediately after the visit of Deputy Foreign Minister Firyubin to Hanoi [your deputy, Gro-

myko!], it can only be assumed that the Soviet Union was aware of and acceded to the decisions involved. Therefore, your Government must share a major responsibility for what is happening now in South Vietnam as well as for the broader implications.

In March 1975 Kissinger is counting even less on the Soviets than on the Chinese.

Two years earlier, in March 1973, Anatoly Dobrynin, Soviet ambassador to Washington, gave Kissinger—"for what it was worth"[9]—his assurance that Moscow had ceased shipping arms to Hanoi after the signing of the Paris Agreement. Dobrynin confirmed or claimed that Soviet supplies arriving in Vietnam had probably been delayed in transit through China.

In his letter to Gromyko, Kissinger reminds him of "the special responsibility of our countries to do everything in their power so that conflicts or situations will not arise which would serve to increase international tensions." Of course, he also asks Gromyko to advise the North Vietnamese to halt their offensive.

The Soviet interest in March 1975 is not the same as in March 1973. Yesterday Moscow was dealing with a strong and dogged president, Richard Nixon. Today the other player, Gerald Ford, is restrained by Congress and public opinion. Since Nixon's departure relations between the Soviet Union and the United States have altered. Kissinger is hampered in his policy of détente by the Senate, which refuses to grant the Soviet Union most favored nation status commercially and which insists constantly on exit visas for Soviet Jews. Right now détente is not bringing Moscow's leaders much satisfaction. Despite Kissinger's setbacks in the Middle East, the Soviets are losing ground there little by little. They know that whatever the Americans say, they won't support Thieu. In 1975 the Soviets are ready to draw dividends on their investments in Vietnam, especially in naval strategy. They have their eyes on the base and port installations of Cam Ranh.

Kissinger's whole Vietnam policy seems a casualty of Watergate. If Nixon had yet been in power, he would never have stood still for the offensive on Phuoc Long or Ban Me Thuot. He would have sent B-52s, legal or not. The Soviets would have had a serious stake in easing the conflict. It's too late to hope that Beijing's or Moscow's leaders can, or want to, halt the North Vietnamese offensive. Kissinger suspects, moreover, that Hanoi can resist a fair amount of pressure from its two big brothers.

On March 25 he addresses Hanoi directly in a "message to Special Adviser Le Duc Tho," his old adversary in the Paris negotiations. A brief letter:

Mr. Special Adviser:

I am shocked and outraged at the attacks of your forces
in South Vietnam and across the demilitarized zone. This
is blatant aggression of the most overt kind. It represents
an abrogation by force of the Paris Agreements.

If you continue and intensify these attacks, you will pre-
clude any further discussion of the implementation of the
political provisions of the Paris Agreements. You must
bear full responsibility for this and for all consequences.

Kissinger concludes:

You must not underestimate the reaction of the United
States nor the impact of your actions here and all over the
world.

This threat, this necessarily vague allusion to an eventual U.S. reaction,
seems a poor gambit. Hanoi's leaders have had over two months to weigh
the advantages and risks of continuing their offensive. From diplomats of
people's democracies posted in Washington, and simply by reading American newspapers that reach Hanoi, they know that the United States will
not intervene militarily. They are just as sure that they won't be officially
disinherited by Moscow or Beijing.

When he receives Kissinger's message, Le Duc Tho is about to depart
for the front in South Vietnam. Le Duc Tho, winner of the Nobel Peace
Prize with Kissinger, principal author and engineer of the "Paris Agreement on Ending the War and Restoring *Peace* in Vietnam" (official title
of the Paris Agreement), is going to see to it personally that the *war*
continues. Until final victory.

On March 25 in Hanoi the Politburo delivers an important announcement: "Our general offensive has begun with the campaign in the Central
Highlands. The long-awaited strategic moment has arrived, and conditions
allow an early execution of our resolve to liberate the South." The Politburo
recommends concentrating "men, arms and materiel to liberate Saigon
before the rainy season."

The political-military organization is in place. The overall operation
will be directed by Le Duc Tho and General Dung, the attack on Saigon
by Pham Hung, party secretary in the South, and General Tran Van Tra.
All North Vietnam's reserve divisions will be thrown into the battle.

Before he leaves Hanoi, Le Duc Tho meets several times with Le Duan.
The special counselor flies out of Hanoi on March 28. During the first night
of his trip, he composes a poem, dedicated to Le Duan:

Your last advice: "Go out, and come back victorious."
How can I reply? Sometimes words are weak,
Through your mouth the whole country spoke to me . . .
What good news on the road to the front!
Everywhere cries of joy celebrating our victories
Encourage me to hurry down the long road.
The opportunity is there, knocking at our door.

In Hanoi they're betting on the military; in Washington they're looking for a diplomatic solution and wooing the Congress, which is to adjourn for a ten-day vacation beginning March 27.

A rather somber Kissinger reappears for a press conference: "We should not destroy our allies," he says. "It will have serious consequences throughout the world."

It will have and not *it would have.* A slip of the tongue? Kissinger has made his bets. With Ford he asks again for supplemental aid from Congress and says the administration would accept a three-year plan for Cambodia and Vietnam. No less. A reporter asks him if he isn't just trying to gain time. Brusquely he answers: "Some problems don't have a terminal date. . . . The situation depends on North Vietnam's actions."

The secretary of state also says: "Since May last year, South Vietnam has received only ammunition and fuel. It has received almost no spare parts and no modern equipment. Under those circumstances, the demoralization of an army is inevitable. And therefore, some of the consequences we now see are not surprising."

A meeting at the White House,[10] Kissinger present, with Brent Scowcroft, General Frederick Weyand, army chief of staff, and Graham Martin. The U.S. ambassador to Saigon has been called back to Washington. A notable absence: Secretary of Defense James Schlesinger. An unexpected auditor: David Kennerly, twenty-eight years old, personal photographer to President Ford, who asked him to remain in the room.

They've at last acknowledged that the situation in Indochina is critical. Nevertheless, Martin recommends "a dose of skepticism" about news from Saigon. They've kissed off Cambodia. In one of his last cables Wolfgang Lehmann is quite pessimistic. He doesn't ask for air support; he knows Ford cannot grant it. He proposes a gimmick: maximum publicity on the plight of Vietnamese refugees, to rouse American public opinion and thus influence senators and congressmen. They don't even answer him.

For the refugees, they'll deploy ships off the coast near Danang with specific orders: these ships will patrol three nautical miles off Vietnam's shores, to steer clear of combat with North Vietnamese and thus keep to the letter of the law.

Weyand will return to Saigon with two jobs to do: write up a report on the military situation, and tell President Thieu that the U.S. government will render all possible aid to South Vietnam, but that Americans will no longer fight in Vietnam, not by land, sea or air.

At the end of the meeting photographer Kennerly asks the president's permission to join Weyand. Ford feels a paternal affection for Kennerly. Permission granted. Smiling, Kissinger says to Martin, "I'm happy you're going too. When it all goes belly up, Phil Habib will identify the guilty party—you."

Martin doesn't find this joke very funny.

Hanoi does not neglect the diplomatic front. They use it to create diversions, to worry their adversaries, especially Americans. They have a good diplomatic launch pad in Paris (at La Celle-Saint-Cloud, to be exact), where, in theory, political talks among the "South Vietnamese parties to the Paris Agreement" have rambled on since 1973. In principle, they're elaborating a political solution viable after the cease-fire.

Dinh Ba Thi, temporary head of the PRG delegation in Paris, holds a press conference, an hour and a half, for American, French, British, German and Vietnamese reporters. Thi's interpreter first reads a long declaration. Communist military operations in Vietnam, he says, constitute "a justified response to alleged violations of the Paris Agreement by South Vietnamese and Americans." Before, Hanoi and the PRG refused to admit they'd attacked. Now, they're justifying their offensive. The PRG demands the ouster of "Nguyen Van Thieu and his men" and raises the new demand detailed in private by the North Vietnamese prime minister to Philippe Richer, French ambassador to Hanoi. The PRG is ready to open discussions on the future of South Vietnam with "a new administration formed in Saigon." An administration, so goes the litany, "favoring peace, independence, democracy and national concord."

The PRG's man in Paris is acting on instructions from a "special cell" set up in Hanoi March 15 to manage the "diplomatic front." This group includes (among others) Nguyen Co Thach, deputy minister for foreign affairs; Pham Hien, press officer in the same ministry; Mai Van Bo, former ambassador to Paris, and Colonel Ha Van Lau, a personal friend of the prime minister who has long been more diplomat than soldier.[11] The colonel was once second in command of the secret police. The Politburo assigns him difficult missions. In liaison with the Politburo, this "cell" must take advantage "of all contradictions in the enemy camp" and give adversaries the impression that there is a slight slippage between the DRV's positions and the PRG's.

After reading his text, the PRG's man in Paris says he'll field questions. They submit one about the presence of NVA divisions in the South. He takes up an old argument, if one can call it that: these are "false and slanderous" reports. Anyway, he adds, the Paris Agreement "refutes the existence of such troops." True, the agreement does not speak of them. It does not deny them.

They press Thi on the political solution. What does he mean by "Thieu's men"? The president and his entourage? Or the whole government? Thi allows as how certain South Vietnamese would be acceptable. Thieu's men are "a very small number." Then Thi sings the praises of the Third Force. In any arrangement, they'll have a role to play. And sure enough, there and then a representative of the Third Force is distributing a manifesto calling for a political conclusion to the war.

After the press conference, North Vietnamese diplomats, PRG delegates and North Vietnamese correspondents offer exegesis all over Paris. Yes, the PRG and Hanoi want a political solution. The current offensive? A way to force negotiations. The PRG people, Thi foremost, as if disclosing a secret, murmur that they even more than Hanoi want a quick political settlement. The Vietnamese communist slogan, "Fight and negotiate, negotiate and fight," has been replaced by "Fight, fight and give the impression that you want to negotiate."

Among Vietnamese communists, diplomacy is the extension of war by other means. The press is just one of those means.

Who'd be prouder of them, Clausewitz or Lenin?

In the shelter of his headquarters, General Dung reviews his plans on the afternoon of March 26. Before he attacks Saigon he needs a delay from Hanoi, to mop up all resistance in South Vietnamese MR 1. The North Vietnamese commander in chief does not want to leave South Vietnamese enclaves behind him along the coast.

That day they confirm "the liberation" of Hue. All resistance has ceased. Dung lights a cigarette: "I had long ago sworn off tobacco, but whenever I solve some thorny problem, or achieve a big victory, or some success relieves me of a burden, I burn one."

At Nha Trang on March 26 General Phu, emerging from his torpor, gives a situation report on MR 2.[12] Phu has lost contact with reality: "Our fighting men in the Second Region," he says, "have completely destroyed the reputation [sic] of two North Vietnamese divisions."

It might have been better to annihilate the divisions themselves. Phu staves off defeat with the ritual phrases of vanquished generals: "troop movements," "halt the advancing forces."

Adapting complacent reports from the general, South Vietnamese radio transforms the debacle of Route 7B into a rather successful withdrawal: "The gigantic advance eastward of 200,000 soldiers and civilians from the provinces of Kontum, Pleiku, Phu Bon and Ban Me Thuot is proceeding in the framework of a regrouping of forces for the defense of coastal territories."

On the radio Phu personally gives details of what he presents almost as a victory: "The caravan of refugees from communism has profited by maximal protection from the military. These latter have repulsed enemy attacks on both the van and the rear guard. All along the march they have constructed [sic] roads and bridges as needed. Engineer units have cleared the road and constructed twenty-eight bridges of all sizes."

The general seems to believe what he says; foreign radio doesn't relay it. In Saigon they know what's going on. There Lieutenant Colonel Le Trung Hien, military spokesman, that day issues "a solemn warning to two press agencies, UPI and AP": "They have broken the rules by broadcasting news about the military situation around Hue."

These agencies announced, the night before, that South Vietnamese armed forces "are said to have" evacuated the city. Hien doesn't care about confirming or denying this information. Those agencies had better watch their step! A good man, incidentally, the lieutenant colonel was about 50 percent credible until then. In time of defeat a military spokesman's job is all but impossible. The lieutenant colonel, masking the truth despite all evidence, lost his cool during the daily briefing ten days before. He told the journalists, "The government has not decided to abandon Pleiku. Based mostly on speculation, your reports have sown panic among the townspeople there."

Following the lead of certain American authorities before 1973, South Vietnam's higher-ups are only too happy to see the press as the cause of their failures. In 1975 as in 1965, relations between reporters and the top brass are often strained. The South Vietnamese brandish threats—and foreign reporters keep reporting.

Saigon's rules and regulations for the foreign press are plenty hazy. The press must not threaten the security of the State. That can cover all journalistic sins. They must not reveal positions of units in combat. That goes without saying. Vietnamese of the political, military and police structure are impressed if not terrorized by the American media's huge machine. They know that any retaliatory measure, like the expulsion of an American correspondent, quickly balloons to a major scandal back in the States. Any difference of opinion between Saigon officials and American correspondents provokes a perverse boomerang effect and always turns to the disadvantage of the Saigon government.

A number of quarrels, public or latent, divide the U.S. Embassy and the American press corps. Nevertheless, when a conflict arises between these last and the South Vietnamese structure, the embassy flies to the rescue of its own nationals. Whatever their disagreement with Americans, the Vietnamese are almost always wrong. The Americans certainly did not fight a colonial war in Vietnam. But the correspondents' privileged position, and South Vietnamese officials' trepidation, almost create a colonial situation. The North Vietnamese don't have these problems. Thousands of journalists covered the war in the South, traveling freely. The North is stingy with visas, except to reporters from "safe" newspapers, communist or sympathetic. And special envoys leave Hanoi for the countryside only with a strong escort. In the DRV since the war began there have never been more than fifteen noncommunist Occidental correspondents at one time. So control of the news is absolute. There is no risk of "false reports," as in Saigon.

At his headquarters in Danang, General Truong draws up a balance sheet for his MR 1. It is less optimistic than Phu's. The evacuation of Hue was a mess. Very few units managed to reach Danang intact. Only most of one infantry regiment of the First Division and 600 marines made it with their weapons. Adding to the confusion, staff officers up from Saigon insist that the marines must head back to the capital.

Truong has neither the time nor the necessary resources to organize the defense of Danang. Reports confirm, moreover, that North Vietnamese troops are maneuvering superbly in the field. What progress since the last great battles of 1972, especially in the use of tanks! In 1972 also they advanced on Hue. But then the tank units rolled alone through the long valleys, barely coordinating their movements with the infantry and artillery. NVA tank drivers always kept the turrets closed and so lacked visibility; under such conditions a tank is almost blind. In 1972 the T-54s were easy prey for South Vietnamese antitank weapons and artillery. That is no longer true.

Meditating on the phenomenon of retreat after a lost battle, Clausewitz wrote:

> Loss of a battle breaks an army's morale even more than its ranks. Barring a favorable shift in circumstances, a second battle will end in complete defeat, that is, annihilation. This is a military axiom. In the nature of things, retreat continues until an equilibrium of forces is reestablished, by reinforcements, or by the protection of strongpoints, or by good cover and position in the countryside, or by the dispersal of enemy troops. The losses sustained, the extent of the defeat, but still more the nature of the enemy, accelerate or delay that moment of equilibrium.

He also says:

> To profit by the enemy's weaknesses or mistakes, not to yield an inch more than necessary, and above all to keep morale as high as possible, it is absolutely necessary to withdraw slowly offering constant resistance and to execute bold courageous counterstrokes whenever the enemy seeks extravagant advantages. The retreats of great generals and seasoned armies have always been like those of a wounded lion, and that is incontestably also the best theory.

Which South Vietnamese general will recast himself as a lion?

12

The Bell Tolls
for Danang

Who are these conquerors surging
south?

Tough, frugal, tenacious, often courageous, for the most part rigorously
disciplined under fire, the North Vietnamese soldier travels without his
family. He is between sixteen and thirty-five. After fifteen years of losses,
some of the army's age groups are severely depleted. A South Vietnamese
soldier carries bric-a-brac; a North Vietnamese soldier carries ammunition.
His basic training lasted eight months. It isn't enough to say that he makes
do with the minimum; rather, the minimum is his way of life. His daily
ration? Six or seven hundred grams of rice; biscuits baked from bean flour;
sometimes fifty grams of dried fish or Chinese tinned meat; rarely, chicken.
Cigarettes are not a right but a privilege granted as deliveries allow. In
combat, throughout the campaign, his officers—who wear no insignia of
rank—share the same rations. Among civilians in the North, rank has its
permanent privileges in housing, food and cigarettes. Those privileges are
known and accepted as inevitable. In the military they disappear almost
entirely when the troops cross the 17th parallel or arrive in the South via
the network of the Ho Chi Minh trail. Of course, General Dung never
lacks cigarettes.

Once upon a time the North Vietnamese soldier tramped south along
the Ho Chi Minh trail knowing that two or three years would go by before
he had a chance to return. If badly wounded, he had no chance of surviving;
a wounded South Vietnamese regular could hope for evacuation by helicopter. NVA recruits can now glimpse the war's end. Before, they moved

on foot, ordinarily at twenty or thirty kilometers a day; today the troops are motorized.

These men have known only war and party propaganda. Even at the officers' level, indoctrination is constant if simplistic. During this 1975 campaign, the units' political commissars have little time for lectures. In primary and secondary school, and during their military training, the soldiers have absorbed, accepted and internalized some basic principles: Vietnam must be reunified; our brothers in the South are poor and oppressed; they are waiting for us to liberate them. A North Vietnamese soldier does not ask and is not asked what right the platoon, company, battalion, regiment or division of which he is a part has or has not to be in the South. We are all Vietnamese even if our accents are different. The tank commander doesn't ask why his tank clanks forward with the PRG's blue and red flag on the turret and not the DRV's red flag. Especially since the taking of Ban Me Thuot, the vast majority of soldiers, most often simple peasants, see the end of military service within reach. Most of them want peace: to have it, they must end the war. No need for political commissars to explain that.

These commissars' role is much less important than previously. For one thing the long quarrel between "experts" and "ideologues" has been, for practical purposes, resolved in favor of the professional military. Debate raged in the Party and on the staff: in the making of a soldier does political conviction or military skill come first? The question perhaps made sense for small resistance units without modern weapons, meeting heavily armed U.S. or ARVN units in the swamps of the Delta or in forests along the Cambodian border. But in waging a classic war with conventional divisions, the question seems absurd. No Marxist intuition, no sharp dialectic helps fathom the complexities of a T-54 tank, or of a MiG-21 fighter. Good Leninists, the Northern leaders have at times feared that the Vietnamese revolution may be swallowed up by the military, like the French Revolution or many modern revolutions in the Third World. For the Vietnamese Politburo, "the Party aims the rifle." Revolutionary good will or political conscience as the army's mainspring? Idle chatter to please the Chinese comrades. Here they've avoided contradictions and tensions between civilians and the military, between party and general staff needs, while integrating military principals into party leadership. Here Giap and Dung rule. They've long understood that in a war of large units authority cannot be divided between political and military commands. In theory the distinction exists. In practice it is tenuous. These days officers decide and political commissars follow their lead. At the very top, on the other hand, dual controls survive; only look at Le Duc Tho/Van Tien Dung and Pham Hung/Tran Van Tra.

A North Vietnamese soldier marches rather awkwardly in the streets of Hanoi or Haiphong, like the Israeli soldier in Tel Aviv. Vietnamese communists spent long years learning guerrilla warfare. Then they came to know conventional war, and they've made progress in all its aspects. Only their air force lags behind. The North Vietnamese soldier and guerrilla are famous, even legendary, for their "Ho Chi Minh" sandals, carved out of bald tires, and their AK-47 assault rifles. But it's not the sandals or AKs that bring them victory now. It's the machineguns, the SA-7 missiles to defend them against aircraft, the cannon often plugged into radar systems, the whole panoply of modern armament.* During the Spanish Civil War the Nazis and Fascists tested their arms in preparation for World War II. In Vietnam, the Soviets are testing theirs, especially their anti-aircraft. To prepare for a conventional third world war? The Soviets are prudent: they have not supplied their latest-model tanks or missiles to the Vietnamese. Those must not fall into the hands of the South Vietnamese, who'd send them on to the Americans. The North Vietnamese, like so many Arab factions, make splendid guinea pigs.

It is not rag-tag guerrilla groups with kitchen knives and muzzle-loaders who are surging south, but North Vietnamese army corps. "The rice is already in their mouths. They'll have no trouble chewing it up and swallowing it down," say plenty of South Vietnamese, military and civilian.

The French called it Tourane. After Saigon, Danang is the second largest city in the South. Its name tolls like a bell. It holds so many military memories and hopes for Saigon's men, the nationalists! On its beaches, ten years before, because 6,000 "Vietcong" resistance fighters had been spotted near its air base, President Johnson decided to send massive numbers of U.S. troops into combat. So 40,000 American advisers were replaced by 500,000 soldiers, whose mission was not confined to the protection of U.S. installations.

In 1965 the marines landed on the beaches of Danang, with triumphant smiles, flags and fanfare. The Vietnamese psychological warfare people prepared a welcome. Beneath banners, girls with armsful of leis awaited the armed and helmeted fighting men.

No city anywhere in Indochina, not even Saigon, has been so marked by the war. A strategic roundhouse, Danang has two military ports and three airports that accommodate thousands of planes and helicopters. The city's charm vanished under the ugly disorder of ammunition and gasoline dumps, camps, hospitals. The soldiers had to be entertained. Onto this jumble messes were grafted, and cinemas, and, outside the military perimeter, bars, cheap eateries, bordellos. Danang counts 600,000 inhabitants. As many refugees are now camping in the city. Their columns trickle in slowly over several days, and Danang absorbs them like a sponge. Many have settled in schools; there are, happily, a hundred of these. The prime minister's promises have been broken: the government cannot provide a welcome. The refugees organize, with the aid of charitable groups. Rice

* See Appendix IV.

Top left: Vo Nguyen Giap, North Vietnamese defense minister. Code name "Battler." *(Photo Roger Pic/ Gamma)*

Top right: General Van Tien Dung, North Vietnamese commander in chief. Code name "Excellent." Only in April will the Americans learn of his presence in the South. *(Photo Sygma)*

Right: General Tran Van Tra, commander of NVA Zone B-2: "What 'tin soldiers' you are!" *(Photo Associated Press)*

Pham Van Dong, prime minister of the Democratic Republic of Vietnam: "My dear friend, we shall respect South Vietnam's particular features and characteristics." *(Photo Marc Riboud/Magnum)*

Top right: All over North Vietnam, posters and wall paintings issue the call to arms. "Fight off enemy aircraft." *(Photo Marc Riboud/Magnum)*

Bottom right: North Vietnamese regulars entering Hue. *(Photo Associated Press)*

Pham Van Dong receives the author at Hanoi in 1967. *(Photo Agence d'Information du Viet-nam)*

MÁY BAY GIẶC

South Vietnamese strategic withdrawal, retreat, collapse along the Ba River. *Photo Jean-Claude Francolon/Gamma)*

The bell tolls for Danang. One million residents, refugees, deserters, civilian and military. *(Photos Associated Press, Sygma)*

Photo of aerial image with the following labels:

PHOTO DATE: 19 MARCH 1975

SOUTH VIETNAM
ABANDONED VNAF AIRCRAFT
AT PLEIKU AIRFIELD

N

DERELICT C-7

DERELICT C-47

FOUR O-1s
ELEVEN O-2s
TWENTY-ONE A-1s

DERELICT C-119

27

SCALE APPROXIMATE
0   FEET   300
0   METERS   90

Pleiku. Photo of the airport taken March 19 by an observer from Air America, the CIA's airline.

Top right: At right, near Hue on April 8. Estimated North Vietnamese booty on May 1: 312 planes, 502 helicopters, 550 tanks, 1,330 cannons, 90,000 pistols, 791,000 rifles, 15,000 machine guns, 47,000 grenade launchers, 63,000 antitank guns, 12,000 mortars, 42,000 trucks.

(Photo U.S. Dept. of Defense)

Bottom right: Army chief of staff General Frederick Weyand, President Gerald Ford, and Secretary of State Henry Kissinger at Palm Springs, California, on April 5. "The United States is facing a moral problem."

(Photo UPI/Bettmann Newsphotos)

SOUTH VIETNAM
ABANDONED SVN EQUIPMENT NEAR HUE
APPROXIMATELY 150 VEHICLES

PHOTO DATE: 8 APRIL 1975

AMMUNITION

LST RAMPS

SCALE APPROXIMATE
FEET

0   200

METERS

0   60

is supplied, and blankets, but never enough for the thousands of men, women and children who arrive on foot or pour out of ancient buses. Small groups of soldiers, falling back from Hue and wearing the gloomy faces of defeat, mingle with the refugees. Discipline melts away. Soldiers no longer salute officers. Many of the isolated don't even try to rejoin their units: the tragic ballet begins again. Officers and men look for their families.

A double problem for General Troung at his headquarters in Danang: the masses of civilians are not arriving only from the North; they're coming up from the South, too. Route 1, the broad pulsating coastal artery, is cut: civilians, and eventually the military, will be unable to escape from Danang except by sea. There are North Vietnamese units to the south and west of the city, as well as to the north.

Food is in short supply. Depots are taken by storm, shops gutted. To survive, men must plunder. Brawls break out among the military, and between soldiers and civilians. A few more Air Vietnam flights are announced, leaving from the civil airport to the west. A ticket for Saigon jumps from $50 to $140.

The North Vietnamese command prepares its enveloping movement, a simple maneuver in three parts.

Divisions 324B and 325C, supported by two artillery regiments and an armored regiment, will attack Danang from the north. From the south will come Divisions 404 and 711. They'll meet at Elephant Valley, west of Danang, and press on the city as if on an abscess, squeezing the pus into the sea. Dung does not know how short Thieu is of reserves. But he makes sure that if there are any, they won't be able to join the defense of Danang. Even if Thieu were to send reinforcements, they could not reach Truong over land.

NVA artillery pounds Danang on March 27 and provokes a panic.

Doubly impossible job for Truong: restore order in the city, and reorganize military units. At noon J2, Saigon staff intelligence, sends a message: the North Vietnamese will launch their assault on the city during the night.

2 P.M.: the regional forces, a cordon around Danang, are scattering; personnel of arsenals and fuel farms are fleeing. A fresh order from Saigon: Evacuate the helicopters and military aircraft. These may be saved, but cannot be used to halt the North Vietnamese advance or to cover an evacuation by sea. Warships are in formation offshore. North Vietnamese artillery fire, which a few South Vietnamese 175 mm. howitzers are still trying to answer, is concentrated on headquarters of the First Corps and the naval base.

Under heavy shelling, in a bunker a hundred meters square, officers assemble around General Truong and Vice Admiral Ho Van Ky Thoai, commandant of the coastal region. At 10:30 P.M. Truong orders his adjutant, General Lam Quang Thi, to board an offshore naval vessel and set up a new command post. Truong has made up his mind. He has not enough men to establish entrenched defenses in the city. He may have enough time to save the units still operational. Truong plans an evacuation to commence at 6 A.M.

Emerging from the bunker, Thi sees that even the main navy yard has been invaded by civilians: they hope to board the warships. Among the civilians three NVA observers have been discovered; they were directing artillery fire by radio.

Truong telephones joint staff headquarters in Saigon and the presidential palace. He proposes to begin the evacuation by sea. Thieu hesitates.

Sun Tzu: "He whose generals are capable, and who does not interfere with them, will be victorious."

Thieu cannot bring himself to issue the order.

Sun Tzu: "Upon occasion, the sovereign's orders need not be respected."

During the conversation between Truong and Thieu, shells hit the communications center in Danang. Contact with Saigon is lost. The evacuation option drawn up by General Truong and Vice-Admiral Thoai provides three embarkation points.

From Saigon, Deputy Prime Minister Phan Quang Dan has sent messages to the United Nations, the High Commission on Refugees, and the International Red Cross, soliciting their help in evacuating 100,000 people a day. At the United Nations, the secretary-general will not even receive Nguyen Huu Chi, the South Vietnamese observer.

An armada of South Vietnamese, Korean and Taiwanese ships is gathered off Danang. Australia, Great Britain and the Philippines have promised to lend a hand in the operation. Six Australian planes loaded with food and medicine are waiting at airports in Malaysia.

President Ford has dispatched U.S. warships, naval units and chartered cargo ships, the *Dubuque*, the *Frederick*, the *Blue Ridge*, the *Durham*, which join the *Pioneer Contender* and the *Andrew Miller*. A navy frigate, the *Lowestaff*, patrols the perimeter. Washington announces that none of its merchant vessels is armed. At most a few platoons of marines to maintain order. Absolutely no provocation of North Vietnamese troops. This rescue mission is humanitarian.

Hanoi and the PRG denounce a "new American military intervention." From Bonn, Willy Brandt, whose hostility to U.S. policy in Vietnam is familiar, cautions: "My government has informed the United States that we are ready to participate in humanitarian aid." In Washington, Daniel Parker, director of the Agency for International Development,[1] says, "We are moving with the most extreme prudence." This means that the ships will not berth and will stand off and on in Vietnamese territorial waters.[2] Going him one better, the Pentagon states that only civilians are involved. Mingled civilians and soldiers eddy through Danang's suburbs and streets and quays. Soldiers' families don't want to leave without them. U.S. authorities decide that a soldier separated from his unit and unarmed can be considered a civilian. They offer private assurances that American ships will, if necessary, take aboard several companies of ARVN soldiers, especially if the South Vietnamese vessels assigned by Admiral Cang (now commander in chief of the navy) are not sufficient.

South Vietnamese ships can legitimately dock. But at dawn on March 28 a thick fog hems in the whole coast and makes berthing difficult if not impossible.

Chaos reigns in Danang. Groups of soldiers, some of them drunk, go wild and fire on civilians, fighting them for the last food in the shops. The three NVA observers captured with their radio give rise to a fifth-column syndrome. ARVN soldiers hunt down other agents, real or imaginary.

In the U.S. consulate, a large white building, the personnel wonder how they're going to leave. By sea or by air? At the civilian airport Consul General Al Francis, trying to embark some of his employees, is marched off by ARVN soldiers. Two Britons working for a humanitarian organization intercede to rescue him.

Baggage piles up in disorder on the runways. Refugees and soldiers, dashing to and fro, keep planes from landing. When they do land, thronging refugees prevent any orderly embarkation. Americans from Danang decide to fall back on a smaller airport, at Marble Mountain. Al Francis cannot convince the ambassador in Saigon that the situation is critical. Returning to the South Vietnamese capital on March 27 with General Frederick Weyand and other high U.S. officials, Martin is lofty: No need to dramatize, he says.

Wolfgang Lehmann is losing confidence. Yet only a few days before, he was explaining—to a gathering of Saigon's Chamber of Commerce, including barkeeps as well as adventurers, bankers and industrialists—that Thieu was preparing an "aggressive defense." The main thing was not to run off and demoralize the South Vietnamese. Now Lehmann asks the prime minister to intervene: "We have to restore order at the civilian airport in Danang." Khiem telephones Truong: he will send two battalions of rangers. The Americans from the Danang consulate, concealed in trucks, reach the quays. They leave many employees behind, some of them CIA agents. These Americans have promised to return. . . .

In Saigon a corpulent, truculent American, Ed Daly, who owns a charter company, World Airways, announces that he's going to set up an airlift to Danang. A charter pioneer who owns a fleet of Boeing 727s, he made $21 million in 1974. He delivers arms and rice to Phnom Penh from Saigon. Reports from Danang are firm: the main airport for large aircraft is unusable. World Airways is therefore forbidden to take off. Daly rushes to the embassy, hands his revolver to a marine guard, and bulls into the ambassador's office bellowing, "And what will they do at Tan Son Nhut if I take off?"

"They'll probably fire on you," answers Martin.

"And what will *you* do then?"

"I'll applaud."

The ambassador detests Daly for a vulgar slob; also, the man drinks too much. Martin doesn't want private outfits like World Airways interfering in operations that ought to be his embassy's responsibility. Daly decides to leave anyway with two Boeing 727s. He takes some reporters along for the ride, among them cameramen Mike Marriott of CBS and Tom Aspell of ITN, a New Zealander who also works for ABC. So two of the three big American television networks are present. After a forty-five–minute flight, the Boeings are over Danang and the control tower clears them to land. The runways are swarming with jeeps, trucks, women, children, soldiers. Only one plane can land. Frenzied crowds surround it. They battle to climb aboard. Soldiers fire bursts from M-16s; many of them are Black Panthers, an elite unit of the First Division. Hoping to impress them, Daly fires several revolver shots in the air. A cameraman deplanes and cannot reboard. Later, helicopters will lift him to the safe airport at Marble Mountain. In ten minutes the Boeing bulges with passengers. The landing gear is damaged, the valves are blocked.

During takeoff, soldiers cling to the wheels. Two hundred meters up, one of them lets go and is crushed. Another remains wedged into a wheel housing. The plane lays a course for Saigon, along with its mate that never landed. During the flight a hostess takes care of a wounded soldier: she clears away sawdust from his bulletproof vest and sponges the blood.

Back at Tan Son Nhut, the aircraft unloads its 265 soldiers, 1 woman and 3 children; 40 "passengers" emerge from the luggage bay. The Panthers are disarmed. Jim Eckes, head of Continental Air Services, drives the woman and three children to the terminal. Daly swaggers on the tarmac, explaining that the plane was damaged by a grenade. Checking the damage, Eckes thinks the Boeing must have run into several obstacles on the runway in Danang.

Daly hurries to the U.S. Embassy and dashes toward Martin's office, inadvertently setting off the alarm system in the hallway; while the ambassador talks, a weary Daly falls asleep. There have not been many news features from Phuoc Binh, Ban Me Thuot, Kontum, Pleiku or Hue. Now—thanks to the two cameramen, to photos by a Vietnamese, Vien Huong, and to the reports of a UPI correspondent, Paul Vogle—the whole world sees bits of this "voyage to hell" in Danang. In 1975 events in Vietnam, and often elsewhere, occur only when they've been filmed and broadcast. American public opinion knew things were sliding downhill in Vietnam. Now Americans *see* the chaos.[3]

From World Airways' home office in California, their vice-president David Mendelsohn sends a telegram to the crew of Daly's Boeing: "Our prayers are with you. Remember the words of St. Francis: give me the serenity to accept the things I cannot change, the courage to change the things I can and the wisdom to know the difference."

President Daly objects: "I disagree with St. Francis. And I disagree

with Dave Mendelsohn . . . who is a Jew, incidentally. We can change
things. St. Francis is wrong. We must change things. And I try to keep
trying as long as I'm able."

Daly has scores to settle. "American and Vietnamese agencies shuffled
their feet for a week before they did anything, before they airlifted some
of the four to six hundred thousand refugees jammed into Danang. . . . I
can't stand the stupidity, the ignorance of some American agencies, all
these guys with club ties . . . they're incompetent."

Before this last forbidden flight, the U.S. Embassy canceled its contract
with Daly. He'll pay for this trip, and others to come, out of his own
pocket.

The evacuation of Danang exceeds everything written, photographed
and televised up to then in the way of atrocities.

No possibility now of using planes or helicopters, even to "extract"
Americans. The consul in Danang begs the military attaché in Saigon to
send him two choppers. The military attaché refuses and relays the consul's
plea to headquarters of the American Seventh Air Force in Thailand.
Answer: first, we cannot violate the Paris Agreement; second, the helicopters in Thailand are reserved for the eventual evacuation of Phnom
Penh, which is in danger of falling any day.

Now the only escape from Danang is by sea. On the waterfront there
is weeping and wailing, and they fight to board small craft, sampans, rowboats and barges that can ferry them to the ships. The docks, beaches and
inlets are strewn with weapons, tanks stuck in the sand, artillery caissons,
crates of ammunition, disemboweled suitcases, damaged helicopters. On
the ocean float casks and inner tubes—buoys that soldiers cling to. Dogs
howl. The stench is strong in spots—urine, excrement, dead bodies. On
the flood tide, swollen bodies flow back toward the port. Small craft capsize
trying to reach the open sea. Men, women and children drown. South
Vietnamese marines attack refugees, taking their places in the boats. To
reach the docks, the last soldiers seize cars, ejecting the passengers at
gunpoint. All military police units have vanished, as have the municipal
police. Vehicles burn, shots ring out. A few trucks with loudspeakers roll
through neighborhoods clear of ARVN soldiers: "Be calm. Everything is
all right. The troops of reconciliation will be here soon. The liberation
army is on the way. Decorate your houses with Buddhist flags."

With no command, no morale, no discipline, several hundred drunk or
frightened soldiers keep the panic level high. Many officers are not on their
best behavior. A major of the First Division, asked by a colonel where to
find headquarters, answers: "I don't even know where my wife and children
are. Why should I care about divisional headquarters?"

Refugees jam aboard the ships, 8,000 on a cargo ship with nowhere
near enough toilets or food. In the holds, some soldiers strip civilians of
their money and jewels. They rob, rape, kill those who protest. For trying

to interfere, a priest is slaughtered. Babies and children, adults too, suffocate.

President Ford's photographer, David Kennerly, also in Vietnam now, skims over the armada outside Danang. Aboard an Air America helicopter, he passes above the *Pioneer Contender*. South Vietnamese soldiers fire on the chopper.

With the help of a navy officer, General Truong swims out to a rowboat that ferries him to a Vietnamese ship. Some of the refugees take three days to reach a port, Cam Ranh, Cap Saint-Jacques or one of the welcoming islets. Thieu has issued orders: no refugees in Saigon—they could demoralize the populace as well as the army.

A final count: 50,000 civilians and 16,000 soldiers escaped from Danang. So there remain a million residents and refugees.

On Easter Sunday, March 30, NVA troops complete the occupation of Danang. In Camp Davis at Saigon's airport a persnickety PRG man insists that the city was taken March 29: "Our flag was flying there by the end of the afternoon."

The North Vietnamese round up thousands of prisoners. They have no trouble identifying policemen or those in South Vietnamese special services. Lists are drawn up—by Danang's police chief. A Vietcong agent?

The Politburo meets that day in Hanoi and releases a statement: "The revolutionary war in South Vietnam has not only reached a stage of development by accelerated leaps and bounds. We have reached the strategically propitious moment to unleash the offensive and also widespread insurrections against the enemy's lair. . . . Our revolution is progressing by giant steps." Then: "Our momentum makes a single day the equivalent of twenty years." The leaps and bounds are incontestable. Insurrection, an indispensable element of communist mythology, is still awaited.

In Danang as elsewhere, most residents, whatever they may think, choose to wait and see. In both Vietnams the war touches all lives, but for years now only 3 million at most out of 40 million are involved, or involve themselves, directly in the fighting. This March 30 the Politburo in Hanoi decides "to grasp the strategic opportune moment whatever the cost, issuing this general order: lightning war, audacity, surprise, sure victory." The Politburo "undertakes to complete the victory at all costs, as quickly as possible, some time in April and no later." It will "achieve its vital objectives in the heart of Saigon."

Farther south, the same day, General Tran Van Tra advances to the site chosen for his new headquarters, where he will direct the attack on Saigon. His camouflaged command car advances rapidly through the jungle.[4] "The roads and highways are dry and passable. The month of March has been sunny." From the direction of Saigon, Tra hears the rumble of artillery. Flowers are blooming everywhere. Spring is here. "It was a charming scene of war," says Tra, "and it touched the soul . . . Vietnam was still Vietnam." The general reflects on yesterday's battles and today's. In his diary he notes:

> *Golden apricots embellished the route*
> *The murmuring breeze of the jungle mingled*
> *With the crackle of cannon in the springtime surrounding the town*
> *Yesterday as today, the mountains and flowers are ours.*

For millennia in Indochina March has been the month of war. In March every year the Vietminh launched an offensive, and then the Vietcong, and then the PRG's guerrillas and Hanoi's regulars.

On March 31 in the North Vietnamese capital the *Nhan Dan* publishes an editorial more moderate than the Politburo's statement. For the party daily, the progress of North Vietnamese armed forces represents "a valuable experience allowing soldiers and people to move forward." They announce victories, not yet *the* final victory, to the populace. *Nhan Dan* affirms that "many puppet soldiers have deserted, turned their rifles on the reactionaries and rallied to the people." Nowhere do they mention a rebellion or winning over a single ARVN company. The liberators ask, And how do we explain this flood of refugees? "Thieu's band," comments *Nhan Dan*, "is fleeing in disorder. But they're forcing the people to follow along and serve as a shield, and divert international public opinion." In Hanoi they form committees for support in the South. The one for "people's revolution in Quang Da province and the city of Danang" seems less than optimistic when, in a mimeographed declaration, it exhorts the masses in the South: "The armed forces of liberation *must* attack, Vietnamese of all origins *must* rise up and fight beside our troops . . . , officers and men in Saigon *must* rally the people."

In Hanoi, Tien, the young man with cinematographic ambitions, is already savoring the films and plays he expects to see. Most features shown are still Soviet. The young man still wants to go to the Soviet Union or the German Democratic Republic to study. Nothing's been said about mobilizing him. He goes to class and profits by his privileges. He is under no restrictions. Rations in March are less than in January. The government launches a new campaign: "Save food for the South. Cut yours in half for those in the South." Most citizens receive 250 grams of sugar a month. The young man gets a kilo, and a can of condensed milk. In the capital (depending on deliveries, very irregular these days) the average citizen is entitled to one or two 120-gram boxes of Chinese meat. If the Chinese don't deliver, the authorities distribute powdered eggs. Our young man receives one kilo of fresh meat, usually pork. The elite do pretty well. Tien knows that he has more to eat than his father, a middle-level cadre in the PRG. In January and February, the government must have feared a renewal of U.S. bombing: more and more often, workmen went around touching up individual shelters dug into the sidewalks. No one needed them. It is obvious to the young man that they will never be needed.

His professors comment on the news. Even the fiercest militants speak moderately and not triumphantly. They live in hope. One of Tien's friends is a daughter of Nguyen Huu Tho, president of the PRG. From time to time, the young man goes to 69 rue Nguyen Du, where Tho lives in an old French villa. Many Southerners live in this neighborhood, near Liberation Lake. The young man doesn't always know just what he thinks, politically. Mainly he wants to go back to Saigon, see his mother again— she stayed—and join his old pals. Every victory announced brings his return closer.

They call him out of one of his classes.[5] A captain is waiting: "You have a special mission."

The young man is given orders to pack a bag. They take him to headquarters. He leaves in a jeep. In a "special center" he joins some fifty young men, all from the South. Some of them hiked up the Ho Chi Minh trail with him in April 1971.

"You are going to take part in Operation Ho Chi Minh."

They issue him maps of Saigon, printed in the South Vietnamese capital, and quiz him. Have they altered the course of any streets or boulevards? Are there new buildings? The young man confides that he's fairly familiar with the airport area.

He asks to see his father, who works in a hospital. There Tien realizes that he himself may die. He asks his father to let his mother know if . . . "I'm being sent on a mission as part of Operation Ho Chi Minh."

The accompanying officer reprimands him gently: "Don't even tell your own father what you're up to."

For four days the young man studies the streets of Saigon on those mediocre maps and comments on the city's topography. They dress him in a far from classic uniform, not a private's, not an officer's. Tien is no military expert, but he understands that he's going to serve as a scout. He's excited at the idea of seeing the South again.

No more movies, no more plays—for how long?

Three plays are running in Hanoi's modern theaters. They are all about South Vietnam: *The Sword and the Sea, Living near the Capital, Song of Love.* The official synopsis of that last:[6] "A puppet officer grows to hate war and deserts to seek refuge in a distant coastal region. He would like to find refuge in love, but the police and spies will not leave him alone. Finally he chooses the right path: he joins the rebelling masses to go into battle, singing, *Let's go, up and at 'em, we're off.*" In the DRV everything is oriented to the war in the South—the army, mill hands, peasants in agricultural cooperatives, writers and actors. In socialist realism—certainly socialist, not too realistic—the North Vietnamese are the avant-garde.

With seventeen companions, the young man boards a bus that crosses the old Doumer bridge. At Gia Lam airport the little group, surrounded by officers, is welcomed by the poet To Huu, the regime's official bard and a member of the Central Committee. Like eminent generals, famous writers are cogs in the machine, where you become important because you're a cog. In a solemn, sentimental, emotional tone, To Huu addresses the young men: "Your mission is very important. Good luck . . ."

Photographers bustle. If I'm killed, Tien thinks, they'll publish my picture, a hero's photo. They've issued him a pistol. Now they offer him an AK-47. He doesn't know how to use either. With taciturn older officials, the young men board a C-119, an old South Vietnamese plane. At dusk they take off. No one speaks. Hours go by, the plane makes a stop, the passengers debark. The young man thinks he must be in the Central Highlands because the soil is reddish. Still no one speaks to him.

He travels by car and asks no questions. No one volunteers information. He only knows he's headed south. A lot easier trip than the one he made going north. It was *long*, that hike up the Ho Chi Minh trail! He had a bad attack of malaria, and he marched ten hours a day. For three months: In the jungle he was bored and dreamed of Saigon. He recalls images, the banner at station 94: "This is the end of the NLF Zone. The North begins here, on a highway of the socialist republic, Route 559." He may see Saigon again. They tell him nothing. The trip by car, by truck, by car again, is pleasant. Tien hears talk about fallen cities and provinces.

At last he arrives at Loc Ninh, staff headquarters. Lots of officers, soldiers, antennas on straw huts, tanks. The young man sleeps in a tent. He's treated like a cadre without rank. He's not permitted to speak to soldiers, to the *bo doi*. He waits several days. He examines the camouflaged T-54s beneath the trees and several Southern M-48 tanks in good condition.

One morning he sees Le Duc Tho and his brother, General Dinh Duc Thien.

The young man boards another car. After several hours on trails and paved roads, he arrives at a former South Vietnamese military base on the fringe of a forest.

In Thien Dong, thirty kilometers south of Hanoi, Carpenter Ba is chatting with the other villagers. He's not like our young man, or for that matter most of the peasants. He doesn't believe what the loudspeakers in the village say, relaying Radio Hanoi. He cannot believe that an army as strong as Saigon's, with American support, can be defeated. Southern officers, according to Mr. Ba, are "intellectuals who know their trade." He contrasts the peasant soldiers of the North to the intellectual officers of the South. Mr. Ba is simplifying.

In the North, colonels and generals are older, over forty or fifty. They attended Soviet or Chinese military academies and many are middle-class; some are former teachers like Giap; on the whole they are more cultivated, though also more rigid, than the South's officers, many of whom were once noncoms in the French army. In the South there are colonels of thirty. Despite nepotism and corruption, can the South's army be more democratic than the North's?

Mr. Ba reflects often on these matters. He doesn't like the communists. All he wants is to live, survive, be quiet and be happy just observing. All the same Mr. Ba is uneasy. Things in the village have changed since January. The cadres are recruiting women over eighteen, assigning them to road repair and arms transport. The villagers drew extra rations for the Tet holiday. Shortly afterward, the cadres recommended economies: "You've all sent sons and daughters off to war. If you want to see them again soon, you must accept more sacrifices to liberate the South."

It's obvious to Mr. Ba that most of the peasants are proud to contribute to the victory. They make no distinction between nationalism and communism. Hating the Americans, who bombed their country, is a habit. They also hate the "puppets" who serve the Americans. None of this keeps the peasants from complaining. Some of the old folks say, "Ever since French times the Vietminh have been promising that when the war ended, so would poverty."

Twenty years after the French withdrawal, the peasants are no better off. The cadres who run cooperatives do fairly well. They have more comfortable houses, they own bicycles. Sometimes the peasants speak out and say they seem to be working for the cadres. Patiently the latter explain that after the war there will be no more restrictions. They may very well be right. The peasants don't believe, as Mr. Ba does, that the authorities are exaggerating the number of towns taken in the South. Besides, people who visit families in the village of Thien Dong often say their son is at Ban Me Thuot, or in Kontum, or near Pleiku. The authorities have paired Northern and Southern towns. Ha Tay is paired with Danang. Cadres seek out Southerners who are said to have migrated North after the Geneva Accords in 1954, especially the teachers.

They'll need plenty of cadres in the South, the authorities explain.

The French community in Saigon keeps cool and prepares for great upheavals. Patrick Hays, once a serving officer, has no doubt whatever of the military outcome. To survive at all Thieu's government must find a political solution. The *Courrier d'Extrême-Orient*, a Saigon daily underwritten by subsidies from the French Embassy and local French groups, remains cautious on the matter. Its editor, Marie-George Sauvezon, goes on making her rounds in her Citroën DS driven by her white-gloved chauffeur. Most of the French in Saigon would agree with Hays.

There are several thousand of them. Restaurateurs, hotel managers, insurance men are old residents. Volunteer social workers pass through. Others are there for three or five years, employees or managers of French companies, Michelin, Plantation des Terres Rouges, or Brasseries et Glacières d'Indochine. Rumor has it, and rumor is right, that the Brasseries' plant and warehouse in Danang have been disemboweled and demolished. Les Tabacs, Peugeot, Renault, Citroën, Banque Française d'Asie and Franco-Chinoise, Chargeurs Réunis, and Messageries Maritimes are also big employers. Their officers must plan now, prepare for the future. What will become of French corporations if the communists win? The PRG's plan provides for a mixed economy. Will the French women and children have to be repatriated?

The French ambassador sends for Patrick Hays. Jean-Marie Mérillon is responsible for his nationals. Planters have come in from the provinces, also merchants and priests. Let's think about some sort of continuity between the nationalist rout and the communist takeover. As at Danang, anything can happen. Let's imagine bands of deserters and looters roaming Saigon and taking revenge on French nationals. Let's imagine the city put to fire and the sword. Where will we all regroup? At the Grall Hospital, the Ecole Saint Exupéry . . . We'll set up shelter areas. How do we protect everyone? We have a few French gendarmes here as embassy guards but they're nowhere near enough. Besides, even tough cops can't work twenty-four hours a day. Let's lay in canned goods, rice and drinking water.

Hays is a former lieutenant of the First Foreign Legion Airborne Regiment. Will he take charge of security for these shelters? An ambassador can hardly be allowed to raise a private militia. Hays has a free hand, and circumstances call for just that.[7] He believes, as Mérillon does, that a small group of determined men can make sure Danang's tragedy is not repeated in Saigon.

He gathers some fifteen men he trusts, planters, professors from the cultural center who did hard military service and his own assistant, Michel Hamiaux, an imperturbable colossus whose twenty-seven months in Algeria earned him the Legion of Honor. They'll need vehicles that move fast and freely. Hays takes four plantation jeeps, paints them white, and works up pennants with red crosses. Whatever the situation, cars with red crosses will circulate quicker than others. For weapons Hays turns to a friend, General Le Quang Luong, commander of the First Airborne Division, most of which has fallen back on Saigon. Luong delivers all the weapons Hays wants. Hays obviously doesn't intend to go up against the North Vietnamese with his peacekeeping force. It's just that "if the city goes crazy, or mobs attack the French shelter areas," Hays and his men, notified by radio, will race over in jeeps and "deal with the incident" as discreetly as possible.

Hays sets up a rotation for his group. They wait, they play cards. All the French in Vietnam, all foreigners in or outside Saigon, are waiting.

The Vietnamese too, even more nervously. In courtyards and gardens of villas rented by Americans, baggage is stacked up—the Americans' Samsonite and Vuitton valises, and their Vietnamese employees' suitcases wrapped in plastic sheets and tied shut one way and another.

The U.S. Embassy's agencies draw up lists of potential evacuees, by standards hard to define. Americans are usually good at foresight and options, but the embassy has not prepared a priority list, a master plan for evacuation. What criteria determine priority? First off, of course, come the Vietnamese in danger of death or doomed to concentration camps if the communists come in. Almost everybody who worked for Americans, and their families. A hundred thousand, two hundred thousand, three hundred thousand people? In Saigon and Washington the rumor goes as high as a million candidates for evacuation. After these come Vietnamese who could find jobs in the United States, engineers, doctors, accountants, all those who speak pretty good English. Last on the list, American consuls will have to deal with all the ordinary Vietnamese who want out.

There always seemed to be plenty of time in Vietnam. Now history's speeding up. Vietnamese who want to be evacuated are often torn apart: they're panic stricken but go on telling themselves that there can't be a total collapse. During thirty years of war, the country has known so many battles and lulls. . . . One more time, it will survive.

Americans also wonder and hesitate. Certainly they'll leave if necessary. Many diplomatic and military employees have served several tours in Vietnam, and their years in this country were the most important of their careers. They too can't imagine a total collapse. They're infected by *Vietnamitis*, a profound attachment to Vietnam, aroused by the aroma of a soup or the smell of a street, a landscape of rice paddy, jungle, highlands. How this country grabs hold! In civvies or in uniform, young or old, enthusiastic or cynical, for a conscientious and impatient Frank Snepp, for the blasé old-timer Homer Smith, for all who have Vietnamese friends here, sometimes a wife or mistress, this strange and familiar Vietnam, this enchanting, sometimes abject capital have become the frontier of their youth and the horizon of their maturity. American conscripts served here for a year and then, if they could, forgot Vietnam. Not the career officers, not the diplomats back from Hue, Danang, Saigon, who talk about it all the time.

History is flashing by. The enemy no longer bears the same name. Hardly two years ago they were still talking about the Vietcong, the VC, even when they meant troops from the North. Despite his cruelty, there was a sort of admiration for that enemy. The Vietcong—also called the Cong, Charlie, Charlie Cong or Victor Charlie, or VC—could be cruel but the foreign press was easier on their excesses than on the "crimes" of the South Vietnamese or the Americans. Brass and diplomats alike were furious. Nobody forgave them one atrocity, one burned village, one My Lai. In these Americans' anger and frustration you sensed as much good will as naiveté, impatience and dedication. That seems logical now. The press covered everything except the Vietcong zones. Reporters in the field sometimes came across the bodies of ARVN or American soldiers tortured, crucified, emasculated by the Vietcong, but they mostly saw and chronicled the horrors of American and South Vietnamese warfare. Early and late, correspondents described bombings and defoliations. Who reported the kidnappings or executions of village or hamlet chiefs by the other side? From 1957 to 1973, over 36,000 assassinations and over 58,000 kidnappings.

All that seems so long ago. In Saigon today there's a lot less talk about the Vietcong than about the ten or fifteen NVA divisions in South Vietnam. The NLF and PRG don't matter now. . . . Or is it twenty NVA divisions? There was a shaky familiarity with the Vietcong. Some of its men came back to the fold, maybe as many as 200,000. Will they have to be evacuated, too? The North Vietnamese on the march, even if some have been taken prisoner, are more anonymous, unknowable, more abstract, and they have the conqueror's aura. Over the years, Americans in Saigon—and in Pleiku, Hue, Danang, Can Tho, My Tho, Tay Ninh, in district and provincial capitals—have lived through offensives and counteroffensives. They lost, retook, and lost again a hamlet, a plantation, a hill, a valley, a large but indeterminate tract of jungle, to score points. They played hide and seek with a formidable enemy. Nobody really won. The war was stabilized, or its fluctuations were incomprehensible to the Americans in Saigon. So the Tet offensive in 1968: how was that appalling communist military defeat transformed into an extraordinary political victory on the international scene? American eyewitnesses are still wondering.

The end of an epoch. Entire provinces, cities thought impregnable, always retaken in the end, Danang, Hue, are now in North Vietnamese hands, and this time the Americans know, and so does Saigon, that they won't be retaken. The unthinkable is happening; the point of no return is here.

There's no way to measure the panic, to list statistics about the Southerners' wild desire to leave, to flee. But an irrefutable indicator quantifies fear: the price of a dollar on the Saigon black market. March 29, a $100 bill is worth 5,000 piastres. A few days before, 4,000. Fear is written in the zooming price of gold. From sales you can infer intentions: who buys dollars is ready to leave; who buys gold is taking precautions, but intends to remain.

Easter Monday in Dalat: the last remaining professors and lecturers all prepare to leave town. The evening before, sixty kilometers away, near the Djilin tea plantation, there was a skirmish. They say a French priest had his leg shattered by shellburst. A North Vietnamese doctor operated on him without anesthesia. The North Vietnamese don't have American facilities.

To reach Saigon, the direct route south being cut, they have to go by way of Phan Rang on the coast. Father Jean Maïs loads the professors in his 2 CV.* With them and one of his protégés, an eighteen-year-old Vi-

---

* A tiny tinny Citroën, unimposing but valiant, like an early French version of the VW Beetle. (Tr.)

etnamese orphan, Maïs rolls toward Bellevue Mountain. Beyond the power plant he overtakes refugees, old Peugeot 203s with a dozen passengers, Honda bikes transporting whole families with their cookpots and mats. At the roadside some soldiers are trying to sell the skin of a tiger blown up by a mine. Tiger skins are a scarce item, but no one stops.

Maïs drops off his professors at Phan Rang and returns along the coast toward Nha Trang, against the flow of refugee columns, for news of other fathers from the Overseas Missions.

At Nha Trang, the priests hesitate. Some will leave for Saigon that night. Others feel they must not abandon their parishioners. Father Bianchetti camps in town with Montagnards from a village near Ban Me Thuot.

There are hundreds of thousands of refugees on the roads. If not for the fighting, many peasants would stay. They've lived here for generations, near the tombs of their ancestors. For millions of young people it seems unthinkable to leave their village with its bamboo pale. Even so, many flee.

Returning to Phan Rang at night, Jean Maïs and his protégé stop in Song Pha parish. Hot winds swirl in the dark valley. Around midnight, sleepless, the priest steps outside the rectory for a breath of air. Suddenly, on Bellevue Mountain, Maïs sees hundreds of headlights. A convoy is moving along, soldiers from the Dalat garrison, cadets, officers, militiamen of the regional forces and their families. A jeep halts. A colonel, commandant of the psychological warfare school, steps out. He stops and shakes hands with Jean Maïs: "We were ordered to abandon Dalat."

Another officer says: "We're going to try to regroup at Phan Rang."

Like the radio and newspapers, men speak of "regrouping," of "shortening supply lines," all the euphemisms that cannot disguise what seems to be an irreversible defeat.

The priest goes to bed. In the morning, a communist security committee has been formed in the village. The ex-commander of the ARVN garrison is part of it. Workers from the electric plant are wearing armbands.

Jean Maïs leaves. At Bellevue Mountain, members of another committee demand his papers. Palaver. But a lecturer from the science school comes along. He knows the priest. Thanks to him, the father can go his way.

In Dalat, stores have lowered their blinds and the lakeshore is deserted. In the market stalls, fruit and vegetables are rotting, and chunks of meat and fish. The smell of cabbage is particularly strong. At the Overseas Missions library, looters have torn down the shelves, broken the refrigerator and blown the safe, which was empty. The father gathers up a few books. In town, he meets his assistant in French. With a group of young men, Ngu is cleaning the marketplace. The assistant says, "We're waiting for them. It'll be all right. We want the city to be clean."

At the university, Jean Maïs joins the dean of the School of Liberal Arts, Nguyen Khac Duong, professor of philosophy. His brother, Nguyen

Khac Vien, director of foreign language editions in Hanoi, is well known and meets all the French intellectuals passing through the North Vietnamese capital. Of the two men one, converted to Marxism, has chosen the North, the other, converted to Catholicism, the South.

The dean says to Father Maïs: "South Vietnam is too corrupt; it must accept its punishment."

For the dean, the arrival of the communists will be a purifying fire. And yet Duong knows North Vietnamese brutality; they executed his father in 1956. The dean did not want to flee with those he considered cowards. Nor did Jean Maïs. A missionary, he will work if the university opens again. He tells himself, It's all over for Dalat.

Still, it's not impossible that the South Vietnamese will stop the Northerners.

In Saigon, Writer Duyen Anh mulls over one question: should he leave? The Americans predict a bloodbath if the communists move in. President Ford himself, it seems, has ordered a plan for evacuation of journalists and writers. No question now of articles or news reports, much less starting a novel. Could the writer work abroad, could he find readers? An artist, he thinks, needs a public. The public of his own country. Many of Duyen Anh's writings are anticommunist. If the North Vietnamese take over, he'll be sentenced to death. He thinks of Pasternak's courage, Solzhenitsyn's; fearing they would not be allowed to return home, they refused to go to Sweden to receive their Nobel prizes. The writer puts his name on a list of departures at the U.S. Information Service in Le Quy Don street. Of course he adds the names of his wife and three children.

The loss of all these towns and provinces doesn't faze Engineer Van. What does lost ground matter? The deaths on both sides are what hurt. The engineer still thinks it's not impossible to work out a political solution. At the Ministry of Public Works, he states his opinions. His colleagues approve. Because of his rank? In other agencies there are diehard bureaucrats, who say flatly that you can't parley with communists.

With nine Venerables and twenty bonzes from the Quan The Am pagoda, Thien Hue is taking care of some sixty refugees, the families of religious men. Most of them come from a province near Ban Me Thuot. They mainly camp in the common rooms. Women keep busy with the cooking, infants whimper, weep and shriek. The sound of transistor radios breaks in. Gifts from the faithful buy food for the refugees. They worry about their fields, their rice paddies, their houses and their lost parents. These are simple folk who don't speculate about political developments. They want to go home to their hamlets.

The young bonze is now looking out at the real world. Will his two older brothers, ARVN officers, be slaughtered in reprisals when the North Vietnamese arrive? Communists are atheists. People say they make bonzes do military service. In the North they conscript postulants to bar them from becoming novices. Most of the bonzes are old up there. This doesn't keep the leaders, Pham Van Dong in the van, from telling their foreign visitors, "We're Buddhists, in our fashion." In the PRG zones too the bonzes are old. Helping refugees but in general withdrawn, draped in robes and prayers, the superiors in the pagoda contemplate current events rather calmly. This is karma, retribution for our acts, this North Vietnamese eruption; so thinks the young bonze.

His parents suggest that he flee. One of their brothers-in-law, a lieutenant colonel in the air force, has confirmed that field officers will be allowed to take their families. The young bonze refuses. He cannot escape his karma, he must accept the sufferings to come. So the problem no longer exists. His parents remain. They await the return of a son, a sublieutenant of intelligence in the infantry division defending the town of Xuan Loc east of Saigon.

Tankers no longer come upriver from Saigon to Newport, near the highway to Bien Hoa. Gasoline has grown scarce. Long lines form at service stations. A thousand rumors fly around town. It is now sure that the hostile camps will proceed to a new partition of the country. There were two Vietnams, there will be three. The North Vietnamese communists will retain all their territory, from the Chinese border to the 17th parallel; the Southern resistance regrouped up north, the *tap ket*, will control all between the 17th and 13th parallels. The nationalists will have a third Vietnam between the 13th parallel and Ca Mau point. There they'll set up a two-party government, both nationalist and communist. People solemnly swear that the Americans, especially the CIA, are advising colonels, generals and ranking civilians to leave. The Americans, it seems, have forced general officers to evacuate by helicopter. These officers wanted to defend Kontum, Pleiku, Hue, Danang. The U.S. government has other ideas. Everybody in Saigon can stay. Wish becomes fantasy. French planters make the case that their interests will be protected. People want to, people can, people have to stay in Saigon. Thieu appears on television to justify himself: the Americans don't want to sell us arms, we have to be stingy with bullets. Sometimes the president is funny and colloquial in his speeches: "We never planned to fight the communists with our teeth." People float all probable, possible, impossible, solutions. If Thieu resigns . . . if he's replaced . . . by the vice-president . . . by the prime minister? By Bao Dai . . . The ex-emperor of Annam is close to the French. They may intervene with the communists. . . .

Patrick Hays notes:

(1) The situation: hard to say exactly what's going on, because for once things are moving fast and reliable spokesmen are scarce; furthermore, all kinds of rumors are circulating in the general confusion, which is not conducive to cool analysis. I keep hoping that we're reaching a plateau—supposing the

North Vietnamese staff's most optimistic plans for this phase
of the offensive are fulfilled or surpassed, and the supply
corps needs time to move in. We could have a breathing
space then when we could take steps to secure people and
property. . . .

(2) What's going to happen now? With the new balance
of power, the military issue is no longer in doubt. Not even
if everybody left stands fast before Saigon; it would take de
Lattre or Sainte Geneviève.

Hays thinks about Thieu's departure, but not in terms of the man's
character. An optimistic hypothesis:

The North Vietnamese don't try to take Saigon before the
presidential elections in September. Thieu doesn't run. Afterward, a government that "implements the Paris Agreement," etc.

(3) How to react: I'm getting used to the idea of a
communist conquest of Saigon (chances of a miracle are at
most 5% even in Vietnam). The question is when, and above
all how. I hope we'll have a delay for North Vietnamese
logistical and maybe political reasons. . . .

At the factory, work goes on as usual. But I've provided
(on paper, for the moment) for security teams with VN cadres
in charge if work has to be interrupted. . . .

Saigon is calm.[8]

13

---◆---

Three Red Stripes

To welcome General Weyand's mission in Saigon, President Thieu ordered new banners devised and hung out, proclaiming in English, "The people of Vietnam are ready to fight if there is help."

Weyand landed at 3 A.M. March 27, with Ambassador Graham Martin; Erich von Marbod, assistant secretary of defense; Ted Shackley and George Carver, two CIA VIPs; a swarm of aides and President Ford's photographer. Some felt they were performing in a small ballet: punctilious about rank, Martin is said to have insisted on being first off the plane. He considered reports from Danang exaggerated: "I'm going to see for myself."

"That's out of the question," Lehmann answered.

General Weyand meets with Vietnamese chief of staff Vien, whom he's known for a long time. Frederick Weyand held several commands in Vietnam. He led the 25th Infantry Division. Later he replaced General Creighton Abrams, commander in chief. Weyand speaks Vietnamese. He knows the strengths and weaknesses of the military hierarchy in Saigon. At the same time—this is his strain of *Vietnamitis*—it seems almost impossible to him that the United States should be defeated with Vietnam as proxy. Thieu and his generals distrust politicians like Kissinger, but distrust soldiers like Weyand and Haig less. In any country under any regime most generals distrust politicians.

Men like Weyand concentrate on serious problems, arms and ammunition, not political prisoners or other "foolishness." Vien outlines his

problems: the United States will have to send up B-52s to knock out North
Vietnamese troop concentrations. Weyand replies that any new U.S. military intervention must have congressional approval; there's almost no
chance that any such request will be granted.

There follow open and private meetings between Americans and Vietnamese. Weyand would like to confer with Thieu alone, but Martin
usually insists on being present. The largest gathering takes place in a vast
chamber, its walls covered with maps. Thieu presides in a safari outfit,
with Martin on his right and Vice-President Huong on his left, these two
in business suits. Weyand, von Marbod, Carver sit to Martin's right, across
from the South Vietnamese chief of staff, the prime minister, and Nguyen
Tien Hung, minister of planning and economic affairs. The people must
be told that President Ford cares about South Vietnam's fate: the press
covers the start of this conference in full force.

The conferees address themselves to a variety of questions. The Americans insist on resolving the refugee problem and especially the matter of
soldiers' families—these last must not stay in combat zones. Vien protests,
that's out, forget it, no separating soldiers from their families. They'd lose
interest in fighting. "During the Tet offensive [in 1968]," says the chief of
staff, "we saw women and children in outlying positions helping the soldiers, passing ammunition, evacuating the wounded and even firing
machineguns."

Some of the Americans are stunned: This can't be, we're dreaming.
One of the CIA men, Carver, small, round and owlish behind his big
glasses, wonders, What are they arguing about? The art of arranging chaises
longues on deck while the *Titanic* sinks.

The U.S. delegation wants the Saigon government to detail the situation
more clearly to the public. You can't let them be forever victimized by the
communists' false rumors. South Vietnamese leaders have to use television
more. These Americans believe in television.

They also insist on a victory, however modest. It would help justify a
few hundred million dollars in aid. Couldn't they strike a sharp blow against
the NVA Fifth Division near the Parrot's Beak west of Saigon? The Fifth
isn't a crack division, after all. The government does indeed need a victory.
Not only to impress American lawmakers and public opinion, but first and
foremost to stop the North Vietnamese. Tough luck: the chief of staff has
no reserves and would have to strip Saigon's primary defenses. There's
more talk about B-52s. The Americans present are far from convinced that
bombers would be enough at this point. Anyway it can't be done. . . . The
South Vietnamese chief of staff tells them that C-130As, each carrying
twenty-four bombs, are dropping their loads onto enemy troops from
15,000–20,000 feet. South Vietnamese soldiers call these C-130As "mini
B-52s." One salvo annihilates a square quarter-mile.

Von Marbod asks that ARVN troops' ammunition not be rationed. At
Martin's urging he confirms that supplies will be delivered fast if Congress

accepts President Ford's proposals: "We have large stocks available in Okinawa and Korea."

Von Marbod is also in Vietnam to evacuate materiel. They've lost too much during recent retreats.

The Vietnamese are looking for a miracle weapon. Can they have the daisy cutter, a terrifying 15,000-pound bomb?* The Americans used it to clean up the jungle and prepare landing zones for their helicopters. The Paris Agreement forbids the introduction of new arms in Vietnam. So what? Weyand promises to have twenty-seven daisy cutters delivered, and any necessary American specialists.[1]

Carver expounds a parallel between the British army in 1940 and the ARVN in 1975. A Dunkirk lies ahead, he says. Carver gets on Ambassador Martin's nerves. With Thieu there they sidestep a burning issue, a way to give ARVN staff a dominant role. They need greater powers and freedom from short-circuiting by the president. Weyand's mission emerges from this meeting uneasily aware that Thieu doesn't know how serious the situation is.

In another meeting Thieu explains, enthusiastically and in detail, that after he's reelected in the presidential elections of October 1975 (he has no doubt of the outcome) he'll authorize new political parties. This time they'll really develop democratic institutions. Thomas Polgar admits that's all interesting and promising, but they have to solve their military problems first. And he stresses the point—emphasizes the North Vietnamese advances, the weakness of South Vietnamese command and control, the chaos at Danang. . . . Abruptly, before the Saigon chief of station and Ted Shackley of the CIA in Washington, the president of the South Vietnamese Republic breaks into tears.

Members of Weyand's mission run lightning inspections, in the South's Delta and up north. At Nha Trang they find General Phu incoherent.

Many meetings between Americans and South Vietnamese are tense and acrimonious. The former think the Vietnamese are unrealistic, the latter that the Americans don't understand their problems. The U.S. mission will do its job in Vietnam until April 4.

Minister Hung gives von Marbod photocopies of certain letters from Nixon to Thieu. Ford must see them, insists the minister.

General Weyand writes a twenty-eight–page report.

In a two-page introductory memo the general says, "The current military situation is critical, and the probability of the survival of South Vietnam as a truncated nation in the southern provinces is marginal at best. The government of the Republic of Vietnam is on the brink of total military

---

* Two sorts of bombs were called "daisy cutters." The better known was an antipersonnel fragmentation bomb that flung thousands of sharp shards at body height. Those here referred to were "fuel air explosive" bombs and were also nicknamed "cheeseburgers." They released gases that were then ignited; the blast was enormous, and the combustion depleted oxygen for hundreds of meters around. (Tr.)

defeat. However, the South is planning to continue to defend with their available resources." The Americans must help. U.S. planes would be useful materially and psychologically, but, says the general,

> I recognize, however, the significant legal and political im-
> plications which would attend the exercise of this option.
>   One other matter you should consider. For reasons of
> prudence, the United States should plan now for a mass
> evacuation of 6,000 U.S. citizens and tens of thousands of
> South Vietnamese and Third Country nationals to whom we
> have incurred an obligation and owe protection. The lessons
> of Danang indicate that this evacuation would require as a
> minimum a U.S. task force of a reinforced division supported
> by tactical air to suppress North Vietnamese artillery and
> anti-aircraft.

Weyand recommends a clear warning to Hanoi "at the appropriate time" that the United States have the "intention to use force to safely evacuate personnel." Ford should obtain the necessary authority to use "military sanctions against North Vietnam if there is interference with the evacuation." Weyand ends his introduction with the customary clash of cymbals: "United States credibility as an ally is at stake in Vietnam." That should satisfy Kissinger.

In the body of the report, Weyand sums up the last three months. "Some South Vietnamese units have conducted themselves in a remarkable manner." The retreat from Kontum and Pleiku? "Sound in concept and Thieu's estimate of its necessity was probably correct" but "disastrous in execution." Apropos of the civilian population taken during the fighting, Weyand speaks of "carnage."

According to Weyand the NVA has 152,000 men in the South, true front-line fighting men organized into seventy-four regiments of infantry, five of armor, fourteen of artillery, thirty-three of anti-aircraft. These figures do not include auxiliaries. The South Vietnamese can now assemble 59,000 men, nineteen infantry regiments, two brigades of armor, five ranger groups, four airborne brigades and two marine brigades. Saigon has an air force, a navy and auxiliaries in the popular and regional forces. But, Weyand notes, these last are not as effective as the PRG troops. All in all, North Vietnamese superiority in combat troops is three to one.

Weyand crosses out MR 1 and MR 2. There remain the two southern-most regions. Despite pressure on Tay Ninh and Xuan Loc, the Saigon government must hold MR 3 "as it stands on April 1, at least for the immediate future." The same goes for MR 4 if no new NVA units move forward.

At his level, the general must think in military and political terms. He sees two possibilities: (1) the communists could exploit their tactical advantage to the full to win a "total military victory," or (2) they could consolidate their tactical gains by adding a major victory in Tay Ninh province, "then urging negotiations." Here Weyand's reflections are on the order of "a woman is pregnant or she isn't."

Weyand tells Ford what he doesn't dare suggest to Thieu: "The situation requires the kind of leadership and effective administration Churchill and his war cabinet gave Great Britain after Dunkirk and the fall of France." So far this kind of leadership is not "evident." Moreover, there's no English Channel to allow a delay for regrouping. ARVN officers say troops' morale in MR 4 is good. If attacked, they'll fight "partly because they have no place to retreat." Privately the senior commanders caution that "their troops' morale could not stand the news of MR 1 and 2 type defeat in MR 3."

Weyand explains that at all levels of civil and military society the South Vietnamese are convinced they have been "abandoned, and even betrayed" by the United States. The higher the level, the stronger the conviction.

Soldiers have fired on the helicopter carrying Ford's photographer. But until now, with a few exceptions, the South Vietnamese have not turned on Americans. Latest rumor from Saigon: South Vietnamese officers are prepared to shoot down American helicopters and planes if the United States evacuates its personnel.

Weyand was not favorably impressed by Thieu and his senior advisers, "the true government" (chairman of the JGS, prime minister, security adviser General Quang). According to the American general, for most South Vietnamese, these men are "felt to be disgraced . . . demonstratedly incompetent or worse."[2]

No Churchill on the horizon. In Saigon there's a lot of talk about a coup d'état. For Weyand, this would be a "disaster." But he foresees that the generals who really control the army will, in weeks to come, tell President Thieu that "he has to go." Weyand says that the South Vietnamese general staff, obviously overwhelmed, has no real strategic plan. Thieu cannot command the army from the palace, and no one else, it seems, is authorized to do it. The whole Saigon bureaucracy seems to be in a state of shock.

On the other hand, the North Vietnamese seem to have no serious problem: they can transfer existing divisions to South Vietnam faster than the South Vietnamese government can create new divisions.

Weyand thinks it will take $722 million in military aid, folding in losses over the last few weeks. He lists those losses:

Ground munitions (depot only)	$107.0 million
Individual crew service weapons	24.6
Artillery	16.0
Track vehicles	85.0

Wheel vehicles	77.0
Communications equipment	15.6
Gasoline, oil, and lubricants	4.8
Medical	7.9
Engineer	1.8
General supply stocks	67.4
Total	$407.1 million.

Furthermore, the South Vietnamese air force has left behind 268 planes, $68.6 million in spare parts and $48 million in aircraft ammunition. The South Vietnamese navy has lost three ships and assorted equipment. Weyand's lists don't include the value of munitions transported then abandoned by different units, or military installations, ports or airports. At the U.S. Embassy in Saigon some people—like Frank Snepp—keep saying that the South Vietnamese debacle is not primarily a matter of arms and ammunition. The lists supplied by General Weyand lend support to these statements.

Seemingly more to be thorough than because he believes in it, Weyand details the South Vietnamese plan. It consists of saving a bit of the southeastern part of MR 2, two-thirds of MR 3 and all of MR 4.

Setting out the old argument, the general writes that "the territory to be held contains the bulk of the population" and can constitute "a viable political and economic entity." Rather oddly, the general goes on, "Once the military situation has been stabilized, the GVN plans to rapidly reorganize and reconstitute its armed forces." How can they stabilize the front without reorganized forces? The general presents Thieu's arguments: if the South Vietnamese regroup, their lines of communication will be shorter and less vulnerable. Having extended themselves over considerable territory, their adversaries will be "vulnerable to guerrilla warfare and raids staged by the RVNAF [the South Vietnamese air force]."

The reorganization of South Vietnamese troops becomes a theoretical exercise. ARVN headquarters claims to be reconstituting four infantry divisions, converting twelve ranger groups into four more divisions and transforming twenty-seven regional force groups into several infantry divisions. The Americans have explained unsuccessfully that it's better to include seasoned troops in freshly formed units.

The conclusion of the report to President Ford is wonderfully cautious. Weyand cannot guarantee "that any of the actions I propose, or all of them, will be sufficient to prevent or even long delay, total North Vietnamese victory." This report applies a principle familiar to all levels of the U.S. military: Cover your ass. Don't take too many risks, don't commit yourself too firmly, think of your future.

Leaving Saigon, General Weyand holds a brief press conference. To the stunned journalists he announces that the government's forces "are still strong and still have the spirit and capability to defeat the North Vietnamese."

An army intelligence report[3] predicts that the Republic of South Vietnam will fall "in less than thirty days."

General Weyand joins his president in California. With a formidable lack of tact at this critical and tragic moment, Gerald Ford has gone to Palm Springs to play golf in the sun. His fellow citizens see him on television hitting the little ball, and a few seconds later they watch scenes of evacuation from Vietnamese cities. Some widely seen footage shows Ford in shirtsleeves, at Bakersfield airport, running fast to avoid journalists.

A reporter says to Ron Nessen, the president's press secretary: "He runs almost as fast as the South Vietnamese army."

Surrounded by specialists in public relations, gurus of communication, Ford commits one gaffe after another. Thanks to Bob Hartmann, one of his advisers, who writes his speeches, the president barely avoids a dinner with . . . Frank Sinatra. The actor's reputation is doubly sulphurous: he hung out with Nixon and is said to know mafiosi.

Ron Nessen makes it known that Ford does not foresee further bombings in support of the ARVN:[4] "The law forbids it. The President's inclinations are against it. And he has no plan to do it." Nessen adds: "The President has a great deal of sympathy and compassion for the Vietnamese people."

Ineffectual compassion. Returning from a junket around Southeast Asia and Chiang Kai-shek's funeral, Vice-President Rockefeller says publicly: "I really think it's too late to do anything about it."

Most of the time Rockefeller plays no role in Vietnamese affairs.

So here is Hanoi agreeably alerted, forewarned and reassured: the B-52s will not come back. Kissinger is present at the meeting in Palm Springs; not his rival James Schlesinger, secretary of defense.

The participants wax enthusiastic over an aid program that would make it possible to supply Saigon with 744 artillery pieces, 100,000 rifles, 6,000 machineguns, 11,000 grenade launchers, 1,300 assorted guns and 120,000 tons of ammunition. During these discussions Weyand, faithful to the waffling tone of his report, implies that they can still save the situation militarily—and, on his return to Washington, he will pass this on to Bui Diem. Kissinger has no illusions. But even in tough times you must behave *as if* you have a grip on things. As if we can save South Vietnam. So let's ask Congress for $722 million. Sincere or hypocritical, there's one advantage to that gambit. If Congress refuses to vote aid, and if things go belly up in Indochina, the senators and representatives can be blamed. A process already begun, in whispers, through leaks and confidences.

Ford's advisers, Robert Hartmann and Ron Nessen, don't like this approach at all. They don't want to save *Vietnam*, they want to protect Ford *from* Vietnam. Kissinger wins. The president asks Congress for $722 million in military aid and $250 million in economic and humanitarian aid, underlining the atrocious fate of the populations involved.

David Kennerly brings back many photos of Indochina. He shows them to Ford, who hangs some in the White House. Kennerly tells the president: "Cambodia is gone, and I don't care what the generals tell you; they're bullshitting you if they say that Vietnam has got more than three or four weeks left."

At the end of the minisummit in Palm Springs, Kissinger tells reporters that the United States is facing "a moral problem." When you have been tied to an ally for ten years and he wants to defend himself, is it suitable to suspend deliveries of materiel?

American leaders are sure the South Vietnamese won't retake the lost provinces. At most they could hold a defense perimeter around Saigon and force Hanoi to negotiate. The job at hand is to plan the evacuation of Americans and Vietnamese.

On television James Schlesinger, for his part, seems to offer a minimalist interpretation of events in South Vietnam: "It is plain that the great offensive is a phrase that probably should be in quotation marks. What we have had here is a partial collapse of South Vietnamese forces."[5] He explains that there have been few big battles since Ban Me Thuot. It's not a matter of a North Vietnamese victory, but rather of a South Vietnamese defeat. Interesting semantic nuance. With the implied suggestion also that Saigon's troops don't deserve aid, a widespread opinion in the United States, Schlesinger is no help to the president and Kissinger.

Who's responsible for these military disasters? In political circles that's an important question. Schlesinger says a simple and easy answer is impossible. He seems to be alluding indirectly to the president and Kissinger, rather loftily, when he says the country really doesn't need a "major confrontation between the executive and the legislature" at this point. A government whose most important figures seem to contradict one another in public can't manage crises very well and doesn't inspire confidence.

Multiplying the White House's problems, people have begun to murmur—and rumors spread quickly—that Nixon made secret promises. There are letters from Nixon to Thieu. The American presidential election looms on the 1976 horizon. Anything goes in politics. Erich von Marbod has mentioned the letters to his boss, Schlesinger. The secretary of defense has discussed them with Senator Henry Jackson, who says openly[6] that besides the Paris Agreement, there were "secret agreements."

Reading the letters, Ford is troubled.

General Phu, dug in at Nha Trang after the collapse of his MR 2, swings from dejection to euphoria. He too is plotting a new line of defense, north of Nha Trang. But with which of the units under his command?

The city of Nha Trang is calm.

One morning[7] the provincial chief—without telling Phu, without alerting the Americans—orders his agencies to shut down. Phu has set up his new headquarters in the same building. At first he doesn't notice that all the civil servants have vanished. Late in the morning he suddenly appears, dashing around the army's offices and shouting, "Out! Everybody out! Move it!"

Haggard, he shouts to his personal helicopter pilot, "We're leaving!"

And he leaves. By one in the afternoon the stupefying news is all over. Nha Trang has not been attacked. Some swear that NVA units are at the city gates, others that an ARVN division is "giving Nha Trang to the communists." Civilians pack and head for the airport, hoping to find seats on a plane, or for the docks, looking for a sailboat or motor launch. In town, soldiers open and plunder shuttered shops or, guns in hand, attack passersby, demanding their food, money and jewels. Soldiers from the Nha Trang garrison mingle with others just in from Hue and Danang. There are so many people on the waterfront that some are waiting waist-deep in the sea. Babies, women and old people have been smothered; their bodies lie where they fell, more or less hidden by ponchos.

A new Danang.

The panic grows. U.S. consul-general Moncrieff Spear confides to French vice-consul Henri Strahlheim that he can no longer accept any responsibility. The French are evacuated on aircraft chartered by their embassy. Three fathers of the Overseas Missions and one nun volunteer to stay behind; she will not leave the Vietnamese Carmelites in her charge. In the U.S. consulate's ambit are 200 American citizens, and even more Vietnamese employees. Civilians from Pleiku, Hue and Danang have joined the officers stationed at Nha Trang. They're waiting for planes from Air America, Bird Air, World Airways and Continental Air Services.

Hundreds of employees and their families are jammed into the courtyard of the U.S. consulate. They want to leave, and to be paid. Unfortunately the treasurer has fled, alone, with the treasury. To repulse assaults on the consulate by other Vietnamese aspirants, U.S. marines have to use force; they beat the crowd back, injuring some. It requires a helicopter shuttle to ferry refugees to the airport, six kilometers away.

Howard Archer, a CIA agent, goes around the fourth floor of the consulate with four colleagues and destroys a transmitter and documents. Despite his efforts the CIA, here also, leaves documents behind, as well as files—and employees. The evacuation is so badly organized that the last plane to take off, a C-46, leaves half empty. Another CIA agent, John Lewis, searches courageously and indefatigably for his Vietnamese colleagues in Nha Trang.[8]

The head of the CIA in Nha Trang is primarily concerned with Americans. His justification? For weeks now the fleeing Vietnamese have been leaving the Americans in the lurch.

The embassy in Saigon is partly responsible for the chaos. At 5:30 P.M. on the day of Phu's departure, George Jacobson, a special assistant to the ambassador, ill informed or losing his cool, instructs the consul general, "Get out of town now, you and the other Americans."

When the last helicopter is leaving the consulate, a pleading old man holds a child toward the Americans aboard. A passenger kicks the old man in the face. The child falls to the ground.[9]

This evacuation was unnecessary, at any rate premature. There were no North Vietnamese units at the gates of Nha Trang. The NVA commander in chief, bolder now, decides this time to leave a pocket in the rear and bypass Nha Trang. He orders Divisions 316 and 320 to advance directly on the port and bay of Cam Ranh, thirty-five kilometers south of Nha Trang.

The base at Cam Ranh is 260 kilometers from Saigon.

Various U.S. agencies proceed with unofficial evacuations. So the wife of the head of ARVN intelligence will be sent to Hawaii under the name of Mrs. W. LeGro, with the ambassador's approval. Vietnamese hector their friends and acquaintances at the embassy. International flights are functioning normally, but domestic Air Vietnam flights fall from forty to four a day. The republic is dwindling.

Long lines form before headquarters of the country's largest bank, Vietnam Thuong Tin. They want currency, or gold. The dollar is rising. "We're not freezing accounts, we still have 150 million piastres in reserve," says the governor of the Bank of Vietnam.

The price of rice, vegetables and spices doubles. Markets are out of tea and coffee; these come from the Central Highlands. Avocados too; they come from Ban Me Thuot. Thieu orders a solid cordon set up around the capital. Refugees are halted by barricades and isolated soldiers disarmed—if they're still carrying a rifle or revolver. Spyitis is rampant—they see Vietcong agents everywhere. The military government announces that anyone resisting arrest will be shot on the spot.

Chinese from Cholon throng outside the Formosan embassy, seeking visas. Word goes out that the Australians are issuing visas freely. The Australian consulate calls in police to disperse the mob around its offices.

Flights to Europe and the United States are booked solid. Not a seat left for Bangkok, Singapore, Hong Kong, Taipei.

Ambassador Martin gives orders aimed at curbing the panic. American firms back him fully. They take their precautions—women and children were evacuated at the end of March—but they announce officially that they are not leaving. The American Trading Company says, "We're on hold." IBM: "We'll stay as long as possible." Mobil continues its oil exploration in the China Sea; Exxon and Caltex employees stay on the job.

Newspaper ads reveal that some Vietnamese are liquidating their assets. So in the *Saigon Post*:[10]

The supply of apartments is well in excess of demand. Yet there was
frenzied construction well into March. And at the embassy they've just
given up those long sessions on the major problem of siting the new Hyatt
Hotel.

The ads reflect the times. Again in the *Saigon Post*, under his picture,
bearded and turbaned:

Also, the professor "corresponds with Marcos." He might be charged with
the indirect dissemination of false news reports. Among his references is
a letter of thanks from the Philippine president. The professor can be
contacted at the Hotel Pasteur, room 401, tel. 91236, from 10 A.M. to
6 P.M. He will see people for two weeks. "Professor Singh has made
predictions in the following countries: India, Thailand, Malaysia, Singapore, Indonesia, the Philippines, Ceylon, Pakistan, Hong Kong, Japan,
and Cambodia." Everybody in Saigon knows that Phnom Penh is encircled
and Marshal Lon Nol, chief of state, is preparing to leave "for treatment
abroad."

The South Vietnamese capital is abuzz with confused and contradictory
rumors, denied and revived. Big Minh himself says certain Vietnamese
officers suspect that President Thieu and the Americans in Washington
have concluded a secret agreement with the communists. "In demanding
Thieu's ouster," says the putative head of the Third Force, "the communists
tried to confuse the Americans, who fell into the trap. In fact, Thieu's
presence suits them [the communists] very well. The Americans are taking
what the communists say at face value and are keeping Thieu in power."
Rather tortuous.

They say a number of officers have confided to Big Minh, "One of these days we'll see Thieu in a communist uniform." Absurd, of course.

There's fresh talk of a military coup. Usually sparing of public statements, the chief of staff announces that "the battle for survival" has begun, "the historic moment has arrived. If we are resolute in battle, it is certain that we can win." Everybody listens for news from Washington. His interest in Vietnam renewed, Kissinger has postponed a trip to South America. He was to visit Argentina, Chile, Brazil, Peru and Venezuela. During a CBS morning broadcast, the South Vietnamese ambassador to Washington stated, "The United States has not honored the Paris Agreement. The world will probably conclude that it is better to be an ally of the communists than of the Americans." Reacting to this, Kissinger shows understanding: "We must have compassion for the South Vietnamese."

Splits yawn in the South Vietnamese government, this time in the legislature.[11] Usually more docile than the Chamber of Deputies, the Senate passes a motion hostile to the government, accusing Thieu "of abuses of power, of corruption." The president, say the senators, is also responsible for social injustices. Religious dignitaries fall in line. The archbishop of Saigon, Monsignor Nguyen Van Binh, demands the president's ouster. From Europe comes painful news: a vice prime minister, Tran Van Don, returning from Africa (where he had been trying to mobilize public opinion behind Saigon), stops over in Paris and acquires the firm conviction that "the three superpowers [the United States, USSR, China] have agreed that the two Vietnams should be unified under Hanoi's control." Principal source of this confidence? A friend of . . . Jacques Chirac, French prime minister. Chirac never saw Don.

Despite lack of contact with the Chinese communists, some Saigon politicians hoped they'd have had a moderating influence on Hanoi. Don has also stopped over in Hong Kong, where he's conferred with the U.S. consul general. Together they've worked out the number of South Vietnamese to be evacuated: a million will need help. The consul transmits Don's suggestions to Washington, where, unfortunately, they've settled on another figure: 250,000. The confusion, which could be seen from Mars, is noted by Moscow, Beijing and Hanoi.

Hong Kong is home to the best China-watchers. Many communist officials work there in Peking's banks and business houses. They speak more freely than elsewhere and their information is often reliable. On April 4 Leo Goodstadt, editor-in-chief of the *Far Eastern Economic Review*, one of the best weeklies in Asia if not the best, lunches with the U.S. consul general. Goodstadt has regular contacts with Hong Kong communists who reflect Beijing's point of view. The Chinese communists are worried about the territorial integrity of Cambodia and Laos. They disapprove highly of Hanoi's claim to be spokesman for all of Indochina. The North Vietnamese prime minister has never responded to a request by Beijing that Hanoi guarantee the independence of all countries in Indochina. The Chinese communists hear plenty of requests from Hanoi, which needs food and clothing for the zones "liberated" by its armies, but Beijing has never talked Hanoi into a meeting to discuss the full range of Asiatic problems, including the status of the Paracel and Spratly Islands, which China and South Vietnam dispute.

On Chinese maps the Spratlys are part of China. The Paracels are equidistant from the Chinese and Vietnamese coasts. The islands' main crop is guano. But there may be major offshore oil reserves in the area. The South Vietnamese garrison holding the tiny island of Song Tu Tay, in the Spratly archipelago, showing no sign of life, North Vietnamese ships landed troops to plant the PRG flag.[12] Many months earlier[13] there were skirmishes between the South Vietnamese and the Chinese communists. These latter occupied several islands after sinking South Vietnamese ships. To complicate the situation still further, Filipinos and Nationalist Chinese have also landed symbolic garrisons on other islands in the archipelago. Several Asiatic nationalisms are scrapping over these islands.

The main point: Vietnamese and Chinese communists are competing here. Thieu has never exploited these dissensions—these contradictions, as Hanoi and Peking would say. And now, when tensions between Hanoi and Peking are strong, they're saying in Saigon that the Chinese communists are ready to deliver South Vietnam to the North.

On April 4 Thieu receives his prime minister and Dr. Vien, vice prime minister without portfolio and chief of the South Vietnamese delegation in the negotiations at La Celle-Saint-Cloud. Khiem says a shake-up isn't enough to solve domestic problems.

Dr. Vien says,

> Mr. President, if you leave now, there's a good chance of real trouble. If you stay on and continue the same policy, the government will be isolated. . . . With your permission, we suggest you take three steps. To quiet rumors, say flatly that you won't run in the next presidential election, that you won't seek a third term. To reestablish confidence in the army, call a council of generals. Delegate full power to it. Let it direct military operations! And last, to make the government more efficient, allow more autonomy.

Thieu answers calmly, "Let's take them in order. You want me to leave. I am elected by the people and will not leave unless the people ask me to. No resolution by the Senate, or some small group that wants me out, can make me leave. You may ask, how can the people express their opinion? We'll set up a referendum."

Dr. Vien shakes his head and murmurs, "In times like these it's hard to hold a referendum."

Thieu:

> Then we'll hold it when we can. You tell me to say I won't run for a third term. That would be possible in Europe or the United States. Johnson was president of the United States until the last day of his mandate. But today in Vietnam if I say I won't run, do you know what will happen? Tomorrow nobody will go to work and nobody will obey my orders. I couldn't even ask Binh [chief of police] to break up a demonstration. There'd be chaos everywhere. I might as well quit! A council of generals! Why? [Air Marshal] Ky is talking about it. And you suggest the same thing to me! What do you all want? For military matters we have the Joint General Staff; that's enough. A council of generals would complicate everything. It reminds me of the council of generals in 1964 and 1965, with one coup d'état after another. Don't bring it up again! Let the chief of staff do his job. Until now he's done it well.

Thieu rarely lavishes such praise on his chief of staff. And the civil government?

"The government," says the president, "already has full powers. It doesn't know how to use them. It doesn't do what has to be done."

The prime minister doesn't raise his voice to the president, but ventures, "Mister President, we've lost fourteen provinces. No government anywhere else could stand after a catastrophe like that. There's been no punishment, either in the government or on the general staff. I'd be happy to play the scapegoat."

Thieu, without hesitation: "You want to resign? I accept. I'll announce it this evening on television. What shall I say? I'm not going to tell them you can't form a new government."

Khiem smiles. Thieu continues: "Why give a reason anyway? I have to name your successor, or there'll be speculation. In this country they speculate about everything. Let's check out the prime-ministerables."

Thieu takes out a list of people, drawn up by Khiem:[14] "First, there's Doctor Do. He'd accept. Ky would like that, because Ky wants my job, and if Doctor Do becomes prime minister, he'll support Ky's candidacy in the next elections. Those two are very close. No, not Do!"

Thieu knows that Ky and Father Thanh have been meeting at the Air Officers Club for ten days or so. They want a coalition government. Clever Ky does not serve on the committee that considers this. He's busy establishing "liaisons" with politicians.

"Professor Huy, then?" asks the president. "A good theoretician. No experience, he never ran a ministry, he wouldn't make a good prime minister. Lam [president of the Senate]? He could do it, but God knows what the Americans whispered in his ear on his last trip to the United States. From the moment he got back he schemed to have the Senate pass a motion of defiance against me. He wouldn't mind being prime minister; it would help him in the next elections. . . . He doesn't fool me. . . . There remains Mr. Can. Well, he's all right. . . . Honest, and he has experience. He's run the Chamber [of Deputies] for two years, a hard job. And he's a well-trained administrator. I'll call him."

Thieu goes into the next room and returns smiling. "Can is really surprised! He's coming."

A bit later, an aide de camp comes in: "The president of the Chamber of Deputies."

That evening, Thieu announces the nomination of Can, an unexpected candidate and a colorless personality. Thieu promises to "retake the lost provinces." He will never agree to a coalition government with the communists. There's only one way to bring about peace: general elections in conformity with the Paris Agreement. The military defeats of recent weeks are due to cowardice and defeatism in the army, to the treachery of the Montagnards, to the machinations of communist agents, and, the president adds, to broadcasts by the BBC and the Voice of America.

And above all, to the Americans, who have not kept their promises.

Two hours and fifteen minutes after this meeting, a tragic event overshadows ministerial shuffling altogether.

One of the last letters Khiem receives as prime minister is from one of his assistants for public health, Doctor Pham Quang Dan:

Subject: Emigration of 1,400 Orphans to the United States.

Mr. Prime Minister,

There are at present 1,400 orphans in Saigon sponsored by international charitable organizations and waiting for departure overseas where adoptive parents are ready to take them in charge. The Minister of Public Health and the International Rescue Committee want to resolve this problem immediately in order to attend to other more important problems. Moreover, the emigration of these orphans will shock the world, especially the United States, and will be beneficial to the Republic of Vietnam.

At this moment, two World Airways Boeing 727s are available. Mr. Daly, president of that airline, is well known in political circles. . . . Mr. Daly has pointed out to us that their [the orphans'] emigration and that of a million

inhabitants fleeing regions occupied by the communists
would provide good propaganda for Vietnam, especially by
the in-depth coverage that American television and newspapers will give it.

I therefore beg you, Mr. Prime Minister, to agree to this
proposal.

In law no Vietnamese adult, child or baby has a right to leave the
country without an exit visa. So for the orphans there has to be an excep-
tional collective decision. Tired of Daly's badgering, Ambassador Martin
arranged for a U.S. army Galaxy, a C-5A, the biggest transport plane in
the world. On arrival, the Galaxy unloaded arms and ammunition.

At Tan Son Nhut airport, 243 orphans, some handicapped, wait in
overheated buses for a formal decision authorizing their departure. Officials
decree that the letter from Dr. Dan to the prime minister has the value of
a collective visa. The press has been alerted. A good story: they unload
arms, they load orphans. A great name for the front page: *Operation Baby-
Lift*. To accompany the orphans, the U.S. Embassy assigns medical personnel and spouses of American employees. Trying to send families out
inconspicuously, they grasp at all sorts of pretexts, illness, home leave. . . .
More than sixty adults will board the plane. One hundred and sixty children
throng the plane's upper deck, attached two by two to the seats. Wrapped
warmly in blankets, the others are locked in the baggage compartment.
The little ones suffer from the heat and cry. The men and women escorting
them are kept busy. Cameras roll. Close-up on a pretty little head. Pull
back to reveal the Galaxy taking off heavily.

Aboard the plane, they hear an explosion ten minutes later. One of
the crew cries that the rear doors have blown out. The Galaxy loses altitude,
banks above the sea. The oxygen masks drop from the overhead. But there
aren't enough of them. Anyway, how could a baby use one alone? The
nearest airport is at Cap Saint-Jacques, but the plane heads back toward
Saigon and crashes in a rice paddy. Concrete dikes break up half the
Galaxy. A helicopter pilot maneuvering above the airport alerts the base.
Other choppers rush to the scene of the tragedy. Some of the children
have been flung into the muck of the paddy. About sixty are recovered.
All the others are dead.

At Tan Son Nhut, Jim Eckes, manager of Continental Air Services,
asks the Galaxy's copilot, "Why didn't you land at Cap Saint-Jacques, at
Vung Tau?

"Vung *what*?" the pilot answers.

Nurses pass muddy children along, washing them clean: "This one is
dead. . . . That one is alive. . . . This one?"

Ambassador Martin phones Eckes: "Jim, try to find out how many
people were aboard that plane."

Eckes checks out civil and military offices, and passenger manifests.

All the passenger lists are different. At the last minute, they took on escorts whose names weren't listed. Eckes calls the ambassador. "I can't give you an official list."

Eckes' hangars and offices are at the airport, near the French Aéro-Club. Like many experts, he wonders. Why didn't the Galaxy's crew know there was an airport at Vung Tau? Why had the captain agreed to take these children aboard an ill-equipped aircraft? Why didn't they bring a Pan Am Boeing to Saigon? A well-equipped 707 is waiting in Guam with personnel and volunteer hostesses.

Was Operation Baby-Lift more attractive symbolically if carried out by military Galaxies? In television news all across the United States, Americans see the horrible drama. They will also see President Ford welcome other orphans from other flights at the San Francisco airport. A new high in bad taste: Ford is present for the arrival of the first flight of the new Baby-Lift. In Saigon, bitter and desperate or cynical, a Vietnamese tells some Americans, "These children are nice souvenirs, like the porcelain elephants you love so much. Too bad some were broken. Don't worry about it: there are more."

General Khiem holds his last cabinet meeting, then goes to the palace for lunch with the president and several other guests. Thieu is relaxed, even playful.

Former vice-president Huong fulminates: "The firing squad for colonels and generals who abandoned their posts these last weeks!"

"Even if they've deserted," Thieu answers, "we can't execute men just like that, in cold blood. We have to open an investigation, and try the guilty parties by court-martial."

Dr. Vien suggests they publicize the government's intention to punish officers responsible for the series of retreats. They could announce a commission including senators and deputies from the lost provinces. With the reflexes of a general who doesn't like civilians sticking their noses into army matters, Thieu answers, "It's the chief of staff's problem. He's looking into it."

Several investigations are indeed under way, but they're aimed more at evaluating losses than at naming those responsible for, or guilty of, the debacle.

Luncheon ends. A few guests follow the president. Thieu halts under a second-floor veranda, before a Vietnamese flag, three wide red stripes on a yellow background; he points. "You see, all is written. I don't know who had the idea of putting three red stripes on the flag. There will be three Vietnams."

Thieu does not mean the three regions, the three *ky*, the North, the Center, the South. . . .

14

Not a Thread, not a Needle

"There will be no evacuation until I authorize it," Graham Martin tells Jim Eckes.

Ambassadorial injunctions or no, dozens of networks are in play, set up by civilians or the U.S. military. There are those who feel that the ambassador is shying from his responsibilities on the pretext of avoiding panic.

Near the Continental Air Services hangars, Jim Eckes sees a black van whose driver wants to cross their area. CIA vans are easy to spot. Eckes halts the vehicle. From the front seat a haughty U.S. air force captain says arrogantly, "I'm authorized to go wherever I want."

"You seem to be on my turf," says Eckes.

The two men proceed to a violent argument. Eckes takes the captain's name. Then he follows the van, which heads for a C-130 on an off-ramp. About twenty girls in flashy clothes and heavy makeup, obviously not from the Convent of the Birds, spill out of the van and board the C-130. When the report reaches Martin, he lays into the air attaché, who at first denies everything and is then shown proof—and is officially evacuated at the ambassador's request.

Alexandre Casella, a Swiss citizen, half journalist, half international civil servant, is a consultant to the High Commission on Refugees in the North Vietnamese capital. Hanoi is calm, almost gloomy.

The HCR, in the North as in the South, helps scattered populations to return to their original villages. The HCR buys tractors from the Soviets and textiles from the Chinese and gives it all to Vietnamese. Its primary goal now is preparation for a flood of refugees if the South falls. Casella is concentrating on fertilizer, chickens, small patched-up carts, so the peasants can settle in—or rather resettle. In Hanoi, Casella deals mainly with the Ministry of Foreign Affairs or the Ministry of Agriculture, and PRG people. No one is making any predictions. Casella notices a slogan on a wall: "Vietnam, the conscience of the world." Sartre's phrase. Casella has never seen Tran Duc Thao, graduate of the Ecole Normale, philosopher, Marxist-phenomenologist, whom French visitors often ask about. Whenever a foreigner wants to meet him, the authorities make excuses, from the prime minister down: the philosopher is sick, he lives too far away, the roads to his village are cut, flooded, the philosopher has no bike, you'll see him another time, during another trip.

At the Thong Nhat Hotel a Russian, correspondent for *Pravda*, tells Casella, "These Vietnamese are crazy. They're going to stir up the Americans. And the Americans may take it out on us, and say the Russians egged the Vietnamese on."

Is the Russian sincere? Or is he performing an elementary exercise in disinformation?

In Saigon the political pot is boiling. The new prime minister, who impresses nobody, will take ten days to pull together a government. Ten days during which the Republic of Vietnam will have a president and no government. In this power vacuum the opposition—veteran politicians trained in the French school and younger ones more Americanized—searches for identity, quarrels, lays out projects that would seem unrealistic even in peacetime. They set up committees, they scheme, they seem utterly incapable of forming even the embryo of a coalition. Take two South Vietnamese politicians and you end up with three contradictory opinions and a public wrangle. Take a hundred North Vietnamese leaders and officially you have *one* opinion, or rather, the party line.

Opposition to President Thieu, whether or not its aim is to establish a Third Force, is a nebula with Big Minh its center. Undeniably, it lurks in the urban middle and lower classes. But at this point, what cities can the Republic of Vietnam claim? Saigon, Tay Ninh (which the North Vietnamese are harassing), Can Tho, My Tho. . . . The opposition is a multitude of groups and subgroups without much influence in the countryside. And in just these last days, some new parties have filed their bylaws!

Among Thieu's opponents the Catholics, highly anticommunist, distrust the Third Force—according to them, it's playing the communist game. Since the archbishop of Saigon called for Thieu's resignation, some of the Catholics have slipped into opposition. A majority of Buddhists remains apolitical, cautious and patient. The most active of them gather around the An Quang pagoda and the Venerable Thich Tri Quang. Another influential Venerable, Thich Tam Chau, has supported Thieu; now he too is calling for resignation. Father Thanh, creator of the People's Movement Against Corruption, is still hurling invective. But Thanh isn't supporting Big Minh.

The Third Force doesn't bother Thieu. Some of them, like Senator Vu Van Mau, irritate him at most. In the president's view, his most dangerous and powerful opponent is the former air force commander in chief who was vice president and Thieu's own prime minister, the dashing Air Marshal Nguyen Cao Ky. Here's a serious rival.

Ky lives at the Tan Son Nhut base, where he has a villa near the air operations center. Every day he has pilots in for a drink. He's maintained all his contacts in the "mafia of Tonkinese generals and politicians," born in the North. Ky always seems to have a coup d'état on hold. He's been pawing the ground since January. During the NVA attack on Ban Me Thuot, he was on his experimental farm near that city. He keeps one last bauble from his past splendor, a personal helicopter. He saw General Phu at Nha Trang, then Vien in Saigon. With Hollywood swagger, he challenged the chief of staff: "Give me twenty M-48 tanks, two marine or ranger battalions, artillery and air support, and I'll try to liberate Ban Me Thuot." Unable to make that decision himself, Vien telephoned Thieu. The president sent his compliments to the aviator, adding: "I'll think about it, and talk to my advisers." The two men are bound by an open hostility and complicity. Ky served under Thieu. Impulsive, courageous, a blunderer if not worse—no one has forgotten that he wanted a Hitler for Vietnam— Ky, even more than Thieu, distrusts foreigners, though his first wife was French. Trained in France and Morocco, he abhors what he sees as a sort of anti-American Gaullo-communism. He detests the Americans almost as much, with their real or imagined arrogance and their refusal to let him carry the war to the North.[1]

Of the general officers who emerged during the second Indochinese war, Ky enjoys hearing it said that he is in war one of the most effective and in politics one of the clumsiest. In his own way, Thieu can count on every element of Vietnamese society; the air marshal, mostly on the military castes. Thieu is superstitious; not his rival.

Ky ought to have been named Ho Chi Minh—in Vietnamese, "he who shines." In his forced retreat, he's calmed down. The actor has no more audience. He's given up the sparkling white jumpsuits that made foreign correspondents laugh but drew votes when he ran for office.

Family ties count enormously in both Vietnams, but political-military and military-political alliances, often established along family lines, count just as much. Right now the important people in Saigon, or those who want to be, share a past and especially an old conspiracy—which, despite mistrust and hatred, unites them all. Thieu and Ky, Khiem and Don, Big Minh and others, all acting in concert, overthrew President Diem twelve years ago. That's a strong common bond. In 1963 Big Minh promoted little Ky, intelligent but not cultured, to head up the air force. Impatient, embittered because spurned, the air marshal sometimes pretends to think the generals are too political. But way down deep he believes a coup d'état is a revolution. Now in early April he believes the war must be won or the front stabilized before he can afford the luxury of political machinations. His anti-Americanism is his capital. He's been sounding out the military for some time, insisting that Thieu must go. The president knows this, but doesn't dare arrest Ky. Relations among the 1963 conspirators are often expressed in code. Thieu sends Ky a warning by imprisoning men close to the frisky aviator—several superior officers and a civilian, Nguyen Thien Nhon. Immediately afterward, to give the impression that he's purifying society, Thieu jails others, or places them under house arrest: Huynh Thanh Vi, president of the Journalists Association, and Nguyen Van Ngan, a member of his own party and moreover a former adviser to the president. No strong leadership without ritual purification. No purification without arrests. He leaves it to the minister of the interior to explain these arrests: "Several mean-spirited elements have exploited the people's present state of confusion to sow subversion, create disorder behind the lines, support an attempted military coup and satisfy their personal ambitions. These elements have been arrested and detained by security agencies. An investigation is under way." More than the arrests, the communiqué itself encourages the idea, already current in Saigon, of a putsch. Ky makes no headway. His generals drop away; worse yet, he senses that the Americans would not support him. At a certain level everybody knows what's happening; there are agents everywhere, paid or not. Alerted by his branch in Saigon, William Colby, director of the CIA, sends instructions from Washington on April 6. The company wants to prevent Thieu's fall. Colby cables: "If the CIA were to take part in Thieu's destabilization, it would be an institutional and national disaster." He harped on the theme in several cables to Polgar: "Whatever you do let's not lose Thieu." All the same they have to allow for the worst, the president's ouster. Colby says, "If things become complicated, your job is to give advice. For my part, my recommendation would be to do everything possible so Thieu and his family can get out safe and sound." Every CIA director since 1963 has been haunted by the ghost of the assassinated Diem. The U.S. Embassy more than acquiesced in his overthrow.

The situation seems sufficiently serious for the Americans to violate the Paris Agreement a bit and again become "military advisers." Officers around General Homer Smith feverishly concoct plans to help the ARVN reorganize. The old quarrel resurfaces: the Americans want to mingle fresh recruits and seasoned troops. They think they can re-equip eighteen infantry battalions and three artillery batteries by about April 15. They draw diagrams for May 20 and September 30. The ARVN wants to form brand new battalions, regiments and brigades. General Vien has submitted a desperately unrealistic project—KBC 4 002—to the U.S. military attaché.[2] On paper an army springs to life as if by spontaneous generation: the 3rd

Airborne Brigade, the 22nd Infantry Division, the 7th Ranger Group, military police companies, engineer battalions, field hospitals. The ends are set forth, not the means. Vien writes complacently that "the militia units of the Regional and Popular Forces in MR 1 and MR 2 will have to be broken up to compensate for the shortage of manpower in the new infantry divisions." Most of those units were "broken up" during the retreats from Kontum and Pleiku and the stampedes from Hue and Danang. Those who managed to escape are scattered around Saigon with their families. Document KBC 4 002 stipulates that at battalion level the reorganization should be completed "in two weeks." And the shortage of warm bodies, the manpower? "They will be replaced later, or drafted." Officers of the central logistic command lay plans as if they could operate without transport, mobilizing recruits in the traditional manner, with time to train them and fling them into the imminent battles. Because, despite rumors of haggling and negotiation, of a voluntary halt by the North Vietnamese divisions, the latter continue to advance. On the highest South Vietnamese military level, they fantasize as much as, if not more than, in the government and the opposition.

The general staff is paying a stiff price for twenty years of mistakes, their own and their American allies'. Vien fell into the habit of agreeing to plans drawn up by the Americans. It's a bit late for innovation.

Do South Vietnamese soldiers lack what Clausewitz calls "warlike virtue"? Certainly not. From 1960 to 1974, 250,000 South Vietnamese soldiers were killed in action, and they were not all shot in the back. The international press more often underlined their faults and their routs than their virtues and their victories. Clausewitz defines warlike virtue:

> It is distinct from simple bravery and even from enthusiasm for the cause. The former is certainly a necessary component; but just as bravery, a natural tendency in an individual, may arise in a soldier (as part of an army) from habit and training, it must take on a different aspect than among civilians. It must reject the impulse to unbridled individual activity, and respond to higher demands—obedience, order, rule and method. Enthusiasm for the cause lends life and fire to an army's warlike virtue, but is not an indispensable element.

Soldiers North and South are mostly of peasant origin. Collectively, their morale is very different. South Vietnamese soldiers know roughly what they're fighting *against*, but rarely what they're fighting *for*. The North Vietnamese are indoctrinated; even if they're far from unanimously persuaded of the socialist system's value, most believe in the need to liberate the country.

The communists have been able to exploit a latent natural xenophobia, based on one conviction: We have to throw the foreign devils out. In general the North Vietnamese and Vietcong have confidence in their chiefs at all levels, from the cell of three fighting men, base of the military pyramid, all the way to the top. Not so the South Vietnamese. They're too aware of nepotism in appointments, for one thing.

In the North the generals never show any possible doubt of the war's result, or of one another. They mask their rivalries and hatreds. Never in the South. All the way up to the presidency—Thieu is commander in chief—conflicts are out in the open. Since January how many foot soldiers have wondered if the president and the prime minister are really in harmony? Not to mention the chief of staff. The crisis in command at the upper echelons is profound.

In the North, a totalitarian opacity reinforces discipline.

From 1965 to 1973, in every operation from the simplest to the most complex—patrols, opening and interdicting highways, attacks along a front or in depth, search and destroy missions, parachute drops or helicopter transport—South Vietnamese superior and general officers called in massive artillery fire, extensive helicopter gunship support, and fighter bombers when they couldn't rely on heavy bombing by B-52 squadrons from Thailand, Guam or the Philippines. They're still counting on all that. They can't imagine fighting the war without it. Their enemy wages war with no air support in the South.

Encysted in this mode of thought, or rather *non*-thought, the general staff has adopted the habit of executing to the letter—after translation—offensive or defensive plans detailed by American officers. They've lost all sense of initiative. That's what strikes Israelis come to observe the ARVN. Vien acknowledges that the general staff plays only a consultative role.[3] If they weren't so aware of it, one might say that South Vietnamese officers suffer a double inferiority complex, across the table from the Americans and across the lines from the North Vietnamese.

Whatever the numbers on paper, why are the South Vietnamese short of fighting men in 1975, just as they were five or ten years before?

Is the ARVN in 1975 short of arms and ammunition as Ford, Thieu, Vien and others claim? Some American diplomats, like Frank Snepp, don't think so. The truth seems complicated. Supplies are plentiful—the North Vietnamese turn them up as they advance—but not always appropriate. At the beginning of April 1975, there was a shortage of spare parts for tanks and planes, but there were plenty of expensive radios, state-of-the-art but useless. The army's been rationing mortar and howitzer shells for two years. During big battles in 1972, the 105s fired an average of 180 shells a day. These last three months, 10. The high command and the decentralized provincial arsenals are misers with their ammunition. Distribution is bad and there's a lot of pilferage. Since January 1975 the army has experienced spot shortages of gas and oil. In any South Vietnamese village you can see young men on a street corner selling military fuel, easily recognizable in its red can—so it won't be stolen or resold. Everywhere civilians can buy small military supplies and goods: batteries for cars or helicopters, spare parts for trucks, tires, khaki blankets and mosquito netting. Ponchos, small-sized jungle boots, fatigue pants and jackets, underpants, socks, caps, even helmets. They're all swiped from army stocks with the authorization or connivance of the chain of command.

Tran Van Don, now minister of defense, estimates that about one-third of the superior officers and generals are *clean*, an elegant way to say that two-thirds are crooks and embezzlers. Father Thanh, elaborating his war on corruption, estimates that ARVN officers have dealt M-16s at 20,000 piastres apiece to the Hoa Hao paramilitary forces in the Delta. At least the arms stay on the nationalist side. Since 1973 there hasn't been much sign of small arms sold indirectly to the Vietcong. ARVN soldiers, even worse paid than the officers—a soldier earns around 20,000 piastres a month, a division general five times that—can't live on their pay. The temptation to steal and sell spare parts is great. It seems almost built-in.

Military discipline and good citizenship can only be weak in this context. It's too late to change matters, to make vanished trucks run on fuel that can't be found. Vien and his staff send useless recommendations into a void.

Graham Martin thinks the ARVN can still hold and counterattack if it pulls itself together. The American officers around General Smith are more pessimistic. Intelligence chief Colonel William LeGro considers that even with supplemental aid from Congress it's "already too late." He's told General Weyand how he feels. Even B-52 raids won't stop the North Vietnamese.

They're moving forward along the great axial routes, passing through small market towns and big cities. A renewal of strategic bombing would kill tens of thousands of South Vietnamese civilians. The B-52s have become a symbol. The U.S. military and well-informed South Vietnamese don't forget that the bombers never did succeed in closing the Ho Chi Minh trail, or cutting North Vietnamese supply lines.

Like Thieu but from a position of strength, the North Vietnamese are fighting on the military front and the political-diplomatic front. Hanoi's simple strategy: We have to win in the field before the monsoon, giving the impression all the while that we're ready to negotiate. The diplomatic factor seems as important as the military. In the real diplomatic campaign under way, the PRG has to be in the foreground. The military front is in Vietnam, the diplomatic front all over the world but mostly in Paris.

These days it would be hard to claim that "revolutionary forces," in reality NVA divisions, are instruments of peace. So on French television and in several interviews with the print media, Mme. Nguyen Thi Binh, the PRG's charming and indomitable minister of foreign affairs, explains that Saigon's enemies are on . . . the defensive.[4] "If we're attacking South Vietnam right now [a reality rarely admitted], it's only because we're forced to by the Americans' and the Thieu government's violations of the Paris Agreement. We want the United States to put an end to their interference in South Vietnam's domestic affairs." And she asks, as usual, for a government in Saigon "that favors peace, independence, democracy," etc.

In the DRV democratic communist principle rules. On April 6, citizens elect the National Assembly: 529 candidates for 499 seats. With two exceptions, all candidates are from the national front, which includes the Communist Party, the Democratic Party and the Socialist Party, these last two theoretically representing the middle classes and the intelligentsia. The democratic process provided by the Paris Agreement and the North's democratic centralism, with the Communist Party absolutely preeminent, are not quite identical.

The Hanoi party daily explains the spirit of this election: "Each voter is expressing his sympathy for—and his confidence in—the leadership of the Party and its socialist state." That is not reassuring to the South Vietnamese in general and the Saigonese in particular. In one sense, the ordinary people of South Vietnam are perhaps more attached to religious liberties than to political liberties. Interviewed by Hanoi's "progressive Catholic" newspaper, the *Chinh Nghia*, one of the Communist Party secretaries, Xuan Thuy, says the workers' party respects freedom of religion, adding, "We are opposed to superstition and to those who use religion against the interests of the people and the country, and to obstruct socialist construction."

In Hanoi, the special cell assigned on March 15 to conduct "a diplomatic offensive" has clarified its directives. Ambassadors of the Democratic Republic and PRG representatives must state flatly that a coalition government is the order of the day and imply that, once established in Saigon, it would have a certain independence. A broad and effective maneuver.

On April 5 in Paris the ambassador of the DRV and the PRG representative met separately with François de Laboulaye, director of political affairs at the Quai d'Orsay. The French diplomat and the PRG envoy are agreed: there must be a coalition government with the PRG in control. The French government believes that Thieu will not last long. The Quai d'Orsay has ordered its vice-consul in Danang to contact branches of the PRG. French material aid will be distributed by the PRG.

De Laboulaye says that France hopes the coalition government will develop along the lines of Yugoslavia's, with some slack for independence. It should not identify itself entirely with the DRV.

In these exchanges, four venerable hypotheses of French diplomacy are implicit: (1) North Vietnamese communists are nationalists first, then communists; (2) in Southeast Asia Hanoi represents a sort of suspended Titoism; (3) the PRG is a separate entity, even if (4) most of its important men are old communists, avowed or not. In the PRG there exist Catholics, Buddhists, enlightened bourgeois who are not Marxists, socialists. . . .

Meetings like this, official or unofficial, are held everywhere over the following weeks, in Hanoi and Saigon, in Stockholm, East Berlin, Warsaw, Prague, Algiers. . . . In their homes over a cup of tea, or in Vietnamese restaurants, the DRV's men and the PRG's, diplomats and journalists, driving in the same nail, happily repeat what their listeners want to hear. In confidential tones that make questioners feel rather privileged, these Vietnamese allow, "We know that there are real differences between North and South and we have to take them into account."

Sometimes, as if inadvertently, PRG people sigh, "We and our friends in the North don't agree on everything." This is occasionally true. A PRG man in Paris, Phan Van Ba, small and swarthy, little educated but decisive, is doubtless sincere when he talks about differences between North and South, between the DRV and the PRG.

While this remarkable diplomatic offensive develops, Hanoi is deciding that it's time to loose the communist cadres: speeches about the formation of a coalition government are a "smokescreen." The point is to take power via revolutionary violence. Even Churchill said: "In time of war, truth is so precious that it must be surrounded by a guard of lies." In Saigon, a few Americans glean information about the "smokescreen." One of his agents told Frank Snepp about it several times beginning April 7, an agent in the heart of communist headquarters in the South, COSVN (Central Office for South Vietnam), who has always supplied accurate information. He's categorical about this: the communists will not negotiate under any circumstances. Neither the head of the CIA, Polgar, nor the head of the embassy, Martin, takes this report seriously. The Americans are no longer paying much attention to disagreements between the French ambassadors in Saigon and Hanoi. The CIA has everything in hand, not only because diplomats pass word along to their American colleagues, but also because the Company has broken the French code and opened a lot of mail. Some of the gurus at the Quai d'Orsay think, more than Ambassador Mérillon does, that they can play one card, Big Minh: establishing a coalition government is the policy laid down by President Valéry Giscard d'Estaing. Philippe Richer, in Hanoi, does not share that view. Despite soothing Leninist statements by high officials in the North Vietnamese Ministry of Foreign Affairs, and by the prime minister himself, Richer is convinced that one political force will win the South, the Communist Party. It's not pleasant, but that's the way it is. There is only "one rock to which we must attach our policy, the Vietnamese Communist Party," says one of his cables.[5] Mérillon thinks they can still avoid the worst. Classic phenomenon: a Richer, socialist, puts no trust in communist sweet talk, but a Mérillon, classic moderate-conservative, thinks it can be useful.

On April 8 Pham Van Dong receives Richer. The prime minister approves of what the French "are doing in South Vietnam." Of course, they want to oust Thieu! Persuasive, articulate, Pham Van Dong evokes the idyllic ties that could be established between Paris and Hanoi. The Quai d'Orsay laps it up, in the name of the common colonial past and of the

French-speaking community. "We'll do great things," Pham Van Dong promises.

The prime minister explains that French technicians and investors can help the North Vietnamese develop their oil reserves. A tempting prospect for the Quai. They can imagine French companies taking over American businesses, drilling in South Vietnamese waters. Pham Van Dong opens vast economic horizons. Richer is not fooled but nevertheless thinks there is much sincerity in this prime minister who speaks good French and who feels a cultural attachment to France.

Reinforced everywhere, but originating in Hanoi's diplomatic offensive, the assumption that the PRG must play a role, is *going* to play a role, takes hold in Saigon, too. Convenient assumption! Of course they also count on traditional divergences between Northerners and Southerners, Tonkinese and Cochin-Chinese. These communists aren't crazy. They will not collectivize agriculture and socialize South Vietnamese industry. Besides, the NLF's program, before it became the PRG, allowed for a significant private sector. Saigon will become an economic enclave, like Hong Kong, a kind of Singapore holding tight to its capitalist privileges. The last hopeful argument: we're in Asia, estranged brothers will be reunited. Even some of the French community in Saigon suppose there will be a way to stay on. Not forever, but for five, ten, perhaps twenty years. There's proof of Hanoi's intelligence and good will, like Pham Van Dong repeating to his French interviewers, diplomats or journalists, that South Vietnam's "particular features and characteristics" will be respected. Moreover, the leaders of a united Vietnam or, better, of the two Vietnams, will need Western credits, financial support and European technology. You know, these fellows in Hanoi don't want to depend altogether on Moscow and Beijing. It's in the Vietnamese communists' interest to build bridges to the West, and thus to show moderation in South Vietnam. . . . Proof of communist good will—from Moscow to Hanoi—is mainly palaver.

At the Elysée Palace (where foreign policy is always in the domain reserved to the head of state) as at the Quai d'Orsay, they pay more attention to Saigon's ambassador than Hanoi's. Valéry Giscard d'Estaing has always had the feeling that an accommodation with Vietnam's leaders was possible. He said as much to Kissinger and Ford late last year, during the Antilles summit. Hints accumulate reinforcing the idea of a PRG with vague leeway. The PRG is setting up a governmental infrastructure. In Paris, Pham Van Ba cancels a trip he'd planned for mid-April. According to one of his assistants, the PRG and the French government must—urgently—examine three problems in depth. First, a detailed sketch of economic aid *to the PRG*. Then, a close survey of telecommunications between France and the zones officially controlled *by the PRG*. Last, and most important, review the status and functions of the *PRG mission* in Paris. How shall it issue visas? Here is a sudden suggestion of sovereignty. At the very least, it seems, the PRG mission to Paris will comprise a consulate. The Democratic Republic of Vietnam has one. So another consulate should represent another government. The Quai's diplomats adore legal constructions. They don't foresee total independence for the PRG in the months and years to come, but they hope the coalition government will retain a certain autonomy. Word on the PRG's relative independence buzzes over a number of circuits, particularly Sweden, always in the forefront of Hanoi's defenders. Prime Minister Olaf Palme takes part in demonstrations "against the American war." In Stockholm Western and Eastern diplomats are in contact with another PRG head of mission, Tran Huu Kha. He tells everybody how astonished he is at the speed of "the revolutionary troops' " advance.

When his questioners mention NVA infantry divisions, Kha neither confirms nor denies. He smiles. How many misunderstandings arise from that smile! If you speak to him about the Third Force and Big Minh, Kha smiles again. He insists on one point: "We'll need our European friends."

The PRG's object is not to take Saigon by force, Kha also emphasizes: Thieu must go, Thieu must resign. Afterward, with the Third Force, the PRG will establish an independent government. Western diplomats and reporters study their information and summaries of conversations, send off cables and articles. The most optimistic are still wondering whether the PRG's rose-colored notions reflect Hanoi's desires. The most pessimistic, many of them American, call it all maneuvering.

In Hanoi the PRG issues a "ten-point declaration"[6] about its policy in the newly liberated zones. Declarations from Hanoi and the PRG are often in ten points, a no doubt pleasing number, quasi-magical. The promising last point "guarantees the life and property of foreigners." Much of this property is private. . . . For the rest, a policy of reunion and reconciliation, etc., equality among majority and minority peoples, between men and women, freedom of belief also but—no doubt an oversight—not of religion. The PRG will help peasants, fishermen, "forestry occupations and salt production." As for ARVN officers and men, "those who leave enemy ranks to cross to the liberated zones or who remain voluntarily in the liberated zones" should report to the revolutionary government. "They will be assisted in their search for work." It may be assumed from this that they will not be imprisoned. Where few South Vietnamese soldiers choose to remain in PRG zones, other conclusions may be drawn. The PRG declaration cancels "the puppet government" and creates a "revolutionary government of the people at all levels." All chancelleries pore over this information and cables and documents from North and South—dissect and analyze them.

The communist diplomatic offensive also surfaces in Saigon on April 11 when Tran Van Du, director of a medical lab, who says he speaks for the PRG, meets an emissary from Don, defense minister in the new cabinet. The PRG, says Du, wants to negotiate. But Thieu's presence "is not negotiable." The PRG, Du continues, is open to all suggestions. But alas, he cannot deal with the new team in power. A government that might succeed it, had at its head "a neutral person," and comprised elements of the Third Force, could also include "pro-American politicians." Who? Du can't supply any names, except . . . Don's! How encouraging!

At the Cercle Sportif they're saying that Colonel Vo Dong Giang, PRG man at Camp Davis, has tried to contact Big Minh to negotiate precisely that issue, the formation of a coalition government. True? False? Pious hopes? No one knows. Not many Saigonese frequent the Cercle Sportif, but most listen to Radio Liberation, the voice of the PRG. It calls for all to lay down arms and cease killing one another: "Because we are all Vietnamese . . . , the government will take not so much as a thread or a needle from the people."

Many families in the South have a relative, a *tap ket*, a Southern resister gone North. Often he was not communist when he left. Perhaps he still isn't. Perhaps a large number of those about to arrive aren't communists.

The lab director's approach is favorably received—the more so because he's said that "for the moment, PRG strategy is to cut off Saigon from the rest of the country. . . . The PRG doesn't want to attack Saigon." It's only a matter of isolating the city to effect a change in government. The ultimate solution will be delicately political. Du went so far as to state, "There will be no uprising and no bloodbath in the capital."

Don tells everybody that he's staying in the government to prepare negotiations with the other side. He's sorry, but he hasn't had the courage to ask Thieu to step down. Combining intelligence and naiveté, craftiness and sincerity, exuberant, speaking perfect French, born in the Bordeaux area fifty-eight years ago, Don is the most Frenchified of the Vietnamese general officers and a fine specimen of the military politicos always stirring the capital's pots. He was a corps commander, minister, senator, deputy. He would happily be prime minister, even president. Misfortune encourages him, success does not overly excite him. Like Ky, he has a complicated relationship with Thieu, whom he knew as a colonel when he himself was a divisional general. Because he is clever, he is one of President Thieu's *missi dominici* abroad. Don has long believed that the nationalists must come to an arrangement with the PRG. But this new minister of defense in a new government does not help the regime by telling whoever will listen that the cabinet will last two weeks.

In Dalat, Father Jean Maïs waits. A North Vietnamese cadre, a *can bo*, floating in too-large trousers, about fifty, small, thin, brown, with a short haircut, crosses the university's doorsill, greets Maïs in strongly accented French full of banalities, and departs again.

Dalat is rapidly taken in hand. A hairdresser presides over the administrative military committee that sits in the movie theater over the central marketplace. As Father Maïs speaks Vietnamese, the headmaster of the French lycée asks him to make contact with the committee.

A fourth-year student who is on the committee answers Jean Maïs: "We have other things to do."

Organizations flourish: Liberated Women, Patriotic Intellectuals. . . . If you're not with them, you're considered against them. Rector Duong helps draw up a speech of welcome to the revolutionary fighters. In Vietnamese, the words "happy" and "welcome" are traditionally coupled. The rector replaces "happy" with "unhappy." He is violently criticized. He explains: "I have many friends among South Vietnamese officers. I am welcoming revolutionaries in a divided country."

After a few more thoughtless follies, he is arrested.

The administrative military committee contacts Monsignor Lam, bishop of Dalat. He asks Jean Maïs to take inventory at an agricultural training center of the Overseas Missions, far from town. With another priest, a Lazarist, Jean Maïs leaves in a Land Rover. Looking for a way across a torrent where a bridge has been blown, near a road that crosses a plantation, they come upon some sixty camouflaged tanks under the trees. Squatting or lying beside the armor, soldiers pay them no heed.

They reach the agriculture training center and Maïs meets representatives of the administrative committee. Politely, they ask permission to carry away iron sheets stored in a workshop: "So the tanks can cross," they explain.

15

The Black Cuckoo

Lan, a girl of sixteen, the fourth of eight children in a Chinese family, has very light skin and a smiling oval face. She lives in the village of Ngoc Hai, fifteen kilometers from Cao Bang and forty-five from the Chinese border.

Her father makes bamboo chairs or freights sacks of rice in a cart. Her mother, a seamstress at the cooperative, now and then crosses the border, bribing the guards. She sells Vietnamese chemical sugar and buys Chinese jade jewelery. Last year the young woman won her diploma from secondary school. So she can replace her mother at the cooperative, she attends college only three times a week. The handiwork is not hard. Swatches of garment are ready, precut from Russian cloth. It's piecework, sewing together shirts, pants, blouses, dresses. The more she sews, the more she earns. A blouse pays 7 hao, 70 centimes; double that if she works for a private contractor who supplies his own material.

Lan's mother is pregnant. To earn her food ration, she has to be present and working twenty days a month. When necessary her daughter fills in for her, to guarantee the ration. Lan earns 15 kilos of rice a month. Her father has the right to a supplementary 500 grams of pork. The rationed rice costs 40 hao a kilo. On the black market, 16 dong. A kilo of pork is worth 2.70 dong at the official price, 25 dong on the black market.

In her college history class, Lan has heard of victories by the "popular armed forces of liberation." The professor, a woman, said, "We hope Vietnam will live in peace and independence. That North and South will be reunited. That there will be neither American interference nor Chinese meddling."

The teacher repeats often that the country has been conquered by fourteen foreign powers, among them the Chinese, the French, the Germans, the Italians. They were all thrown out. Only the Americans are still there. She also says, "We must fight on to the final victory, even if that takes another fifty or hundred years. We must fight to the last member of our family."

Lan does not like war. She has relatives in Saigon, down South, her paternal grandmother's little sister and her children. Lan feels strong bonds to her whole widespread family. She thinks many young men don't understand why they have to fight. They're required to do their military service. She knows a Montagnard deserter who's been sentenced to forced labor. She sees young men conscripted who weep, and go off. During their basic training at Cao Bang, many Sino-Vietnamese leave the barracks and desert. Lan sees the wounded, the maimed. To one soldier who's lost both legs, the state has offered artificial limbs and a modified Honda. Another, armless, has a pedal-cart and prostheses.

Lan likes to follow the singing lessons at 2:30 on the radio. The teaching proceeds verse by verse. She also likes courses in social behavior, moral conduct and hygiene, during the same broadcast. Lan knows many of the songs and poems by heart, especially To Huu's:

> *Never mind the world's lies;*
> *Keep your heart steady as a tripod.*

She understands these verses well. In village kitchens they use tripods. The three feet of the poem represent the North, Center and South of Vietnam. Lan likes to gaze into the clear water of the Bang Giang River, near the village, and at the varying greens of mountain, hill and paddy.

She doesn't care about politics. She doesn't read the newspapers that reach her village. Yet even in the solemn *Nhan Dan* are stories that the simplest peasant can understand. In the April 5 issue, "Stories for Here and Now" column, she can read,

> The sign of the Mouse in the Year of the Cat: Thieu is under the sign of the mouse. A mouse naturally passes from one sewer to another, from the French sewer to the American. Attacked at Ban Me Thuot, the mouse Thieu runs toward Hue and Danang, tail between his legs, before plunging into the China Sea to swim back to South Vietnam and be swallowed up in the sewers of Saigon. According to the lunar calendar, this is the year of the Cat. When the cat meets the mouse, he eats him. The cat has eaten a lot of mice in the last month. How can the mouse Thieu escape from the cat's

mouth? All is written: when you're born a mouse, you die by the cat.

In his report on the offensive, General Dung stops now and then to express (he too) his love of countryside, his pleasure at hills washed in sunshine, at the tender green of tall grass, at the endless dense vaults of rubber trees, at the immense majesty of hundred-year-old trees, at the fragile beauty of fresh-blown orchids. His account lingers on the cooks. On the banks of streams they prepare the usual fare over *hoang cam* fires, fireboxes smokeless thanks to an ingenious arrangement of the chimney. The general sees soldiers asleep in their hammocks after a night's march; sees road signs "of all sizes and shapes, all manner of letters, and in every color" pointing the way for this or that unit, or service, or column. It would take a shrewd outsider to decipher these signs. The NVA's commander in chief loves moralistic anecdotes as much as he does nature. Dinh Duc Thien, a logistics expert who's been checking storage areas and personnel, relays one to him: One day in a car park near Duc Lap, he saw two slovenly drivers repairing a truck. "What unit do you belong to?" he asked them. "We're about to win this war and you look like tramps. Have you no shame?" And these two men answered him: "But sir, we're POWs!"

"On all fronts and in all units," writes Dung,

> our men were using former military or civilian specialists of the Saigon army for the management and upkeep of different categories of vehicles. We had them explain the characteristics of American arms and materiel for proper use, and in our convoys you could see M-113 armored cars, M-48 and M-41 tanks, 105 mm. and 155 mm. cannon and PRC 25 tactical switchboards, *made in USA*. Our pilots quickly learned to handle the A-37 and F-5 fighter planes. Never before had we hit the enemy so hard with his own weapons. All this booty multiplies our firepower tenfold and speeds up the pace of our deployment.

Dung keeps up his campaign journal:

> After liberating Danang, the Second Army Corps . . . is racing south along the coast. It has been ordered to reach Bien Hoa [the large base north of Saigon] in at most eighteen days. In the 900 kilometers it must cover, a number of bridges have been destroyed. Between Danang and Quang Ngai we counted six. . . . To run a convoy of 2,000 vehicles and cross six rivers, not to mention skirmishes along the way, was a complex problem in command and organization.

Dung always analyzes the problems of 1975 in relation to the past: "In 1962, when the 308th Division was on maneuvers with only 400 vehicles, they piled up along the road until it was impossible to move." The commander in chief and his staff have made sure that in 1975 combined operations would run more smoothly. "The Second Army Corps was deployed in columns for the advance: engineers went first, to repair damaged bridges and roads at once, and tanks followed them to fight wherever they found the enemy. Each advancing column had an anti-aircraft regiment for protection, with infantry and artillery behind them."

Dung doesn't hesitate now to send out detached armored units, far from any infantry. "Alongside the road many old aunts and uncles, many mothers and children, stood waiting for a long time to bring tea, coconuts and sugar cane to give the soldiers." Dung does not note that often the civilians *sold* glasses of tea, coconuts and the pieces of sugar cane. "But the soldiers in their trucks, with the slogan 'Lightning speed and daring' affixed to their helmets, could not stop even a minute to talk with the people. They had only time to wave as they sped singlemindedly toward the front."

General Dung arrived at Loc Ninh, fifteen kilometers from the Cambodian frontier and a hundred kilometers north of Saigon, after crossing "vast stretches of rubber plantation damaged by air raids, then pepper plantations, durians and jacquiers and coconut palms recently planted." Dung is jotting little propaganda notes. Loc Ninh was taken by the North Vietnamese three years earlier. At the time of the Paris Agreement, it was considered the official capital of the PRG. For a long while there'd been an air link between Saigon and Loc Ninh. "On both sides of the repaired and widened roads, new straw huts," writes Dung with a revolutionary enthusiasm as peasant as it is warlike, alternate "with fields of manioc and beautiful rice paddies." Dung sees workers uprooting stumps and weeding among the rubber trees.

The general relaxes. Never weary of kitchen gardens and orchards, he takes time for a nap after admiring a banana plant. He dreams of the moment when his divisions will reach southernmost South Vietnam, at Ca Mau. And of course he recalls some lines of the inevitable To Huu:

> O Binh Long, here in our Nam Bo,
> This morning for the first time I meet you face to face.
> I hold a clod of your red earth in my hand,
> My heart chokes as if intoxicated with strong wine.
> As I clasp you, liberation brother, to my heart,
> I dream of running all the way to the plains of Ca Mau.

West of Loc Ninh, at headquarters of the southern zone, Dung first meets Pham Hung. This broad-shouldered little man has been directing the fight in South Vietnam since 1967. South of the 17th parallel, he is the most important man politically. Secretary for the South in the Vietnamese Communist Party's Central Committee, an old militant, he led strikes in 1930. Often arrested, condemned to death, pardoned, deported to the penitentiary of Poulo Condor, he was liberated from French prisons for the last time in August 1945. He has worked with Le Duan before in this South he knows so well. Now he is political commissar for the campaign, topped only by Le Duc Tho.

Pham Hung's military counterpart, General Tra, comes to inspect the Fourth Army Corps. It will attack the South Vietnamese line of defense east of Saigon, around Xuan Loc. Tra reports to General Dung.

Around headquarters are tents set up for staff officers, shelters dug against air attacks, trenches under the trees. They keep activity to a minimum during the day. South Vietnamese planes may appear suddenly. The forest comes alive at night. You hear vehicles grinding down the trail, generators humming, radios crackling. The various services are scattered to avoid air raids. Meticulous, sometimes seated on the baggage rack of a motorcycle, Dung inspects everything. His guards wear black and white checked kerchiefs around their necks. The staff has parked its transmitter vehicles deep in the jungle, at the end of winding roads, to avoid electronic interception of its broadcasts by aircraft and subsequent raids by South Vietnamese commandos.

Pham Hung asks about the ammunition supply. An officer answers, "I guarantee that we have enough to strike fear into three generations."

After that, every time there's a question about ammunition they pick up the joke, laughing: "And fire fast enough to strike fear into three generations!"

They hold a meeting at headquarters. A motorcycle stops in the courtyard of the house where part of the staff is billeted: Le Duc Tho arrives, in a blue shirt and khaki pants, and wearing a light helmet. There he is in the South for the third time in thirty years. He has traveled by plane, car and finally motorcycle.

Of those now directing the campaign, Le Duc Tho is the most important. He has all the parameters in his head, political, diplomatic, military, national and international. On April 8 he presents the resolution adopted by the Politburo in Hanoi on March 22: "Forward to final victory."

The first rains fall on the forest, disturbing the cadres' sleep. How to fight insomnia? By writing. Le Duc Tho sets down a poem which, according to General Dung, "well describes the atmosphere of the moment." To judge a communist's place in the hierarchy, Vietnam watchers check his rank on lists published in Hanoi during a congress; the number of his published articles; and his position on the platform during a demonstration. They can also judge his importance by the number of poems he composes that his colleagues quote. In his memoirs, when Le Duc Tho is there General Dung—let's say it aloud—sucks up. Le Duc Tho is boss for this phase of operations in the South. Moreover, he could succeed Le Duan, secretary general of the Party, as number one. So you can't quote too much of Le Duc Tho, who writes, there in the forest:

> *I hear the call of the black cuckoo.*
> *At sunrise in the Loc Ninh jungle.*
> *All night long I couldn't sleep,*
> *Lying, counting drops of falling rain,*
> *Worried for our army brothers*
> *Mired along the flooded roads;*
> *First come tanks and then come cannon,*
>
> . . . .
>
> *The battlefield awaits them, minute to minute.*
> *Oh rain, please rain no more!*
> *Let the road dry off quickly*
> *So our trucks can reach their places.*
> *In this final historic battle*
> *The sound of guns has already begun.*

North Vietnamese leaders write poems as fluently as they imprison or execute their enemies.

Le Duc Tho and Pham Hung issue instructions for "liberated" areas. "Soldiers must behave properly. But South Vietnamese cadres, especially the police, must be arrested." The Politburo wants the general offensive to start "at the latest in the last ten days of April."

In Southeast Asia, especially Thailand and the Philippines, there are fighter bombers and B-52s on U.S. bases. Now at the beginning of April, the NVA command isn't afraid U.S. ground troops will come back but can't be 100 percent certain that U.S. aircraft won't intervene. At NVA headquarters, Dung explains, they've also been "following operations in Cambodia very closely since the beginning of April." Dung is more specific: "Even though there is no agreement between us [North Vietnamese and Khmer Rouge], our tactical and strategic actions [are] tightly coordinated." The general exaggerates. Relations between Hanoi and the Cambodian revolutionaries are at best complicated, at worst strained.

Dung persuades his political bosses in Hanoi. In March, often uneasy, they bombarded the commander in chief with cables recommending caution. In his memoirs Dung, a disciplined communist, refers constantly to the Politburo's decisions, neglecting to add that the military allowed themselves plenty of leeway for independent action during the last weeks. The Politburo agrees to Dung's suggestions. In a cable of April 8, they urge "unremitting vigor in the attack all the way to the heart of Saigon." They also say "in combining attacks from the outside in with vice versa, we will create conditions for a popular uprising." The Politburo still admits, implicitly, that this uprising, which the communist radio and papers make much of, has never eventuated.

The same day at Loc Ninh, Le Duc Tho gives one of those little speeches which communist orators if not audiences are so partial to:

> The Central Committee has ordered the party's Southern bureau and the whole of our armed forces to complete the liberation of the South. . . . Let us go forward to attack Saigon, now when the enemy, in utter disarray, has lost his strength. . . . He has five divisions, we have fifteen, not to mention our strategic reserve. There is no excuse for not winning: that is the Central Committee's view. When I left, my friends at the Politburo said to me, "You must win, you can only come back victorious."

If they can wind it all up in the month of May, for Uncle Ho's birthday, the victory will take on great symbolic value.

Every military campaign bears a name. Loc Ninh headquarters suggests one to Hanoi. On April 14 at 7 P.M., headquarters will receive telegram 37/TK from the Politburo, signed by Le Duan: "Agree that the Saigon campaign be called 'Ho Chi Minh campaign.' " Almost proof positive that up to then Hanoi's leaders were uncertain, if not indecisive, about the final outcome.

For the first time since the beginning of the year, shells fell on greater Saigon on April 7. About sixty 75 mm. shells, mortar shells and many rockets hit the oil refinery at Nha Be, fifteen kilometers from the center of the city.

Operations proceed in a classic and traditional cycle: in February, March and April the communists deployed enough men and munitions to mount their major offensive for the year. "Infiltration" slows. The rains begin in Laos. In April, the defenses of greater Saigon are tested. Any large-scale offensive must end in July, for then most of South Vietnam will be saturated. Tanks, the cutting edge of the North Vietnamese deployment, need dry land.

Back in Saigon, some believe the capital can defend itself and hold out, mainly thanks to the planes still operational. Holding out until July will do it. Later, in October, the cycle will recommence. Americans and South Vietnamese alike fear the union of the North Vietnamese attacking down the coast with the divisions assembling around the capital and the regiments gathering in the Delta. Out of Ambassador Martin's earshot, some American diplomats are muttering that these North Vietnamese divisions remind them of the Allied armies racing toward Berlin in 1945.

On April 8 at 8:25 A.M. the Japanese ambassador meets with Jean-Marie Mérillon at the French Embassy. A difficult conversation: the Japanese does not know much and the Frenchman does not want to elaborate.

He cannot really promise, as the Japanese hopes and believes, that "France will take care of everything."

An enormous explosion! Bombs fall a few hundred meters away, beyond the cathedral. A great din of machineguns and small arms. In one wall of his office Mérillon has installed a superb, immense glass window. If it shattered it would be dangerous. But dignity and diplomacy oblige: the ambassadors go on chatting, the Japanese with the calm of a samurai.

Coming from the South, gliding above the river, a South Vietnamese air force F-5E has swooped down on the presidential palace and, at 1,000 feet, dropped two 250-pound bombs. They've exploded in the palace courtyard, killing two gardeners, barely damaging the buildings. The fighter climbs to 3,000 feet and dives again. The last two bombs are duds. In passing the F-5E strafes—with its 20 mm. guns—a Shell fuel depot in Nha Be and hits two intact tanks. The plane climbs and heads north-northwest.

This sort of attempt on the presidential palace is part of Vietnamese political folklore. In February 1962 two South Vietnamese pilots bombed and gunned another palace, hoping to liquidate President Diem. They demolished one wing of the building. No one in the president's family was killed. In Vietnam, as in parts of Asia and Africa today, and in Europe yesterday, there are those who bet on the assassination of major figures to change the course of history radically. Is this one of the childhood diseases of underdevelopment?

In the capital they're wondering if the bombardment signals the start of a coup d'état. Marshal Ky is a schemer, and the air force is his up to a certain point. Everybody knows that the communists are calling for Thieu's ouster. Some claim Ky wants to negotiate with them. So if Thieu is eliminated, one communist condition is met. Cars with mounted loudspeakers roll through the capital, announcing that a curfew is reestablished as of noon. The loudspeakers belch patriotic songs.

As far as the Ky hypothesis goes, the president of the Senate and others note that the brilliant aviator is no more in a position to negotiate than Thieu. Some swear they saw a MiG; so it was a North Vietnamese incursion. Still others, more imaginative and perverse, maintain that Thieu mounted the operation. It will give him a pretext to arrest his opponents. At 10 A.M. at the press center, a spokesman says there were explosions "along the perimeter of the presidential palace." Then, a slave to habit, business as usual, the spokesman distributes the daily communiqué: "In the last twenty-four hours the communists have committed 142 additional violations of the cease-fire."

At noon the streets downtown are deserted, stores closed. All over town everybody seems to be on the phone. The battle for Saigon has begun, the North Vietnamese are coming, Thieu is dead, the generals have taken over, Big Minh is going to be president. . . .

Thieu shows he's alive by speaking on the radio. No member of his family has been wounded, he assures all. The South Vietnamese armed forces are loyal to him, and there has been no putsch. Thieu remains head of state. Improvising, the president adds: "This was an isolated attack by a group that wants to assassinate me, and to change the constitutional and legal form of this regime."

The truth leaks out at the end of the afternoon. Taking off from Bien Hoa base to shell communist positions, Nguyen Thanh Trung, a South Vietnamese air force lieutenant, reported engine trouble and radioed that he was returning to base. He bombed the palace. Then the lieutenant landed at an airport in North Vietnamese hands. North Vietnamese authorities immediately announce that this officer has been one of them for a long time. This suggests that the South Vietnamese armed forces are collapsing, and even that they're going to revolt. Some have the impression that Trung, whose fidelity to the regime was never indubitable, was depressed because his family hadn't been able to leave Danang, a motivation more personal than political. He's incorporated into the North Vietnamese air force and posted head of a squadron of captured South Vietnamese planes. Promoted to captain, he's decorated with the Order of Liberation second class.

Relieved, the Saigonese joke: "If he'd killed Thieu, he'd have won the Order of Liberation first class!"

At 6 P.M. curfew is lifted.

Spectacular but insignificant, the attack draws unfavorable reaction in Washington. At a minimum, they note, Saigon's anti-aircraft defenses had better be reinforced. A centrifugal swirl starts in the South Vietnamese capital, a good gauge of unrest: departure of the branch managers of the Bank of America, First National City Bank, and Chase Manhattan—who also halted all foreign currency transactions in their establishments without notice. They have no desire to accumulate piastres. Ambassador Martin shows his displeasure. His office lets it be known that the managers' absences "are temporary."

Air Marshal Ky can be acquitted of this crime, but they worry about his other projects. On the evening of the bombing, during a dinner, Wolfgang Lehmann listens attentively to the South Vietnamese chief of staff. Vien seldom speaks; his thoughts are distilled, but Lehmann senses that the chief of staff would like to know if a coup against Thieu would be acceptable to the United States. Enough of these children's games!

"No," says Lehmann, "the United States is against any operation of that kind."

U.S. ships are on course for the Vietnamese coast. Abruptly, the barometer of optimism rises in Saigon. These aircraft carriers, *Coral Sea* racing from the Phillipines, *Midway* in the Sea of Japan, *Enterprise* halfway between Manila and Saigon, *Hancock* nearing Subic Bay[1]—are they coming to defend South Vietnam? Le Duc Tho has good reason to keep an eye on the whole of Southeast Asia from his headquarters in the South.

Off Cambodia, in the Gulf of Siam, the helicopter carrier *Okinawa* is already cruising. In Washington the fall of Cambodia is considered imminent. Since April 7, 360 marines of Amphibious Readiness Group Alpha have been in a state of alert, ready to leave in three hours. Eight hundred people must be evacuated from Phnom Penh. This operation has a name, too, "Eagle Pull," less bracing than "Ho Chi Minh Campaign." At the U.S. Embassy in Saigon they know the American armada will protect an evacuation and that's all.

Tension grows at upper levels of the embassy. The higher in the hierarchy, the more optimistic. Thomas Polgar bypasses Martin and cables the CIA in Washington on April 9: "COS [Chief of station, i.e., Polgar] still has to spend an inordinate amount of time arguing about the validity of intelligence which contains bad news, and debating need for administrative decisions which embassy is reluctant to make for one reason or another." So much for Martin.

Polgar is annoyed by the humdrum routine, by business as usual. In these dangerous days you might think they could man their desks overtime. "The ambassador is spending the bulk of his time trying to generate support for increasing economic and military assistance to South Vietnam, and to maintain orderly attitudes in the face of what is clearly a worsening situation." If Martin were to lay hands on this cable he'd appreciate the good manners. Polgar denounces the South Vietnamese government, not yet completely formed: "has not managed to gather itself for effective action." What's the most probable outcome, according to Polgar? Intelligence suggests "that the North Vietnamese have made a determination to continue and expand military pressure aimed at the isolation of Saigon, with the ultimate military objective being total victory in 1975." The isolation of Saigon: despite Snepp's mole, Polgar believes the communists may stop after cutting off the South Vietnamese capital. Polgar is a philosophical soul. Speaking of himself—majestically—in the third person, he goes on: "COS is well aware that history seldom moves along the line of straight-line projections. Nevertheless, it is certain that we are heading for a debacle of historic proportions unless the necessary changes are effected in time." At the beginning of this second week in April, Polgar does not rule out saving changes: "It remains COS judgment that the military situation cannot be stabilized without decisive American moves. If no decisive American moves are made, then we believe major and useless bloodshed can be avoided only if Thieu steps down and a national union government offers to implement the Paris formula as defined by the communists." Thus the CIA's boss in Saigon goes into mourning for Thieu.

Polgar does not accept Frank Snepp's analysis. The latter writes in a draft for a cable: "The indications are that the North Vietnamese have altered their plans and timetable to include attacks against Saigon possibly as early as mid-April." Snepp is categorical: there is "no provision for negotiations or a tripartite government." Polgar and Martin read this report. They both find it "too alarmist." It will be sent to Washington, but edited by Polgar. Snepp wrote "attacks against Saigon." In Polgar's version this becomes "some attacks in and around the Saigon area."

In Washington CIA director William Colby, briefing the National Security Council, tells them the military situation in Vietnam is highly charged. The CIA's rewrite men and analysts have taken Snepp's report into account. They say flatly that "all talk of a negotiated settlement" is "a sham."

Who will sing the danger and importance of rewrite men in the diplomatic bureaucracy, intelligence services and journalism? At high levels of the U.S. Embassy in Saigon, the idea of possible negotiations thrives.

The French Institute in Saigon screens a film with the appropriate title *Closed Eyes*. South Vietnamese also rally to or revert to the idea of eventual political negotiations. In journalistic circles An, one of the Three Musketeers, speaks with authority. He tells his two friends Vuong and Cao Giao, "The communists want to negotiate."

Tall, with regular features, courteous, impeccable in English and excellent in French, An is impressive. Always well informed, a full-time staffer at *Time*'s Saigon bureau, he has entrée to military and political high places. He has reported for the *Christian Science Monitor* and worked for Reuters. In Diem's time he lived in the United States thanks to a grant from the Asia Foundation, which, rightly or wrongly, was reputed a seedbed for potential CIA agents. An loves dogs and birds. He supplies at least 80 percent of *Time*'s Vietnam copy. He tells Cao Giao, "The communists don't bother with sentimental considerations. It's in their interest to set up a provisional government. So that's what they're working toward."

An concentrates on fact, doesn't he? He rarely expresses opinions; only alone with Vietnamese. He hints to Mme. Nga, who also works in the *Time* bureau, that he doesn't much like Americans. He advises her to leave the country. He'd like to send his mother out. For the moment, *Time* is preparing to evacuate spouses and children of its people first of all. Just the same, An explains to Cao Giao, there's no cause for alarm: "I can easily imagine a third Vietnam. But of course Thieu must go."[2]

An's information and analyses are picked up by a number of foreign correspondents. In the past, An has often proved prophetic.

Even with all the grave news, cinemas, bars and restaurants are jammed. The Central Market and Thieves' Market are crowded despite the rise in prices. People who were saying yesterday, "Giap's divisions are about to enter Saigon," are saying today, with the same peremptory certitude, that "whatever happens, Saigon will be spared." A stiff upper lip can mask anguish. Vietnamese newspapers are full of want ads. The prices of apartments and villas to buy or rent are dropping. Marriage brokers are doing good business. Young Vietnamese girls are looking for U.S. passports in the form of husbands. Sometimes the Americans propose.

Advertisement in the *Saigon Post*, April 6:

> American army colonel wishes to meet pretty young woman, refined, with a view to marriage and residence in Paris, France. The lady should have some knowledge of French and English and be of distinguished origin. Write Col. Mark Broman, 200 N. Howard, appt. 24, Clarksville, Indiana, USA 47130.

Cynics say, "The price of Vietnamese girls is dropping like the price of villas."

The Saigonese are crowding into banks and withdrawing piastres to convert to dollars. Exhausting procedures. To leave, a Vietnamese must obtain a passport, an exit visa and clearance from the Internal Revenue. Exit visas are selling for 10 million piastres, $14,000 at the official rate. South Vietnamese bureaucrats raise their price for speeding things up. American bureaucrats are worried about real problems. What are Hanoi's military and political projects? What's happening in Cambodia? Will President Ford win his bid for additional aid?

In this second week of April, nine NVA divisions are converging on Saigon. The ARVN chief of staff has no doubts about an attack. General Vien no more believes in a political solution than Thieu does. When Vien is not meditating karma or the nature of Truth and Beauty, he is of two minds. He wants to be loyal to the president. But his new defense minister has confided that Thieu is becoming dead weight. Vien also keeps an eye on army morale. Too many majors, colonels and generals are holding the president responsible for the disorganized evacuation of Hue and Danang. Vien doesn't wonder *whether* the North Vietnamese will attack Saigon, but from *where*. Masters of diversion and feint, the NVA general staff manipulated its enemy perfectly in the Central Highlands. They rely on Mao's precepts, indeed all his strategies: "When you want to attack from the west, make a fuss in the east." Intelligence, under Colonel Luong,[3] predicts that the next big attack will hit Xuan Loc, a provincial capital of 100,000, nestled among rubber trees between two ranges of hills, a hundred kilometers east of the capital. There is only one large base between Saigon and Xuan Loc: Bien Hoa and its military airport.

The South Vietnamese have guessed the North Vietnamese maneuver, a classic pincer movement. General Tra is going to throw three divisions of his 4th Corps into the battle of Xuan Loc. The 341st is coming from the northwest after crossing the Dong Nai River. The 7th is coming down from the north-northeast. The 6th, to the west, is moving along Route 333, but will attack from the southwest. Full of young recruits, the 341st is not an elite division. Some soldiers aren't even sixteen.

Xuan Loc, like Hue, Danang and Tay Ninh, has entered American military mythology. Colonel George Patton, Jr., son of the swashbuckling general, had his command post at Xuan Loc and headed a famous armored regiment, the Eleventh Cavalry. American officers posted to Xuan Loc said approvingly that the city was far enough from Saigon to retain its provincial charm and close enough to the capital to feel secure.

The NVA's 341st Division leads the advance, preceded by an artillery barrage and supported by T-54 tanks. It pushes into the city of Xuan Loc, dominated by the spire of the Catholic church. North Vietnamese units drive as far as Market Square and the bus depot. They are repulsed by men of the ARVN 18th Infantry Division under General Le Minh Dao. Soldiers of the ARVN 43rd Regiment, after horrific hand-to-hand combat, force back the first elements of the NVA 6th Division. The fighting, says General Dung, in this case a good loser, is "hard, bloody," during the first days. NVA artillery saturates the suburbs with almost 10,000 shells in twenty-four hours. The NVA loses many tanks and begins to run short of artillery and shells. For the first time since January, the North Vietnamese supply corps faces serious trouble. The T-54s run out of fuel and ammunition. Tra has to call up reserve regiments of the 6th and 7th Divisions. And still the ARVN holds the ruined town. They don't suffer from the "family syndrome." For the most part, the women and children of the 18th Division's officers and men have been evacuated, the lucky ones by helicopter. Here the fighting men think mainly about fighting. But they're hampered by refugees, residents of Xuan Loc and surroundings who want to flee and make Saigon. Many escape by crossing North Vietnamese lines. Bypassing routes and roads cratered by artillery, some refugees will indeed reach the capital by shoving through the *cordon sanitaire* deployed by Thieu.

On April 10 the South Vietnamese staff has to make a serious decision. Xuan Loc's defenders aren't retreating, but they need reinforcements. The argument pertinent to Hue and Danang—we can't strip Saigon's defenses—is inadmissible because Xuan Loc is part of Saigon's defenses. Vien fears yet other attacks on Saigon, but the chief of staff seems suddenly to reject his passive role and decides to throw reinforcements into the battle of Xuan Loc, naturally with Thieu's concurrence. Even the South Vietnamese air force, which hasn't shown much skill at combined operations these last weeks, shoots up the NVA infantry and armor to serious effect. Vien throws in his paratroopers. Near the Michelin factory on the Xuan Loc road, Patrick Hays sees them off with a connoisseur's eye. In great spirits, brave, even swaggering, the paratroopers swap their helmets for their red berets. Morale is high here. About two brigades of airborne were "consumed" before Nha Trang and Phan Thiet to slow down the enemy—30 percent dead.

At Tan Son Nhut airfield, American officers around General Homer Smith believe that the battle of Xuan Loc, though not decisive, will stop the North Vietnamese advance and, who knows? stabilize the front. This may be the victory Weyand's mission needed. South Vietnamese soldiers show the world they can hold fast and counterattack—and so deserve U.S. aid. Helicopters are made available so foreign reporters can at last witness a South Vietnamese victory. Vien's staff discovers there's no shortage of either arms or ammunition. They can equip every man of the 1st Airborne Brigade's two battalions with a light antitank weapon, the Law. They're going to tighten the noose around the North Vietnamese. F-5 fighter bombers and A-1 Skyraiders scatter North Vietnamese concentrations, particularly regiments of the 341st Division. C-130 transport planes drop 750-pound bombs at low altitude through their rear doors. The North Vietnamese high command hurls two more divisions at Xuan Loc, the 325th and 312th.

The defenders' morale is high. Communications are excellent. The paratroopers and rangers arrive. The road from Saigon is cleared and reinforcements roar in. Helicopters evacuate the wounded. Attack helicopters also play a part in the battle. The South Vietnamese are fighting one against three, but their enemy has no air support. North Vietnamese artillery shells the base at Bien Hoa, where most of the aircraft take off and land, but the fighter bombers are diverted to Tan Son Nhut airport, where they take on fuel and ammunition. In the rubber plantations around Xuan Loc, supporting artillery emplacements are well stocked and well commanded. Observer helicopters signal coordinates of NVA artillery or tanks. ARVN infantry officers call up artillery or air support quickly and accurately. We're almost back in the golden days of the American war. Optimism is so contagious that General Homer Smith cables from Saigon to General George Brown, chairman of the Joint Chiefs of Staff in Washington, top man in the U.S. military hierarchy, that the South Vietnamese have won the first round, that the ARVN's courage and aggressive push seem for the moment to settle one question: Are the armed forces of the Republic of Vietnam going to fight?

On April 10, the consolidated intelligence report in Washington judges that the North Vietnamese will still not be strong enough "to launch a general offensive against Saigon" the following week. Less enthusiastic than General Smith, the intelligence gurus back home think the NVA is waiting for fresh reinforcements.

A stabilized front + a will to negotiate on both sides = a political solution. On tour in Africa, Mme. Nguyen Thi Binh declares that the PRG is trying to attain its objectives in South Vietnam "if possible by nonmilitary means."

16

---◆---

Flowers
Behind Their Ears

The U.S. Congress reconvenes on April 7. In their home constituencies senators and congressmen found their voters distrustful of the Saigon regime. Few Americans will be impressed by photographs of ARVN soldiers at Xuan Loc in well-fortified positions or waving captured flags. A Lou Harris poll quantifies voter sentiment. Two out of three Americans oppose military aid for Cambodia and South Vietnam even if it would "spare the populations of these countries a bloodbath."

Committees and subcommittees crank up the ponderous but traditional democratic procedures. Senators and congressmen are kept closely informed about disagreements at the heart of the administration. The White House and the State Department have, officially at least, a common political line: South Vietnam *can* be saved. Unofficially the Pentagon implies that there's no hope. But James Schlesinger loyally defends Ford's policy again, and in public; that's his style. The secretary of defense doesn't go so far as to claim that supplemental military aid would save the South Vietnamese army. He says the United States' credibility worldwide is at stake: "We cannot be the country that abandons its friends, betrays its allies, goes back on its promises."

In Washington there's increasing gossip about secret agreements by President Nixon. More: Didn't he also offer "oral" guarantees? Senator Henry Jackson demands that Kissinger appear before the Congress and explicate any guarantees given "without notifying Congress." With the majestic indignation of an outraged senator, Jackson says he's ready to

launch an investigation. Like his colleagues, he wants any U.S. commitments out in the full light of day. It's also in his own interest to diminish
Ford through Kissinger. Testily aware of their prerogatives, allergic to
diplomatic secrecy since President Wilson praised the merits of "open
covenants openly arrived at," the legislators are in no mood to coddle the
administration. The fallout from Watergate has not dissipated. More than
ever, the president and his administration are presumed guilty until they
prove their innocence.

In long public hearings and "executive sessions," the lawmakers question officials from State, Defense, the CIA and other government agencies.
Committee meetings become almost brutal and take on the air of litigations
or trials; in these imposing wood-paneled and marbled rooms, the legislative and executive branches thrust and parry. The officials who testify
can hardly disguise their skepticism.

Daniel Parker, head of the Agency for International Development,
declares before the House Foreign Affairs Committee, "I cannot tell you
what the fate of South Vietnam will be in the weeks and months to come,
but I can tell you what the fate of its people will be . . . if we . . . do not
grant them the necessary resources."

The committees distinguish clearly between military assistance, to which
they are more and more hostile, and humanitarian aid. Senator Hubert
Humphrey, former vice-president and former Democratic presidential candidate, says in the corridor, "They're all walking around with flowers
behind their ears saying everything's going to be all right. It will not be
all right. It is a disaster. I'm not prepared to appropriate another dime for
people who won't pull themselves together and fight for their own survival."

President Ford addresses a joint session of Congress in a solemn atmosphere. Out of conviction for the most part, but for some out of fear
of displeasing their constituents, a number of lawmakers have already let
slip—to congressional aides and to special envoys from the White House
who sound them out—that they're inclined to vote humanitarian aid and
of course the necessary money to proceed with an evacuation, but not a
dollar more for the war. Ford has to beat against this current.

A bit more than half his speech is devoted to Indochina. On Cambodia,
the president recalls that he asked for supplemental aid three months ago.
This very evening, "it is perhaps already too late." In fact, Ford is preparing
to shut down the embassy at Phnom Penh. For him Cambodia is lost but
not Vietnam. On the latter he repeats—according to many congressmen,
he recites in a drone—his administration's arguments: the Paris Agreement
is viable only if America supports Saigon. Congressional refusal to vote
massive aid is encouraging Hanoi to intensify its attacks. The lawmakers
are far from happy at this obvious attempt to saddle them with responsibility
for the South Vietnamese debacle.

The president sees several possible solutions. Two are extreme: do
nothing at all, or declare war to implement the Paris Agreement. Two

seem more moderate: to grant the $300 million in military aid initially requested or to increase military and economic aid. Ford recommends the last solution.

At best, it would help South Vietnam stabilize the military situation and reach a political settlement. At worst, it would permit the evacuation of some 6,000 Americans still there and a certain number of Vietnamese. Reading his speech in a monotone, drawing from General Weyand's report, Ford asks Congress for $722 million in military aid and $250 million to help the refugees. The president implores the legislators to grant these funds and to vote before April 19.

Ford also raises a complicated problem: What are the president's powers in using the armed forces to evacuate Americans from Vietnam, "if that should prove necessary"? Ford is thinking of all the legislation drawn up under Nixon limiting presidential powers. Ford is cautious. He wants authority to send U.S. troops to "protect and escort" U.S. citizens; he does not want to be accused in any way of renewing the war. Constitutionally, Congress "shall have the power . . . to declare war." No president, not Kennedy, nor Johnson, nor Nixon, called on Congress to do so—doubtless a serious psychological error. The truth is that since World War II the U.S. Congress has never declared war. This has not kept presidents from sending U.S. forces into Greece, Korea (under the aegis of the U.N.), the Dominican Republic and Libya. Sometimes they could claim it was a large-scale police operation. Tacitly, and especially since 1965, the lawmakers have conceded to the president the right to *wage* war without declaring it. And every year they voted the necessary funds. But that's all over now.

In July 1973 Congress voted a law canceling funds for all "combat activities" in Indochina. Despite President Nixon's veto, that same Congress approved a War Powers Resolution, which became the War Powers Act the following November. By its terms the president must submit a report every time he sends U.S. combat troops abroad. The law does not provide for events like the evacuation of South Vietnam. What "authority" has the president to introduce "United States Armed Forces into hostilities, or into situations where imminent involvement in hostilities is clearly indicated by the circumstances"? The resolution and act are not monuments to judicial clarity. Ford wants to clarify certain aspects—and to cover himself. Another problem: the law makes no provision for the evacuation of Vietnamese who are not U.S. citizens. The legislators agree on aiding endangered Americans, of course, and some Vietnamese. But how many Vietnamese?

To put an end to the rumors of secret commitments by Nixon, Ford meets with congressional leaders on April 11 at the White House. In sum, Ford says that "private exchanges between Nixon and Thieu do not differ from what has been said publicly." Fine subject for a doctoral thesis, the question remains unanswered: Does the personal commitment of an ex-president commit the sitting president and more particularly the Congress? But the president and the Congress are on a tighter schedule than doctoral candidates.

Gerald Ford orders John Dean, U.S. ambassador in Phnom Penh, to close the embassy.

On April 12 at 7:45 A.M. three waves of helicopters take off from the helicopter carrier *Okinawa* in the Gulf of Siam. Others will take off from *Hancock*. The marines are armed with M-16s and grenade launchers. In preparation since February, operation Eagle Pull begins. John Dean, a highly competent diplomat who immersed himself in Indochinese affairs in Paris and Vientiane before his posting to Phnom Penh, informs Cambodian political and military officials. Any who want to take advantage of the evacuation are welcome. To deliver this message, Dean himself goes to the residence of the prime minister, Long Boret. All the ministers— except one and the interim president—refuse the offer.

After overflying 170 kilometers of Khmer Rouge terrain, the first helicopters of Amphibious Group Alpha land. The marines deploy on the embassy's perimeter.

Dean receives a letter from Sirik Matak, a government adviser:

> Dear Excellency and friend,
>
> I thank you very sincerely for your letter and for your offer to transport me toward freedom. I cannot, alas, leave in such a cowardly fashion. As for you, and in particular for your great country, I never believed for a moment that you would have this sentiment of abandoning a people which has chosen liberty. You have refused us your protection, and we can do nothing about it.
>
> You leave, and my wish is that you and your country will find happiness under this sky. But, mark it well, that if I shall die here on the spot and in my country that I love, it is too bad, because we are all born and must die one day. I made only one mistake, which was to believe you and to believe the Americans.
>
> Yours most faithfully and cordially,
>
> > Sirik Matak

With curiosity, without hostility, Cambodians near the U.S. Embassy watch the evacuation—which goes well. Captain Cyril Moyher and his marines do their job. In two hours the helicopters evacuate 82 Americans, 159 Cambodians and several Filipinos, Nationalist Chinese, Australians, Thais, French, Spaniards, Swedes, British, Canadians and Italians. The Americans are mostly diplomats and journalists. Sydney Schanberg, of the

New York Times, and his Cambodian colleague, Dith Pran, choose to remain in Phnom Penh.[1] At 10:15 A.M. John Dean, his expression serious, even brooding, leaves with the American flag under his arm. By 10:41 all civilians have been evacuated. Mortar shells fall around the embassy, where an American corpsman tends two wounded. Still on the ground, the marines radio the C-130 that serves as flying command post. No U.S. plane or helicopter succeeds in spotting the Khmer Rouge mortars. The dozen fighter bombers patrolling between the coast and Phnom Penh do not intervene.

On the high seas off the port of Sihanoukville the U.S. fleet has been deployed since yesterday: *Vancouver, Thomaston, Henry D. Wilson, Knox* and *Kirk*. U.S. aircraft based in Thailand can also—if needed—respond to Khmer Rouge attacks.

After several hours aboard the warships, the Phnom Penh evacuees reach Thailand.

Eagle Pull is gratifying to the U.S. military: a mission well prepared and well executed. A logistical masterpiece that succeeds because (among other reasons) the Khmer Rouge were powerless to oppose it. But mainly, perhaps, because the people of Phnom Penh had no desire to flee en masse aboard the helicopters. In short, a fine rehearsal for Saigon, should it come to that. Newspapers around the world will run similar headlines: "Americans Leave Phnom Penh," "Army Takes Over in Phnom Penh," "Military Committee Formed by General Sak Suttsakhom." President Giscard d'Estaing is very fond of the word "suitable." Immediately, the French government recognizes the new state—that is, the Khmer Rouge regime. Is this headlong embrace quite suitable?

The French Embassy at Phnom Penh is directed by consul Jean Dyrac, temporarily demoted to vice-consul: thus France keeps her distance from the new regime. On April 17 at 5 A.M., Khmer Rouge troops cross in front of the embassy. A bit later government armor clanks through the city flying white flags.

The Khmer Rouge "liberate" Phnom Penh before the North Vietnamese take Saigon. It's a race between enemy brothers; the Khmer Rouge want to show that they can advance on their own, without North Vietnamese help.

The Khmer Rouge empty the capital.

Messages from the French in Phnom Penh are relayed to Paris through Saigon and often interrupted. Four thousand refugees are camping on embassy grounds, among them East Germans and Russians. The "KR," as the experts say, have breached the wall of the Soviet Embassy with rockets. Prince Sirik Matak and members of Norodom Sihanouk's family, among them two grandchildren, are also at the French Embassy. The next day KR officers, their escort armed with bazookas, come for the prince. Dyrac refuses to let them enter and gains some time.

"We'll be back tomorrow," the KR say.

Dyrac assigns Fathers François Ponchaud and Bernard Berger to the "psychological welfare" of the refugees. They raise morale by relaying news items; a line to Saigon will be open until the electricity is cut altogether.

At 11 A.M. a U.S. plane flies over the embassy. A group of Americans, two journalists and some stringers, make contact with a walkie-talkie and ask for a helicopter operation to "pull them out." At U.S. headquarters in Thailand, and at the Pentagon, they study the problem. Such an operation might lead to the massacre of all the refugees there.

On April 19, Matak and other Cambodians decided to give themselves over. The Khmer Rouge arrive at the embassy with a jeep and two trucks. Matak will be glimpsed some twenty kilometers from Phnom Penh; then he will disappear.

Cambodia's agony under the Khmer Rouge has begun.

Thieu is discussing the fall of Phnom Penh with his cousin Nha.

"The same thing could happen in Saigon," Nha says.

"You think so?"

"Yes, if the communists throw all their forces against us."

"I still don't think so. There's too much at stake," Thieu insists. The president is clinging to the belief that he can galvanize the Americans.

Nha is about to take a quick trip to Singapore. He admires Prime Minister Lee Kuan Yew, the authoritarian social-democrat who runs the little city-state. Lee Kuan Yew has given the people of Singapore what the communists always promised—work, education, housing. Nha finds this system of muscular democracy quite appealing. So the cousin is very happy when a British reporter tells him that Lee Kuan Yew wants to see him. Nha emplanes for Singapore and registers at the Raffles, the famous and charming old hotel. Then he goes to dine in a restaurant at Newton Circus. Singapore is an orderly, civilized and puritanical city, and its police are low-profile but effective.

An inspector in civilian clothes approaches Nha: "Mr. Nha?"

"Yes."

"The prime minister would like to see you. Now."

Nha admires the police for spotting him immediately. At the prime minister's he also finds the foreign minister and a political adviser. They use English. Nha knows about a junket by U.S. Vice-President Nelson Rockefeller. The latter took advantage of funeral services for Chiang Kai-shek (who died on April 5) to make a tour of Southeast Asia. He's dropped a few bricks. Asked about Vietnam, he answered in terms of the U.S. presidential elections of 1976: "If two or three thousand Americans are killed or taken prisoner, that'll cause a number of problems." Asked about Cyprus, he suggested that the Greeks ought to be very happy about the Turkish invasion, which led to a resurgence of democracy in Greece: "If I were Greek, I'd kneel down and pray—I don't know what gods the Greeks would pray to in this case." Does President Ford intend to use his vice-president more often in foreign affairs? "That depends on who dies."

Jumping right in, the prime minister says to Nha, "Let's not waste time. I've asked you here because the end is coming [in Vietnam]. Rockefeller has asked me, and other Asian leaders, if we'd approve some process to oust Thieu."

Apparently, Rockefeller's idea—his own? Ford's? certainly not State's or the CIA's—would be to install a junta in Saigon. Ex-Prime Minister Khiem, Chief of Staff Vien and the fiery Marshal Ky would play a part in it. Later a coalition government would be formed and the junta would head it up. Lee Kuan Yew doesn't say whether he judges this plan reasonable or lunatic; Rockefeller may bear full responsibility for it.

The prime minister of Singapore says to Nha, "Warn your cousin. You stay here. Don't go back to Saigon. I'll fetch your family out of Vietnam. You know, the Americans have already chosen a place for Thieu's exile."[2]

Ignoring wiretaps, Nha calls the South Vietnamese president. The news is consistent with other reports. From his friends, young colonels, Nha knows about discontent at the ARVN's highest levels. He advises Thieu to resign: "Don't wait to be deposed or dismissed. Take the initiative. Make a move."

Nha returns to Saigon via Bangkok. He telephones the presidential palace. An aide asks him to call back later: "The president is working on an important speech."

Kissinger asks Martin: can they use Cap Saint-Jacques for a massive evacuation? To avoid chaos in this matter, he cables, we have to collaborate "very closely with President Thieu."[3] Kissinger is worried about Vietnamese who have worked with Americans: "We would like to know if Thieu is prepared to allow some of them to leave now."

Martin is warming to the idea of a negotiated solution. He has always defended the South Vietnamese president, but now he can imagine Thieu's departure. The latest rumors, attributed by Americans to the French Embassy, say the North Vietnamese will bomb Saigon if Thieu doesn't quit immediately.

In Washington, Kissinger makes a statement to the Senate Appropriations Committee.[4] "The North Vietnamese offensive, and the South Vietnamese response, did not come about by chance—although chance is always an element in warfare," he says in a Clausewitzian manner.

He reviews events of the last three months. He admits that South Vietnam has not always respected all the clauses of the Paris Agreement. Nevertheless, he insists, Saigon's record is better than North Vietnam's. There is a military imbalance today in the North's favor. Saigon has sought a political solution through discussions with the PRG in Paris: "There was no progress toward a compromise political settlement because Hanoi intended that there should not be."

Kissinger justifies the Paris Agreement. Neither the United States nor South Vietnam expected that the North Vietnamese would respect it entirely, he repeats. If they had been implemented by Hanoi, the principal clauses would have allowed a swing from the military to the political. Everything was based on a military parity that no longer exists: "North Vietnam's combat forces far outnumber those of the South, and they are better armed. Perhaps more important, they enjoy a psychological momentum which can be as decisive as armaments in battle."

Senator Joseph Montoya (D., N.M.) asks the secretary of state reasons for South Vietnamese defeats. Kissinger repeats his and the administration's arguments: "While Hanoi was strengthening . . . aid levels to Vietnam were cut . . . worldwide inflation . . . a fourfold increase in fuel prices."

Kissinger salutes the courage of the South Vietnamese army, which, he says, counted 30,000 dead in 1974. According to Saigon there were 21,000.

With the matter of Nixon's letters lurking in the background, Senator Montoya broaches the problem of U.S. obligations, legal and moral: "How long are we to sustain this moral obligation, assuming that we had it since our initial involvement in Vietnam?"

Kissinger:

> Senator . . . it would be extremely tempting to give a terminal date. But the fact is there are many situations in the world where the threat is constant and where a terminal date cannot be given unless the possible aggressor decides to give up his aggression. We have had a commitment to Europe, in the entire postwar period, and we cannot give that a terminal date. We have a commitment to Israel and we cannot give that a terminal date.

The senator: "Can you tell us of any other country in the world that has a moral obligation . . . to South Vietnam?"

"There are few other countries; . . . only the South Koreans, the Australians and the New Zealanders have sent contingents."

Another Democrat, Senator Henry Bellmon of Oklahoma, addresses Kissinger: "You sometimes have been called a 'modern miracle worker' in diplomacy, and you brought about more normal relations with China and—"

Kissinger interrupts the senator amiably: "If I may say so, not by me, but I may sometimes not have protested sufficiently loudly."

Senator Bellmon: "Also you helped bring about the agreement with Russia [sic], these . . . nations that have supplied the North Vietnamese. It is hard for us to understand if our relations with China and Russia are being improved, or being used here."

Kissinger, whose whole policy is here in question, replies: "When people say we have been used, one has to ask the question of what have we given them. . . . The principle objective of détente with the USSR was to minimize the danger of nuclear war and to lessen tensions in general." And this is what has happened, he goes on: the level of military supplies from the Soviet Union to North Vietnam has remained almost constant these last years. The level of military supplies from the United States to South Vietnam has dropped. The Soviet Union does not seem to have considered the ultimate use of these arms as carefully as we have.

Kissinger does not refer to any renewal of bombings. Democratic Senator Walter Huddleston asks: "Americans want to know yes or no, after so many years, will these supplemental funds [that the government is requesting] result in a better conclusion. Is there an answer to that question?"

"There is no certain answer," says Kissinger. "If only there were one!"

Moved, and also a good actor, the secretary of state ends his testimony by reading to the senators, in absolute silence, Sirik Matak's letter. The lawmakers are overcome. Kissinger makes the most of it: "Mr. Chairman, Ladies and Gentlemen. I suspect that neither Ambassador Dean nor I will ever be able to forget that letter, or the brave man that wrote it. Let us now, as Americans, act together to assure that we receive no more letters of this kind."

Maintaining an elevated tone in defending himself, Kissinger scarcely even touches on the fundamental cause of the North Vietnamese push to a total and final offensive. To start with, there was the Watergate affair, for which Nixon is to blame, and Nixon alone. As intolerable as it was absurd, that shabby little break-in at Democratic Party headquarters initiated a process that Kissinger could not have foreseen while constructing the delicate framework of the Paris Agreement. If Nixon were still in power, he would probably, even certainly, have sent B-52s after the attack on Ban Me Thuot. In bombing Cambodia and Hanoi, Nixon had already shown his scorn for congressional or public opinion. Would the resolution and the War Powers Act have stopped him? If the flyers had received orders from the president, commander in chief of the armed forces, would they have obeyed? Or would they have called their lawyers, refusing to obey, citing the resolution and the act?

Ford's financial requests activate eight committees in the House and Senate. James Schlesinger and General Weyand also testify.

The numbers shrink: $515 million, $449, $401, $370 then $350. They play with the idea of $165 million for military assistance and the same sum for humanitarian aid. Congress, especially the senators, is very close to granting $200 million for humanitarian aid and for evacuation operations. Ford doesn't compromise: he wants $972 million altogether.

The exhausting confrontation between administration and Congress is also shown on television, on the radio and in the print media. During a press conference, Ford tries to put his requests into perspective: he's not asking much, less than a billion dollars. What is that "compared to the $150 billion that we've already spent?"

Hanoi's leaders, and Le Duc Tho down south at the front, keep abreast of all this.

Evidently, despite their good will and sympathy for Gerald Ford, a majority of Congress is not prepared to follow him in the matter of military aid. Naturally, he can have all the money he needs to evacuate Americans. How many are there, really, 5,400 or so? They will also vote the president substantial credits for the now famous humanitarian aid, and to keep Vietnamese who served the United States from falling into communist hands.

For an hour and a half Ford receives the whole Senate Foreign Relations Committee.[5] Republicans and Democrats alike want the president to promise a quick evacuation of Americans in Vietnam. The Vietnamese are a secondary concern. How many does he propose to take out? Ford answers: "All in all there must be between 175,000 and 200,000. We're morally responsible and we have to help the people who helped us."

The president doesn't want to set an exact date for the senators. To pull the embassy out immediately would create panic and endanger the lives of compatriots still there: "We need to gain time, even if it's only a few days."

Some in Washington have talked about evacuating a million Vietnamese, transshipping them onto warships at Cap Saint-Jacques. How many soldiers and marines would you need to protect such an operation? Several divisions. The lawmakers prefer the figure of 200,000 Vietnamese.

They take up the case of Ambassador Martin. Before seeing the president, most of the senators read a report by Richard Moose and Charles Missner, aides to the delegation just back from Vietnam. In their view, Martin still won't acknowledge that the momentum of military developments is irreversible.

From Saigon the ambassador follows the skirmishes in Washington.

To whoever will listen, he vigorously denounces "the fiscal whores in Congress." Expecting a negative vote on military aid,[6] Martin suggests to Kissinger that "it would be highly preferable to find some way to delay the final vote." No sense in demoralizing the South Vietnamese government; they need time to turn around. Thieu has finally understood: with his minister Hung, he's working out another plan and another maneuver to acquire American dollars. Saigon could ask Washington for a long-term loan of $3 billion, over three years, coupled with a ten-year moratorium. The repayments would begin in 1985. The U.S. Congress could set the interest rate. The loan would be guaranteed by agricultural and oil resources. They've even found a winning name for it, which should charm American public opinion: The Liberty Loan.

Hung submits this idea to Martin, who asks embassy economists to study it. Hung will go to Washington and set up a lobby to get the "Liberty Loan" off the ground. On the telephone Martin seemed vague to him. Hung remembers one question from the ambassador: "By the way, is your president going to resign?"

On the military side Martin emphasizes, in his cables to Kissinger, that the battle of Xuan Loc west of Saigon is going well, with the ARVN inflicting "well over 2,000 KIAs. . . . Some captured are in their mid-teens. One yesterday said he 'thought' he was fourteen." So he thinks Hanoi has no more reserves. . . . The ambassador remains confident: "I do not think that the [ARVN] will necessarily fold."[7]

The new government has at last been installed in Saigon.[8] Martin, still to Kissinger,[9] whom he cables several times a day: "It seems clear that [Thieu], as well as everybody else, is unsure of what comes next."

In Washington, the Senate Foreign Relations Committee gives provisional approval to a request for urgent legislation. It will grant the president the necessary authority to use force if needed while evacuating Americans and certain Vietnamese. The senators demand that Martin speed up the withdrawal of Americans. Republican Senator Charles Percy asks Ford to make sure that every seat on every plane leaving Saigon is occupied. The president confirms that Kissinger has so ordered. Martin sees just how unfavorable the attitude is in Washington.

Above and beyond the immediate problems, a hunt for scapegoats has begun. That's how democracies work.

How many Vietnamese can be airlifted out and how can it be done in conformity with U.S. law? You can leave the United States without showing any identification at all. Entering the country is much tougher, considering the rules and quotas that apply to Vietnamese as to all other candidates for immigration. The State Department is fighting hard. It alerts the Saigon embassy (on April 14 at last) that it has won some limited concessions. A certain number of Vietnamese will enter the United States under oath, on parole. This is not pure altruism. They want to invalidate one of the reasons Americans are giving in refusing to leave Vietnam—the existence of Vietnamese wives or children. The U.S. Justice Department, which handles immigration, defines the criteria.

To emigrate to the United States, one must be: (1) legally married to a male or female American; (2) child of a male or female American; (3) mother or father of a U.S. citizen (including a Vietnamese become American by marriage); (4) mother or father of a foreign spouse of a U.S. citizen (for example, of a Vietnamese married to an American and who is not yet a U.S. citizen); (5) unmarried minor sibling of a foreign spouse; or (6) unmarried minor sibling of a U.S. citizen. Each candidate for departure must document his status and fill out form I-94.

Officials in Washington feel they've set out clear, just and generous rules. Unfortunately they fail to take into account Vietnamese realities. An undetermined number of American civilians in Vietnam—workers,

foremen, engineers working for private firms, reporters, photographers—
have been cohabiting for some time with Vietnamese and have fathered
several children. Some of them have simply neglected to get married.
Officials in Washington are thinking of the American nuclear family, husband, wife, one or two children in time, and maybe one or two grandpar-
ents. The Vietnamese families who apply at the consular agencies often
count fifteen to thirty persons; in the case of certain Sino-Vietnamese from
Cholon, fifty.

In Saigon, U.S. officials know what's what and are more flexible. On
the planes taking off from Tan Son Nhut every day, seats are limited.
Painful decisions: How can anyone know who should stay and who should
go? A heartbreaking choice, especially when the Vietnamese say to U.S.
consular employees, "You choose."

One man in charge of this sad triage, Ken Moorefield, decides to bend
the rules. When he cannot accept a whole family, he operates on one firm
and sensible principle: Leave no old people in Saigon without a son or
daughter to help them survive.

In theory the U.S. consulate, before granting visas, must confirm that
candidates have been cleared by the Vietnamese authorities. Obtaining a
passport is no small matter, not to mention the fiscal formalities. Americans
break Vietnamese rules more easily than U.S. laws. Since early April the
consulate has been accepting a sort of laissez-passer issued by the Vietnamese Ministry of the Interior, whether legitimate, falsified or bought.
To grease the wheels they promise bureaucrats in the ministry or police
to evacuate their families if they're more cooperative. Normally in Saigon
even when you bribe an official it takes weeks, sometimes months, to obtain
a legal document. When tens of thousands are clamoring there's no hope
that passports, exit visas, tax clearances and laissez-passer will be provided
rapidly. A flourishing trade in forgeries springs up, supplying the whole
range of printed documents and rubber stamps. The Americans learn not
to examine too carefully. In Washington they talked of a million potential
evacuees, and the president spoke of pulling out 200,000. No number has
yet been specified to the embassy in Saigon. Only on April 26 will Graham
Martin be authorized to allow 25,000 Vietnamese to leave legally.

Alongside the official evacuation traffic, or pipeline, parallel unofficial
lines are created, supported by businesses, by American airline operators,
by the CIA, by private citizens. Larry Johnstone and Lionel Rosenblatt,
two Foreign Service officers in their early thirties working in Washington
after a stint in Saigon, are appalled by dilatory officialdom. They take
"annual" leave and fly to the South Vietnamese capital at their own expense, without notifying their superiors.[10] They set up headquarters at the
Hotel Caravelle, then in an empty apartment. For six days, hardly sleeping,
they streak around Saigon in an old Citroën or a Pan Am bus. They collect
false papers, go to secret rendezvous at the central post office or the ca-

thedral and assemble *their* refugees. It was all very "melodramatic, not very Foreign Service," says Johnstone.

The main problem is to filter the clandestine passengers into the airport. The police are strict, as are the military guards, even when offered substantial bribes. Some refugees sneak through in the Citroën's trunk. Rosenblatt works with Jim Eckes of Continental Air Services. In all Johnstone and Rosenblatt evacuate about 200 Vietnamese, among them 20 adult males who, the two officers say, would be in mortal danger in North Vietnamese hands.

At his pagoda the bonze Thien Hue has decided to stay in Saigon whatever happens. His older brother, a second lieutenant, is escorting NVA troops captured at Xuan Loc. The second lieutenant takes advantage of his trips to Saigon and advises his parents to leave. They urge him to desert. He refuses. He tells his brother about the battle of Xuan Loc: "When the communists broke into the city for the first time, some of our wounded soldiers struggled to their feet so they wouldn't be taken, and trudged back holding plastic bags over their exposed guts."

The second lieutenant thinks the North Vietnamese have unlimited stocks of mortar and artillery shells.

Some deputies from the National Assembly friendly to the pagoda's superiors assure them that the Americans and Chinese have agreed to establish a buffer zone under PRG control. That's why the Americans have ordered ARVN units to withdraw. More wild stories circulate in the capital: a military coup d'état has broken out in Hanoi and Giap has been killed; NVA divisions are pulling out and heading north to halt the Chinese, who are attacking the Democratic Republic of Vietnam; obviously everything that's happening, including the battle of Xuan Loc, is part of a very complicated and highly subtle overall plan jointly conceived by the Chinese and the Americans. Or by the Soviets and the Americans. Or by the North Vietnamese and the Americans.

The European and American communities still hang out at the Cercle Sportif, where the rules are still in effect: no bathing suits except at the swimming pools, white tennis shoes required on the courts. They stroll among the tamarind trees, they play a game of boules. The number of women has dwindled these last weeks; they're still smearing themselves with Ambre Solaire or Monoï. Waiters in white jackets serve whiskeys or gin-and-tonics. Quartered lemons gleam on the saucers. A page rings his bell: "Telephone, Mr. Hien! . . . Mr. Polgar! . . . Mr. Brochand!"

The fans stir up a false gaiety and a true uneasiness. Americans and Germans, French and Australians exchange the latest news and old gossip, or glance through the papers. Once in a while they have a good laugh: Ed Daly, the president of World Airways, has called reporters to his hotel suite in Tokyo and read them a telegram he sent to President Ford. Daly ordered a DC-8 and a Boeing 727 to Saigon to be filled with refugees. No one was allowed to board. The two planes flew back to Tokyo empty. Daly claims that the U.S. Embassy threatened to shoot down his planes on takeoff. The embassy has denied it. No one knows whether President Ford has read Daly's telegram: "Keep your fucking CIA men out of the action and let those who are immediately interested do a job. . . . Get some loyal and dedicated men in who can make a contribution. Being one of your largest personal and corporate taxpayers, I have a right to an opinion. Let's get moving."

The foreign establishment in Saigon finds this language shocking, but through its vulgarity Daly is telling a truth: to avoid a panic, Graham Martin is still holding up the evacuation.

Near the Cercle Sportif, on the lawns of the presidential palace, soldiers are setting up anti-aircraft guns, digging trenches, building redoubts of sandbags, emplacing heavy machineguns. To oppose the North Vietnamese if they arrive, or other South Vietnamese soldiers, rebels, if there's a coup?

The palace emits general statements, mainly incantatory. The president[11] announces that his new team is full of "good will," ready to negotiate with the communists. The government "will not surrender." Thieu hopes the communists in La Celle-Saint-Cloud will return to the conference table and establish the National Council of Reconciliation and Concord.

The new cabinet consists mostly of civilians chosen by Prime Minister Can, who is amazed at the room to maneuver Thieu has granted him. Among the ministers is Ton That Niem, a moderate Buddhist. Civilians in the government are saying openly that they have no more faith in a military solution and are as tired of the war as most of their fellow citizens. Many want Thieu to resign but don't dare tell him. General Don, minister of defense, is busy. On the president's authority, he places several field officers and generals under close arrest, among them General Phu.

Don, who claims to have serious contacts with the PRG, is cooking up a plan: he'll assume presidential powers and in forty-eight hours will issue the order for a cease-fire. He'll form a new government. In return, the PRG will guarantee the security of Americans in Saigon. Except for a small nucleus at the embassy, most will be evacuated. After an interim period, the PRG will take control of the city. They will do nothing to impede those Vietnamese who want to leave. They will freely grant . . . exit visas. These can be applied for in Hue, Danang and Saigon.

So, barely on its feet, the new government is distancing itself from President Thieu. In a last-ditch effort to influence American leaders and public opinion, Thieu publishes one of Nixon's letters, dated January 23, 1973. Excitement runs high in Washington. The State Department enjoins Martin to emphasize that a letter does not constitute a treaty. Thieu doesn't realize that the very mention of Richard Nixon's name is unfortunate, even with many Republican voters and elected officials.

The Vietnamese president is asking everyone to fight, to counterattack, to stabilize the rear as well as the front. As its contribution to the war effort, the municipal government publishes new regulations concerning . . . traffic: doubtless to avoid delays, the city sets speed limits of fifteen kilometers per hour for bicycles, twenty-five for motorcycles, trucks and buses, forty for scooters and cars.

In case of alert, "the public should not panic."

17

---◆---

Filling up the Ocean
with Stones

At the Quai d'Orsay they always say serious questions are not settled in public. French diplomacy is discreet, not secret.

In Saigon it is hardly discreet. Too many go-betweens, too many well-intentioned meddlers, too many real and imaginary envoys, too many double and triple (and trouble) agents circulate in political and military circles.

Distorted or not, the French position is known to all: Ambassador Mérillon has decided to bank heavily on the Third Force and Big Minh.

In the French view, the South Vietnamese have lost the war but the Saigon regime is not going to collapse within weeks. The essential is to assure the survival of a diminished South Vietnam, a kind of Cochin China. The North Vietnamese are in no great hurry; they'll accept a neutral government headed by Big Minh.

This is what Pierre Brochand explains to Thomas Polgar on April 13 beside the swimming pool at the Cercle Sportif. Second counselor at the French Embassy, Brochand is a specialist in Indochinese affairs, as handsome as he is tanned, with a trace of a Midi accent; he is in practice deputy ambassador for political affairs. The first counselor takes care of cultural affairs and his offices are two kilometers from the French Embassy. Brochand and Polgar have seen a good deal of each other these last weeks.

For some time Brochand has been delicately reproaching Mérillon for not spending more time with Third Force people. The French ambassador knows it would annoy Thieu if he saw too much of Big Minh.

Polgar is now leaning toward a political solution involving Thieu's departure; Thieu will have to be replaced. Why not by Big Minh? The French counselor proves himself a realist, moreover, by saying that France is ready to take in 50,000 Vietnamese refugees. Brochand is applying his ambassador's policies.

Jean-Marie Mérillon is rather small, a trifle nearsighted, a graduate of the Ecole Nationale d'Administration who speaks elegantly and much. He is a distant relative of the Giscards through the Carnots and was named to Saigon by Georges Pompidou. While presenting his diplomatic credentials to Thieu, Mérillon heard "La Marseillaise": they were playing it for the first time in ten years in South Vietnam. According to Mérillon, people here take the French for more than they are. He says some Vietnamese see the French representative as almost a viceroy. Mérillon has several objectives. To watch over the safety of the French in Vietnam (about 10,000 nationals); 300 were rescued from the Central Highlands by private planes. Should the NVA take Saigon, he must protect the community, especially during a turbulent transition period. Mérillon is thinking of 1945. The Japanese were leaving. In Saigon, the French of one enclave were massacred atrociously—babies flung on fires, women raped, men tortured. Mérillon wants to spare the capital Danang's fate. He must do what is best for France. In the two Vietnams, French policy, if there is one, is a mixture of nostalgic memories and vague desires. For the Quai d'Orsay, Vietnam does not take priority. After anti-American Gaullism, Pompidou has eased off, and Giscard is feeling his way, basing policy on Hanoi's hypothetical flexibility. So many Vietnamese in Saigon, at least those over forty, keep saying they're so much closer to the French than to the Americans! These Americans are rude and blunt. The French have an exaggerated sense of their own importance. Historical importance—after all, they created Indochina. Diplomatic importance—the 1973 agreement was signed in Paris. When Mérillon left Paris for Saigon, he asked for instructions from his minister. Michel Jobert answered: "An ambassador needs no instructions; he instructs himself." He added: "How're the digs in Saigon? Keep an embassy that looks like an embassy."

In Saigon the French Embassy is charming. In the residence, Mérillon admires the spiral staircases hung from mailed turrets, which date back to the era of admiral-governors. On the whitewashed walls, collections of blue china from Hue hang like motionless waterfalls. The other collection, of champagne coolers bearing the arms of the Second Republic, and of the Government-General, and of the high commissioner of the republic, is superb. Some of the silverplate, and the Christofle, is even stamped with the imperial crown.

In his lovely embassy, Mérillon would like to implement grand policies. He receives often, listens well, offers encouragement. He's told Nha,[1] "You must speak to your cousin. He should be more accommodating, bring the Third Force into action, make contacts with the PRG."

Nha replied, "You think Hanoi will let him talk to the PRG!"

Mérillon also hinted, "You yourself might play a large role in the new government."

"That doesn't interest me. I have no confidence in this so-called coalition government."

What a narrow view Thieu's men take!

Mérillon is one of the few ambassadors welcome at Martin's table; there is great mutual esteem. On Polgar's advice, Martin doesn't put much stock in French political or military intelligence. The French certainly have planters, businessmen and priests scattered about the provinces, but nothing comparable to the CIA's powerful network. On the other hand, Martin pays attention to Mérillon in diplomatic matters. At the very least, the French may be useful. The two embassies adjoin on the boulevard Thong Nhut. The ambassadors have had a gate cut in the common wall. In case the Saigon telephone system breaks down, and to maintain close ties, Martin and Mérillon have a hot line at their disposal, a direct phone line between their offices. At the French end the phone is in a little room just off Mérillon's office. An apostolic nuncio, visiting the French ambassador and seeing him dash to and fro, noted with some distress that Mérillon seemed colicky.

Martin is looking for a political solution and is more and more inclined to listen to the French diplomat. In mid-April they agree: Thieu is truly an obstacle.

Martin toys with several formulas. One of them seems attractive at this point: additional aid + political negotiations. Unfortunately on April 16 Kissinger cables bad news about the marathon of committees and debates in Congress: "We must anticipate we will end up with a negative vote." According to the secretary of state, the debates in the Senate and the House are polarized on a *totally phony* issue. Kissinger knows how to handle Martin, and compliments him, telling him that he is doing his job in Saigon as admirably as a "field commander." Kissinger then asks him how he'd reduce the American presence to 2,000.

That same day President Ford commits a gaffe, saying carelessly that he has ordered all Americans evacuated "who are not essential." Kissinger almost apologizes to Martin: "I know that this will make your task more difficult." Reluctantly the ambassador agrees to the idea of an evacuation in a stable situation and with ARVN cooperation. According to recent reports, some South Vietnamese officers are warning that if the Americans let them down and pull out, they'll stop the aircraft from taking off. They're even prepared to shoot them down. So on April 16 at 1:30 P.M., with Admiral Hugh Benton, sent in by CINCPAC, Martin is studying an evacuation plan for 200,000 Vietnamese. The admiral proposes to embark them at Cap Saint-Jacques. From there, they'll head for Thailand, the Philippines, Singapore. A skeptical Martin expresses his doubts in a cable direct to Brent Scowcroft at the White House. In the table of organization Kissinger is Martin's superior, but the ambassador likes to prove to himself, and show others, that he is also the president's personal representative. Anything but modest, an intelligence officer during World War II, Martin believes himself more competent than any general or admiral. And more competent than anyone when it comes to evacuation problems: in Paris, he laid out evacuation plans for Americans in case of Soviet attack on Western Europe. He would have sent his personnel toward Brussels, against the current of the inevitable flood of refugees rushing south. He surely doesn't plan to send his Americans or Vietnamese up toward Hanoi. But in his view the admiral's plan will not hold up and would be costly. It would mean chartering sixteen ships at $250,000 a day.

But some of his colleagues are relieved that he's finally zeroing in on the problem of evacuation.

Now that he's finally accepted the idea of retreat, with a heavy heart, Martin receives a disturbing cable "for his eyes only" from Kissinger on April 17, written after a meeting of top officials from various departments and agencies:[2] "You should know that . . . there was almost no support for the evacuation of Vietnamese, and for the use of American force to help protect any evacuation. The sentiment of our military, DOD [Department of Defense], and CIA colleagues was to get out fast and now." Kissinger agrees with Martin that he must prevent panicky chain reactions, but the secretary of state requires that by April 22 the number of Americans in Vietnam be reduced to 2,000.

Returning from a trip abroad, itinerant ambassador Bui Diem asks to meet with Thieu. A colonel answers: "The president is most distressed by the loss of his natal province. The prime minister will see you."

Bui Diem has no desire to see that politically impotent unknown. In Vietnam only the president matters. Bui Diem's phone rings. Prime Minister Can himself says, "The president wants me to meet with you."

Bui Diem hesitates. At that point Don walks in. The minister of defense, a busybody, insists. After all, Can *is* prime minister. Bui Diem is irritated: "Why should I waste my time?"

Don leaves, comes back, finally drags Bui Diem to Can's. There they find a vice prime minister, Hao. A gloomy general survey follows. Moreover, these men have no power to make decisions.

"The plain truth is," Bui Diem says, "that there's nothing more to be done."

The prime minister and the vice prime minister are dumbfounded. They're aware that Bui Diem knows a lot about Americans and the mechanics of power in the United States. Don seems a little less stunned. Hao cries, "Well, we have to organize the defense of the Delta!" Don points out some difficulties there. What do the Americans in Saigon think?

Bui Diem goes to the embassy. Martin and Bui Diem respect each other, but candor is not the order of the day. Martin: "Are you going to see the president? Will you tell him the truth?"

"Yes," answers Bui Diem. "The truth is that for the United States the war is over."

Martin has no comment on that remark. He lavishes vague encouragements on Bui Diem. He does not tell him that the United States ambassador, himself, personal representative of the president, is thinking hard about the departure of the president of the Republic of Vietnam. Martin freely admits that a diplomat has to be an actor.

The worst news of the day comes in: the Khmer Rouge control all of Phnom Penh, 190 kilometers from Saigon. Big Minh hears this while taking a meal with several friends in a restaurant owned by General Mai Huu Xuan, near a rubber plantation at Thu Duc on the outskirts of Saigon. Minh shows no surprise and no worry. One of his friends, political observer Ton That Thien, says, "Now the communists will go all out and march on Saigon."

Minh protests: "They'll need six months to reach Saigon. You don't know anything about it. You're not a soldier."

According to him, the communists will call a halt because—familiar tune—they haven't the necessary cadres to control and run the capital. Minh looks around for support and keeps French and American diplomats up to date. His liaison with the U.S. Embassy still runs through General Charles Timmes, the retired officer who's joined up with the CIA; liaison with the French is secure thanks to Brochand. Mérillon instructed Brochand to reestablish contact with Minh. One of Minh's close colleagues, Senator Vu Van Mau, would like to send six or seven deputies of his party, the Force for National Reconciliation, into their communist-occupied constituencies. There the deputies could woo the PRG. Minh repeats that the communists do not intend to attack the capital, that they only want to isolate Saigon. If the government deploys enough units on the outskirts of the city, particularly to the east toward Xuan Loc, and if they negotiate quickly, they'll be able to avoid the establishment of an "unacceptable coalition government." They must reach some agreement that preserves a small South Vietnam. They can see about a coalition government later.

But why would the communists accept that plan?

"Because they don't have the means to govern all of South Vietnam," Big Minh repeats.

PRG authorities in Hanoi have organized a visit to "liberated" Danang for April 17. They've invited Alexandre Casella to join a group of foreign correspondents. They told this consultant from the High Commission for Refugees, "You can go in because you're a journalist, too. You won't be going as a delegate of the HCR."

The group includes correspondents from Le Monde, the AFP, Pravda, the New China agency, and Swedish and French television crews. The Yak-40 that flies them in lands at the big airport in Danang, for a reception with a buffet beneath a large portrait of Ho Chi Minh.

The city seems calm. There are few NVA soldiers in the streets. The PRG is directing traffic. Chinese shops display the flag of the People's Republic of China, which the New China correspondent finds prodigiously interesting. This is a guided tour. The general impression is good. Inspection of an orphanage run by Vietnamese sisters. One of them says, "There was no fighting in Danang. We were liberated by the North Vietnamese army. We keep busy with our orphans."

Back in Hanoi, Casella writes a report for the United Nations that the secretary-general makes public. This report states that the food situation seems normal, that displaced people are drifting home, that the shantytowns seem to be emptying. They need some emergency aid, and over the short haul they'll surely need various kinds of help to repopulate villages.

The Hanoi papers rejoice: "A United Nations official has visited Danang. The situation is normal." A charming turnaround: now, for the North Vietnamese, Casella went to Danang as a representative of the HCR. Casella notices no triumphant elation in the North Vietnamese capital over military developments in the South.

On the first day of Casella's excursion to Danang, Frank Snepp meets with his best agent in a suburb of Saigon. The agent is categorical: the North Vietnamese have decided to fight to final victory; there will be no diplomatic-political solution. Martin and Polgar attach no importance to Snepp's report. In the fullness of time it arrives on the secretary of state's desk in Washington, while Kissinger is renewing pressure on the Soviets— a strategy that Martin likes. He cabled Kissinger: "It does seem to me that there should be at least a small price for détente, and perhaps some way could be found to make the Soviet Union and China believe it would be to their advantage in their future dealings with us to exercise the most massive restraint on Hanoi to back away from Saigon and resume the negotiating track."

In Washington at about noon on April 18, Kissinger meets the Soviet ambassador, Anatoly Dobrynin, wholly at home in the United States and very popular on the Washington circuit. Kissinger hands him a note from Ford intended for Brezhnev: "Our principal concern is that the evacuation of Americans and important Vietnamese take place in good order." The president wants a "controlled evacuation," avoiding confrontation between the NVA and supervisory U.S. detachments. If the NVA will cease fire, the Americans will halt deliveries of materiel to Saigon and will be ready to resume political discussions. Kissinger warns Dobrynin specifically that the North Vietnamese must not touch the Saigon airport. Should they bombard it, there would be very unfortunate consequences for Hanoi. Kissinger indicates that Washington is dealing directly with Moscow—not with Hanoi, much less with Beijing. All in all, the secretary of state is threatening Hanoi and implicitly tossing détente into the pot by addressing himself exclusively to Moscow. A necessary but futile procedure. Kissinger knows from experience how hard it is to talk with communists in Moscow or Hanoi except from a position of strength. He seems to suppose, or pretends to believe, that Brezhnev can issue orders to North Vietnamese divisions. Kissinger is unaware, and Dobrynin as well, that four days earlier, on April 14, from his headquarters in Loc Ninh, the North Vietnamese commander in chief had prepared the final assault on Saigon.

There, informed political circles—often badly misinformed on political matters—have not ruled out an NVA campaign to encircle and isolate the capital. Ambassador Jean-Marie Mérillon has a political strategy: to put pressure on Minh and Martin.

The French diplomat meets Minh for the first time April 17, apologizing that he has not visited earlier.

Mérillon assures Minh of France's support. In Vietnam France has obligations, rights or interests. The voluble ambassador outlines the setting for a large-scale political operation. The plan centers on Minh. Of course they must see that Saigon is not put to fire and the sword. If the communists occupy the capital, it is almost certain that a way of life will vanish. The two men converse in French. They are emotional, Minh the more so; with tears in his eyes he shakes Mérillon's hand for long moments: "Yes, it must be so. You are a man of great heart, Mr. Ambassador. I'm going to try, I'll see."

Mérillon follows instructions. He has received an astonishing cable from the Quai d'Orsay. The gist: force Thieu out, install Minh as president. Mérillon thinks he can work out an "honest transition." The only possible solution is to negotiate.

The South Vietnamese government publishes an announcement in English and Vietnamese in the newspapers: "Repulsing massive communist attacks on Xuan Loc and Long An, the armed forces of the Republic of Vietnam have shown their willingness to defend their country and their capacity to overcome the communist aggressors."

Perhaps less convinced than it says of its "capacity to overcome," the same government is preparing to send its gold reserves to the United States. If the vote in the U.S. Congress turns out negative, Thieu will say the gold must be sold in order to buy arms and munitions.

Rumors of peace, rumors of war: the North Vietnamese will never attack Saigon; small North Vietnamese units, sappers and engineers in civilian clothes, have infiltrated the capital; putsch in Saigon, coup d'état in Hanoi. . . .

Most of the Americans still in Vietnam are anticommunist, but some among them are sympathetic to the PRG and the North Vietnamese— particularly in the humanitarian and charitable organizations that live day after day in close contact with the miseries and misfortunes of war. For these Americans the North Vietnamese advance is neither an invasion nor an occupation, but liberation, an assurance that the fighting will finally end. For them, the end of the war is naturally peace.

Claudia Krich belongs to a Quaker humanitarian organization.[3] She has worked tirelessly among the civilians. She speaks Vietnamese and she has been working in a center for physiotherapy and corrective surgery at Quang Ngai, north of Saigon. There they supply the handicapped with artificial limbs, crutches and wheelchairs. Believing that Quang Ngai would be bombed, she returned to the capital in March.

She keeps a diary:

> Saigon, April 17, 1975, Thursday.
>
> The rumors fly again, that Saturday will bring liberation, or at least an attack on Saigon. One tidbit I learned today is the "secret code" the U.S. Embassy will broadcast over the radio when they decide to evacuate. Someone will say: "The temperature in Saigon is 105 degrees and rising." Then they'll play "I'm Dreaming of a White Christmas."

All the Americans in Saigon know the code.

> We listen to the radio every night to count the provinces as they "fall" [writes Krich]. Quang Ngai was liberated on March 24 . . . with hardly a shot being fired. Danang was liberated on March 29. By now, there's very little GVN area left at all. Saigon will be soon. An American friend said today that the Hong Kong Shanghai Bank won't take dollar checks anymore.

Admiral Cang's sailors and regional forces stop the NVA's Fifth and Seventh Divisions at Ben Luc, on Saigon's river. North Vietnamese losses are heavy; the South Vietnamese sailors are firing 20 mm., 40 mm., and 105 mm. pieces. Nevertheless, morale at South Vietnamese headquarters sinks lower and lower. In a letter to his ambassador, Homer Smith wonders if even Chief of Staff Vien doesn't favor Thieu's ouster—which confirms Wolfgang Lehmann's impressions.

Thieu is at his lowest ebb. He retreated first to his private apartments, then to the concrete shelter in the palace basement. He learned that marines and rangers, before pulling out, razed the tombs of his ancestors in a village near the coastal town of Phan Rang. A terrible and oppressive forewarning . . . Thieu refuses to answer phone calls even from the U.S. Embassy.

Aware of Saigon's uneasy gloom, Martin decrees that the populace be reassured. He orders Alan Carter, head of the USIS, to appear on television. Martin's decision is not altogether free of malice; he doesn't like this bearded man whose notion of information differs greatly from his own. Perhaps Martin feels a certain satisfaction in handing Carter this difficult assignment. At any rate Carter doesn't seem fully at ease when he appears on television, questioned by a Vietnamese: "There is a rumor that if no positive decision is taken about appropriations the Americans will be evacuated . . . by April 19."

Carter answers loftily that no one knows *when* Congress will make its decision, adding: "There is no truth to that rumor. If you were to visit Mrs. and Ambassador Martin's home, you would see that nothing has been evacuated. The same is true of my house. . . ."

"Another rumor says that the consulate issues passes to certain Vietnamese for purposes of evacuating them . . . so there are long lines at the consular offices. . . ."

Carter gestures and protests: "Another rumor! We are really talking first about normal functions; filing of marriage papers, reporting of births, visas. . . ."

To hear him you'd wonder about the sudden rise in the birthrate among Americans in Saigon.

Carter knows that many viewers have seen the lines at the consulate: "It is true that some Americans have been leaving," he concedes. "Given the circumstances, it is normal that some Americans should have been leaving somewhat earlier than they had planned."

These Americans just moved up the start of their summer vacations.

The information officer's performance is unconvincing. Even provincial viewers feel that an evacuation has begun. Carter did what he could. To show that his embassy is working hard at counterpropaganda, Martin sends Kissinger the text of the televised interview and cables doggedly: "If there is a negative vote, I hope you and the President will calmly announce you are going all out to win the fight for the fiscal year '76 appropriation." The ambassador knows it's a bit far-fetched: "As unrealistic as this may seem, it will have great effect here." They'll tell the Saigon government, Not a dollar in 1975, but you watch, in 1976 the manna will fall again! Martin is afraid of highly disagreeable reactions among South Vietnamese, civil and military: "There must be no panic in Washington. The one thing that would set off violence would be a sudden order for American evacuation." According to him, "The ARVN can hold the approaches to Saigon for quite a while." He doubts that Hanoi "desires a frontal smash at Saigon." The ambassador is worried about interpretations, all over the world, of decisions taken in Washington. The word "betrayed" appears frequently in the cable. No one must think that the Americans are betraying the Vietnamese. Above all, Martin wants to persuade Kissinger not to send in the marines until he asks for them: "I will not hesitate in the slightest to do so if public order begins to crumble." Then, for the first time, Martin cables: "It seems to me that the essential process of negotiations cannot be started with Thieu in power."

Unless ordered not to, Martin will discuss this possibility with Thieu. The ambassador outlines his proposed approach to the South Vietnamese president. He'll talk to him as a friend. Thieu's place in history is assured. If he does not leave, his generals will force him to. He must preserve the legitimacy of the South Vietnamese constitution. That will be an act of courage. Thieu will place his country's interests above his own. Martin's advice will be strictly personal, and *not* on instructions from the president or the secretary of state.

With marvelous diplomatic skill the ambassador is asking his secretary of state for authorization to lean hard on Thieu, but is also freeing Kissinger and Ford from responsibility. Hypocrisy or self-sacrifice?

Written by a man under severe strain, this cable 710 is not tooled like a dissertation. Martin reverts to the problem of evacuating Americans: if "U.S. armed forces come in here in force under the present circumstances, they will be fighting the South Vietnamese on the way out." On the other hand, if Washington "[plays] it cool," Martin can get these people out, "in a way that will not, repeat not, add a rather ghastly mistake to the thousands the Americans have already made in and about Vietnam. Warm regards." Lucidity, at least.

The cable will remain confidential. In Saigon, only his secretary and Martin's code clerk will see it. Kissinger's answer: "I have discussed your cable 710 with the President. There is no objection to your proceeding along the lines of paragraph 9." A brief and discreet funeral oration for Thieu.

In a cable widely distributed, from Washington to Honolulu and Saigon, Kissinger says:

> We had a very sober interagency meeting today to review the state of our planning on the evacuation of Americans and Vietnamese. . . . There is strong domestic and congressional concern that we must put a higher priority on insuring the safety of Americans. . . . Is it realistic to believe that Vung Tau can be used for mass evacuation? Do you believe that certain South Vietnamese forces could be counted on to help secure evacuation zones?

On April 18, Kissinger issues further orders:

> Despite your best efforts and my own instincts, the perception in Washington of the military situation around Saigon, and of Hanoi's own intentions, has reached the point where I must ask you to reduce total American presence to the level of 1,100 by [Tuesday evening, April 22]. This is the number of people whom [sic] we estimate can be evacuated in one helo lift.

Kissinger is afraid they'll accuse him and Martin of "dragging our feet."

Congress may at any moment order immediate evacuation of all Americans from Saigon: "I know that this decision will come as a blow to you. It is so for me. I can assure you that once we reach this level, I shall not press you again for further reductions except on the day, God forbid, if and when you are instructed completely to close down the mission. Warm regards."

There was the problem of sending a 350-man security force to protect General Smith's agencies. A reconnaissance team had sent a message to CINCPAC in Honolulu and to the command of the marine amphibious force in Okinawa. The missions outlined, says this message, "require at least a batallion of infantry."

Martin reacts with dry irony to Kissinger's last cable: "We are glad to note that the interagency meeting yesterday was a sober one. It should have been, but it is necessary to avoid the tendency of always assuming the 'worst case' which will lead to decisions which may endanger the situation here. We also assume the 'worst case' and plan for it." The pessimism in Washington, even catastrophism, angers the ambassador.

In Hanoi on April 18 the prime minister receives a Frenchman, Dr. Roussel, who tells him of Pham Van Dong's recent statement to the French ambassador; the North Vietnamese prime minister said, "There is not much chance of a political solution."

Contradictions arise pretty well everywhere in the American camp. No one speaks seriously of evacuating a million Vietnamese. Kissinger's estimates fluctuate around one figure, 200,000. In Washington a special organization is set up by representatives of various government agencies. Its activities will be coordinated by Bill Brown, a retired ambassador and a friend to Martin.

They have to provide for the evacuation of 50,000 Vietnamese refugees in the next ninety days. Facilities to process and welcome them, under the base commander at Camp Pendleton in California, must be operational by April 29. All humanitarian organizations and federal agencies will collaborate in the preparations. Martin replies that he can't evacuate so many refugees directly from Saigon. He's thinking of Ford's figure of 200,000. "We will instruct our own local employees to make their way to designated spots on the coast where they may be evacuated. Many may not make it, but we do owe those who do the chance to escape."

The State Department, other departments and the White House are swamped with appeals from businesses wanting to evacuate their employees from Vietnam. Their demands are passed along to Saigon, where they infuriate Martin. He says if they don't stop they'll create "chaos." The ambassador begs Kissinger to use his influence with "your colleagues" to keep them from talking or anyway talking too much "over the next ten days when coolness will be absolutely essential."

Martin wants to retain control of events in Saigon. They're talking about

Marshall Ky again; he's been meeting constantly with generals, air force chief Tran Van Minh, airborne commander Le Quang Luong, top marine Bui The Lan, and with other officers, like the commander of armored units in MR 3, Saigon's. The topic of their discussions is clear: Thieu must go.

Ky has a plan: all he has to do is take the presidential palace, the main post office, military headquarters, the radio and television transmitters. The generals agree that if something isn't done, South Vietnam is finished. But they all shrink from it: "I can't do a thing, myself."

"You, Ky, you can do it."

Chief of Staff Vien says to Ky, "Go to it. Let me know the day and the hour. I'll open the gates at headquarters."

The air force chief confides, "Go ahead. You can even arrest me; I won't resist. Thieu knows what's going on, you know. After our last meeting, the Americans sent me a message. They told me to sit tight. They guaranteed that if anything happened, they'd send me to the United States and take care of me."

The commandant of marines, Ky's friend, tells him, "I can't give you troops, but if you move, my men won't put up any resistance."

Ky is exasperated. Even his closest friends, generals of Northern origin, Tonkinese, are following the American lead! What do these generals want? Do they want Ky to march into the palace with a handful of soldiers and pull his revolver and arrest Thieu? Ky can't be sure of one single battalion.

In his villa at Tan Son Nhut, Ky receives a phone call from Charles Timmes on April 18. The general, "with a *very* important person from the American Embassy," wants a meeting with Ky. They set a rendezvous for that afternoon. Timmes arrives in an old Volkswagen; with him is Graham Martin himself.

Martin is uneasy about all this unrest around Ky. He's been told that if the Americans pull out, South Vietnamese pilots are really prepared to fire on the evacuation planes. He has to sound Ky out, and eventually calm him down.

In the South—as in North Vietnam—you rarely cut to the heart of the matter at the beginning of a conversation. First you exchange courtesies. A courteous man, Martin asks Ky for news of his very pretty wife, Mai, a former flight attendant.

Later, over a map, the two Americans and the Vietnamese try to clarify the military situation. So far the three are in substantial agreement. Now they diverge. Timmes brought along a tape recorder. It breaks down. Ky and Martin are speaking English; a linguistic misunderstanding is always possible. General Timmes later seems to admit that Martin's message did not come across clearly. Martin will confirm that his informal visit had a formal object: to let Ky know that he had best not commit himself to a coup d'état. And according to Ky, Martin asked him: "What will you do with Thieu if you form a government?"

Answer: "We won't liquidate Thieu. It will be up to the people to decide."

The common *Rashomon* effect: an interaction perceived differently by each participant.

Then the three men come back to military matters. On the map Ky traces the outline of a reduced area that regrouped South Vietnamese forces could hold around the capital, with the Delta for support. Another possibility: try to reestablish the front from Tay Ninh, near the Cambodian border, all the way to the coast, perhaps hanging on to Phan Thiet.

Martin seems tired. Ky finds his remarks vague and ambiguous. The ambassador will see what he can do, he needs time, the situation is extremely complicated. . . .

When they break up, Martin has the feeling that Ky won't instigate a coup. Ky has the feeling that they only asked him to postpone it. Obviously Martin could not tell Ky just yet that he planned to ask Thieu to resign. And that consequently they could all save themselves the trouble of a coup d'état.

To discourage aficionados of coups, the minister of defense gives orders that same day to place under house arrest (or rearrest) a dozen generals and provincial heads.

Claudia Krich's diary:

April 18, 1975 (Friday)

I've been working on "adopting" two children—my little friends Van and Tu. These boys are four and six years old, and their mother, Chi Yen, is my good friend. She asked us to take them to Laos so they could be sent to their grandfather in Hanoi to go to school. At the Embassy two weeks ago, I told an official that I wanted to adopt them, but was told it was too late. Today, I went again, and this time I decided to tell the truth. I said, "I don't want to take these children to America. I want to take them to their grandfather in the north." "Well, that's nice to hear," the Embassy official said. "I'm so fed up with this wholesale export of children I could scream!"

An ad in the *Saigon Post*, April 18:

> legally to enable to continue her college
> studies outside Vietnam at her own ex-
> pense. Please telephone: 45470.

Not everyone can contemplate life abroad at his own expense. Same paper, same day:

> Vietnamese chef specialized in prepar-
> ing American meals and making pastry
> . . . volunteer to go to whatever place
> away from home.

The U.S. authorities go on evacuating children. Many are orphans, others belong to South Vietnamese officials who want to send them to safety. On April 18 in Geneva, 101 countries are discussing ways to improve Red Cross conventions. The two Vietnams argue fiercely. Hanoi denounces the airlift snatching Vietnamese children from their country, "a farcical version of humanitarian law." Saigon's delegate replies, citing "summary executions" and "collective massacres" in the PRG zone.

The congressional machine hums. Henry Kissinger appears in room 2172 of the Rayburn House Office Building, before the thirty-four members of the House Foreign Affairs Committee. No preliminary statement. The secretary of state thinks the honorable members of the committee would prefer proceeding directly to questions.

The chairman: "Are there any lessons to be learned from the situation in Cambodia that might apply to a possible communist takeover in South Vietnam?"

Kissinger: "First of all, of course, we don't want to speculate at this moment on a Communist takeover of South Vietnam, but the various lessons indicate there is simply no substitute for some kind of military balance, that without that there can be no negotiation that is effective, and under some circumstances it may be in the interests of the communist forces not to have a negotiation."

Kissinger denies any parallel with Cambodia. There are more arms in Vietnam. A congressman congratulates the government on the well-conducted evacuation of Phnom Penh. He hopes that the evacuation of Saigon, should it become necessary, will be as successful. Kissinger takes a moment to speak a little piece about unanimous solidarity: there must be confidence between the executive and the legislative branches. He repeats one of Martin's favorite words, *panic*: it must be avoided at all cost. Some in the capital are suggesting that by proceeding so slowly with the evacuation, the government wants to leave Americans hostage to the North Vietnamese. Such idiot tittle-tattle is unworthy of this debate.

They move along to the president of the Republic of South Vietnam.

Question: "Mr. Secretary, some members of Congress—and I might

say I am not one of them—advocate the resignation of President Thieu. . . .
What is your assessment of their claim?"

Kissinger asks that certain aspects of this problem be postponed to
executive session. But he does say: "The United States supports the government in South Vietnam. It does not support particular individuals."
He's obviously letting Thieu slide while defending the South Vietnamese
government: "We believe that in Saigon today there is a great readiness
to negotiate with considerable flexibility."

Kissinger offers no proof of this great readiness. Indeed, there are many
in Saigon who want to negotiate, but President Thieu is certainly not one
of them.

The minutes of all committee meetings go out as usual on press service
wires and shortly reach Hanoi, and then general headquarters of the Ho
Chi Minh offensive.

Australia has recognized Sihanouk and the Khmer Rouge. Other countries are ready to follow suit. What will the United States do? Kissinger
sees no reason to rush. Diplomatic recognition would be premature. Will
Sihanouk be head of the new government?

Kissinger: "I am sure he would like to know that, too."

"There are newspaper reports that the Khmer Rouge military were
applauded and commended upon entering Phnom Penh. Was this performance expected?"

Kissinger: "The reaction of populations to victorious armies, particularly in civil wars, tends to have a certain uniformity."

"Has the PRG been recognized as the legitimate government of South
Vietnam by North Vietnam?"

Kissinger: "No . . . It will be very interesting to see how that relationship
develops."

Representative Donald Fraser, one of the congressional delegation to
Saigon some weeks earlier: "There is a general impression . . . that the
conflict in South Vietnam represents a lost cause."

Kissinger: "There are many intermediary stages between military success and total collapse, and to achieve these intermediary stages—that is
to say, to achieve possibilities for controlled outcomes—I think a vote of
some military assistance would be extremely helpful."

Fraser agrees but he detects no flexibility in Saigon. Even the French
president, Valéry Giscard d'Estaing, is calling for new leadership in Saigon.
They come now to Martin's role. Kissinger remarks that an ambassador
should not publicly criticize the government to which he is accredited.
Fraser sets his banderilla: "There has been a lack of confidence on the part
of many of us in our ambassador there based on some experiences with
him. . . ."

Kissinger defends Martin: "Of course, it is not an opinion we share or
he wouldn't still be ambassador, but in any event, under the conditions
that now obtain it is obvious for the United States to change its ambassador

and for the South Vietnamese Government to change its leadership simultaneously . . . is not the best way to maintain a controlled situation. . . . Ambassador Martin is a disciplined Foreign Service officer who will carry out his instructions with great competence."

Fraser had met a PRG representative in Geneva: "My impression is that their demands keep escalating. . . . I was told it was important that President Thieu be removed . . . there was a discussion that we stop all military assistance."

Kissinger: "And before long it will be to stop all assistance."

In executive session Kissinger talks about Ford's approach to Brezhnev.

Isolated, Kissinger feels he's facing a country swayed by Senator McGovern's antiwar progressivism. Ford is not an elected president. In Congress, Kissinger thinks, conservatives as well as liberals "have developed a theory that détente is a great favor we are doing the Soviets, for which we can ask a price. Why don't you let one hundred thousand Jews out of the Soviet Union? Why don't you do this, why don't you do that? . . . It is a miracle that the Soviets have not used Nixon's collapse to follow a more aggressive policy. . . . We cannot obtain anything much by menacing them."[4]

There was an armada assembled off Cambodia. They will do the same off the Vietnamese coast. But Kissinger knows he can't use it for military purposes. The Soviets know it too. When Kissinger met with Dobrynin, a formidable professional, he was bluffing. In Ford's inner circle men like Rumsfeld and Nessen have hatched a "nutty" theory, says Kissinger: that everybody will give Ford the credit for pulling the Americans out of Vietnam.

The Pentagon wants a rapid pull-out, Martin a slow pull-out. Kissinger thinks the best way to evacuate Vietnamese from Vietnam is to keep some Americans in there for a while. If they evacuate all the Americans, as many in Defense and State want, they won't save any Vietnamese, and they may see ARVN soldiers firing on Americans. They will then be unable to evacuate more Americans. A vicious circle. To complicate an already difficult situation, two heavyweight senators, Jacob Javits and Edmund Muskie, on two very popular television shows, "Face the Nation" and "Meet the Press," say bluntly that the president has the authority to use a small contingent of marines to help evacuate Americans but will need congressional authorization before evacuating 200,000 Vietnamese. From Saigon Martin protests: "It will not be pleasant to be an American in Saigon."

On April 18, American radio beats television, announcing that the Senate Armed Forces Committee has rejected the request for supplemental aid for Vietnam. The House Foreign Affairs Committee agrees that Ford can use U.S. armed forces, in a limited and prudent manner, to evacuate Americans. The lines are drawn.

Henry Kissinger draws conclusions from the legislative decisions: "The debate on Vietnam has ended. . . . The government will accept Congress' verdict with no spirit of recrimination or reprisals."

Later at Tulane University President Ford will go further: "Today America can regain the sense of pride that existed before Vietnam. But it cannot be achieved by refighting a war that is finished as far as the United States is concerned."[5]

At Camp Davis during his regular Saturday morning press conference, Colonel Vo Dong Giang, head of the PRG delegation, jabs hard at Martin for the first time. The American ambassador, says the colonel, "looks like an American diplomat" but "is directing military, political and economic operations. He is responsible for all the crimes of Thieu's regime."

The advance guard of Hanoi's diplomatic offensive is doing good work. Giang accepts the presence of a thousand "American civilians," but maintains that even one U.S. military adviser constitutes a major violation of the Paris Agreement.

A few hundred meters from Camp Davis, in the buildings of the U.S. military mission, a movie theater has been converted to a triage center for potential evacuees, and the last picture show has been canceled. The ad for that film, *Phase IV*, shows a spider crawling across a bloody hand, "the day the earth became a cemetery."

U.S. officials are screening candidates for departure. To regularize the situation of some Vietnamese, they don't force impromptu marriages but write and stamp "documents of engagement." The American future husbands sign a declaration of intent to marry. In the long waiting lines people joke and read newspapers.

An ad in the *Saigon Post:*[6]

> Dear Americans, you are ordinary Americans, unemployed for the moment. If you need a respectable profession, come see us immediately, we are ready to advance money if necessary. Good salary. Please contact Miss Lan. Phone 96052.

In town, the price of an American, French or German husband or fiancé is on the rise. They say the families of some young women are paying $150,000 in cash. In the *Saigon Post* again, Professor Nguyen Huynh Duc, "specialist in secret passion," offers a brochure in English, attractively printed. It will teach its buyers to "control their ejaculation of sperm for three or four months."

The U.S. ambassador doesn't know exactly how many Americans are in Vietnam. He wants them all out on time. Businessmen, engineers and foremen follow instructions. But what about the oddballs (including deserters) who have no contact with the embassy, and all the dropouts that Martin calls "lotus eaters"? Too many American civilians, in his view, are taking things lightly, believing this is just another offensive. Martin will both cajole and threaten the lotus eaters. He is not proceeding, he cables to Kissinger, on any supposition that State "wishes to keep the mission open as long as there is hope that there can be a negotiated settlement." Martin will reduce the American colony to 750 in three weeks. Of course he'll hang on to Air America's pilots. He's going to close the consulate at Bien Hoa, twenty-five kilometers from Saigon. And for pity's sake, no loose talk in Washington! "I don't propose to risk another Danang." Martin feels that the Americans are not yet in danger. There is still "a month to six weeks." He must wait until he's seen Thieu before he makes important decisions. If Martin finds Thieu "obdurate and in a Götterdämmerung mood," the ambassador will speed up the evacuation. He knows the North Vietnamese could bombard Tan Son Nhut with artillery or use SAM-7 rockets around the airport. They have not chosen to do so. The manipulator that sleeps in every diplomat wakes up in Martin. He explains to Kissinger that he's going to meet with the Polish ambassador to the ICCS. If there are so many rockets around Saigon, he'll tell him, it's surely to protect the new North Vietnamese headquarters. He will also remark that he, Martin, hopes the North Vietnamese will try to shoot down an American plane "because nothing could be more certain in my mind that if they do that they will provide an excuse for the U.S. Air Force to take out Hanoi."

Claudia Krich's diary:[7]

April 19, 1975, Saturday

> The PRG would like a negotiated settlement. That requires Thieu resigning. Thieu doesn't seem to be planning to resign. Therefore the prediction is an attack on Saigon. . . . Keith [another Quaker] pointed out to me that many Saigon soldiers have never had to fight—they've bought positions in safe Saigon—and hopefully these inexperienced soldiers will just give up without a fight.

Martin assembles his staff for a general survey. Hanoi may try to take Saigon for Ho Chi Minh's birthday, May 19; but more probably, if they nail Thieu's hide to the wall Hanoi will try for a weak, neutral government in Saigon that they can dump later. The ambassador has seen Bui Diem, fresh from a meeting of generals at Ky's. There was plenty of moaning and groaning about the future. Martin has asked Bui Diem to restrain his military friends. The main thing is, no coup! Martin wonders about Colonel Giang's statements. The PRG man talked about a thousand Americans who could stay. So some sort of negotiation is possible. That's what Minister of Defense Don, says, too. They have to play all these cards—marked cards?

Polgar—like Martin and despite warnings from his subordinate, analyst

Frank Snepp—also thinks more and more that negotiations are possible. The CIA chief takes a phone call from the Hungarian Colonel Toth. Can they meet?

They lunch at Polgar's house.

"Do you agree with me that the war is lost?" asks the Hungarian. "Do you also agree that when a country loses a war there are bound to be certain political consequences?"

"Yes," Polgar concedes.

"Obviously the consequences for South Vietnam and for your country cannot be favorable."

"Are you speaking for your friends?" asks Polgar.

"No. I don't think anyone wants the destruction, the bloodshed and . . . the humiliation of the United States."

Toth lets it be known that his information comes from Hanoi and not just the PRG. He knows that to Polgar the PRG is a fiction. Toth wants to pass along the prerequisites for negotiation. The word "prerequisite" comes up often. Polgar is suspicious. He knows about disinformation. But on the military level it's obviously all over. They have to find a political solution. Keen observers like Malcolm Browne of the *New York Times*, with whom Polgar is in contact, confirm that the PRG wants to negotiate. A chorus of encouragement.

"Okay," says Polgar. "Where do we go from here? Who does what to whom?"

Toth runs through the prerequisites. Thieu will have to resign unconditionally. There must be a new government, people acceptable to the North Vietnamese. The United States will supply no military aid to this government. The U.S. Embassy must limit its activities. Nothing very new in all this except that the enemy, if Toth is really speaking for them, foresees the survival of the U.S. Embassy in Saigon. Can the colonel ask "the other side" for the names of acceptable Vietnamese?

The Hungarian will try, but, he emphasizes, time is short. It's a matter of days, not weeks.

Polgar, highly excited, reports to Martin, who cables Kissinger on April 19 at 6:10 P.M. All this seems very interesting. Can Kissinger clarify certain issues by sending a "message to Le Duc Tho"? Whatever Toth's real motives are, the ambassador finds the survival of his embassy an enticing notion.

In his cable Martin complains about various people. The officers in charge of the evacuation are saying now that they need 800 marines. Martin doesn't want more than 300. He's obsessed by the bureaucracy. "Everybody has completed the CYA operation in Washington," *cover your ass*. Arrange to escape your responsibilities and avoid blame. Martin says intelligence "has drawn the absolutely worst possible case, which is unrealistic but which protects them." The military and the DOD have their planes ready. "So that if the worst case happens it can be said by defense they did their part and if anything happens to Americans it couldn't have been their fault. . . . The only one whose ass isn't covered is me. . . . There is no way I can come out of this without criticism." Then, the art of the diplomatic dispatch requiring a mix of the tragic and the comic, Martin passes along news gleaned from radio interceptions of NVA units: "Eighty percent of the sixth company has conjunctivitis, and it could spread through the entire second battalion. Suggest a medic be sent down for immediate treatment."

Martin orders Polgar to keep in touch with the Hungarian colonel. Never mind the opinions of an underling like Snepp. . . .

Kissinger puts no stock in secret meetings between the CIA mission chief and a Hungarian colonel. The communists don't usually engage in serious negotiations through secondary personnel.

The battle of Xuan Loc ends badly for the South Vietnamese, and the military situation seems disastrous again.

Kissinger's answer, Sunday morning, March 20: "My ass isn't covered." When this is all over, he says, the critics will blame him more than Martin. Martin should sound out Thieu on his eventual resignation. Its timing will be highly important. Kissinger is in contact with the Soviets. Martin must not mention that to the South Vietnamese president: "We can use Thieu as a bargaining chip."

Pentagon brass are worried that materiel and munitions may once again fall into North Vietnamese hands. During interagency meetings in Washington, Kissinger ventures, "I know that, if any Americans are killed, it will be my fault. I know that, if a single American remains there, it will be my fault. Now, gentlemen, you have all taken your precautions. Let us proceed. . . ."

At the Ministry of Foreign Affairs in Moscow many foreign diplomats, mostly Westerners, especially French, German, and Swedish, are given audience. After conversations with representatives of the DRV and PRG, high Soviet officials repeat blandly that the Vietnamese communists have no intention of taking Saigon or winning the war with the present offensive. The Vietnamese, say the Soviets, are fully aware of logistical problems and food shortages. The proof: rations have been cut in the Hanoi area.

Latest arguments advanced by the Soviets: the rapid advance of their troops has taken the North Vietnamese command by surprise, and they will have great difficulty smashing Saigon's last, well-equipped divisions. And finally, the PRG doesn't want a devastated capital.

The same general line from intelligence out of Paris. There the South Vietnamese delegates are asking that the North Vietnamese as well as the PRG resume talks without "preconditions." The PRG answers: "No political progress possible as long as Nguyen Van Thieu remains in power."

At Graham Martin's request several months earlier, Thieu named General Nguyen Van Toan—very fat, very corrupt, and a very good soldier—

commander of Military Region 3, which includes Saigon and Xuan Loc.

Toan informs the president: the battle of Xuan Loc is lost. The communists can crush the last defenders or bypass the city. North of Saigon, they're regrouping not just divisions but whole army corps. They're popping up all over the Delta. In the presence of Chief of Staff Vien, Toan—whom Thieu trusts—reports, "We have no more reserves. We can't go on fighting. In the military sense, the war is over. We have to negotiate with the communists."

On political levels of Saigon familiar with French history, they're saying that there should be a transfer of power as legitimate as de Gaulle's ascension in May 1958. Some, like Bui Diem, believe that any maneuvering by anyone at all is useless. Martin telephones Bui Diem and asks, "Have you seen Thieu?"

"Not yet. I can't just break down his door." Thieu has apparently shut himself into his private apartments, overwhelmed.

"I may have to go over there myself," Martin sighs.

In the morning of April 20 Martin, accompanied by an aide, Brunson McKinley, goes to the palace. He's already checked the latest intelligence reports.[8]

The ambassador explains to the president that analysis of the order of battle and a comparison of present forces result in grim conclusions. If Hanoi wants to finish off the South Vietnamese army, Saigon cannot hold out over a month, probably not more than three weeks, even with a skillful and determined defense. Hanoi surely wants to take Saigon intact. If negotiations are not undertaken, we cannot rule out seeing the North Vietnamese occupy a capital in ruins. What are the prospects for more aid? asks Thieu. Murky, answers Martin.

Thieu seems calm and dignified while Martin sketches likely details of a crushing defeat. Leaders in a position like Thieu's in Saigon, Martin says—at 10 Downing Street in London, at the Elysée, in the Kremlin or the White House—have a problem in common: they never know if they're being told the whole truth. People can lie to them, "shave reports" for personal or bureaucratic advantage, or to avoid offending the powerful—either because they fear power or because they don't want to be bearers of bad news.

Thieu listens patiently.

Martin says he's speaking personally, not as the U.S. ambassador but as a man who has observed events in Southeast Asia for a long time, a man who has worked long and hard these last two years to understand the complexity of Vietnamese problems.

Martin is in full flight.

The older he grows, he says, the more he knows that he does not know it all, and a reasonable doubt is always present. But in these difficult times perhaps his perceptions are as accurate as those of any other Westerner. The military situation is very bad and the Vietnamese people are holding

Thieu responsible. The political class, both his supporters and his enemies, don't believe he can lead the country out of this crisis. His generals may go on fighting, but they need a respite that can only be won by offering negotiations. Martin thinks that unless Thieu moves fast his generals will ask him to step down.

A strange scene, over and above the two men's preternatural calm. Thieu's questions show that on one point at least he has, like the ambassador occasionally, lost touch with reality: Would his resignation affect the voting in Congress?

Perhaps several months ago, Martin answers. Now, he doubts it. The important thing would be the effect his departure would have on "the other side." Martin does not know just what that would be, but thinks that Hanoi would oppose *any* strong leader. All Thieu's colleagues, his whole government, feel that his departure would buy time. Martin thinks there's a dim hope for the survival of an independent Vietnam.

Thieu answers that he will decide in the country's best interests. Martin expects no less of him. Thieu will think it over.

The conversation lasted an hour and a half.

On his return to the embassy, Martin reports to Kissinger:

> [Thieu] may very well try one of the maneuvers that kept him ahead of his opponents, but the time for pulling rabbits out of the hat is rather short. On balance my guess is that he will leave rather shortly. . . . If his generals give him a few more days, he may well come up with a dramatic resignation. . . . I went home and read the daily news digest from Washington and took a shower using the strongest soap I could find. It did not help very much. Warm regards.

That afternoon the French ambassador goes to the palace alone. Thieu gives him a private audience. Mérillon is well aware that his approach is bizarre, even weird: "I have come to see you, Mr. President, because the situation is extraordinarily grave. There is no military solution." Thieu does not answer. Mérillon goes on: "I see only a political solution . . . a political process must be permitted to develop."

Usually talkative, Thieu is silent. It is more a long monologue by the ambassador than a conversation. Mérillon lists facts that Thieu is becoming familiar with. Three-quarters of the country is irretrievably lost. Which big cities are still in government hands? Saigon, Can Tho. Except for the gravity of the situation Mérillon would never have allowed himself . . . Considering your position, it is clear that . . .

The ambassador speaks of personal relationships, a sense of history, honor, the ties between Mme. Mérillon and Mme. Thieu. The president can render his people a great service. By means of the inevitable negotiations, we all hope certain South Vietnamese interests can be safeguarded.

Thieu speaks of necessary regroupings, of the American betrayal, of his defeatist generals. The president remains calm but, Mérillon notes in his cable to the Quai d'Orsay, "now and then he looked haggard." The ambassador feels he must mention the anti-French attacks in Saigon these last days. He must protest even the most polite expression used to characterize the French approaches, "interference in internal affairs." After all, the Paris Agreement was solemnly guaranteed in the French capital.

Thieu listens, and raises no objection. The interview ends with a banal remark by Thieu: "Come what may."

Like Martin, Mérillon leaves convinced that Thieu will step down. Happily the president has not asked for political exile in France!

Mérillon returns peacefully to his embassy. At the Quai d'Orsay some bureaucrats were afraid Thieu would expel the ambassador. Even worse, have him assassinated.

That same evening, Thieu reads excerpts from Nixon's letters to cabinet ministers and several senators and deputies. In the restaurants, bars and brothels of Cholon they're giving three to one on the president's departure. Ten to one. This week. In ten days.

At 8:20 on April 21, Polgar makes contact again with Colonel Toth. The American tells the Hungarian that *they* have taken his remarks under consideration. Before commenting on their substance, the Americans would like clarification of the other side's position. Particularly, what sort of statement do the communists expect from the United States? The two review the military situation over the last forty-eight hours. Further bloodshed makes no sense. It's in everyone's interest to avoid chaos. Polgar asks where and when negotiations might commence.

While Toth and Polgar rebuild Vietnam, Colonel Vo Van Can of President Thieu's personal staff drives to 9 Hong Thap Tu, the studios of Vietnamese television. He asks another colonel, Le Vinh Hoa, still director of radio-television and cinema, to set up a live broadcast. The director goes to the palace with a mobile unit and about twenty technicians. A relay van will feed the broadcast to the studio.

During a brief meeting, Thieu informs his ministers of the decision he has taken. At 2 P.M. the president comes to see the director of television, who is setting up: "Can we broadcast tonight at about six? To line up your cameras, choose a man of my height."

At 3 P.M. the commandant of the national police announces that the president will speak. At 5 P.M. Thieu calls the director into his office: "At the moment of the transfer of power, hold on me with Huong."

Thieu wants a live broadcast so he can speak freely. If he taped the broadcast in advance, the Americans could create technical difficulties. The transmitter is next to the American radio station.

Thieu issues last instructions to the director: "I will speak at 7:30 P.M. At the end, freeze on a picture of me. And show the broadcast every two hours."

There are—before the offensive, there were—five broadcast centers, in Saigon, Can Tho, Nha Trang, Qui Nhon and Hue. Of the 400,000 South Vietnamese television viewers, half are in the region of the capital. The speech will also be broadcast by radio, which covers practically all of Vietnam.

Aware of Thieu's intentions, Martin warns Kissinger: "You may therefore wish to inform Dobrynin on what is to take place in order to transform this into an advantage with whatever you are trying to accomplish with Hanoi through the Soviets. . . . While I do not know what he [Thieu] will say this evening, I would not expect it to be too rough on the United States."

Kissinger responds immediately: "Should Thieu wish to leave the country you should of course offer him every assistance. . . . Whatever he may have said about me, I have the greatest respect for him."

Thieu has assembled the senators and deputies in a large room on the ground floor of the palace. Two cameras are set up on a podium. There are officers in the room too, among them the chief of staff. The public is uneasy, troubled, relieved. Thieu has been in power for some ten years. He has persisted, and against many enemies. He is going to leave. Can they change horses in midstream?

"Ladies, gentlemen, patriots, dear brothers and sisters," says Thieu, "the communist strategy is as follows: when they are strong militarily, they fight vigorously while holding talks perfunctorily. And when they are weak militarily, they fight that way but come on strong in the talks."

Thieu is embroidering a historic tapestry. His voice rises. Sometimes his gestures seem uncoordinated. He apologizes for the informality of the setting.

> There was collusion between the communists and the United States with a view to reaching the agreement of 26th October 1972. . . . I had enough courage to tell Secretary of State Kissinger at that time the following: if you accept this agreement, it means you agree to sell South Vietnam to the North Vietnamese communists. As for me, if I accept this agreement, I will be a traitor.

Thieu refused to sign for three months. For the first time in public, he says now that to force him to sign Nixon threatened to cut off all aid in 1973.

He did not polish this speech, as he usually did, with his cousin Nha. Thieu is reading and also improvising, at length and tortuously. Often uncomfortable, his studio audience listens solemnly to the historic oration.

In a safari jacket, nervous, occasionally showing anger, the president halts from time to time to grope for the thread of his discourse. How long they spin out, those televised seconds of silence! Thieu is much harder on the Americans than Martin expected:

> I have therefore told them [the Americans]: you have asked us to do something that you failed to do with half a million powerful troops. . . . If I do not say that you were defeated by the communists in Vietnam, I must modestly say that you did not win either. But you found an honorable way out. And at present, when our army lacks weapons, ammunition, helicopters, aircraft and B-52s, you ask us to do an impossible thing like filling up the ocean with stones. This is like the case in which you give me only three dollars and urge me to go by plane, first class; to rent a room in the hotel for thirty dollars per day; to eat four or five slices of beefsteak and to drink seven or eight glasses of wine per day. This is an impossible, absurd thing.

Television viewers—in Vietnamese homes and press agencies, at the U.S. Embassy where the speech is translated as it goes along—sense that this is more a testament than a diplomatic talk.

Agitated, his brow sweaty, Thieu is not smooth but seems sincere. He rails against the Americans: "You have let our combattants die under the hail of shells. This is an inhumane act by an inhumane ally."

He hammers out his words and repeats himself: "Refusing to aid an ally and abandoning him is an inhumane act."

Then he returns to his notes: "The United States is proud of being an invincible defender of the just cause and the ideal of freedom in this world and will celebrate its two hundredth anniversary next year. I asked them: are U.S. statements trustworthy?"

Thieu says he is ready to take any criticism, from the entire world, from his allies, from the Vietnamese people.

> I admit that some, but not all, of our military leaders were cowardly . . . in recent battles. In some areas, our combattants fought valiantly. . . .
>
> I could stay on as president, to lead the resistance of all our armed forces and people. However, I am not in a position to supply adequate means for the army to fight. Moreover, I might also be misunderstood by the people as an impediment to peace. . . .
>
> The second solution is to resign . . . my resignation is a very small sacrifice.

Thieu asks everyone to rally to Vice President Tran Van Huong, who will accede to the presidency as the constitution provides. At Thieu's side Huong seems much moved, behind his dark glasses.

"It is not due to the pressure of our ally," Thieu continues,

> or the difficult and hard struggle against the communists that I have to avoid responsibility and leave my office. The presidents of some big countries are proud of the fact that they have undergone six, seven or ten crises. They have written books in which they proudly offer themselves as heroes and outstanding politicians. As for me, over the last ten years, all years, months, days and hours in my life have been bad, as my horoscope forecast.

The audience wishes Thieu would finish. He continues, reverting to his primary themes: "I am ready to accept judgements and accusations from my compatriots. . . . The life of a people should not be sold like fish in the market." At last he cries, "I am resigning but not deserting."[9] He has spoken for an hour and a half.

New President Huong has something to say. They have to help him to the microphone. Seventy-two years old, stooped like a rheumatic, he tells the military, "As long as you go on fighting, I'll be at your side. If the worst befalls our nation, my bones will rest with those of our brother combattants. It is my dearest wish." To the people, Huong explains, "In unity is life, in division is death."

After the new president is sworn in, the chief of staff and the police chief promise that the troops will fight and that order will be preserved.

Writer Duyen Anh listened to Thieu. He says to himself: Thieu was no genius but the Americans had confidence in him. If they're dropping him, the party's over.

The writer's name is on a list, and for several days he's been waiting for a phone call to leave for the United States. They told him to keep his line open for this urgent call. Between the call and the rendezvous, he may have no more than five minutes.

Surrounded by refugees, the bonze Thien Hue listened to Thieu at the pagoda. They are all overjoyed. Thieu has lost both his ally and his compatriots' confidence. It's a good thing he's leaving. Under another leader the situation may improve.

Engineer Van feels no pleasure. How can the nationalists negotiate from a position of weakness? New President Huong is a diehard anticommunist. To negotiate they needed someone more flexible.

At Dalat Father Jean Maïs retreated to the university refectory to listen to the president, all the shutters closed. The priest felt rising anger. Thieu said he was going back to work as a general. But Jean Maïs is sure he has a plane ticket for foreign parts in his pocket.

Two hours after the transfer of power, Radio Liberation and Radio Hanoi announce, "This is Thieu's regime without Thieu . . . another puppet regime."

Thieu meets his cousin Nha in his private apartments. The ex-president is as serene now as he was tense during his speech. He's even wearing a smile—or is it a grimace?—as he says, "Perfect! Okay. If they think they can solve the problems, find a way out . . ." Then with a sigh: "I did all I could for my country."

He is no longer at the helm but he does not abandon ship. Nor does he think about leaving Vietnam: "I'm ready to advise, but I'm not the boss any more."

While Thieu was resigning, the last elements of the ARVN 18th Division escaped from Xuan Loc. The divisional commander, General Dao, baptizes his retreat Operation Surprise and Diversion. Dao had help—briefly— from a "daisy cutter" dropped at night six kilometers northwest of Xuan Loc, near the headquarters of the NVA 341st Division. The shock waves rocked the city of Xuan Loc like an earthquake. Wild rumors: the ARVN has tactical atomic bombs. Several hundred NVA officers and men were killed by this low-pressure bomb that uses up all the oxygen for 250 meters around, killing on the spot by suffocation and leaving no wounds.

Erich von Marbod promised twenty-seven "daisy cutters." Three were delivered on April 16, together with an American bomb expert. He trained the South Vietnamese in the art of priming the bomb and securing it to a C-130. It wasn't easy to find an experienced South Vietnamese pilot to drop that first bomb. The promised American pilot never showed. They'll drop no more "daisy cutters."

The retreat from Xuan Loc is well planned and well executed. The last elements of the Eighteenth Division, of the First Airborne Brigade, of various regional and popular forces, pull out during the evening of April 23. The Eighteenth, which has lost 30 percent of its men, regroups with its artillery around the bases at Long Binh and Bien Hoa. The paratroopers, who sustained smaller losses, move into position on Route 15, which protects access to Cap Saint-Jacques.

The North Vietnamese commander in chief has decided to bypass the city and harry Bien Hoa, between Xuan Loc and Saigon. Dung lost thirty-seven T-54 tanks in the battle of Xuan Loc.

In Saigon, French diplomats are busy. They want to spare the city destruction and leave Big Minh's calling card on the North Vietnamese. Will Hanoi accept it? Saigon, a city drifting, disabled, desperate, seems to be disappearing into a void. Mérillon and Brochand think they must provide some psychological and political stability. The French are convinced that the Americans only want to save *their* hides.

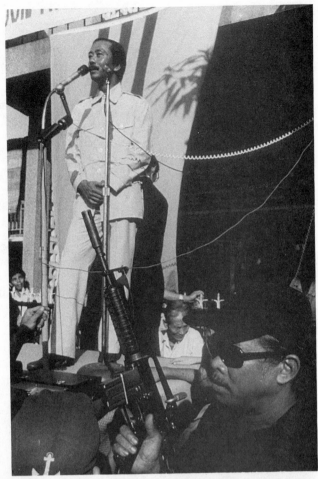

Air Marshal Nguyen Cao Ky: "What do they expect me to do? March into Thieu's office pistol in hand?" *(Photo Dieter/SIPA Press)*

President Thieu resigns: "I am stepping down, not deserting." *(Photo Pavlovski/Sygma)*

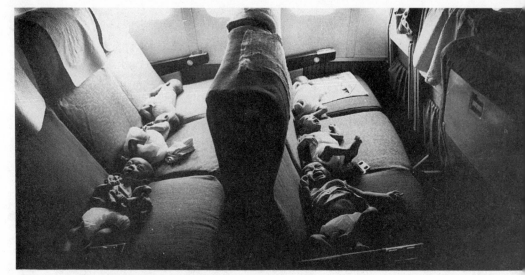

South Vietnamese orphans en route to the United States. "These children are nice souvenirs, like the porcelain elephants you love so much. Too bad some were broken. Don't worry about it: there are more." *(Photo Jean-Claude Francolon/Gamma)*

Top right: ARVN soldiers on the Newport Bridge over the Saigon River on April 28. Eighteen North Vietnamese divisions are converging on the capital. *(Photo Dieter/SIPA Press)*

Bottom right: Devil take the hindmost at Nha Trang. *(Photo UPI/Bettmann Newsphotos)*

Ritual press conference by the PRG's delegation in Camp Davis at Tan Son Nhut Airport: "The Americans must stop violating the Paris Agreement. We want the people's happiness, independence, peace, national reconciliation. . . ." *(Photo Wheeler /SIPA Press)*

U.S. Marines boarding helicopters. *(Photo U.S. Dept. of Defense)*

Top left: Take to the foxholes in Saigon. *(Photo Associated Press)*

Bottom left: Xuan Loc: "We'll see if the South Vietnamese Army can fight." *(Photo Associated Press)*

In Saigon, assemblymen and senators wage debates.
(Photo Naythons/SIPA Press)

Troops fighting in the suburbs. *(Photo Associated Press)*

Top right: Outside the U.S. Embassy. "A lot of fleeing people won't be able to leave. A lot of people who are staying ought to come out with us."

Bottom right: North Vietnamese tanks smash through the wrought-iron gates of the presidential palace. "Like the petals of a lotus, our five columns have just blossomed." *(Photo Françoise Demulder/Gamma)*

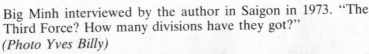

Big Minh interviewed by the author in Saigon in 1973. "The Third Force? How many divisions have they got?" *(Photo Yves Billy)*

The roof of the Embassy. "There are 1,500 to 2,000 people left."
(Photo UPI/Bettmann Newsphotos)

Last cable from the Embassy received by Kissinger.

Department of State

TELEGRAM

SECRET   9456

PAGE 01 2919292

51
ACTION EA-10

INFO OCT-01 ISO-00 OC-05 CCO-00 INRE-00 SSO-00 NSCE-00

     USIE-00 PM-03 NSC-05 SP-02 SS-15 CIAE-00 INR-07

     NSAE-00 DODE-00 H-02 AID-05 FORE-00 SR-02 ORM-01 VO-03

     SCA-01 PRS-01 SAM-01 A-01 OPR-02 SY-05 PER-01 /073 W
     ---------------------   096246

7 2912152
FM AMEMBASSY SAIGON
TO SECSTATE WASHDC 0000

S E C R E T SAIGON 0000
    PLAN TO CLOSE MISSION SAIGON APPROXIMATELY 0430
SAIGON TIME, DEPENDENT ON PERFORMANCE OF MILITARY EVALUATION
CHANNELS.

    DUE TO NECESSITY TO DESTROY COMMO GEAR, THIS IS THE LAST
SAIGON MESSAGE TO SECSTATE.
S E C R E T

EOT

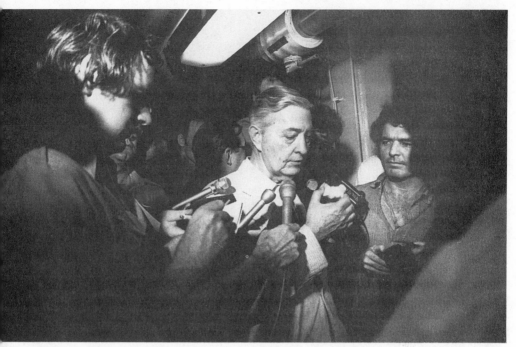

Graham Martin aboard the *Blue Ridge*: "This is not how I saw American honor." *(Photo Bryn Campbell/Magnum)*

1987: Soviet Strategic Bear Bombers at Cam Ranh Airport.
(Photo Indochina-Report, Singapore)

18

Big Minh's
Big Moment

After Thieu's resignation, France volunteers her good offices. President Valéry Giscard d'Estaing salutes the ex-president's "sense of duty." To the French Embassy in Saigon the scheme seems simple: they just plug General Minh into the political circuit and then everybody can negotiate.

Senator Sam Nunn (D., Ga.) sees "a possibility, not a probability" of negotiations in Thieu's departure. At the White House they say with a straight face that Thieu was not asked to leave. Of course someone in Saigon may have talked to him. . . . In his public statements Ford does all he can to saddle Congress with responsibility for developments in Vietnam.

On April 21 he appears on television, interviewed by Walter Cronkite, Bob Schieffer and Eric Sevareid. Presidential logic is simple: the South Vietnamese had to beat a retreat because Congress did not vote sufficient military aid. No retreat, no disaster. Ford is beyond Vietnam. He's worried about the danger of war in the Middle East and fears an oil embargo. Encouraging signs in the domestic economy: the inflation rate has stabilized, retail sales are up. Saigon is so far away!

Still, there remains the problem of evacuation. The differences between State and the Pentagon are obvious. They fight a war of news leaks. The secretary of defense points out that it will be hard now to use planes, either civilian or military, and that they'd better plan a pull-out by helicopter, a more delicate operation. The problem of evacuating Vietnamese hasn't been solved. In Saigon, furthermore, requests for evacuation are momentarily but officially suspended. Vietnamese who troop to the U.S. Embassy are greeted by a typed message:

Requests concerning relatives.

Given the importance of the matters at hand, we have temporarily stopped accepting requests for parents, brothers and sisters. DO NOT LINE UP IF THAT IS WHY YOU ARE HERE. We hope soon to be able to accept requests concerning parents, brothers and sisters.

Kissinger cables Martin: "As soon as Tan Son Nhut comes under fire, the DAO [General Smith and his staff] should be immediately evacuated by plane . . . not repeat not rely on helicopter extraction."

Kissinger stresses that he is not involved in the French diplomatic maneuvers. Eventual Soviet intervention? "We have suggested a temporary, about two-week cease-fire . . . in order to evacuate Americans and some Vietnamese." There seems to be "some indication of serious interest . . . no reply as yet."

In Honolulu Admiral Noel Gayler, commander in chief of the Pacific theater (CINCPAC), decides to launch an airlift to Saigon. C-141s shuttle in daylight, C-130s at night. In Congress a new financial battle is under way; finally the administration wrings $165 million in economic and humanitarian aid from the Appropriations Committee. At the White House, Ron Nessen says the president thinks it's still possible and necessary to appropriate $1 billion for South Vietnam.

In Saigon soldiers are digging individual foxholes, unrolling barbed wire, installing zigzag traffic barriers, filling sandbags, setting up batteries of automatic rifles, machineguns and a few mortars. The presidential palace and its gardens are still illuminated and the fountains are still spouting.

On April 22 Le Duan cables Dung and Le Duc Tho on behalf of the Politburo: "Every day counts. . . . We have to push the offensive rapidly on all fronts. Any delay may have unfortunate consequences on political levels as well as military." The Party's first secretary fears a political solution that would once more deprive the North Vietnamese of complete military victory. No leader with any sense of history can forget 1954 and the frontier imposed at the 17th parallel between the two Vietnams.

For the assault on Saigon, General Tra concentrates his troops in the usual protected and privileged areas: war zone C northwest of Saigon, war zone D in the northeast, iron triangle in the north, the forest of U Minh, and in the south, PRG units on Ca Mau peninsula.

On April 22 in the presence of Le Duc Tho at Loc Ninh, Dung, as commander in chief, and Pham Hung, as principal political officer in the South, solemnly affix their signatures to a map. The North Vietnamese army corps' advances on Saigon are annotated in red. Le Duc Tho and

Pham Hung, the politicians, stay at Loc Ninh. Dung and Tra, the soldiers, have set up forward headquarters at Ben Cat, north of Saigon.

At Loc Ninh, the young film buff Tien sees Le Duc Tho again. He recognizes this leader. He's pleased. Around Le Duc Tho he sees many people whose importance is obvious from their manner of speaking. An officer tells him now what his mission will be: "You will lead a group of tanks and guide them, particularly when we reach Saigon."

In Saigon, Huong presides . . . slowly. He can hardly see. He suffers from high blood pressure and heart trouble. A colorless man, he was virtually invisible as—almost honorary—vice-president. Once a teacher, he was also mayor of Saigon. Prime minister briefly and candidate for the presidency in 1967. Thieu named Huong vice-president in 1968, dumped him a year later and took him back two years after that. A devoted legalist, even ritualist, now that he's president Huong is primarily interested in nominations and elections within the Senate and Chamber. He wants all in order there before he chooses a prime minister. He's happy the day after he takes power, when Deputy Pham Van Ut, head of the republican bloc, is elected head of the Chamber, which has been leaderless since the former head became prime minister. President Huong is upset: Why was no worthy candidate nominated to be secretary-general of the Assembly? Regrettably, the only serious candidate is at Can Tho. Ah! but here's something that deserves the new president's undivided attention: the Sultan of Oman has agreed to send an ambassador to Saigon beginning April 26. Who can be assigned to Oman? Huong seems more concerned with the shape of his government than with its weight, its eventual program and its prospects.

Communist artillery shells the Long Binh base. Never before have NVA 130s struck there, one of the biggest bases during the golden age of the Americans.

An ecumenical *Te Deum*, a thanksgiving or requiem ceremony assembles members of the four great religions, Catholics, Buddhists, Hoa Hao and Cao Dai, in the cathedral. A striking scene—Hao Hao chiefs all in black around the archbishop in white chasuble and the Buddhist venerables in saffron robes. The leading Cao Dai representative couldn't reach the capital because Route 22 from Tay Ninh to Saigon was cut. In Tay Ninh province, the ARVN repels several attacks, so Thieu's departure hasn't affected the military much.

In commentaries on his resignation observers note odd contradictions. Some who disliked him admire him now for his anti-American tirade. Others detested his autocratic rule and are wondering whether Huong will wield any real authority. Still living in the palace, Thieu offers his services and advice to the new president, who seems testy about it.

A teacher's vice: Huong seems to confuse words and action. He makes a speech on television, in which he simply authorizes women and children to leave the country if they want. The men must stay in Vietnam and fight.

At Tan Son Nhut airport, cargo planes shuttle in and out. U.S. evacuation officials are working in and around the gymnasium, screening refugees. Officially 3,300 refugees leave Saigon by U.S. military aircraft on April 22. In Washington, Kissinger has won suspension of immigration laws for over 130,000 Indochinese, of whom 50,000 are "high-risk" Vietnamese. This is an unprecedented concession: by the quota system, no country is entitled to more than 20,000 visas a year. After the Bay of Pigs fiasco the immigration services made an exception and granted 60,000 visas to Cubans. Now Kissinger realizes that Martin has slowed the evacuation inordinately. Is it realistic to believe that any great number of South Vietnamese will be able to escape or be pulled out? Aware of the problems posed by the size of Vietnamese families, Ford tells a joke during a discussion at the White House: "A Vietnamese went to the American consulate in Saigon with four wives. 'Which one do you want to take out with you?' they asked him. 'The youngest.' "

In Saigon, nothing is worth more than an American visa.

Another ad in the *Saigon Post*:

> Seeking adoptive parents. Poor diligent students:
> • Chu Thi My Ho, born on October 2, 1954, in Nam Dinh, identity card no. 00113070.
> • Chu Thi Tuan Hoa, born October 12, 1958, in Khanh Hoa, identity card no. 10796374.

The papers are full of want ads. Vietnamese try to find Americans they know, civilian or military, who could sponsor them, who might help them leave Saigon:

> Need to meet J. T. Slotberg . . .

> Where is Tom Westerling?

There seems to be a sudden lull in the fighting. With Thieu gone, one condition set by the communists is fulfilled, so there should be a military pause. Kissinger passes the Soviet reply to Martin, indicating incidentally that this is certainly the first time he's communicated details of his negotiations to one of his subordinates. After receiving Ford's message of April 19 to Brezhnev, the Soviets say they have taken

> appropriate steps to get in touch with the Vietnamese side. . . . The position of the Vietnamese side on the question of evacuation of American citizens from South Vietnam is definitely favorable. . . . They have no intentions to put any

obstacles in the course of military actions to evacuation of
American citizens . . . now, in fact, favorable conditions have
been established for such an evacuation.

The Soviets specify that the Vietnamese side "will proceed from the Paris
Agreement" for any political settlement. Hanoi has no intention of hu-
miliating the United States. They are counting on Ford not to exacerbate
the situation in Indochina. Kissinger is mildly perplexed. He asks Martin
to cable his "interpretation of the Soviet response." The secretary of state
feels that the Americans can proceed to pull out and also to "the evacuation
of Vietnamese, unimpeded." He adds, "I also take the response to indicate
that the PRG is prepared to undertake negotiations in the tripartite formulation." Is Kissinger moonstruck too? The reports jibe, out of Moscow
via the secretary of state and out of Hanoi via the Hungarian colonel.
Kissinger asks the ambassador to reduce the number of Americans in
Vietnam to 800 within four days.

President Huong's and Ambassador Martin's people have noted diplomatic activity by the French government. Jean-Marie Mérillon was the
only member of the diplomatic corps in Saigon to attend the ecumenical
service at the cathedral. In Paris, President Valéry Giscard d'Estaing called
in the minister of foreign affairs, Jean Sauvagnargues, to keep up with the
situation in Indochina. In turn, Sauvagnargues received Vo Van Sung,
ambassador of the Democratic Republic of Vietnam, and Pham Van Ba,
PRG representative. All this with considerable fanfare.

At the Quai d'Orsay some urge immediate recognition of the PRG,
partly to make sure that it will be the South's government. This is subtle.
Prime Minister Jacques Chirac is against it, in part to avoid a South Vietnamese reaction against the French in Vietnam. This is wise. In all Western capitals South Vietnamese diplomats feel more isolated than ever. The
communists refuse to meet them at La Celle-Saint-Cloud; their diplomats
and journalists explain that "Huong is still Thieu without Thieu."

At the ambassador's residence that night Martin writes a long cable to
Kissinger: "1. Tran Van Don, Minister of Defense, visited me last evening.
He is the past master of the glide, the two step, the waltz. . . . When he
is finished one may not notice where one has been but it will have been
an active session."

A few days before, Don had explained to the ambassador that once
Thieu left and was replaced by Huong, he, Don, would make an excellent
prime minister.

2. Last night, he had a different scenario. Big Minh is the
man Hanoi wants, with Don to advise him of course. Authority: Big Minh and the French ambassador. . . . had he
[Minh] just inherited the mantle of heaven? Don did not
know how a succession was to be arranged. Minh could be

appointed prime minister with full devolution of military and civilian powers from Huong. . . . The other way would be for Huong to turn over all powers to Big Minh, who would immediately start negotiations and would form the National Council.

Don said the Catholics, Buddhists and sects would accept this. "Was Don sure that Big Minh was acceptable to Hanoi? Yes, he said, but he couldn't or wouldn't give any specific evidence." What did the Americans think? "I said that the Congress was in the throes of making it evident that it cared very little who were the players in Vietnam . . . I had no authority to approve or disapprove what must be essentially a Vietnamese arrangement." Martin had explained to the Vietnamese minister of defense that it was no longer an American problem. Perhaps Don should consult the French, who claimed to have some influence over Hanoi.

"3. I saw Mérillon at noon after he had an appointment with the president," Martin goes on.

The French ambassador said he had pointed out to Huong the necessity of quick action. The President seemed slow, ill and an old man and had given no specific reaction. He confirmed that the Quai was pushing Big Minh. I asked if he had received specific indications through Hanoi that Big Minh would be accepted. I never received a direct response. I am under the impression the French had presented Big Minh's name in Hanoi and gotten no specific response but have interpreted lack of answer as tacit assent. French say they requested cease-fire at the departure of Thieu to work out some new political modalities and see current lull as result of this initiative. Believing Big Minh susceptible to their influence they are anxious to get him in power hoping that once he is in, Hanoi will find it difficult to disown him. My own guess is that Hanoi wished French pressure to destroy legitimacy of the regime by forcing an unconstitutional succession, perhaps accepting Big Minh for a short while as the Vietnamese Kerensky, then move to make the revolution irreversible.

Big Minh has been in contact with General Timmes. Ky still has irons in the fire.

4. Big Minh informed one of his regular American contacts [Timmes] in the afternoon that some of the Northern generals [men around Ky] were planning a move against him. Since my own desire is a quiet, tranquil Saigon through to-

morrow and the weekend I did send a messenger to Ky with word that if this rumor were true we thought it would get nowhere.

Martin can be devious: "Assuming that he would deny any connection I said that he should be told that we accepted this as true but no one else would believe it so he had some vested interest in seeing that it did not happen." Martin can be more Vietnamese than a Vietnamese.

Huong has asked the prime minister named by Thieu to stay on the job for the time being. Can wants to leave. He appeals to the ambassador. "I said no transportation would be available until the weekend." Martin cannot permit the political process to ravel.

Jean-Marie Mérillon besieges the president. He goes to great lengths to make it appear that Huong summoned him. The president's office says Mérillon asked to see him. Martin follows these events carefully.

"6. Mérillon went back to see the President at 4 P.M. Told me afterwards by phone there was nothing new. President summoned me at 5 P.M. . . . respite only respite of military activity. Didn't know how long it would last."

Mérillon asks Martin to pressure Huong to step down.

Huong is fading fast. Receiving the American ambassador, Huong talks to him as to a friend. Martin says his own view is that the communists see Huong as an extension of Thieu.

Huong says, "Thieu without Thieu? If I have to be the Pétain of Vietnam, I will do so with honor and dignity."

The president wants to know what Martin thinks of Big Minh. The ambassador has never met Big Minh. There are many rumors circulating about his ambitions. Some say it would be a good thing if Big Minh were named prime minister in the traditional way, others that he'd rather be chosen by the National Assembly and the people, and will demand full powers. Huong talks about his old friendship for Minh. The general always called Huong "Teacher." Huong had once advised Minh to go abroad. Huong had called him back from Bangkok in 1968. "There are many ties between us."

Martin reminds him that Minh is acceptable to the Third Force and certain generals. To Huong, the ambassador's impressions seem reasonable. The essential question, Is Minh acceptable to Hanoi? Huong knows nothing about that. He asks Martin to query the Polish ambassador to the ICCS.

Still from Martin's cable:

> 8. Polish ambassador came to see me at 2000. He is a hard-line communist but also a professional diplomat. We understand each other. I told him my impression the new head of state squarely faced the realities and thought destiny had

made him play the role of a Pétain. . . . he had no way of knowing whether Hanoi would accept Big Minh in a temporary role of Laval.

The Pole will try to find out. Martin: "He is a cautious man and Warsaw must give him permission to move. I doubt he will have an answer in time. I'm certain he will report in the morning that he has heard nothing. I can report that to the President and leave it at that." Martin thinks "Big Minh would be as good as any at this period," but Americans should play no part in this affair. "Do we have any indication in Washington whether he [Minh] would be acceptable to Hanoi?"

In this great game of chess there is one pawn missing. No one knows what role Minh *could* play, no one knows if the North Vietnamese will even sit down at the board with him.

In Paris, President Giscard d'Estaing calls in Paul d'Ornano, senator for overseas Frenchmen, former planter in Indochina, who is going back to Saigon. The president of the republic thinks the PRG has good chances. At any rate, the French presence must be maintained. D'Ornano must pass the word to Frenchmen: stay in place.

The president can instruct officials and only advise civilians.

Kissinger and Martin are in constant touch. Kissinger explains on April 23 that there are

> two ways to proceed with respect to the political situation in Saigon. We can try to maintain a viable governmental structure [structure, a favorite Kissinger word and concept] which means preventing further unravelling of the government as it is now composed, or we can seek what is in essence the French approach: seeking to induce changes until we can find a governmental structure acceptable to the North . . . the only practical hope for the amelioration of the inevitable is through the Soviet route.

They must wait for a response from Moscow and until then preserve the present political structure. "If we do not hear within a couple of days or if the present response is negative we can then reconsider our position. In the meantime I suggest you do whatever possible to bolster Huong and his government without telling him about our Soviet initiative." In his turn, Huong becomes a bargaining chip. Like Kissinger, Martin still faces the same dilemma about the evacuation—the Pentagon is in a hurry; in case of an attack on Saigon, they don't want to let materiel and munitions fall into communist hands; but if they ship out the materiel, the South Vietnamese will panic.

Thieu's men prepare to depart. Former prime minister Khiem sends several tons of baggage abroad. Thieu's special security assistant is received by the new president, who tells him that he is too closely identified with Thieu and must resign. Quang does so on the spot, then asks Huong to take care of Thieu's faithful. Huong will see . . . he'll talk to Thieu about them shortly. The important thing right now is negotiating with the enemy, isn't it? "The nations's welfare comes before individual happiness."

A few hours later, at the end of the afternoon of the 23rd, Ky's helicopter lands on the roof of the presidential palace, where Huong waits him.

Ky: "The communists may reach Saigon in a few days or a few hours."

Huong: "We have to negotiate. Mérillon and many others are pressuring me to transfer power to Minh. The army can't hold out. Is it true we're out of ammunition?"

Ky thinks the army needs an energetic leader: "With what we have, we can hold on for a year or two. Appoint me chairman of the joint general staff."

Huong sidesteps this: "A man of your stature, who has been prime minister and vice-president, cannot become simply chief of staff. Very shortly I will name you special military adviser to the government."

"But there isn't much time, Mr. President."

Ky leaves. All these weaklings and waverers! Like the French, the Americans are going to bet on Minh, another weakling. If Minh takes power, or rather if he's given power, because he'll never take it himself, things will fall apart. Perhaps Ky regrets not having instigated a coup. A few days before Thieu's departure, a squadron leader had proposed dropping a "daisy cutter" on the palace.

The French are encouraging Minh to take over as prime minister, at least to begin with. That evening Minh calls his advisers together. This "constitutional" nomination, he says, would make him a weak prime minister: "I'd prefer to receive the job directly from the people. For example, by public approval of the principal religious groups, and of others."

Minh imagines that the various groups will grant him a sort of popular mandate. He asks one of his advisers, Deputy Nguyen Van Binh, to make contact with professional associations—lawyers, professors, businessmen, journalists. With the army, Minh is sure of himself. Some hours earlier the generals met at staff headquarters, in the presence of Vien, who thought the Constitution should be suspended and Minh should be named head of state. Named by whom? By the people, Minh replies. Mandate of the people, mandate of religious leaders, mandate of professional associations, mandate of heaven. Minh now knows at least that the chief of staff is at his service. If Minh is given full power, many generals and superior officers now preparing to flee will stay on and follow his orders.

From the neighborhood committee in Dalat, Father Jean Maïs obtains a permit to move about. On a red Honda, with one of his protégés, Maïs rides down Route 1 among a flood of refugees and North Vietnamese convoys. In mid-afternoon near Can Cu, a village about twenty kilometers from Xuan Loc, Maïs and his protégé are halted by civilians with armbands: "Where are you going?"

Maïs answers in Vietnamese: "To Gia Kiem to see a wounded priest."

Under the curious gaze of several pistol-packing civilians and two North Vietnamese soldiers, the questioner examines the priest's French carte d'identité and Vietnamese residence permit. A civilian invites the travelers into a home, where they're offered tea and bananas. An hour passes. They're taken to another house, where they're not asked to sit down. A fifty-year-old civilian, who introduces himself as a security officer, interrogates them dryly. He keeps his distance and addresses the priest, calling him "mister," *ong*: "Who are you, *ong*? Where do you come from? Where are you going? *Ong*, you don't want to gad about like this. I can't guarantee your safety."

A second civilian arrives and calls Maïs "professor," *giao su*. The travelers wait. They sit on stools. A third interrogator joins them, polite and even respectful. With Maïs, he uses "father," *cha*.

They confiscate the two travelers' papers and take the men upstairs in a house where they find the village chief, a peasant who interrogates them. Night falls. They're brought cold rice, vegetable soup, two mats. Guards in khaki or black, fifteen year olds, watch the house. By their accents Maïs knows they come from Central Vietnam. They release a few prisoners, who are quickly replaced by others. Jean Maïs asks questions.

He is told: "Your case has not yet been decided."

April 24. From the base at Plesetsk, the Soviets launch a high-resolution photoreconnaissance satellite that can spot military units as small as a platoon and pick out tanks clearly. The satellite's inclination: 81°. A week earlier they'd launched another, inclination 65°. The two overlapping satellites will give the Soviets superior photographic reconnaissance of Vietnam for six days, until April 30.

These second-generation satellites send back photographs that can be developed quickly. The results are relayed to Hanoi within hours. And from there to Dung's headquarters immediately. So the commander in chief knows what he's up against.[1]

In Saigon everybody's hoping for an imminent cease-fire. A scheme, a fantasy, is drifting through the air: three Vietnams, one in the North, communist, one in the Center with a coalition regime, one in the South where an augmented government will negotiate with Hanoi.

April 24, in the morning: President Huong and Big Minh meet secretly in former prime minister Khiem's home at Tan Son Nhut airport. Secretly? Everybody who's anybody in Saigon, and everybody who's nobody in Saigon, will know all about it within hours.

The new president says he's ready for direct discussions alone with Big

Minh; but Minh wanted the interview—which will last two hours—to take place in the presence of former Senate president Nguyen Van Huyen.

Huong draws a very somber picture of the military situation. The government can count on at most five divisions to face five NVA army corps. At best, they could make a last stand. Huong tries to persuade Minh to accept the post of prime minister, which would certainly be constitutional. Calmly Minh refuses: that would compromise him. The communists would accuse him of accepting authority and legitimacy from one of "Thieu's clique." This would render Minh powerless in negotiations. He suggests that Huong resign in his favor. Unpredictable, this Minh! In serious crises, braggarts often collapse, the meek assert themselves, and the modest become demanding. Minh knows that the Catholics and Buddhists are preparing public statements, separate or joint but saying the same thing: Minh must assume supreme power. This very day the bonze Tri Quang, most active venerable of the An Quang pagoda, will espouse that position in a press conference.

The old president hears Minh out without indicating approval. The former president of the Senate supports Minh. Huong doesn't want to give in. He jokes: "The simplest way to get rid of me would be a coup d'état. It would be more natural."

They consider ways and means of appeasing the communists, primarily the freeing of political prisoners. Minh discussed it the evening before with the chief of national police, General Binh, still on the job. Huong seems by turns irritated and relieved by Minh's many contacts. No question, Minh is accepted everywhere and by everyone, even the police. When President Diem was overthrown, Big Minh saved Binh. The latter was a loyal Diemist, then became a Thieuist. If he must, he'll follow Minh.

When he leaves, leaning heavily on his cane, old President Huong seems shaken, but he hasn't come to a decision.

As many political and military bigwigs are visiting Minh as they are the president. Either in the conviction that he must face the PRG and Hanoi alone, or by misplaced arrogance, this placid man Minh is now uncompromising, a far cry from the Vietnamese proverb, "If someone else comes in first, I'll be second. And if someone else comes in second, I'll take third with pleasure."

Minh sketches a provisional constitution or charter which he proposes to promulgate as soon as the present constitution is suspended and Huong resigns and fades away. Minh lists a provisional government. President: Minh. He'll keep military affairs as well. Vice-president will be Senator Huyen, who was present at the meeting with Huong: his primary duty will be to negotiate with the enemy. The ministerial balance shows wisdom. Huyen is a Southerner, a moderate and a Catholic, and should reassure the nationalists. Prime minister and minister of foreign affairs: Senator Vu Van Mau, assisted by a vice prime minister, Deputy Ho Van Minh. Those two between them will rally the members of both houses. Nguyen Vo Dieu, a banker, will become minister for economics. Big Minh also introduces people clearly acceptable to the communists: in the Ministry of Justice Mme. Thanh, a well-known neutralist whom Thieu had practically placed under house arrest, and in the Ministry of Social Affairs and Refugees a leftist Catholic, deputy Ho Ngoc Nhuan. Of course, the list can be altered, but it shows promise and proves Minh's good will. A combination as ingenious as any ministry under the French Fourth Republic. But how to persuade the communists?

Separately, President Huong and Big Minh send emissaries to Camp Davis. They are received quite courteously by the PRG delegates, who refuse to commit themselves. In Paris and in Hanoi that day, the PRG issues a statement: "There must be a new administration in Saigon [and] in that administration there must be no one who was part of Nguyen Van Thieu's clique." That's aimed at Huong but also at an overwhelming majority of civilian and military figures in South Vietnam.

The nimble minister of defense Don plays middleman, working toward a Huong–Minh compromise. Suppose the president offered Minh the position of "head of government" rather than "prime minister," with full civil and military powers? In bad times words weigh heavier. The more Frenchified a Vietnamese—and Don is, extremely so—the more he values phrases and legal constructions. By Don's scheme Huong, a new kind of president, would play an honorary role, like a Scandinavian monarch. He would not interfere in governmental matters. He'd exercise a function comparable to Emperor Bao Dai's before he vested full powers in President Diem. Huong's honor would be preserved and they could begin negotiations. Don pushed his luck telling Mérillon he might be top man in a vast political shakeup and the Americans were behind him. He made the same suggestion to Martin, saying the French were behind him. The two ambassadors had fun swapping versions.

Now Don is ready to play the Minh card with good grace, but thinks Minh is dreaming if he supposes he'll be drafted for the presidency by popular demand. Statements by a few religious figures, however eminent, will not confer legitimacy. Minister of Defense Don feels, moreover, that generals and superior officers still fighting and commanding would not easily accept Big Minh, who would be taking power only to raise the white flag. In the eyes of many ranking military men, the negotiations Minh is talking about look more like surrender.

How can Saigon's politicians and generals meet the demands trumpeted by the PRG? *All* the generals, colonels, majors, senators and deputies are part of the Saigon administration. What the PRG really wants is to dismantle the civilian and military machines both.

At 4 P.M. the Nguyen Ba Can cabinet resigns officially. Reduced to greater Saigon and part of the Delta, the Republic of South Vietnam has only a president and some acting ministers. At the request of the minister of defense, the chief of the joint general staff orders South Vietnamese troops to take up defensive positions. They are to refrain from attacking the NVA and the Vietcong. Another token of good will—instructions broadcast to all personnel: "In all news bulletins, we must take a more conciliatory tone." Employees of the Ministry of Information are to remove or deface anticommunist signs and banners in the capital and its suburbs. Huong examines lists of political prisoners to be freed immediately.

At 5 P.M. Minh calls in several reporters: "I have refused the post of prime minister offered me by the president of the republic. If I accepted, I would be unable to negotiate with the other side, which is demanding his ouster."

A leak from Minh's colleagues to the reporters: "Old Huong will resign soon. It's the only way out."

At the U.S. Embassy, Martin and Polgar are monitoring the labyrinth of discussions and negotiations hour by hour. Polgar gives better odds on Big Minh than Martin does.

On April 24, at last, Martin officially authorizes evacuation of Vietnamese personnel at the embassy. A massive departure of Vietnamese by way of Cap Saint-Jacques still seems logical. Polgar keeps in touch with the commanding general of Vietnamese marines, General Bui The Lan, who says he's prepared to protect an evacuation of 40,000–250,000 refugees. Polgar cables Washington: If Saigon falls, General Lan will cut the road to Cap Saint-Jacques by blowing the bridges. That will keep a flood of refugees from swamping Cap Saint-Jacques. The Vietnamese marines will cooperate with the Americans. To maintain order, the South Vietnamese can be brutal if they must; "U.S. marines," he cables primly, "could not take the required measures. His [General Lan's] marines would have no such restrictions." In a nutshell, if refugees have to be battered or killed in the shambles, better it be done by South Vietnamese marines. The Vietnamese general did not ask to have his men evacuated, but it goes without saying that they too would like to leave.

Jim Eckes comes and goes at will at Tan Son Nhut. The military and police guards are used to his white Volkswagen.

Planes take off every half-hour, carrying refugees with or without papers. On one runway a Pan Am plane, the last announced flight, is to take out 600 people, company employees and their families. Eckes spies a group of Vietnamese women, all in Pan Am flight attendants' uniforms. Some are floating in their skirts, others are spraining their ankles in high-heeled shoes. They seem to be afraid, especially when they file past the police. Suddenly at the bottom of the ladder one of them removes her shoes and takes the steps two at a time. Eckes understands: one real Vietnamese Pan Am hostess has distributed more or less suitable uniforms to her sisters and friends to get them out of Saigon. Six hundred passengers for three hundred and fifty seats: on board, an American federal aviation inspector says nothing. They close the doors. Al Topping, head of Pan Am in Saigon, realizes that two white American hostesses have been forgotten in the terminal. Someone runs to find them.

The plane waits on the runway. The control tower will not authorize it to take off. Jim Eckes sees a South Vietnamese soldier, walkie-talkie in hand. Jim hands him two hundred dollars: "Ask the tower to let that plane take off. Offer them this money. Let 'em drink our health. Let 'em do what they want with it."

The officer speaks to the controllers. Take off authorized.

"Now all my pals are gone, all my friends," Eckes says, and weeps softly.

19

---◆---

Half-Price Sale

P ham Van Ba, the PRG man in Paris, notifies the Quai d'Orsay that a political formula including General Minh as head of state would be acceptable, provided he front a government genuinely desirous of national reconciliation. It's a matter of finding acceptable people. Does "acceptable to the PRG" mean "acceptable to Hanoi"?

The Quai d'Orsay relays this news to the U.S. Embassy in Paris, which relays it to Washington, where it is relayed to the U.S. Embassy in Saigon by Kissinger himself. According to the same Pham Van Ba, "the United States must resolve South Vietnamese problems with the PRG and not with Hanoi. For its part, the PRG is ready to open a dialogue."

Pham Van Ba seems frank and open to those who have met him. He's a "moderate" in the PRG, they say. In Paris he holds talks with Bui Kien Thanh, assistant secretary general for international affairs of a tiny forgotten party affiliated with the Second International, the Vietnamese Socialist Party. European socialist parties ignore it. To the PRG Thanh proposes forming a government comprising heads of the principal religions: He maintains that only these religious leaders represent most of the Vietnamese population. No politician, no statesman, Big Minh no more than others, is truly representative. Only delegates from the great religions, the Vietnamese socialists humbly aver, could lead the population into a dialogue with the PRG. In Paris the latter seem to find the idea interesting. Immediately the Vietnamese socialists, also inspired by the ecumenical ceremony at the cathedral in Saigon some days earlier, send a telegram to the archbishop, Monsignor Binh. He never receives it. At that the Vietnamese socialists ask the U.S. Embassy in Paris if they can guarantee communication with the religious chiefs. The PRG in Paris encourage the socialists but make it clear that they can't promise a cease-fire even if an acceptable government *is* established in Saigon.

In some diplomatic circles in Paris, they believe there's dissension between the PRG and Hanoi, and even in the PRG itself.

At first Mérillon thinks it's a joke. A central operator in Saigon said, "The president of the republic wants to speak to you. Not *our* president, *your* president."

Valéry Giscard d'Estaing encourages Mérillon: "What you're doing is very good. I congratulate you. Don't take too many chances." He adds amiably, "All your initiatives are very good initiatives."

"I'm not taking the initiative, I'm following your instructions."

Politics by media: in Paris and Saigon, they announce the presidential phone call officially, to show that Paris is backing Minh. French diplomacy is trying to move up to the front lines. Jean Sauvagnargues assures all that "the French move is totally disinterested."

Mérillon is received by Huong and strongly advises him to give way to Minh. South Vietnam is dying. An operation is essential. The old man hangs on, arguing about constitutional difficulties. He receives Tran Van Lam, president of the Senate, who says he's ready to take charge of the government as the constitution provides, should Huong renounce his position and functions.

"President Huong can resign," Lam tells reporters. "He can't transfer power to just anybody. If he passed it to General Minh, it would violate the constitution."

Journalists ask him about France's role. Lam replies rather vaguely: "I hope France will have some influence on the other side . . . that she can play a part by interceding with the great powers, and more particularly with the communist powers."

Lam was minister of foreign affairs in 1973 and one of the negotiators of the Paris Agreement. Like many realistic political Saigonese, he counts more on Moscow's intervention than on Hanoi's good will.

In Washington the House of Representatives, resuming debate on Vietnam, has voted $327 million for humanitarian aid, $77 million more than the Senate. Congress authorizes Ford to use American soldiers to protect the evacuation. At the White House Ford has announced to a committee of businessmen who sponsor public service advertising campaigns, "America is going to make a new start. She is going to move forward."

Airman Ky and Father Thanh speak before 10,000 people at a meeting in a Saigon suburb. Pell-mell the orators demand the formation of a new government; resistance; a cease-fire; and negotiations.

At the embassy, Martin is betting on Huong, and Polgar even more on Minh. Lehmann reassures his visitors: everything will be all right. Greeting the Canadian chargé d'affaires, Lucien Hébert, who has come to say good-bye—he's leaving the next day—Lehmann protests: "No, you don't really have to go. We're staying. The North Vietnamese aren't going to take Saigon; there'll be an arrangement."

Then, after a slight pause: "At any rate, if things turned bad, there'd be room for you."

Understood: in one of our aircraft.

Polgar feels encouraged because he's had another meeting at his home with his favorite Hungarian. Colonel Toth assures him that all messages from the U.S. Embassy have been relayed rapidly "to the other side and to Budapest, and—I suppose—to others." According to Toth, the PRG and North Vietnamese at Camp Davis consider recent political develop-ments to be of a "constructive nature." Optimists, they think they'll find "mutually satisfactory" solutions. Guardedly, Toth insists: he is not speak-ing for the DRV or the PRG. Nevertheless, he can supply Polgar with items of intelligence "from the other side." Because he has a lot of trouble with Vietnamese names, he's taken notes.

He pulls out a notebook. According to "the other side", no one person is essential in the context of moves toward peace. A number of South Vietnamese would be acceptable. General Duong Van "Big" Minh is one of these. He is not the only one. The PRG's main concern is that nobody unacceptable play a role in South Vietnam.

"Entirely aside from who will run the new government," Toth contin-ues, "it would be good to include—for example—Mme. Ngo Ba Thanh, and Father Chan Tinh."

The PRG could get along with many figures. Toth even names interim Prime Minister Can, who yet belongs clearly to "Thieu's clique"! The PRG would like most of all a declaration from the Americans, stipulating that the United States will no longer interfere in South Vietnam's internal affairs and will cease all military support to the Saigon government.

Two very different messages from the PRG: in Paris they will not guarantee a cease-fire and at Camp Davis they say they're ready to accept one if there's a "satisfactory development in the political process." At least that's the official word relayed by Toth. His friends at Camp Davis, he says, would like to know if it's true that U.S. marines have landed at Cap Saint-Jacques. If so, why? Polgar denies it.

"Why," Toth then asks, "are there so many American ships offshore, when there've been mass evacuations of Vietnamese for over two weeks?"

Polgar answers that that fleet is there only to serve in evacuation op-erations. He wants Toth to make the "other side" understand that Huong's government has "emotional and psychological problems," and so will any successor government. They can't move too quickly. They have to think of all those South Vietnamese, especially the soldiers, who are casting a cold eye on political developments. "We don't want to see F-5 pilots bombing the presidential palace to protest what they consider a betrayal of the nationalist cause."

Admirable! "We"! We, Americans, Hungarians, Hanoi and the PRG. Polgar continues, repeating Martin's and Mérillon's hackneyed theme: "We don't want a collapse of law and order in Saigon. We have to avoid individual acts of violence and mob rule."

Polgar has no doubt that the police will execute the new government's orders. No one knows when it will be complete. Anyway the Huong government will publish decrees before then that "will clearly indicate that national reconciliation is the order of the day." His evidence? A few hours earlier interim Prime Minister Can announced that several hundred political prisoners would be released. Some will be indeed, but South Vietnamese security forces will take advantage of the moment to liquidate certain very important North Vietnamese agents in their hands. So Nguyen Van Tai, one of these agencies' prize catches according to Snepp, will be flung from an aircraft.

With Martin's assent, Polgar asks Toth to tell his friends at Camp Davis that the embassy would like to explore certain problems with a PRG representative, officially but in secret. Toth takes copious notes and hopes to have a rapid response. Perhaps even this evening.

Kept abreast of this whole discussion, Kissinger can hardly believe a word of it. A cease-fire with the Vietnamese communists should really not depend on approaches by a Hungarian colonel. Kissinger informs Martin imperiously that any negotiations with the PRG will take place in Paris and not in Saigon.

For some, among them Jean-Marie Mérillon, the Minh plan is evolving nicely. Apparently Martin is beginning to favor this solution too. The American ambassador naturally thinks the French want to reestablish themselves in Indochina, but he has a certain confidence in Mérillon. Why not play the Minh card? Big Minh, the perennially retreating general, doesn't work too hard, they say. What's he doing after all these years, this sage? He's playing tennis, and taking care of his collections of orchids and tropical fish. So! To succeed in politics, high intelligence is not essential. Still, it takes energy and character. Minh has a *nice* character. Has he *real* character? Some say he's "an elephant with the brains of a sparrow." Martin and Mérillon are agreed on one point: a 100 percent communist solution would be the worst of all. If the NVA takes Saigon, any continued fighting will mean total seizure of the South by the communists.

The French, and especially Pierre Brochand, have a real liking for Minh. Like his entourage he's a Francophile, in contrast to many Vietnamese generals trained by the Americans. He's a general, which will please the military. That's not true of Huong. The South still has four or five divisions. So in the political game Minh has all the trumps. He must be given a chance to fuse the political and religious elements. If the PRG deems him acceptable, why not support him to the maximum? The French diplomats are profoundly gratified to see Polgar and even the hawk Martin swinging gradually into line. At worst, a hypothetical coalition government in a position to negotiate would avoid a battle for Saigon, the Stalingrad that hothead Ky is calling for. The Americans think the French are incurably naive; on the contrary, the French diplomats harbor few illusions over the long term. They know well enough that the Vietnamese communists have wanted to unify Vietnam for thirty years and Indochina for forty-five.[1] The French today, like Kissinger yesterday, are banking on Vietnamese common sense: it would be in Hanoi's interest, at least for a transition period of one to five years, to accept a government under the flag of a Third Force that the communists would not dominate entirely. A "presentable" regime in Saigon, more democratic than North Vietnam, would win them Brownie points in the West and allow them to keep their distance from Moscow and Beijing. The French are counting equally on traditional rivalries between North and South. Minh is really the man for the situation. Hanoi's communists are, up to a point, independent of Moscow's. Why shouldn't South Vietnam's show a similar independence of Hanoi, at least for a while?

Senator Paul d'Ornano arrives in Saigon. He will pass Giscard's instructions to one and all: stay where you are. Almost in spite of itself, the French community in Saigon radiates a certain optimism. Some Americans, among them Snepp, feel that attitude is influencing many Vietnamese. If the French don't leave, it means there will be an arrangement, perhaps the embryo of a noncommunist South Vietnamese state. A sort of Cochin-Chinese solution. The French Embassy in Saigon is working toward it. The French Embassy in Hanoi does not believe in it at all.

At Camp Davis, General Hoang Anh Tuan knows that there will be no negotiation, that the climax of "revolutionary violence" is at hand. In the battle shaping up, Tan Son Nhut airport will be bombarded.

On April 25 Tuan sends Hanoi a telegram in the heroic style of North Vietnamese communiqués and films. Headquarters may ignore his and his men's presence at Camp Davis: "We will dig bunkers and hold fast to our fighting positions here. If the enemy are obstinate, have our artillery intensify its barrage and don't worry about us. We are prepared to accept that sacrifice for the total victory of the campaign, for the total victory of the revolution. We would consider it an honor."

Honored or not to be doomed to sacrifice, NVA and Vietcong officers and men feel somewhat exposed in their wooden tin-roofed barracks. With shovels and pickaxes, and sometimes stakes and daggers, they dig shelters and improvise sacks to fill with earth. These measures could never protect them from a direct hit but will shield them from explosions.

In his campaign planning Dung takes note of the delegations at Camp Davis. The North Vietnamese commander in chief writes: "When we drew up plans for shelling Tan Son Nhut, we repeatedly warned those responsible about the location of the compound our delegation was in, to guarantee their security."

South Vietnamese sentinels calmly keep guard over the North Vietnamese and the PRG. The latter have only small arms and a few machineguns. Nothing to ward off a serious attack. A few companies of South Vietnamese paratroopers could take Camp Davis in no time.

President Huong summons Ambassador Martin. Thieu is complicating his life, he explains. The former president continues to bombard the new one with advice. Huong feels that Thieu's presence is a hindrance to negotiations. Huong would like Thieu to leave. "Would the United States take him in?"

"Yes, I'm sure of it," Martin says.

Like most high-ranking generals, Thieu has a residence at Tan Son Nhut airport. He could stay there. At least, Martin thinks, he'd be in less danger there than elsewhere. After a Thieu Resigned, the ambassador doesn't need a Thieu Assassinated on his hands.

Martin sends for a C-118 held at his disposal in Bangkok. By Martin's order, General Timmes proposes to Thieu that he leave Vietnam. Thieu accepts. He'll go to Formosa, where his brother is ambassador. At 7:30, after nightfall, the expresident leaves the palace in a Mercedes and goes not to his own villa but to ex-Prime Minister Khiem's, also at the airport. Martin orders Polgar to type up parole documents for Thieu's party, authorized by the Department of Justice and delivered by order of the president. These grant them the right to enter the United States as refugees. In his hurry, Polgar forgets the documents. Mme. Thieu, like Mme. Khiem, left several days before. Thieu will travel with about fifteen people. At 8:30 General Timmes, Frank Snepp and two officials head for Khiem's residence. Timmes presents Snepp to Thieu: "An outstanding embassy analyst, therefore a high-class chauffeur."[2]

They laugh. Thieu, Khiem and Polgar get into the cars. Before driving through the military airport, Timmes advises Thieu to scrunch down, "for your own sake, Mr. President."

Timmes asks after Thieu's wife and daughter.

"They're in London shopping for antiques."

Diplomatic plates win them quick passage through the roadblocks. Martin is waiting for Thieu near the plane. The ambassador notes that around these two men, the former president and the former prime minister, cluster only a few obscure officers. The travelers have almost no baggage—valises, overnight bags, cameras. Martin orders the pilot to douse the lights in the cabin.

Only then does he tell the pilot his destination: Taipei, on Formosa. Thieu thanks Snepp with a friendly clap on the shoulder. He climbs into the plane. Martin follows him.

"Thank you," says Thieu, very calm.

"Godspeed," says Martin, in the charming old-fashioned term.

The plane takes off. Martin slips back into his car, relieved. It was work well done. Thieu is safe and sound. Now, how to squeeze a delay out of those sons of bitches in Hanoi? So Martin can complete the evacuation. Like Polgar, the ambassador heads toward a villa in a residential neighborhood west of Saigon, where the Poles are giving a cocktail party. Ambassador Ryszard Fijalkowski takes him aside. Martin asks Fijalkowski the million-dollar question: "After Huong, would the people in Hanoi agree to Big Minh?"

The Pole will make inquiries. He asks a question for the Vietnamese communists: "We're all working toward negotiations, so can you tell me why there's an American armada in the South China Sea?"

"I sure as hell hope that neither you nor I will learn why," Martin answers. "Apropos, can you tell me why are there so many NVA rocket batteries so close to Saigon? Tell your damn friends in Hanoi that if they try to block our evacuation they'll find out in a hurry why that armada's there."

Martin thinks his Polish colleague will pass the warning to Hanoi quickly. Martin has no liking for polite small talk, and soon departs. A good enough day, all in all. With or without papers, a thousand Americans, their wives or mistresses and their children, have left.

And a president.

To complete the evacuation, Martin needs time most of all.

Locked into a house, Father Jean Maïs hears a girl shouting, "Every day she washed herself in a bathtub full of 33 Beer. He's gone abroad with tons of gold. They can play musical chairs all they want—we're going to take Saigon."

The girl is talking about Mme. Thieu, and the president, and his successors. Jean Maïs and his friend have been shuttled from one house to another. Now, the priest is called *anh*, brother, to show him that he's in no way superior to his captors. "*Anh*, I must tie your hands."

"Why?"

No one answers. His friend is not tied up. On the floor beside him, two men are seated. One has his hands tied, the other not. The mats have disappeared, like the deferential tone. They all wait. One day, two nights . . . They hear tank treads on the highway. Through cracks between the boards Maïs watches traffic. He sees SAM missiles towed by Molotova trucks. The priest knows that the South Vietnamese will not counterattack now, and it is not the PRG that's taking power in the South.

North Vietnam is conquering the South.

Despite rumors circulating in communist areas as well as Saigon, Thieu has not fled with the Bank of Vietnam's gold.

Of course, everyone is interested in that gold, Saigon's leaders as well as Washington's. If the communists must march into the capital, it would be preferable that they not take the gold with it. Two men study the problem closely on April 26—Hao, former vice prime minister in charge of the economy, and an adviser from the U.S. Embassy, Dan Ellerman. The gold could be deposited in Switzerland in the Bank of International Settlements or in the United States in the Federal Reserve Bank. Hao does not want this gold under American control in the United States. Martin insists that the ingots be evacuated. He goes to see the president. Huong seems distraught.

Martin leaves with the impression that Huong has approved shipping the gold out. He cables to Kissinger the same day. "The shipment"—he doesn't mention gold—worth many millions of dollars, can be insured up to about $60 million. The insurance will be good only if shipment is made before April 27. Hao is in charge of the transfer, but he has doubts and makes them known to his president. Whether Huong stays on or Minh takes power, if the gold leaves, all concerned could be accused of treason. They have to think it over. The American idea is to load the crates of ingots on a military plane, which would settle the insurance problem. The military have no need of such precautions. The operation will take place tonight. A telephone call to the embassy: Hao says Huong has not authorized the shipment.

The crates of gold bars stay in the basement of the bank where they were stored.

Shaken by conflicting advice, legalistic President Huong addresses a joint session of the South Vietnamese legislature. He asks a serious question: "Can I resign and transfer power to General Duong Van Minh so he can open negotiations with the enemy?"

The honorable senators and deputies debate for ten hours.

In the corridors Pierre Brochand watches the debates. Verbal rows and temporary adjournments punctuate the speeches at once tragic, comic and pathetic.

The senators and deputies finish by voting a resolution: they reaffirm their confidence in President Huong. They leave all necessary decisions to that same president, including the one on handing over power "to a personage of his choice." This resolution violates the constitution, but retains a faint juridicial aroma.

Toward noon, while these discussions rage in the Senate, Colonel Vo Dong Giang holds a press conference at Camp Davis. He is not very encouraging on the subject of negotiations. He says only, "Our troops continue their advance; there will be no cease-fire."

The colonel enumerates nine conditions that the Americans must fulfill. He demands the departure of all members of the CIA, the withdrawal of the fifty U.S. warships cruising in territorial waters and the 6,000 marines aboard, the withdrawal of 200 U.S. aircraft poised, he says, to intervene. He adds seven preliminary conditions aimed at the Saigon government. They come down to completely eliminating the government.[3] While the communist representative is speaking at Camp Davis, Pierre Brochand telephones Thomas Polgar. According to him, Saigon's politicians, dilatory and byzantine, are wasting their time: it is unquestionably too late to negotiate.

The Poles of the ICCS must think the same thing. The CIA learns that an Ilyushin will land at Tan Son Nhut in a few hours to evacuate 280 Poles to Warsaw via Bangkok. This can mean only one thing: the Poles foresee an assault on Saigon and have no desire to hang around waiting for the liberators. Just this once the Poles didn't exchange information with Snepp or Polgar.

The evacuation proceeds, fairly well organized and disciplined. CINC-PAC offers Martin latest impressions: "The morale of the Vietnamese armed forces has dropped because their families have not been evacuated with the other refugees. . . . In Da Nang, ten intelligence officers of the 1st Air Division have been executed. . . . In general the Vietnamese think they will be killed if we do not let them escape." Martin is irritated: intelligence in Honolulu is doing its job, but he has no need to be told from that distance what's happening on his doorstep in Vietnam.

Kissinger is worried. How is Martin granting permission to leave? Is it true that South Vietnamese pilots are ready to shoot down American evacuation planes? Where did we hear that the communists have drawn up a list of people to liquidate, a million of them? And these stories of Americans arrested, attacked or turned over to the communists? Martin answers that sorting out rumors is an art. The ambassador says confidently there's increasing evidence that Hanoi "tacitly acquiesces to evacuation . . . while political evolution in Saigon continues in a direction they deem favorable." Another proof of North Vietnamese good will: they could capture the port of Cap Saint-Jacques, eighty kilometers south of the capital, but they're not doing it. General Homer Smith has run a reconnaissance there. We're going to ask for two C-130s to evacuate the families of 250 South Vietnamese marines, at their commander's request. The formalities will be taken care of efficiently. The planes will land and take off in a few minutes. No South Vietnamese air units down there. So no danger of an aggressive move by South Vietnamese pilots. This operation will serve as a test. We'll see if Lan can really protect the airport on the Cap.

All day, French diplomats besiege the president. In private, Jean-Marie Mérillon and Pierre Brochand worry a bit. They begin to doubt whether even a negotiated surrender is possible. In public, they radiate confidence. By now Polgar has more faith than Brochand in the Minh solution.

Le Courrier d'Extrême-Orient, almost the official sheet of the French Embassy, has four notes in its issue of Saturday April 26:

(1) President Giscard d'Estaing talked by telephone with the French ambassador in Saigon.
(2) Jean-Marie Mérillon has been received for the third time by President Tran Van Huong.
(3) M. Paul d'Ornano has arrived, bearing a message from the President of the Republic to the French community in Vietnam.
(4) There will be a de facto armed truce.

Translation: French diplomatic steps are bringing about a cease-fire situation which is bound to lead to a negotiated political settlement.

Le Courrier speaks of the rumors sweeping Saigon: five North Vietnamese divisions are returning to Hanoi and—one more time—a coup d'état has taken place in the North Vietnamese capital.

The Vietnamese press has modified its vocabulary. It speaks of "adversaries" or of "brothers," and less of "communist enemies."

Foreign airlines—Pan Am, Singapore Airlines, Thai International, China Airlines, Cathay Pacific—will no longer serve Saigon. On the other hand, Air France and UTA are studying the possibility of laying on supplementary flights for Sunday and Monday, April 27–28. Two American banks, Chase Manhattan and First National City Bank, close their doors and wickets with no notice to their clients. At the clearinghouse they think the Bank of America will follow suit. Marshall Ky says he intends to support General Minh if the latter succeeds Huong. Contradictory rumors circulate about the situation in the provinces, especially south of the capital.

A notice in *Le Courrier*:

Denial.

In recent days extravagant rumors of a nature to damage the reputation and honor of our family, concerning alleged LOOTING AND RAPE said to have been committed at the Auberge des Roches Noires, located at Bai Dua Vung Tau, have been intentionally circulated by evil tongues.

In response to this gossip, which is only ignoble tittle-tattle unworthy of honest folk, in the name of my family I deny it categorically and state formally that there has been neither looting nor rape. We are at present living, like so many of you, in safety, in the full sense of the word.

Despite the circumstances, despite the wild imaginings quoted above, our inn is functioning and continues to serve our gracious clientele as in the past.

As a gentleman, I forgive these inaccurate allegations formulated in a moment of aberration and beg the author or authors to show an ounce of good sense and above all honesty and withdraw these lying words circulated with a view to sullying my family and sabotaging our business.

> M. Lam Van Ho Gustave
> Manager of the Inn of the Black Rocks
> (Vung Tau, Cap Saint-Jacques)

An obvious indicator for Saigon's populace, the post exchange, that immense tax-free supermarket for the Americans, announces that it is going to close. Employees empty the shelves and repack cases of whiskey, gin, rum. All the rest, cartons of cigarettes, packages of potato chips, jars of jam, tape recorders, is for sale at half-price. In town they begin to hear that many U.S. marines who aren't embassy guards deplaned the night before at Tan Son Nhut airbase. Many Vietnamese politicians have no faith in a negotiated solution. Bui Diem phones Martin: "I can do nothing more for my country. I've decided to leave Vietnam. Can you help me? I want to leave with my elderly mother."

A diplomat, Josiah Bennett, comes to fetch Bui Diem. Martin puts a small eight-seat Marine Corps plane at his disposal. The control tower will not authorize them to take off. An American colonel grows impatient: "We have to take a chance. Let's go."

The plane reaches Bangkok.

Generals Dung and Tra order their men at Camp Davis to dig in. Tra thinks about sending in special units to bring them out. He decides against it, fearing "regrettable losses." The men at Camp Davis reinforce their trenches to protect themselves "from enemy artillery and our own 130s." At Tan Son Nhut, in this Camp Davis encircled by twelve watchtowers erected by South Vietnamese, Colonel Ngo Van Suong is stiffening his defenses. Officers and men are still digging, filling metal lockers with dirt and placing them on the roofs of bunkers. They set up an underground infirmary and connect the two delegations' barracks by a passageway.

Tra is about to order his divisions to begin the assault on Saigon. The order of battle is perfect: to the northwest of the capital, the 3rd Corps, to the north the 1st, in the east the 4th and 2nd, in the southwest the 232nd Tactical Force. (See map page 380.)

In all, eighteen divisions.

Even more useless than the closing of Saigon's banks is a message from the U.S. secretary of defense on April 26. James Schlesinger addresses all in the Department of Defense and members of the armed forces: "As the last withdrawal of Americans from Vietnam takes place," Schlesinger sends the military, men and women, some words of comfort.

For many of you, the tragedy of Southeast Asia is more than a distant and abstract event. You have fought there; you have lost comrades there; you have suffered there. . . . In combat you were victorious and you left the field with honor. . . . It will be stated that the war itself was futile. In some sense, such may be said of any national effort that ultimately fails. Yet our involvement was not purposeless. . . . I salute you for it. Beyond any question you are entitled to the nation's respect, admiration and gratitude.

Almost a requiem! The U.S. armed forces are always subject to the civil power. There is no violent reaction among them in 1975 any more than in 1973. No rebellion remotely comparable to that of the French army in Algeria. The majority of American career officers are convinced that their hands were tied by the civil power; a few career military have resigned in silence.

The entire world knows that soon there will not be a single American left in Vietnam. Many Americans of varying political opinions do not believe that, as Schlesinger affirms, the U.S. armed forces have been "victorious." Or that they are leaving "with honor."

With luck, this final departure will be at least methodical and dignified.

20

Brothers
of the Same House

Erich von Marbod is roaming Vietnam with one aim, to save all possible materiel and destroy what can't be pulled out. On the morning of April 27 he reaches the huge base at Bien Hoa. Idle or indifferent, ARVN soldiers are wandering the runways. Where are their officers?

The Vietnamese air command's electronic equipment, the mechanical and electrical repair shops, the radio installations, the state-of-the-art meters and gauges are intact. It would take days to pack it all. A furious von Marbod returns to Saigon. He protests vigorously to General Dang Van Khuyen, who has replaced General Vien as chief of the joint general staff. Vien persuaded Huong to accept his resignation; fearing assassins, he donned civilian clothes to flee. Von Marbod talks to the pilots, Ky among them. Could they destroy the abandoned materiel? They tell him that North Vietnamese anti-aircraft, and even more the new Strella rockets, are too dangerously accurate. To demolish the materiel the aircraft would have to fly very low; they'd be shot down.

Next day von Marbod meets Martin, who's dubious about this destruction. Another busy bee creating panic. Martin hasn't canceled an order prohibiting the removal of any South Vietnamese plane or helicopter. Like the Pentagon brass, von Marbod is radically pessimistic; not Martin, who confides that matters are edging toward a cease-fire in place and a coalition government headed by Minh. So Martin believes the Americans have time, a month at least, to take inventory, classify, label and load military materiel, safe and sound behind the cease-fire lines.

Von Marbod pays no attention to the ambassador's impressions. He asks the U.S. air force command in Thailand to prepare their landing fields for a large number of South Vietnamese aircraft. Two hundred of them reach the Thai runways.

Orders become more and more contradictory between Americans and Vietnamese. At Tan Son Nhut airport, 2,000 Vietnamese refugees are ready to leave, among them some military officials in civilian clothes. But President Huong forbids their departure and even demands that soldiers and officials abroad return to Vietnam within thirty days. Dotting his i's, the president lets them know that if they do not do so, they'll lose their citizenship and their assets will be confiscated. Huong moves the curfew up from 7 P.M. to 6 P.M.

The indefatigable Minister of Defense Don, surrounded by generals of the joint staff and the Saigon regional command, assembles the senators and deputies, calling them in by radio and television. Behind closed doors, he gives a detailed military summary to 138 legislators. His intelligence is so precise that they wonder if NVA headquarters hasn't deliberately sent messages in clear to worry the ARVN staff. Map in hand, Don traces communist lines of attack and possibilities for South Vietnamese resistance. "Here, southeast of Tay Ninh, to oppose four North Vietnamese divisions, the 320th, the 316th, the 70th and the 968th, we have only our 25th."

And so it goes, for all fronts around Saigon. A shocking appraisal: five divisions against at least eighteen. The road to Cap Saint-Jacques is cut, impassable to troops. Even the refugee convoys can't get through. The night before, 122 mm. rockets hit Saigon's suburbs.

The president of the Senate agrees that Minh should take power, full power. Fresh debate in the Assembly. Pierre Brochand is still there. He's helping one of Minh's advisers, Ly Qui Ching, clarify certain phrases. A degree from the Ecole Normale d'Administration has its uses. They vote at 8:30 P.M.

Question before the house: Are senators and deputies agreed that the president of the Vietnamese republic shall transfer all presidential powers to General Duong Van Minh so that he may find ways to restore peace in Vietnam? Ayes, 136. Abstaining, 2. A quorum is 106. The resolution is adopted. One little hitch, but a great loss of time—Huong wants the transfer to take place next day, not on the spot. He wants to be able to say that he was president for a week.

French policy has achieved its goal. Martin cables to Kissinger: "The French, the Poles, the Hungarians have all passed the word to the other side" to halt the attack. To prove that he's not the only optimistic American, Martin adds, "The unanimous opinion of all seniors here is that there will be no direct attack on Saigon." Which may imply that lower-level diplomats don't share that comforting belief. All the more so as Honolulu intelligence passes the word that they've picked up North Vietnamese messages in clear, orders about artillery fire aimed at Tan Son Nhut airport.

That doesn't impress Martin. Specialists in radio monitoring have told him that in the last fifteen years no order of that importance has ever been transmitted uncoded. So Martin decides it's an attempt by NVA headquarters to intimidate their enemies.

The ambassador reports on the progress of the evacuation. All in all, things are going well. By noon on April 27, 35,245 people have been pulled out. Now they're just waiting for Minh's enthronement. Kissinger authorizes contact with the tenants at Camp Davis, but only to deal with "the local situation." The men at Camp Davis are more than cool. Never mind, that can be handled at a higher level. At the Pentagon as at CINCPAC in Honolulu, no one is deluding himself about Hanoi's intentions. Only a few politicals now, like Martin, are still thinking about a cease-fire. The Pentagon takes a crucial decision without consulting the ambassador. The moment Tan Son Nhut airport is attacked, evacuation by plane will cease. They'll fall back on helicopters to transport refugees to ships at sea. It is General Homer Smith—not Ambassador Martin, technically his superior—who will give the order to evacuate the U.S. military from Saigon. For several days the brass in Honolulu thought there might be a truce. A cable to Martin on April 27 indicates that's no longer true: "Communist forces have launched what may be the final assault on Saigon." A delicate position for General Homer Smith, as he's also under Honolulu's command.

Martin meditates on a long cable from Kissinger:

> My thinking regarding the political evolution in Saigon is that following the formation of a Minh government there will be negotiations which will result more or less rapidly in an agreement on a tripartite government. That government will be two-thirds communist and one-third controlled by them [the communists]. Our problem at that point will be what to do with the embassy.
>
> At some juncture, perhaps soon, the north will decide to prevent the further evacuation of Vietnamese. When that happens, I think we should cut down to very bare-bones operation at the Embassy. The question then will be whether or not we should pull out altogether or maintain a token presence with a handful of Embassy personnel.

What is the United States' interest in maintaining an embassy? There is only one immediately obvious: the return of the bodies of American soldiers and the search for MIAs.

Martin can't accept the idea of Saigon's military and political annihilation. The French are staying. Why shouldn't the Americans do the same? Martin did not consider the departure of his colleague, Ambassador John Dean, from Phnom Penh a shining hour. Martin has faith in—or pretends to have faith in?—the Minh solution.

During the evening of April 27, Erich von Marbod is drinking green tea and cognac at Ky's. They hear artillery in the distance and sirens in the city. Ky is pondering a redeployment: "We can fight in the Delta and perhaps hold out for a few months. Will the American government support us, not with men, but with arms?"

"I'm sorry, the answer is no," replies von Marbod.

He advises Ky to leave Vietnam with him, in two or three days. Ky can start fresh in the United States. He ought to send his family out right away.

Tran Van Huu, the former prime minister who besieged the State Department in January, has sent emissaries to Saigon, among them Le Quoc Tuy and the former pilot Hanh. They make contact with the navy's commander in chief, Admiral Cang, at naval headquarters between the Hotel Majestic and the Arsenal. Without informing the joint chiefs, Cang prepares to pull out all operational seagoing vessels. He loads fuel, stores, ammunition, officers' and mens' families. He proposes to land the women, children and old folks on the island of Phu Quoc, in the Gulf of Siam near Sihanoukville. A fully defensible South Vietnamese base is manned there. Afterward Cang will lead his ships and men back toward the Delta. He'll set up headquarters on a coast guard cutter, the HQ 03, a large patrol boat of the type used by the French colonial navy.

Cang and Huu's two envoys proceed to Minh's: "In Paris, we saw people from Hanoi and the PRG. They agreed to a transition government."

Tuy says, "You'll have to invite Tran Van Huu back into the country and give him full power to negotiate with the communists."

Minh doesn't find that too tempting.

"How are you doing in your talks with the other side?" Admiral Cang wants to know.

Minh: "The Camp Davis people don't want to negotiate at all. They say they're only a military mission, and have no power to negotiate political questions."

Tuy: "Then why did you take power, with no guarantees and without being sure what the North Vietnamese want? Now you have to invite Tran Van Huu back to work out a solution."

Minh: "The French government pressured me into it and set it all up. Mérillon and Tran Van Don kept telling me they had a plan, and I had six months to arrange it all. And now there's *nothing*. I know you represent Huu and I think probably he can do something. . . . I respect him. . . . What do I do now to get him to help?"

Cang: "Don't worry, I'll take care of it. I have people. In the meantime, whatever happens, we must hold on at any cost. If the situation deteriorates, I suggest you leave Saigon and fall back on Can Tho [capital of the Delta]. General Nguyen Khoa Nam is in command of the fourth region, and phoned me last night to say the situation in the Delta is normal. He has three good divisions, an air force and all the naval forces. Plus the

Hoa Hao and Cao Dai, and the militia. We can stand fast, and negotiate from strength."

Minh: "Go on back. As soon as the studios are ready, I'll go on the air. In about an hour."

Cang: "Well, what's your plan?"

Minh: "I don't have one."

"As long as we stay in Saigon," the admiral insists, "we'll be surrounded. We . . . you have no room to maneuver if we stay here. You have to declare Saigon an open city and transfer the government to Can Tho. Your position won't be strong there, but at least it will be a position. While you're on the air, you ought to order all military units to fall back on the temporary capital."

Weary, Big Minh answers: "The war! Always the war! When will we be finished with this war?"

Obviously he's against the project. Cang asks a question: "Then everybody prepares his own plan?"

"Do what you want."

In an admirable display of eternal bureaucracy, and proof that the administration is still on the job, the president's secretariat announces that "public services will operate normally on May 1st, Labor Day." The dollar is worth 4,000 piastres.

Ky's advisers suggest he get in touch with Minh. He telephones Colonel Dau, Minh's assistant. "Thank you for calling," says the colonel, "but the president can't talk with you now. He is making up his government. We'll call you back."

When they leave Minh, Admiral Cang and Huu's two envoys return to naval headquarters. Huu's solution seems interesting. No one can accuse him of being part of "Thieu's clique." And in Saigon they say that once upon a time Huu might have become president of the National Liberation Front. He was even the preferred candidate of Le Duan, secretary general of the North Vietnamese Communist Party himself.

Cang and his companions wait for Minh. He never shows up. The admiral cannot get through to him. Cang tries to contact Mérillon and ask him to relay a message from Minh to Paris. In vain.

Cang notes then, "I did what I could, but we have no useful political leader now. Even if Minh were deposed by a coup, which would be easy because he has no real command over anyone, I don't see a solution. I have one more mission to carry out: to evacuate and rescue thirty thousand people with my ships."

The Huu solution is stillborn.

Shortly before midnight, about twenty officials of the U.S. Embassy meet. They have to go over the lists of Vietnamese who absolutely must be evacuated, especially those at greatest risk if the North Vietnamese take Saigon. They must evacuate at least 10,000 tomorrow. Impossible? Well then, 2,000.

In Washington at the same hour, Dobrynin is considering the questions Kissinger asked him to transmit to Hanoi: (1) Are the North Vietnamese ready to negotiate with Minh? (2) To accept a reduced American presence in Saigon? (3) To facilitate the American evacuation by leaving open (a) an air corridor to Saigon and (b) the road from Saigon to Cap Saint-Jacques?

They want frank, straight answers. A bit later Radio Liberation announces in a bulletin that "maintaining the American Embassy in Saigon with reduced personnel does not amount to an American disengagement." What does that mean?

Washington like Saigon fears a future bloodbath. In Danang, it seems, policemen were beheaded, and in Ban Me Thuot officials were shot. In other places South Vietnamese officers, bound hand and foot, were executed by grenade. High officials note that in the 1950s, after they took power in the North, the communists executed 50,000 people. Wolfgang Lehmann thinks that in the long run there will indeed be executions and liquidations.[1]

Lately the embassy has been arm-wrestling with the press. *Newsweek* correspondents interviewed a lot of refugees and concluded that there was little eyewitness testimony to atrocities. To contradict this, Martin orders that reporters be shown cables summarizing executions at Danang, Ban Me Thuot and elsewhere. Diplomats admit that only the most alarmist cables were selected. All the reports don't speak of atrocities. Some even cast doubt on the matter. Whatever the truth, it's obviously necessary to evacuate Vietnamese who work for the Americans in Saigon and Can Tho, and especially CIA employees and agents. Nothing seems to have been said about the Information Service. Alan Carter is worried about the fate of his 150 Vietnamese USIS employees.

The other embassies, with the exception of the French, have been all but emptied, primarily by plane.

Sir John Bushell, Britain's ambassador, wanted to stay in place after sending out his employees and the dozen Gurkhas that guarded his mission. British Prime Minister James Callaghan orders him to clear out. Sir John asks for a torpedo boat. What style! But if it were sunk on the Saigon River, what a lamentable effect! Four RAF Hercules are sent, by way of Singapore. Abandoned, the British Embassy now shelters South Vietnamese civil servants, among them some policemen. Many embassies, "forgetting" their Vietnamese employees who want to leave, behave less elegantly than many private companies.[2] The most considerate are the press agencies, radio and television networks, daily and weekly papers. Their managers made plans, some since February. Many rented planes from Eckes' company, Continental Air Services. The media need planes to film the action and send out photos and reels, but also to evacuate their employees at the last moment. The media will not abandon either personnel or their families. CBS, ABC, NBC have made provision for an airlift to

Singapore or Hong Kong. The Associated Press sent a light plane to Phnom Penh, during its last hours, to evacuate its Cambodian stringer. An NBC vice president personally watched over a chauffeur and his numerous children.

At the airport, all willing help is welcome. Volunteers like Jim Eckes make lists and escort refugees to the planes taking off every forty-five minutes. When refugees don't have official papers, volunteers and even civil servants escort them to planes for Guam or any airport on U.S. territory. Once landed, these refugees cannot be expelled. But arriving in the Philippines, for example, a refugee without papers may have serious problems entering the United States.

During the day of April 28, the U.S. marines assigned to protect the evacuation finally feel the embassy is taking it seriously. A detachment of marines—a lieutenant, a sergeant, thirty-six men and two nurses—is at Tan Son Nhut by order of the Pentagon. Since their arrival these marines have been frustrated. Several days earlier the four officers and one noncom of an advance team discovered on the spot that preparations for an evacuation were "nebulous." The marines are walking a tightrope. They're answerable to their military command, but the embassy is responsible for the evacuation of its personnel. Martin doesn't want any emphasis on departure plans; he's still trying to avoid panic. There was a lot of negotiation between civilians and the military before the marines could prepare helicopter landing zones at Tan Son Nhut, raze tennis courts, hang barbed wire. Martin's in the way. The high command in Honolulu sorted out the options a long time ago.[3]

The order for a massive evacuation of Americans by plane went out on April 22. The marines have to prepare for an evacuation based solely on the use of helicopters, according to the option Frequent Wind. The first code name, Talon Vise, was changed. There were leaks. The plan recommends thirteen assembly points in town to "extract" the last Americans and transport them to the airport. Professionals, the marines would like to set up beacons on roofs at these thirteen points. The ambassador is against that, still for the same reason. In his final report, General Richard Carey, commanding the marines involved, will say: "Much of what was accomplished was done with unofficial sanction" (translation: without Martin's authorization). An important detail: at no time did the evacuation plan foresee large helicopters landing on the embassy roof. They proceeded as if they had permanent use of the runways at Tan Son Nhut, and therefore of planes. One almost feels that Martin, clinging to the idea of a cease-fire, has in mind an evacuation protected by a security force comprising marines, docile South Vietnamese soldiers and, why not, North Vietnamese police and soldiers, each group more obliging than the others.

Minh has a call put through to Ky: "The general wants to see you tomorrow morning at the palace."

Ky has changed his mind. Most of the officers in his entourage advise him not to accept that invitation. Suppose they took him prisoner to neutralize him? Suppose they handed him over to the North Vietnamese? Ky's and Minh's personalities are truly so different that they never agree on anything. Impulsive, bubbling, Ky cares more about fighting than about a negotiation he doesn't believe in. Slow, a dawdler, Minh is aiming at a cease-fire. In the twisted world of Saigon politics, Ky and Minh manage to get along, the younger ritually respecting the older. They don't care for each other at all. Now they've reached the point of absolute distrust. Ky will not see Minh.

The transfer of power from Huong to Minh is set for 9 A.M. At Huong's request, the ceremony is postponed until afternoon. Huong wants it to take place amid a certain pomp. "We cannot hand over the responsibilities of power like a handkerchief," he says. The two men are behaving as if they have weeks before them.

In Saigon's suburbs, soldiers are still piling up sandbags for low walls and emplacing machinegun and mortar nests. Refugees are filtering into the city by thousands. On the Saigon–Bien Hoa highway, military convoys and civilian cars are immobilized, mingling with cattle-drawn carts. Military police units, those still operational, receive orders and counterorders.

The jewelry shops in the rue Catinat are closed. It's more and more difficult to buy gold. At the airport, Americans walk around with rolls of dollars and piastres to bribe sentries and police. Mail delivery is normal.

At Minh's the telephone rings nonstop. At 3 P.M., Minh tells General Timmes he thinks the communists will negotiate with him. A little later, Minh takes a phone call from Ngo Cong Duc in Bangkok; editor of the newspaper *Tin Sang*, he is en route from Paris and is late reaching Saigon: "You must not accept the presidency. It's too late. The communists have not the slightest intention to negotiate."

The transfer of power is accomplished at 5 P.M. The gates of the palace are wide open, hardly guarded. Deputies, senators, soldiers, reporters come and go at will. On the chairs before the dais sit officers, former ministers and high officials, Catholic prelates and Buddhist dignitaries, uniforms and severe business suits alongside flashy costumes. Colonel Hoa supervises his television crews. The hot air is becoming very humid. The wind that always precedes storms excites the palms on the lawn and the white damask curtains in the big reception room. Leaning heavily on his cane, supported by a colleague, Huong speaks first, at 5:15. "My age and infirmity prevent me from leading the country in these difficult moments. . . ."

Rain begins to fall. Huong addresses Minh: he must seek peace without compromising his country's honor. Tears in his eyes, Huong says, "General, your burden will be heavy."

A long silence follows. The dais stands empty. No one moves. Everything is happening as if protocol did not cover such occasions. Minh remains seated. The audience gazes at him. One of his entourage rises and steps toward the platform. A young soldier has removed the flag of the republic and replaced it by a plaque showing a stylized apricot-flower opening itself to the Chinese characters for *yin* and *yang*, the two complementary forces of the universe—the opposing forces in Vietnam on the road to reconciliation? Minh rises, speaks, in a voice that seems all the firmer after Huong's faltering:

> We have no vengeful intentions, and there is no reason that forbids brothers of the same house to reconcile. . . . It is my responsibility to seek a cease-fire. . . . Lawyer Nguyen Van Huyen is vice-president, and has agreed to help me in negotiations. . . . Vu Van Nau is prime minister. . . . Citizens, my brothers, in the last few days a situation so serious has risen that numerous religious groups and many generals have asked me to assume the presidency. . . . One urgent political decision is to free all political prisoners and to cease all harassment of the press.

Minh raises his voice over thunderclaps and the sound of fat raindrops splashing outside the open windows:

> This government's success will depend on the steadiness and support of the people. I call on all political parties and on all religions. Let them forget their hates and their suspicions. . . . Soldiers, my comrades, I have spent most of my life in the armed forces. More than anyone, I understand your difficulties these last weeks. Today, an old page of history is turned. You have a new task, to defend what territory remains and to defend the peace. . . . Do not throw down your arms; obey your officers absolutely. Any breach of discipline will be punished immediately. And now a few words for our friends on the other side, the Provisional Revolutionary Government of South Vietnam.

Minh avoids mention of Hanoi or the North Vietnamese divisions, as the communists have never acknowledged their presence in the South. He must not give offense.

> Sincerely, we want reconciliation. You know that. Reconciliation demands that each in this country respect the rights of all. . . . Citizens, my brothers, in these last days you have wondered why so many have calmly deserted their country. I want to tell you, my fellow citizens, that this is our beloved land. Take courage, I beseech you. Stay here and accept the fate decreed by heaven. I beg you: stay here and stay united.

Rebuild an independent South Vietnam, democratic and prosperous, so Vietnamese may live with Vietnamese in fraternity.

President Minh speaks for twenty minutes.

For many in the Vietnamese television and radio audience, the rain and thunder before the monsoon are bad omens.

Some take heart. Engineer Van tells himself: militarily, we are in a position of weakness, but the communist victors will be humane.

Minh finishes his speech at 5:48. An hour later, while diplomats, politicians and reporters are dissecting his discourse, Radio Liberation notes the transfer of power:

> After the departure of the traitor Nguyen Van Thieu, those who are replacing him, namely the clique Duong Van Minh, Nguyen Van Huyen and Vu Van Mau, are holding fast to their war, to keep their present territories while calling for negotiations. It is obvious that this clique continues stubbornly to prolong the war in order to maintain American neocolonialism. But they are not fooling anyone. The fighting will not stop until all of Saigon's troops have laid down their arms and all American warships have left South Vietnamese waters. Our two conditions must be met before any cease-fire.

Big Minh's son tries unsuccessfully to take over the South Vietnamese embassy in Paris.

For the first time, Radio Liberation states clearly that Minh and his colleagues are *not* acceptable leaders of the Third Force: "Supporters of the Third Force must carefully consider the PRG's appeal . . . must spot traps set by the lackeys of the United States government. . . . They must join the revolutionary forces."

Translation, understood by all: no one in South Vietnam can support Minh *and* be recognized as a partner by the PRG or Hanoi.

Huong telephones Ky: "They forced me out. You're free to do what you want."

What do those bitter words mean? That the old, legalistic, punctilious Huong cannot himself mount a coup d'état?

At 6:15, after Minh's inauguration, five A-37 fighter bombers of the South Vietnamese air force buzz the main runway at Tan Son Nhut. The control tower asks, "What squadron do you belong to?"

A pilot responds oddly: "These planes were made in the United States."

The planes dive and loose their bombs. Near the gym and Homer Smith's offices, where 3,000 Vietnamese are waiting, there is panic. Jim Eckes is out by Continental Air Services' hangars. He's had a small plane, a Baron, come in from Bangkok, and is ready to leave. He takes shelter in a hole full of water. Rifle fire and bursts from heavy machineguns ring out all over. Anti-aircraft fire commences from the presidential palace and from ships moored at the Quai Bach Dang. The pilot of the Baron urges Eckes to move out: "Jim, *let's go*."

There's major damage at the airport. South Vietnamese helicopters and military planes, three AC-119s and four C-47s, are destroyed. The Baron is waiting on a short runway near the Air America hangars. Its pilot and Eckes hop into a car and race toward it. South Vietnamese soldiers fire on them. They think the airport is being attacked by NVA infantry. The enemy planes return. The Baron takes off. Anti-aircraft shells burst around it. The light plane rises quickly, veers and heads toward the racecourse and Cholon.

Two South Vietnamese pilots have taken off in their F-5As to pursue the attackers, but the enemy is gone.

Minh just asked for a a cease-fire, and the North Vietnamese answer is to escalate the war a notch; now they're using planes. The attack squadron was led by the South Vietnamese deserter who bombed the presidential palace some days earlier. "It was magnificent coordination, the best combined operation by our forces," says General Dung. The North Vietnamese commander exaggerates. Many bombs fell in the fields. Just the same, the deserter-lieutenant has taught North Vietnamese MiG pilots how to handle A-37s. That operation, baptized Determined To Conquer, has a double impact, political and military. It is now clear to all doubters that there will be no negotiations. The chief of South Vietnamese aviation, now in full agreement with Erich von Marbod, orders South Vietnamese aircraft to Thailand.

A few hours after Minh's speech, the PRG man in Paris announces that "there has been a massive uprising of the people of Saigon. . . . Saigon's troops are laying down their arms and surrendering."

A lie for a lie: in Saigon, some are claiming that French troops have landed.

In the French capital, North Vietnamese Ambassador Vo Van Sung and the PRG delegate Pham Van Ba have been received by Jean Sauvagnargues, the foreign minister. As he leaves the Quai d'Orsay Sung is asked why Big Minh is not an acceptable partner. A reporter remarks that he fulfills two requirements set out by the PRG in the last forty-eight hours: implementation of the Paris Agreement and abolition of the Saigon regime.

"That is not the case," the ambassador responds dryly.

The French foreign minister exclaims: "All conditions for a political solution seem to have been met. We're surprised that it isn't under way."

Around Saigon and in the Delta, ARVN units make contact with Saigon headquarters, asking for direct control and orders. Among these units are armor, rangers and airborne. North of Saigon, arsenals and fuel dumps are burning, the flames streaked purple, brown and red.

The bureaucratic machine grinds away. General Smith's accounting officers meet. To balance the books, the head auditor needs 300 million piastres. He must obtain them at the embassy. Foreseeing layoffs of Vietnamese employees in General Smith's service, they've arranged ways and means of compensation. Part of the accounting office was transferred to Honolulu five days before with stacks of unpaid bills and pending contracts. The last, signed April 17, is for 45,000 ponchos worth $220,500.

In the evening Martin decides that 10,000 people will be evacuated next day. He's received a cable from Kissinger: "The judgement of all agencies at the Washington Special Action Group this morning was that we could have as little as one to three days before a military collapse and Tan Son Nhut becomes unusable." Kissinger wants Martin himself to leave Saigon on the last airplane, "the last 130." The secretary of state is worried about the fate of personnel at the U.S. Embassy. He's not in favor of maintaining a considerable presence under a government dominated by communists. The diplomats and employees who remain "could end up as hostages." They should all be very careful: "I think we should not miss the point at which Saigon slides from neutralism into communism . . . at that point our obligations are terminated and a new look is needed."

Late that night, American C-130s crammed with arms and ammunition land at Tan Son Nhut. Each takes off again with 180 passengers, for the most part Vietnamese refugees.

In Bangkok, where he arrives after skirting Cambodia, Jim Eckes, with other Americans, is reminiscing about Vietnam in deep sorrow. He remembers all the Vietnamese, hundreds of them, that he couldn't evacuate. He remembers especially Tan Son Nhut, one of the busiest airports in the world, and the hangars with mechanics still at work only a few minutes before the North Vietnamese pilots attacked, and the barracks and sheet-metal huts, and the military, the police, the indolent smiling customs men, the smudged notices, the ringing telephone, all that his life was for many months.

Like thousands and tens of thousands of Americans, civilian and military, who've passed through Vietnam, Jim Eckes wonders now how he might have helped this or that friend to flee, this or that Vietnamese who had no chance to escape.

21

———◆———

April 29:
Put out the Lights

At 4 A.M. on April 29, the NVA opens an artillery barrage, zeroing in expertly on Tan Son Nhut air base, South Vietnamese general staff headquarters and navy headquarters. Fuel and ammunition dumps, trucks, jeeps and civilian cars are burning at the airport. The NVA infantry can't be far; mortar and rocket shells also burst in flashes of red, blue and green. Two marines, Charlie McMahon and Darwin Judge, are killed on the defense perimeter. General Homer Smith and American field officers are driven from their beds. Among the 1,500 Vietnamese in the gymnasium, several are wounded. A C-130 is hit after it lands.

Dawn comes up. The pilots of the last F-5s and A-37s take off, never to return. Like the few pilots who want to stay on and fight, they're hampered by the hundreds of ARVN soldiers cluttering the runways and taxiways. Air traffic controllers can no longer do their job. One South Vietnamese AC-119 pilot is a true diehard. He takes to the air, flies off on a sortie, attacks communist positions he spots around Saigon, returns to refuel, takes off again. At 6:46 he's shot down by an SA-7 rocket.

U.S. Army Colonel John Madison, one of the officers on the surveillance commissions established by the Paris Agreement, fires off a message to the visitors at Camp Davis, sheltering in their trenches and bunkers. The colonel protests the bombardment of the airport, which constitutes—to say the least—a violation of the ICCS's and the Two-Party and Four-Party Commissions' diplomatic immunity. The DRV and PRG men at Camp Davis answer blandly that they don't know what's going on. Furthermore, they saw no need to forewarn the Poles and Hungarians at Tan Son Nhut, who are now asking the Americans for information. The Hungarians make contact with Polgar, who went back to the operations room at the embassy during the night. CIA people there are worried about the fate of their Vietnamese colleagues.

The 130 mm. fire is directed by North Vietnamese observers less than four kilometers north of the airport. For General Dung, and for Le Duc Tho, the situation is delicate. On the one hand, they must let the Americans pull out, therefore not hinder the evacuation too much. On the other hand, the two communist officials, following Hanoi's directives, want to keep the pressure up so Americans in both Saigon and Washington understand that there's no question of negotiations. North Vietnamese troops receive orders not to attack planes or helicopters unless attacked by them. With very few exceptions, the orders are obeyed. Dung always has to worry about intervention by U.S. aircraft based in Thailand. At this stage, a lot of dead and wounded Americans might provoke the Pentagon to massive retaliation. North Vietnamese leaders have never really been sure how far military power in the United States is subordinated to civil power. In the same way Americans, always looking for factions and rifts in Hanoi's leadership, haven't always appreciated the politico-military symbiosis among them.

Marshal Ky takes to the air in his personal helicopter, circles Saigon, sees North Vietnamese batteries firing one shot a minute. Over his radio he monitors messages from a formation of A-1 Skyraiders coming from Can Tho: "This is Nguyen Cao Ky. You must take out those batteries."

"I hear you loud and clear. I have only one bomb left," answers the lead pilot.

The time has come for a pathetic last-ditch struggle.

At 5:45 Saigon time Graham Martin returns to the embassy. Last order from the South Vietnamese air command: all operational aircraft should leave South Vietnamese territory.

6:00 Saigon time, 5:00 Hanoi time. In his headquarters at Ben Cat, forty kilometers north of Saigon, General Dung receives a message from the Politburo congratulating his troops on their progress in the last few days. The Politburo orders a rapid advance to "strike with the greatest determination straight into the enemy's final lair."

In quick succession come many cables and phone calls among the White House, the State Department, the Pentagon, CINCPAC in Honolulu, the embassy and the military attaché's office in Saigon. Events move faster than the cables. A State Department cable says: "Intercepted radio communications from various North Vietnamese commanders indicate a three-pronged attack on Saigon on an unspecified date with provisions for individual troop initiatives if opportunity presents itself." This information was checked by National Security Council analysts. Another forecast: the North Vietnamese may take Saigon on Ho Chi Minh's birthday, May 19, "with a likely kickoff date late April." The evening before, a radio intercept revealed that the NVA 7th Division was assigned to seize Saigon's broadcasting station.

7 A.M. Saigon time, 7 P.M. Washington time, the National Security Council meets, Gerald Ford presiding. Present are Henry Kissinger, James Schlesinger, their aides, the chairman of the Joint Chiefs of Staff, General George Brown, and CIA Director William Colby, who says that for three days there's been no hope of stabilizing the military situation. Now, finally, everyone agrees. But what orders to send Saigon? Kissinger hesitates. He feels that for the moment they must continue to evacuate Americans and Vietnamese by plane. Schlesinger and Brown feel they must switch immediately to evacuation by helicopter. Kissinger is adamant. The North Vietnamese might misunderstand.

And embassy personnel? They must cut down to 150 within twenty-four hours; of these one-third will be CIA agents and employees. Frank Snepp learns that he'll be part of the rear guard.

Knowing Martin's touchiness, Admiral Noel Gayler cables from Honolulu, "My recommendation . . . is that you now evacuate the entire American population less those mission people you propose to keep indefinitely." Gayler authorizes General Smith to board both Americans and Vietnamese on his planes. The admiral wants to avoid at all costs the political embarrassment of general and flag officers falling into communist hands. He orders them out of Saigon. The admiral emphasizes that the military situation is critical. He's read Polgar's cables about a possible political arrangement: "My intelligence does not support the rather euphoric view given me by Mr. Polgar."

In Mr. Polgar's case, the admiral uses an antiquated and elegantly scornful expression: "I have the impression he may not be current." According to the admiral's intelligence, NVA troops are about a mile from Tan Son Nhut airport. They're firing their SA-7 rockets "effectively, having shot down three aircraft in the last couple of hours."

North Vietnamese artillery continues to pound the airport area.

A messenger from President Duong Van Minh delivers a letter to the U.S. Embassy:

> Dear Mr. Ambassador:
>
> I respectfully request that you give an order for the personnel of the Defense Attaché's Office to leave Vietnam within twenty-four hours beginning April 29, 1975, in order that the question of peace for Vietnam can be settled early.

Martin is suffering the after-effects of bronchitis. He dictates his reply in a hoarse voice:

Dear Mr. President:

    I have just received your note. . . . This is to inform
Your Excellency that I have issued orders as you have
requested.

Reports from Tan Son Nhut indicate that there is haphazard fire at
Americans by ARVN troops. So Martin adds:

    I trust Your Excellency will instruct the armed forces
of the Government to cooperate in every way possible in
facilitating the safe removal of the personnel of the DAO
[General Smith].
    I also express the hope that Your Excellency may inter-
vene with the other side to permit the safe and orderly
departure of the Defense Attaché and his staff.
Sincerely yours,
Graham Martin, U.S. Ambassador.

As soon as the news leaks out, people say there was a complicated
arrangement between Minh and Martin: the embassy solicited Minh's
request.

Martin orders General Smith to prepare to evacuate all his personnel.
For once the general receives the same order from his two superiors in the
chain of command, Ambassador Martin and Admiral Gayler. Only the
marines assigned to security are to remain at the airport. Martin asks
Kissinger to let him stay in Saigon "at least for a day or two, to at least
give some dignity to our departure." The ambassador will keep two Air
America helicopters for a quick departure when the time comes. Afterward
the French Embassy will represent U.S. interests. Martin hopes for
"prompt approval."

Martin has found a political-diplomatic advantage in Minh's request:
they can announce the Americans' departure "at the request" of the South
Vietnamese. That way, he thinks, the final evacuation will not seem a
response to panic. Kissinger orders a situation report by Lawrence Eagleburger, special assistant to the secretary of state. Eagleburger writes an
unambiguous note: leaving American diplomatic personnel in Saigon will
imply informal recognition of the incoming government, whatever it may
be. Kissinger makes his decision: they'll close the embassy.

At 8:15 A.M. Saigon time, Martin meets with his ranking colleagues,
among them Thomas Polgar, Alan Carter and Colonel George Jacobson,
an assistant to the ambassador. Polgar seems to think that all is not lost
politically. He told Snepp that the bombardment of the airport constituted
a positive "important signal." Right, think several CIA officials like Snepp,
"a signal as important and significant as a bullet in the head."

They pay particular attention to the military situation. The night before, they were hoping to evacuate about 10,000 people today and counting on better than fifty C-130 runs. How should they proceed? NVA artillery fire on the airport has slackened. They'll be able to resume flights. American officials have discovered that there are also motor barges tied up at the docks in Saigon, specifically at Newport. From Tan Son Nhut, General Homer Smith sends word that the runways are now unusable for fixed-wing aircraft, jet or prop. He's ordered convoys of buses and helicopters into Saigon to pick up Americans and Vietnamese assembled at different spots and ferry them to the airport. Martin doesn't accept General Smith's view. These career soldiers are always pessimistic. This wouldn't be the first time planes landed and took off under shelling by mortars and artillery. The ambassador decides to go inspect the runways. He asks for a CIA helicopter. None is available; at the moment all the Air America choppers are carrying CIA personnel from Can Tho to the fleet offshore. At Tan Son Nhut, the helicopters not being used in the evacuation in town have been crippled by North Vietnamese fire. Polgar admits, "We don't have a machine for the moment, Mr. Ambassador."

Martin's glare is icy: "I'll go to the airport by car. That way I can get the feel of the atmosphere in town. Call my car and driver."

Colonel Jacobson interrupts: "Mr. Ambassador, it's dangerous. We have reports that Vietcong units have infiltrated the city."

Martin's armored black Chevrolet is ready. Even those who don't like him, or who hold him responsible for the dilatory evacuation, say the old man has guts.

The Chevy rolls along without its pennant, between two vehicles full of marines, arms at the ready. A halt at the edge of Tan Son Nhut. A U.S. ambassador forced to wait? ARVN officers and men are jumpy and ask for instructions on their walkie-talkies.

The convoy passes through.

Part of the South Vietnamese air force staff is shut up in a building with its commander, General Tran Van Minh. Some thirty of these officers marched on General Homer Smith's quarters, revolvers in hand, demanding to be evacuated. Lieutenant Colonel Richard Mitchell, assistant to the air attaché, disarmed them without trouble. These officers know him. Mitchell has been evacuating their families for some weeks.

In Honolulu Admiral Gayler is impatient and phones Washington. What about this fighter escort? Should they be ordered in? General Brown, chairman of the Joint Chiefs, answers, "No."

9:30 A.M. in Saigon. A group of officers including Colonel William LeGro and Colonel Le Van Huong, head of South Vietnamese intelligence, shows Martin the airport littered with the carcasses of aircraft and trucks. Several disorderly groups of ARVN soldiers add to the chaos. Martin speaks to Colonel Huong: "Telephone headquarters. Tell them to do what has to be done to restore order on this base!"

At Vietnamese headquarters no one answers. Erich von Marbod appears, in a flight suit, submachinegun slung, not the usual getup for an aide to the secretary of defense. Martin says, "You have friends at Seventh Air Force headquarters in Thailand, Erich. Can you ask them for a plane for my wife?"

Von Marbod explodes: there's no question of planes. Anyway if they landed now, all these Vietnamese at the airport would take them by storm.

Martin goes to General Smith's office. On the special scrambler telephone, he calls the White House and talks to Henry Kissinger and Brent Scowcroft.

He comes back: "Washington agrees. If we can restore order on the base and clear the runways, we'll continue the evacuation by plane. If we can't, too bad. Homer: you ought to know that everybody—the Pentagon, Schlesinger, the chiefs of staff and CINCPAC—is going to ask us to get the Americans out fast and leave the Vietnamese. We have thousands of high-risk Vietnamese here; we have to pull out as many as possible."

In the city, Operation Strip Mine, with choppers looking for the assembly points in Saigon, is going badly. All the helicopters aren't ready. Four have been taken by Vietnamese paratroopers. The sixteen making shuttle runs have plenty of trouble; their landing zone at the airport has been hit by the bombardment. The bus shuttle has problems, too. Some of the buses, without drivers, are immobilized in the embassy garage. Others prowl slowly through town, crawling toward the assembly points.

At the vast airport, Vietnamese soldiers and police watch the ballet of buses and choppers with more curiosity than antagonism. The military are preparing to defend the base. Sergeant Le Van Thuong, twenty-four years old, bronze complexion, a transmitter repairman for three years,[1] hasn't left the base since April 1. His officers have told him he'll have to fight. He's issued a .45 automatic, later an M-16 rifle, finally an antitank weapon, the M-72. The officers explain to their men that two rings of paratroopers have been stationed around the airport. Sergeant Thuong is now in combat.

At the U.S. Embassy, diplomats and employees are burning shredded documents, destroying typewriters, radio receivers, and transmitters. The CIA has files stored in Snepp's office, in the radio monitoring room, and in a prefab building outside. Nobody remembers the duplicate files in Vietnamese intelligence offices at the headquarters of the National Police.

Snepp continues to study fresh intelligence and tries to collate it. One obvious fact: the communists intend to take Saigon quickly. On embassy grounds Vietnamese are wandering by the pool in small groups. Some are well-known people but others are domestic help and their families, chauffeurs, cooks, maids, nursemaids.

Martin has called his agency heads to the embassy. Alan Carter doesn't want to, or doesn't dare, go back to the USIS. His employees are waiting there for evacuation lists that never come. These Vietnamese have no time now to reach the waterfront on foot; barges are leaving half empty. A weird atmosphere prevails, of indifference and disorder, incompetence and cowardice. This is the panic the ambassador feared so badly for so long.

Martin can telephone his French colleague directly or step through the breach in the wall between the two embassies. He meets with Mérillon, who has talked with Big Minh. Any good news?

"Nothing new," says Mérillon. "Minh is sounding out the PRG but there's still no answer."

Martin asks Mérillon if he, the U.S. ambassador, could meet with the PRG.

"I'll find out."

Martin offers Mérillon—or leaves it with him for safekeeping, there seems to be a misunderstanding on the point—a Chinese porcelain, a small pagoda.

10:10 A.M. Saigon time. The dollar has risen from 4,500 to 5,000 piastres in two hours. The people of the capital heard the new prime minister, Vu Van Mau, call for the departure of Americans, as did President Minh. The U.S. ambassador's presence at the airport was noticed. They thought he was pulling out. The crowd around the U.S. Embassy is growing.

10:40 A.M.: from the airport Homer Smith calls Admiral Noel Gayler in Honolulu: "There's no way we can use the runways for fixed-wing aircraft."

"I've seen that coming for a while," Gayler answers. "I'll call the Joint Chiefs at the Pentagon and tell them we have to switch to Option IV."

Option IV: evacuation by helicopter.

A pathetic, absurd, protocolish debate proceeds by telephone—Saigon, across the Pacific, North America. In simple courtesy General Smith must let Martin know that he's recommended switching to Option IV. Now the ambassador thinks it's inevitable because of the chaos that would hinder a methodical evacuation.

"It's not for the Joint Chiefs to make the decision on this option," Martin says.

10:48 A.M. Saigon time. 10:48 P.M. Washington time. Martin calls Kissinger: "I think we have to go to Option IV."

10:51 A.M. Saigon time. 10:51 P.M. Washington time. Start Frequent Wind in one hour. The order comes from Kissinger.

On the USS Blue Ridge off Vietnam Admiral Donald Whitmire, commanding Task Force 76, also has problems. He has eighty-five helicopters available.[2] First he has to verify the sequence and intent of his orders; then, because they're not all on one ship, he has to transship marines to choppers or choppers to marines. Then he has to synchronize helicopter take-off with fighter escort take-off from Thailand.

When he gave the order to go to Option IV at 11:51, the secretary of state was thinking of Saigon time. The various military commands—CINC-PAC in Honolulu, Admiral Whitmire on the high seas, the air force in Thailand, General Smith at Tan Son Nhut, the U.S. Embassy in Saigon—

wonder which time he meant, Washington, Greenwich or Saigon? Questions, orders and counterorders crisscross on the telephones, telex and radio.

11:13 Saigon time. The American radio, as arranged, plays "I'm Dreaming of a White Christmas." The tape repeats regularly. The head of Vietnamese TV, Colonel Hoa, sees all the American technicians and a number of Vietnamese agency chiefs leave. The colonel decides to stay put. A company of paratroopers takes up position around the station.

11:30: Polgar has given up on a political solution. He's received several significant phone calls, one from President Minh himself: "I would like to ask a last favor of you: to evacuate some of my family."

"Certainly," says Polgar.

Another call, from the Hungarians in the ICCS. Several dozen of them are stuck at the airport. The NVA bombings have damaged some of their cars. Others have been stolen by South Vietnamese soldiers. The few still in running condition are out of gas. "We have no transport. We'd like to get to our hotels in Saigon," the Hungarians say.

Vietnamese celebrities show up at the embassy. Thieu's former national security adviser, Fat Quang, strolls the top floor in a vast raincoat. He sits down a few yards from Colonel Toth, the Hungarian, come to push requests to evacuate his men from the airport. Polgar is magnanimous, operating on the principle "whoever asks my help deserves it." And then tit for tat—you never know if this Hungarian son of a bitch will be useful in an hour, a week or a month. Wolfgang Lehmann has a soul less sensitive or provident than the CIA chief; he refuses to intervene on behalf of the last Poles, who, in a tearing hurry to leave Saigon, plead with him. Polgar arranges a convoy of three buses to pick up the Hungarians and Poles at the airport and take them to the Hotel Majestic in town.

The political coup de grâce for Polgar: reporter Malcolm Browne, on good terms with the PRG at Camp Davis—he's been talking to them every two or three hours—informs the CIA chief that the Vietcong are less and less "receptive."[3] Their courtesy has turned to morose surliness. President Minh's four advisers at Camp Davis have the same impression. The president's envoys have suggested two rounds of negotiations to the PRG. One, about military problems, would take place in Saigon; the other, about remaining political problems, would take place on a higher level in Paris. Evasive, the PRG people say again that they aren't competent to deal with these questions. They offer their guests tea and bananas, noting that they raised the banana plant themselves near their barracks.

Still on the job, Snepp is handed an urgent intelligence report: it seems the North Vietnamese have received orders to fire on the presidential palace this evening at 5:00 Hanoi time, 6:00 Saigon time. Two hundred rounds! Enough to destroy the whole center of Saigon, with the American and French embassies, too. Snepp rushes to Polgar. "To the ambassador! Now!"

The ambassador relays the message to General Timmes, who telephones Minh. Can the president intercede with the communists so they don't bombard Saigon?

At which point, a call from Kissinger for Martin: "You must all evacuate. *All*. Orders from President Ford himself. And before nightfall."

The deputy commander of the South Vietnamese navy, Admiral Diep Quang Thuy, meets Minh. He urges the president to leave Saigon, so as to flee Vietnam altogether or lead the resistance from the Delta. Minh refuses.

General Lam Van Phat, named commander of the Saigon region, proposes to organize a route march to Thailand through Cambodia! This general took part in five coups d'état in the 1960s with the famous Colonel Pham Ngoc Thao, manipulated by the Vietcong and liquidated by Thieu.

Noon in Saigon. No evacuation helicopters in sight.

Scouring the city, the American buses go on picking up passengers. To be sure of their help, police and airport officials have, once more, been promised evacuation with their families. The first buses of Mission White Christmas reach Tan Son Nhut at 12:10. The atmosphere at the airport is more tense than around the docks, where there are few people. Some Vietnamese ship captains are selling passages at $4,000–$12,000 each.

12:15: Intelligence reports grow worse and worse. Two NVA divisions, the 70th and 968th, have wiped out the ARVN 25th Division near Cu Chi, hardly thirty kilometers west of Saigon. Three NVA divisions, the 3rd, 9th and 16th, have isolated the ARVN 22nd. It's holding out but can't fall back on the capital. Dung's strategy is clear and flexible. He's leaving some of his divisions around the encircled ARVN but sending the others straight into Saigon.

12:30: Thirty-six big transport helicopters take off from the *Hancock*, escorted by Cobra helicopter gunships.

Evacuation helicopters fly toward Saigon in three waves of twelve. They overfly Bien Hoa, northeast of the city. Each wave proceeds in V-formations of three choppers. The pilots' orders are first to shuttle between the fleet and the airport bringing in marines of the security detachment. General Richard Carey, the marines' commanding officer, agrees with General Smith: they must gain time. All the helicopters fly out loaded with refugees. Up from three air bases in Thailand, Phantom fighters are ready to join the choppers in the air corridor between Saigon and the fleet. All ships will keep station just outside the twelve-mile limit off the Vietnamese coast. A grand armada is deployed at sea in a hundred-mile arc. The flagship is seventeen miles offshore. There's been no operation like it since Dunkirk in 1940. Thirty-five ships of the line are surrounded by dozens of tenders and reconnaissance ships.[4] Some have been on station for several days, others have just come from Okinawa and Pearl Harbor, still others from San Diego.

From one command post to another, from ship to planes and helicopters, radios hum, telephones and telexes sputter incessantly. In command of the task force, Admiral Whitmire bears a code name of the utmost simplicity: Jehovah. At Tan Son Nhut airport, General Homer Smith is Jacksonville Bravo. The marines around him are Baritone. Blue Chip is the Seventh Air Force in Thailand. The civilians at the U.S. Embassy in Saigon are simply Embassy.

Many South Vietnamese ships, minesweepers, patrol boats, armed junks are running down the Mekong or already on the high seas, where they cause radio interference.[5]

Another confusion in the timetable: the helicopters are piloted by marines and in their command L-hour—for landing—is the time a helicopter must reach its landing zone. For the carrier aircraft it's launch-time. They used that designation in evacuating Phnom Penh. The necessary adjustments are made, after several colorful rebukes.

The chopper pilots run into unexpected trouble. They'd been told that the weather would hold, but it turns bad. For three days visibility is limited. They figured on doing the whole job by daylight, but it becomes obvious that they'll have to fly at night, on instruments, a tougher job.

At least the two corridors to Saigon, "Michigan" at 6,500 feet for going and "Ohio" at 5,500 feet for return, are clearly indicated. Below these corridors a number of NVA anti-aircraft units are noted, equipped with heavy machineguns and SA-7 rockets. The U.S. fighter bombers must protect these corridors. At the last moment everybody realizes that the one-ton laser-guided bombs these fighter bombers carry are very effective against batteries of 130 mm. guns but not against machineguns and rockets. The same for 500-pound bombs, generally used against bunkers. They're better off using AH-1J attack helicopters with their rockets and powerful 20 mm. guns and A-7 planes to mark targets with phosphorus. Luckily all the Cobra pilots are also qualified air controllers, so they can both patrol and help direct the transport helicopters.

The chopper pilots are warned: since the night before, South Vietnamese have taken over a number of helicopters and small planes and crammed them full of family and will be heading out for the fleet and sowing monstrous confusion. A Chinook CH-47 will land on the quarterdeck of the *Blue Ridge*. Its pilot, Lieutenant Truong Ma Quoi, tells *Newsweek* correspondent Ron Moreau: "The generals, colonels, majors and captains have pulled out. I said to myself it was time lieutenants did the same."

Helicopters weave through the American armada. Sometimes, even if ordered to hold, the South Vietnamese pilots land. They unload their refugees. They're asked to go and "crash" their planes in the sea. Some refuse. Others make a specialty of it—landing the helicopter on the water, quickly exiting and climbing aboard a lifeboat. The American crews applaud the South Vietnamese pilots who suddenly become champions at this maneuver. Two helicopters crack up on the *Blue Ridge*; a third will botch his landing and "plow in."

The planners intended that the great majority of refugees be picked up at the airport. Gradually General Carey realizes that he's going to have to "extract" between 1,000 and 2,000 people from the embassy. He was assured there would be no more than 200. Three or four UH-1E light helicopters from Air America would have sufficed for that number. Now they'll have to use CH-53 heavy helicopters at the embassy as at the airport. Carey will also be obliged to reinforce the security detail at the embassy.

1:12 P.M. Air Marshal Ky—with General Truong, who came back to the capital after the Danang debacle—arrives on the *Midway* by helicopter. Mrs. Martin lands a little later on the *Denver*.

2 P.M. A cable from Kissinger to Martin confirming their last telephone conversation: "We have studied your request to keep small staff behind and the president insists on total evacuation. Warm regards."

3 P.M. At the airport marines are protecting three landing areas carefully cleared on a baseball diamond, the tennis courts and the parking lot of General Smith's annex building. There are about 3,000 refugees. The marines methodically divide them into groups of 50–70.

Major William Melton arrives at the airport with three platoons of G Company, 2nd Battalion, 4th Marines and the first transport helicopters at 3:06 P.M.[6] They've followed the Saigon River, flying at 9,000 feet. Above 10,000 feet, you need oxygen. Below them his men saw hundreds of small craft, boats and ships heading to sea. The first chopper flies off with its passengers. The rotation of CH-46s and CH-53s goes well. News from the embassy is worrisome. To protect it there's only a detachment of 44 marines. General Carey decides to transfer immediately 130 of the 840 protecting the airport.

Major William Melton, thirty-eight years old, five children, a death's head butterfly tattooed on his arm, from California, a marine for twenty years, commissioned from the ranks, was one of the first marines to land ten years ago at Danang. For him, the politicians are responsible for "all this shit." His men are dug in close to General Smith's buildings. Most of them are setting foot in Vietnam for the first and last time. They're full of beans, highly disciplined and—some of them—shaky. They hear rifle fire and the crump of mortar shells. Orders are strict: do not return fire unless absolutely necessary. Melton watches the Vietnamese civilians and soldiers swirling around the perimeter his men hold. Melton thinks: we've come here to shut the doors, put out the lights and go on home. And he says it aloud to the officers leading his men. He remembers his two tours of duty in Vietnam, in 1965 and 1968. A South Vietnamese colonel approaches him, salutes him and hands him his .25 automatic pistol: "Major, here is my personal weapon. . . . What's going on? This isn't possible, it isn't right. Twenty years ago, I was a lieutenant and I was fighting in the suburbs of Hanoi."

What can you say to him? The colonel changes to civilian clothes before boarding a helicopter. Melton keeps an eye on his marines, who are sorting out the evacuees and searching them. A group of young women addresses the major: "Should we leave?"

"Do you have any relatives in the United States?"

"I have a boyfriend in Chicago," says one young woman.

Why are they asking me that? Melton wonders. There must be plenty running out who'd be all right if they stayed and plenty staying who ought to come out with us.

Vietnam, his Vietnam, comes back to him in countless memories. Melton has never hated these North Vietnamese converging on Saigon, the enemy, soldiers. The Vietcong are something else. Around Danang, Vietcong booby traps blew up marines. You were blown to bits and there was nothing you could do about it. You never saw that enemy. In a way, in all ways, the NVA regulars were more . . . *regular*. Ground troops like us. We have things in common. We're both far from home. Sometimes the Vietcong were only a hundred yards from their villages. The marines like the NVA troops lived in the mud, the spongy rice paddies, the thick rain, with the black ants and the leeches. Melton once took a wounded North Vietnamese officer prisoner and shook his hand. The nearby ARVN officers and men were scandalized. What the hell, this North Vietnamese had fought well. Melton doesn't regret his handshake. Or serving more than one tour in Vietnam. Or leaving. He's doing his job, and around him his young marines are doing fine.

Escorted by several marines, Martin goes home and pulls files from his safe. The marines toss a thermite grenade on them; they burn well. Martin goes back to the embassy, through the improvised gate from the French Embassy. Mérillon tells him the PRG has no desire to meet with him.

General Timmes ran into Minh and still feels that the president thinks he can parley and negotiate with the communists. But by this time Minh has no illusions. To the very end, the history of the second Vietnam war will be, among other things, an accumulation of misunderstandings and doubts.

3:30 P.M. To evacuate the Americans and Vietnamese still within the confines of the embassy, Martin decides to operate on the simple principle, "First come, first served."

General Carey observes that the means of evacuation and embassy security are both insufficient. He has one landing pad on the roof and another in a cleared parking lot. If the crowd surging around the embassy manages to break in, the whole evacuation will be endangered. As military reports politely say, "the parameters have changed."[7] The helicopters are going to maintain the shuttle all night. Landing on the embassy roof will be risky. Three men—Wolfgang Lehmann, Colonel John Madison, head of the U.S. delegation to the Joint Military Team at Camp Davis, and a priest, Reverend Thomas Steddins, are sorting and regrouping refugees near the parking lot and the swimming pool. In the buildings, refugees, diplomats and reporters are busy.

Some of the personnel raid the reserves of Scotch and Cognac, some go after fresh food in the—medical—refrigerators. Iranian diplomats on the ICCS have arrived, by way of the French Embassy. They've lost their codes. Telephones are ringing on every floor. Rumors circulate: bus convoys were attacked in town, there are still plenty of places on barges and ships at the waterfront. At 4 P.M. there are 5,000–10,000 Vietnamese besieging the embassy. They're jammed against the gates to a depth of thirty feet, with sacks, suitcases, boxes more or less tied up. In the crowd is writer Duyen Anh, with his wife and children, come from the USIS. He looks about him at his terrified compatriots and recognizes generals, senators, deputies, sees U.S. marines pulling back refugees trying to climb over the gates. Now and then the marines club them. There are Japanese and Koreans in the crowd as well. If you're white, someone will help haul you over the walls. Vietnamese police from nearby headquarters also make it over. The embassy struck a bargain with them: if they'd maintain order, they'd be evacuated. The Americans there know that they're leaving whatever happens. Under the ballet of helicopters, young people on motorbikes or scooters watch the spectacle from the street. Sometimes a Vietnamese fights his way into the embassy. Often his father, his mother, his wife are left outside. They all shout and weep, begging the marines and U.S. officials to let them in.

The evacuation involves tens of thousands of Vietnamese. Many others would be happy to leave but no longer even dream of it. They go about their business. In many neighborhoods children are still playing on the sidewalks and old people are still gossiping.

4:30 P.M. CIA officials realize that 250 Vietnamese agents have been forgotten at a distant supply depot and 100 at the Hotel Duc. Seventy translators never do reach the embassy. Some of the Air America helicopters can no longer fly; their batteries have been stolen. There are no more buses available. The agents, the translators and their families have no way and no time to reach the port.

Northeast of Saigon, NVA troops fire several SA-7 rockets at American Phantoms, which respond with missiles.[8]

On the whole, General Dung's order—do not attack American planes—continues to be respected.

Toward 5:15 dusk begins to fall. General Smith at the airport and General Carey at marine headquarters offshore add up the figures. There remain about 1,300 people to evacuate from Tan Son Nhut. It will take two to three hours to "extract" everyone, including the marine security detachments. In one hour the dollar rises from 6,000 to 7,000 piastres. Matters are confused at the embassy. To Admiral Whitmire, who asks for precise numbers, Martin answers, "There are still fifteen hundred to two thousand people."

General Timmes phones President Minh again. Have the communists replied? Are they ready to cancel their planned 6 P.M. barrage on the presidential palace? No answer.

At 5:30 President Minh sends a new delegation to Camp Davis: lawyer Tran Ngoc Lieng, Professor Chau Tam Luan and Redemptorist Father Chan Tinh, the known neutralist. After the meeting, the PRG people send a radio message to the North Vietnamese command:

> Comrade Vo Dong Giang received them and confirmed our views outlined in the April 26 statement [total abolition of the Saigon government]. After the talk they asked for permission to leave the camp, but when we told them our artillery was now bombarding Tan Son Nhut airport and it would be better for them to spend the night with us, they agreed to stay.

Near General Smith's buildings at the airport ARVN troops open fire. U.S. marines return fire. ARVN soldiers are infiltrating the marines' perimeter and interfering with the evacuation. They are pushed back. Near Smith's office, American officials are burning bundles of bills, several million dollars' worth.

At the same time a fire breaks out in front of the U.S. Embassy. Everybody thinks an artillery shell burst in the street. Actually a Vietnamese dropped a lighted match into the gas tank of a Volkswagen, which thereupon exploded.

The flood of refugees continues to beat against the embassy walls. Americans, including Polgar, help certain refugees to climb over. Polgar is weeping. He can't find his driver, Ut. Air America helicopters have ferried well over a thousand passengers during the day, in dozens of flights. The U.S. military count more and more refugees every hour to "extract" from the embassy.

7 P.M. At naval headquarters on the Saigon River Admiral Cang supervises the staggered departure of his ships. He receives a call from the presidency. The navy's chief of staff is expected at the president's house. Minh requests him to escort his son-in-law, Colonel Dai, and one of his colleagues, General Mai Huu Xuan, kingpin of the coup d'état against Diem in 1963.

"I cannot leave, myself," the president sighs.

At the palace Minh is still waiting for news of the delegation sent to the PRG. His advisers, his prime minister most of all, urge him to make a unilateral declaration. He must surrender unconditionally. Minh refuses. It would accomplish nothing morally, militarily or politically. It would only be an admission of weakness.

Admiral Cang's convoy is running down the Saigon river. Along the way, naval personnel watch U.S. helicopters—or South Vietnamese?—attack ammunition depots with rockets.[9]

At the U.S. Embassy the helicopters, guided by automobile headlights, are taking off with sixty to eighty passengers on each trip. Vietnamese have formed a long line in the corridors, on the stairways and on the roof. The air conditioners are no longer working. The heat is overwhelming. The air stinks of urine and burnt paper. Making their rounds the marines learn with some surprise that all the young men in shirtsleeves, most of them armed, walking the corridors nonchalantly, are CIA agents, *spooks*.

7:15 P.M. By accident or sabotage, electricity blacks out in the airport buildings.

"Time to go," General Smith decides.

He's about to climb into a helicopter when a last group of refugees rolls up. They board the general's chopper while he waits for another.

Reinforcements are needed at the embassy. They'll be drawn from Major Melton's command. One platoon, under Lieutenant Jay Roach, will proceed to the embassy by chopper. The major calls his officer: "Jay, go see the colonel; he'll brief you. Meanwhile your men can assemble."

The lieutenant goes to find the colonel. When he comes back his platoon has taken off. "And how do I get to the embassy?" he roars.

There's no chopper to fly him over. Roach is furious. Many marine officers are holding back cold anger, here at the airport, and at the embassy, and on the ships at sea: this is a shambles. The civilians never prepared properly. They made their move too late. Lieutenant Alan Broussard, a marine who served in the evacuation of Phnom Penh, says it was much better organized. The refugees there wore labels of different colors indicating the first, second, third groups to embark. . . . The officers are used to chaos on the battlefield, but this operation should have been better blueprinted.

"Well, what do I do?" asks Lieutenant Roach.

"You can't make the embassy on foot," Major William Melton answers, and shrugs.

Off Cap Saint-Jacques, Captain Cyril Moyher with the men of Detachment India, fifty-two marines, are loading refugees on the *Pioneer Commander*, a large chartered civilian cargo ship. The soldiers have installed latrines and set barrels of fresh water everywhere. Moyher gives his young marines their orders: "Help the refugees, but no familiarities. Respect the old people. Keep your distance. Don't fall in love. You're marines, the best of the best."

The marines are trained to defend the *Pioneer Commander* if soldiers, NVA or ARVN, should try to take it by force. The holds are full of rice sacks, powdered milk and cans of tuna and sardines.

Near the accommodation ladder, two men are searching the refugees as they board. The marines are up to here in orders. You will do this, you will not do that. You will preserve order among the evacuees, you will be constantly aware of security, you will note evacuees who speak English and any suspect individual. You will not touch anyone on the head, you will not react to any provocation, you will not let the young men brawl. You will confiscate all arms and explosives.[10]

The refugees have already been searched, but the marines discover revolvers and knives. The passengers are directed to different decks. Some come from the beaches of Cap Saint-Jacques, others from the U.S. Embassy in Saigon. Still others have made a long journey, since Danang, passing from boat to boat. In the crowd the marines find three doctors, seven chefs and a South Vietnamese general who says he's commandant of their marines. And a senator. The last two don't want to perform any duties even when requested to by Moyher, who has to take care of several thousand refugees.

Small craft and boats circle around the *Pioneer Commander*. Some of them are on fire.

The Americans are also evacuating their last consulate, at Can Tho.

Consul Francis McNamara now rejects helicopters. He decides to load his men on boats. Intelligence says groups of North Vietnamese and Vietcong armed with recoilless cannon are scattered the length of the river. McNamara wants to assemble his people on the docks. He's wearing a cap with a sprawling legend, "Commodore, Can Tho Yacht Club."

Once at the port, he finds neither the pilots he expected nor the CIA agents. Those agents will be rescued by Air America helicopters, despite several attacks by South Vietnamese soldiers.

Under way by noon, the U.S. flotilla is boarded by a South Vietnamese naval patrol. Their commanding officer asks the consul if he's carrying any Vietnamese of draft age. Of course: McNamara has boarded 298 Vietnamese, among them several officers in civilian clothes. Without waiting for an answer, the patrol commander smiles: "I see that everything is in order. Steady as you go. Good trip and good luck!" A few days before, McNamara helped that particular officer, a corvette captain, to evacuate his family.

An emotional moment, immortalized by photographs: an old man beside the consul recognizes his son among the naval patrol. They embrace. One is leaving, the other staying.

9 P.M. From the roof of the U.S. Embassy, harshly lit by white floodlights, you can see tracers in the distance, streaks of fire in the storm. You can hear artillery boom. The big CH-53 helicopters land in the courtyard, the smaller CH-46s on the roof. Each passenger is allowed to carry one suitcase. In their enormous helmets strung with wires and plugs, the pilots look like Martians in a comic strip. Alan Carter, who was unable to evacuate his USIS employees; the ambassador's secretary, Eva Kim; and the reporter George McArthur climb into a helicopter. There are only a dozen

or so CIA people at the embassy now. They will destroy the last communications gear.

"We're losing 5 million dollars' worth of equipment," mutters Polgar, pacing, revolver in a shoulder holster.

Frank Snepp joins General Timmes on another chopper. They take off. Flying over Saigon, Snepp sees an ammunition depot blow up. Stunned, he sees thousands of bright headlights on the roads from Xuan Loc: triumphant convoys of North Vietnamese trucks and tanks.

10 P.M. Saigon, 10 A.M. Washington: at the Pentagon, they're recapping the evacuation. It's going well enough at Cap Saint-Jacques. At Can Tho also, probably. The secretary of defense thinks disaster looms in Saigon. In the first place, they've evacuated too many Vietnamese. What Schlesinger wants is to terminate the U.S. presence, halting all other operations at midnight Saigon time and resuming the exodus of other nationals in the morning. Schlesinger telephones his last orders to Saigon. He asks help from the White House, especially Brent Scowcroft, who cabled Martin fifteen minutes ago: "Understand there are still about 400 Americans in embassy compound.[11] You should ensure that all, repeat all, Americans are evacuated in this operation ASAP."

An immediate reply from a hopping mad Martin: "Perhaps you can tell me how to make some of these Americans abandon their half-Vietnamese children, or how the president would look if he ordered this." Martin complains: "For more than fifty minutes there have been no CH-53s here. And only one CH-46."

After a message from Admiral Whitmire, who'd like to close down at 11 P.M. Saigon time and resume operations next morning at 8, Martin adds: "I replied that I damned well didn't want to spend another night here. Four hours ago, I told Noel [Gayler, supreme commander in Honolulu] the number of sorties we need. Now the number is thirty CH-53 sorties."

Various companies are asking the State Department or the White House to intercede on behalf of their employees in Saigon.

10 P.M. again: Martin wires that he has a priest beside him, head of Catholic Relief Services. The priest doesn't want to leave without his Vietnamese. Martin wonders about relations between President Ford and American bishops if this priest is left behind.

Pierre Brochand asks Minh by telephone to order a cease-fire. The general says he'll think about it.

Brochand realises that fuel reserves for the generator are stored against the common wall with the U.S. Embassy. He wakes some young men of the "village," the jumble of houses within the French Embassy compound, where employees live with their hordes of kids, ducks and chickens: "Come on," cries Brochand, "we're going to move the fuel drums to the middle of the garden and cover them with a wet canvas."

Brochand and a dozen young men move the drums.

11:06 P.M. From the White House, Don Rumsfeld cables Martin that he should take care of the 150 IBM employees somewhere in Saigon with their families.

The ambassador says: "Shit."

11:30 P.M. At the airport, the marines destroy buildings and particularly communications equipment, 200 machines, 60 computers, a data bank, a satellite spotting station and the huge ARVN computer installed as if by chance in the cluster of U.S. military buildings. They also destroy many files. That goes well: the officer assigned the task laid his charges six days before. He puts the finishing touches on the job. They use three barrels of thermite, a hundred grenades and about twenty inflammable plates. They set the final explosives on delayed action. Then the marines race for the tennis courts, where the last helicopters are waiting.

Here for ten years stood the center, the heart, the engine of U.S. military power in Indochina. Here a U.S. commander in chief, General William Westmoreland, proclaiming victory, announced that there was "light at the end of the tunnel." At the end of the tunnel of this long war, the only light is this gigantic bonfire: roofs collapsing under the explosive charges and buildings burning fiercely in the white glow of magnesium and aluminum powder.

11:45 P.M. Cable from Martin to the White House: "Since my last message, nineteen, repeat nineteen, CH-46s have come and gone. I needed thirty CH-53 sorties capacity. I still do. Can't you get someone to tell us what is going on?"

Fifteen minutes later, Martin to Gayler: "Nothing in last twenty minutes. . . . It now seems I will spend part of April 30 here—a very small part I hope. But I sure don't want to spend May Day here." In a joking moment Martin told Kissinger that if things turned bad he'd go through the wall to the French Embassy and ask hospitality of Mérillon, who would surely take him in. He would sleep in Mme. Mérillon's room, "wishing that she were there and not in Paris."

The last marines leave the airport a little after midnight. In destroying the airport communications center, they destroyed the embassy's most advanced means of transmission.

Claudia Krich, the Quaker, will write up her diary for the evening of April 29. Before midnight, two neighbors came to see her:

> They are doctors from Danang, married. They had fled Da-
> nang, terrified by the stories they had heard about the com-
> munists. They asked us if we knew how they could attract
> the attention of a helicopter. They thought of painting an
> SOS on their roof. We begged them to do nothing, remarking
> that, if a helicopter should land in our alley, we would prob-
> ably all be killed by the South Vietnamese.

Colonel Hoa issues orders to break off all television broadcasts at midnight. The paratroopers around the station melt away. The prime minister told the director of radio and television, "Minh's going to surrender tomorrow. We don't want any paratroopers in Saigon."

North Vietnamese headquarters orders all artillery batteries to cease firing. Dung writes: "At midnight April 29, the whole of our attack force was ready to march on Saigon, like a divine hammer held aloft."

Rough days for the helicopter pilots. The formidable U.S. military machine, ready for anything, forgot one detail: for every chopper in the air, there's only one crew assigned. No one even planned a rotation, maybe three eight-hour shifts for the crews! The chopper pilots and gunners did their job on no sleep.

Second Lieutenant Richard Van de Geer was assigned to the 21st Special Operations Squadron, based at Nakhon Phanom in Thailand. He participated in the evacuation of Phnom Penh. He sends a letter-cassette[12] to his friend Dick. The lieutenant first went to Utapao, 500 kilometers south, where he was briefed:

> They told me that I was going to fly my airplane . . . to a
> Navy carrier. Well, that was not really a surprise . . . and
> we knew that the Seventh Fleet was doing some weird thing
> out there. But I didn't know that the goddamn carrier was
> 500 miles away—off the coast of South Vietnam. Well, obviously, I did manage to find the carrier, the USS *Midway*.
> I assure you that they are not as large when they are on the
> ocean as they appear to be when they are tied up at the dock.
> I landed on the carrier and was quickly indoctrinated into
> the way of the navy. I didn't like it one goddamn bit.

Every day the lieutenant attended intelligence briefings:

> We were there to evacuate American citizens, selected Vietnamese and other delegated third country nationals at the
> last possible moment if the situation deteriorated to the point
> that they couldn't use Tan Son Nhut airfield. . . . I made
> four sorties into Saigon. The situation with 150,000 [enemy
> troops] around the city, of course, was not the most salubrious situation in which to take a big, lumbering aircraft
> with nothing but defensive weapons to take people out. . . .
>   I could tell you about how real the fear was that I felt,
> since from the time we crossed the Delta and made the run
> into Saigon we were over enemy territory. We were being
> fired upon by anti-aircraft guns. The VC had commandeered
> Air America Hueys and they were flying them around, which

simply made for a very interesting chess game.[13] I mean, it was bad. We thought that they were going to call off the operation when it became dark, because we never expected them to send us into such a bad situation to begin with, even if it was daytime. But, as you probably know, they continued the mission until nearly 5 o'clock in the morning. The night sorties were the worst, because we flew lights out. The tracers kept everybody on edge. To see a city burning gives one a strange feeling of insecurity. Tan Son Nhut was being constantly shelled, and when I see you I will show you some pictures. . . .

Let me throw a couple of facts your way, which may conflict with what you have been reading in the papers. I call them facts in that I saw them happen. . . . [T]he morning of the 29th of April . . . a Vietnamese Huey flew out toward [the] sea, and found a carrier. It was nearly out of gas. It made an emergency landing on the carrier. . . . [A]nybody who had an ability to fly anything commandeered aircraft from whatever source. They flew out their families and their children. . . . This aircraft that landed—landed about 50 feet away from mine—and the man who got out of this aircraft [had been] quoted approximately a week earlier as saying that any South Vietnamese who left the country [was a] coward and that everybody should remain in South Vietnam and fight to the bitter end. This very same man was the first person to arrive on the USS *Midway* and, to my knowledge, the first to be recovered by the 7th Fleet. This man was General [Nguyen Cao] Ky. . . . Now I really don't have any personal feelings about the war over here. I really don't care one way or the other in regard to who is right and who is wrong, because that's a waste of time. . . . But I did find myself feeling that I wish he had been shot down. We pulled out close to 2,000 people. We couldn't pull any more because it was beyond human endurance to go any more.

22

———◆———

April 30:
The Last Lotus

At the Pentagon, at U.S. head-
quarters in Thailand, on the flagship, they're losing patience with Martin.
How many evacuees are still on line at the Saigon embassy? No more
games, no more guesswork, no more pick-a-number!

At 2:30 A.M. Saigon time the ambassador reports 726 people at the
embassy: 500 Vietnamese, 53 American civilians and 173 marines. The
military make a quick calculation. It will take nine CH-53 sorties to empty
the embassy.

Shortly afterward, phoning the White House, Martin revises his figures.
There are almost twice as many Vietnamese as predicted.

In fact, 1,100 people are waiting, mostly Vietnamese citizens, also a
German priest and a dozen South Korean diplomats including General
Rhee Dai Yong, former deputy commander of the 40,000 Korean soldiers
serving in Vietnam. In Washington and Honolulu people are getting
worked up: "Martin started the evacuation too late and now he doesn't
want to end it! They did it at the airport too: at Tan Son Nhut, they told
us first there were 500 refugees, then 1,000, then 2,000."

Political considerations come into play. In Washington they want a
quick announcement that all Americans have been evacuated. Kissinger
has promised to hold a press conference at 2 P.M. Washington time, 2 A.M.
in Saigon. He postpones the conference until 4 P.M.

They have to get it over with. At 3:15 A.M. in Saigon a Ch-46 lands on
the embassy roof. The pilot shows a hand-copied message signed by CINC-
PAC: "On the basis of the reported total of 726 evacuees, CINCPAC is

authorized to send 19 helicopters and no more." The words "no more" are underlined twice. "The President expects Ambassador Martin to be on the last helicopter."

The secretary of defense wants the last helicopter to take off at 3:45 A.M. Martin is asked to acknowledge this "presidential message."

They try to reassure the Vietnamese refugees in the embassy courtyards. Polgar figures he himself will shut down all transmission at 3:20 A.M. Oddly enough for the time and place, the CIA chief of mission indulges in general considerations. He cables: "This experience unique in the history of the United States does not signal necessarily the demise of the United States as a world power. The severity of the defeat and the circumstances of it, however, would seem to call for a reassessment of the policies . . ." As if to mark the moment well, Polgar blames a niggardly Congress: "Those who fail to learn from history are forced to repeat it. Let us hope that we will not have another Vietnam experience and that we have learned our lesson."

At 3:30 the flying command post circling over Saigon, a C-130, sends a coded message. From now on, only Americans will be evacuated, and Ambassador Martin will board the first available helicopter. When he's in the air, the helicopter will broadcast a simple message: "Tiger, tiger, tiger."

On the telephone, Kissinger says to Martin: "You and your heroes must return home now."

Kissinger postpones his press conference another hour.

At 3:45 Martin inspects the crowd in the embassy courtyard and says, "From now on the helicopters on the roof are reserved for Americans."

All the Vietnamese in the embassy buildings are to gather in the court-yard. Martin says CH-53s will pick them up there.

At the White House, Brent Scowcroft receives an urgent message, a flash from Martin: "Plan to close mission Saigon approximately 0430. . . . Due to necessity to destroy commo gear, this is the last Saigon message to SecState."

At 4:42 a CH-46, its name "Lady Ace 09" painted on its flank, lands on the embassy roof. The pilot presents a presidential order: ". . . for helo limits, only Americans plus crews will be carried. The ambassador should get on *Lady Ace 09.*"

Martin climbs aboard with his press attaché, John Hogan, Polgar and Colonel Jacobson. On the helicopter they find the last marines from the airport. If the ambassador refused to leave, there was a reserve order, to arrest Martin, signed by CINCPAC Admiral Noel Gayler. There are still several Americans at the embassy, Wolfgang Lehmann among them. Two officers are quarreling. Colonel John Madison thinks all the Vietnamese are going to be evacuated. Major Jim Kean, chief of the marine detach-ment, answers that he's had orders to leave. He's going to ask his men to fall back toward the roof.

Behind the embassy walls, Vietnamese jostle and stamp and shout:

"Please, evacuate me."

"Take my child."

"I have gold, dollars."

"My wife and children have left. Take me too."

They beg, they weep. For many Americans the dilemma is excruciating. If more Vietnamese are allowed into the embassy those already inside will never be able to board and leave. The marines use their rifle butts, find it hard to hold a shrinking perimeter and fall back from the outer wall. Some Vietnamese climb over the wall. Some start up a truck and break down the gates. Colonel Madison is appalled. Now there are 400–500 people, mostly Vietnamese, many of them embassy employees, including firemen; also the German priest, also Koreans. They've all abandoned their baggage. The firemen offered to be of some use. The refugees are organized into six groups. Two officers, Colonel Madison and Colonel Harry Summers, of the Four-Party and Two-Party Joint Military Commissions of the Paris Agreement, feel helpless. The Vietnamese understand that they're going to be left behind. The marines fall back to the embassy stairs.

Landing on the *Okinawa* shortly afterward, Colonel Madison begs that six helicopters be sent to pick up the six groups in the embassy courtyard. His request is denied. The first diplomats reaching the ship "forgot" to say that there remained 420 refugees in the embassy courtyard, before it was overrun by the outer throng of Vietnamese.

5:10 A.M. Two hundred Americans, among them one hundred and seventy marines, are waiting in the embassy. Time drags. At Major Kean's order the last marines go upstairs. They block the doors behind them with steel bars. They dump dressers, tables, anything that comes to hand, into the stairwells and elevator shafts. The marines take two hours to make it from the ground floor to the roof. They throw tear gas grenades. And one of them tosses a combat grenade. The Vietnamese cannot follow them up.

Armed Vietnamese soldiers roam the embassy. On the roof an unlimbered machinegun covers the perimeter. The marines are applying rule D on engagement: no random fire—commence firing only by order of an officer or a noncom in command.

5:47: aboard *Lady Ace 09* an exhausted Martin consoles himself. In the end it was a good job of work . . . they did their best. . . . Some of his colleagues think he took too many decisions too late. Martin feels he avoided panic and even fooled the North Vietnamese. All Americans are out; the marines were not forced to fight. Martin might have stayed longer, but he's been a disciplined diplomat for forty-five years.

To him the president's order was a terrible ordeal. He thinks the president was misled by Schlesinger. Headquarters officers think Martin gave misleading responses. Martin thinks he himself has been misled.

So it goes in war. So it goes in any debacle.

In Washington they weren't ready for any of this, the ambassador reflects. They were coasting on the successful evacuation of Phnom Penh—

300 evacuees, mostly Americans! In Saigon, in Vietnam, by ship, plane, helicopter, they had to evacuate 130,000 Vietnamese. And surely even more by unreported flights.

On the embassy roof Corporal Stephen Bauer wonders whether he and the other Marines won't have to take cover in the French Embassy. Mortar shells are crumping closer. Dawn is clear, without fog or haze. Finally the last chopper arrives. It sets down. Its blades turn slowly, stirring up gusts of air, sucking up tear gas from the grenades tossed down the stairwell. On the roof, the marines are blinded and choking. Ten marines still to board the helicopter. The last, pushing his men, is named Juan Valdez. A master sergeant, he knows each of his men would rather have followed him—to say what he himself will be able to say: "I was the last one."

7:53 A.M. This last helicopter flies off, escorted by Cobras. For the first time in ten years, there are no American fighting men in Vietnam. A few deserters are holed up in the suburbs. When the chopper reaches the coast, the marines on board applaud and take pictures.

In the embassy courtyard the Vietnamese and the South Korean general are milling and pacing. Official U.S. reports will speak of "about 420 persons." Out front, a crowd is screaming. Communist propagandists are shouting slogans: "The Americans have gone, the country is free, independent, democratic." Inside the embassy looting has begun. Then suddenly the crowd streams away. Someone cried, "The embassy's going to blow up."

Once on the flagship *Blue Ridge*, Martin passes briefly through the press room, where Polgar is talking to reporters. Martin says a few words: ". . . we did not have to leave Vietnam in the way we did. If we had done what we said we would do in the first year after the Paris Agreement, if we had kept our commitments . . ."

The phrase races over press agency telexes. The ambassador receives a cable from Kissinger suggesting firmly that he save his impressions for the president of the United States. Martin has a small breakfast, scrambled eggs and sausage. A physical examination and an X-ray confirm congestion in both lungs. When he thinks back over the evacuation later, Ambassador Graham Martin says: "That is not how I saw American honor."[1]

On *Blue Ridge*, the ambassador is given three cables at once. The senders address him in very different styles:

President Ford to Ambassador Martin:

> I want to express my deep appreciation to you and your entire staff for the successful evacuation of Americans and Vietnamese from Saigon. The tireless dedication of your mission and its skillful performance under the most severe pressure was vital to the accomplishment of this most difficult and delicate operation. Please accept as well

my sincere personal compliments. Your courage and stead-
iness at this critical period enabled us to evacuate our own
citizens and a very large number of endangered Vietnamese. I hope you will convey to your entire staff my deep
gratitude and that of the American people for a job well
done. Sincerely.

The secretary of state is more familiar:

To Graham Martin from Henry Kissinger.

I'm sure you know how deeply I feel about your performance under the most trying circumstances. My heart-
felt thanks. Warm regards.

From the White House, Brent Scowcroft cables simply: "Graham, you
were superb."
The helicopters, with Major Melton's marines, have scattered. The
major's lands on *Midway*, his second-in-command's on *Vancouver*.
South Vietnamese helicopters arrive, half empty or crammed with soldiers and civilians, women, old folks, children, baskets of fruit, weapons
and ammunition. Major Melton even sees passengers debarking with
trussed live chickens.
It is appropriate and maybe even symbolic that the American war, so
mechanized, should end by helicopter. In 1965 American staff planners
decreed that the helicopter would be the decisive offensive weapon. Today
it's the way out. Mobile and maneuverable, the helicopter is perhaps emblematic of four American character traits—four weaknesses too?—optimism, aggressiveness, impatience and confidence in modern technology.
This April 30, while the last aerial ballet dances above the fleet, the world
notes that the helicopter has become truly an instrument of flight.
Midway maneuvers. Officers inform Major Melton that the aircraft
carriers are headed for the Thai coast to take on South Vietnamese fighter
planes. A small plane appears out of the blue and radios: "I am a South
Vietnamese major. I have my wife and children with me. I want to land."
Reply: "Impossible. We're not equipped for it. We don't have re-
straining cables nets for your type of plane."
"I am landing."
The machine glides into line with the carrier's runway, lands, brakes.
A successful landing. Sailors and marines, including Melton, cheer the
pilot.
Melton is rather pleased. None of his men were killed or wounded.
Marines are trained to attack, hit the beaches, take enemy positions. These
last days they've successfully protected a retreat. Melton is a career officer
and obeys orders. Leaning on the handrail, he contemplates the small boats

around the aircraft carriers and watches sailors help refugees clamber aboard.

General Richard Carey sums things up for these three days, April 28–30. Successful evacuation by sea: eight ships took aboard 29,783 refugees, mostly from Cap Saint-Jacques; 2,500 were taken from the islands of Phu Quoc and Con Son. The *Pioneer Commander* collected 4,669 of them at the mouth of the Saigon River.

The marine pilots flew an average of thirteen hours a day, some more than eighteen hours straight. The evacuation helicopters alone flew 689 sorties, 160 of them at night. Two marines were killed at the airport. And two pilots. A CH-46, trying to land on the *Hancock*, hit the sea and capsized, with no passengers aboard. The pilot and copilot were drowned, the two machinegunners were saved. The pilots of an AH-1J, a Cobra, with trouble in the fuel line or out of gas, set it down in the sea four miles from the *Okinawa*. The men are safe and sound. In all, four Americans killed in action.

From the landing pads near General Smith's complex at Tan Son Nhut airport, the marines pulled out 5,600 people. No one ever dreamed that there'd be 2,206 people, among them 1,373 American citizens, ferried from the courtyard and roof of the U.S. Embassy.[2]

On the ships, marines were occasionally insulted and sometimes shoved by refugees, mainly during distribution of food. Minor brawls, and a few refugees punched out. On some ships armed ARVN soldiers, in uniform or in civvies, created tense situations, but the marines managed to disarm the troublemakers and reestablish a semblance of order.

Problems of sanitation are multiplying. Sometimes there is not enough water. The holds stink of vomit and excrement.

The surprising thing is not that there were incidents but that there were so few.

Colonel Le Vinh Hoa did not want to leave Saigon. At 6 A.M. he's on the job as head of TV. He wants to go out with the mobile unit. The police stop him: "You're under arrest."

"By whose order?"

"By order of President Minh."

To depart is to flee, to desert. The president forbids his officials to leave Saigon.

At Tan Son Nhut all the soldiers are hunched over their transistor radios; Sergeant Thuong, like his comrades, is waiting for a communiqué from the new government.

A meeting in the prime minister's offices, in an old French house on the boulevard Thong Nhut. Holding on around the president are Prime Minister Vu Van Mau and several general officers and high officials. A Minh adviser, Ly Qui Chung, returns from Camp Davis. The PRG will not agree to negotiate with the new president. They are not prepared to make any concession, military or political: "They demand 'the dissolution of the puppet army and police.' They're ready to issue safe-conducts to the president and his men."

Minh's advisers are divided. Should they take a firm stand? But on what power base? The last divisions of the line, the 5th, 18th, 22nd and 25th, have scattered, like what remains of the marine brigades and paratroopers, according to the latest military intelligence. Some advisers urge surrender. Minh thinks it over. They send a new emissary to Camp David. They telephone here and there. The Buddhists, Catholics and French diplomats all admit they have no idea now just what the communists want. Suddenly French General François Vanuxem, a die-hard, an extremist in French Algeria with an advanced degree in philosophy, comes forward in civilian clothes. He has already proposed a number of plans. Now he suggests another: they should ask China to invade North Vietnam. Then Paris could serve as mediator. They could thus maintain a neutral or neutralized Cochin-China.

Minh writes a speech and submits it to his prime minister, then goes to the palace to tape it. Radio broadcasts the text at 10:24 A.M.:

> The policy line we back is reconciliation. I believe firmly in reconciliation among Vietnamese to avoid unnecessary shedding of the blood of Vietnamese. . . . I ask the soldiers of the Republic of Vietnam to cease hostilities in calm and to stay where they are. I ask the brother soldiers of the Provisional Revolutionary Government of South Vietnam to cease hostilities. We wait here to meet the Provisional Revolutionary Government of South Vietnam to discuss jointly a ceremony of orderly transfer of power so as to avoid any unnecessary bloodshed in the population.

In this speech Minh still doesn't mention North Vietnamese troops. He accepts the fiction of the PRG and shows clearly that he is not out to retain even an appearance of power. He is going to "transfer" it. Shortly afterward, radio also broadcasts a communiqué from the South Vietnamese general staff:

> Soldiers, regimental commanders, unit commanders, Regional Forces, People's Forces, Self-Defense Forces. I, General Nguyen Huu Hanh, Deputy Chief of General Staff, in the absence of General Vinh Loc, Chief of General Staff, ask you, generals and soldiers of all ranks, to strictly obey the order of the President of the Republic of Vietnam concerning the cease-fire. The military command is ready to enter into contact with the military command of the army of the

Provisional Revolutionary Government of South Vietnam in
order to effect a cease-fire without bloodshed.

The prime minister has also taped a brief declaration: "In a spirit of
concord and reconciliation, I, Professor Vu Van Muu, Prime Minister, call
on all levels of the population to salute with joy this day of peace for the
Vietnamese people. I call on all employees of the administration: return
to your workplaces and resume your activities."

At the airport, Sergeant Thuong weeps.

At home, Engineer Van concludes that Minh's negotiations were unsuccessful. The communists, he thinks, will not stand still for a neutral
regime. Then Van pulls himself together. At the least he wants to trust in
the conquerors' clemency. He goes to his office. Of his colleagues who
answered the prime minister's appeal, most are fearful.

Around the bonze Thien Hue, most of the refugees in his pagoda are
saying: "It's over. We're going home."

In Washington, Gerald Ford is finishing dinner with King Hussein of
Jordan. Ford is told of Minh's declaration. No one talks about this surrender or of Vietnam.

The NVA command hears Minh's speech on the radio. General Dung
says they will not chance being deprived of victory "by sleight of hand."
The Politburo issues orders: "Continue the attack on Saigon according to
plan, advance as powerfully and quickly as possible, liberate and take over
the whole city, disarm enemy troops, dissolve the enemy administration
at all levels and thoroughly smash all enemy resistance." Dung immediately
dispatches the order of the day to his troops: "To all army corps, all military
zones, all units: (1) Continue the advance as rapidly as possible to the
assigned objectives in the city and the province. (2) Call on the enemy to
surrender and hand over all its weapons. Arrest and assemble enemy officers from the rank of major on up. (3) Wipe out any attempt at resistance
on the spot."

There is pillage throughout Saigon, especially in offices and villas abandoned by Americans. Men, women, children carry off lamps, radios, wash-
basin faucets, typewriters, tables, chairs, sofas, mattresses. The halls and
stairways of the U.S. Embassy are strewn with papers, brochures, reports
and files. On all floors air conditioners are yanked and refrigerators dis-
mantled. Some try to open safes. Everywhere you can see chairs ripped
open, pictures and portraits smashed. Barefoot shirtless young Vietnamese
in shorts, working by twos and threes, make off with couches. For thirty
years the Vietnamese have rebuilt, refurbished, mended with patience and
skill. They're still doing it. The former owners have left and the new ones
haven't moved in yet.

The phone rings all day at the presidential palace. Nguyen Van Hao,
former economics minister, says in pompous tones,

Those who have borne a certain responsibility for their country cannot leave. Whatever happens, they must stay. The North Vietnamese know what they want. They have been fighting for thirty years and they deserve to lead Vietnam. . . . With a unified and independent country, the future is assured. The South is rich in agriculture and oil. The South can help the North.

The new prime minister has named a minister of information, Ly Qui Chung, who announces: "We have no surrender complex. . . . Let us no longer talk about the Third Force. It has no proper place in politics. It mainly represented a people who wanted a unified and peaceful country."

In the city, flags are flying. Residents hang the blue and red PRG flag in their windows. On public buildings they most often settle for a large swatch of white cloth or a sheet. Some use French flags, thinking they'll grant a sort of immunity. The weather is superb.

Patrick Hays makes a tour of Saigon. Some streets are deserted, others thronged. Hays runs across armed and disciplined paratroopers in the rue Cong Ly and rue Pasteur. He arrives at the Grall Hospital. A lot of civilians and a fair number of soldiers in civvies are dawdling around the building.

Captain Pham Thin[3] is working at police headquarters. His superiors have vanished, including General Binh, national commander and head of counterespionage, three other generals, four colonels and assorted officers. Thin has stayed on, with the task of "maintaining order and honor." He sent his wife and children to France two days ago. He had helped Air France plenty and was given a 50 percent discount on his tickets. Thin asked his superiors to destroy all the files. No one's so much as touched them. He decides to hide in the British Embassy, left in charge of Mr. Sam, the Indian concierge. There, Thin finds a colonel and a dozen police officers. They go by car to the Grall Hospital. They think they'll be protected by the French flag someone's run up. The captain gets rid of his revolver. He thinks often of the files still in place at headquarters, from yellow and powdery sheets with notes in violet ink that go back to the French era to the typed sheets that are copies of CIA reports. The captain hates the communists, but he tells himself they'll be understanding. They talk about concord and reconciliation. All regimes need policemen. He'll be downgraded a bit, maybe. He'll win his stripes back later.[4]

Groups of ARVN soldiers are wandering around town. Many ditch their weapons and throw away their uniforms. Sidewalks here and there are strewn with shirts, combat pants, jungle boots, caps and cartridge belts. Once again contradictory rumors spread. Some Saigonese say the communists are going to "punish" the capital by bombing it. Equally sure, others insist communist tanks won't enter the city. Saigon will be a free port, a sort of Hong Kong. Hanoi needs a window on the West.

In the place Lam Son, at the foot of the monument to the Vietnamese soldier, a body is sprawled. After the broadcast of Minh's declaration, a police lieutenant colonel came there. He saluted, stood at attention for several moments, and then put a bullet through his head. Many officers commit suicide on April 30, among them General Phu, former commander of the Second Army Corps.[5] Once upon a time, mandarins who failed in their mission were expected to kill themselves.

North Vietnamese units are spotted in the suburbs. Elements of the NVA Third Army Corps reach the perimeter of the airport. Dung is throwing 150,000 men at Saigon. Several ARVN units hold out near the Newport Bridge on the Saigon River. The Saigonese watch tanks and infantry pass. Most of the men are transported in trucks, followed by half-track cannon and anti-aircraft batteries. The tank crews seem to have a hard time finding their bearings. Sometimes they ask their way, like lost tourists.

At the airport Sergeant Thuong receives orders from his commanding officer, Major Le Xuan Huyen, at 11 A.M. To the sergeant and twenty or so soldiers, the major says: "It's all over. Lay down your arms and go home. I'll stay here, for the transfer."

No one leaves.

At the palace President Minh, weary, the shadow of a beard on his jowls, is surrounded by his prime minister and several reporters.

"I'm waiting for the other side," the president says.

To Jean-Louis Arnaud, head of the AFP office, he confides, "I don't know if they'll come today or tomorrow. . . . Somebody has to do it."

When the NVA troops move in, Vietnamese agents left at the Hotel Duc by the CIA fire several shots from a revolver and a submachinegun. Heavy machineguns and rockets reduce them to silence. Behind the cathedral, a paratrooper platoon tries to stop some tanks. All the paratroopers are killed or wounded.

The Saigonese observe the victors with relief, fear, astonishment. Most of them seem as young as they are disciplined. The officers seem to be at least forty years old. Tank turrets are often open, the armor camouflaged with palm fronds.

At 11:45 ARVN Sergeant Thuong sees some North Vietnamese soldiers armed with AKs. They speak loud and clear, with Northern accents: "Who's in command here?"

Major Le Xuan Huyen steps forward. "I am."

The North Vietnamese order the South Vietnamese to undress. The soldiers obey and stand there waiting in their underpants. All of them, victors and vanquished, seem fearful. Are the former afraid of a trap? Are the latter wondering if they're about to be executed?

The North Vietnamese soldiers tell them, all except the major, "Go home."

Sergeant Thuong leaves with the other soldiers.

Jeeps are racketing around the center of the city, full of students waving M-16s decorated with red ribbons.

Tien, the young film buff from Hanoi, arrives with six NVA tanks in front of South Vietnamese General Headquarters. The tanks fall in line on the wide street, turrets aimed at the buildings. This group of tanks was heading for the Chi Hoa Prison, and received orders at the last moment to close in on South Vietnamese headquarters. The prisoners in Chi Hoa have been liberated.

The young man is pleased; the war is over, and he'll see his mother and brother again.

Tank 879, of the 203rd Brigade, driven by Bui Duc Mai, rumbles down Thong Nhut Boulevard, passing the U.S. Embassy and proceeding on its way. Shortly the tank officer realizes he's gone too far, backs up and makes a three-point turn on the boulevard, and heads for Independence Palace. He arrives before the gates and lawns. Symbolically, because no one's resisting and the guards would have opened up without demur, tank 879 staves in the heavy wrought-iron gates and advances right to the large building. Bui Quang Thuan, squadron commander, climbs out of the tank, marches up the stairs and reappears on the balcony. A soldier has scaled the façade to take down the South Vietnamese flag. Now the blue and red PRG flag floats over the palace. It is 12:15 P.M. Saigon time, 11:15 A.M. Hanoi time. Plowing up the lawns, other tanks move into position. Infantrymen deploy on the lawn. They hear several shots in the distance, over by the prefecture, and explosions too. Many civilians, kids and reporters crowd around the NVA troops and tanks. Officers and men scatter through the ground floor, then mount to the first floor, where they find President Minh and his entourage. An employee of the Saigon Electricity Company, Mr. To Van Quang, seems to be serving as go-between. Nervous, the North Vietnamese ask if they have any weapons: "If you have, lay them down and surrender."

Minh gets the good-guy-bad-guy treatment. First, friendly: Colonel Bui Tin, normally a journalist, is the highest-ranking NVA officer present and must therefore receive the surrender. "You have nothing to fear," he says. "Among Vietnamese, there are no victors and vanquished. Only the Americans have been conquered. If you are patriots, consider this a moment of joy. The war is ended for our country."

Minh replies to the North Vietnamese: "I have been waiting since early this morning to transfer power to you."

Then a certain Tung—sublieutenant or lieutenant—answers harshly: "You have nothing left to turn over. You can only surrender unconditionally. I invite you to come to the radio station to announce an unconditional surrender."

Head bowed, Minh descends the palace steps and goes to the radio station. There he reads a statement written by a North Vietnamese officer: "I declare the Saigon administration entirely dissolved, from the central level to the regional level. From the central level to the regional level, it has surrendered to the revolutionary government."

Minh returns to the palace; out front are now about forty tanks, cannon aimed outward, as if they were to defend the place. Several prisoners are seated on the ground; they rise and go, escorted by North Vietnamese guards, to join the columns forming in the city.

There is a holiday atmosphere outside the palace. Curious children scamper everywhere. Standing, or squatting on their heels, with or without helmets, North Vietnamese soldiers chat with civilians.

Minh and his men have lunch. The presidential meal, fried crabs and noodles, was hot and ready. But the president is served a military ration of rice and canned meat.

Young men—"the April 30ths," last-minute liberators—more or less armed, crisscross the city in requisitioned vehicles.

Sergeant Thuong, in civilian clothes, goes to the rue Lang Cha Ca. The house is empty. He takes his bicycle. On rue Truong Minh Giang, he sees the bodies of ARVN soldiers stretched on the ground. The sergeant arrives near the Grand Market, which is surrounded by tanks and Molotova trucks. The April 30ths, with red armbands, are bustling about, giving orders to the crowd: "Applaud!"

Women and children nip into shops and run off with cassettes, lamps, radios. The April 30ths shout: "Don't loot, those are the people's goods!"

Resistance fighters in black pyjamas and short hair, often with scarfs tied around their necks as sweatbands, armed with AK-47s and rocket launchers, mingle with North Vietnamese regulars.

At his headquarters, General Dung exults:

> On our map, our five columns of troops seemed like five lotuses blossoming out from our five major objectives. The First Army Corps had captured Saigon's general staff headquarters and the command compounds of all the enemy armed services. When the Third Army Corps captured Tan Son Nhut they met one wing of troops already encamped there—our military delegation at Camp Davis; it was an amazing and moving meeting. The Fourth Army Corps captured Saigon's Ministry of Defense, the Bach Dang port, and the radio station. Group 232 took the Special Capital Zone headquarters, and the main police headquarters.

There the special units uncover thousands of files and computers, which intrigue them mightily.[6] Dung goes on, "The Second Army Corps seized 'Independence Palace,' where [the American puppets] had sold our independence cheap."

At North Vietnamese headquarters the brass meet happily, hugging and congratulating one another. Le Duc Tho, Pham Hung and General Dung embrace all around. A great moment, so the Northern commander in chief lights and savors a cigarette. "The sound of applause, laughter and happy, noisy, chattering speech was as festive as if spring had just burst upon us," he writes. This General Dung, former militant, soldier all his life, who hid in a Buddhist monastary thirty-six years ago, alludes in strange terms to the Buddhist cycle of births and rebirths: "This historic and sacred, intoxicating and completely satisfying moment was one that comes once in a generation, once in many generations, certainly not twice in a single life."

One of his officers says: "Now we can die happy."

Dung recalls the classic image of the lotus, first among flowers, first sign of life in troubled waters, a beautiful, pure flower. Dung is emerging from the muddy waters of war, of the resistance, of failed offensives then successful offensives. One of his bodyguards, Vo Xuan Sang, photographs these first moments of jubilation. Of course, communist officials and soldiers express their joy freely. In his memoirs Dung leaps into the sentimental-political mix of lyricism and cliché obligatory in Hanoi: "And we wept. . . . Our first thought in that first moment of victory was for Uncle Ho. . . . We expected to hear the bell ring at his house on stilts, announcing the good news. We imagined him behind the awnings, writing a poem to celebrate the event."

Uncle Ho said he'd wait ten, twenty, thirty years if necessary. The army is the Party, and the Party is like a lotus with four, six, twenty and a thousand petals. The lotus with a thousand petals is the total revelation, and the Party is the whole truth. It only remains to bring home this truth to the often indolent, laughing, corrupt Southerners. Dung thinks Saigon and the South, like Hanoi and the North, deserve "peace and happiness at last." Only they don't know which happiness it is that they need. Hanoi knows. Happiness is earned and worked at. In Saigon, this troubled, suspicious city, many must first atone. Beyond special interest and individual suffering, a collective joy will spring up transcending mean, personal, egotistical, bourgeois ambitions.

Now on the shady square before Independence Palace there must be 2,000 smiling, polite North Vietnamese soldiers. As they moved in they never saw the predicted mass demonstrations of joy. Some rifles sport flowers. The soldiers are eating sticky rice and canned food.

The Grall Hospital is full of refugees, among them Koreans and Taiwanese. Men, women and children have overrun the lawns and are camped among the large metal-framed buildings. Many, more foresighted, hospitalized themselves some weeks ago. An old antique dealer and opium addict, Thanh Anh, rented the Grall's dovecote, a room at the end of a footbridge, with a number of verandas. In the old days the admiral-governors would recuperate in the dovecote. There, lounging on a rice-straw mattress, the antiquarian draws on his pipe.

Patrick Hays has not had to use his weapons. His aide, Hamiaux, crosses the city full of North Vietnamese to take them to Grall in his jeep; its canvas top is gone, unneeded. The weapons will swell the heap at the gate surrendered by those hoping to shelter beneath the French flag. Hays hears the first orders broadcast by Radio Liberation. Henceforth Saigon will be called Ho Chi Minh City. Women must dress decently, wear modest peasant clothes, black or brown. Communist happiness is gray. Ho Chi Minh City radio announces that there has been an uprising, that enthusiastic crowds are welcoming the liberators. Some in Saigon are in truth cheering; others are silent. Trucks crisscross town, loudspeakers blaring: "The forces of the National Liberation Front are now masters of Saigon. Do not be afraid. You will be well treated if you respect order and discipline."

Radio Liberation, quickly echoed by the capital's radio, broadcasts the PRG's ten-point program.[7]

Little by little, NVA troops take traffic in hand. In the distance, ammunition depots are blowing up. Columns of black smoke rise in the sky over Cholon.

Father Jean Maïs hears about the fall of Saigon from the adolescents guarding him.

"*Anh*, your case is serious," they tell him. "You are an international spy. You are going to be held a long time."

Maïs buys a school notebook, a pen and some Basto de luxe cigarettes. He kills time, rewriting his lecture on metaphors or inventing spoonerisms.

"What am I guilty of?" he asks now and then.

"*Anh*, don't you know?"

"No."

"What? You dare to say you're not guilty when the revolution has put you in prison!"

Maïs waits, his place of detention changes, he goes from house to a shed. Here they hood him, there they fetter his legs. One day a guard reads him regulations: "*Anh*, you are called number 31. It is forbidden to use your name. It is forbidden to say who you are. It is forbidden to speak of your past. It is forbidden to raise political problems. It is forbidden to speak of religion."

Hanoi's power takes over quickly but discreetly in Saigon, more slowly in the Delta provinces, because there are fewer communist troops, only some Vietcong and NVA regiments, in the south of MR 4. Until the beginning of March, they were dispersed, *so tan*ized at company and platoon level. General Tra had issued orders to regroup PRG "divisions" that existed mostly on paper. He had to impress the Saigon government, persuade it that the PRG commanded huge detachments.

In the Delta the war was a guerrilla war, often bloody on both sides. Tra undermined the infrastructure of the Saigon government. The Vietcong made raids on the rice harvest. In MR 4 the hardest fighting always took place north of the capital. There the NVA and Vietcong could be supported by their rear bases in Cambodia. The NVA generals would have liked to

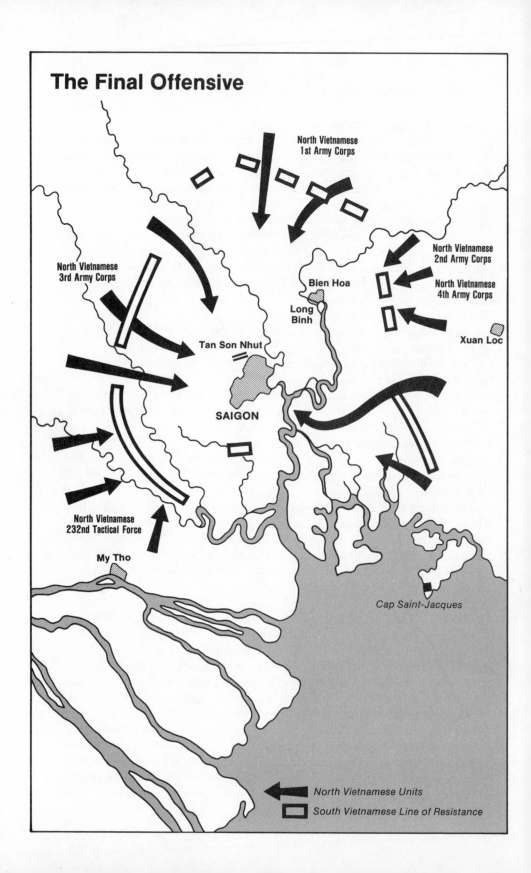

The Final Offensive

North Vietnamese
1st Army Corps

North Vietnamese
3rd Army Corps

North Vietnamese
2nd Army Corps

North Vietnamese
4th Army Corps

Bien Hoa

Long
Binh

Xuan Loc

Tan Son Nhut

SAIGON

North Vietnamese
232nd Tactical Force

My Tho

Cap Saint-Jacques

North Vietnamese Units

South Vietnamese Line of Resistance

take Can Tho toward the end of March. But the ARVN 21st Division was well supplied with armor, and the town remained impregnable. Reaches of the Mekong served as the South Vietnamese line of defense.

The revolutionary government takes over in Can Tho during the afternoon of April 30, more by evaporation of the bureaucracy and the ARVN than by any arrival en masse of Vietcong or NVA troops.

The NLF and PRG were never strong in that region. Wilfrid Burchett, an Australian journalist and militant communist,[8] shows this unintentionally. Nguyen Thi Muoi Be, president of the people's revolutionary committee of An Nghiep, one of the city's twelve districts, describes the liberation of Can Tho for Burchett. In her quarter, a district of 19,000 people, Mme. Be confesses candidly that on April 28 the "revolutionary core consisted of only fifteen patriots." She adds four underground militia and forty South Vietnamese police, "patriots ready to come over to our side as soon as we gave them the signal." We can extrapolate: at Can Tho there were at most a few hundred activists working for the PRG. On April 30 until 9 A.M. they distribute tracts quietly and stick notices up on walls and trees. A bit later, they offer their tracts to ARVN troops at food and transport depot No. 4, in the An Nghiep quarter. Most of the ARVN troops are casting off their uniforms, donning civilian clothes and drifting away.

The communists occupy the radio station. At 3 P.M. South Vietnamese General Nguyen Khoa Nam, discovering that the PRG has almost no weapons, orders his remaining soldiers to retake the station. He asks for reinforcements, which do not arrive. Thereupon the general and one of his aides, Colonel Tran Huu Tien, commit suicide.

Nguyen Ha Van, a member of the regional communist party committee, a graying man with a wrinkled face, will explain to Burchett, "Later in the night, our regular troops began to arrive. They'd been delayed by fighting all along Route 4."

Capturing the radio station will be decisive. In the surrounding villages and hamlets civilians and soldiers alike, hearing the station is in communist hands, figure it's useless to resist. In groups of twenty or thirty, ARVN officers and men head for the deep South. Some hope to join nests of resistance. Others think they may be able to reach the marshy areas of Ca Mau point. Still others look for sailboats, rowboats, junks, to head for the vast American and South Vietnamese armada at sea. Some of these groups wind around the towns of Soc Trang, Can Tho, Vinh Long, Ben Tre and My Tho.

At My Tho, the South Vietnamese garrison lays down its guns around 6 P.M.

Units of the national navy fire salvos, running down the Mekong toward the sea. The South Vietnamese resist at several strong points, hardest at headquarters of the rural pacification corps. Here one company refuses to surrender. The entry gate is flanked by double rows of barbed wire. The revolutionary forces—according to Burchett—use a ruse. They disguise themselves in ARVN uniforms, approach the buildings, knock out the sentinel and penetrate headquarters.

At the same time, on the island of Poulo Condor, seventy-eight prisoners revolt. Since colonial times Poulo Condor and its penitentiary embody a history and a symbol. The infamous tiger cages are there. Ambassador Graham Martin said they were healthy. . . . The tiger cages are pit cells with access from above. There is no roof, just an iron grill one can raise to drop a prisoner in and through which food and water are passed. A number of communist leaders had a taste of Poulo Condor. Most of its prisoners are political. The prison guards ran off, or have been neutralized. That evening Radio Liberation announces that Poulo Condor's prisoners have set up an eleven-member committee "under the presidency of Comrade Le Cau."

The PRG radio also announces that "twenty-seven ships of the puppet fleet" have been stopped off the Vietnamese coast. These vessels have been surrounded by North Vietnamese naval units at the latitude of Danang, where there are no more U.S. ships.

All along the South Vietnamese coast innumerable refugees, the first boat people, are embarking.

The North Vietnamese navy never intervenes where the U.S. navy is deployed.

In Saigon, the French ambassador drafts a cable to the Quai d'Orsay. Jean-Marie Mérillon explains that "the afternoon has been rather warm. . . . The Vietcong have subdued the last resistance."

The ambassador identifies North Vietnamese units mopping up in the capital by the word "Vietcong," confirming despite himself the fiction that the PRG took Saigon. "The Vietcong," he continues, "entered Saigon toward noon, about two hours after the appeal, actually a surrender, broadcast by General Minh." Poor unfortunate Minh is no longer president even in official cables. "There was practically no fighting. The only obstacles were some isolated snipers, rapidly eliminated." Often, information lacking, the paratroopers and rangers who fought are denied the dignity of mention in dispatches. "Out beyond the U.S. Embassy, submachineguns are still stuttering away."

At least one objective of French and ambassadorial policy has been achieved: there were none of the atrocities in Saigon that occurred in Danang. "Saigon will have seen a little less than forty-eight hours of chaos. Relative chaos, moreover, if we allow for a few episodes of looting," Mérillon cables.

Responsible for their safety, an ambassador must think of his nationals: "I believe I can assert that the French community has not suffered. . . . Our people seem to be safe and sound."

Mérillon picks up the receiver of the hot line to the U.S. Embassy. The line is dead.

Captain-major of the North Vietnamese army Tran Ba Doai is at headquarters of MR 4 in Quang Binh when he learns of Minh's surrender on the radio. The captain-major is in the 28th Battalion of Unit 559. He's in command of a convoy of seventy trucks transporting munitions, dried fish and rice. So—the war is over, and reunification has begun.

How long this war was! Doai has been a soldier for sixteen years. He wanted to be a doctor. Before his assignment to transport, he'd been with the 305th Airborne Brigade. Trained by the Chinese and Russians, he'd jumped twenty-five times. He served cheerfully in those days. He had to liberate the country, reunify the nation. His head was full of slogans: "Vietnam is our country," "The Vietnamese are one people," "Nothing is as precious as independence and liberty." The slogans were as much a part of him as the anchor tattooed on his arm. He spent many days and nights on Route 1, which runs from Haiphong to Hanoi and then heads south. He led his convoys of fifty to eighty trucks in the cabin of a Molotova. When all went well, he took two and a half days to cover 700 kilometers. Sometimes a third of his men were wounded or killed.

For a long time he wondered how the war would turn out. In December 1974 his superiors told him the struggle would be long, they could not soon liberate the whole of Vietnam. They needed the "correct perspective," they could not mount a frontal attack on Saigon, there would be too many losses on both sides. Saigon was a pearl, it should not be destroyed in an assault. In January the captain-major attended a meeting with 700 officers from all the services, in Hanoi near the place Ba Dinh. He was stunned. They were told they had an opportunity that would not come again in a thousand years.

They grasped the opportunity, and the war is over.

In Hanoi the people as well as the leaders hear Minh's surrender on the radio. Several government offices have telephoned AFP correspondent Jean Thoraval to obtain the full and exact text of General Minh's speech. They're preparing a May Day celebration. For the Labor Union Federation the theme of the workers' festivities will become "incomparable and brilliant perspectives on the Vietnamese revolution." May Day becomes Victory Day.

Toward three in the afternoon local time they hear officially that the South Vietnamese capital has fallen. Work continues for a while then stops. Workers spill into the streets. The real explosion of joy takes place that evening. Some foreigners celebrate the great event before many North Vietnamese citizens do. Cuban volunteer workers and diplomats parade around with a makeshift band in the rue de la Soie, in the old section of Hanoi. The Swedish Embassy gives a reception in honor of the king's birthday, a Swedish national holiday. All the East European embassies are decked with flags. A civil servant in the Ministry of Foreign Affairs reproaches the French ambassador for not doing the same. Philippe Richer answers: "I follow customary usage and hang out flags only for *our* national holidays."

In the camp at Phong Quang the prisoners, criminal and political, busy themselves at their work. It's hot. Like many of the detainees, Nguyen Ky believes that one day ARVN troops will liberate them. He did not believe in the fall of Ban Me Thuot, or Hue's, or Danang's. The camp loudspeakers announce the fall of Saigon. Propaganda! Lies! Disinformation! They're trying to demoralize the prisoners, destroy all hope in them. A South Vietnamese soldier, a ranger here for several months, believes the "information" no more than the other prisoners.

How does poet Nguyen Chi Thien react in the same camp? They know only that he's still memorizing the poems he composes:

> *Painful, this century's great error*
> *In a thousand years*
> *History will never stop talking of*
> *The many decades of blood and tears*
> *What have the people gained—*
> *Only a vocabulary to delude idiots?*
> *Painful, this century's great error*
> *In a thousand years*
> *History will never stop talking of*
> *The coolie promoted to worker*
> *Soldier promoted to fighter*
> *Porter or stevedore—*
> *They labor under the same load*
> *Forever starving*
> *Forever poor*
> *Always ready for sacrifice on the field of battle.*[9]

The prisoner Nguyen Ky will admit six months later that Saigon has become Ho Chi Minh City. The news will be confirmed by Southern prisoners, one of them a lieutenant colonel born in the same village as Ky.

In Washington, agencies under Ambassador Bill Brown, who's supervising the task force assigned to refugees and their problems, have installed a toll-free line: (800) 368-1180 rings constantly.

At the State Department a special command center has been in operation for several days. The personnel catch a few hours' sleep on quickly improvised camp beds. Like most of his colleagues, Douglas Pike is almost literally in shock. The whole thing passes understanding.

At the Pentagon career soldiers have no comment, or send reporters to a spokesman at the Defense Department or, preferably, the State Department. Most of the officers think responsibility for the outcome of the war lies with politicians and not soldiers. The politicians often attribute that responsibility to the press.

While the last wave of helicopters is evacuating the last Americans, White House press aides announce that President Ford has been meeting with a delegation of sheep and turkey ranchers. Coyotes are giving them a lot of trouble.

"It must have eased the tension," some of his staff explain; he's spent an hour and ten minutes with the ranchers.

Ford issues a soothing statement for the media. The evacuation is complete; the U.S. marines and Ambassador Martin have done their duty, done it very well, under difficult conditions. "I ask all Americans to close ranks, to avoid recrimination about the past."

Henry Kissinger holds his televised press conference in the Executive Office Building near the White House. During the last four months, and especially in the last forty-eight hours, a major element of *his* Vietnam policy has collapsed.

"Until Sunday night [April 27]," says Kissinger, "we thought a negotiated solution was highly probable. But sometime Sunday night, the North Vietnamese obviously changed signals." They then pressed to a quick military solution. "We succeeded in evacuating something on the order of 55,000 South Vietnamese."

The secretary of state goes to great pains to show that the enemy continually modified his diplomatic position: "The communist demands have been escalating as the military situation has changed in their favor."

At first the communists said there could be no negotations unless Thieu departed. Then, unless Huong departed. Later, Duong Van Minh seemed acceptable. In the end, he was rejected.

The "cell of the diplomatic offensive" in Hanoi has done its work well.

A reporter asks Kissinger, "Do you now favor American aid in rebuilding North Vietnam?"

The secretary of state slips the question a bit; a qualified no.

"How about South Vietnam?"

"We will have to see what kind of government emerges; and, indeed, whether there's going to be a South Vietnam."

On April 30, Henry Kissinger writes to Mme. Lioanaes, secretary for the Nobel Peace Prize. The secretary of state wants to return his prize, the title and the money. The Norwegian committee will refuse. Later events do not at all diminish their esteem for Kissinger's sincere efforts in trying to establish a cease-fire in 1973.

For Kissinger, the man and the stateman, the fall of Saigon represents the most important, very painful and public failure of his career.

Since May 1968 the Provisional Revolutionary Government of South Vietnam has occupied a villa at Verrières-le-Buisson, near Paris. There, Mme. Nguyen Thi Binh, La Pasionaria of the resistance, impresses and charms the international media. The minister of foreign affairs now holds a press conference. A Frenchman brings up the problem of settling scores in South Vietnam. Mme. Binh answers,

> There will not be any. We know that in France and other European countries there was a settling of scores with Nazi collaborators. A natural, human reaction. Our enemies have committed bloody crimes. They have tortured, killed and violated the families of their victims. Those who would have the most scores to settle are the revolutionaries. We have taught our people not to succumb to vengeance.

For the skeptics she adds: "In the last thirty years, we have made so many sacrifices that to deny ourselves vengeance is a little thing by comparison—especially when the price is national reconciliation. We are drawing a line through the past."

With friends from the General Association of Vietnamese Students in Paris, Tran Van Ba goes to the embassy of the former Republic of South Vietnam on the avenue de Villiers. The ambassador, Nguyen Duy Quang, is going to resign. Ba tells him: "I am going to carry on the fight, with the other students. Help us!"

The ambassador gives him a check—drawn on an account that has no funds. Ba knows that the embassy will soon be handed over to authorities from Hanoi. Going from floor to floor with his friends, he sorts through the archives, burns some dossiers. He talks about fighting, not about accepting defeat.

It is his first action as a member of the resistance. Because their mother lives in Saigon, Ba's brother Tran Van Tong in Paris cautions him: "The communists can take it out on her."

From that day forward, between the apartment in the ramshackle building in Bourg-la-Reine where he lives and the office of the association, rue Monge in Paris, Ba makes contacts, writes, hopes, reflects, and despairs. He wants to whip up resistance among the Vietnamese in France and the worldwide diaspora. A socialist former schoolfellow of his at the Lycée Yersin asks him, "How can you go up against the whole machinery of a military police state with fifty years of experience?"

Ba's brother plays devil's advocate: "Is this the right time for that kind of resistance? You're trying to swim the ocean."

Ba smiles: "It's not the hardest way to cross. When Ho, Giap and Dong began their work there were only four or five of them. The communist movement was feeble. The common people encouraged them."

Ba doesn't accept the fall of Saigon. He doesn't want to be stripped of his future. If the Vietnamese won't help one another, who'll help them? Today abroad, as yesterday in Vietnam, the Vietnamese are divided. Too often they refuse to unite. Resist they must. But how? Must they take up arms again, Ba wonders, and inflict more suffering on the people?

23

Breaking Stones
To Mend the Sky

Exactly twenty-five years ago, on May 1, 1950, President Harry Truman signed documents that "authorized" the first official U.S. military aid for Indochina.

Five months later, in September 1950, a group of U.S. military advisers landed in Saigon.

Since 4 A.M. this May 1, 1975, the Saigonese have been gathering or are being gathered in front of the presidential palace. The new authorities have decided to celebrate "the victory of the Vietnamese people."

Writer Duyen Anh walks around. Here North Vietnamese soldiers, the *bo doi*, chat cheerfully with civilians. Farther along, at headquarters of the Association of Vietnamese Writers, rue Doan Thi Diem, a banner covers the façade: "Association of Patriotic Vietnamese Writers." At the Vietnamese Journalists Union, rue Tu Do, the Champs-Elysées of Saigon, another banner: "Union of Patriotic Journalists." How many writers and journalists, Duyen Anh wonders, are going to change sides? How many would rather live new lives as masons or pedicab drivers than write for the new press? Farther along, Duyen Anh notes a dozen coffins containing *bo doi*.

The new authorities have not invited civil servants to celebrate May Day. Engineer Van goes to his office. The only perceptible change, aside from a number of absentees, is the presence of *bo doi* armed with AK-47s, and everywhere the *can bo*, North Vietnamese cadres. A *can bo* and several *bo doi* flank each agency chief or manager at the Ministry of Public Works. With distinct Northern accents, the cadres claim to be qualified

388

engineers or doctors. Some went to Hanoi after the Geneva Accords in 1954. They ask how the former ministry used to operate.

Everybody gets down to work. The *can bo's* incompetence surprises the engineer. They're ignorant of certain mathematical formulas. When the engineer talks about metals from up North, these cadres mention minerals unknown in Vietnam.

Other cadres proceed to the Quan The Am pagoda. "Go home," they tell the refugees. The bonze Thien Hue notes differences between the PRG guerrillas and the North Vietnamese regulars. The former wear motley uniforms, the latter are better dressed. The *bo doi* are polite; talking to adults, they refer to themselves by the familiar term *con*, child. The guerrillas are distant, even arrogant.

Sergeant Thuong is pedaling along the road to Cap Saint-Jacques. In the torrid heat he passes burned out vehicles and tanks, corpses too. Weapons, shoes, pieces of South Vietnamese uniform are scattered everywhere. On his baggage rack the sergeant has taken up a girl and a younger child, both unknown to him. They're stopped every ten kilometers. The April 30ths are setting up barricades and checking everyone who comes through. The sergeant has left Saigon for good and now wonders what he's going to do. He spends 500 piastres for a cup of coffee and 500 for a glass of milk for the child. The sergeant has drawn his last pay, 18,000 piastres. A ferryboat crosses near a collapsed bridge. The sergeant separates from the girl and child, who switch to a Lambretta.

Colonel Hoa returns to the radio and television center in Saigon, where some fifty employees are gathered. Many of them are wearing their uniforms, navy blue pants and sahara jackets. Outside the gate armed civilians are on guard. In his office, the former head of television meets a civilian and the former second in command of MR 2, General Pham Dinh Thu, who announces to the surprised director: "I am part of the Saigon Revolutionary Committee."

North Vietnamese soldiers are roaming the corridors. The colonel introduces himself to some North Vietnamese officers as friendly as they are astonished. Hoa is in civilian clothes: "I'm a colonel, director of television, radio and cinematography. I'm here to transfer power."

"Good," they answer. "Can we broadcast?"

"I'll go see. I'll check out the equipment."

The equipment is in working order. There are enough technicians. So they can broadcast. The director has come back to protect his employees. Perhaps the conquerors will be understanding. Why not try to cooperate?

At North Vietnamese general headquarters, Dung and his staff are celebrating the liberation of the South and International Labor Day at one time. There's a buffet with cakes, candy, sodas and syrups. Pham Hung spies a bottle of spirits. One of the commander in chief's aides explains its presence: "We're celebrating Van Tien Dung's birthday at the same time."

There is no gunfire whatsoever. This part of the forest is calm. Pham

Hung proposes a toast: "I raise my glass to all those to whom we owe this day of glory. All praise to President Ho Chi Minh! All praise to our heroic party, its central committee . . ."

The commander in chief heads for Saigon in his car. He's amused by the South Vietnamese motto on the barracks' pediment: "Honor. Responsibility. Country."

At ARVN staff headquarters, as at the Directorate-General of Police, Dung notes, "We found the files of the enemy commanders' top secret documents. Their modern computer with its famous memory containing bio-data on each officer and soldier in their million-plus army was still running. American computers had not won in this war. The intelligence and will of our nation had won completely." Dung proceeds to Camp Davis, where, in the press room, he calls together the commanders and political commissars of all four NVA corps.

From his command post General Tra "continues to direct mopping up of the last [South Vietnamese] troops regrouped in companies, and sometimes batallions, in the jungle and scrub around Saigon."

Tra receives a message: "Brother Ba"—Le Duan—announces . . . that Tra will preside over the military committee of Saigon–Gia Dinh. Tra must hurry to the capital.

On his arrival in Ho Chi Minh City, he goes to the presidential palace. But before starting work, he takes a tour of the capital. Back at the palace he gives orders, by command of the Politburo, to release the leaders of the last short-lived South Vietnamese government, President Minh, Vice-President Nguyen Van Huyen, Prime Minister Vu Van Mau. He gives them a short moralizing lecture explaining that the political line of "the revolution is just, dignified, moderate and tolerant. It uses justice to counteract brutality and replaces cruelty by humanity." Let bygones be bygones. General Tra has the feeling that his listeners are "moved." According to him, Minh said, "I am happy to be a citizen of independent Vietnam." Minh maintains he never did.

And Nguyen Van Huyen affirms, "As a citizen of Vietnam, I am proud of the nation's glorious success and victory."

Et cetera. In his memoirs General Tra exaggerates. A man like Huyen had never been able to stomach expressions like "glorious success." In their desire to standarize history, North Vietnamese leaders never lend enough importance to simple realism. General Minh simply said: "The Front deserves its victory. We've all worked for the same cause, reconciliation and concord of the Vietnamese people, and for peace in Vietnam."

The new authorities don't quite trust the last president's enthusiastic good wishes. He is placed under house arrest. No reporter is allowed to see him. The same conditions apply to the former vice-president and prime minister.

The first television broadcast is at 7 P.M. and lasts half an hour: several shots of PRG men while the new national anthem plays, and some news.

They didn't hire the woman announcers Colonel Hoa tried to find jobs for. They told him, "You're a technical adviser now. Come in every day."

Later in the week he sees the arrival of a man (surrounded by guards) whom one addresses as *anh Chin*, or "Ninth Brother." It is the poet To Huu, a member of the central committee. Huu chats with the former director of television and tours the studios. He asks Hoa, "What do you think of the music we're turning out in Hanoi?"

"Your music seems Chinese."

One of To Huu's aides jumps up. Another goes to a piano and plays a tune: "That's Chinese?"

"Yes," says Hoa.

He tinkles another tune.

"And that?"

"No. Not that one."

To Huu leaves.

The *bo doi* wander all over the city buying Bic pens, watches, transistor radios; they're discovering the consumer society. The Saigonese are reassured; these *bo doi* are kind and rather naive. Civil servants from Hanoi are cataloguing and classifying businesses. Plantations are classed K1, factories K9. . . .

A North Vietnamese officer introduces himself to Doctor-Colonel Fourré at the Grall Hospital: "I am General Hung. Will you agree to take care of our sick?"

"Of course."

"How much will it cost us?"

"For you, no charge."

Delighted, the general asks that his wounded be placed aside, in a special pavilion. They are assigned a young French military doctor. In the hospital's morgue lie the corpses of Generals Phu and Nam.

Many South Vietnamese neither sick nor wounded, and many police, crowd the gardens of the Grall Hospital.

Le Duan and Vo Nguyen Giap land at Tan Son Nhut. They embrace the political victor, Le Duc Tho, and the military victor, General Dung.

The radio has announced that the city "should be a revolutionary city, civilized, clean, healthy, cheerful and fresh." By the old rule of obligatory volunteer service, students go to it, armed with shovels, buckets and rice-straw brooms. Previous inscriptions are covered by cloth banners: "Long Live Free Saigon." "Peace, Independence, Democracy, Prosperity." "Long Live the People and the Army United To Build Socialism."

In the disciplined rejoicing of this liberation, which a number of Saigonese (a number hard to estimate) see as only an occupation, see as the entry of Northerners, Tonkinese, early omens in the takeover go unnoticed. Many of the Third Force, like Father Chan Tinh, who sent Amnesty International the files on South Vietnamese prisons, are kept isolated. An Italian journalist, Tiziano Terzani, meets a twenty-two-year-old student,

Nguyen Thi Man, who had been deported to Poulo Condor.[1] She is taking "classes." Evidently liberated members of the Third Force are not free.

Slowly, meticulously, bureaucratically, Saigon's arrondissements are divided into sectors, quarters, groups, families. At each level a leader is designated. A security (*cong an*) agent keeps vigil. The population is divided into categories, from 9 to 12 years old, 13 to 16, 17 to 33, 34 to 60, 61 to 88. Everyone arriving in Ho Chi Minh City must be registered. If they spend a night, they need permission. Police-state control clamps down on the city like the grid of a waffle iron.

"Liberation families" join the Hanoi cadres, move into hotels and villas and hang their laundry around the swimming pools at the Cercle Sportif. The Provisional Revolutionary Government has dropped the word "provisional," but it doesn't seem to be governing. Everywhere, at the power station as well as the post office, PRG people are backed up by one and sometimes two North Vietnamese stand-ins. There's no shortage of gasoline; there's a six months' reserve. There's a shortage of money: no one can withdraw more than 10,000 piastres from his bank. Sugar is selling for 2,000 piastres a kilo. The North Vietnamese discover four treasures: bikes, television sets, electric fans and refrigerators. The boats tied up at Saigon's docks fill up with furniture, appliances, mopeds, motorcycles, air conditioners.

A well-known actress, Kim Cuong, shows up in an NVA colonel's uniform. An, the *Time* reporter, perfectly at home, hobnobs with dignitaries of the military committee running the city.

Foreigners, diplomats, reporters and people from aid organizations hunt for but never find the PRG, the phantom revolutionary government. Military government has set up in the former South Vietnamese Directorate-General of Police, guarded by the security service in orange-pink uniforms. These police are less friendly than the rank-and-file *bo doi*. Ambassador Graham Martin's residence is converted to headquarters of the Revolutionary Committee of the first arrondissement, and the Hotel Star to a military brothel, despite the calls for virtue spilling from loudspeakers all day long.

Some Saigonese wait patiently. After all, the new leaders have problems: they have to repatriate refugees and repair the administrative machinery and the economy. You've got to trust them and wait. Overvalued the first weeks against the South Vietnamese piastre and the dollar, North Vietnamese money, the *dong*, drops. The dollar holds firm. At the official rate, 1.85 dong equals $1 American. On the black market, $1 buys 20 dong.

Other Saigonese note signs of communization. Nationalizations are announced. Puritanical regulations are published about the length of your hair. No one can fight the nationalizations, but the Saigonese very quickly reject or ignore the hair code.

The North has conquered the South. The South is resisting, and will slowly "corrupt" the North.

On the morning of May 7, the *Pioneer Commander* makes port in Guam.

On her voyage, three children die and three babies are born. An eleven-year-old girl on board, a handicapped orphan, Vu Le Thu, is adopted by the marines. Supervising the debarkation of his 4,670 refugees, Captain Moyher draws up his report. The children's deaths were the worst aspect. The ship was ravaged by an epidemic of conjunctivitis that infected a number of sailors.

The refugees present Detachment India with a set of lacquered trays accompanied by a letter:

> May 7, 1975
> To: the Seventh Communications Battalion Marine Corps
> From: The refugees from South Vietnam aboard the
>   *Pioneer Commander*
>
> This is a very modest emblem of our deep appreciation
> for the act of knighthood as proved by this Battalion in the
> utmost emergency occasion when a cry for help has been
> answered. . . . No words would be enough for us to ex-
> press our thanks. . . . The marines were always there when
> we needed them most. . . . They were there to hold the
> babies when their parents were stepping up aboard. . . .
> They were there when somebody was sick and needed im-
> mediate doctor's care. . . . And most of all, their smile
> was on their face even though they had been working
> around the clock. There was no question whatsoever on
> race discrimination or on superiority complex. . . . We
> would like very much to have them as our friends . . .
> please accept this simple gift as a souvenir from your
> friends in the most crucial period of friendship.

The marines board buses.[2] They will leave for Okinawa three days later.

During a prerecorded interview on NBC's *Today* show May 8, Henry Kissinger says he will not resign: to leave in a time of unrest, when we are searching for a line of conduct, while foreign nations watch—he thinks it would be no service to his country to bow out, inasmuch as the president has confidence in him and has asked him to stay. After a good look at the accomplishments of recent years with China, with the Soviet Union, in the field of energy, in bringing troops home from Vietnam, in bringing back POWs and in initiating a process that will lead to peace in the Middle East, he doesn't think it would be fair to say that his foreign policy has failed. . . . Most American setbacks, many reverses, are due to problems of domestic politics.

Whatever their setbacks, great modern states go on living and survive their failures. The next day Philip Habib writes an "action" memo for the secretary of state. The United States has asked France to represent them in Vietnam. The French have agreed but are waiting for approval from the Saigon authorities before making the decision official. Ho Chi Minh City's government assigns Algeria to take charge of South Vietnamese assets in the United States.

Habib discerns three categories of immediate problems: (1) the 900 military listed as missing and the 1,400 American dead whose bodies have not been found; (2) about 50 Americans who remain in South Vietnam: 9 civilians taken prisoner at Ban Me Thuot and Phan Rang, as well as the missionaries, reporters, doctors and nurses who voluntarily remained in Vietnam; (3) the U.S. government and American businesses have assets of about $100 million in South Vietnam.

Also, $50–100 million has been deposited in American banks by Vietnamese banks. There are other South Vietnamese deposits in foreign banks, probably about $40 million worth. The South Vietnamese Embassy in Washington and the consulates in New York and San Francisco, including their bank accounts, are worth about $3 million.

Shall they agree to the Algerians' taking charge of South Vietnamese property in the United States? Among the arguments for the arrangement: Americans would preserve a line of communication with ex-Saigon, the Algerians would be pleased, the United States would keep its options open "with a view to a future resumption of relations."

Against the arrangement: the United States would implicitly recognize that the authorities in ex-Saigon legitimately represent South Vietnam. In the United States and abroad this would perhaps be seen as a hasty and inappropriate decision.

At any rate from May 9 the State Department, in the person of Philip Habib, is not excluding a normalization of relations, in time, with the new Vietnam. Among modern states, cold monsters all, the United States is the least vindictive.

May 15 is the eighty-fifth anniversary of Ho Chi Minh's birth. Celebrations of Ho Chi Minh City's liberation begin. They are to last several days. A grandstand is erected before the presidential palace, framed in flags and green plants.

Under a brilliant sun at eight in the morning you can see the elderly Ton Duc Thang, honorary president of the Democratic Republic of Vietnam, former mutineer in the Black Sea, now sheltered beneath a parasol on the grandstand. At his side are PRG Prime Minister Huynh Tan Phat, with short gray hair, Nguyen Huu Tho, president of the NLF, and Mme. Binh, minister of foreign affairs. Le Duc Tho is smiling, like General Tra, beside officers in dress uniforms of light gray, caps with red bands, chests covered with medals in the Soviet style. The archbishop of Saigon pales beside several Buddhist venerables. Pierre Brochand, the French diplomat, is at the foot of the grandstand. Riding around on his bike, he saw President Tho of the NLF in an official car, driving around the capital like a tourist.

Before the parade PRG president Phat makes a speech in which the world learns that the new government in the South will be democratic, will build friendly relations with all countries and will respect differences of opinion and belief.

There is a superb military parade. Some PRG guerrilla units lead the march with assorted armament. There are not many of these PRG men. On the stand Truong Nhu Tang, PRG minister of justice, is bewildered: "But where are our divisions?"

Around General Tra they burst out laughing: "Reunification is complete; the soldiers from the Front have been integrated."

T-54 and T-56 tanks, PT-76 amphibious tanks, SAM missiles towed by tractors gleam and glitter; so do the soldiers and sailors in white gloves.

People are still saying, "Vietnamese from Hanoi are our own kind, and the PRG even more. We'll come to an understanding."

"It will be to their advantage to accept a pluralist and neutralist South Vietnam."

Others temporize: "We have to wait. We'll see. You can't make an omelet without breaking eggs."

Still others: "Socialism, and therefore communism, has begun."

For reasons the authorities never explain, the liberation festivities are cut short.

Some who hated Thieu remember his slogan: "Don't listen to what the communists say, watch what they do." Many South Vietnamese and Saigonese, like General Vien in exile, are experiencing "what a mother must feel when her child dies accidentally."

A few *bo doi* are assassinated in the suburbs, most knifed. North Vietnamese patrols are reinforced. The security police patrol with radio sets or walkie-talkies taken from the enemy. Sometimes when they capture a thief they execute him and leave his body in public view, as an example.

Western literature, once sold in bookstores and sidewalk stalls, disappears. It will be burned later. Gradually volumes by *Mac* (Marx) and *Engel* (Engels) appear. By Lenin and Stalin too—Hanoi has never repudiated Joseph Stalin. And works by Northern thinkers appear, Le Duan first. Schools open. In each class Uncle Ho's five recommendations to children are posted: Love the country, love the people. Study well, work well. Cooperate well and observe discipline well. Respect rules of hygiene well. Be modest, frank, vigilant.

Vigilance often consists of denouncing your parents, neighbors, friends.

Officials, policemen and soldiers of the former regime are assembled. They will be sent to *hoc tap* centers, schools for reeducation. It is announced officially that privates will spend three days there, noncoms two weeks, field officers three months. Security agents, torturers and certain generals could stay on, they say, for as long as three years.

As for the refugees fled abroad, the leaders in Ho Chi Minh City are torn between good riddance of a large number of potential dissidents and a desire to see this strayed flock return to their "democratic" and "pluralist" fold. They try to retrieve certain refugees. On May 25 Huynh Cong Tam, director of the PRG liaison office with the United Nations in Geneva, writes to the high commissioner for refugees, Sadruddin Aga Khan:

> Dear High Commissioner,
>
> You are no doubt aware that some tens of thousands of Vietnamese left South Vietnam a short time before the complete liberation of our country.
> Among these Vietnamese many were evacuated against their will, or were led to leave their country by lying propaganda. Also hundreds of Vietnamese children were uprooted from their country, this in violation of current international law. . . .

At various reassembly centers a few hundred refugees, in Guam for example, ask to go back. The United States is ready to repatriate them. Curtly the authorities in Ho Chi Minh City refuse them.[3] Hanoi's men may have spurned a historic opportunity to normalize their relations with the United States.

Which does not keep Pham Van Dong from calling for normalization on June 3. The prime minister sets conditions: the United States must grant economic aid to the two Vietnams. With cynical humor, the prime minister insists that the United States implement fully the cease-fire agreement of 1973.

History swallows up or scatters its vanquished. In Vietnam the victors knew how to wage war but not how to wage peace. The so-called democratic republic of Vietnam, aligned with the Soviet bloc, supported by the Soviet Union, is now one of the three poorest countries in the world and one of the tightest police states in Asia.

Among the exiles, the young do not trust their elders; and the latter too often denounce one another instead of working together: "He was a communist." "She worked for Thieu." "These were leftist Buddhists." "Those backed the die-hard Catholics." "He was a PRG minister." Like so many exile communities, the Vietnamese must recreate, or perhaps create, their nationalist and democratic unity.

Nguyen Van Thieu lives a middle-class life in London, though he has held a U.S. resident's card since 1985. He "keeps a low profile," as Americans say. On Thieu's arrival in Great Britain, a British Special Services agent assigned to investigate his fortune verified $200,000 and Mme. Thieu's many pieces of jewelery. Thieu travels, visits the United States and France, follows political developments in the Vietnamese diaspora. In particular he watches a rather unreal campaign by a group of Vietnamese jurists under the leadership of Professor Vu Quoc Thuc to "resume implementation of the Paris Accords [sic]." If by some chance there was serious talk about the agreement, Thieu might again become de jure president of half of Vietnam—in theory, of course. There are those who forget too easily that Thieu resigned. The Vietnamese diaspora, which can't even resolve its temperamental differences, sometimes undertakes wildly absurd projects, and other times approaches realism.

The bloodbath predicted before the fall of Saigon took place not during but *after* the takeover. Two researchers, Jacqueline Desbarats and Karl Jackson, have proved that there were at a minimum 65,000 executions, not to mention men and women who were virtually condemned to death when they were sent into appallingly unhealthy areas or used, without detectors, in minesweeping operations.[4]

Thieu's colleagues are scattered over all inhabited continents when they are not surviving or dead in the Vietnamese Gulag.

Cousin Hoang Duc Nha works for an American company in Chicago. He trades on a grand scale, an activity that takes him often to Beijing. Most of the South Vietnamese generals are living in the United States. Ex-prime minister Tran Thien Khiem and the ex-chairman of the Joint General Staff, Can Van Vien, have no material worries. Contrary to legend, that is certainly not true of a majority of field officers and generals. So Admiral Chung Tan Cang, last head of the navy, and General Le Quang Luong, brilliant airborne commander, live modestly in Bakersfield, California. Holding down jobs in the oil industry equivalent to foreman, they put in long hours. The ebullient Nguyen Cao Ky, quieter than he used to be, has not succeeded in business, but he has several attentive Arab friends. The last president of the senate, Tran Van Lam, owns a restaurant in Australia. Bui Diem, the itinerant sage, has published his memoirs. In Virginia, the last military governor of the Saigon region, who spent seven years in a reeducation camp, ponders his association with ARVN Colonel Pham Ngoc Thao, posthumously named Hero of the Liberation for having tried so often to destabilize the Saigon government.

Civilians and soldiers, men and women, known and unknown, have accepted their lot with dignity. A once-important colonel may be a night watchman. To their political problems are added private woes, often painful. Many South Vietnamese freed after ten years in camp discovered that their wives had divorced them unilaterally and legally.

After his surrender, Big Minh was not reeducated. Communist authorities authorized him to emigrate in 1981. Often accused of having stashed away thick rolls of bills in France, Duong Van Minh lives discreetly and almost in poverty in a Paris suburb. Poetic justice: this often hesitant (perhaps too scrupulous) politico lives in the rue du Téméraire—"street of the Reckless."

Until July 1975 engineer Van, come Stalinist hell or Leninist high water, goes on hoping that neutralists will win power in Ho Chi Minh City. He was sent to a camp, like so many civil servants. In 1977 he reached Paris.

Writer Duyen Anh, considered by the communists "as one of the ten most dangerous authors," is denied publication, then arrested and interned, of course without a trial. Official number 239 D TH6 TCT CTXM, Anh will be freed in 1981, thanks to the efforts of the PEN Club and Amnesty International. Arriving in France like the bonze Hue, Anh published *A Russian in Saigon* in 1986, his first book translated in the West, and then *Fanta Hill*. During a visit to the States he was attacked and seriously wounded by Vietnamese hecklers. The best Vietnamese literature—for how many years?—will be a literature of exile. Every totalitarian state has its Kundera. Anh was first translated by Jean Maïs. This missionary found himself imprisoned for nine months. Charge: "For traveling on a road without permission." Later, like all foreign priests, he was expelled from Vietnam.

At this writing over a million Vietnamese have dared the terrible adventure of the "boat people." At one time Hanoi claimed they were all middle-class, *compradores*, or embezzlers. Evidently in the North as in the South, peasants, small businessmen and workers also fled, an exodus without precedent in the history of Vietnam, where an attachment to your land, your village, your "stand of bamboo" is a fundamental value. Sergeant Thuong is also a "boat person." At Cap Saint-Jacques he learned to be a fisherman, married, embarked illegally in 1976, lost his family at sea, found it at last in Switzerland. Bearing laissez-passer #11 2517 TH1, police captain Pham Thin dropped from 65 to 49 kilos before he was liberated. He is manager, or rather cook, in a small restaurant in Pierrefitte, near Paris.

Two of the Three Musketeers are dead: Cao Giao, a refugee in Belgium after his time in prison, and M. Vuong, who settled in the United States. The third Musketeer, An, never said a word when the communists imprisoned Cao Giao. This third Musketeer, who was such a fine reporter for *Time*, was a North Vietnamese agent and some say a colonel in intelligence. Cao Giao nevertheless remained his friend, seeing in him "a deceived and disenchanted idealist." Even wounded and betrayed, friendship is often thicker than political quarrels. "We are Vietnamese," Cao Giao used to say, stroking his goatee.

Time resettled Mme. Tran Thi Nga in New York. In 1986, with Wendy

Wilder Larsen, she published a collection of poems in two voices, clear and shattering, deeply moving to all who had lived through Vietnam, dove or hawk. Mme. Nga writes of her life, her Vietnam and the United States:

> *We took the jobs available.*
> *My son-in-law, who had a law degree,*
> *sold the Electrolux vacuum cleaner*
> *demonstrated door to door.*
> *American people are afraid of Asians.*
> *They would not let him in.*

Mme. Nga writes to her mother:

> You always loved autumn in Hanoi. You like the chill. Not us. We've just had the coldest winter in the last hundred years. . . . Your grandson is three years old. . . . He speaks English so well it makes us sad. We've made a rule: we must speak Vietnamese in the house so the children don't forget their mother tongue.
>
> We've set up an altar to our father. We try to keep up the traditions. . . .
>
> We're well off here, but spiritually famished. We miss our country. We miss you most of all. If Buddha exists, we must pray, pray to be reunited.

Vietnamese generally adapt well in exile, better than Cambodians or Laotians. They integrate professionally, not socially. Almost all are haunted by return to their native country, like Mme. Nga.

In June 1987 Pham Van Dong gave up his post as prime minister at the age of eighty-one. He occupied it for thirty-one years. Le Duc Tho left the Politburo in 1986, at seventy-five. Both became "advisers to the Central Committee." Le Duc Tho did not succeed Le Duan as party secretary at the latter's death. But Le Duc Tho's brother, Mai Chi Tho, who ruled the Saigon region following the "liberation," is today on the Politburo. Sclerotic and almost mummified, Vietnamese communism has adapted many features of world communism. A government of old men, it is also familial, like Albanian, Romanian and North Korean communism. In Hanoi you can reconstruct vast families behind different identities or pseudonyms in the power struggle. Cut off from the outside world, primal Marxists, communist leaders in Hanoi reject *facts*. Yuri Zhivago, or rather Boris Pasternak, wrote: "Marxism is too little master of itself to be a science. . . . Marxism and objectivity? I do not know a movement more inward-looking and remote from facts than Marxism."

Men like Pham Van Dong, Le Duc Tho and especially Le Duan fell back within themselves, within their schemes and their prideful ignorance.

The least cultured *bo doi* arriving in Saigon soon discovered that the West and the capitalist system of free enterprise worked better for the dispossessed than did rigid Northern socialism. And the *bo doi* went home aware that they'd been duped, and introduced doubt in the North, even into the party machinery. You don't persuade the "masses" any more when you tell them that *all* the country's misfortunes today are due to the "rottenness" of "imperialism," or to the war, or to the weather. Vietnamese socialism was so disorganized that sometimes after the "liberation" there were shortages of cress and carp in Saigon's markets. The one grew in profusion in the countryside; the other pullulated in ponds everywhere. During the war there was never a shortage of either. Vietnamese socialism is not, as Lenin's formula had it, "electrification plus soviets," but production and distribution broken down by an insane theory of centralization and an automatically ineffective bureaucracy. You can't succeed by decreeing nationalization or collective farming one day and rescinding it a few years later.

The Vietnamese Republic is currently a beggar state at the mercy of a single sponsor, the Soviet Union, and its good will.

In unified Vietnam, "there is a great lack of essential goods and medicines. . . . Inability to fulfill many major objectives of the last five-year plan has affected all aspects of economic activity. . . . In general the economy is operating at half-capacity. . . . Natural resources have been wasted. . . . The environment is being destroyed. . . . Millions of workers are unemployed or underemployed. . . ."

Those are not the observations of nostalgic South Vietnamese or bourgeois journalists. They were made officially by Truong Chinh, next-to-last general secretary of the Communist Party, and by the authors of reports to the party congress in December 1986. The failure of economic reform is attributed "above all to the Central Committee, the Politburo and the government."

The reunifiers, the Vietnamese and communist conquerors, are consenting victims of their own dogmatism. The program of the Indochinese Communist Party in the 1930s provided for the unification of all Indochina. It was achieved. And to all the governments of Southeast Asia, Hanoi's men became the region's Prussians. Panzer-communism has always known the uses of force. Soviet tanks went into action in Berlin, Prague and Budapest: you could say these were large-scale police actions, intimidations. But the Vietnamese communists can claim one incontestable stroke of originality, backed by maniacal endurance: in a great historical first, they will have been the first communist country to wage war—with infantry, armor, heavy artillery, planes and helicopters—on another communist country. In Cambodia, by a logical boomerang, conventional Vietnamese units faced guerrilla warfare by the Khmer Rouge, Sihanouk's partisans and Son Sann.

Some in Hanoi say Vo Nguyen Giap opposed this lurch into the Cambodian quagmire; that may be one reason why he was superseded. But mainly he was a sick man. His successor, General Dung, hero of the Ho Chi Minh Campaign, went up the ladder and then stepped aside—or was set aside, à la Vietnamese, gently and without fanfare—long after he published his picturesque account of the fall of Saigon. His subordinate, General Tra, took retirement earlier. He also published his *Memoirs*—volume 5 before the others, 10,000 copies printed in 1982 but never reissued in Ho Chi Minh City because Tra, a relatively free mind by communist standards, gave the PRG too fat a part and questioned some of Dung's theories, even the image of the blossoming lotus. Tra lived in a housing complex for cadres near Saigon. He was seen at the festivities commemorating the tenth aniversary of "liberation" in 1985. He was not "available for interviews." Pham Hung, the politico who worked with Tra in the South during the last months before the fall of Saigon, was number two in the Politburo and prime minister before dying, number one being the new secretary general, Nguyen Van Linh, known as The Tenth, Muoi Cuc, to his close friends.

After seventeen years in prison camp, Nguyen Ky made it to Ho Chi Minh City and then, he too a boat person, to the United States. A typographer, he barely gets by at Westminster in Orange County, California. He's still dreaming of "socialism with a human face." Young film buff Tien became bodyguard for his brother, a former PRG cadre; since 1977 Tien too has been living in Westminster. Very soon there were as many former communists or apoliticals as nationalists in the Vietnamese diaspora. A number of ruling dignitaries' relatives have left Vietnam: Truong Chinh's nieces sought shelter in France, the daughter of NLF president Nguyen Huu Tho in Canada. . . . So many repudiations.

Poet Nguyen Chi Thien has spent twenty-three of the last twenty-nine years in prison or in a camp. In June 1978 he was pardoned. He collected his works, sent them to the British Embassy in Hanoi and was in consequence arrested. He was still alive in January 1990, most likely in the Hoa Lo prison in Hanoi, the "Hanoi Hilton," where American prisoners of war were imprisoned and tortured.

Captain-Major Tran Ba Doai, after repairing the trucks that had to be restored to the Soviets and Czechs, was demoted to second lieutenant for "lack of enthusiasm" and expelled from the Party. He went to China. There he refused to join the new Vietnamese revolutionary army sponsored by the Chinese. In 1981 he went to Hong Kong, then to Great Britain.

Of all the Vietnamese communities around the world, Great Britain's seems saddest. No one can easily forget the forlorn look of these Sino-Vietnamese peasants drinking tea in sparsely furnished rooms in low-rent housing projects, watching television programs they don't understand. Vietnamese adapt well—sociologists acknowledge it—but some less well than others. How they dream of the California sun in England, and even of the pale winter sun in North Vietnam!

Today Gerald Ford is less praised than Richard Nixon. The one comes off badly in history for presiding over the fall of Saigon; the other comes off better as a venerable geopolitician. History doesn't pay moral dividends to men of state.

When you meet him in the offices of Kissinger Associates on Park Avenue, Henry Kissinger doesn't seem altogether reconciled to his exile from the corridors of power, from affairs that never were or will be foreign to him. He once said that "power is the supreme aphrodisiac." Interviewed, published, consulted, received with enthusiasm even by Gorbachev in Moscow, Kissinger talks about Vietnam gravely and sometimes with a subdued perplexity.

Graham Martin still seemed very bitter in 1984. He was not given a new post after he left Vietnam. No doubt he had reached retirement age, but to succeed to another embassy he'd have had to appear before the Senate. That was to be avoided at any price so soon. At Winston-Salem in North Carolina, Martin brooded over his memories, still believing he was right all along. After his ordeal he saw Kissinger once, for half an hour. And, he said with grating humor, "Henry spent twenty-five of those thirty minutes talking on the phone with [columnist] James Reston."

On Christmas Day in 1985, the phone rang at Martin's home: Thieu was on the line, to offer season's greetings. He assured Martin of his friendship.

Martin is on bad terms with Thomas Polgar, who worked in Rome, Bonn, Mexico and Washington, where he ended his thirty-eight-year career as head of personnel in the CIA. Polgar was extremely uncomfortable with William Casey's style—a favorite of Ronald Reagan and in his turn director of the CIA. Polgar became a "consultant" in Washington. He was appointed an investigator in the Irangate scandal in 1987. Lehmann became a consul-general in West Germany.

The CIA persecuted Frank Snepp when he published *Decent Interval*. Snepp violated the oath of secrecy and was too critical of U.S. authorities. In a classically petty move the CIA initiated judicial proceedings, as a result of which Snepp received no book royalties. He teaches [1987] at a small California university. Sometimes he opposes William Colby, head of the CIA in 1975, in courteous public debates.

Old Saigon hands from the U.S. Embassy go through life trailing clouds of disputation.

All the Americans involved in the fall of Saigon were entitled to two extra weeks of vacation. Most of them continued their careers. Some are ambassadors. Many keep in touch with Vietnamese abroad. Some are still trying to help friends or acquaintances leave communist Vietnam legally.

Philippe Richer stayed in Hanoi until May 1976. President Valéry Giscard d'Estaing didn't take to him at all, and complained: "Who is this man who keeps saying the same thing?" The right wing shelved Richer. He served on the Conseil d'Etat (France's highest administrative court) and published important works about Asia. His counterpart in Saigon, Jean-Marie Mérillon, left Vietnam in May 1975. On leaving he was searched. He was given fine embassies, Athens, Algiers. Mérillon then went to Berne, and a promotion. Now he is in Moscow, a superb post. Pierre Brochand is now a very active delegate to the French mission at the United Nations.

In Singapore, Patrick Hays supervises shipments of natural rubber to the Michelin group. He revisited Saigon in 1987 and visited Hanoi for the first time.

All these people have heard about one another, or know each other somewhat, or have met. Some, a long time ago, met the resister Tran Van Ba.

Since his recall to Moscow in April 1986, Anatoly Dobrynin is on the Central Committee as secretary for relations with the West. Observers detect his hand in Gorbachev's policies and notably in the introduction of *glasnost*. Well-informed, Dobrynin remains a master of disinformation.

Who is responsible for the fall of Saigon, for that dizzying debacle in the first four months of 1975? For an even worse defeat than Dien Bien Phu, since this time all Vietnam falls into the hands of Ho Chi Minh's heirs? Major historical events are always the result of many forces, of innumerable combined causes. For forty-five years the Vietnamese communists had one aim, and only one: to control all of former Indochina. During the second war in Vietnam, they used the NLF as a political screen, then the PRG. That let them distort or conceal an essential truth: they had appropriated the fight against colonialism. They were well armed by the Soviets and Chinese. Despite sometimes bitter dissension among Moscow, Beijing and Hanoi, the goal remained the same: to communize all of Vietnam, Cambodia and Laos, a grand design formulated by Ho in 1930.

Lost in the labyrinth of their internecine quarrels, divided by personal ambition, often treated as children by their American advisers, the South Vietnamese ruling class was never able to rally the people and the army to the cause of a democratic nationalism.

The Americans pressured the South Vietnamese to build a traditional regular army from 1954 to 1960, when the problem was to fight a guerrilla war. Later these same military strategists, one war behind, labored to create counterinsurgency units when the problem was more and more to fight conventional North Vietnamese divisions. Furthermore, the South Vietnamese army was never independent. Even when at its most bellicose it was not autonomous. It never had confidence in itself. Almost always it lacked morale. Clausewitz: "We must expressly emphasize that in speaking of the enemy's combat strength, nothing requires us to limit that notion to simple physical strength. On the contrary, it implies moral strength just as much, because both, down to the smallest details, are tightly merged and cannot be separated." To use an overused word, even between 1973 and 1975 Saigon's troops, tied by an umbilical cord to the U.S. military attaché's agencies, never felt themselves "Vietnamized."

On the other hand, the U.S. military commands in Saigon, Thailand, Honolulu and the Pentagon were unquestionably limited and "restrained" in the use of *traditional arms* by Washington politicians. Unquestionably military power must be subordinate to civil power; but can the latter demand the impossible of the former? Can one ask that a war be won with limited means, and without taking battle to the enemy? Clausewitz again: "You cannot introduce a moderating principle even into the theory of war without committing an absurdity."

In Washington a shilly-shallying Congress sidetracking or shackling the executive, and the media reporting well or badly what they saw of the war, discouraged American public opinion, at first in favor of intervention. Posing as David up against Goliath, Hanoi manipulated world opinion admirably and always fought on three fronts, military, political and diplomatic. Vietnamese communists profited by innumerable advocates, purposeful or unthinking; that was never true of Saigon. Hanoi could sow discord in the enemy camp. Democracies are badly equipped to fight that kind of war. Totalitarian regimes are always ready for it, whatever the human loss. In Hanoi there was no public opinion forcing leaders to include humanitarian considerations among the parameters of their decision-making processes.

Again Clausewitz: "Accident and hazard, and good luck too, play a large role in war." In 1974, the accident was Watergate, which stripped the U.S. presidency of its powers and destroyed Kissinger's work in Southeast Asia. Watergate was Cleopatra's nose. If Nixon, an unappealing personality but a great statesman, had remained in power, the Soviets would no doubt have played détente against the immediate interest of the North Vietnamese—these latter would not have abandoned their ultimate objective but at least Saigon would not have fallen in 1975. Now we can see rather clearly that neither Moscow nor Beijing was ready to risk a third world war for Hanoi.

Among the democracies, the Vietnamese conflict was badly analyzed in both its local aspects and geopolitical perspective. Today Laos, Cambodia and Vietnam are communist.

Should the United States have replaced the French in Vietnam after 1954? Probably not, and certainly not alone. The other democracies were no help to the United States. Before the fall of Saigon in 1975 the democratic parties to the Paris Agreement of 1973, France and Great Britain, did not support the United States and that demi-democracy which was South Vietnam.

The United States should have fought their war differently. Forbidding the bombing of Hanoi, refusing to invade the North, declaring unilateral cease-fires, halting aerial bombardment, the United States condemned itself to failure. From 1965 to 1968 President Lyndon Johnson ordered nine unilateral cease-fires and ten bombing halts.

Hanoi's communist leaders proclaimed that they "beat" the Americans. In a sense, the United States beat itself. This is not to suggest that they should have used tactical atomic weapons. But it should be pointed out that they never used the full range of their conventional weapons in waging an undeclared war, the longest and least understood in all their history, and the best covered—in the South—by the media.

Washington's limited military policy was based in part on errors of political analysis. To begin with, American geopoliticians believed that Hanoi was only an extension of Beijing. Later they persuaded themselves that if American and South Vietnamese armed forces intervened in the North, China and the Soviet Union would react violently. They did not want to risk a third world war over Vietnam.

For a long time, some American analysts said Ho Chi Minh and his successors were primarily nationalists. Major Archimedes Patti of the OSS, ancestor of the CIA, armed some of Ho Chi Minh's first 300 resistance fighters. A detachment of uniformed Americans, OSS men, entered Hanoi on August 25, 1945, alongside Vietminh troops. In his reports, Patti said Ho's partisans were "nationalist first and party members second."[5] At that time, the Americans considered Ho an honorable scout for the OSS, under the code name "Lucius."

During the nineteen years of the second war in Vietnam, Saigon's enemies were portrayed as a swarm of guerrillas. It was not jungle fighters in bare feet or Ho Chi Minh sandals that took Saigon but perfectly equipped North Vietnamese divisions with hundreds of armored vehicles.

The South Vietnamese army, they said, always lost ground through lack of courage. The battle for Xuan Loc shows how untrue that was, right up to the last moment. They said the South was swimming in corruption, in contrast to the so virtuous North. There was doubtless plenty of that in military as well as civilian circles, but it was not institutionalized and structural as in the North. They said the Republic of South Vietnam was a dictatorship. The Democratic Republic of Vietnam was the dictatorship. In the South—and the first four months of 1975 prove it even if by caricature—there existed a parliament, a press and a judicial system, all very imperfect but unquestionably superior to what could be found in the North. Politicians in Saigon like Senate president Lam insisted that the republic in the South was capable of developing its democratic institutions. Half-democracy, half-dictatorship, certainly an authoritarian regime, this South Vietnamese republic had neither the time nor often the will to prove it. Recent history, especially in unified Vietnam, proves that no communist regime ceases being communist, or democratizes itself, except by very temporary fits and starts, with or without *glasnost*. On the other hand, authoritarian regimes of the right are biodegradable. Salazar's Portugal, Franco's Spain, the colonels' Greece, and most recently almost all of Latin

America have passed or are passing from authoritarianism to liberal democracy. Even General Pinochet's days are numbered. This is one of the fundamental differences between communist totalitarianism and right-wing authoritarianism. During the fall of Saigon, Solzhenitsyn[6] shocked the left by stating that one was freer under Franco than in the Soviet Union. And yet it was true. It's one of the truths the noncommunist left hasn't yet accepted or integrated into its analyses—a left-wing that includes, among others, those Americans who militated for the Hanoi Politburo, generously and in good faith, right up to April 30, 1975, and thought they were defending a PRG that proved its pluralism. A number of Vietnamese, too, including political experts, were seduced by the communist sirens and the PRG's noisy good intentions, as Professor Tran Van Dinh[7] has demonstrated so clearly.

When we consider the war in Vietnam and especially its last episode, the fall of Saigon, a revisionist history is essential. It is not a matter of choosing between totalitarianism and authoritarianism, one as unacceptable as the other. Nor of denying the errors, even the crimes, of the United States or of Saigon's successive governments. It is a matter of dispelling the cloud of disinformation that obscures the history of Southeast Asia in the second half of the twentieth century.

South Vietnamese resistance up to April 30, 1975, will not have been useless. Without it a number of countries in Southeast Asia, among them Thailand, Malaysia and Singapore, would have had no time to develop economically and so reduce chances of a communist takeover. Today in Southeast Asia no citizen, no peasant in the most remote hamlet, is unaware that the present regime in Vietnam is economically ineffectual, especially for the underprivileged, and a perfect police-state for all.

We can speculate and ask questions that no one can answer. What would have happened if President Woodrow Wilson, in Versailles, had agreed to see an Indochinese in a morning coat who was calling for Vietnamese independence? Ho Chi Minh—it was he—was then *perhaps* more nationalist than communist. A dozen years later Ho, steeped in Leninism, would react first and always as a communist.* In democracies political consciousness is a fluctuating variable. It took forty years to see the Gulag in Russia, thirty to recognize it in China. Three years were enough to reveal concentration camps all over Vietnam.

During that second Vietnam war, two peoples, the Americans and Vietnamese, met in the worst possible historical circumstances. Despite their good will, sometimes frank and sometimes brutal, Americans in Washington knew next to nothing about Vietnam or its culture. And the South Vietnamese knew next to nothing about American culture or institutions. Americans appeared to be first and foremost anticommunist crusaders. But they were incomprehensible behind their democratic and liberal

* See Appendix VI.

talk. President John Kennedy upheld idealistic notions yet shrugged off the assassination of President Diem. To many South Vietnamese the United States represented mainly the godsend of a sort of eternal Marshall Plan—dollars, Coca-Cola, blue jeans and study grants.

And also the horrors of the war, waged at first with enthusiasm, then with rising skepticism, sometimes with cynicism in the face of suffering and atrocities. Many Vietnamese remember the folkloric epigrams of war. Rhetoric from an officer after a battle that razed a small town: "We had to destroy Ben Tre to save it." The black humor and slogans of the U.S. Special Forces: "If you kill for money, you're a mercenary. If you kill for pleasure, you're a sadist. If you kill for both, you're a Green Beret."

Richard Nixon[8] has written that Vietnam was a tragedy for the Americans. No doubt, but it was first—and still is—a tragedy for the Vietnamese. When Saigon was about to fall, Ambassador Graham Martin said that it would not be "all that pleasant to be an American in Saigon." It was most difficult of all to be South Vietnamese. For the astonishing Vietnamese people, that war is still a festering wound, a poison still toxic.

For the living, the survivors, there are memories, dreams, bitterness. No one can forget either the bravado of well-known politicians or the bravery of unknown soldiers. Too many Vietnamese had neither childhood nor adolescence. Of American civilization and culture many Vietnamese still in Vietnam, especially rural folk, have retained only wartime codewords—M-16 rocket, C-4 explosive, a few words of American jargon, *mama san, papa san, gooks*.

Full of remorse and frustrations, the U.S. military, career or conscript, rarely tackled the logical problem of a people's war as waged by the communist enemy. Women, children, old people were killed and sometimes massacred. For the communists, each woman, child, oldster was a potential soldier. Many American soldiers who killed civilians, in cold blood or hot rage, thought—consciously or not—It's a goddam shame to kill these people but it will be a worse goddam shame if you don't kill them and the grenade the woman hid in the basket explodes in your face, or your buddy's blown to bits by a land mine.

In the West they glorified the communist war effort. They played down communist massacres, especially those in Hue in 1968, or tortures and executions in the villages. There were no Western eyewitnesses, as when American, French, British, Italian and German reporters, doing their jobs at great personal risk, cameras often in hand, testified to the excesses of U.S. or South Vietnamese troops. The North Vietnamese often spoken of their own "clemency." Only with the return of American prisoners would we learn how they had been tortured morally and physically; and *their* accounts were given no publicity in Europe. Only with the appearance of the film *Platoon* in 1987 would we see an American soldier crucified, literally, by communist soldiers.[9]

In the heart of Washington, not far from the Potomac River, almost

equidistant from the State Department and the Lincoln Memorial, lies the
most moving of monuments to the dead. It does not *rise*, pompous or
grandiloquent. It is half buried in an immense lawn. Squirrels scamper
here and there. In springtime tulips, jonquils and cherry trees bloom all
about. On seventy slabs of black marble are engraved the names of 58,022
Americans dead in Vietnam or reported missing. Simple, almost discreet,
this monument does not glorify the war. It recalls it, reminding us above
all that war kills. To win approval for this too modern and simple masterpiece, the authorities had to erect a more conventional sculpture a bit
farther on: three soldiers, one of them black, wearing bulletproof vests
and carrying machineguns.

When you walk along those black marble slabs, you hear planes landing
and taking off constantly. Washington's National Airport is nearby, and
you cannot help remembering the aerial ballet of planes and helicopters
at Tan Son Nhut—where today Bears, Soviet strategic bombers, sit waiting.

New names are still being engraved on the black marble slabs. On Slab
11W appears the name of Second Lieutenant Richard Van de Geer. His
helicopter was shot down on May 15, 1975, by the Khmer Rouge, who
had taken the American merchant ship *Mayaguez* by force.

In Ho Chi Minh City the monument to the Vietnamese soldier, near
the theater where the National Assembly sat, was demolished. Communist
authorities raised monuments to their dead elsewhere.

There does not exist a monument commemorating South Vietnamese
soldiers—much less, of course, a monument reminding us of a new
resistance.

After five years of reflection and preparation, Tran Van Ba, former
president of the General Association of Vietnamese Students in Paris,
weary of discussions in exiles' living rooms in London, Washington and
elsewhere, decided to commit himself further, to carry his resistance to
Vietnam itself.

On June 6, 1980, he takes off for Thailand. From Bangkok he disappears
into the underground, which leads him to Cambodia and Vietnam. Ba is
not an intellectual, but he has elaborated his own political philosophy. It
doubtless expresses the hopes of a majority of Vietnamese today. Ba advocates a "Swedish sort of social-liberal" system. Romantic, sure of himself, reckless, he sends a letter from Ho Chi Minh City on June 6, 1982:
"I am well. It's a hard life. That's true: it's a very hard life. But I am at
ease with myself and committed to our poor, unhappy, starving country."
For Ba the future of Vietnam "will be the work of resisters at home . . .
and not of politicians in exile." In another letter he asks to be sent a book
by Gérard Chaliand "on guerrilla strategy." He's forgotten the title, but
on the cover, a Goya, "there is a man who has been shot."

For the long run Ba is betting on the decay of the Vietnamese Communist Party and its privileged leaders. He worries about the aberrations

possible in any resistance, the risks of terrorism, white or red. How do you keep your hands clean? To his companions, a handful of resisters, he says, "Resistance can't solve all problems. It helps us to face the enemy, and not live on our knees. We have to try to make fireworks with little candles."

To his brother Tong, come to meet him at the Thai border, Ba says—half smiling half melancholy—"I'm breaking stones to mend the sky."

Despite the red-wine birthmark on his temple, which makes him easy to spot, Ba travels everywhere in occupied South Vietnam, sometimes by communist army jeep.

Incautious, or betrayed, he is arrested with some companions in September 1984, probably on the 11th.

A trial. Ba is charged with high treason, he and the pilot Mai Van Hanh—one of the two men who, in the last days of the fall of Saigon, tried to persuade General Minh to transfer power to former prime minister Tran Van Huu. Inviting foreign journalists, communist authorities make much of the trial. The tribunal sits in the heart of Ho Chi Minh City, in the municipal theater, across from the former Hotel Continental. The twenty-nine articles of indictment, read on December 18, are badly drawn. Their true indictment is of the regime; they expose its struggles in a South Vietnam where police control, ideological bludgeoning and reeducation camps have not subdued the people. Vietnamese communist leaders seem to be reinventing the Stalinist trial. The procedure does not permit the accused access to the evidence, the debates are not adversarial, the twenty-one accused are limited to two designated lawyers. Strange lawyers who, at the very start, announce that proof of their clients' guilt is overwhelming. It must be said in their defense, explain these lawyers, that the accused were largely ignorant of the situation in revolutionary Vietnam. The lawyers beg the tribunal for clemency. Part of the trial is televised.

Defendant Mai Van Hanh, emaciated and exhausted, states: "I acknowledge that my activities are negative. . . . I am a henchman of China and Thailand . . . I sincerely repent."

All the wooden language of extorted, dictated and repetitious testimony is dredged up, alpha to omega. Moscow, Prague, Budapest, Tirana, Ho Chi Minh City: errors, crimes, police methods, justice, terror all compounded. It's a long way from the reconciliation and concord preached by the late PRG.

Ba is the second defendant in this badly staged farce, more political than juridical. Height of the absurd, the improbable, the impossible—the defendants are accused, among other things, of having prepared the "kidnapping of consular agents and French technicians."

The clemency implored by the lawyers results in five death sentences, including Ba's. He refuses to sign an appeal for pardon.

Proud and lordly, Ba says to the presiding judge, "I'm sorry to meet you under such difficult circumstances."

And Ba's last rejoinder to the court is heavy with meaning: "A foreign friend once said, 'When you've lost confidence, you've lost everything.' "

Starting in Paris, a worldwide campaign on behalf of the condemned embarrasses Hanoi a bit and irritates Hanoi a lot. Televised and broadcast in the East as well as the West, the judicial masquerade does real harm to the regime in unified Vietnam. In an unforeseen and perverse effect, by this trial the Vietnamese communists spread an idea everywhere: in Vietnam, there was a first resistance, against the French, then a second, against the Americans. Now, more than ten years after the fall of Saigon, a third resistance—impossible to quantify—is emerging, this one anticommunist. The trial surely terrorizes the Vietnamese in Vietnam. But more than that it arouses international public opinion, which has tended to forget Vietnam. This third resistance cannot be laid to the garrulous, muddled bustle of small emigré groups in France or the United States. The authorities heap up some confiscated weapons at the door to the theater-courtroom in Ho Chi Minh City, to support the charge of high treason. The question arises immediately: if Ba and the other guilty men could transport so many rifles, tommy guns and grenades across South Vietnam, don't they have widespread support, even networks?[10]

Ba's mother, in France, asks to be received at the embassy of the Democratic Republic of Vietnam. The ambassador, Colonel Ha Van Lau, one of the shrewder heads in the North Vietnamese delegation to Paris in May 1968, and in the "diplomatic offensive cell" at Hanoi in 1975, refuses to see the elderly woman.

The French government will win a pardon for Mai Van Hanh, who had a French passport, too; not so Ba.

On January 8, 1985, drawing on a newspaper article published in Ho Chi Minh City, a dispatch announces the execution of Tran Van Ba. There is no positive proof of that execution. Communist authorities refuse to hand over the body. Witnesses attend an execution January 9 at the military cemetery in Thu Duc, fifteen kilometers from Ho Chi Minh City. The faces of the men shot were covered by hoods. Some say Ba died under torture. Others that he may not even have been killed.

So despite themselves the communists assure Ba's place in legend—which almost always simplifies and dehumanizes. Part of the new generation of young Vietnamese, everywhere in Vietnam and in exile, recognize themselves in Ba. Vietnamese publications abroad set him beside Kinh Kha, the chevalier who 2,000 years ago went to fight the tyrant who erected the Great Wall, burned books and liquidated intellectuals and mandarins. Ba is also compared to that militant anticolonialist who, condemned to death by the French, demanded to lie on his back and see the guillotine drop, saying: "I want to be looking at the sky." To the exasperation of Hanoi's leaders, Vietnamese commentators do not hesitate to see in Ba "a new and anticommunist Ho Chi Minh."

Was Tran Van Ba, like several other new and unknown resisters, a realist, an idealist, or an adventurer? Was he an exemplary hero or a futile martyr? He believed in the values of Western democracy. The freedoms that Hanoi's Marxists-Leninists-Stalinists call abstract, Tran Van Ba believed to be very real. Is the fight he was committed to, and that others are continuing, a desperate fantasy or a moral wager meriting respect, understanding and support?

When you remind Vietnamese resisters that to this day no country that went communist ever ceased to be communist, they answer quickly,

> We know that. But Vietnam today is a long way from the Soviet Union geographically. In the North it faces a permanent enemy, China. Civil and military circles are discouraged, corrupt, pessimistic. For us it's not just a matter of military combat. We're fighting mainly a political war. Sooner or later the people will rise up. Five years, ten years—that's not much in the history of Vietnam. Nothing is irreversible, not even communism.

After the fall of Saigon as much as before, during all that cruel month of April 1975 and today, Vietnam—communist and nationalist, left and right—struggling to see the face of its own destiny, has never lost patience, confidence, hope or heroism.

Notes

———◆———

1 HANOI–SAIGON: 1789 KILOMETERS

1. National Intelligence Estimate (NIE), December 1974.
2. Notebooks of Patrick Hays, Saigon, December 25, 1974.
3. Cao Giao, interview with the author, Brussels and Paris, 1985.
4. Central Intelligence Agency. From 1965 to 1973, when the United States had combat troops in Vietnam, the CIA varied in its appraisals, in contrast to those of army intelligence, which tended to optimism. CIA reports very soon became rather pessimistic. In 1966, one of its documents states explicitly: "Setting aside a general invasion or a nuclear attack, there is probably no form of naval or air operation, whatever the scale, that would seem insupportable to Hanoi, to the point of constraining North Vietnam to put an end to the war." CIA Archives, Langley, Virginia.
5. Defense Intelligence Agency (DIA).
6. Bureau of Intelligence and Research (BIR).
7. Director of Central Intelligence (DCI).
8. Saigon, December 14, 1974, State Department Archives, Washington, D.C.
9. Saigon, December 2, 1974, CIA Archives.
10. Douglas Pike, interview with the author, Berkeley, California, 1986.
11. Henry Kissinger, interview with the author, New York, 1986.
12. Ibid.
13. Nguyen Duc Cuc, alias Nguyen Van Linh, is today general secretary of the Vietnamese Communist Party.
14. Nguyen Ky, interview with the author, Westminster, California, 1986.
15. Foreign Office Archives, London.
16. Nguyen Ky, interview with the author, Westminster, California, 1986.
17. *Prison Songs*, supplement of *Que Me*, review of Vietnamese abroad, Gennevilliers, 1982, French translation by Phuong Anh.

413

2 EVEN THE GODS WEEP FOR PHUOC LONG

1. Cao, *The Final Collapse*.
2. William LeGro, Defense Attaché Office Report, Saigon, January 1975. See also LeGro, *Vietnam from Ceasefire to Capitulation*.
3. Washington Special Action Group (WSAG).
4. Douglas Pike, interview with the author, Berkeley, California, 1986.
5. In 1967, while a professor at Harvard, Kissinger served as a mail drop between President Lyndon Johnson and Ho Chi Minh, with the help of Frenchman Jean Sainteny.
6. See Kissinger's memoirs.
7. Reports of Cao Van Vien, chairman of the Joint General Staff, December 1974 and January 1975.
8. Ibid.
9. There are eighteen active Vietnamese banks (Vietnam ngan hang, Vietnam cong-thuong ngan hang, Vietnam thuong-tin, Nong-cong thuong ngan hang, Tin nghia ngan hang, Nam-do ngan-hang, Dai-nam ngan-hang, Dong-phuong ngan hang, Dai-A ngan hang, Dong-A ngan hang, Dong-nai ngan-hang, Ky-thuong ngan hang, Nai-ham ngan hang, Trung-Viet ngan hang, Mekong, Saigon tin-dung, Nam-Viet ngan-hang, Ngan hang phat-trien nong-nghiep) and fourteen foreign banks (France: French Commercial Bank, French Bank of Asia, BNP; Great Britain: The Hong Kong and Shanghai Bank Corp., The Chartered Bank; Thailand: Bangkok Bank; Formosa: The Bank of East Asia, International Commercial Bank of China, Bank of Communication; United States: The Chase Manhattan Bank, Bank of America, First National City Bank; Japan: The Bank of Tokyo; South Korea: Korea Exchange Bank). The presence of all these banks is *one* indicator of the commercial, industrial and financial activity in South Vietnam in 1975. The Republic of Vietnam is moving ahead economically. Ministries of foreign affairs often keep embassies in certain countries for show; banks, never.
10. Ordinance No. 53 of September 6, 1956, promulgated by President Diem. Still valid in 1975.

3 NIXON'S LETTERS

1. For propaganda purposes, Hanoi regularly states that there are 25,000 Americans in Vietnam.
2. At Danang, Pleiku, Qui Nhon, Nha Trang, Bien Hoa, Long Binh, Nha Be, Dong Tan, Binh Tuy, Can Tho.
3. JCS, Joint Chiefs of Staff in the Pentagon. The four services—army, navy, air force and marines—are represented. It is the supreme military authority, subordinate to the secretary of defense and the president, who is constitutionally the commander in chief.
4. Dillard, *Sixty Days to Peace*.
5. Ibid.
6. Dega, *W. Pokojowej Misji*.
7. Van, *Our Great Spring Victory*. Most of the Dung quotations here are from Spragens' translation, verbatim or freely adapted.
8. All of Nixon's letters to Thieu have been published in *The Palace File* by Nguyen Tien Hung and Jerrold Schecter (New York: Harper & Row, 1986). That work was written with Thieu's collaboration. Copies of the letters are also in both Nixon's and Ford's archives. Thieu did not show the authors *all* his correspondance with the American presidents.

4 THE FLAMES OF HANOI

1. FitzGerald, *Fire in the Lake*.
2. Article by Frances FitzGerald in *The New Yorker* (April 1975).
3. Ibid.
4. Memorandum 37 (Hanoi), Australian Ministry of Foreign Affairs, Canberra.
5. January 27.
6. The Democratic Republic of Vietnam has many active listening posts in the West (France, Belgium, Luxemburg, Holland, Great Britain, Denmark, Norway, Sweden, Finland, Switzerland, Italy, Canada, New Zealand). Both the DRV and PRG send numerous missions throughout the Third World. North Vietnamese journalists accredited in the West or East report to their embassies several times a week for instructions. In January 1975 communist diplomats and journalists explain everywhere that there is *no* question of a general offensive in South Vietnam.
7. COSVN, Central Office for South Vietnam: the name given by U.S. agencies to communist political-military headquarters in the South. Perpetually searching for it, the Americans imagined it as a headquarters. In fact, it was quite decentralized. Cf. *Memoirs of a Vietcong*, by Truong Nhu Tang.
8. Policy Planning Council.
9. War Powers Act.
10. State Department Bulletin, January 1975. Sixteen dailies are "firmly opposed" to any aid, including a couple of powerful West Coast newspapers, the *Los Angeles Times* and the *San Francisco Chronicle*. Thirteen "are sympathetic" to aid, among them the papers in the Scripps-Howard chain. Also in this category are the two best-known dailies, the *New York Times* and the *Washington Post*, often accused by the government of showing no understanding of or "sympathy" for its positions or decisions. Seven papers, among them the very respectable *Wall Street Journal*, take no very decided position. Several rightly considered bellwethers would favor increased aid to Saigon if President Thieu proved more disposed to seek a political settlement: that is the position of the *Washington Post* and the *New York Times*, the two guardians of the American conscience. With the *Christian Science Monitor*, a number of editorial writers call for diplomatic initiatives: the U.S. government should put pressure on Moscow and Beijing to reduce their aid to Hanoi. What can, what should Washington's leaders do? "Nothing that has not already been tried, without success," the *Chicago News* announces somberly.
11. The right-wing Americans for Constitutional Action, which "grades" elected officials, gives Ford 77 out of 100 for his votes in the House. The left-wing organization Americans for Democratic Action awarded him a 67 in 1966 and a 52 in 1973.
12. Henry Kissinger, interview with the author, New York, 1986.
13. Order of magnitude: in the following year, 1976, Ford will be ready to give Israel $1.5 billion in military assistance, of which only half must be repaid.
14. Ford is in a difficult situation vis-à-vis Congress. Deliberating on foreign aid at the end of 1974, Congress showed clearly that it wants to diminish the U.S. commitment in Indochina. At the beginning of this session of Congress, the administration—the government—asked for $1.6 billion in military aid to South Vietnam alone. After debate, Congress reduced the figure to $700 million. Later, Congress put a ceiling on all aid to Saigon, military and economic both, of $1.26 billion. In economic aid, Laos, the permanent forgotten man of that war, receives only $40 million, Cambodia $100 million, Vietnam $339.9 million. To nail it down, Congress specifies that during fiscal year 1975 the president can in no way "play" with the

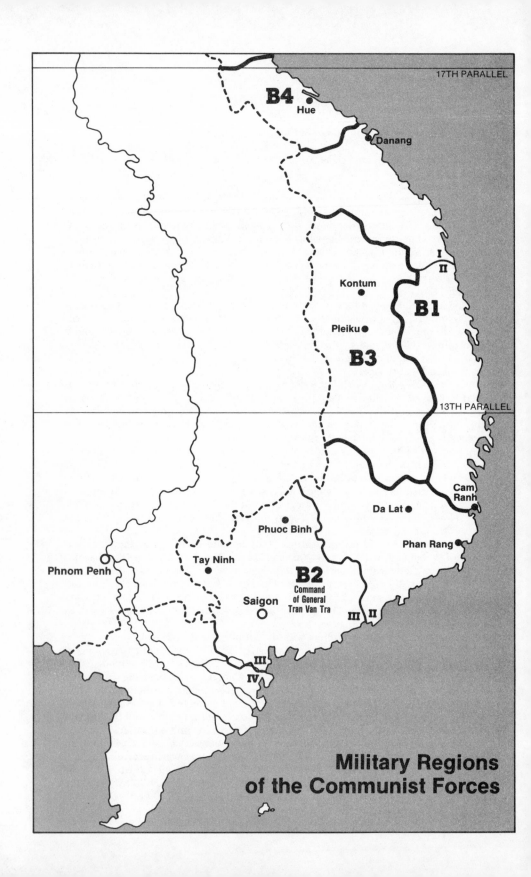

17TH PARALLEL

B4
Hue

Danang

I
II

Kontum

B1

Pleiku

B3

13TH PARALLEL

Cam
Ranh

Da Lat

Phuoc Binh

Phan Rang

Phnom Penh

Tay Ninh

B2
Command
of General
Tran Van Tra

Saigon

III
II

III

IV

Military Regions
of the Communist Forces

funds: that is, he may not transfer sums destined for Cambodia to another country in Indochina, to Vietnam or Laos, and Congress prohibited the purchase of any war materiel without authorization. Congress also decided that the number of official Americans present in Vietnam should be reduced to 4,000 in six months, and to 3,000 in a year. It is in this atmosphere, hardly favorable to the administration, that the president requests *supplemental* funds for the Republic of Vietnam.

5   A STROKE OF THE AX AT THE BASE OF THE TRUNK

1. The communists divided Vietnam south of the 17th parallel into four military regions. B1 (which they often called zone 5), B2, B3 and B4. Region B2 was commanded by General Tran Van Tra. It extended from the province of Gia Nghia (today Dar Lac province), to the southern end of Vietnam, the Ca Mau peninsula. Saigon was at the center of zone B2. The B2 region covered about half the territory of South Vietnam, where about two-thirds of the population lived. Three-quarters of the Vietnam–Cambodia border lay in region B2. Tran Van Tra speaks of the "B2 theater of operations," subdivided into "military regions."

2. Van, *Our Great Spring Victory*.

3. Report by Le Duan on the fiftieth anniversary of the Russian Revolution, Hanoi, 1967. Partially in code language, it is extremely hard on the Soviets and the Chinese.

4. Tran, *Vietnam: History of the Bulwark B2 Theatre*.

5. Ibid.

6. General Tra will not be given all that he asks. Headquarters will not allocate extra T-54s to his B2 zone. His troops will have to be satisfied with M-41 tanks and M-113 armored vehicles taken from the South Vietnamese. The modern materiel will go to the divisions engaged in B3, the Central Highlands, and B4, just below the DMZ at the 17th parallel. On the other hand, headquarters does agree, early on, to grant Tra infantry reserves for diversionary operations in the Delta.

7. Historians and journalists owe much to this photographer, who is moreover a prolific writer.

8. Whatever the North Vietnamese generals say, everybody who performed this hard labor was not a volunteer; but very few deserted.

9. When Robert McNamara was secretary of defense the Americans set up a special group, Task Force 728, to neutralize the Ho Chi Minh trail. Under a bland title, Defense Communications Planning Group, it occupied an old building near the British Embassy in Washington. There they perfected dozens of acoustic, seismic, magnetic and infrared detectors under various names—Acubuoy I, Commike III, Sars III, SOSID, UVID. . . . The idea was to sow the Ho Chi Minh trail and its edges with gadgets that would pinpoint North Vietnamese convoys. So as not to be discovered in their turn, the detectors were camouflaged. Some took the form of dog turds, others looked like leaves or plants. Project Igloo White cost $1 million a year from 1968 to 1972. To store the millions of data, an IBM 360–65 computer was installed at air force headquarters in Thailand. The data gathered by detectors on the trail were relayed by specially equipped planes, ERC-121 R Constellations. Some reconnaissance helicopters could identify trucks' lighting systems from several hundred meters' altitude. At least they thought so. The Pentagon thought they destroyed 12,000 trucks in 1971. According to Washington, 8 million tons of bombs were dropped on the Ho Chi Minh trail, three times the tonnage dropped on Europe and Japan during World War II. Cf. Paul Dixon, *The Electronic Battlefield* (London: Marion Boyars, 1976).

10. Unpublished study by Thai Quang Trung, Singapore, 1986.

11. Van, *Our Great Spring Victory*.

12. The text of this conference has been published in *Tap Chi Quan Doi Nhan Dan*, Hanoi, March 1975.

13. Lenin, *Complete Works* (Moscow, 1947). "Clausewitz, one of the greatest military historians, whose ideas were enriched by Hegel" (vol. 21); "That author whose essential ideas have today become incontestably the inheritance of every thinking man" (vol. 24).

14. Sun Tzu, *The Art of War*, translated by Samuel Griffith (New York: Oxford University Press, 1963); slightly adapted here.

15. Karl von Clausewitz, *On War*.

6 ASLEEP ON THEIR FEET

1. Hoang Duc Nha, interview with the author, Chicago, 1986.

2. The Indochina Resources Committee, a very active pacifist organization.

3. State Department Archives, 1975.

4. Douglas Pike, interview with the author, Berkeley, California, 1986.

7 THE DRAGON'S VEIN

1. The minister of public works and communications was Duong Kich Nhuong.

2. This horoscope reader had been consulted by Agence France-Presse on the future of Vietnam and its president.

3. *Saigon Post*, February 4, 1975.

4. The minister of the interior was Ho Van Cham. The national commander of police, Nguyen Khac Binh, kept a firm hand on the intelligence service, the CIO, in charge of espionage and counterespionage.

5. The *Dien Tin*, the *Dong Phuong*, the *Song Than*, the *But Thep*, the *Tia Sang*.

6. The *Dan Chu*, the *Quat Cuong*, the *Tien Tuyen*.

7. Duong Van Minh, conversation with the author, Saigon, 1973.

8. *Daily Intelligence Publication*, limited distribution, to officials in the National Security Council, the State Department and the Pentagon.

9. Broadcast of *Issues and Answers*.

10. Ford's letter is dated February 24, 1975. Thieu's letters of January 24 and 25, 1975, have not been published.

11. Daily Intelligence Publication.

8 CAMPAIGN 275

1. *A* is the general code name for the North; *B*, for the South.

2. General Vo Nguyen Giap is minister of defense and secretary general of the Central Military Committee.

3. Senator Bartlett leaves on February 21, the commission members on the 25th.

4. Thieu remembers especially assurances given by the new president when he took over after Watergate the year before. On August 10, 1974, Wolfgang Lehmann gave Thieu a letter in which Ford said that "the existing agreements that this nation has taken in the past are still valid and will be fully honored in my administration." Thieu translates: Ford is aware of the commitments made by Nixon in his letters.

On October 24, 1974, in another letter, Ford wrote: "American policy towards Vietnam remains unchanged under this government." The new American president also said: "I give you my firm assurances that this government will continue to make every effort to furnish you with the assistance you need." Isn't this an echo of Nixon, who promised to "furnish . . . the most complete support"?

5. In the United States there is constant talk of the KIA (killed in action), and even more of the MIA (missing in action). From August 1973 to February 1975, Americans submitted 107 cases of missing men to the DRV and the PRG. With no result.

6. Cao Giao, interview with the author, Paris, 1985.

7. Analysis prepared by the CIA and the BIR (State Department Bureau of Intelligence and Research) jointly, March 5, 1975. Next day the *Daily Intelligence Publication*, recalling the battles in the Central Highlands, says the North Vietnamese have begun their spring campaign in that region. The city of Kontum is particularly threatened.

8. Actress Jane Fonda and her husband Tom Hayden were serious militants in the peace movement.

9. But the greater part of the funds went to the Christian Democrats. In 1968 Graham Martin published an article in *Annals of the Academy of Political and Social Sciences* that defined his idea of an ambassador's role. According to Martin, an ambassador abroad must control *everything* his agencies do.

10. In regard to corruption, Martin says in a cable to the State Department that the average degree of corruption in Vietnam was about the same as what prevailed in the state of Massachusetts and the city of Boston in the first decades of the century. He adds that they've probably hit bottom, and it's not impossible that they'll turn things around quickly.

9 "LITTLE HEAD, BIG BUTT"

1. Ethnologists list more than thirty ethnic minorities in the Central Highlands. The largest groups are the E De, the Jarai, the Ba Na, the Xe Dang.

2. At the time the military infrastructure of the PRG had been decapitated. Hence, in part, its weakness in 1975.

3. General Dung is selectively candid. Almost everything he tells us is true, confirmed by other sources, American, South Vietnamese and North Vietnamese, but he doesn't tell us everything. His lapses are useful to Hanoi's propaganda and the long march of the Vietnamese communists.

4. For his part General Tra dislikes that image, and criticizes it. All through his narrative Tra is more frank or realistic than Dung. He downplays the hardships of war far less than Dung, and the disagreements in the North Vietnamese high command, and the reservations among the rank and file. So for the period 1973–1975 he writes that here and there in the PRG zones they applied "five strict bans: on attacking the enemy in general, on attacking Saigon's troops that retake terrain, on encircling posts, on attacking artillery, on fortifying the villages in combat zones." That phase was rapidly terminated. In the summer of 1973 resolution 21 of Lao Dung and resolution 12 of COSVN advocated "a return to revolutionary violence." It remains true that certain PRG units in the South, not many, wanted to implement the Paris Agreement. They were quickly called to order.

5. Cf. Snepp, *Decent Interval*.

6. After the war, a sequence from the Hanoi army film bureau will even show large Soviet helicopters transporting cannon, but there is no way to tell whether that happened during the war or on maneuvers afterward.

7. During the whole war North Vietnamese planes never intervened south of the 17th parallel. The Politburo had decided that the United States would not accept that escalation.

8. A fifty-kilo sack of rice was worth 14,000 piastres at that time, around $20, or 110 francs. It was just enough to feed a family of five for one month. Often a

South Vietnamese soldier, sometimes with the help of his wife and older children, had to feed ten or a dozen people.

9. The Americans realize only on March 14 that the city has fallen. Photographs taken by an Air America plane lead them to believe that Ban Me Thuot is still in South Vietnamese hands: cyclists are pedaling peacefully in the streets. Several pockets of resistance hold out until March 18.

10. These civilian prisoners will be released quite late, in Hanoi on October 30, 1975, partly because the North Vietnamese are convinced that Struharik is a CIA agent.

11. March 7, 1975.

12. Until 1973 reporters who had been accredited by the South Vietnamese press office automatically obtained American accreditation. It entitled them to a priority equivalent to a major's for seats on planes and helicopters. Easy and free transport, guaranteed lodging in press camps, officers' mess, easy contacts with fighting men: the press has *never* been so well treated by a government and an army during a campaign. Of course, there was plenty of friction. Even so, thousands of reporters took advantage of that "open war." It was totally different in North Vietnam, which admitted fewer than a hundred noncommunist Western journalists. After U.S. combat units left in 1973, "access to the war" was more limited. The right to know was not one of the Saigon government's doctrines—and it lacked the means of transportation.

13. March 20, 1975.

14. The conversation between Dan Ellerman and Nguyen Van Hao took place March 9, 1975, but the idea of a strategic withdrawal had been in the air for a long time.

15. The prime minister has vassals and his networks. He controls lucrative posts in the capital and the provinces. The title, function and perquisites of a provincial or district head are negotiated to the tune of hundreds of millions of piastres. Once on the job, the beneficiaries can rule and tax at will. In Vietnam some consider these posts a bit like being a notary or stockbroker in Europe. Khiem "is interested" in the oil industry. His wife has the Coca-Cola concession for the whole country.

10   ROUTE 7B

1. Kissinger is in Riyadh March 19, 1975, and returns to Washington March 23. Thieu thinks King Faisal favors a long-term loan to the Republic of Vietnam. But the king is assassinated. His successors will be far less sympathetic to Saigon.

2. A journalist from the daily *Szabada Nep*, disguised as an Hungarian officer.

3. Thomas Polgar, interview with the author, Maitland, Florida, 1986.

4. March 9, 1975.

5. This is a fundamental element in all American political history.

6. VOA, the Voice of America. This radio station seems to have almost as many listeners as the BBC in Southeast Asia.

7. Personal communication from Dr. Nguyen Luu Vien.

8. Tran Van Do, a former minister, has a certain reputation in Saigon.

9. Some in the South Vietnamese government are also counting on the Arab emirates.

10. General Tran Van Cam will protest in vain against this "organization."

11. For a long time the CIA has noticed that North Vietnamese attacks often follow close on the departures of Polish and Hungarian members of the ICCS. "The Poles are leaving, the VC arriving," U.S. "consular agents" sometimes said. The Poles and Hungarians were not told about the attack on Pleiku by their

Vietnamese comrades. The civilian Poles on the ICCS were not directly aware of their delegation's espionage. The Hungarians were all soldiers.

12. In Pleiku, a Hungarian from the ICCS will be saved and evacuated by a CIA agent who—a unique example—will be decorated for his bravery by the Hungarian government.

13. Some strategists, Clausewitz, Bulow and Lloyd, recommend retreat in divided order, "thus by separate groups, that is, in eccentric directions."

11   WHAT ARE MOSCOW AND BEIJING UP TO?

1. March 12, 1975.

2. March 18, 1975.

3. This ingrained French habit of calling all Saigon's enemies "Viets" helps confound North Vietnamese soldiers and PRG guerrillas.

4. State Department Archives.

5. State Department Archives and Ford Foundation Archives.

6. Kissinger, New York, 1986, and Smyser, former member of the National Security Council, Geneva, 1985. Interviews with the author.

7. The South Vietnamese CIO officer does not want to be directly involved.

8. Sino–American rapprochement is more suspect in Hanoi than in Saigon despite everything. In November 1971 Prime Minister Pham Van Dong tried to persuade Mao that he should not receive Nixon. The Great Helmsman tried unsuccessfully to show Pham Van Dong that he must in the end compromise with the Americans. A first letter from Nixon to Thieu, December 31, 1971, before the U.S. president's trip to Beijing, aims at reassuring Thieu: "If the question of the Vietnam war is raised in Peking, I must reassure you that I will explain forcefully and clearly the position of the United States and the Republic of Vietnam according to which the war in Vietnam must be terminated by direct negotiations with Hanoi or, lacking that, by an increased capacity of the Republic of Vietnam to defend itself against Hanoi's aggression." Nixon wants to make it perfectly clear to the Chinese leaders "that our two governments remain firmly side by side in this vital problem." At that time the interests and objectives of Washington and Saigon seem to coincide.

9. The phrase is Kissinger's, from his memoirs.

10. March 25, 1975.

11. Colonel Ha Van Lau is a key personality in Hanoi. He is as much politician as soldier, if not more. A member of the first North Vietnamese delegation to Paris, in May 1968, he is also assigned to very special missions by the Politburo and the prime minister. He had, for example, met secretly in Rangoon with Secretary-General U Thant of the United Nations when the North Vietnamese, a year earlier, seemed ready to compromise. In 1987 Ha Van Lau was ambassador to Paris.

12. Bulletin of *Vietnam Press*, no. 8776.

12   THE BELL TOLLS FOR DANANG

1. AID.

2. For the occasion, the Americans set the traditional three-mile limit to Vietnamese territorial waters.

3. Press agencies cover these events, in particular Richard Blystone for the Associated Press and Lim Thanh Van, a photographer, for the United Press, who do a fine job documenting the progress of operations and especially the retreat on Route 7B.

4. Tran, *Vietnam*.

5. The third week in March.

6. *Nhan Dan*, the party daily, March 2, 1975.

7. Jean-Marie Mérillon, Paris, 1985, Geneva, 1986. Patrick Hays, Singapore, 1984, Mougins, 1986. Interviews with the author.

8. Notebooks of Patrick Hays, March 30.

13 THREE RED STRIPES

1. Six "daisy cutters" will be delivered and three used. One of these bombs is on display today in Hanoi.

2. "Demonstratedly": General Weyand is so dismayed by Saigon's ineffectiveness that he will not shrink from any barbarism.

3. DIA.

4. April 3, 4, 5, 6, 1975.

5. *Face the Nation*, April 6.

6. April 8.

7. April 1.

8. In his book *Decent Interval*, Frank Snepp loyally uses a pseudonym, Lew James, for the CIA agent whose real name is John Lewis. The Poles and Hungarians will tell the North Vietnamese that Lewis is an important CIA agent—or a major in the U.S. army. Taken prisoner, he will be freed in Hanoi in October 1975.

9. Snepp, *Decent Interval*.

10. April 3.

11. Tran, *Our Endless War*, and interviews with the author, Washington and Paris, 1986.

12. April 12.

13. In January 1974.

14. March 25, 1975.

14 NOT A THREAD, NOT A NEEDLE

1. When he was running the CIA outpost in Saigon, William Colby—head of the Company in Washington in 1975—authorized Ky to train paratroops for commando operations in North Vietnam. No president, Johnson no more than Nixon, would allow the war to be carried to the North, despite repeated demands by U.S. and South Vietnamese military.

2. The project was drawn up on April 5.

3. Cao Van Vien speaks rather calmly of an "advisory role."

4. Mme. Binh is one of the better disinformation agents in Hanoi's "diplomatic cell."

5. Philippe Richer, Paris, 1986, interview with the author.

6. April 6.

15 THE BLACK CUCKOO

1. Subic Bay, U.S. base in the Philippines.

2. Cao Giao, Paris, 1986, interview with the author.

3. Report of April 9, 1975.

16 FLOWERS BEHIND THEIR EARS

1. See the excellent film, *The Killing Fields*. French critics complained that it *normalized* the role of the French at Phnom Penh—in the way philologists

standardize a text for beginning students. In an hour and a half no one can show all the complexities of an historical situation.

2. Hoang Duc Nha meets Lee Kuan Yew April 19, 1975.

3. April 13.

4. April 15.

5. April 9.

6. April 15.

7. April 15.

8. April 14.

9. April 15.

10. April 14.

11. April 20.

17 FILLING UP THE OCEAN WITH STONES

1. Snepp, *Decent Interval*, and Hoang Duc Nha, Chicago, 1986, interview with the author.

2. WSAG, Washington Special Action Group.

3. AFSC, American Friends Service Committee.

4. Henry Kissinger, New York, 1986, interview with the author.

5. April 23, 1975.

6. April 19.

7. Claudia Krich published her diary. Extracts from *Notes from Abroad* (Philadelphia: American Friends Service Committee, 1975).

8. Apropos of the report for Ambassador Martin, Polgar says to Snepp, "Make it as bleak as you can. . . . The Ambassador is going to use it to convince Thieu that it's time for him to go." In his last report, Snepp wrote very accurately: "With the collapse of government defenses around Xuan Loc and the continuing NVA build-up in MR 3, the balance of forces in the greater Saigon area has shifted irreversibly in favor of the North Vietnamese and the Viet Cong." Martin himself expresses the gist of Snepp's conclusion: "Although the government might be able to reinforce one of the major target areas now in imminent danger of attack—Bien Hoa/Long Binh to the east of Saigon; Long An and Hau Nghia Provinces to the west; or Binh Duong Province to the north—it does not have the strength to defend them all equally." Polgar and Snepp argued over that appraisal. The former found it too pessimistic, the latter, too optimistic. Obsessed by the possibility of negotiations, Polgar thought there was a lull in the fighting. That was not Snepp's opinion at all.

9. The press will not report all that Thieu says. To his compatriots he had also said, "You must remember that in 1968 American pressure was strong. . . . At that time, I said to you that if you agreed to the Americans' plans you'd be lost. Now you're going to see what I meant in 1968." Like other passages in his speech, this one seemed incoherent to many of his listeners. The words meant: in 1968, certain Americans wanted to assassinate me. Now, in April 1975, they've assassinated me politically and you're going to see, you South Vietnamese, how they'll abandon our country.

18 BIG MINH'S BIG MOMENT

1. This double coverage was used during the 1973 war in the Middle East. The Soviets then had six Flint satellites in permanent orbit. Each one transmits information, generally twice a year—the usual rhythm during periods of crisis. U.S. intelligence noted the same kind of satellite activity during the Indo-Pakistani war in December 1971 and during the Vietnamese communist offensive in April 1972.

The U.S. services involved tell the State Department there "are no grounds for international alarm." But it's obvious then that the Soviets are concerned about satellite observation of Southeast Asia.

19   HALF-PRICE SALE

1. Cf. Appendix VI, Agenda of the Indochinese Communist Party.
2. Graham Martin, Winston Salem, 1986, interview with the author. Snepp, *Decent Interval.*
3. Colonel Vo Dong Giang recalls nine conditions set for the Americans by the PRG: (1) respect for the independence, sovereignty, territorial unity and integrity of South Vietnam; (2) absence of any political pressure on the population; (3) cessation of all military activity; (4) departure of all CIA agents; (5) withdrawal of all military personnel camouflaged in civilian clothes; (6) withdrawal of fifty warships cruising in territorial waters; (7) withdrawal of U.S. planes ready to intervene; (8) withdrawal of the 6,000 marines stationed on those ships; (9) the end of all aid to South Vietnam, military or other. To the South Vietnamese government, the PRG set seven preliminary conditions for negotiations. Clause 3 is the most important; it negates the whole idea of negotiations: (1) formation of a new administration in favor of peace, independence, democracy and national concord; (2) implementation of the Paris Agreement; (3) *removal of all men connected with Thieu's clique*; (4) abandonment of warlike, fascist policy and oppression of the population; (5) abolition of all antidemocratic laws; (6) guaranteed respect for democratic liberties; (7) liberation of all people arrested and imprisoned for having fought for peace and national independence.

20   BROTHERS OF THE SAME HOUSE

1. Jacqueline Desbarats and Karl Jackson, "Vietnam 1975–1982: The Cruel Peace," *The Washington Quarterly* 8, no.4 (1985).
2. The Australian press will denounce this scandal.
3. The Pentagon has been studying options and evacuation plans since July 1974. On April 8, 1975, the chairman of the Joint Chiefs of Staff in Washington sends a long message (no. 3698), to CINCPAC, the State Department and the commander of the U.S. Seventh Air Force in Thailand. CINCPAC is asked "to develop a detailed plan with appropriate options to evacuate from Vietnam the following numbers of people: (A) 1,500, (B) 3,000, (C) 6,000. These plans must be completed before April 19. (D) 200,000. This plan must be ready as soon as possible." CINCPAC develops plan 5060-V, operational name "Talon Vise," which will become "Frequent Wind." The American planners must have been worried: the evacuation of MR 1, conducted the end of March following the plan Fortress Journey, was not a great success. It is symbolized by the chaos of Danang. But far from the site, the planners are very pleased with the results of another large operation. Eagle Pull, the evacuation of Phnom Penh.

At first the planners study four possibilities:

Option 1: An evacuation using all forms of transport, including commercial planes and ships. It would be controlled by the U.S. Embassy. Military aid would be limited to extra help in aerial or naval evacuation. This option all but implies a calm departure, during something like a real cease-fire.

Option 2: Evacuation by planes and landing a security force—that is, marines— to protect the operation; and even, if necessary, an amphibious force.

Option 3 provides primarily for a mass evacuation by sea from Cap Saint-Jacques and/or Saigon, with evacuations by plane, a security force and an amphibious force.

On April 5, *Option 4* is completed. It includes mainly an evacuation by helicopter from the Saigon region and also elements of Options 2 and 3—security and amphibious forces. This is the option accepted.

On April 24, *Option 5* also is finished: it provides for evacuation by planes and helicopters from the Saigon airport; by boats and helicopters from Newport; and no less than the seizure of the Vung Tau peninsula. It provides for some 200,000 evacuees. It would require, besides a brigade of marines, two batallions air-lifted in, one of army and one of marines. As General Carey says, "Option 5 would have been a big undertaking if it had come to pass." That option will be just ready the evening of April 28. (Report of General Richard Carey. Marine Corps Historical Archives, Washington, D.C.)

For a long time it's been taken for granted that marines would be the spearhead of the operation. On March 26, the Ninth Amphibious Brigade of marines is put on alert. Its commander, General Richard Carey, arrives in Okinawa April 3 and at Subic Bay April 4. The elements of the different units are assembled and the Ninth Brigade, after several typically military orders and counterorders, finds itself aboard ship off Cap Saint-Jacques. The first ships of the U.S. armada arrive in the waters of the China Sea south of Vietnam on April 10. Officers from the military attaché's group come aboard the flagship *Blue Ridge* to brief their marine colleagues. The latter return the courtesy and spend the next day in Saigon. Back aboard the flagship they report to their commander, General Carey. They get the impression that diplomats in Saigon don't care too much about the problem of evacuation. They note "a general lack of concern." General Carey decides to visit Saigon himself on April 13. In Saigon they plan three evacuation points: one far from the capital at Can Tho, another even farther away at Cap Saint-Jacques and a third in Saigon itself. In the capital they're apparently counting on the docks and quays at Newport, from which they think 100,000 people could be evacuated by the river route. This dock site will be considered a possibility until April 29.

The second Saigon site will be the complex used by General Smith and Air America at Tan Son Nhut airport. They plan seven landing zones for helicopters: LZ 40, close to the Air America buildings. Then to the right of these buildings, around the group named The Alamo, LZ 37 and LZ 38, which must take care of the wounded. Still farther to the right, by General Smith's offices, LZ 34, LZ 35 and LZ 36. Finally, a little more isolated in the parking lot, LZ 39.

They don't really expect that the U.S. Embassy will be the site of a mass evacuation.

21 APRIL 29: PUT OUT THE LIGHTS

1. The sergeant is attached to the ICS, Integrated Communications System.

2. Carey has forty-four CH-52 helicopters, twenty-seven CH-46s, six UH-1Es and eight AH-1Js. He has ten landing areas on *Midway*, seven on *Hancock*, five on *Okinawa* and eight on other ships.

They allow an hour and a half to make the round trip between the fleet and the evacuation sites. They also allow for a certain percentage of breakdowns: 10 percent on the first run, 15 percent on the second, 25 percent on the third.

3. The communist soldiers at Camp Davis will suffer few losses during the fall of Saigon. At Camp Davis there are a few wounded, including a lieutenant colonel.

4. This is not the equivalent, far from it, of the fleet deployed for the Normandy landing, but just the same there are thirty-five very big ships. The evacuation fleet is in position off Cap Saint-Jacques. Three ships, *Peoria*, *Barbour County* and *Cochrane*, are a few miles from the coast. The flagship, *Blue Ridge*, stands seventeen miles out. And behind it, in three lines, the largest units: first, *Mount Vernon, Vancouver, Dubuque, Denver, Duluth, Mobil, Anchorage*; then *Hancock, Oki-*

nawa, Thomaston; and last, *Durham, Frederick, Tuscaloosa, Midway*. All ship captains have orders to report immediately by telephone and telex any incursion into Vietnamese territorial waters.

5. In 1973 the Vietnamese navy had 672 amphibious ships, 20 minesweepers, 450 patrol boats, 56 supply ships and 242 armed junks. But for reasons of economy, in 1975 622 units are in drydock.

6. The Second Battalion, Fourth Marines, Ninth Amphibious Force (MAB) is at sea off the coast by April 20. On April 21, it is to go in six hours; on the 27th an hour before dawn the next day; on April 28, six hours again. Then three hours. Then one hour. On April 29 the order to execute Frequent Wind arrives at the command of the Ninth MAB at 12:15 P.M. L-hour, that is, time of landing, is set for 3 P.M. The marine helicopters are only six minutes late.

7. Report of General Richard Carey.

8. No official communiqué speaks of these skirmishes, or of the five South Vietnamese aircraft, two planes and three helicopters shot down at dawn.

9. Perhaps these helicopters were trying to neutralize the NVA anti-aircraft batteries or missile sites. They probably hit ammunition dumps by secondary impact. There was no mention made of them in official U.S. communiqués. Admiral Chung Tan Cang, Bakersfield, California, 1986, interview with the author.

10. Mimeographed instructions were distributed to the marines:

(1) The physical condition of the evacuees may be bad. . . . It is also probable that there will be wounded. . . . Given the aforementioned physical conditions, it is probable that their state of mind will not be very good. Many of them will be fearful and in a state of shock. We must suppose that these people will be excited, frightened, in a state of panic, and hungry and thirsty. In consequence, extreme care must be taken in relations with the evacuees. (2) Respect the culture of the evacuees. You will have contact with people of all social levels, that is with farmers, doctors, professors, diplomats and even Buddhist monks. If cultural and social norms are violated, our work could be very difficult.

11. 9:41 A.M. Washington time.

12. *Dear America—Letters Home from Vietnam* (New York: Norton, 1984).

13. No official report makes note of communists flying helicopters during the fall of Saigon. They were more probably helicopters commandeered by fleeing South Vietnamese pilots.

22 APRIL 30: THE LAST LOTUS

1. Graham Martin, Winston Salem, 1986, interview with the author.

2. During the war they jammed as many as ten ARVN soldiers into UH-1Bs, designed for six passengers. Even with their arms and ammunition and pots and pans, they were lighter than American soldiers. The Chinook helicopter is designed for fifty passengers: during the evacuation up to seventy were crammed aboard.

3. Pham Thin, Pierrefitte, 1986, interview with the author.

4. The National Police had 100,000 men in uniform and 25,000 plainclothesmen.

5. Among the military suicides were General Le Van Hung, hero of the battle of An Loc in 1972, and aide to Phu; General Nguyen Khoa Nam, commander of the Fourth Corps; Generals Le Nguyen Vy and Tran Van Hai, divisional commanders.

6. The new Saigon authorities will have a Vietnamese technician come from France to operate them.

7. In the afternoon of April 30 Radio Liberation, now set up in Saigon, broadcast a ten-point program several times: (1) All existing agencies must apply the policies of the revolutionary government (the word "provisional" is dropped). The old system is abolished. All reactionary parties and all organizations serving imperialism and the puppets are abolished. (2) Equality of the sexes, freedom of thought and religion are guaranteed. (3) Any activity promoting divisiveness is forbidden. The united country is called upon to reconstruct the liberated zone and to build a new life. (4) The right to work is guaranteed. Everyone must support the revolution. (5) All assets of the puppet administration become the property of the revolutionary government. (6) Helping orphans and the handicapped is a national duty. (7) Country folk are urged to increase production. (8) Cultural establishments, hospitals and schools managed by foreigners must devote their activities to the service of the people. Talents useful for the reconstruction of the country must be well treated. (9) Soldiers who deserted the enemy ranks are to be treated with kindness. (10) With the exception of those who are opposed to the revolution, and who will be punished, foreigners will be well treated and their property guaranteed.

8. Burchett, *Vietnam: Un + Un = Un.*

9. Nguyen Chi Thien, *Prison Songs*, supplement of *Que Me*, review of Vietnamese abroad, Gennevilliers, 1982. French translation by Phuong Anh.

23 BREAKING STONES TO MEND THE SKY

1. Tiziano Terzani, *La chute de Saigon* (Paris: Fayard, 1977).

2. On May 13 Captain Moyher finishes his report on the operation for the Third Marine Division. He says there were not enough men: fifty-four men were insufficient, especially with twenty of them suffering from conjunctivitis, flu and dysentery. Moyher lacked "sugar, salt, vegetables, instant rice, sanitary napkins, baby bottles with nipples, powdered formula, and body bags for burial." Moyher needed a communications officer. He had great problems in the assignment of frequencies and the use of code words. He recommended better placement of water barrels on the ship. They should have had large pieces of canvas to rig for better protection from sun and rain.

3. Document of the High Commission for Refugees, Geneva, 1975.

4. Desbarats and Jackson, "Vietnam 1975–1982." A fundamental study on the problem of a "bloodbath" after the fall of Saigon, this work represents three years of research. Desbarats and Jackson used very sophisticated statistical techniques and in weighing their results most carefully arrive at the conclusion that the total number of people executed in Vietnam between 1975 and 1982 was 65,000 at a minimum. This result is independently corroborated by Vo Van Ai, editor in chief of *Que Me*, who after ten years' work drew up maps of the Vietnamese gulag—and by the cortradictory statements of North Vietnamese leaders about the population of the camps. So the prime minister himself, Pham Van Dong, declared in 1978: "In three years, we have returned to civilian life and to their families more than a million people who collaborated with the enemy one way or another." The widespread refusal to admit that there was a bloodbath in Vietnam can be compared to the inability of citizens of the democracies during World War II to accept the idea that Jews were being exterminated in Eastern Europe. By July 1942 more than a million Jews had been exterminated. The Holocaust had begun, but at that time the State Department itself spoke of "foolish rumors inspired by Jewish fears."

5. Patti, *Why Vietnam?*

6. In France on April 11, 1975, interviewed by Bernard Pivot during a broadcast of *Apostrophes*, Aleksandr Solzhenitsyn said, "All Vietnam will be transformed into a concentration camp." Solzhenitsyn was reasoning by analogy. Now, after

the testimony of boat people, it is hard not to be aware that an archipelago of camps covers Indochina and that in them are a considerable number of former Third Force and PRG people.

7. In a very autobiographical novel, *Blue Dragon, White Tiger, a Tet Story* (Philadelphia: Tri Am Press, 1983), Professor Tran Van Dinh shows his hero studying in the United States for a long time, rejoining the PRG, then leaving the communist regime after the "liberation." His support of the PRG is approved by his father, an elderly respected man of letters.

8. Richard Nixon, *No More Vietnams* (New York: Arbor House, 1985).

9. This film was so successful in the United States in large part because Vietnam veterans, grunts, recognized their day-to-day life in the field. The American right saw it as an attack on the U.S. army or on the government's policies: cf. *The American Spectator* (April–May 1987). At the same time, left-wing critics in France had reservations because the film is "antiwar" but not "anti-American." We should probably distinguish the content of the film from statements by its producer, Oliver Stone, after he won an Oscar for it.

10. We cannot describe or quantify the new Vietnamese resistance any more than we could count European resistance in 1943 or 1944. The best-organized and most active Vietnamese resistance groups in Vietnam itself are surely not the most visible or the noisiest. Vietnamese exiles, though encouraging or supporting them, are cautious and sometimes distrustful. The head of one of these groups who filmed his guerrillas on the Vietnam–Cambodia or Vietnam–Laos borders and then sold videocassettes of this short subject in California earned, they say, over a million dollars. Some of this leader's adversaries say it was a pure swindle. In all resistances there arise true and false fighters, truly committed men and women, and others who are racketeers. Anyway, Vietnamese exiles are divided, as were so often the citizens of the Vietnamese republic. Vietnamese communities all over the world—in the heart of the 13th arrondissement in Paris or in Westminster, Orange County, California—never achieve political unity. A classic phenomenon among émigrés, whether Russian, Afghan or Vietnamese. The old divisions, rancors and rivalries resurface, denying the diaspora a distinct, united stand against the Hanoi regime. Suspicions flourish. In a word, the mechanisms of exclusion come into play. The multiplicity of resistance movements, at home and abroad, reflects the same antagonisms that marred European resistance networks. Then, too, the younger generation vigorously opposes the "politicians and soldiers, authors of the 1975 debacle."

Toward the end of 1987, certain leaders were groping toward a worldwide confederation of resistance movements.

APPENDIX I

———◆———

The Paris Agreement

The agreement on "ending the war and restoring peace in Viet-nam" was signed in Paris on January 27, 1973. The official texts were in Vietnamese and English.

It was ratified on identical and separate pages (the Saigon government did not want to seem to be recognizing the PRG by signing beside it) by U.S. Secretary of State William Rogers; Tran Van Lam, minister of foreign affairs of the Republic of Vietnam; Nguyen Duy Trinh, minister of foreign affairs of the Democratic Republic of Vietnam, and Nguyen Thi Binh, minister of foreign affairs of the PRG.

The text of the final act was signed on March 2, 1973. It was in French, Russian, Vietnamese, English and Chinese, all the texts being official and equally authentic. Signing were: for the French republic, Maurice Schumann; for the PRG, Nguyen Thi Binh; for the Hungarian People's Republic, Janos Peter; for the Republic of Indonesia, Adam Malik; for the Polish People's Republic, Stefan Olszowski; for the Democratic Republic of Vietnam, Nguyen Duy Trinh; for Great Britain, Alec Douglas-Home; for the Republic of Vietnam, Tran Van Lam; for the Soviet Union, Andrei Gromyko; for Canada, Mitchell Sharp; for the People's Republic of China, Ch'i P'eng-Fei; for the United States, William Rogers.

The agreement comprised nine chapters and twenty-three articles. Rereading most of them today is black comedy. For example:

ARTICLE 1:
The United States and all other countries respect the independence, sovereignty, unity, and territorial integrity of Viet-Nam as recognized by the 1954 Geneva Agreements on Viet-Nam.
[The Geneva agreements state that there were two Vietnams, separated by the 17th parallel.]

ARTICLE 2:
A cease-fire shall be observed throughout South Viet-Nam as of 2400 hours G.M.T., on January 27, 1973.

At the same hour, the United States will stop all its military activities against the territory of the Democratic Republic of Viet-Nam by ground, air, and naval forces, wherever they may be based, and end the mining of the territorial waters, ports, harbors, and waterways of the Democratic Republic of Viet-Nam. The United States will remove, permanently deactivate, or destroy all the mines in the territorial waters, ports, harbors, and waterways of North Viet-Nam as soon as this Agreement goes into effect.

The complete cessation of hostilities mentioned in this Article shall be durable and without limit of time.

At the insistence of Hanoi's negotiators, their American counterparts agreed to be the first party named in the first phrase of Article 1 and throughout Chapter 2 concerning the "withdrawal of troops."

ARTICLE 3:
The parties undertake to maintain the cease-fire and to ensure a lasting and stable peace. . . .

ARTICLE 9:
The Government of the United States of America and the Government of the Democratic Republic of Viet-Nam undertake to respect the following principles for the exercise of the South Vietnamese people's right to self-determination:

(a) The South Vietnamese people's right to self-determination is sacred, inalienable, and shall be respected by all countries.

(b) The South Vietnamese people shall decide themselves the political future of South Viet-Nam through genuinely free and democratic general elections under international supervision. . . .

ARTICLE 12:
(a) Immediately after the cease-fire, the two South Vietnamese parties shall hold consultations in a spirit of national reconciliation and concord, mutual respect, and mutual non-elimination to set up a National Council of National Reconciliation and Concord of three equal segments. The Council shall operate on the principle of unanimity. . . .

ARTICLE 15:
The reunification of Viet-Nam shall be carried out step by step through peaceful means on the basis of discussions and agreements between North and South Viet-Nam, without coercion or annexation by either party, and without foreign interference. The time for reunification will be agreed upon by North and South Viet-Nam. . . .

ARTICLE 7 OF THE FINAL ACT STATED:
(a) In the event of a violation of the Agreement or the Protocols which threatens the peace, the independence, sovereignty, unity, or territorial integrity of Viet-Nam, or the right of the South Vietnamese people to self-determination, the parties signatory to the Agreement and the Protocols shall, either individually or jointly, consult with the other Parties to this Act with a view to determining necessary remedial measures.

The communist diplomats were very clever. The Act continued:

(b) The International Conference on Viet-Nam shall be reconvened upon a joint request by the Government of the United States of America and the Government of the Democratic Republic or upon a request by six or more of the Parties to this Act.

Hanoi was certainly not going to point out its own violations of the Agreement, and it was mathematically impossible to find six parties, signatories of the Act, ready to protest the annexation of the Republic of Vietnam. Among the dozen signatories of the Act, only four represented true democracies, the Frenchman Maurice Schumann, the British Alec Douglas-Home, the Canadian Mitchell Sharp and the American William Rogers. The impossibility of a diplomatic reaction was structured into the final Act, even if Indonesia had voted against North Vietnam.

Of course, de facto quickly won out over de jure.

Immediately after the fall of Saigon, the French government seemed embarrassed. On May 6, President Valéry Giscard d'Estaing stated, "In the last weeks of the conflict, our objective was to avoid a useless and bloody battle over Saigon. Our action has contributed to the prevention of such a battle. We have also made an effort to find a political solution conforming to the Paris Agreement, with institutions comprising representatives of the three political groups in South Vietnam." After that indirect homage to Jean-Marie Mérillon's work, the French president said: "We note that statements made at this time in South Vietnam provide for the participation of diverse tendencies in the government." What statements? What institutions?

More realistic, the Quai d'Orsay had already handed representatives of the new authorities the keys to the South Vietnamese embassy in Paris, deposited at the Quai by the former occupants. An ephemeral French envoy to the PRG never reached Ho Chi Minh City. He waited for a long time in a hotel room in Hanoi.

APPENDIX II

——◆——

Military and Economic Aid to the Two Vietnams Before the Final Offensive

The problem of aid to Hanoi from communist countries came up constantly during the war and in particular during the first months of 1975. A memorandum prepared jointly by the CIA and Army Intelligence (DIA), and concurred in by the State Department's BIR, is put out on March 5, 1975. Memoranda of this type were drawn up by these three services to avoid fallacious interpretations and overestimates.

This memo says: "North Vietnamese forces in South Vietnam, supported by record stockpiles of military supplies, are stronger today than they have ever been. The Communists are expected to sharply increase the tempo of the fighting in the next few months." The memo continues: "Given the present military balance in the South, the GVN's forces will not be decisively defeated during the current dry season." Then, on the customary bureaucratic principle—always cover yourself when you make predictions—the same document adds that current levels of U.S. aid will later place "the Communists in a position of significant advantage." Translation: South Vietnam can hold in 1975, but the North may win in 1976.

The memorandum takes up the question of "Communist military and economic aid" to Hanoi from 1970 to 1974.

The types of equipment supplied to the South by the United States have always been more sophisticated, and thus more expensive, than what Hanoi needed. To redeploy forces rapidly throughout its territory, Saigon needed very costly land and air transport. South Vietnam required greater logistic support—one of the reasons why, the report emphasizes, it is difficult to compare the aid given by the two superpowers to their protégés. American analysts know their limits: "On the matter of accuracy, our information on North Vietnam has always been incomplete, although coverage on civilian imports is substantially better than for military aid . . . and our estimates for the part we cannot see have a wide margin of error."

In 1973, aid to North Vietnam decreased considerably. But in 1974, "total Communist military and economic aid to North Vietnam in 1974 was higher (in

433

current dollars) than in any previous year." In 1974 especially, the North Vietnamese received a lot of ammunition. Also, economic aid to Hanoi from socialist countries increased: they had to rebuild, and make up for losses in the 1973 autumn rice harvest due to typhoons.

Here are some of the tables drawn up—with many reservations—by American specialists. They show *estimates* of all the military aid supplied to Hanoi:

Military Aid (in millions of dollars)

	1970	1971	1972*	1973	1974
TOTAL	205	315	750	330	400
Military materiel	140	240	565	230	275
Anti-aircraft	20	85	310	100	55
Equipment for ground troops	45	80	110	40	45
Munitions	70	60	130	85	170†
Miscellaneous	5	15	15	5	5
Transport (trucks, helicopters, etc.)	20	15	30	35	25†
Other shipments, spare parts, gas, oil, medical supplies)	45	60	155	65	100

* April offensive.
†Note especially.

It should be noted that the only strong increase from 1970 to 1974 was in munitions. The North Vietnamese, say the Americans, never had so much before. In 1974, these munitions represent 40 percent of all military aid. Even taking inflation into account, these numbers are startling.

What do you prepare for by stockpiling ammunition?

It may also be noted that transport represents a relatively large part of this aid, with minor variations of the maximums in 1972 and 1973.

What do you prepare for by accumulating transport?

Economic aid—food, fertilizer, gasoline, machine tools, metallurgic products, technical assistance—has almost doubled in four years:

Total Economic Aid (in millions of dollars)

1970	1971	1972	1973*	1974†
635	645	360	540	1,145

* Year of the Paris Agreement
† Preparation for the offensive. The Soviets tell the Americans they've increased economic aid but reduced military aid.

What matters is aid to North Vietnam by *all* the communist countries, from the Soviet Union to Cuba, from China to Albania. By reports from Western embassies in communist bloc countries, reports usually based on confidences from diplomats, journalists and advisers in those countries, everyone knows that the citizens of her sister nations are up to here with feeding and arming their valiant North Vietnamese comrades. When not obligatory, collections in Poland or Czechoslovakia, in Romania or Hungary, are unsuccessful among the people. The Polish and Hungarian members of the ICCS in Saigon do not hide their annoyance.

Conscientious, the American analysts remind us to subtract from the total $125 million representing rather seedy exports from North Vietnam. This militarized nation is also a nation existing almost wholly on aid. Its unfavorable trade balance, especially with the Soviet Union, is huge.

What interests the American researchers most is comparing communist aid to the North and U.S. aid to the South. The comparisons are even more difficult because the U.S. fiscal year is not the calendar year. But we can attempt a parallel.

Military Aid to South and North Vietnam
(in millions of dollars)

	To the DRV 1974		To the RVN 1975	
Total military aid	400	(100%)	700	(100%)
Military materiel	275	(69%)	268	(38%)
Anti-aircraft	55	(14%)	negligible	
Ground troop equipment	45	(11%)	negligible	
Munitions	170	(43%)	268	(38%)
Other	5	(1%)	negligible	
Military transportation equipment	25	(6%)	negligible	
Delivery costs	20	(5%)	74	(11%)
Other military-related support (spare parts, fuel, oil, misc.)	80	(20%)	358	(51%)

U.S. dollar aid to Saigon is greater than communist aid to Hanoi. But aid to the North in war materiel is a bit greater and represents a much higher percentage of total aid. In dollar value, the South Vietnamese receive more munitions, but they represent a smaller part of the total aid—and factory costs in the Soviet Union are lower or kept artificially low where war materiel is concerned.

We note that the last two categories make up 62 percent of U.S. aid: a service and consumer society like South Vietnam has different needs from an almost spartan communist state.

American experts don't try this in their analysis, but if we deduct these last two categories from the totals for both Vietnams, we arrive at a curious result: subtracting the costs of shipping, spare parts, medical supplies, etc., we find a total of $300 million in aid to North Vietnam and $260 million to South Vietnam in a twelve-month period.

Obviously the North Vietnamese received considerable military support in 1974. No less obviously, if the Americans had been able to establish estimates of this kind at the end of 1974, they would not have been so surprised in Washington in January, February and March 1975 by the size of the communist offensive.

Of course, it may be assumed that the various American services contributing to this memo tried to influence congressional committees in order to win supplemental aid. Possibly they managed to underestimate aid to Saigon and overestimate aid to Hanoi. But the last ten years of the war proved that American studies *almost always* underestimated Hanoi's strength in men and materiel.

APPENDIX III

◆

On the South Vietnamese Armed Forces

On the eve of the great offensive, South Vietnamese armed forces comprised eleven infantry divisions, one airborne division, one division of marines and fifteen groups of rangers. Even now it is still impossible to say how many units were really operational. For these regular troops, estimates may range from 150,000 to 550,000 soldiers. In January 1975 no infantry battalion had more than 400 soldiers and no ranger battalion more than 300.

Add to this the regular support units: artillery with 1,492 cannon or heavy mortars; anti-aircraft units with 168 guns; 4 armored brigades with 2,074 tanks and armored personnel carriers.

The air force counted 41,000 men divided into 6 air divisions forming 66 wings. It owned 510 fighters or fighter bombers, of which 30 were F-5Es, 900 helicopters, 360 reconnaissance planes, 80 transport planes—on paper.

The navy counted 39,000 men. The South Vietnamese said they had 1,611 ships or armed boats. The Americans thought they actually had only 1,440 (cf. Chapter 21, note 5), To obtain aid, the South Vietnamese inflated their lists.

To these regular troops in the three arms were joined 140,000 men in regional forces and 300,000 men in popular forces. Regional and popular forces were commanded by provincial and district chiefs, while the regular units were run by divisional and military region commanders.

These numbers are supplied by General Lam Quang Thi, one of the best South Vietnamese officers, in *Autopsy: The Death of South Vietnam.*

Order of Battle of the South Vietnamese Army, January 1, 1975, according to Lam Quang Thi:

MR 1: 1st, 2nd, 3rd infantry divisions; four ranger groups; four artillery battalions; one armored brigade.

MR 2: 22nd, 23rd infantry divisions; six ranger groups; six artillery battalions; one armored brigade.

MR 3: 5th, 18th, 25th infantry divisions: six ranger groups; two artillery battalions; one armored brigade.

MR 4: 7th, 9th, 21st infantry divisions; eighteen ranger groups; three artillery battalions, one armored brigade.

General reserve troops: one division of paratroopers, one division of marines and special forces.

The regular troops and the South Vietnamese paramilitary units, regional and popular forces, are distributed over all of South Vietnam. The general deployment is static. The command is not ready to face a massive invasion.

The South Vietnamese army is twenty-five years old. It was formed by the French, then by the Americans. The majority of its general and field officers have never attended a major war academy. Few among them are capable of coordinating combined operations at the divisional or army corps level. They have been too long dependent on Americans. Nevertheless, despite all its faults, the enemy recognizes the ARVN's warlike qualities when its training and command hold up. Vietnamese CIA agents obtained copies of reports written by Polish and Hungarian soldiers on the ICCS, asserting that in 1973 and 1974 no PRG unit equalled the South Vietnamese regulars. And even the best North Vietnamese units, those that proved themselves in the heroic epoch of Dien Bien Phu, Divisions 304, 308, 312, 316, 320 and 325, are not at the level of the South Vietnamese elite outfits, the airborne division and the marine division.

The South Vietnamese army is abundantly supplied with arms, but they're not necessarily superior in quality to what the Soviets send the North Vietnamese. The South Vietnamese adopted the famous semi-automatic M-16 rifle only in 1968. At that time it replaced the M-1, the Garand—which French soldiers who did their military service in North Africa know well. In theory, the M-16 has a clip of twenty cartridges. But its spring seems weak and most soldiers load eighteen cartridges to a clip. American and South Vietnamese soldiers agree that the M-16 jams more easily than the AK-47. At headquarters they say that ARVN troops don't clean their weapons properly. General Westmoreland, when he was commander-in-chief in Vietnam, made the same remark apropos of U.S. troops when they complained about the M-16. According to a stubborn legend, the communist guerrillas showed their scorn for this American weapon by not always carrying off the M-16s they found on a battlefield. Also, in contrast to the theoretical twenty cartridges in the M-16 clip, the Chinese version of the AK-47 had a clip of thirty cartridges. In practice they loaded only twenty-eight, again to keep from fatiguing the spring and to avoid eventual firing accidents.

The ARVN 81 mm. mortars were just as accurate as the NVA 82 mm., and a little less powerful. The ARVN 105 cannon cannot counter the NVA 130s with their longer range and greater power. But on the eve of the general offensive, the problem at Saigon headquarters is primarily one of munitions. From 1973 to 1975, South Vietnamese soldiers were rationed: before the Paris Agreement, a soldier leaving for the front was issued seven offensive grenades. Afterward, two. ARVN staff, at the divisional and corps level, hoard. Hanoi is counting on unlimited supplies from Moscow; Saigon notes that U.S. aid is decreasing. From 1968 to 1970, the war cost the United States $25 billion a year. In 1970 and 1971, $12 billion a year. In 1973, military aid will total $2.2 billion. In 1974, the South Vietnamese army had to be content with $943 million and in 1975 with $475 million. Thieu feels that he must "fight a poor man's war" and to fight "with 60 percent of his former firepower" and "with 50 percent of his former mobility." Or so say the South Vietnamese experts. A commonplace on all levels of the military machine, the idea that the South Vietnamese army will lack munitions in the near future, creates the conviction that they lack them already.

Analyst Frank Snepp, who disagrees with the theory that arms and ammunition are short, writes soon after the fall of Saigon that the South Vietnamese army had all it needed to fight for "six to eight months," with stockpiles comparable to what it had during the hardest battles of 1972. (Frank Snepp, *End Game: An Inquiry Into Saigon's Last Rites, 1975*).

The great and incontestable South Vietnamese superiority lay in its aviation. But not wanting to engage their own, quantitatively and qualitatively inferior, the North Vietnamese eased this difficulty by heavily reinforcing their anti-aircraft. The fear of this very modern weapons system played a large part in the South Vietnamese defeat.

Beginning at the end of February, South Vietnamese general officers no longer count on aerial mobility. They can no longer ferry reinforcements rapidly from one point to another. On March 20, 1975, General Homer Smith's office in Saigon reported that of seven South Vietnamese C-130 air transports, only one was in condition to fly. And of the large Chinook helicopters, one out of six.

Few South Vietnamese officers thought they were as proficient as the American advisers who left in 1973.

On the evidence, the unquantifiable factor of morale worked in Hanoi's favor.

APPENDIX IV

◆

On the North Vietnamese Armed Forces

In Hanoi, most notably when visiting the War Museum, where almost a whole room is now devoted to the final offensive of 1975, the visitor hears constant mention of the "several thousand–year history of Vietnam." Officials emphasize that throughout its history Vietnam has had to repel invaders, Chinese, French, Japanese, Americans. The Vietnamese, and most of all the communists—Douglas Pike stresses this in his excellent book on the Vietnamese army, *PAVN: People's Army of Vietnam*—perceive themselves as a martial nation. All through the ages they have been obliged to *defend* themselves. In their insistence they forget that by other peoples' lights they are aggressors, not only aggressees. They invaded the Cham, the Khmers. To the various ethnic Montagnards of the whole Indochinese peninsula, to the Siamese and the Burmans, these Vietnamese are warriors, not simple peasants forced to take up arms to defend themselves.

The communist Vietnamese army is rooted in that history, which the Party has standardized for propaganda purposes. The North Vietnamese armed forces have now been in existence almost half a century. The first unit of 200 men was commanded by Tran Dang Ninh in Lang Son province in 1940. This was the "Bac Son Guerrilla Unit." In 1944 Vo Nguyen Giap headed the "Armed Propaganda Liberation Brigade," thirty-four men, in Cao Bang province. Van Tien Dung attracted notice in 1945, when he commanded the "Quang Trung Resistance Platoon," active in the provinces of Hoa Binh and Thanh Hoa. Soon enough, despite legend, the resistance groups became regular units.

Tanks played a very important role in the fall of Saigon. The first armored unit, the 202nd Tank Regiment, consisting of thirty T-34s, appears officially in 1959. In March 1963 for the first time the NVA command throws six PT-76s into a limited night attack on Ben Het in the Central Highlands. Two tanks are knocked out. A second big battle is fought in 1968 near Khe Sanh on Route 9, against a camp of U.S. Special Forces. A disastrous battle for Giap: the North Vietnamese PT-76s are up against American M-48s.

The PT-76, fourteen tons, had armor 14 mm. thick. Its 76 mm. guns did not have great penetrating power. The M-48, forty-seven tons, had armor ten times thicker in certain spots. Its 90 mm. guns could blow up a PT-76 like a paper bag. In 1971, T-54s faced M-41s: 100 mm. guns against 76 mm. guns.

Echelons of North Vietnamese officers go through Soviet schools. Now the North Vietnamese train with T-54s and T-55s, and in the field in Vietnam they do their on-the-job training. During the 1975 campaign, headquarters did not encourage its tanks to roam the countryside alone like mobile artillery pieces. The armored were almost always accompanied by infantry and units of anti-aircraft artillery equipped with 12.7 mm. or 14.5 mm. heavy machineguns and 37 mm., 57 mm., 85 mm. and 100 mm. cannon. The North Vietnamese offensive sees the appearance of a sort of tank with ZSU 57.2 anti-aircraft guns mounted on a modified T-54 chassis, which fired by eye or through a radar system. Supplying units with fuel and ammunition is the principal problem for armor in a lightning campaign. Most of the North Vietnamese tanks were T-54s. A T-54 uses an average of 80 liters an hour (about 17.5 gallons). General Dung is a logistician. Bernard Fall said of Giap that he was a "logistical genius"; his heir, Dung, was aided significantly by the network of pipelines laid down long before and, later, by the Soviet heavy trucks at his disposal, Aurochs, ZIL 555 or 130, and a large number of tank trucks.

There is considerable North Vietnamese artillery in the South: at least 400 85 mm., 100 mm. and 130 mm. pieces. Twelve meters long, a little less than eight tons, with a range of twenty-six kilometers, the 130 mm. M-46 is one of the most powerful cannon in its series. In the West, only the 155 mm. M-188 and the 175 mm. M-107 can answer it. Trapped in their own rut, the Soviets taught concentration of artillery batteries. Fearing aerial attacks—they suffered them for years—the North Vietnamese dispersed their cannon during the Ho Chi Minh campaign. With its radar, their 57 mm. S-60, seventy rounds a minute, is formidable.

North Vietnamese aviation, which consisted of several hundred fighters and fighter bombers in 1975, did not join battle but to the South Vietnamese command constituted at least a potential menace which had to be taken into account. Against South Vietnamese aircraft Dung's infantry units were equipped with a very large number of SA-7 missiles, with a range of ten kilometers. One soldier easily carried the missile launcher, very effective against small aircraft. Some time earlier, during the Yom Yippur War, half the Israeli A-4s hit by SA-7s had managed nonetheless to regain their bases. In the Soviet army, each infantry platoon had one SA-7. In 1975 most North Vietnamese platoons had two and sometimes three.

Against enemy tanks, the North Vietnamese have RPG-7 grenade launchers, effective at 300 meters. The Soviets have also supplied rather old-fashioned antitank guns, the SD-44s.

Except for the tank drivers, North Vietnamese regulars and many if not most Vietcong irregulars are armed with the famous Kalashnikov assault rifle. In the hands of the Vietnamese, that semi-automatic weapon eighty-seven centimeters long seems almost too large. The AK-47, in different models, is no doubt the most manufactured, used, copied and exported single weapon in the world. Since the end of World War II, the Japanese have exported Sonys, the Germans Volkswagens, the Americans Coca-Cola, and the Soviets Kalashnikovs. Easily recognized, sturdy, effective at 200–300 meters, the AK-47 is in the hands of every revolutionary in the world, civilian, paramilitary or military; and above all in the hands of communist troops in Indochina. According to certain specialists like Edward Clinton Ezell, there are some 30 million AKs in circulation. Few regular soldiers have used the AK as effectively as the troops of Giap, Dung and Tra. In 1974 the Soviets delivered a certain number of AK-74s to the North Vietnamese, the latest improved model of the Kalashnikov. Among themselves South Vietnamese soldiers armed with the M-16 speak often of the AK's superiority. They acknowledge only one advantage to the M-16: the lighter weight of its 5.56 mm. ammunition compared to the 7.62 mm. of the AK-47. The North Vietnamese soldiers prefer the Soviet model AK to the Chinese model, even to the bayonet-equipped AK-56.

All the Vietcong and North Vietnamese generals should erect a monument to Master-Sergeant Mikhail Timofeyevich Kalashnikov, former employee on the railroads, who invented the AK, inspired by the German Sturmgewehr. In 1975 Kalashnikov, creator of the Kalashnikov Automatic, is directing a factory in the Soviet Union.

During the 1975 campaign North Vietnamese generals usually command divisions that include support units. Infantry, artillery and armor do not move with relative independence as before. All the imperfections have not been ironed out. Example: not every tank has a radio. But the South Vietnamese are now and then surprised by North Vietnamese progress in tactics. The latter show a boldness lacking in the great offensive of 1972. Running down Route 1 toward Hue and Danang, NVA tanks avoid grouping up. In 1972 in Binh Long province, a hundred North Vietnamese armored vehicles, among them T-54s and PT-76s, all tagging along together, were "massacred." In 1975—especially after the conquest of Phuoc Long—communist infantry, preceding the armor, bars ARVN infantry with its grenade launchers and its RPG-72s from close approach to the North Vietnamese tanks. Sometimes, as around Hue and Nha Trang, the T-54s bypass solidly entrenched South Vietnamese positions. The South Vietnamese, in their successive retreats in the Central Highlands or along the coast, have no time to dig antitank ditches or lay mines, much less to set ambushes. Radio traffic proves North Vietnamese staff have learned one lesson that goes back at least to 1940: tanks must be commanded from up front, in the lines, and not from some remote headquarters.

In their 1975 advance the North Vietnamese were really stopped only three times. North of Hue, at the My Chanh River, they were slowed down by water and well-organized ARVN resistance. There Dung's men faltered and even retreated. And north of Hai Van Mountain a North Vietnamese division fought a very hard battle. The North Vietnamese also experienced great difficulties before taking Xuan Loc.

Never during the campaign was there a serious battle of tanks against tanks.

In MR 1, before, during and after the fall of Hue, the South Vietnamese abandoned quantities of armor, too often without putting it out of commission. In the streets of An Loc in 1972, the South Vietnamese were treated to long files of North Vietnamese tanks just a few meters apart; also in 1972, ARVN tank gunners armed with M-72s went to write their names on destroyed T-54s, to win a bonus. But when the ARVN fell back on Danang in 1975, Radio Hanoi explained that special units were taking possession of South Vietnamese materiel and restoring it to working order. Actually, the North Vietnamese do not have the improvisatory talents of the Israelis, who during the Yom Kippur War, having captured Soviet armor from the Egyptians in the Sinai or across the Suez Canal, repaired it very quickly.

Analyzing the offensive as a whole, some experts say today that it was less a lightning advance and a North Vietnamese victory than it was a disastrous retreat and a South Vietnamese defeat. Be that as it may, it is difficult to deny a victory to the victorious.

A North Vietnamese infantry division counts about 10,500 men. Between 1965 and 1975 Hanoi's army went from thirteen to twenty-five divisions. In 1986 Hanoi has fifty-one—and a million men under arms. . . . The air force has gone from one to five divisions, including one of helicopters. Under the circumstances we can understand that their military experts, writing and rewriting the tale of the Ho Chi Minh campaign, speak less and less of a "people's war" and almost not at all of the quarrel between the professionals and the ideologues. An army of that size needs specialists first and party members afterward.

Vietnamese society is unquestionably demoralized by the successive wars it has been obliged to wage and is still obliged to undergo. Even at Moscow's expense, Hanoi's armed forces swallow up more than half the state budget, but Vietnamese society is more militarized than ever.

APPENDIX V

North Vietnamese
Military Booty

All through April 1975 American high officials and soldiers try to recover materiel to keep it out of the invader's hands. Planes are the easiest to evacuate since there are a large number of South Vietnamese pilots available. So on May 1, 125 planes land in Thailand, some at airports, others on roads. CINCPAC asks all services to update a list of recovered materiel every twenty-four hours. The Americans want to repair and evacuate materiel from Vietnam but also from Thailand "to avoid having the government [Thai] appropriate this materiel or, eventually, hand it over to Vietnam or Cambodia" (State Department report). With that in view, the aircraft carrier *Midway* will be ordered to the port of Sattahip, in Thailand, where it will load mostly aircraft, F-5s and A-37s. It will head for the Philippines on orders from CINCPAC. But the State Department would have preferred that *Midway* head for Guam (U.S. territory) "to avoid having the Philippine government claim to exercise jurisdiction over this materiel." The State Department also orders that eight C-130s of the South Vietnamese air force, at the Utapao airport, be sent to Clark air base—and repainted in U.S. colors.

On May 1, according to American agencies, the North Vietnamese laid hands on—among other materiel—300 M-41 tanks and 250 M-48s; on 1,000 105 mm. cannon, 250 155s, 80 175s; on 791,000 M-16 rifles; on 15,000 M-60 machineguns; on 47,000 M-79 grenade launchers; on 63,000 LAW antitank weapons; on 90,000 .45 pistols; on 12,000 60 mm., 81 mm. and 90 mm. mortars; on about 50,000 radio transmitter-receivers; on 312 planes (F-5A, F-5E, A-37, A-1, C-130, C-119, C-47); on 502 helicopters minimum; on 42,000 trucks, and, at the lowest estimate, on 130,000 tons of ammunition.

These prizes of war represent billions of dollars. To give an order of magnitude, in 1975 an M-16 was worth $142, an 81 mm. mortar $4,500, an M-4 tank $280,043. . . .

To this day, the Americans can only make a rough overall estimate of North Vietnamese booty. In 1975 it made the army of unified Vietnam potentially the second strongest military force in Asia. The United States worried about that for some time. Memorandum 322 of the National Security Council, dated March 31, 1976, signed by Brent Scowcroft, outlined the broad lines of U.S. policy on the resale of materiel by the Vietnamese. The United States "should cooperate peacefully" with countries "friendly" to the United States who are potential buyers. Nevertheless the United States should not encourage acquisition of this materiel. When these countries demand spare parts, requests will be examined case by case. American businesses are barred from participating in these transactions. In regard to this materiel, any request for spare parts or technical cooperation must be submitted to the White House.

In September 1975 Romania put in a bid for construction materiel and metals recovered in Vietnam. In the same month French, British and Argentine arms merchants showed interest in light and heavy weapons in North Vietnamese hands.

The North Vietnamese had great trouble "digesting" their spoils, in particular the planes. The North Vietnamese army was short of qualified mechanics. In September 1975 it placed ads in newspapers seeking "mechanics and technicians for the bases at Bien Hoa, Tan Son Nhut and Nha Trang."

APPENDIX VI

Agenda of the Indochinese Communist Party

In July 1932 Ho Chi Minh set out this agenda, staking his claim to represent all of Indochina.

In ten points—an already rooted habit—the program listed the fundamental tasks of the revolution:

    1. Full economic and political independence for all Indochina. An end to French domination; expulsion of all military land, naval, air and police forces from the territory of the workers' and peasants' Indochina.

    2. Removal of indigenous dynasties, the Annam court, the Cambodian and Laotian kings with all their mandarins and nobles. Confiscation of all their goods.

    3. For a revolutionary government of the worker and peasant. For the creation of soviets and a workers' and peasants' revolutionary army. Arms and the right to military training for all workers and the working classes.

    4. Ownership by the workers' and peasants' state (nationalization) of all banks and French and foreign industrial enterprises, of all plantations, railroads, shipping industries and irrigation canals.

    5. Confiscation without indemnity of all lands and forests, and of all assets of imperialists, Catholic missions, landowners and usurers, royal families, mandarins and nobles.

    6. Cancelation of all obligations reducing workers to a state of slavery to usurers and banks. Cancelation of all debts and obligations of the state vis-à-vis banks and French capitalists.

    7. Fraternal union of all the people of Indochina. Right of self-determination for Cambodians, Laotians and other Indochinese nationalities.

Since 1932 Cambodians and Laotians have been considered "other nationalities," like the Montagnards of diverse ethnic origins living in Vietnam.

> 8. An eight-hour day and a radical amelioration of working conditions. Health, old-age, unemployment, disability and pregnancy insurance paid for by the bosses and the state. Freedom of organization and action for labor unions.
> 9. Complete political, economic and legal equality of the Indochinese woman.
> 10. Fraternal union with the workers' and peasants' revolutionary China and with the Hindu revolution.

In the whole program, Indochina is the primary entity. This is Greater Vietnam as it exists today, with its Cambodian and Laotian satellites. Naturally, the program ends with the slogan always on the mind of a Le Duan: "Long live world revolution!"

There should be no doubt about it: for the Vietnamese communists, the fall of Saigon in 1975 is only one step.

Selected Bibliography

Arnaud, Jean-Louis. *Saigon. D'un Vietnam à l'autre*. Paris: Gallimard, 1977.

Aron, Raymond. *Sur Clausewitz* (collection of articles). Preface by Pierre Hassner. Brussels: Éditions Complexe, 1982.

Barron, John and Anthony, Paul. *Peace with Horror*, London: Hodder and Stoughton, 1977. Published also as *Murder of a Gentle Land* (New York: Readers Digest Press, 1977).

Boudarel, Georges et al. *La bureaucratie au Vietnam*. Paris: L'Harmattan, 1983.

Bowman, John. *The Vietnam War*. New York: World Almanac Publications, Bison Books, 1985.

Braestrup, Peter. *Vietnam as History*. Washington, D.C.: University Press of America, The Wilson Center, 1984.

Bui Diem and Chanoff, David. *In the Jaws of History*. Boston: Houghton Mifflin, 1987.

Burchett, Wilfred, *At the Barricades*. New York: Times Books, 1981.

———. *Vietnam: Un + Un = Un*. Paris: François Maspero, 1977.

Butler, David. *The Fall of Saigon*. New York: Simon and Schuster, 1985.

Cao Vao Vien. *The Final Collapse*. Washington, D.C.: U.S. Army Center of Military History, 1983.

———. *Leadership*. Washington, D.C.: U.S. Army Center of Military History, 1981.

Cao Van Vien and Dong Van Khuyen. *Reflections on the Vietnam War*. Washington, D.C.: U.S. Army Center of Military History, 1980.

Dega, Czeslaw. *W. Polojowej Misji*. Warsaw: Mon, 1977.

Dillard, Walter Scott. *Sixty Days to Peace*. Washington, D.C.: National Defense University, 1982.

Dougan, Clark and Fulghum, David. *The Fall of the South*. Boston: Boston Publishing, 1985.

Dreyfus, Paul. . . . *Et Saigon tomba*. Paris: Arthaud, 1975.

449

Druiker, William. *The Communist Road to Power in Vietnam*. Boulder, Colo.: Westview Press, 1981.

Elliott, David et al. *The Third Indochina Conflict*. Boulder, Colo.: Westview Press, 1981.

Ezell, Edward Clinton. *The AK 47 Story: Evolution of the Kalashnikov Weapons*. Harrisburg, Penn.: Stackpole Books, 1986.

FitzGerald, Frances. *Fire in the Lake*. Boston: Little, Brown, 1972.

Ford, Gerald. *A Time To Heal*. New York: Harper & Row, 1979.

Franck, Thomas and Weisband, Edward. *Foreign Policy by Congress*. New York: Oxford University Press, 1979.

Gallucci, Robert. *Neither Peace nor Honor*. Baltimore: The Johns Hopkins University Press, 1975.

Goodman, Allan. *The Lost Peace: America's Search for a Negotiated Settlement of the Vietnam War*. Stanford, Calif.: Hoover Institution Press, 1978.

Haley, Edward. *Congress and the Fall of South Vietnam and Cambodia*. London and Toronto: Fairleigh Dickinson University Press (Associated University Presses), 1982.

Hallin, Daniel. *The "Uncensored War."* New York: Oxford University Press, 1986.

Hartmann, Robert. *Palace Politics: An Inside Account of the Ford Years*. New York: McGraw-Hill, 1980.

Herring, George. *America's Longest War*. New York: Knopf, 1979.

Hersh, Seymour. *The Price of Power*. New York: Summit Books, 1983.

Ho Chi Minh. *Selected Writings: 1920–1969*. Hanoi: Foreign Language Editions, 1973.

Hosmer, Steven, Keller, Konrad, and Jenkins, Brian. *The Fall of South Vietnam: Statements by Vietnamese Military and Civilian Leaders*. New York: Crane, Russak, 1980.

Isaacs, Arnold. *Without Honor*. Baltimore: The Johns Hopkins University Press, 1983.

Kalb, Marvin and Kalb, Bernard. *Kissinger*. Boston: Little, Brown, 1974.

Karnow, Stanley. *Vietnam*. New York: Viking Press, 1983.

Kinnard, Douglas. *The War Managers*. Wayne, N.J.: Avery, 1985.

Kissinger, Henry. *White House Years*, Boston: Little, Brown, 1979.

———. *Years of Upheaval*. Boston: Little, Brown, 1982.

Lam Quang Thi. *Autopsy: The Death of South Vietnam*. Phoenix, Ariz.: Sphinx, 1986.

Lam Thanh Liem. "De Saigon à Ho Chi Minh-Ville." Unpublished ms.

Landau, David. *Kissinger: The Uses of Power*. Boston: Houghton Mifflin, 1972.

Laqueur, Walter. *A World of Secrets: The Uses and Limits of Intelligence*. New York: Basic Books, 1985.

Lartéguy, Jean. *L'adieu à Saigon*. Paris: Presses de la Cité, 1975.

LeGro, William. *Vietnam from Ceasefire to Capitulation*. Washington, D.C.: U.S. Army Center of Military History, 1980.

Miller, Carolyn. *Captured!* Chappaqua, N.Y.: Christian Herald Books, 1977.

Millett, Allan et al. *A Short History of the Vietnam War*. Bloomington: Indiana University Press, 1978.

Momyer, William. *Air Power in Three Wars (WWII, Korea, Vietnam)*. Washington, D.C.: Government Printing Office, 1983.

Nguyen Cao Ky. *Twenty Years and Twenty Days*. New York: Stein and Day, 1976.

Nguyen Duy Hinh. *Vietnamization and the Ceasefire*. Washington, D.C.: U.S. Army Center of Military History, 1980.

Nguyen Ngoc Huy and Young, Stephen. *Understanding Vietnam*. Bussum, Netherlands: DPC Information Service, 1982.

Nguyen The Anh et al. . . . *1975 . . . Vietnam . . . Vérités et réalités*. Paris: Duong Moi, La Voie Nouvelle, 1985.

Nutter, Warren. *Kissinger's Grand Design*. Washington, D.C.: American Enterprise Institute for Public Policy Research, 1975.

Palmer, Bruce. *The 25-Year War*. Lexington: The University Press of Kentucky, 1984.

Patti, Archimedes. *Why Vietnam?* Berkeley: University of California Press, 1980.

Pham Kim Vinh. *In Their Defense: U.S. Soldiers in the Vietnam War*. Phoenix, Ariz.: Sphinx, 1985.

Pike, Douglas. *PAVN: People's Army of Vietnam*. Novato, Calif.: Presidio Press, 1986.

Porter, Gareth. *Vietnam: The Definitive Documentation of Human Decisions*. 2 vols. Stanfordville, N.Y.: Earl M. Coleman, 1979.

Richer, Philippe. *Jeu de quatre en Asie du Sud-Est*. Paris: Presses Universitaires de France, 1982.

Salisbury, Harrison et al. *Vietnam Reconsidered*. New York: Harper & Row, 1984.

Santoli, Al. *Everything We Had: An Oral History of the Vietnam War by Thirty-three American Soldiers Who Fought It*. New York: Random House, 1981.

Snepp, Frank. *Decent Interval*. New York: Vintage Books, 1977.

Stanton, Shelby. *The Rise and Fall of an American Army*. Novato, Calif.: Presidio Press, 1985.

Summers, Harry. *On Strategy*, Novato, Calif.: Presidio Press, 1982.

Sutsakhan, Sak. *The Khmer Republic at War and the Final Collapse*. Washington, D.C.: U.S. Army Center of Military History, 1980.

Thomson, W. Scott and Donaldson, Frizzell. *The Lessons of Vietnam*, New York: Crane, Russak, 1977.

Trager, Frank et al. *Marxism in Southeast Asia*. Stanford: Stanford University Press, 1959.

Tran Thi Nga and Larsen, Wendy Wilder. *Shallow Graves*. New York: Random House, 1986.

Tran Van Don. *Our Endless War*. San Rafael, Calif.: Presidio Press, 1978.

Tran Van Tra. *Vietnam: History of the Bulwark B2 Theatre. Vol. 5. Concluding the 30-Years War*. Arlington, Va.: Joint Publications Research Service, 1983. Originally published as *Ket Cuoc Chien Tranh 30 Nam* (Ho Chi Minh Ville: Ed. Van Nghe, 1982).

Truong Nhu Tang, Chanoff, David and Doan Van Toai. *Mémoires d'un Vietcong*. Paris: Flammarion, 1985.

Van Tien Dung. *Our Great Spring Victory*. Translated by John Spragens, Jr. New York: Monthly Review Press, 1977. First serialized in *Nhan Dan* (April–May 1976).

Vo Nguyen Giap. *Unforgettable Months and Years*. Data Paper 99. New York: Cornell University, 1975. First published by Foreign Language Editions, Hanoi, 1975. Translation of *Nhung nam thang khong the nao quen*.

Warner, Denis. *Certain Victory: How Hanoi Won the War*. Kansas City: Sheed Andrews & McMell, 1977.

Watson, Peter. *War on the Mind: The Military Uses and Abuses of Psychology*. London: Hutchinson, 1978.

U.S. GOVERNMENT PUBLICATIONS

Congressional Record
Congressional Hearings

Department of State Bulletin
Weekly Compilation of Presidential Documents

ARTICLES

Bundy, McGeorge. "Vietnam, Watergate and Presidential Powers." *Foreign Affairs* 58, no. 2 (Winter 1979–80).
Carey, Richard and Quinlan, D. A. "Frequent Wind." *Marine Corps Gazette* (February-March-April 1976).
Herrington, Stuart. "The Third Indochina War, 1973–1975: A Personal Perspective." Air Command and Staff College, Maxwell Air Force Base, Alabama, May 1980.
Kissinger, Henry. "The Vietnam Negotiations." *Foreign Affairs* (January 1969).
McCloskey, Paul, Jr. "The North Vietnam–South Vietnam Confrontation." *Congressional Record*, March 14, 1975.
Szulc, Tad. "Behind the Vietnam Ceasefire Agreement." *Foreign Policy* (Summer 1974).
Timmes, Charles. "Vietnam Summary: Military Operations After the Ceasefire Agreement." *Military Review* (August-September 1976).
Tobin, Thomas. "Last Flight from Saigon." USAF Southeast Asia Monograph Series, vol. 4, monograph 6, Office of Air Force History, 1975.

PRINCIPAL PERIODICALS

Newsweek, Time, New York Times, Washington Post, Boston Globe, Los Angeles Times, U.S. News and World Report, The Times (London), Far Eastern Economic Review, Le Monde, Le Figaro, Der Spiegel, Saigon Post, Stars and Stripes, Le Courrier d'Extrême-Orient, Nhan Dan, Quan Doi Nhan Dan, Hoc Tap, Vietnam Courrier, Song Than, Dien Tin.

A researcher can no longer ignore the innumerable audiovisual documents stocked by television and radio networks and by photo agencies.

I particularly thank the personnel of four institutions: the Marines Historical Department and the Department of Defense Still Media Depository, both in Washington, the Center for Research Library in Chicago, and the Institute of East Asian Studies of the University of California at Berkeley.

I cannot thank here all those who helped me in my research.

Nevertheless, I must express my gratitude to Jean-Louis Arnaud, "Ba," Bach Thai Ha, Carol Becker, Edward Behr, Joyce E. Bonnett, Pierre Brochand, Malcolm Browne, Bui Diem, Georges Buis, Sir John Bushell, Buu Lich, Cao Giao, George Carver, Alexandre Casella, Chung Tan Cang, William Colby, John Cole, José Courbil, Steve Denney, Jacqueline Desbarats, Ross Dunham, Du Tu Le, Duyen Anh, Jean Dyrac, Jim Eckes, Penelope Faulkner, Jean Fourré, Dalia Grumbach, Ha Vinh Quang, Patrick Hays, Lucien Hébert, "Hien," Hoang Duc Nha, Christian Jelen, Piotr Kaminski, Henry Kissinger, Lam Ngoc Diep, Lam Ngoc Loan, Lan, Branko Lazitch, Wolfgang Lehmann, Le Kim Hung, Le Quang Luong, Le Vinh Hoa, Jean Maïs, Mai Thao, Graham Martin, William Melton, Jean-Marie Mérillon, Ron Moreau, Cyril Moyher, Ngo Quang Truong, Nguyet Anh, Nguyen Cao Ky, Nguyen Thi Kim Dung, Paul d'Ornano, Dr. Pham Kim Vinh, Pham Thin, Phuong Anh, Douglas Pike, Thomas Polgar, François Ponchaud, Melinda Porter, Muri Rajaretnam, Philippe Richer, Henry Shaw, Jack Shulimson, W. R. Smyser, Frank Snepp, Betty Sprigg, Robert Stalter, Thai Quang Trung, Thanh Phuong,

Thich Thien Hue, "Thuong," Frank Tonini, Ton That Thien, Tran Ba Doai, Tran Mong Huong, Tran Thi Nga, Tran Van Don, Tran Van Tong, Tri Dang, Truong Nhu Tang, Katherine Turpin, Van, Vo Van Ai, Vuong, David Wigdon, Frank Wisner, Peter Wyro, Elio Zarmati, Hannah Zedlick, and especially to Sylviane Labes-Degombert.

Index

Page numbers in *italics* refer to illustrations.